# The Evil Inclination in Early Judaism and Christianity

One of the central concepts in rabbinic Judaism is the notion of the Evil Inclination, which appears to be related to similar concepts in ancient Christianity and the wider late antique world. The precise origins and understanding of the idea, however, are unknown. This volume traces the development of this concept historically in Judaism and assesses its impact on emerging Christian thought concerning the origins of sin. The chapters, which cover a wide range of sources including the Bible, the Ancient Versions, Qumran, Pseudepigrapha and Apocrypha, the Targums, and rabbinic and patristic literature, advance our understanding of the intellectual exchange between Jews and Christians in classical Antiquity, as well as the intercultural exchange between these communities and the societies in which they were situated.

James Aitken is Reader in Hebrew and Early Jewish Studies at the Faculty of Divinity, University of Cambridge. Publications include *No Stone Unturned: Greek Inscriptions and Septuagint Vocabulary* (2014) and *The T&T Clark Companion to the Septuagint* (2015).

Hector Michael Patmore is Associate Professor in the Faculty of Theology and Religious Studies at the KU Leuven. His research focuses on the interpretation of the Hebrew Bible and the development of Jewish beliefs in Antiquity. Publications include *Adam, Satan, and the King of Tyre* and *The Transmission of Targum Jonathan in the West.*

Ishay Rosen-Zvi is Professor in the Department of Jewish Philosophy and Talmud at Tel Aviv University. A scholar of rabbinic literature, he was elected to the Israel Young Academy of Sciences in 2013. He is author of several books, most recently, *Goy: Israel's Multiple Others and the Birth of the Gentile.*

# The Evil Inclination in Early Judaism and Christianity

Edited by

JAMES AITKEN
*University of Cambridge*

HECTOR M. PATMORE
*KU Leuven*

ISHAY ROSEN-ZVI
*Tel Aviv University*

CAMBRIDGE
UNIVERSITY PRESS

**CAMBRIDGE**
**UNIVERSITY PRESS**

University Printing House, Cambridge CB2 8BS, United Kingdom

One Liberty Plaza, 20th Floor, New York, NY 10006, USA

477 Williamstown Road, Port Melbourne, VIC 3207, Australia

314–321, 3rd Floor, Plot 3, Splendor Forum, Jasola District Centre, New Delhi – 110025, India

79 Anson Road, #06–04/06, Singapore 079906

Cambridge University Press is part of the University of Cambridge.

It furthers the University's mission by disseminating knowledge in the pursuit of education, learning, and research at the highest international levels of excellence.

www.cambridge.org
Information on this title: www.cambridge.org/9781108470827
DOI: 10.1017/9781108557153



First published 2021

*A catalogue record for this publication is available from the British Library.*

*Library of Congress Cataloging-in-Publication Data*
NAMES: Patmore, Hector M., editor. | Aitken, James K. (James Keltie), 1968– editor. | Rosen-Zvi, Ishay, editor.
TITLE: The evil inclination in early Judaism and Christianity / edited by Hector Patmore, James Aitken, Ishay Rosen-Zvi.
DESCRIPTION: Cambridge ; New York, NY : Cambridge University Press, 2021. | Includes bibliographical references and index.
IDENTIFIERS: LCCN 2020028438 (print) | LCCN 2020028439 (ebook) | ISBN 9781108470827 (hardback) | ISBN 9781108557153 (ebook)
SUBJECTS: LCSH: Yetzer hara (Judaism) | Good and evil – Religious aspects – Judaism. | Good and evil – Religious aspects – Christianity. | Sin – Christianity – History of doctrines – Early church, ca. 30–600.
CLASSIFICATION: LCC BJ1286.Y48 E95 2021 (print) | LCC BJ1286.Y48 (ebook) | DDC 296.3/6–dc23
LC record available at https://lccn.loc.gov/2020028438
LC ebook record available at https://lccn.loc.gov/2020028439

ISBN 978-1-108-47082-7 Hardback

# Contents


*Acknowledgments* — *page* vii

*List of Contributors* — viii

1 Introduction
*J. K. Aitken, H. M. Patmore, and I. Rosen-Zvi* — 1

2 Reconsidering the Semantics of the "Inclination" (*yeṣer*) in Classical Biblical Hebrew
*Noam Mizrahi* — 13

3 The "Inclination" (*yeṣer*) as Rendered in the Septuagint
*James K. Aitken* — 33

4 "Fleshly Spirit" and "Vessel of Flesh" in 4QInstruction and the Thanksgiving Hymns
*Benjamin Wold* — 49

5 Theological Anthropology in the Enochic Tradition
*Loren Stuckenbruck* — 65

6 The Perils of Philosophical Persuasion: Philo on the Origin of Moral Evils
*Sharon Weisser* — 95

7 The Evil Inclination (*yeṣer ha-ra'*) in Tannaitic Literature: Demonic Desires and Beyond
*Ishay Rosen-Zvi* — 115

8 Conflicting Intrapersonal Powers in Paul's Letters
*Daniel Schumann* — 126

9 The "Two Inclinations" and the Double-Minded Human Condition in the Letter of James
*George van Kooten* — 143

10 An Evil Inclination in the Early Targums to the Pentateuch and Prophets?
*Hector M. Patmore* 159

11 "Gnostic" Theologies of Evil
*Timothy Pettipiece* 176

12 The Rabbinic "Inclination" (*yeṣer*) and the Christian Apocrypha
*Monika Pesthy-Simon* 186

13 Origen on the Origin of Sin
*Riemer Roukema* 201

14 Augustine on the Diabolical Suggestion of Sin
*Sophie Lunn-Rockliffe* 212

15 Jerome and the "Inclination" (*yeṣer*): The Evidence of the Vulgate
*C. T. R. Hayward* 232

16 Rabbinic Inclinations and Monastic Thoughts: Evagrius Ponticus' Doctrine of Reasoning (*logismoi*) and Its Antecedents
*Augustine Casiday* 247

17 "Inclination" (*yaṣrā*) in the Syriac Tradition
*David G. K. Taylor* 262

18 Evil, Sin, and Inclination (*yeṣer*) in Jewish and Christian Poetic Disputes between the Body and Soul
*Ophir Münz-Manor* 280

19 The Wizard of Āz and the Evil Inclination: The Babylonian Rabbinic Inclination (*yeṣer*) in Its Zoroastrian and Manichean Context
*Yishai Kiel* 294

20 The Evil Inclination in the Targums to the Writings
*Leeor Gottlieb* 315

*References* 331

*Index of Names* 358

*Index Locorum* 360

# Acknowledgments

We would like to take this opportunity to express our thanks to the organisations and individuals whose contributions made this volume possible. First and foremost, we are grateful to the contributors for their willingness to participate in this project and their patience as it made its long way to publication. The costs of the original conference and preparation of the indicies were generously covered by an anonymous sponsor. In addition, Fitzwilliam College provided us with a congenial setting and ensured a smooth running of the conference. We note too the contribution of La Fondation du Judaïsme Français, which funded Hector Patmore's research stay in Strasbourg, during which time he was able to prepare his contribution to this project. That this project has finally come to fruition in the form of this edited volume is thanks to the Syndicate of Cambridge University Press and to the editorial and production teams of the Press, among whom Beatrice Rehl, Eilidh Burrett, Caroline Morley, Sudarsan Siddarthan, and Mathivathini Mareesan. We note with particular appreciation the contribution of our copy-editor, Mary Starkey, who carefully weeded out the last remaining infelicities and inconsistencies. In addition to the team at Cambridge University Press, Sophia Johnson helped us prepare the indices. To all these we extend our warmest thanks.

# Contributors

**James Aitken**, Reader in Hebrew and Early Jewish Studies, Faculty of Divinity, University of Cambridge.

**Augustine Casiday**, Honorary Senior Research Fellow, School of History, Archaeology and Religion, Cardiff University and Affiliate Lecturer, Department of Theology, University of Glasgow.

**Leeor Gottlieb**, Lecturer, Zalman Shamir Bible Department, Bar-Ilan University.

**Robert Hayward**, Professor of Hebrew (retired), Department of Theology and Religion, University of Durham.

**Yishai Kiel**, Research Fellow, Faculty of Law, Hebrew University of Jerusalem.

**Sophie Lunn-Rockliffe**, Lecturer in Patristics, Faculty of Divinity, University of Cambridge.

**Noam Mizrahi**, Associate Professor, Department of Bible, Hebrew University of Jerusalem.

**Ophir Münz-Manor**, Associate Professor of Rabbinic Culture, Department of History, Philosophy and Judaic Studies, Open University of Israel.

**Hector M. Patmore**, Associate Professor in Biblical Studies, Faculty of Theology and Religious Studies, KU Leuven.

**Monika Pesthy-Simon**, Independent Scholar and Doctor of the Hungarian Academy of Sciences, Budapest.

**Timothy Pettipiece**, Instructor, College of Humanities, Carleton University, and Department of Classics and Religious Studies, University of Ottawa.

**Ishay Rosen-Zvi**, Professor and Head of the Talmud and Late Antiquity Section, Department of Jewish Philosophy, Tel Aviv University.

**Riemer Roukema**, Research Professor in Early Christianity, Protestant Theological University, Groningen.

**Daniel Schumann**, Marie Skłodowska-Curie Fellow, Faculty of Theology and Religion, University of Oxford.

**Loren T. Stuckenbruck**, Professor of New Testament, Faculty of Protestant Theology, Ludwig-Maximilians University, Munich.

**David G. K. Taylor**, Associate Professor of Aramaic and Syriac, Faculty of Oriental Studies, University of Oxford.

**George van Kooten**, Lady Margaret's Professor of Divinity, Faculty of Divinity, University of Cambridge.

**Sharon Weisser**, Senior Lecturer in Ancient Philosophy, Department of Philosophy, Tel Aviv University.

**Benjamin Wold**, Associate Professor of Early Judaism & Christianity, School of Religion, Faculty of Arts, Humanities, and Social Sciences, Trinity College Dublin, the University of Dublin.

1

# Introduction

## J. K. Aitken, H. M. Patmore, and I. Rosen-Zvi

> Rabbinic [language] has no literal equivalent for the Pauline "flesh and spirit" (σάρξ and πνεῦμα), but in many cases it corresponds to the "Good and Evil Inclination," which occurs extremely frequently in Rabbinic literature.[1]

So Strack and Billerbeck began their excursus on the *yeṣer* in their influential *Kommentar zum Neuen Testament aus Talmud und Midrasch.* They attempt to trace the origins of the rabbinic concept of an internal struggle between two forces within the human being, one inclination that is good and one that is evil, finding an equivalent in earlier Hellenistic concepts. Their comments exemplify two of the major methodological weaknesses that dogged earlier scholarship on the Evil Inclination – a tendency on the one hand to read rabbinic sources from different times and places as an undifferentiated synthesis, and an overenthusiasm for perceiving in superficial similarities concrete parallels and the marks of direct borrowings, on the other.

The work of Rosen-Zvi on the *yeṣer* over recent years (cited frequently in this volume) has set about remedying particularly the first of these two deficiencies by carefully unpicking the chronological layers of rabbinic literature and differentiating between the two principal geographical settings of early rabbinic Judaism, Roman Palestine and Babylonia.[2] This work opened up new possibilities for identifying the origins of the concept of an "Evil Inclination" and its development in pre-rabbinic Judaism; for comparing Jewish ideas with thought patterns

[1] "Fur das paulinische 'Fleisch u. Geist' (σάρξ and πνεῦμα) hat das Rabbinische kein wortliches Aquivalent, es deckt sich aber vielfach mit dem in der rabbinischen Literatur ungemein haufig vorkommenden 'bosen u. guten Trieb'" (Str-B 4: 466–83).

[2] See, e.g., Rosen-Zvi 2008, 2009, and 2011.

in nascent Christianity; and for exploring the uses of the *yeṣer* in important Jewish works from Late Antiquity outside the classic rabbinic corpus (e.g. Targum and *piyyut*).

It was with these three aims in mind that an international conference was convened at the University of Cambridge in September 2014. The contributors were carefully selected, and each was asked to examine afresh a corpus of materials in which she or he has particular expertise. Some additional papers were commissioned by the editors after the conference to ensure a comprehensive, coherent, and integrated treatment of the subject. We are glad to present the results in the current volume. The participants considered how their materials evidenced dependence on earlier traditions, how they differed from or reacted to ideas found in other corpora, how they reflected trajectories that are more fully developed in later literatures, and the extent to which the ideas that they embody were shaped by the cultures in which Judaism and Christianity were embedded (in particular, Hellenistic, Sasanian, and Roman). Many of the contributions find unexpected relations between different compositions, Jewish and Christian, in the context of explanations for human sinfulness, thus necessitating a rethinking of the connection and borders between genres and cultures in Late Antiquity. The results of this collaborative approach therefore mark an important new contribution to our understanding of the development of Jewish and Christian thought on the nature of human sinfulness, a major theological category.

Both Jewish and Christian sources rely on certain key biblical passages as they develop traditions connected to the Evil Inclination, and so a logical place to start our investigation was with a thorough reexamination of the semantics of some of the key terminology in the Hebrew Bible. The fundamental question of the meaning of the Hebrew יצר (*yeṣer*) is addressed by Noam Mizrahi. Mizrahi examines its meanings in Biblical Hebrew before the undoubted development in semantic range that is seen in Sirach, Qumran, and in Rabbinic Hebrew. He suggests that it would be wrong to interpret the word in the key passages in Genesis (6:5, 8:21) as denoting the human mental faculty. Rather, in line with the meaning of the verb as "to fashion" and the uses of the noun elsewhere as a manufactured product, in Genesis 6 and 8 the *yeṣer* denotes the products of human civilization. This is in keeping with the sense of *yeṣer* elsewhere, but in the context it takes on a dark foreboding, as they are products that are specifically condemned by God. It thus can be seen that in Classical Biblical Hebrew the term underwent a semantic change, from denoting the work and products of a potter to the making of objects by other artisans. The psychologized extension in meaning is not attested in the classical corpus, and is to be attributed to post-biblical developments. Therefore, as far as the use of the term *yeṣer* is concerned, the distance between biblical and post-biblical literature is even greater than is commonly thought.

It might be expected that in the Septuagint, the first books of which were translated in the third century and the rest in the centuries that followed, signs of the developing notion of the inclination would be seen. James Aitken notes how the translation was made near to the time when the semantic change is seen in the Hebrew version of Sirach, but that despite this very little scholarly attention has been given to the Septuagint in studies of the *yeṣer*. Greek lexicographic tools have too easily at times opted for meanings in the Greek that seem to derive from the later rabbinic understanding than from a thorough semantic analysis. Throughout most of the Septuagint a standard default rendering of the Hebrew is chosen: words signifying a fashioned product, in accord with the prime meaning in Biblical Hebrew. In the Greek of Sirach a shift is detectable from a fashioned product to an internalized sense of "will, desire." Most striking are the renderings of the two parade passages in Genesis (6:5, 8:21), where the translator clearly sees a connection between the two passages by translating them in similar ways that are interpretative of the Hebrew source text. Although these two passages as rendered in the Septuagint cannot be interpreted in the full rabbinic sense, they already reveal in the third century BCE a recognition of human frailty in controlling the will.

The two chapters on the Second Temple period by Benjamin Wold and Loren Stuckenbruck offer important examinations of some key concepts and terminology in the Dead Sea Scrolls and the Enochic traditions that foreshadow the rabbinic conception of the *yeṣer*. Wold examines in detail two terms appearing in various Thanksgiving Hymns as well as in 4QInstruction: "Fleshly Spirit" and "Vessel (יצר) of Flesh." These two cryptic terms, which appear nowhere else in Ancient Jewish literature, were interpreted as conveying a stark dualistic worldview. Wold rejects this interpretation, claiming instead that the terms express distance between the unenlightened and base human being as a whole and the divine. It thus uses these two unique expressions to rethink Qumranic anthropology. The chapter also uncovers deep connections between Thanksgiving Hymns and 4QInstruction not observed in scholarship. The shared use of rare vocabulary suggests not just a common cultural milieu, but also a direct knowledge of 4QInstruction by the hymns. At the same time, this proximity also reveals the differences in worldview between the compositions, the hymns being much more negative, projecting an anthropology that radically separates "us" and "them."

Given their significance in the development of rabbinic thinking about the *yeṣer*, critical attention needed to be given to interpretations of the first chapters of the book of Genesis in the Second Temple period. In his chapter Stuckenbruck compares, both textually and phenomenologically, the Enochic traditions regarding humans and their place in the cosmos with the account in Genesis 1–9. In respect of the former Stuckenbruck finds clear (if implicit) traces of the Genesis account in the Book of Watchers. As for the latter, he analyzes the differences between the accounts, mainly the presentation of humans as victims rather than as a source of evil. In the Book of Watchers personified forces of evil are held accountable for human suffering. This leads to Enochic overlooking of both the idea of human creation in God's likeness and the divine regret that humanity was created in Gen 6:6. But the major difference between the two accounts concerns eschatology. While Genesis does not show any interest in linking the universal *Urzeit* with a similar *Endzeit*, the Enochic eschatological vision includes all humanity. After analyzing the Book of Watchers (1 En 1–16), Stuckenbruck moves to subsequent parts of First Enoch, showing how these compositions adapted the universal vision of the third century BCE into the turmoil of the second (the rise of Antiochus IV in the 170s and the Maccabean Revolt in the 160s BCE) and later, while preserving much of the Enochic unique worldview.

The focus on the Greek cultural context of Alexandria in Aitken's contribution is picked up again in Sharon Weisser's chapter on Philo of Alexandria, one of the first and most important Jewish interpreters of the Bible. Weisser examines the origins of moral evils in Philo's thought, where we see a conjunction between the naturalistic vantage point of ancient philosophy and that of the particularism of Jewish philosophy. The influence of Greek philosophy in Philo leads to his seeing the origin of vice lying in the passions of the soul, which are connected to the embodied human condition. The existence of the passions is explained by two interconnected reasons: the embodied condition of man on the one hand, and an impaired epistemological state of the agent on the other. In part vice arises from a wrong valuation of the physical realm: the pleasure and pain associated with the senses lead the agent to believe that what is pleasant should be pursued and what is painful should be avoided. Furthermore, improper philosophical argumentation constitutes, in Philo's eyes, one of the main causes of ignorance and hence of irrational and vicious conduct. For the agent to regain rationality and to oppose the recalcitrance of his material condition, the best path is to endorse the true philosophy, that is, the Law of Moses. The Torah, as the best and most detailed expression of the law of nature, is the dogmatic solution provided by Philo for the corrupted characters of both the soul and of philosophy in his time.

As we reach the end of the Second Temple period, Ishay Rosen-Zvi helps set the stage for a comparative examination of the nascent rabbinic and Christian thought-worlds, by sketching Tannaitic characterizations of the *yeṣer* and offering some reflections on the methodological challenges that a project such as this one presents. Rosen-Zvi begins by summarizing his findings on the Tannaitic *yeṣer* and responds to critique of his book on the topic, *Demonic Desires*. His main thesis is that in Tannaitic sources the *yeṣer* is not characterized as a "blind and unbridled passion" but as a sophisticated operator, which entices humans to every kind of sin, sometimes by deploying (quasi-)halakhic arguments. Unlike demons, which account for external dangers (e.g. illness, suffering), the *yeṣer* is therefore answerable for human sinfulness. Humans have the ability to fight the *yeṣer* and prevail with the aid of tools such as adjuration (oaths, vows) and Torah study. In terms of its anthropology, Tannaitic literature presents the *yeṣer* residing within humans, while remaining an independent entity.

Having outlined his main thesis, Rosen-Zvi turns to methodological questions. First, he considers how one should evaluate the a priori resemblances between the *yeṣer*'s modus operandi and the role played by demons in some early Christian writings (e.g. Origen). Rosen-Zvi is inclined to see such resemblances as purely phenomenological, while others would argue for a genetic link. Second, Rosen-Zvi considers how literally or otherwise one ought to take rabbinic descriptions of the *yeṣer*'s physicality. Rejecting the category of metaphor, he argues that they should be read literally and located in the realm of myth. Finally, Rosen-Zvi responds to Kister's critique of his claim about the novelty of the Tannaitic *yeṣer*. Rosen-Zvi acknowledges that components of the rabbinic concept of the *yeṣer* are foreshadowed in Second Temple times, but argues that it is precisely the combining of these components in Tannaitic thought and the integration of the *yeṣer* into a wider rabbinic anthropology that has resulted in something genuinely novel.

With the methodological groundwork in place, we are able to turn our attention to the literature of nascent Christianity, beginning with the works of Paul. Conscious of the risk of "parallelomania," of which much earlier studies on the Pauline corpus fell foul, Daniel Schumann adopts a method of "word field" analysis in order to consider the relevance of the rabbinic concept of the *yeṣer* for Paul's reflections on the human tendency to sin. Focusing on a selection of key texts, he concludes that the language of "desire" (ἐπιθυμία) in 1 Thessalonians and the flesh/spirit antithesis in Galatians are best understood against the backdrop of Greek philosophy rather than rabbinic notions of an evil intrapersonal force. Similarly, he argues that fundamentally different approaches to the Law sharply distinguishes Paul's language of malevolent external forces (particularly "sin") in his letter to the Romans from the rabbinic understanding of *yeṣer:* whereas Tannaitic sources regard the Law as an antidote to the Evil Inclination, Paul identifies the Law as a catalyst. Schumann's conclusion is stark and will doubtless engender further debate, especially among adherents of the "New Perspective on Paul": He writes, "Paul either did not know of the rabbinic יצר concept or, if he knew of the יצר, he chose not to use it in expressing his own thought."

Weisser's chapter on Philo of Alexandria is complemented well by the contribution of George van Kooten, who revisits the notion of the δίψυχος, the double-minded nature of human beings in the Letter of James (1.8, 4.8), which has long been connected in scholarship with the rabbinic notion of "the two inclinations." He suggests that it does not suit well the Hebrew notion of a double heart, which is better translated by other terms; rather, it conveys a notion of the soul and mind. Van Kooten traces the idea of the double soul through Xenophon, Plato, and the Stoics, and observes its adoption in Platonists such as Plotinus. It finds Jewish expression in the writings of Philo of Alexandria, first in a passage on the two spirits or powers, and second in a section where Philo finds confirmation for his Platonic view of the duality of the soul in the Pentateuch. Against these backgrounds the Letter of James can be seen as partaking in a specific Greek discourse of divine simplicity in opposition to the double-minded nature of humans, a discourse deeply influenced by the Platonic notion of the divided self. It may be that, like Philo, James participated in Jewish and Greek discourses, and that if he were familiar with anything akin to the rabbinic notion of the two *yeṣarim* he transmitted it in terms of Greek conceptions of the divided self. Thus, Jewish anthropology proved to be compatible with Greek reflections.

Three chapters focus on Jewish and Christian literature from the second and early third centuries CE. Research on the Evil Inclination has focused mainly on texts from the Talmud and Midrash, with the result that the Aramaic Targums have been largely neglected, despite their importance as repositories of traditional Jewish exegesis. Hector

Patmore focuses his attention on those Targums that have their origins in the Tannaitic period, with a view to shedding light on the date of the Targumic traditions and the nature of their relationship to mainstream rabbinic literature. While Targum Onqelos simply uses the Aramaic cognate noun when it encounters *yeṣer* in the Hebrew, Targum Jonathan characterizes the *yeṣer* as a stumbling block and the source of disturbing thoughts, hinting at its antinomian nature. Both envisage a single *yeṣer,* which they treat as a normal human tendency, rather than a distinct external entity. Patmore concludes that their portrayal of the *yeṣer* reflects the early Tannaitic period. Turning to the Palestinian Targum traditions, Patmore examines an exegetical tradition that holds the *yeṣer* responsible for prompting Cain to murder his brother. He argues that this tradition reflects a more developed understanding of the *yeṣer*, suggesting a late Tannaitic or early Amoraic date.

Careful analysis of Christian literature roughly contemporaneous with these Targums is offered in chapters by Timothy Pettipiece and Monika Pesthy-Simon. Pettipiece examines the rise of theologies in the second century CE that focused on metaphysical explanations for evil rather than the human will as the source. Such "gnostic" theologies inextricably linked evil with their cosmogonic understandings, and address the question of Christian indebtedness to Judaism. They subverted the traditional Judaic notion of a benign creator God, and instead saw the creator, or Demiurge, as an impostor who conspired to prevent humans from acquiring knowledge of the true God hidden in the divine realm beyond the cosmos. This malevolent Demiurge, as he was often called, was said to be the product of a disastrous degeneration of divine being, and the world that he fashioned, including human beings themselves, was seen as deficient if not outright evil. Pettipiece traces this movement to place the responsibility for sin and evil on humanity and not the deity or his creation. It comes at a crucial time for the early Christian movement. In the second century Christianity was increasingly coming to the attention of Roman authorities, which accused Christians of abandoning the ways of their ancestors. As a counter to this claim Christians sought to maintain a link to their Jewish heritage, and especially its scriptures. They put forward a new way to solve the problem of evil, one which exonerated divinity and implicated humanity, and as a result one that made sin and evil not a matter of nature but of will.

Despite recognizing the inherent problem in the definition and scope of the term "Christian Apocrypha," Pesthy-Simon underlines how important a source they are, forming as they do a unique witness to early

Christian literature. She focuses on texts from the second and third centuries, a period constituting the transition between the New Testament and the development of systematic patristic thought. While there is no specific notion of the Evil Inclination, there are some notable passages describing how evil operates in the world. She examines such passages from the Acts of Andrew, the Acts of Peter, the Acts of Thomas, and the Apocalypse of Paul. In most cases there appear to be parallel developments in ideas rather than direct connections with rabbinic notions. If, as Rosen-Zvi argues, the rabbinic *yeṣer* is a phenomenon that is part of a wider development in the placing of demons inside the human psyche, the Apocryphal literature is not fully aligned with such a development. Satan or demons are not yet fully internalized: the enemy remains external, though able to act inside the human being to instigate him to sin from within. A passage in the Acts of Thomas found only in the Syriac version comes the closest to the description of the Amoraic *yeṣer* (*Acts Thom.* 34,1a–f), including as it does sexual transgression. Its origins in East Syria would have allowed for influence from Jewish sources.

A volume considering the influence of Jewish concepts on the emergence of Christian ideas could hardly neglect Origen, who is well known for his (often quite detailed) familiarity with Jewish interpretations of Scripture and for his direct contacts with Jews in Alexandria and Caesarea. Riemer Roukema takes on this task, reconstructing Origen's views on the origin of sin and the human proclivity to evil, principally on the basis of his systematic exposition of the Christian faith, *On First Principles*. Roukema argues that Origen took the view that God had first created creatures that were both spiritual and rational; later these fell away from God as a result of negligence and became attached to material human bodies (a view for which he was later anathematized), with the result that the soul now finds itself between the spirit and the flesh, and can orient itself to either of them. There is certainly a prima facie resemblance to the rabbinic concept of the two *yeṣarim*. Yet as Roukema shows it is Plato, Paul, and to a lesser extent Philo and the Gospels, that provided the basis of Origen's anthropology, not nascent rabbinic models.

Equally essential to any discussion concerned with the overlap of Jewish and Christian traditions in Late Antiquity is Jerome. Robert Hayward carefully combs through the fine detail of the Vulgate to bring to light Jerome's understanding of the word *yeṣer*. Hayward delves into Jerome's commentaries and the works of his contemporaries, both Jewish and Christian, as well as the other ancient translations (Septuagint, Aquila, Symmachus, etc.) in order to demonstrate how Jerome wrestled with the Hebrew text in order to bring out its *sensus*: Jerome's is no mechanical translation, but a diligent and skillful work of philology and exegesis. Although the genre precludes a systematic presentation of the concept, Hayward is able to show that Jerome places the word *yeṣer* primarily in the semantic domain of human meditation and thinking, though he also connects it with human volition and, on one occasion, with idolatry. The possibility that some of Jerome's thinking was shaped by direct engagement with Jewish conversation partners is an important result. It certainly suggests that, were the massive task of sifting Jerome's other writings for evidence of the *yeṣer* to be undertaken, this could well turn up further exciting results.

Important and unexpected results are brought to light by Augustine Casiday, in his study of Jerome's contemporary, Evagrius Ponticus. Casiday analyzes Evagrius' concept of the eight *logismoi.* He develops and qualifies Antoine Guillaumont's radical argument, in his 1971 edition of Evagrius' *Praktikos*, that the doctrine of *logismoi* should be compared not to Greek philosophy (where *logismos* has only positive meanings), but to the biblical and post-biblical concepts of *yeṣarim* (along with concepts of penetrating demons, as developed by Christian predecessors such as Origen and Anthony). The author builds on his previous studies of Evagrius, arguing for his deep interest, mostly unacknowledged by scholarship, in Hebrew language and Jewish practices. Casiday develops and sharpens similarities and differences between Evagrius' *logismoi* and rabbinic *yeṣer* suggested by Rosen-Zvi. For Evagrius, unlike the early rabbis, the *logismoi* are not inherently evil, but neutral, and even, in and of themselves, good, before being taken over by demonic forces. Casiday's nuanced and critical return to Guillaumont's thesis demands no less than a reevaluation of the relationships between Jewish and Christian anthropologies in Late Antiquity.

The thought of Origen (perhaps also Evagrius) may well have left its mark in the writings of Augustine, whom Sophie Lunn-Rockliffe examines in her contribution. Unlike his famous account of "original sin," Augustine's narration of the individual, personal sins is much more conflicted and ambiguous. These two spheres are for him both separated and causally connected, on the grounds that original sin had had various weakening effects on post-lapsarian humans. Lunn-Rockliffe narrates the various accounts in Augustine of personal sins, concentrating on the place of demonology in them, in particular Augustine's claim that emotions could be stirred up by demons. Augustine combines Stoic language with biblical stories (Adam and Eve, Judas), in an attempt to account for the diabolic side of sinfulness without however compromising human agency. Lunn-Rockliffe locates Augustine's different explanations in their polemical contexts: first with Manicheism and then with Pelagianism. Against the former, he was keen to repudiate anything reminiscent of Manichean anthropology, which suggested that from the moment of his creation there had been something rotten in the matter of humanity. Against the latter, he stressed that Adam and Eve's sin did indeed affect humans by weakening their ability to will the good, and thus they are in a constant need of God's grace. The combination of these two contexts leads to his dialectical and conflicted account. Lastly, Lunn-Rockliffe compares Augustine's solution to the rabbinic *yeṣer*, uncovering both similarities and differences between the two solutions, to the shared problem of human sinfulness and its psychological and demonological origins.

The examination of Christian sources is completed by the contribution of David Taylor, who examines Syriac sources ranging chronologically from the second century to the medieval period. Taylor focuses in his study on the term *yaṣrā* (a Syriac translation equivalent for Hebrew *yeṣer*) in early Syriac Christian literature. He begins his analysis with the Peshitta, which played a key role in establishing the early Syriac understanding of *yaṣrā*, arguing that in the Peshitta *yaṣrā* functions as a technical term borrowed from Jewish anthropology. Taylor's broad survey of Syriac sources shows that the term was rapidly taken up in the Syriac tradition and, with a few exceptions, is found in almost all early Syriac writers. Taylor goes on to discuss the use of *yaṣrā* in a selection of important early Syriac writers (e.g. Aphrahat, Ephrem). He pays particular attention to the works of the poet and theologian Narsai, for whom *yaṣrā* was a key anthropological and philosophical concept, reflecting a particular interest in the term among writers of the Church of the East. Taylor shows that, in contrast to medieval sources in which the *yaṣrā* was normally treated as an author of evil, the earliest Syriac texts generally regard the *yaṣrā* as morally neutral. Yet, although the *yaṣrā* is capable of inspiring both good and bad behavior, it more commonly provokes the bad. The *yaṣrā* therefore is something with which human free will must wrestle; like the rabbinic *yeṣer*, it can ultimately be controlled and defeated. Of particular importance in the context of this volume is Taylor's conclusion that, while the Syriac texts reflect a distinctive development within the context of Christian exegesis and theology, there are many striking points of contact with post-biblical Jewish thought.

Taylor's contribution dovetails perfectly with that of Ophir Münz-Manor, who examines a group of liturgical poems written in Hebrew,

Jewish Aramaic, and Syriac, which focus on the issue of human accountability for sinning. It concentrates on one specific genre: the debate between body and soul after death. This is the first English translation of the Jewish poems of this genre, discovered and published only recently. The poems, Jewish and Christian alike, share the same verdict: both body and soul are responsible for sins, and both should be punished. Münz-Manor uses these poems to uncover the proximity of Jewish and Eastern Christian liturgies, as well as the plurality of anthropologies available to Jews and Christians in Late Antiquity. An additional contested issue discussed by the author is the relationship of *piyyut* to Midrash. In a departure from the common scholarly attitude, Münz-Manor argues for a reciprocal relationship in which liturgy affects Midrash, rather than just being affected by it. The author offers a new method of reading *piyyut* in the context of both Late Antique liturgy and rabbinic literature. Lastly, Münz-Manor analyzes a few poems written for the Day of Atonement that mention the evil *yeṣer*. While the presentation of the *yeṣer* is pretty similar to that found in rabbinic literature, it is surprising to find how marginal the *yeṣer* is in *piyyut*. The differences come not only from the different genres, but also the variegated audience. Unlike Midrash, which is formed inside the study hall, the presentation of these topics in contemporary liturgical poems were aimed at a much more diverse audience. This may also explain their special receptivity to non-Jewish materials.

Further important new contributions to our understanding of the *yeṣer* in Jewish literature from Late Antiquity and beyond are made in the chapters of Yishai Kiel and Leeor Gottlieb, both of whom are concerned – in quite different ways – with conceptions of the *yeṣer* in classical rabbinic sources. Kiel discusses the possible impact of Iranian culture on Babylonian rabbinic representations of the *yeṣer*. He argues that the distinctly Babylonian rabbinic constructions of the *yeṣer* may be partially explained in light of Zoroastrian and Manichean portrayals of the demon Āz. Just like the *yeṣer*, an amalgamation of human inclination with demonological traits, the Persian Āz is a psycho-demonic embodiment of human desire, which assumes cosmic dimensions. After comparing phenomenologically rabbinic *yeṣer* discourse and Iranian demonology, Kiel reads one cryptic Talmudic story on the imprisonment of the *yeṣer* (b. Yoma 69b, b. Sanh. 64a) in light of Persian accounts of the imprisonment and final defeat of Āz at the end of days. Kiel shows that the parallel Zoroastrian tradition sheds light on various unique details in the story (the image of the *yeṣer* as a fiery lion cub emerging from the Holy of Holies; the note that fell from heaven with the word "truth" inscribed on it; the imprisonment of the *yeṣer* in a cauldron sealed with metal and the setting of fire under it). More generally, as a reified sexual desire, Āz gives new context to one of the main novelties of the *yeṣer* in the Bavli – its unequivocal sexualization.

While the Targums to the Writings (*ketuvim*) do not themselves belong in the classical rabbinic corpus, Gottlieb demonstrated that they have nonetheless borrowed directly from concepts found therein. The Targums to the Writings are a heterogeneous group of texts that were completed at a relatively late date (some even close to the turn of the second millennium). Gottlieb's analysis found that most of these Targums make no mention of the *yeṣer* at all: the Targums to Psalms, Ecclesiastes, and Chronicles contain twenty-eight of the twenty-nine occurrences. These present an eclectic array of characterizations of the *yeṣer:* as an antagonist of humans, inflamer of sexual appetites, and enticer to sin. The *yeṣer* resides in the heart in some of these Targums and needs to be subdued (or "slaughtered like a sacrifice"). We even find the Good and Evil Inclinations locked in battle in Targum Ecclesiastes. In almost all cases the term is not used as a formal equivalent of the word *yeṣer* in the underlying Hebrew verse. Rather, these Targums imported existing rabbinic concepts and embedded them in their expansive Aramaic translations, sometimes reflecting post-Amoraic concepts of the *yeṣer* and even reworking Talmudic material. As Gottlieb nicely puts it the Targums to the Writings "functioned not as heralds, but rather as echoes." One might anticipate similar results for Targum Pseudo-Jonathan (a study of *yeṣer* in Targum Pseudo-Jonathan still waits to be done).

2

# *Reconsidering the Semantics of the "Inclination"* (yeṣer) *in Classical Biblical Hebrew*

Noam Mizrahi

## 1 INTRODUCTION

It is widely acknowledged that the far-reaching development of *yeṣer* as a theological and anthropological concept has little to do with the use of this word in the Hebrew Bible. Still, it is often asserted that the link between the biblical employment of *yeṣer* and its demonized hypostases in later literature is anchored in a semantic change that took place already in Biblical Hebrew (BH). Following earlier Bible scholars,[1] Ishay Rosen-Zvi has recently summarized the scholarly consensus at the opening of his comprehensive study, *Demonic Desires*:[2] "The root יצר [...] denotes [in the Hebrew Bible] the creating, fashioning, and designing of objects (mostly made of clay). ... The noun indicates the result of this craft: an object or a creature (Hab 2:18). By extension, it also includes the things created in or by the mind, such as thoughts, devices, and inclinations." While the latter, metaphorical usage is admitted to be relatively rare, being attested in only six passages,[3] it supplies the background for the portrayal of *yeṣer* as evil in two passages concerning the Deluge, where they appear to refer to the human mental faculty: the phrase כָּל יֵצֶר מַחְשְׁבֹת לִבּוֹ (Gen 6:5) is thus rendered as "every *plan* devised by his mind" and יֵצֶר לֵב הָאָדָם (Gen 8:21) is similarly translated by "the *devisings* of man's mind." Rosen-Zvi

[1] Especially the entry of Otzen 1990 (with previous literature). Among previous surveys, noteworthy is the systematic exposition of Humbert 1958. See further below, n. 6.

[2] Rosen-Zvi 2011, 3 (with notes on pp. 135–36). Cf. Hadot 1970, 65–74; Anat 1980, 217–18.

[3] Gen 6:5, 8:21; Deut 31:21; Ps 103:14; 1 Chr 28:9, 29:18. (English translation follows the NRSV, often with significant modification; references follow the order and enumeration of the Hebrew text.)

notes that: "Taken alone, the word *yetzer* in these two verses might denote 'what is created,' and thus they might be read as saying simply that 'every *product* of the thought of man's mind' is evil. Other verses (e.g., Deut 31:21 and Ps 103:14), however, indicate a more developed meaning: human thoughts, plans, imagination, or even dispositions and tendencies." These observations reflect the widespread assumption that the term *yeṣer*, at least as employed in the aforementioned passages, practically belongs to the semantic domain of the human mind, and that it may accordingly be rendered as "thought, scheme, plan, purpose," and the like.

Notwithstanding that few if any biblical scholars will disagree with this view, my purpose in the present chapter is to ask: is it necessarily so? Arguably, although the semantics of the verb *y-ṣ-r*, as well as that of its nominal derivative *yeṣer*, were previously studied both meticulously and insightfully, a few significant nuances of their usage were not fully appreciated. To put it provocatively, the dynamic development of the post-biblical notion of יצר הרע, or the Evil Inclination, depends, at least to some extent, on a seemingly slight – but semantically significant and ideologically decisive – misreading of the biblical sources (especially of the Flood story), which has had sweeping consequences as far as the history of this idea is concerned.

From a theoretical point of view, close reading of the biblical texts, on their own terms, suggests that the common understanding of BH *yeṣer* does not take into sufficient account the recognition of modern semantics that words are not to be treated as isolated concepts explicable on the sole basis of their immediate contexts. In natural languages, words seldom have single meanings; more often they display a semantic range, and their usage is significantly conditioned by a complex set of both linguistic and paralinguistic variables, including contextual and pragmatic factors. Moreover, language is an aspect of a broader cultural matrix, which may manifest itself even in very particular niceties of usage and turns of phrases.

It is important to recall, in this context, the standard semantic distinction between the "sense" of a word (or expression) and its "reference." Sense is a lexical property, which depends on the relation to other vocables that can be compared to (or contrasted with) the vocable under scrutiny. Reference, by contrast, is an indexical property, which relates to the identification of a given entity in the broader context (which is not necessarily only linguistic). Thus a single lexeme may be used to indicate different referents, depending on the context; while a referent can be referred to by a whole range of various lexemes.[4] The relationship between the lexical meaning and the referential one is intricate, and requires sustained scholarly attention.

Obviously, when dealing with the language of a dead civilization, such as BH, we have no access to the full range of cultural reverberations of each and every word used in the texts handed down to us. Nor can we be certain of the actual referents of numerous expressions, even if their sense can be fairly easily defined. Nevertheless, our interpretation of individual lexemes in given contexts is significantly amplified by unfolding of the rhetorical strategies of the contexts into which such words were integrated, and close attention should also be given to the tracing of the literary traditions that form the background of particular texts. An integrative approach can help us approximate the range of meanings that each such word might have had for native speakers of ancient Hebrew.

A final word of introduction needs to be said on the corpus to be examined. In my judgment, there are significant differences in the use of the lexeme between Classical and Late Biblical Hebrew, that is, pre- and post-exilic varieties of the language (CBH and LBH, respectively), and they should be carefully distinguished from one another. This chapter focuses on the early variety, thus largely excluding passages from Chronicles, Sirach, and the Qumran scrolls. On the other hand, despite numerous attempts by literary-historical critics to argue for a late, post-exilic date for most Pentateuchal texts, their language is by and large Classical; Genesis and Deuteronomy are therefore included in the present analysis. As far as the semantics of *yeṣer* is concerned, texts produced in the transitional, exilic period (especially Deutero-Isaiah) usually display essential continuity with respect to the classical language, so they are integrated into the first part of the following discussion.[5]

Although the general range of uses of *y-ṣ-r* and *yeṣer* has been described time and again in the past, it is necessary to begin with an outline of what might be called the standard usages of these words. This brief overview does not intend to be exhaustive or replace existing surveys, but rather to highlight those nuances that are pertinent for the present analysis (§2).[6] The discussion then moves to consider several passages that belong to the corpus of Classical Biblical Hebrew (CBH) and allegedly employ the term

[4] See Lyons 1977, 1: 174–229. [5] But see below, n. 21.

[6] In addition to previous studies already mentioned, see also de Liagre Böhl and Brongers 1975–78, 92–97; their discussion places the verb יצר within the context of its semantic domain, alongside other verbs such as עשה, ברא, etc.

in a different, broadened or extended, abstract sense. Particular attention shall be paid to the passages from Deuteronomy (§3) and Genesis (§4), with an additional short excursus on Jeremiah (§5), as these are the most conspicuous examples for the "psychologized" or "internalized" usage of the term *yeṣer* within CBH.

## 2 OVERVIEW OF PRIMARY USAGES

**2.1** Both the noun *yeṣer* and the related verb *y-ṣ-r* denote the forming or shaping of ceramic vessels, and are thus part of technical terminology from the realm of the arts and crafts.[7] This is most evident in the famous descriptive passage of Jeremiah 18:

> 1 The word that came to Jeremiah from the LORD: 2 "Come, go down to the *potter*'s house (בֵּית הַיּוֹצֵר), and there I will let you hear my words." 3 So I went down to the *potter*'s house (בֵּית הַיּוֹצֵר), and there he was *working* (עֹשֶׂה מְלָאכָה) at his wheel. 4 The vessel he was making of *clay* (בַּחֹמֶר) was spoiled in the *potter*'s hand (הַיּוֹצֵר בְּיָד), and he *reworked* it (וַיַּעֲשֵׂהוּ) into another vessel, as seemed good to him to *make* (לַעֲשׂוֹת).

The form יוֹצֵר, an active participle of the verb *y-ṣ-r*, is clearly used here as technical term denoting a professional potter.[8] His workshop is accordingly termed בֵּית הַיּוֹצֵר "the house (or place) of the potter" (vv. 2a, 3a). But the verb denoting his actual work can also be עָשָׂה, which usually has the more general sense "to make" (vv. 3b, 4). The typical product is termed כְּלִי "vessel" (v. 4),[9] and it is made of חֹמֶר "clay" (v. 4a). Since the latter term is often collocated with עָפָר (Job 4:9, 10:9, 27:16, 30:19), it apparently denotes mud derived from the earth (cf. Isa 41:25).

**2.2** These terms form a phraseological complex, which is often employed, wholly or partly, in numerous other passages that allude to the notion of the potter and his handiwork. They often do so as a rhetorical device aiming at demonstrating a theological stance. The most

7 Cf. Kelso 1948, 6–9.

8 For the evidence, see Otzen 1990, 258; Huehnergard 2008, 134. That the technical usage indeed reflects the primary meaning of the verb – and not a secondary narrowing of a broader sense such as "to form, shape, create" – is confirmed by comparative evidence from related Semitic languages of the third and second millennium BCE, such as Ugaritic and Eblaite, in which one finds cognate forms of *yoṣer* in the sense of "potter."

9 The phrase כְּלִי יוֹצֵר (2 Sam 17:28; Ps 2:9; cf. נֵבֶל יוֹצְרִים in Isa 30:14) literally translates as the "potter's vessel," but it is an idiomatic expression denoting ceramic vessels. This expression thus connotes the fragile nature of the objects so termed, as suggested by the verbs that collocate with it (נפץ "shatter" in Ps 2:9; cf. שבר "break" and כתת "smash" in Isa 30:14).

common use of this kind is by equating the relation between the potter and his products to that between God and his creation in general or the people of Israel in particular. Thus in Deutero-Isaiah (Isa 45:9): "Woe to the one who quarrels with his Maker (or better: potter, יֹצְרוֹ), an earthenware vessel (חֶרֶשׂ) among the vessels of earth; Will the clay say to its potter (לְיֹצְרוֹ) what you (i.e. he) should be making (מַה תַּעֲשֶׂה)?!"[10]

2.3 An additional depiction of a dialogue between the human vessel and the divine potter, similar to that of Isa 45:9, is to be found in another prophetic passage, Isa 29:16: "You turn things upside down! Shall the potter (הַיֹּצֵר) be regarded as the clay? Shall the thing made (מַעֲשֶׂה) say of its maker (לְעֹשֵׂהוּ), 'He did not make me'; or the thing formed (וְיֵצֶר) say of the one who formed it (לְיֹצְרוֹ), 'He has no understanding'?"

This passage makes use of the terminology surveyed above: the potter is termed יֹצֵר, his material is חֹמֶר "clay," and the verb that denotes the making of the vessels is עשה (cf. Isa 64:7). At the same time, the potter's product is denoted by two additional words that are evidently related to the verbs we have encountered. From the verb עשה we get the verbal noun מַעֲשֶׂה, which can function as a *nomen actionis* "making"; but like all nouns of this type it may also denote the result of the action, that is, "the thing made." Similarly, the noun יֵצֶר is evidently a *nomen actionis* of the verb יצר,[11] and it too denotes the result of the action and is properly rendered by "the thing formed." Both מַעֲשֶׂה and יֵצֶר thus signify earthenware created by the potter.[12] Contextually, however, these concrete objects are to be taken

[10] In such contexts, the image of the potter and the vessels he produces may be linked to another image, that of a parent and children. Thus the Deutero-Isaianic passage quoted above continues immediately with the related, parental image (v. 10), and then amalgamates both of them (v. 11).

[11] For the *qétɛl* pattern (originating in **qitl*) see Bauer and Leander 1922, 460, §61*f*″. This usage also supplies adequate explanation for Ps 103:14 (among the six passages allegedly demonstrating the "psychologized" use of יֵצֶר; cf. above, n. 3). The term יֵצֶר in this passage has nothing to do with "planning, devising," but should be interpreted in the light of the explicit mention of עָפָר in the parallel hemistich, both evidently referring to the divine potter's making of living creatures. Thus, the medieval commentator Isaiah of Trani rightly renders the biblical form יֵצֶר by the more transparent verbal noun יצירה (*Mikra'ot Gedolot "Haketer": Psalms*, ed. Cohen 2003, 2: 103). Contextually, as far as its reference is concerned, this noun apparently refers to the human body (as was suggested to me by Dr. Leeor Gottlieb, following the oral presentation on which this chapter is based).

[12] The clauses וְיֵצֶר אָמַר לְיֹצְרוֹ and יֹאמַר מַעֲשֶׂה לְעֹשֵׂהוּ of Isa 29:16 parallel הֲיֹאמַר חֹמֶר לְיֹצְרוֹ of Isa 45:9 (discussed above), demonstrating the material essence (i.e. the clay) from which the product (i.e. the יֵצֶר or מַעֲשֶׂה) is composed. Cohen Stuart 1984, 100, has noted a telling variant reading attested in 1QIsa[a] for Isa 29:16: while the MT reads וְיֵצֶר אָמַר לְיֹצְרוֹ לֹא הֵבִין, 1QIsa[a] reads ויצר חמר ליוצריו לוא הבין. The words יצר חמר were evidently read as a construct phrase, "a product of clay" – an expression that becomes very common in the sectarian

metaphorically as referring to humans, who were created by God but now dare to deny their origin and ignore God's authority over them.

**2.4** Another usage that deserves attention in this passage is the verbal phrase לֹא הֵבִין "he has no understanding," presented as the argument made by the *yeṣer* against the potter, its *yoṣer* (cf. Ps 33:15). Like עשה, the verb הבין is of a general sense, and it is used in BH in a variety of contexts. Yet again, like עשה, when used in conjunction with other terms that belong to the phraseological domain of the arts and crafts, it has a more specific sense, referring not to "understanding" things in general but rather to the noticeable expertise of the artisan's work.[13]

This specialized sense is not unique to הבין. It can be found with respect to another, very common verb of mental perception, namely, חשב. While in most occurrences the verb and its derivatives, especially מַחֲשָׁבָה, denote "thinking, accounting, planning, devising," etc., in several passages they clearly function as technical terms that refer to concrete objects, skillfully produced by expert artisans.[14] The clearest examples come from Priestly texts that prescribe the manufacturing of cultic objects.[15] Thus the chief artisan Bezalel is described as having been granted a divine spirit of wisdom so that he would be able "to *produce dexterous works* (לַחְשֹׁב מַחֲשָׁבֹת), to *skillfully work* (לַעֲשׂוֹת) in gold, and in silver, and in brass" (Exod 31:4; cf. 35:32), and the list of artisans includes the active participle חֹשֵׁב as well (Exod 35:35; cf. 38:23): "to work all manner of work, of the *engraver* (חָרָשׁ), and of the *dexterous workman* (חֹשֵׁב), and of the embroiderer, in blue, and in purple, in scarlet, and in fine linen, and of the weaver, even of them that do any work, and of *those that produce dexterous artisanal work* (חֹשְׁבֵי מַחֲשָׁבֹת)." As such, it is also integrated into the standard phrase מַעֲשֵׂה

work *Hodayot* (e.g. 1QH$^a$ ix 23 [Suk. 1:21]: ואני יצר החמר ומגבל המים, "I am but a product of clay and kneaded with water"). It appears, however, that it originates in a scribal mistake: MT's אמר was replaced by 1QIsa$^a$'s חמר due to the weakening of the guttural consonants in Qumran Hebrew; see Kutscher 1974, 505–06.

[13] Cf. the designation of the professional singers among the Levites as כָּל מֵבִין בִּכְלֵי שִׁיר (2 Chr 34:12; cf. 1 Chr 25:7).

[14] Cf. BDB, 363, s.v. חשב *qal* I.5. The NRSV often represents חשב by the adjective "cunning" (e.g. Exod 31:4, לַחְשֹׁב מַחֲשָׁבֹת "to devise cunning works"), but such a rendition may carry a negative connotation, suggesting deceptiveness and trickery. On the semantics of חשב see Saydon 2010, 2013, 89–100.

[15] Although such occurrences are witnessed mostly by P, they are to be regarded as part and parcel of CBH; cf. Amos 6:5, "those who improvise on the harp, like David, have *skillfully produced* (חָשְׁבוּ) musical instruments for themselves" (cf. n. 13). In 2 Chr 26:14–15 the phrase חִשְּׁבֹנוֹת מַחֲשֶׁבֶת חוֹשֵׁב appears to refer to sophisticated weaponry devised by King Uzziah.

חֹשֵׁב "an artisan's workmanship."[16] This expression, incidentally, also exemplifies the specialized use of the term מַעֲשֶׂה.

**2.5** The depiction of God as a potter (*yoṣer*) and of Israel – or humans in general – as an earthenware (*yeṣer*) is a common trope in biblical poetic diction, from prophetic to hymnal contexts. It should be noted, though, that while *y-ṣ-r* primarily denotes the work of the potter, its semantic scope eventually extended to include skillful work performed by artisans of other types. This is most clear in a passage of Deutero-Isaiah that describes the artisan (in charge of producing a cult image – that is, an idol) as making use of hammers – evidently not the typical tool utilized by potters but rather by smiths (Isa 44:12): "The ironsmith fashions it and works it over the coals, *shaping it with hammers* (וּבַמַּקָּבוֹת יִצְּרֵהוּ) and forging it with his strong arm." Earlier in the same context (Isa 44:10), the verb *y-ṣ-r* is juxtaposed to *n-s-k* "to cast," suggesting that the former refers again to the work of an ironsmith:[17] "Who would *fashion* (יָצַר) a god or *cast* (נָסָךְ) an image that can do no good?"

Furthermore, the depiction of God as a potter was gradually becoming a dead metaphor. The verb *y-ṣ-r* was eventually joined by other terms that refer to God's creative power, thus losing its distinct, technical sense and gradually broadening its meaning to "create" or "make" in general.[18] This semantic change is particularly evident when the object of the verb is something that is not easily likened to any ceramic product, as in Isa 45:7:[19]

[16] Exod 26:1, 31; 28:6, 15; 36:8, 35; 39:3, 8. Cf. מַעֲשֵׂה רֹקֵם "an embroiderer's workmanship" (Exod 26:36; 27:16; 28:39; 36:36; 38:18; 39:29), מַעֲשֵׂה אֹרֵג "a weaver's workmanship" (Exod 28:32; 39:22, 27), and מַעֲשֵׂה רֹקֵחַ "a perfumer's workmanship" (Exod 30:25, 35; 37:29). And again, although such phrases are attested mainly in P, they are not specifically Priestly; cf. מַעֲשֵׂה אֹפֶה "a baker's workmanship," i.e. pastries (Gen 40:17).

[17] It is reasonable to similarly interpret the term יֹצְרֵי פֶסֶל "those who fashion idols," used earlier in the same context (Isa 44:9; cf. Hab 2:18). Yet, if taken in isolation, this expression may also refer to potters who create ceramic figurines: cf. Isa 54:17.

[18] Isa 43:7, 10; 45:18; Ps 94:9, 20. Cf. Ps 104:26, "and Leviathan that you *created* (יָצַרְתָּ) to sport in it"; *y-ṣ-r* in this context is best interpreted in light of the preceding v. 24, which employs synonymous terms for things created derived from the verbs עשה and קנה that are often used in contexts of creation.

[19] Perhaps one can say that in such cases the specific member of the word-pair (i.e. the B-word יצר) has undergone a process of semantic broadening, motivated by assimilation to its counterpart of a general sense (i.e. the A-word עשה). The loss of specificity seems to be interconnected to the change in word order: Isa 45:7 is the only passage in which יצר takes the position of the A-word; this is a direct result of its function as a general rather than a specific term.

> I *form light* (יוֹצֵר אוֹר) and create darkness,
> I *make weal* (עֹשֶׂה שָׁלוֹם) and create woe;
> I the LORD do all these things.

Accordingly, the noun *yeṣer* can also refer to various things made or produced, from earthenware to living creatures and human beings.[20]

The above outline of the semantics of *y-ṣ-r* in Classical and transitional BH is far from exhaustive, but it should suffice to illustrate the typical phraseology, which is essentially drawn from the realm of artisanal work. The verb *y-ṣ-r* and its derivatives primarily denote the production of ceramics by a potter. This usage expanded to encompass first other types of artisanal work and secondarily "making" in general, particularly in contexts that refer to God's creation of the world.[21] The examples adduced above also illustrate the semantic link with verbs of mental perception, such as חשב and הבין. These facts allow us to move forward and review the key passages in which it was argued that the noun *yeṣer* refers to abstract plans, purposes, or human inclinations, and especially passages that appear to assert the inherent inclination of humans toward sin.

## 3 DEUTERONOMY 31:21

3.1 One such passage is Deut 31:21: "For I know its (i.e. the people's) *yeṣer*, which it commits even now (אֶת יִצְרוֹ אֲשֶׁר הוּא עֹשֶׂה), before I have brought them into the land that I promised them on oath." The NRSV renders the phrase יִצְרוֹ אֲשֶׁר הוּא עֹשֶׂה by "what they are inclined to do," but such a rendition faces both linguistic difficulties (see §3.2) and exegetical incongruities (§3.3).

[20] This broadened sense fits well the expression יֵצֶר סָמוּךְ (Isa 26:3). This interpretation is confirmed by its usage in the Qumran scrolls, as demonstrated by Qimron 1995, 314–15, §I.

[21] Most examples are found in Deutero-Isaiah – that is, in an exilic work whose language is placed between CBH and LBH. But because of the paucity of evidence, it is not safe to conclude that the process must be situated chronologically in the exilic period. In any case, it was internally motivated and there is no need to assume here an influence from languages with which Hebrew was in contact during the exilic period. There are some grounds for suspecting that the narrow senses of *y-ṣ-r* were rendered obsolete in LBH. Note, for instance, that the Chronicler replaces ויצר of 1 Kgs 7:15 with the more general וַיַּעַשׂ in 2 Chr 3:15; the former is vocalized in the MT as √ צור > וַיָּצַר, but apparently it was read by the Chronicler as √ יצר > וַיִּצֶר.

3.2 Before anything else, one must translate the phrase in a way that does justice to its syntax. It consists of a noun (יֵצֶר) modified by a relative clause, which consists of a pronoun (הוּא) plus an active participle (עֹשֶׂה). In BH the predicative participle encodes a durative aspect, and in terms of the Information Structure of the text, the construction employed here is a normal way of supplying background information, inserted at strategic points into the main chain of events.[22] In all comparable cases there is a clear and simple relation between the noun and its clausal modifier: the subordinated verbal clause denotes an action that is ordinarily and habitually being done with respect to the modified noun.[23]

The exact relationship between the noun and its clausal modifier in our case is best perceived when compared to a parallel passage, which utilizes a virtually identical relative clause. Tellingly, this is none other than Jeremiah's depiction of the potter at his workshop:

| | | | | | |
|---|---|---|---|---|---|
| Deut 31:21 | הַיּוֹם | עֹשֶׂה | הוּא | אֲשֶׁר | יִצְרוֹ |
| Jer 18:4 | בַּחֹמֶר | עֹשֶׂה | הוּא | אֲשֶׁר | הַכְּלִי |

The wording of the relative clause in both passages is virtually identical, suggesting that the *yeṣer* of Deut 31:21 precisely corresponds to the "vessel" of Jer 18:4. In both cases, the noun (יֵצֶר or כְּלִי) functions as the direct object of the verb employed within the relative clause (עֹשֶׂה). If so, the term *yeṣer* refers to something concrete, a thing made or in the process of being produced at the time of the divine speech.

The abstract notion of "inclination" or "purpose" does not fit into this context. The actual referent of the word is to be sought among other things that the context unambiguously identifies as being made by the same agent, namely, the people of Israel. These things are, of course, nothing but transgressions, which are enumerated in two parallel lists: one describing the Israelites' sins to be committed immediately upon Moses' death (v. 16), and the other listing the sins that they shall commit even after God fulfills his part of the covenant and brings them to the Promised Land (v. 20).

22 See, e.g., Joosten 2012, 245.

23 See, e.g., Gen 39:6, הַלֶּחֶם אֲשֶׁר הוּא אוֹכֵל, "the food that he ate" (i.e. his daily meals); Exod 18:5, הַמִּדְבָּר אֲשֶׁר הוּא חֹנֶה שָׁם, "wilderness where he (i.e. Moses) was encamped"; Num 13:19, וּמָה הָאָרֶץ אֲשֶׁר־הוּא יֹשֵׁב בָּהּ ... וּמָה הֶעָרִים אֲשֶׁר הוּא יוֹשֵׁב בָּהֵנָּה הַבְּמַחֲנִים אִם בְּמִבְצָרִים, "and whether the land that they live in and the towns that they live in are unwalled or fortified."

Despite their different formulation, both lists essentially contain the same three major offenses, which are logically interconnected as successive stages of exhibiting disloyalty, on the part of Israel, toward her divine partner.

(a) Considering alternative deities, and then straying after them:

v. 16: וְקָם הָעָם הַזֶּה וְזָנָה אַחֲרֵי אֱלֹהֵי נֵכַר הָאָרֶץ אֲשֶׁר הוּא בָא שָׁמָּה בְּקִרְבּוֹ, "This people will begin to prostitute themselves to the foreign gods in their midst, the gods of the land into which they are going."
v. 20: וּפָנָה אֶל אֱלֹהִים אֲחֵרִים וַעֲבָדוּם, "They will turn to other gods and serve them."

(b) Leaving behind the original partner, God, thus effectively rebelling against him:

v. 16: וַעֲזָבַנִי, "They will forsake me."
v. 20: וְנִאֲצוּנִי, "They will despise me."

(c) The final breaking of the legally binding covenant with God:

v. 16: וְהֵפֵר אֶת בְּרִיתִי אֲשֶׁר כָּרַתִּי אִתּוֹ, "They will break my covenant that I have made with them."
v. 20: וְהֵפֵר אֶת בְּרִיתִי, "They will break my covenant."

Significantly, both lists vary in their wording of the first and second stages but are practically identical with respect to the third (וְהֵפֵר אֶת בְּרִיתִי). This is a discursive strategy, which highlights the last element and marks it as the most crucial item of all, most probably because of its legal implication of finality. Since this is the single most important offense mentioned in this Deuteronomic paragraph, it is not unreasonable to propose that this is also the reference of the direct object of the verb עֹשֶׂה in the immediately following v. 21. In context, then, the term *yeṣer* most probably refers to the breaking of the covenant, which is presented as being done continually or habitually by the disloyal people of Israel.

If this interpretation is correct, then the employment of the pottery phraseology (namely, the use of the noun יֵצֶר accompanied by the verb עשה) might well be interpreted as a rhetorical device that underscores the irony inherent in the people's actions. The literal sense of עשה יֵצֶר is "to produce earthenware," but according to Deut 31:21 the only thing that the Israelites normally produce is not constructive but destructive: rather than forging their covenant with God, they break it.

Interestingly, this argument makes use of *p-r-r*, which can also be said of the shaking and collapsing of the earth.[24] A comparable word-play is at

[24] Note, however, that *p-r-r* (literally "to split, divide") can also be used with respect to the sea (Ps 74:13).

work in the Isaiah Apocalypse, in which the description of the transgression in Isa 24:5 is matched by the corresponding punishment described further on (v. 19):

| **Isa 24:5** | **Isa 24:19** |
|---|---|
| The earth lies polluted under its inhabitants; for they have transgressed laws, violated the statutes, *broken the everlasting covenant* (הֵפֵרוּ בְּרִית עוֹלָם). | The earth is utterly broken, *the earth is torn asunder* (פּוֹר הִתְפּוֹרְרָה אֶרֶץ), the earth is violently shaken. |

3.3 This line of interpretation is further confirmed by close inspection of the exegetical problems encountered by the view that *yeṣer* is to be rendered as "inclination" or the like – problems posed by the literary characteristics of the passage in its contexts. The core of the entire paragraph in which it is embedded (Deut 31:16–22) is a legal argument, which is not concerned with psychological diagnosis but rather with assigning direct liability for actual actions.

The paragraph serves as an introduction to the Song of Moses (Deut 32).[25] It presents the Song as an incriminating piece of legal evidence to be brought, in due time, against the people of Israel. In the face of future calamities the people will complain that God has inexplicably forsaken them, but the Song shall prove that they were indeed warned in advance that such disasters would befall them – if they break their covenant with God and worship other deities. The paragraph may well be a retrospective reflection, made from a point of view subsequent to a national catastrophe. But regardless of its historical identification (which will surely remain controversial), it seems clear that the point of its argument is not to inform the reader of God's power to foretell the future, but rather to demonstrate that the legal responsibility for the pending disaster lies not with God but rather with the people. Its insistence is not at all on an abstract inclination toward sin, but rather on the actual commitment of concrete transgressions, namely, the breaking – rather than the expected forging – of the covenant.

3.4 In terms of its lexical sense, Deut 31:21 can therefore be conveniently interpreted within the usual semantic range of the verbal noun *yeṣer* without any recourse to an alleged "psychologized" or "internalized"

[25] Pentateuchal criticism has long ago recognized that Deut 31 is not a literary unity (e.g. Driver 1902, 333–44). My understanding of the passage is indebted to the analysis of Rofé 1979, 75–76.

usage, as referring to a "product of the mind, purpose, thought," etc. In terms of its contextual reference, the term *yeṣer* is applied to a patently negative action or its result (in this case, legal or contractual offenses). In Deut 31:21, then, *yeṣer* is not the cause of wrongdoing but rather its effect.

## 4 GENESIS 6:5 AND 8:21

The above conclusion enables one to reevaluate the common interpretation of the two most important passages adduced in support of the contention that *yeṣer* has shifted, already in CBH, to refer to human mental faculties, thus preparing the ground for the birth of the post-biblical Evil Inclination. Both passages, Gen 6:5 and 8:21, are part of the Flood story, which famously consists of two narrative threads, now intertwined but originally independent of one another. One of them is known to reflect Priestly phraseology and concerns, but it is universally acknowledged that the two passages that employ the word *yeṣer* belong to the other, non-Priestly component of the story, identified as J by the Documentary Hypothesis.[26]

4.1 A methodological comment is in order here. Leaving aside the ongoing debate concerning the exact degree of narrative integrity of – and continuity between – the traditions belonging to the P and J materials, it requires no particular sophistication to realize that within Genesis 1–11 (the so-called Primeval History), the two narrative strands conspicuously differ not only in style and phraseology but also in their ideological outlook. The difference most pertinent for our concern relates to their contrasting interests in nature vs. civilization. The Priestly traditions seek to establish a ritual *Gestalt* for natural phenomena – arguing, for instance, that the division of time is a natural feature ordained by God, or explaining the rainbow as a symbolic discharging of the divine weapon taken as a sign of a legally binding covenant. In contradistinction, the non-Priestly

[26] See, e.g., Skinner 1910, 147–81 (with references to earlier literature); cf. Schwartz 2007. Although it has been obvious for more than a century now that the Documentary Hypothesis does not supply a satisfactory solution for the entire range of the mysteries posed by the compositional history of the Pentateuch, the basic distinction between Priestly and non-Priestly materials is well established and commands broad consensus among critical scholars. Moreover, as far as the Flood story is concerned, the analysis of this text as being composed of two originally independent narratives remains, in my view, the most compelling philological solution for the literary complexity evident in the canonical story. For the sake of convenience, I retain the traditional designation "J" for the non-P strand of the Genesis 1–11, without necessarily implying full adherence to all strictures of the Documentary Hypothesis.

traditions supply etiological explication of human society and civilization, tracing the origins of social institutions such as intimate partnership; differentiation of communal organization into rural, nomadic, and urban ways of life; economic specialization to diverse professional occupations, and so on.[27]

One need not convert to the source-critical orthodoxy of the Documentary Hypothesis in order to admit that the J version of the Flood story is not well served by isolation from its broader narrative matrix, but is better interpreted with an eye opened to the other non-Priestly traditions of the Primeval History. Even if they do not necessarily all stem from the very same hand, some of them are clearly interrelated, and many of them evince a common conceptual outlook and a similar texture of mythological motifs that have their background in ancient Near Eastern lore.[28]

**4.2** In light of this observation, I propose that in order to properly appreciate the meanings of the term *yeṣer* in its original context, it is better to begin with another non-Priestly narrative, namely, the J account of the Creation (Gen 2:4b–3:24). Admittedly, the image of God that governs this story is that of a landlord in search of a capable gardener. However, the first scene of the drama[29] depicts God as a divine potter who fashions the first human being out of the earth (Gen 2:7):

> The LORD God *formed* (וַיִּיצֶר) man, *dust out of the ground* (עָפָר מִן הָאֲדָמָה), and breathed into his nostrils the breath of life; and man became a living soul.

In this, of course, humans were not very special; under the same capacity, God has created all the other animals (Gen 2:19):

> The Lord God *formed* (וַיִּצֶר), *out of the earth* (מִן הָאֲדָמָה), every animal of the field and every bird of the air

Evidently, this is an amplified manifestation of the same image we have already seen operative in biblical poetry (§2.2): living creatures, especially humans, are conceived as earthenware vessels that contain a breath of life;

[27] The importance of this motif in J has been aptly emphasized – albeit from a somewhat different point of view – by Westermann 1994, 56–62.

[28] See, e.g., Hess and Tsumura 1994. For the Flood story in particular cf., e.g., Noort 1998; Day 2013.

[29] As usual in Hebrew prose, the text is demarcated by means of verbal syntax; the opening exposition is marked by the use of non-preterite verbal forms (Gen 2:4b–6), whereas the proper story is marked by the use of preterite forms (Gen 2:7ff.).

as such, they owe their form and content alike to their creator, the divine potter. Here, however, the basic image is given full mythological force, matching similar traditions well entrenched in the cultures of the ancient Near East.[30]

4.3 Within the specifically mythological matrix of the non-Priestly traditions of the Primeval History, the image of the potter plays a double role, as it signifies the achievements of civilization as well as its fragility.

On the one hand, the image of the potter introduces into the early days of the world the notion of cultivated life, illustrating the benefits of expert artisanship whose role model is God himself. This theme is carried on by J's etiological accounts of the occupations of Adam's descendants, who are presented as the eponymous founders of various fields of expertise.[31]

On the other hand, the image of the potter also implies that humankind originates in lifeless earth, and its existence is thus as fragile and limited as that of earthenware. This is underscored by the curses that end the first, all-too-short episode of human existence in the Garden of Eden (Gen 3:17–19):

> [17] And to the man he said, … cursed is the earth (אֲרוּרָה הָאֲדָמָה) because of you; in toil (בְּעִצָּבוֹן) you shall eat of it all the days of your life; … [19] in the sweat of your face shall you eat bread, until you return to the earth; for out of it you were taken; you are dust, and to dust you shall return.

Significantly, the very same emphasis is to be found in another verse considered to be a segment of J, now integrated into the Priestly genealogy of Adam's descendants which bridges between the Creation and Flood stories (Gen 5:29):

> He named him Noah, saying, "This one shall bring us relief from our work (מִמַּעֲשֵׂנוּ) and from the toil (וּמֵעִצְּבוֹן) of our hands out of the earth (הָאֲדָמָה) that the LORD has cursed (אֵרְרָהּ)."

[30] This is the standard positon of critical commentaries on Gen 2:7; see., e.g., Skinner 1910, 56; Gunkel 1997, 6–7. But see the different assessment of Westermann 1994, 203–7.

[31] Thus Abel is the first keeper of sheep, while Cain is the tiller of the ground (Gen 4:2); Cain's son Enoch initiates urban architecture (v. 17); the latter's offspring, Jabal, is designated as "the ancestor of those who live in tents and have livestock" (v. 20), while his brother Jubal "was the ancestor of all those who play the lyre and pipe" (v. 21), and their half-brother Tubal-Cain "made all kinds of bronze and iron tools" (v. 22).

The peculiar form עִצָּבוֹן, as well as the repeated use of the *Leitwörter* אֲדָמָה and ארר, all allude to God's curse to Adam, hinting that the image of the potter is about to play a part in the forthcoming story, in which Noah is the protagonist.

4.4 When viewed against this background, one can better appreciate the diction of the J account of the Flood. In this version the use of *yeṣer* frames the narrative, with its two occurrences being located at the strategic points of the opening and closing paragraphs of the story. Furthermore, the term is clearly loaded with theological import, since in both cases it is presented as the motivation for the dramatic decisions taken by God with respect to his creation. The first occurrence comes at the very beginning of the narrative and supplies the motivation for God's determination to annihilate all beings (Gen 6:5; see below, §4.5–6). The second occurrence is integrated into the very end of the narrative, and interestingly enough it explains God's opposite resolution never to attempt again such a total destruction (Gen 8:21; see §4.7).

In my opinion, these seemingly contradictory statements are contingent on the J account of the Creation, implying a comparison between God, the divine *yoṣer*, and his human equivalents in terms of the products they produce. Humankind is considered as God's *yeṣer* – that is, as the product he himself has fashioned out of the earth; but humans are also able to fashion their own products, following the model set by God, the primeval artisan. As mentioned above (§4.3), this is the grain of civilization as portrayed by J.

Unfortunately, as God learns gradually (and not without difficulty), human products fundamentally differ from divine ones. The difference between the two is effectively expressed by the contrast between טוֹב וָרַע, "good and bad." The term רַע is often translated as "evil," but this rendition loads it with a strongly metaphysical burden that it does not necessarily carry in the original Hebrew. According to J, at least up to this point, the paired terms טוֹב וָרַע relate to whether or not products are used in accordance with their intended function. In the Creation narrative, J insists that whatever God created was good (e.g. the creation of the trees, as described in Gen 2:9), or at least created with good intentions (e.g. the creation of the woman, as described in v. 18), i.e. it was meant to be useful. By contrast, human achievements, as it turns out, are carried out in violation of the manufacturer's instruction (Gen 3:11). Even worse, they are often the outcome of uncontrolled, lethal violence that hopelessly damages the divinely produced artifacts (Gen 4:7–8, 23–24).

4.5 Interestingly, though, the adjective רַע is never employed by J to characterize human deeds – up to the beginning of the Flood story, where it is said twice in a single verse, as part of the astounding statement that opens J's Flood narrative (Gen 6:5): "The LORD saw that the wickedness of humankind (רָעַת הָאָדָם) was great in the earth, and that every יֵצֶר מַחְשְׁבֹת לִבּוֹ was only bad (רַע) continually." The complete abstention from employing the adjective רַע up to this point reflects J's perceptive narrative technique, which offers here a penetrating insight into the divine psyche: God continually attempts to repress the obvious conclusion that his flagship product is determined not to follow his instructions. Eventually, however, proofs amount to a critical mass, at which point he overreacts emotionally (v. 6): "And the LORD was sorry that he had made humankind on the earth, and it grieved him to his heart (וַיִּתְעַצֵּב אֶל־לִבּוֹ)." He then impatiently decides to reboot the entire line of production (v. 7): "So the LORD said: 'I will blot out from the earth the human beings I have created – people together with animals and creeping things and birds of the air – for I am sorry that I have made them'." I propose, therefore, that it is precisely the narrator's total avoidance of רַע beforehand that charges the characterization of human deeds as רָעַת הָאָדָם with its overwhelming weight at the beginning of the Flood narrative, thus leading inevitably to the final verdict.

The expression רָעַת הָאָדָם (Gen 6:5) does not refer to an abstract notion of wickedness. Rather, it refers to actual, harmful deeds and their concrete, destructive outcomes. Similarly, the statement that וְכָל־יֵצֶר מַחְשְׁבֹת לִבּוֹ רַק רַע כָּל הַיּוֹם, "every יצר מַחְשְׁבֹת לִבּוֹ was only *bad* continually," contextually indicates that the term *yeṣer* too should be interpreted as referring not to abstract thoughts but rather to a concrete object. The most plausible interpretation, so it seems to me, is to take this noun as a collective reference to the entire range of products of human civilization, such as the handiworks innovated by the mythological forefathers of the various professions described in Genesis 4.[32] This interpretation also explains why the term מַחֲשָׁבוֹת was employed in this particular context (see §4.6).

[32] This is contrary to most commentators, whose position can be illustrated by Skinner 1910, 150: "It is difficult to say whether יֵצֶר is more properly the 'form' impressed *on* the mind (the disposition or character), or 'that which is formed' *by* the mind (imagination and purpose – *Sinnen und Trachten*)," and similar comments are made by many others. To be sure, their understanding of *yeṣer* may well be applied to several contexts in LBH, but I see no reason to assume that it is applicable for any passage composed in CBH. Projecting a late sense to the passages under review runs the risk of seriously distorting the meaning of the narrative as a whole by injecting into it anachronistic concepts.

If so, Gen 6:5 comes very close to the use of *yeṣer* in Deut 31:21. In both cases the noun *yeṣer* is used in keeping with its lexical sense, "things made." Contextually, though, these actual products are colored with dark, negative overtones, as they refer specifically to actions (or their results) that are passionately condemned by God.

**4.6** This reading of Gen 6:5 is reinforced by the employment of the word מַחְשְׁבוֹת. As mentioned above (§2.4), מַחֲשָׁבָה can function as a technical term designating a piece of work characterized by the skillful expertise invested in it. If this sense is applied to our context, it follows that God is not concerned by human deeds in general, but more specifically by the skillful products of their expert craftsmen. What makes him furious is his sudden realization that humans constantly invest their best efforts and hard-achieved technical expertise in producing things that are "bad" – that is, not in accordance with his original plans. If so, the clause וְכָל יֵצֶר מַחְשְׁבֹת לִבּוֹ רַק רַע כָּל הַיּוֹם does not intend to assert the existence of an innate inclination toward evil. Rather, it visualizes God's shocking insight that he had thus far been naïve: the typical products of human civilization reflect their conscious decision to put their best energy into realizing their own desires, not those of their divine creator.

**4.7** It is now possible to turn to the closing paragraph of J's Flood narrative (Gen 8:21):

> The LORD said in his heart (אֶל לִבּוֹ, i.e. to himself): I will never again curse the ground (הָאֲדָמָה) because of humankind, for the human יֵצֶר לֵב is evil from youth; nor will I ever again destroy every living creature as I have done.

Significantly, the term מַחְשְׁבוֹת is not employed in this latter context, for an obvious reason: At this point of human prehistory, dexterous, "high-tech" products – which had infuriated God in the first place – are all destroyed. But God, as portrayed by J, is a *deus sapiens*: he learns from his mistakes. As he realizes, even without craftsmen human products are bound to counter his original intention – simply because humans produce them, not God himself. People need not be qualified experts in order to produce bad products (יֵצֶר רַע); they successfully do so as laymen as well.

And indeed, the continuation of the J story confirms God's gloomy view. Soon after the ark opens and Noah resumes the orderly tilling of the ground, he experiments with wine production, ending with a most embarrassing scene of drunkenness and very probably sexual misbehavior as well (Gen 9:20–24). Human civilization after the Deluge is thus as hopelessly destructive as it was beforehand.

According to my interpretation, then, the expressions יֵצֶר מַחְשְׁבֹת לֵב of Gen 6:5 and יֵצֶר לֵב of 8:21 are not to be regarded as mere synonyms, as is commonly done. The subtle – yet decisive – shift from one to another – that is, the omission of the term מַחְשָׁבוֹת – reflects God's learning experience: he realizes that it is not only professional expertise that renders human products evil, but rather human skills in general; his expectation that his products will always follow his instructions and meet his intentions has been unrealistic to begin with, as he is now forced to admit.

## 5 EXCURSUS: JEREMIAH 18:1–11

The subtleties of the employment of the nouns מַחֲשָׁבָה ,יֵצֶר and רָעָה in the J account of the Flood narrative find a partial yet instructive parallel in a passage that was already adduced more than once, namely, Jeremiah 18 (cf. §2.1 and §3.2):

1 The word that came to Jeremiah from the LORD: 2 "Come, go down to the
potter's house (בֵּית הַיּוֹצֵר), and there I will let you hear my words." 3 So I went
down to the potter's house, and there he was working (עֹשֶׂה מְלָאכָה) at his wheel. 4
The vessel he was making of clay (עֹשֶׂה בַּחֹמֶר) was spoiled in the potter's hand, and
he reworked it into another vessel, as seemed good to him.
5 Then the word of the LORD came to me: 6 "Can I not do with you, O house of
Israel, just as this potter has done? says the LORD. Just like the clay in the potter's
hand, so are you in my hand, O house of Israel.
7 At one moment I may declare concerning a nation or a kingdom, that I will
pluck up and break down and destroy it, 8 but if that nation, concerning which I
have spoken, turns from its evil (מֵרָעָתוֹ), I will change my mind about the disaster
(וְנִחַמְתִּי עַל הָרָעָה) that I intended to bring on it. 9 And at another moment I may
declare concerning a nation or a kingdom that I will build and plant it, 10 but if it
does evil (הָרַע) in my sight, not listening to my voice, then I will change my mind
about the good (וְנִחַמְתִּי עַל הַטּוֹבָה) that I had intended to do to it.
11 Now, therefore, say to the people of Judah and the inhabitants of Jerusalem:
Thus says the LORD: Look, I am a potter shaping evil against you and devising a
plan against you. Turn now, all of you from your evil way, and amend your ways
and your doings.

The comprehension of this prophetic unit is somewhat hampered by its literary complexity.[33] The text can be divided to two paragraphs:

[33] The specific delineation sketched above is essentially close to the analysis proposed by Hoffman 2001, 1:407–14. Note that although critical commentators of Jeremiah vary greatly in their assessment of the (lack of) unity of Jer 18:1–12, most of them agree that v. 12 is a later addition to the original prophecy – an opinion with which I concur, and because of which I left it outside the present discussion.

(a) vv. 2–4 depict, in much detail, a scene at the potter's workshop; (b) vv. 5–11 supply a symbolic interpretation of this happening. The latter section is apparently of a composite nature. Only its framework (vv. 5–6, 11) relates directly to the image of the potter and its significance for the future of Israel. The original sequence of vv. 5–6 + 11 is interrupted by a secondary expansion in vv. 7–10 (marked above by indentation), which do not refer to Israel but rather to God's universal rule over all the foreign nations.[34]

The exegetical relation between the image of the potter (as described in vv. 2–4) and its symbolic decoding (unfolded in vv. 5–6 + 11) pertains also to the technical terminology employed in this context: the potter (יוֹצֵר) produces (עֹשֶׂה) a vessel (כְּלִי) made of clay (חֹמֶר), while the prophetic decoding of this image asserts that Israel is for God like a clay at the hand of the potter (v. 6).

This declaration is then given a detailed explication in the form of a parallelism: הִנֵּה אָנֹכִי יוֹצֵר עֲלֵיכֶם רָעָה // וְחֹשֵׁב עֲלֵיכֶם מַחֲשָׁבָה. Taken in isolation, this is a seemingly clear example for a semantic shift in the sense of *yeṣer*: since the second hemistich can be rendered as "I *scheme* a plan against you," so presumably one should understand the first hemistich as "I *devise* an evil plan against you," with the participle *yoṣer* being used as a verb denoting "thinking" or the like. Read in its broader context, however, this parallelism is revealed to rely on the well-known phraseology of artisanal pottery (יוֹצֵר, חֹשֵׁב מַחֲשָׁבָה). It makes clear that the skillfully produced product is nothing but Israel's destruction, which is already set and done – but can nevertheless be overturned upon their repentance.

If so, the term רָעָה is again a designation of actual deeds (this time, Israel's pending punishment) and the verb חשב is used here primarily not in the general sense "to think" but rather in the technical sense "to skillfully produce."[35] The verb *y-ṣ-r*, accordingly, is also to be read as an allusion to the work of the potter, who is able to reshape the (destiny of the) vessel while making it on the wheel.

[34] Interestingly, this division of the content of this prophetic unit closely corresponds to the explicit marking of paragraphs in the MT by "closed paragraphs" (פרשות סתומות). For the exceptional ideology of the expansion, vv. 7–10, which sets it apart from its immediate context as well as from the book of Jeremiah in general, see Hoffman 1997, 236–37.

[35] In this respect, there is a marked difference between the older stratum of the interpretive paragraph (vv. 5-6 + 11) and the epexegetical expansion of vv. 7–10, in which the verb חשב is used in its standard sense, "to devise, scheme" (v. 8).

## 6 CONCLUSION

This discussion focused on a small selection of passages that exemplify the use of the term *yeṣer* in Classical Biblical Hebrew. The term and the related verb evidently underwent semantic changes, mostly in the direction of broadening their semantic scope, from denoting the potters' work and products to the making of objects by other artisans. But a "psychologized" or "internalized" extension of its sense is not detectable within the classical corpus. All such occurrences, including those in the J version of the Flood story, are better interpreted within the perimeters of its original sense. In this respect, the distance between biblical and post-biblical literature, as far as the use of the term *yeṣer* is concerned, is even greater than is commonly thought.

Our results, however, are not only negative. As demonstrated above, the term *yeṣer* is not at all a neutral term in Biblical Hebrew. It rather encapsulates a fully fledged anthropology, shared by a whole range of biblical sources, from prophetic to hymnal and narrative modes of literary writing. The image of humans as earthenware penetratingly captures the intricate interaction between different aspects of the human condition. It can be appropriately rendered with the help of some famous words of another great poet, albeit a much later one:

> What a piece of work is a man! How noble in reason, how infinite in faculties; in form and moving, how express and admirable; in action how like an angel, in apprehension, how like a god – the beauty of the world, the paragon of animals! And yet, to me, what is this quintessence of dust? (William Shakespeare, Hamlet, II.2)

# 3

# The "Inclination" (*yeṣer*) as Rendered in the Septuagint

James K. Aitken

One of the questions in the debate regarding the *yeṣer* is the point in time at which one can speak of a fully developed rabbinic notion of an Evil Inclination in opposition to a Good Inclination. The answer is in part dependent on identifying its forerunners. While there is a concept of a *yeṣer* in the Hebrew Bible, it is not an internal disposition or entity in the way it is in later rabbinic tradition. The noun *yeṣer*, as a derivative of the verb *y-ṣ-r*, denotes in the Hebrew Bible something that is created, and in some passages refers to what is created by the mind or heart, which might simply be interpreted as a thought.[1] Sirach, in the early second century BCE, might well be vital evidence for the development of the notion already in the Second Temple period, where *yeṣer* is apparently used in the context of free will, something given for humans to choose their destinies.[2] This supposition has now been supported by the Qumran discoveries, although the precise interpretation of both these sets of sources continues to be discussed.[3]

Rosen-Zvi has underlined how our understanding of the *yeṣer* in rabbinic tradition – and accordingly our reading of earlier passages – is dictated by scholarly fashions.[4] Early twentieth-century scholarship discussed *yeṣer* in the context of theodicy combined with a focus on sinfulness. This was seen in Sirach's concept of free will and the cosmological determinism of Qumran, along with discussion of Pauline theology. More recently, the shift has moved from theology to anthropology, describing the

1 For the complexity of the Hebrew semantics, see the chapter by Mizrahi, Chapter 2 in this volume.

2 Hadot 1970; Brand 2013.

3 On the Qumran material, see now Tigchelaar 2008.

4 Rosen-Zvi 2011.

inner workings and psychological dynamics behind the *yeṣer* concept. Rabbinic concepts have been placed in the context of ancient philosophers, describing the inner struggle between the rational and irrational parts of the soul. In such narratives the inclination is to be tamed or controlled in an ascetic fashion. Rosen-Zvi himself takes a different path, emphasizing that the *yeṣer* is an external force that must be conquered and defeated. It is to be placed not in the context of self-control but in the biblical context of human sinfulness, linked to the tradition of demonology.

With the turn to the psychological and demonic understandings of evil, Greek evidence should hold an important place, but has been rarely discussed in detail. Comparable notions in the Greek tradition could have played a part in the shaping of the Jewish notion, and the Septuagint would be a natural place to begin to identify this. The Septuagint Pentateuch was translated in the third century BCE,[5] shortly before the time of the Second Temple sources already cited, and therefore is the first witness as to how the Hebrew was being interpreted in Antiquity. Other parts of the Septuagint were translated in the centuries following, and at the same time Jewish Greek compositions were in production. The Greek translations therefore offer an alternative perspective at the very same time that the Hebrew sources appear to be developing the notion of the *yeṣer*.

Second, looking at Jewish Greek sources offers the opportunity to consider whether Greek ideas or philosophical notions had any influence at all in Jewish discussions. Without essentializing "Greek thought," it is fair to ask whether concepts of evil or of human dispositions in Greek writings played a role that might have shaped Jewish ideas in this period or indeed later. In reality, Greek views of evil when presented systematically do not diverge greatly from biblical and early Jewish notions. We should avoid Porter's polemic in which Greek and Hebrew are seen as strongly divergent.[6] In both Platonic and Stoic thought God cannot be the cause of evil since naturally what is good can only beget good (cf. Plato, *Resp.* 379; *Tim.* 69; Stoics, *SVF* 2.1168–86). Human action is the cause, and in philosophical terms this is through ignorance. We will encounter similar notions in Jewish writings.

## 1 THE TRANSLATIONS OF YEṢER IN THE SEPTUAGINT

The Greek evidence has largely been seen as problematic. As early as 1901 Porter identified the concept of sin expressed via the *yeṣer* in the book of

[5] See Lee 1983, 139–44; Evans 2001, 263–64. [6] Porter 1901, 93.

Sirach, whose Hebrew had just come to light. The subsequent finding of the Dead Sea Scrolls in addition to the Hebrew of Sirach naturally contributed to this aspect of the history of development. Porter's discussion of Sirach allowed him to deny that the rabbinic notion was a post-Christian development or under Greek influence.[7] He argued against there being any clear notion in Greek in comparison to the developed themes in Sirach since the Hebrew word had no one Greek equivalent and no uniform Greek rendering is to be found in the Septuagint.[8] On this he seems to have influenced the reflections of Cohen Stuart later. Cohen Stuart's book *The Struggle in Man* is the only work that examines the Greek terms in the whole Septuagint and not merely in Sirach or other apocryphal books.[9] Cohen Stuart's argument is, nonetheless, curious. He recognizes that if there had been a change in meaning of the Hebrew during the Second Temple period, there would be a corresponding change observable in the Greek translations, and therefore rightly devotes some attention to the translations. He notes first how six words are used to render eleven passages, and how the most frequent rendering is πλάσμα, "anything formed or moulded," an equivalent also used by Aquila and Symmachus at Deut 31:21 and Isa 26:3.[10] He concludes, using an argument that is not clear, that his survey of LXX uses shows that only one word, namely πλάσμα, has the probability of being an equivalent for *yeṣer*. He opines that "all other words ... might be related to it, but this is always doubtful." He follows Porter in concluding that this word πλάσμα could never bear the figurative meaning of the Hebrew (though Cohen Stuart sees a possible exception at Jdt 8:29), and he prefers to consider figurative meanings conveyed by the other translation choices as being used "incidentally."[11] In effect he seems to be saying that πλάσμα was the correct translation equivalent for *yeṣer*, but that it could not convey the figurative meaning of the Hebrew. Other translation equivalents, by contrast, are not suitable translations for the Hebrew, and therefore of lesser evidence for interpretation.

Cohen Stuart does proceed to examine other translation choices, especially in his discussion of the Sirach passages. He therefore considers one use of διαβούλιον, "deliberation"; two uses of ἐνθύμημα, "thought, reasoning"; cognates of διανοεῖσθαί, "to intend, have in mind"; and one use of πονηρία,

[7] Porter 1901, 145. [8] Porter 1901, 136–37 n. 3. [9] Cohen Stuart 1984.

[10] Cohen Stuart 1984, 83. Here his data, including the Aquila references, are the same as those laid out in footnote 3 of Porter (1901, 136–37).

[11] Cohen Stuart 1984, 84.

"wickedness." He concludes that it is evident in this period that *yeṣer* means a disposition, the power to choose and the result of that choice; it is never used of an (evil) inclination.[12] Hadot in similar fashion to Cohen Stuart examines a range of terms that can be placed in the semantic fields of Evil Inclination or of free will. He goes beyond the equivalents for *yeṣer*, as he is examining free will as a notion as well. As his focus is on Sirach he primarily discusses the translation equivalents in that book, and therefore does not consider much of the Septuagint material. Indeed, as he is seeking parallels to the concept in Sirach, Hadot must go to non-Hebrew sources of a far later period, namely 4 Maccabees (probably second century CE) and Wisdom (first century BCE or CE), as well as Paul. He also examines 4 Ezra, originally a Semitic work if now in translation, which is also very late (end of first century CE) and the Testaments of the Twelve Patriarchs, which have a complex and confused textual history. His work is illustrative of the problem of finding suitable contemporary Second Temple sources, especially in Greek.[13]

The Greek equivalents are handled sensitively in one recent study by Brand.[14] It is nevertheless a study of the passage in Sirach that leads to a consideration of the Greek rather than an examination of the Septuagint per se, and therefore the results are necessarily limited. She suggests that there is a subtle change in the Greek from the Hebrew in the choice of Sirach's grandson when he uses διαβούλιον to render יצר (Sir 15:5 and 17:6).[15] She suggests that the noun διαβούλιον expresses the ability to deliberate between good and evil, and in that it is to be distinguished from the *yeṣer*, which is the character of the individual that will direct his choices. Accordingly, the translator has subtly changed the meaning of the base text. Surrendering humans to their character (*yeṣer*) may imply that character is determined by God, but the translation by διαβούλιον implies that there is human capacity for free choice, and therefore that that choice cannot be determined. In both the Hebrew and Greek it is not an inborn inclination but a choice, and that free choice is underscored in the LXX.[16]

It can be seen that there has only been occasional consideration of the Septuagint renderings, and more attention has been given to Sirach than to the rest of the Septuagint. Particularly surprising in the discussions of the Evil Inclination is the failure to consider in depth the Greek version of

[12] Cohen Stuart 1984, 93.

[13] Murphy, in an early study of the Qumran material, also resorted to such difficult sources for comparison: Murphy 1958. See the comments of Brand 2013, 104 n. 42.

[14] Brand 2013. [15] Brand 2013, 102–3. [16] Brand 2013, 104.

those passages that are formative in Second Temple literature and the later rabbinic tradition, namely Gen 6:5 and 8:21. It is desirable therefore to consider the Septuagint evidence as a whole, focusing on the translations for *yeṣer*, since it is the history of that word with which we are concerned. Attention to the lexicography of the Greek will also be seen to be of importance.

## 2 THE TRANSLATION OF THE HEBREW VERB

We may begin with brief consideration of the renderings of the verb *y-ṣ-r*, used of fashioning or forming objects.[17] In the majority of the forty-five appearances of this verb in the MT it is rendered by the Greek verb πλάσσω.[18] In similar fashion to the Hebrew, this Greek verb is used of molding, forming, or fashioning objects, especially from soft substances such as clay, earth, or wax (LSJ 1412). It therefore is a fitting equivalent in Jer 40:2 (MT 33:2) for describing the formation of the earth: "Thus did the Lord say, when he was making earth and forming (πλάσσων) it to establish it – the Lord is his name" (NETS). It is also appropriate as the verb for making idols: "all who fashion (πλάσσοντες) a god or cast useless things" (Isa 44:10, NETS). For the same reason it became a natural choice for the fashioning of mankind from the dust of the earth: "And God formed (ἔπλασεν) man, dust from the earth" (Gen 2:7). While πλάσσω is the default equivalent, occasional variation in the translations leads to synonymous equivalents that are unremarkable, both in the MT and in the eight appearances in the extant Hebrew Sirach. Verbs of creating or manufacturing are found a number of times: κατασκευάζω (Isa 45:7, 9), ποιέω (Isa 45:11, 18), κτίζω (Isa 22:11; 46:11; Sir 31[34]:27; 33[36]:10; 49:14), and καταδείκνυμι (Isa 45:18). In similar fashion the verb γίνομαι twice appears to translate the *niphal* of the verb (Isa 43:10; Sir 46:1). In Amos 4:13 the translator is seeking a variation before κτίζω later in the verse and therefore opts for στερεόω, "to establish firmly," which is itself an aspect of the creating act. Meanwhile, the nominal participle is rendered by κεραμεύς, "potter" (Isa 45:9, including in a doublet in the same verse). Other translations in the Septuagint reflect contextual interpretation and therefore do not contribute to the semantic evidence. A similar

[17] Cf. Rosen-Zvi 2011, 3. See too Mizrahi, Chapter 2 in this volume.

[18] Gen 2:7; 2:8, 19; 2 Kgs 19:25; Isa 27:11; 43:1, 7; 44:2, 9, 10, 21, 24; 49:5; Jer 1:5; 10:16; 18:11; 33:2 (40:2); 51(28):19; Hab 2:18 *bis*; Zech 12:1; Pss 33(32):15; 73(74):17; 94(93):9, 20; 95(94):5; 104(103):26; 139(138):16.

interpretation is in Isa 54:1 where the essential nature of being created is clarified as having the property of being "perishable" (φθαρτός). In Isa 44:12 the verb forms part of a series to describe the fashioning of idols from iron, and therefore it has been freely rendered as τετραίνω, "to bore."[19] Finally, the formation of the prophet in his mother's womb is interpreted as his being sanctified for the task (Sir 49:7: ἁγιάζω).

## 3 THE TRANSLATION OF THE HEBREW NOUN

In the nine appearances of the noun in the MT, the equivalent πλάσμα is obviously a natural rendering of the more common meaning of *yeṣer* as something that has been fashioned (a product of the verb *y-ṣ-r*). It is cognate with the most frequent rendering of the verb, πλάσσω, and would be in accord with the understanding of the Hebrew as described by Mizrahi elsewhere in this volume. In fact, this equivalent is chosen only twice (Hab 2:18; Ps 103[102]:14), although we may also note the similar ποίημα (Isa 29:16). In these passages the referent is indeed something that is manufactured and therefore the Greek nouns are suitable equivalents in the context. In one instance (Deut 31:21) *yeṣer* is translated by πονηρία, "evil," and this appears to be a contextual explanation. The one intriguing case where πλάσμα might have some significance is in the expression in Jdt 8:29, "*plasma* of your heart is good" (τὸ πλάσμα τῆς καρδίας σου).[20] As a literal translation of the Hebrew expression,[21] it does not necessarily convey any special sense of inclination, and it may be understood as merely denoting the product of the heart, a sense that Mizrahi argues is original to the Hebrew.

The variety of options for translating *yeṣer* indicates that no one standard equivalent had been agreed. This is significant since for many items of religious vocabulary in the Septuagint the translators appear to have had an agreed and established equivalent that they would use regularly (e.g. διαθήκη for "covenant"; εὐλογέω for "to bless"). These

[19] Three other instances in the MT are not considered here: ἐπιγονή, "descendant" for the nominal participle (Amos 7:1) implying a reading of the Hebrew noun נצר; a minus at Isa 64:7; and the equivalent συντάσσω (Isa 37:26) suggesting a reading of the Hebrew verb צוה. In Sirach, Sir 11:16 and 51:12 do not have Greek equivalents, and Sir 37:3 is reinterpreted.

[20] See Cohen Stuart 1984, 87; Hadot 1970, 73.

[21] We leave open the question whether Judith was translated or an original composition; even if a composition, the phrase is a rendering of the Hebrew expression. On the debate, see Joosten 2007; Corley 2008.

equivalents may well have become common in use before the Septuagint was written down. In the case of *yeṣer*, the Septuagint is perhaps indicative of the fact both that the meaning was changing between the Hebrew text being written and being translated, and also that there was no one obvious equivalent in Greek for the concept. An examination of these other passages will reveal how far the translators have understood the concept of *yeṣer* in their time.

## 3.1 Genesis 6:5 and 8:21

The most explicit passage in the Hebrew Bible linking the *yeṣer* with some sort of inclination to do evil is Gen 6:5. In tradition this came to be the *locus classicus* for the origins of the concept, and it is therefore significant that the Septuagint already translates the verse with some interpretative elements.

| Gen 6:5 (NRSV, modified) | LXX (NETS) |
|---|---|
| The LORD saw that the wickedness of humankind was great in the earth, and **that every *yeṣer* of the thoughts of their hearts was only evil** continually. | And when the Lord God saw that the wicked deeds of humans were multiplied on the earth and **that all think attentively in their hearts on evil things** all the days |

The Hebrew in this passage is itself difficult to interpret. Every *yeṣer*, "fashioning," is evil, but the *yeṣer* is a part of or product of the thoughts of the heart (וְכָל־יֵצֶר מַחְשְׁבֹת לִבּוֹ). The Greek rephrases the sentence providing no obvious nominal equivalent to the Hebrew *yeṣer* and instead rendering the thoughts of the heart alone. The differences are significant enough in the whole verse to make a case for a differing Hebrew *Vorlage*. However, as we shall see, there is close harmony between this verse and Gen 8:21, suggesting that there is intentional interpretation of the two passages.[22] Even if there were a now lost differing Hebrew *Vorlage*, the result would be the same – by the third century BCE these passages had taken on a particular interpretation, irrespective of whether it was by a Hebrew scribe or the Greek translator. Nevertheless, there is more to the text than mere interpretation. We can see that the translator was

[22] Cf. Prestel and Schorch 2011, 168, who raise the question whether there was harmonization here already in the Hebrew *Vorlage*.

working with an understanding of the text through his translation. The first phrase וְכָל־יֵצֶר מַחְשְׁבֹת is rendered by πᾶς τις διανοεῖται, "everyone ponders," with no attempt to preserve the יצר in the translation except for the τις, "anyone," being in the same word position in the sentence. If יצר denotes the product of the thought, then it could be argued that this is a reasonable translation of the sense.[23] The verb διανοέομαι, "to ponder," only appears three times in Genesis: here, then in the very next verse, and finally in 8:21. It thus links closely this passage at the beginning of the Flood narrative with the promise at the end of the narrative in 8:21:[24] "And the Lord God smelled an odor of fragrance, and the Lord God, when he had given it thought (διανοηθείς), said" (NETS). It is clear that in each case "(in) his heart" (לִבּוֹ) is the reason for the translation "pondered." In Gen 6:5 we should see the translator as an accomplished one, and rather than seeing his omission of an equivalent for יצר as a shortcoming, instead appreciate how he has rendered the verse as a whole. For the next phrase expressing the intention on performing "only evil" (רַק רַע) is interpreted in the Greek as "attentively on evil things" (ἐπιμελῶς ἐπὶ τὰ πονηρά).[25] At first sight the adverb ἐπιμελῶς, "attentively," appears to be an interpretative translation of Hebrew רַק, "only," underlining the intent of the action and the human responsibility.[26] Certainly it is in the same word position as the Hebrew, but we also have to account for the addition in Greek of the preposition ἐπί, which is naturally paired with ἐπιμελῶς. It seems more reasonable to examine the whole phrase as a unit. The reading of יֵצֶר מַחְשְׁבֹת as a periphrasis for "thinking," the rendering of רַק as ἐπιμελῶς, and the addition of the preposition ἐπί all point to a careful rephrasing of the expression. The product of the thinking is expressed merely as the verb thinking (διανοεῖται), but it is intently focused on evil, clarifying that the restrictive adverb of רַק is to be understood as denoting exclusive attention to the task of performing evil.

Turning to Gen 8:21, we see some harmonization with Gen 6:5, but, as noted above, it is not necessary to presume a Hebrew version already

[23] Cf. Wevers 1993, 79. [24] Prestel and Schorch 2011, 174.

[25] Brayford's translation of Gen 6:5 ("pondering in his heart only on evil matters") does not do justice to the Greek and appears to be influenced unnecessarily by English versions of the Hebrew in preserving the translation "only" (Brayford 2007, 49). Cf. similarly her translation of Gen 8:21: "because the mind of the human involves itself only on evil matters from youth" (Brayford 2007, 55).

[26] So Harl 1986, 127.

containing the harmonizations.[27] Whether in the Hebrew or the Greek, it shows an attempt to unite the two accounts, but in this case the Greek has translated the Hebrew slightly differently than in Gen 6:5.

| Gen 8:21 (NRSV, modified) | LXX (NETS) |
|---|---|
| I will never again curse the ground because of humankind, **for the *yeṣer* of the human heart** (יֵצֶר לֵב הָאָדָם) is evil from youth | I will not proceed hereafter to curse the earth because of the deeds of humans, for **the mind of humankind applies itself attentively to evil things** from youth |

We lack in the Hebrew of this the passage the "thoughts" from Gen 6:5 and the qualifier רַק, "only." Here the יצר is rendered as a verb, "applies" (ἔγκειται), and the heart as "mind" (ἡ διάνοια), although once more we might see the Greek as a clarifying rendering of the whole phrase.[28] In harmony with Gen 6:5 we once more find the adverb ἐπιμελῶς, "attentively," without an obvious equivalent in Hebrew, along with ἐπὶ τὰ πονηρά, "to evil things," as an equivalent for the simple רַע. Intent toward evil action is thereby underlined. It has been suggested that the use of the verb ἔγκειμαι implies a shift, by which the Greek has changed the nominal clause into a verbal clause and has changed the sense, including the addition of a copulative. The result would seem to be in the Septuagint that the wickedness is not in the mind, but outside it, and is sought by it.[29] However, ἔγκειμαι can mean simply "to be involved" as well as "to press hard," and therefore the phrase ἔγκειται ἡ διάνοια here could simply be a periphrasis for the verb διανοέομαι. At most it might indicate a sense of urgency in that the διάνοια is pressing on to do evil.

Let us look more closely at the vocabulary. The choice of the verb διανοέομαι in Gen 6:5 and the noun διανοία in Gen 8:21 conforms with other parts of the translation of Genesis where the reflexive use of "heart" (לב) is rendered by the noun διανοία "thought, thinking faculty." Speaking in the heart is thus expressed by such phrases as speaking ἐν τῇ διανοίᾳ (e.g. Gen 24:45; 27:41).[30] Distinctive is the use of the verb διανοέομαι only in

[27] The suggestion of Prestel and Schorch 2011, 174.
[28] Harl 1986, 127, who takes whole phrase as having been rendered simply by διάνοια.
[29] So Prestel and Schorch 2011, 174–75.
[30] Cf. Harl 1986, 61. Harl also suggests that יצר is untranslatable and therefore omitted.

these three places, resulting in two realms of thought, humans pondering evil and God pondering the condition of humans.[31] It does also tie in Genesis 6 with the resolution in Genesis 8. This association with διάνοια, though, places the action of the "heart" in the cognitive realm. The combination with the Greek adverb ἐπιμελῶς is striking since it does not appear elsewhere in the Pentateuch, except in the corresponding passage of Gen 8:21. Elsewhere in the LXX ἐπιμελῶς is used of concentrated work where due diligence is to be observed. This may be for ensuring correct punishment (e.g. Prov 13:23), for the proper enactment of orders (e.g. 1 Esd 8:19), or for the proper observance of divine Law (e.g. 1 Esd 8:21, 24). By contrast ἀμελῶς, "carelessly," is used in Jer 31:10 for performing works of the Law indifferently. It thus can have an ethical dimension over ensuring the correct fulfillment of demands and the correct behavior toward those commands. As illustration of the use of these adjectives in an ethical sense, we may compare Plato's *Symposium*:

He (Love) it is who casts alienation out, draws intimacy in; he brings us together in such friendly gatherings as the present; at feasts and dances and oblations he makes himself our leader; politeness contriving, moroseness outdriving; kind giver of amity, giving no enmity; gracious, superb; a marvel to the wise, a delight to the gods coveted of such as share him not, treasured of such as good share have got; father of luxury, tenderness, elegance, graces and longing and yearning; *careful of the good, careless of the bad* (ἐπιμελὴς ἀγαθῶν, ἀμελὴς κακῶν).[32]

Commentators on the Septuagint have made little of these two passages in Genesis, but what they signify is a cognitive approach to evil action, the *yeṣer* representing thought of undivided attention to evil. The adverb ἐπιμελῶς, "attentively," reinforces the evil on which they embark, since such "attention" should be aimed at following God's Law, but instead is aimed at the reverse: continual evil. The importance of this adverb was not lost on Philo, either, who drew attention to it in his commentary:

But since the mind is a potential and principal part of the soul, he introduces that word "diligently"; but that which has been weighed with diligence and care is exquisite thought, examined more certainly than certainty itself. But this diligence does not tend to any one evil, but as is plain, to mischief, and to all mischief; nor does it exist in a perfunctory manner; but man is devoted to it from his youth, not

[31] Wevers (1993, 79) and Brayford (2007, 262) on Gen 6:5 note how God ponders (Gen 6:6; cf. 8:21) in response to humans themselves "pondering" after evil.

[32] Plato, *Symp.* 197d.

only in a manner, but from his very cradle, as if he were in some degree united to, and nourished, and bred up with sin.[33]

In these two Septuagint passages the Greek is well phrased and draws attention to the focus on thinking upon evil deeds. The *yeṣer* is not given a specific translation equivalent or seen as an entity separate from the machinations of the "heart," but the coordination between the two passages indicates that the translator viewed the operation of the *yeṣer* as a single-minded purpose, and in this it is one step toward the view of the *yeṣer* as a guiding principle within.[34] On the other hand, as there is no translation equivalent for the *yeṣer*, it has not become an entity of such importance and exegetical weight that it needs to be specified. It is not yet as important as it comes to be even in Sirach.

## 3.2 Cognitive Translations of *yeṣer*

That the translator of Genesis was not alone in connecting the *yeṣer* specifically with the action of thinking is clear from the other renderings of *yeṣer* in the Septuagint. Continuing in the same tradition as Genesis we first see the same equivalent διάνοια (1 Chr 29:18) as in Gen 8:21, and notably translating the combined expression in Hebrew of יֵ֫צֶר מַחְשְׁבוֹת, "*yeṣer* of the thoughts," as in Genesis. The noun διάνοια renders the Hebrew לבב/לב thirty-nine times,[35] and this indicates the close affinity in understanding between יצר and לב. A second translation choice is the noun ἐνθύμημα, found both in 1 Chr 28:9 (to translate the whole phrase יֵ֫צֶר מַחֲשָׁבוֹת) and in Sir 27:6: "Its fruit brings to light a tree's cultivation – so reasoning notions (λόγος ἐνθυμήματος; MS A יצר) of a person's heart" (NETS). In Greek ἐνθύμημα denotes a thought or the reasoning behind a thought (cf. LSJ 567). For the Septuagint occurrences LEH (*Greek–English Lexicon of the Septuagint*) reproduces the glosses directly from LSJ, such that there is, therefore, little to comment upon.[36] Muraoka, however, seeking to provide a definition based on the appearances in the

[33] Philo, *QG* 2.54d (trans. Yonge).

[34] Prestel and Schorch 2011, 174. They note the suggestions of Siegert (2001–2003, 1: 258) that the free translation is under the influence of Hellenistic psychology.

[35] Cohen Stuart 1984, 86.

[36] LEH (Lust et al. 2003), 204: "thought, piece of reasoning, argument ... invention, device, imagination." Also to be noted is the *Brill Dictionary of Ancient Greek* (*GE*) (Montanari 2015), a translation of Montanari's *Vocabolario della Lingua Greca* (2013), where the entry is similar to LSJ as well, with the first set of meanings given as "thought, idea, rationale."

Septuagint, comes up with his own definition: "that to which one's heart is inclined."[37] The use of the word "inclined" here is suggestive that the noun renders יצר, but may be a misleading definition for all the occurrences of ἐνθύμημα in the Septuagint, especially when they are not all associated with the heart. Another important lexicographic resource is the new *Diccionario Griego-Español* (*DGE*),[38] the most important Greek lexicographic project since LSJ, and the foundation for all future lexicographic work in ancient Greek.[39] In the *DGE* the simple presentation of the meaning in LSJ has been significantly refined, as seen in the first set of glosses in the entry for ἐνθύμημα (here with my own translations of the Spanish):

1 pensamiento, reflexión, consideración [thought, reflection, consideration] ...
2 idea ingeniosa, ocurrencia, plan, estratagema [ingenious idea, occurrence, plan, stratagem] ...
3 plu. argumentos, razones [pl. arguments, reasons] ...
4 pensamiento, modo de pensar, intención [thought, way of thinking, intention] κύριος ... πᾶν ἐνθύμημα γιγνώσκει LXX 1Pa.28.9, ἄδικον τὸ ἐνθύμημα αὐτῶν de los que se apartan de la ley de Dios, LXX Ps.118.118, cf. LXX Si.27.6, Si.37.3.

The entry separates the Septuagint data into its own sub-class of the meaning (item 4), a procedure that runs the risk of imputing unique meanings to Septuagint words, arising from the Hebrew words being translated, rather than recognizing that the standard meanings in Greek could be applicable in the Septuagint too.

It is clear that some have seen the word ἐνθύμημα as conveying a hint of what later became the notion of the inclination, and have imparted this sense to the Greek. By contrast Hadot, who considers the use of this term in Sirach in the wider context of its Septuagintal appearances, proposes that it is an entirely neutral term, except for in one place (Sir 37:3), where it comes close to the sense of evil inclination.[40] In the Septuagint the term appears as many as twenty-eight times, but it is restricted to certain books: once each in 1 Chronicles, Psalms, and Malachi, twice in Jeremiah, four times in Sirach, and an impressive nineteen times in Ezekiel. It can be observed that in the majority of these occurrences it is in a negative context. In Ps 119(118):118 it refers to the faulty (ἄδικον) reasoning of

[37] Muraoka 2009, 238. [38] *DGE* (Adrados 1980–).
[39] "*DGE* en línea": http://dge.cchs.csic.es/xdge/. [40] Hadot 1970, 127–30.

those not following God's Law, and in Mal 2:16 the one who divorces will have his thoughts (ἐνθυμήματα) taken over by ἀσέβεια.[41] In both of these cases, while the context is negative, the meaning of ἐνθύμημα is simply that of thoughts that could be either positive or negative. There is no special sense in the use of the noun here. In Jeremiah (3:17; 7:24) the thoughts are of their evil hearts (τῆς καρδίας αὐτῶν τῆς κακῆς) where ἐνθύμημα is the equivalent of שְׁרִרוּת, "stubbornness," but the negativity is in the heart not in the thoughts. The frequency in Ezekiel is explicable by ἐνθύμημα translating both עלילה, "deed," and גלול, "idol," in Hebrew, objects toward which the people improperly turn their thoughts. What is important is that even in Ezekiel it signifies the thoughts, associated at times with the operations of the heart (Ezek 14:7). In this, ἐνθύμημα seems to differ little from διάνοια, and the reason for it being so often in negative contexts is not necessarily the connotation of the word, but the fact that the biblical writers are most interested in discussing thoughts when they are turned toward wrongdoing. Indeed, in Classical Greek a particular use of the noun is to denote in Aristotelian logic an enthymeme or rhetorical syllogism (LSJ 567), and if the word has such a sense of logical reasoning, it would seem contrary to think it also can mean an inclination. The contextual reference should not impair our seeing the general sense.

Similar considerations can be given to the passages in Sirach (Sir 27:6; 32:12; 35:22; 37:3). In its four occurrences there ἐνθύμημα denotes "thought," which can also imply a decision, but need not do so. Even in the example that resembles most closely the evil inclination, Sir 37:3, caution should be exercised. The translator presumably had in his *Vorlage* יצר,[42] and therefore translated by one of his preferred equivalents ἐνθύμημα: "O evil notion (πονηρὸν ἐνθύμημα), how were you involved, to cover the dry land with deceit?" (NETS). The term here can be translated by "notion" (i.e. thought) without any difficulty. It is once more in a negative context and collocated with a negative adjective as the purpose of the thought is to bring about deceit.

At this point we can consider the one other translation of יצר, διαβούλιον (Sir 15:5 and 17:6). As we have noted above, Brand suggests that this translation by the Greek for "choice" is a shift by the translator to the cognitive realm so that God is not seen as

[41] It is conceivable that ἐνθυμήματα is a corruption of ἐνδυματα, "garments," in light of the MT, but the use of ἐνθύμημα conforms to its appearances in the other Prophets.

[42] MSS D and Bmg both seem to have contained a form of the verb אמר.

creating the cause of evil.[43] While διαβούλιον does imply some action rather than mere thinking,[44] and therefore is one stage further on than either διάνοια or ἐνθύμημα, it still remains in the cognitive realm. These words are, as Hadot had noted, largely neutral. They do not imply any sort of external force imposing itself on the person's actions, nor do they even imply some sort of internal impulse; rather, it is a choice, conceived through rational thinking. The one small step made in the direction of rabbinic thinking is only that the *yeṣer* is now seen as part of the cognitive processes.

## 4 THE INCLINATION WITHOUT YEṢER

Finally, it is worth reflecting whether the notion of an inclination exists in the Septuagint even where the noun *yeṣer* does not appear in the (presumed) *Vorlage*. Cook has suggested there is one such case in Proverbs, where the translator has added the expression "bad counsel" (κακὴ βουλή) to counterbalance "good counsel" (βουλὴ καλή) earlier.[45] Cook presumes it is the translator's addition, but the possibility that it was already in the *Vorlage* does not affect the final result:[46]

Prov 2:11 "good counsel will watch over you"
Prov 2:17 "My son, let not bad counsel overtake you"

The version now witnessed by the Greek draws an opposition between good and bad, and this is certainly intentional. Such opposition, though, is a hallmark of the proverbial form (and found in other passages of LXX Proverbs too) and is not to be particularly associated with the notion of good and evil inclinations. The expression "good counsel" (βουλὴ καλή) is the rendering in the MT of מְזִמָּה, a term also translated elsewhere by διαβούλιον (e.g. Ps 10:2[9:23]; Sir 44:4) and by ἐνθύμημα (Sir 35[32]:22[24]). The Proverbs passage thereby fits into the pattern of discussion of choice in the cognitive realm, and does not appear to reflect a developing notion of inclination.

[43] Brand 2013, 102–04. Cohen Stuart had earlier noted how restrained the Greek is by translating with "choice" rather than a word such as ἐπιθυμία, "desire" (1984, 89).

[44] See Muraoka (2009, 149): "that which one deliberates to do." Brand 2013, 102 and n. 34, observes how some commentators on Sirach (including R. Smend, M. Segal, and A. A. Di Lella) blend the Hebrew meaning with the Greek translation and thereby misrepresent the Greek.

[45] Cook 2007. See also Cook 1997, 137.

[46] See Fox 2005, for a cautious approach to assuming that the translator was responsible for all the differences from the MT.

A more fruitful approach might be to examine the emotions in the Septuagint, such as at Sir 5:2 where the reader is instructed not to walk in the desires of their heart (ἐν ἐπιθυμίαις καρδίας σου). The importance of the passions in Greek thought might well have an influence on how the Hebrew expressions are rendered into Greek. Indeed, Cohen Stuart briefly discusses desire at end of his book as evidence for the developing concept of inclination. Nevertheless, Rosen-Zvi wishes to separate inner Greek struggles and self-control from the causes of sin, and it is not to be equated with the development of the evil inclination. Closer might be the passage in Wisdom of Solomon (from the first century BCE or first century CE). In Wisdom's recourse to biblical history there are only passing references to the wicked persons of the Flood narrative (10:5), and therefore little opportunity is afforded to draw upon the classic texts of Genesis 6 or 8. The author instead emphasizes that God does not create death (1:12–13), but that the wicked have faulty reasoning (2:1), being blind to discern good from evil (2:21–22). It is reasoning, as we have already seen in the Septuagint, that appears to be the cause of human sin – the blame for evil is squarely laid upon humans (cf. Wis 1:16; 14:14). The most puzzling passage, however, is the presentation of the wicked in Wis 2:23, where God is said to make all things perfect (repeating the earlier sentiment), and that instead it was envy of the *diabolos* that created evil (2:24).

2:23 Because God created human beings for incorruption and made them the image of his own nature,
2:24 but through the envy of the devil (φθόνῳ δὲ διαβόλου) death entered the world, and those who belong to his party experience it (πειράζουσιν δὲ αὐτόν). (NETS)

This is a *locus classicus* for the first reference to the devil, but there are many problems with such an interpretation.[47] If Zurawski is correct, there is no obvious allusion here to Genesis 2, and the abrupt introduction of the devil, notably here without the definite article, does not fit the wider context or overall argument of Wisdom. His preferred translation is: "But through an adversary's envy death enters the world, and those who belong to death's party put humanity to the test."[48] An adversary is the one opposing the righteous, perhaps intellectually as much as physically. His envy (φθόνος) is only treated briefly by Zurawski. He notes how in Plato and Philo envy is opposed to wisdom, and therefore places the ideas within the

[47] Cf. Stone 2009. [48] Zurawski 2012, 398.

Alexandrian milieu. Wisdom 6:23 also isolates φθόνος as antithetical to wisdom and, therefore, to immortality.

However, we can go further than this and note how much envy is part of the Greek catalogue of emotions. It becomes a central catalogue of 1 Clement, which reviews biblical history as a catalogue of actions through envy:

> 4:7 Ye see, brethren, jealousy and envy wrought the slaughter of a brother.
> 4:8 Through envy our father Jacob fled from the face of his brother Esau.

A reference to a real *diabolos* would be the first step toward an external force, but without it we are left with merely the concept of wrong decisions and possibly envy from others. This is one seed in the development of the notion of the evil inclination, but it needs much more to germinate.

## 5 CONCLUSION

It has been shown that the evidence of the Septuagint has most often been invoked when discussing the important passages in Sirach. Even in this text, however, the Hebrew seems to be closer to a concept of the Evil Inclination than the Greek. Some lexicographers have imputed a sense to the Greek that suggests a similar notion to the Hebrew, but that is perhaps beyond the evidence of the Greek semantics. The translation and understanding of the *yeṣer* seen in the Septuagint is that it represents a faculty of thought. As a consequence, humans sin because their thinking is either incorrect, or on matters other than on God's Law. The key passages of Gen 6:5 and 8:21, meanwhile, elaborate on this thinking, since they describe humans as wholly intent on doing evil. The most remarkable aspect of the Septuagint in these passages is that the translator does not offer any equivalents at all for *yeṣer*, but instead paraphrases the whole string of words. This is significant evidence that the *yeṣer* has not yet developed associations around it. As a faculty of human thinking it attributes the cause of evil to humans and their thoughts, and this is a tradition that continues for some time, found as late as the Wisdom of Solomon.

# 4

# "Fleshly Spirit" and "Vessel of Flesh" in 4QInstruction and the Thanksgiving Hymns

Benjamin Wold

The Dead Sea Scrolls preserve some of the earliest literature that bears witness to the demonizing of sin and the reification of evil. In two compositions, 4QInstruction (1Q26; 4Q415–18, 423) and the Thanksgiving Hymns, evil *yeṣarim* are found alongside and interwoven with "flesh" language. Early on in the study of 4QInstruction Elgvin, noted a number of distinctive terms shared between these documents, including "fleshly spirit" (רוח בשר).[1] In the hymns, the expression "vessel of flesh" (בשר יצר) occurs twice (1QH$^a$ xviii 25; xxiv 6). These two terms occur in close proximity in the opening column of 4QInstruction (4Q416 1 16; par. 4Q418 2+2a 8), although the fragmentary context leaves conclusions uncertain.[2] Outside 4QInstruction and the hymns[3] no extant references to "vessel of flesh" or "fleshly spirit" are to be found in early Jewish literature. This chapter considers how these two expressions are used in these documents to determine how their shared interest in "flesh" language relate to one another. This assessment shall then be brought to bear on how the evil *yeṣer* (יצר רע) is to be understood in 4QInstruction.

4QInstruction does not share the pessimistic view of human nature as found in the hymns, and yet both use "fleshly spirit" to refer to humanity. Harrington and Strugnell comment that רוח בשר in 4QInstruction "scarcely has any connection with the רוח בשר" in the Thanksgiving

I would like to thank the National Endowment for the Humanities and the Albright Institute of Archaeological Research, Jerusalem for financial support that made this research possible. I am also grateful to Eileen Schuller for valuable comments on drafts of this chapter.

[1] Elgvin 1997, 160–63. See also Goff 2004; Lange 1995, 204–32.

[2] Cf. Num 16:22; 27:16 for יצר בשר.

[3] 1QH$^a$ iv 37; v 15, 30; 4Q416 1 12, par. 4Q418 2, 2 a–c 4; 4Q417 1 i 17; 4Q418 81+81a 2.

Hymns "where the meaning is 'a fleshly spirit'."[4] If, however, "fleshly spirit" is not language for one group of humanity created separately from another, then comparisons with the expression in the hymns becomes much more meaningful.

## 1 4QINSTRUCTION

### 1.1 The Vision of Hagu (4Q417 1 i 13b–18)

4QInstruction demonstrates an interest in the categories of "spirit" and "flesh" and yet there is not a spirit/flesh dichotomy where they function as binary opposites, contrary to the view of those who interpret the Vision of Hagu passage as depicting the creation of two types of humanity, one fleshly and the other spiritual.[5] For those who hold this view, the Hagu pericope expresses a deterministic theology similar to, but less developed than, the Treatise on the Two Spirits. According to this view, the two peoples are found in the terms "spiritual people" (עָם רוח) and "fleshly spirit" (רוח בשר).[6] "Spiritual people" would not only be a *hapax legomenon* in 4QInstruction, but in the whole of ancient Hebrew literature too. The contrasting people are supposedly referred to with a "wonderfully oxymornonic" term that describes spirit as fleshly.[7] Even if these translations are correct, this would be the only occasion in 4QInstruction when these two peoples are explicitly mentioned in relationship to one another.

The address "and you, O understanding one" at the end of line 13 marks the beginning of this passage and the similar expression "and you, son of understanding one" (l. 18) begins a new section.

> 4Q417 1 i 13–18 (4Q418 43 11–14):[8]
> And you, 14 O understanding one,
> *inherit* your reward,
> by the remembrance *of*[]come.
> Engraved is {your} the statute and every punishment inscribed,
> 15 for engraved is the decree by God,
> against all i[*niquities of*] the sons of perdition,
> and a book of memory is written before him,
> 16 for those who keep His word,
> and this is a vision of *meditation* to a book of memorial,
> and He made humanity (אנוש), a people with a spirit (עם עם רוח), to inherit it
> (i.e. the vision?),

[4] Strugnell et al. 1999, 95.
[5] For a recent bibliography on this pericope see Tigchelaar 2009, 103–04.
[6] Following Collins (1999). [7] Newsom 2012, 344.
[8] For a transcription see Wold 2018, 104–05.

> for [17] according to the pattern of the holy ones is *humanity's* fashioning,
> and no longer is the *vision* given to a f[le]shly spirit,
> because it *did not know* the difference between [18] [goo]d and evil,
> according to the judgment of his [sp]irit
> *vacat* and you, O son of an understanding one.

The three words (עם עם רוח), found in line 16, may be read either as the creation of אנוש who are "a people with a spirit," or אנוש "with a spiritual people." Werman suggests reading the first עַם ("people") as the attributive of אנוש, rather than the preposition "with," and the second עִם ("with") as the preposition.[9] Her suggestion is further supported when we observe that a similar combination of "with spirit" is found in the Thanksgiving Hymns: "And you cast for a person an eternal lot with the spirits of knowledge [עם רוחות דעת]" (1QH[a] xi 23–24).[10] If this is correct, then there is no "spiritual people" and instead the emphasis is on humanity possessing a spirit, and a segment of humanity (i.e. בשר רוח) is wayward and dispossessed of revealed wisdom. In line 17 the "fleshly spirit" are "no longer" (ועוד לוא) given Hagu, which implies that they once had it.[11] Therefore, there is no ontological and predetermined distinction between spiritual and fleshly people in 4QInstruction; in fact, there are no "people of flesh," only a spirit that is labeled "fleshly." If the "fleshly spirit" had been created separately, then they would never have possessed Hagu and it would not be possible to state that they "no longer" have it. The "fleshly spirit" is so designated because they are corrupted humanity, and humankind is a people with a spirit.

How אנוש is translated is as important as how the consecutive עם עם are rendered. That "Enosh" (Gen 4:26)[12] is in view here is unconvincing, in part because the supposed reference to Seth, his father, in line 15 (בני שׁוֹת), is best read as "sons of perdition" (Num 24:17).[13] An alternative proposal, that אנוש means "Adam," has been justified on the basis of 1QS iii 17–18, although this reference actually makes explicit that "humanity" and not just "Adam" are tasked with ruling over the world. The translation "humanity" is also not without its problems: rendering עם עם רוח as "with a spiritual people" creates an apparent tautology, since it would be nonsensical to describe the creation of all humanity together with a sub-section of humankind.[14]

9 Werman 2004, 137; Werman 2002, 92.

10 Unless otherwise indicated, references to the Thanksgiving Hymns are from Schuller and Newsom 2012.

11 Following Strugnell et al. 1999, 166. 12 Brooke 2002. 13 Goff 2003, 92.

14 Goff 2009, 385.

In the case of both רוח בשר and רוח עם the author's emphasis is on spirit. The Mēvîn and his community are deficient in pursuing revealed wisdom, found in the "mystery of existence" (רז נהיה), and are concerned with all that threatens their acquisition of it. In 4QInstruction one should take care of one's spirit because it is possible for it to become displaced. One of the best examples of this is found in 4Q416 2 ii 6–7: "and in your speech do not belittle your *spirit* and for wealth do not exchange your holy *spirit* for there is nothing equal in value to it." In the very next column (4Q416 2 iii 6) the Mēvîn is warned of the consequences of borrowing money from a stranger: one's *spirit* becomes corrupted. Indeed, if one successfully guards oneself from such corruption of spirit then future reward will follow (4Q416 2 iii 7–8).

The Vision of Hagu passage is crucial to understanding whether all of humanity or only a specific group is revealed wisdom. However, "humanity" (אנוש) may not be as all-encompassing as first appears. 4QInstruction designates some of humanity as "fleshly spirit" because they did not know the difference between good and evil when they had access to the very meditation that enabled them to do so (l. 17). 4QInstruction describes those who had been tasked with pursuing revealed mysteries, failed in their pursuit, and had this privilege removed. This may suggest a polemical context between fellow Israelites and an accusation that some had gone astray (e.g. CD i 13). If it is correct to translate אנוש as "humanity," then this means that meditation and revealed wisdom – that is, mysteries which are deeply cosmological and focused on the created order – were universal to humankind in the beginning. While this is possible, given the nature of the "mystery of existence," a fair question is whether the author was universally minded or conceived of "us" and "them" in more limited terms despite the language of "humanity." Similar to other sapiential traditions, the author likely thought beyond Israel and the giving of revealed wisdom to Gentiles too. In 4QInstruction the order of being given the spirit so that one may gain insight begins with "spirit," which is equated with access to Hagu, and when not maintained and wisdom is not pursued the wayward are called "fleshly spirit."

## 1.2 4Q418 81+81a

4Q418 81+81a 1–14 form a distinct unit; they are written in direct speech and may be organized into six *stichoi*, each beginning with the statement "and you." The one addressed is an exalted figure who is to act as an intermediary between heavenly angels and his community. The first two lines begin with a description of the exalted figure who has been separated from the "fleshly spirit." While this has been taken at times as reinforcing the view that there are two groups of humanity predetermined from creation, this perspective is much less convincing in light of this reassessment of the Hagu passage.

4Q418 81+81a 1–3:[15]
[. . . by the pouring out of] [1] your lips open up a spring to bless the holy ones.
And you, as an everlasting spring, praise His [name,
sin]ce He separated you from every [2] fleshly spirit (רוח בשר);
And you, keep separate from every thing that He hates,
and keep apart from all the abominations of the soul;
[Fo]r He has made everyone,
[3] and has given to each man his own inheritance,
but He is your portion and your inheritance among the children of mankind,
[and over] His [in]heritance He has set you in authority.

The addressee's exalted status is found repeatedly in this pericope. In lines 3 and 9 he is said to have been placed in a position of authority. Line 4 has him appointed as a "most holy one" (לקדוש קודשים). His lot has been cast with the angels and he is considered to be a first-born (l. 5). Particularly telling is that the addressee plays a role turning away wrath from the "men of good pleasure" (l. 10). This language of elevation describes a member of the community serving in a special role. Again, separation need not be viewed in ontological terms.[16] An uncorrupted spirit (i.e. holy spirit) that permits this Maskil figure to access the heavenlies, pursue revealed wisdom, as well as to participate with and venerate angelic beings (l. 1), distinguishes him from his antithesis, namely "fleshly spirit."

In assessing the addressee's separation from the "fleshly spirit" the singular subject "you" should not be overlooked. It is unlikely that this singular address is a statement reflecting anthropology broadly. Given the characteristics of the addressee here, the second-person singular address does not apply to all within the community. A variety of people in different positions are addressed in 4QInstruction, including a second-person singular feminine address at one point (4Q415 2 ii). The "first-born" and "most holy" individual in 4Q418 81+81a 1–14 may, using the *hiphil*

[15] For reconstruction of the text see esp. Strugnell et al. 1999, 300–01; cf. Tigchelaar 2001, 230–31; Rey 2009, 307–08.

[16] Tigchelaar 2001, 232, suggests that the addressee being distinguished here should be read in relation to Levites being separated from other Israelites (Num 8:14; 16:9; Deut 10:8–9). Elgvin (2004) makes a strong case that Levitical and Aaronic descent play no significant role in 4QInstruction.

followed by *niphal* verb from the root בדל, be described as "distinguished" or "separated" from "fleshly spirit." Being "distinguished" from others underscores that the addressees in 4QInstruction do not all share an identical "lot" or "inheritance" (i.e. vocation, here as sage); instead, they acquire revealed wisdom to different degrees. Throughout 4QInstruction are urgent exhortations to seek the "mystery of existence" and genuine concern that one may succumb to fatigue in the process. Angelic beings are held up as superior in pursuing mysteries and therefore models to be emulated. The distinguishing of the one addressed in 4Q418 81+81a from the "fleshly spirit" reinforces his special status and superior acquisition of revelation in comparison to other members of the community.

## 1.3 4Q416 1 12

4Q416 1 preserves part of the opening column of the document, which is evident from the wide right margin, and here we find references to both the "fleshly spirit" and "fleshly vessel."

> 4Q416 1 10–16 (comp. 4Q418 1, 2, 2a, 2b, 2c):[17]
> [10] in heaven he *declares* judgment upon wicked works,
> and all the sons of his truth shall hasten to [...]
> [11] [...] its end.
> And they shall feel dread,
> and all who wallowed in it shall cry out,
> for the heavens shall fear [...]
> [12] [the s]eas and the depths fear,
> and the fleshly spirit (רוח בשר) will be made destitute,
> and the sons of heave[n ...]
> and in the day of [13] its [ju]dgment,
> and all iniquity will be completed,
> until the period of tru[th] is fulfilled
> ◦*lm*◦◦◦
> [14] in all periods of eternity,
> for he is the God of truth and from before the years of[...
> [15] to understand righteousness,
> between good and evil to *l*[[*r* every judgmen[t ...
> [16] fleshly [v]essel (יצר בשר) is he,
> and understanding[...

4Q416 1 describes the order of the cosmos (ll. 1–9) before turning to the theme of judgment. While judgment upon the "fleshly spirit" is described

[17] For reconstruction of the text see Tigchelaar 2001, 42–43, 175–81; cf. Strugnell et al. 1999, 81–88.

in line 12, where they are "stripped" or "made destitute" (ערער), they are never contrasted with a righteous group of humanity.[18] In line 10 "the sons of his truth" cannot be assumed to be a group of righteous and elect human beings, but rather may be heavenly beings. If the verb at the end of line 11 is read as "they will run" (יָרֻצוּ), then this is a depiction of angelic beings hastening to judgment.[19] The "sons of heaven" in line 12 is a more straightforward designation for heavenly beings.[20] These sons of heaven are not set in contrast with the "fleshly spirit," but rather serve as instruments of judgment upon them, similar to line 10.

In 4QInstruction "sons of heaven" (בני שמים) is only found here and in 4Q418 69 ii 13 where a rhetorical question is posed whether human beings are like angelic beings who do not tire. In 4Q418 69 ii future judgment on the wicked is contrasted with reward for the righteous (cf. eschatological judgment in 4Q418 126 i–ii). 4Q418 69 ii does not refer to the "fleshly spirit," but rather the wicked are the "foolish of heart," "sons of iniquity," and most importantly of all "ones who hold fast to evil" (l. 8). By contrast the righteous are those who "seek understanding" and "watch over all knowledge" (ll. 10–11). Expressions for the righteous and wicked root reward and judgment in human activity. The author justifies judgment on the wicked by asking another rhetorical question: "what good is justice for what has not been established?" and then answers this question with, "you were fashioned, but to eternal destruction you will return" (ll. 4–5). Like the Vision of Hagu passage, these lines underscore that the wicked in the document were originally fashioned and established to pursue wisdom. This resonates well with the description of judgment upon the "fleshly spirit" in 4Q416 1, which begins with a pronouncement against their "evil works" (l. 10) and upon those who "wallowed" in wickedness (l. 11).

The words in 4Q416 1 16 (i.e. יצר בשר הוׄא) could refer to an "earthly vessel" (יֵצֶר בָשָׂר) as an epithet for a base human condition (i.e. "he/it is an earthly vessel") or to a fleshly inclination. One justification for reading this as a fleshly *yeṣer* is found in 4Q417 1 ii 12 where this fragmentary phrase is preserved: "do not let the thought of an evil inclination entice

[18] Line 15 may begin a new section; Strugnell et al. 1999, 83 translate line 15 "So that *the righteous may distinguish* (?) between good and evil"; Tigchelaar 2001, 176, has "to let the righteous understand (the distinction) between good and evil." Here, the righteous would be instructed to draw upon the lesson of judgment in the preceding lines.

[19] Tigchelaar 2001, 180.

[20] Strugnell et al. 1999, 290: בני שמים "is usually a non-metaphorical epithet for a group of heavenly beings." Cf. 1QS iv 22; xi 8; 1QH$^a$ xi 23; xxiii 30; xxvi 36; 4Q181 1 2.

you" (אל תפתכה מחשבת יׄצר רע). Tigchelaar comments on line 12 briefly, since the context is too fragmentary to determine its reference,[21] while Kister locates this line within a broader treatment of *yeṣer* in Qumran literature without giving explicit attention to other possible *yeṣarim* in 4QInstruction.[22] Notably, Rosen-Zvi refers to this use of an evil *yeṣer* as innovative. He describes it as "an active agent that can entice people to evil."[23] Moreover, in his assessment the *yeṣer* is not yet reified, however it features "in a demonological semantic field" even if its precise meaning is rather fluid.[24]

In 4Q417 1 ii 12 the imperative form of the verb פתה is used to exhort the addressee to avoid the thought of an evil inclination. How the *piel* form is translated ("enticed," "misled," "deceived," or even "seduced," are possibilities) has significant impact on our understanding of the evil *yeṣer*. Moreover, the expression "thought" (מחשבה) in construct with the *yeṣer*, were it to occur without פתה, would seemingly locate the inclination within the interior of a human being. In 4QInstruction the *piel* verb occurs only here, and in *qal* form is well known as a description for "being simple" (4Q418 221 2). In *piel* פתה is used in the Qumran literature only twice, in (1) 4Q184 1 17 ("Wiles of the Wicked Woman"), and (2) the Temple Scroll (11Q19 66 8; par. 4Q524 15 22).[25] In 4Q184 the seductress "entices" human beings, and in the Temple Scroll a man "seduces" a virgin. It was Baumgarten who first suggested that the woman of 4Q184 is a demonic figure.[26] If this is correct, then this strengthens the argument that the verb פתה functions in a demonological semantic field in 4QInstruction. The activity ascribed to the Evil Inclination in line 12 helps locate its actions as an external and independent force. This is likely similar to the use of evil *yeṣer* in the Plea for Deliverance and Barkhi Nafshi where it is also, likely, an external force.[27]

While there is an active, evil *yeṣer* in 4QInstruction it seems unlikely that the "fleshly vessel" in 4Q416 1 16 is a synonym for it. The presence of

21 Tigchelaar 2008, 350.

22 Kister 2010, 252 (commenting on 4Q417 1 i); cf. Wold 2018.

23 Rosen-Zvi 2011, 46. 24 Rosen-Zvi 2011, 48.

25 Not a frequently used term. It occurs several other times mostly in *pual* forms (e.g. 1QH[a] xii 17; xiv 22; xxii 27).

26 Baumgarten 1991–92. The most recent discussion of this proposal is Goff 2016.

27 In the Qumran literature the set phrase is found on five occasions, in: the Plea for Deliverance (11QPs[a] [11Q5] xix 15–16); 4QInstruction (4Q417 1 ii 12); 4QBarkhi Nafshi[c] (4Q436 1 i 10); and the so-called 4QSectarian Text (4Q422 i 12).

the pronoun (יצר בשר הוא) indicates that it is not an active agent and the translation "fleshly vessel" is more convincing. Therefore, although this is not an identical description for the wicked as "fleshly spirit," it is closely aligned with it because it uses "flesh" language for them.

## 2 THE THANKSGIVING HYMNS

### 2.1 "Vessel of Flesh"

The majority of occurrences of *yeṣer* in the Thanksgiving Hymns are used to describe scurrilous human nature. That humanity is innately sinful in the hymns, and that this is intertwined with physical aspects of a person (e.g. the heart or eyes), has been noted since they were first studied.[28] Rosen-Zvi convincingly argues that to distinguish between *yeṣer* as part of a person's nature and as a component of cosmology is to make a false distinction.[29] Indeed, in the Thanksgiving Hymns *yeṣer* is used frequently in relationship to anthropology, and yet there are occurrences that suggest it is at times reified (1QH$^{a}$ xiii 8): "you did not abandon me to the devices of my inclination [זמות יצרי]."[30] This echoes "devilish plans" (זמות בליעל) in 1QH$^{a}$ xii 14. However, human nature does not consist of two interior parts; good and evil are not battling within. As such care should be taken not to label the cosmology of the hymns as "dualistic"; they are not identical to the Treatise of the Two Spirits where dualistic tensions between light/dark and good/evil, both internal and external, are found.[31] Rather, the hymns testify to a *yeṣer* as an external actor which serves to explain members' sinful consciousness.

An examination of the different ways *yeṣer* is used in the Thanksgiving Hymns confirms Rosen-Zvi's observation. In 1QH$^{a}$ xv 16 ("for you yourself know the intention [יצר] of every deed") and line 19 ("you yourself know the intention [יצר] of your servant"), *yeṣer* is used in reference to a neutral tendency and generic "intention."[32] "Strengthened *yeṣer*" (יצר סמוך) occurs three times in the hymns (1QH$^{a}$ ix 37; x 11, 38)

[28] E.g. Hyatt 1955–56 ; Holm-Nielsen 1960, 274; Newsom 2004, 219–20; Brand 2013, 59–61.

[29] Rosen-Zvi 2011, 48–51.

[30] Tensions are found in the hymns when the *yeṣer* is both an external actor and an aspect of human nature, one way to resolve this is source-critical; so Rosen-Zvi 2011, 50.

[31] *Pace* Holm-Nielsen 1960, 296, who makes the case for a dualistic cosmology in the hymns.

[32] Murphy 1958, 343–44; cf. Rosen-Zvi 2011, 48.

and has positive connotations, denoting firmness or resoluteness in purpose (cf. יצר מבין in 4Q417 1 i 11).[33] The most frequent and well-known expression is "*yeṣer* of clay" (i.e. "vessel of clay": iii 29; ix 23; xi 24–25; xii 30; xix 6; xx 29; xx 35; xxi 11, 38; xxii 12; xxiii 13, 28; xxv 31–32). The expression "*yeṣer* of dust" (i.e. "vessel of dust": viii 18; xxi 17, 25; xxi 34; xxiii 28) is comparable. Characterizing the human "vessel" as dust, and to a lesser extent "clay" (cf. 1QS xi 22), is an allusion to the creation of man from the earth in Genesis 2 and relates to human nature.[34] The "*yeṣer* of guilt" (i.e. "guilty creature": xiv 35), "*yeṣer* of iniquity" (i.e. "vessel of iniquity": xxi 30), and "abhorrent *yeṣer*" (i.e. "abhorrent vessel": xxiii 37, 38) are also indicative of the psalmist's pessimistic anthropology. However, at least two occurrences indicate that it is used as an "inclination"; these are "*yeṣer* of destruction" (i.e. "destructive intention": xv 6–7) and "*yeṣer* of deceit" ("deceitful inclination": xxi 29).

In the case of "*yeṣer* of flesh" (יצר בשר, xviii 25; xxiv 6), Schuller and Newsom's translation "vessel of flesh" rather than "fleshly inclination" makes good sense because it would be difficult to account for an "inclination" within the context. Among the two occurrences of the term, only 1QH$^{a}$ xviii 25 provides context; here we read: "a vessel of flesh [יצר בשר] you have not set up as my refuge." This description appears to be about the speaker's own corporeal being which is insufficient to protect him. Moreover, in the immediately preceding lines the speaker elaborates that he does not put his trust in wealth and unjust gain. "Vessel of flesh" in line 25 is closely related to his body and tangentially to physical luxury and possessions. In lines 28–29 all humanity is given produce from the land, which is contrasted with the sons of truth, who have intelligence and an everlasting inheritance added to this.

In 1QH$^{a}$ xxiv 6 the term "*yeṣer* of flesh" (יצר בשר) at the end of the first line in the column offers no immediate context. An important theme in this column is judgment upon the wicked and, although the text is only preserved in part, guilt is in some way associated with flesh: "and the mysteries of transgression to change flesh [להשנות בשר] through their guilt."[35] Column xxiv is interested in angelic beings (ll. 8, 11) and depicts the fall of the heavenly angels in lines 11–12: "You cast down the heavenly beings [אלים]

33 יצר סמוך is found elsewhere at Qumran only in the Rule of the Community (1QS iv 5; viii 3) and Barkhi Nafshi (4Q438 4 ii 2). For יצר מבין see Wold 2015, 269–71.

34 Maier 1960, 2: 66; Murphy 1958, 339–40.

35 Translation mine; Schuller and Newsom 2012, 73 translate: "and the mysteries of transgression in order that humankind be changed through their guilt."

from [your holy] place." Line 15 refers to the "bastards" (ממזרים), most likely the half-breed offspring from human–angel relations. That "flesh" imprisons is suggested by line 13: "like a bird imprisoned until the time of your favour." Therefore, "vessel of flesh" in column xxiv is not straightforwardly about human nature, but may also extend to the "bastards." Indeed, it is interesting to note that twin spiritual and fleshly existence is typically only found in the Enochic tradition of the giants; here in the hymns (and 4QInstruction) human beings as "fleshly spirit" are also a combination of what is elsewhere separate.

## 2.2 "Spirit of Flesh"

Although humanity is a creature who is defiled by perverted spirits (cf. 1QH$^a$ v, 31–33 below),[36] here in 1QH$^a$ iv it is not entirely clear whether the psalmist views רוחות as (1) evil spirits possessing human beings and trying to lead them astray (e.g. 4Q444 1 1–4; 2 i 4; 4Q510 1 5–6; 4Q560 1 i 2–3; 1 ii 5–6; 11QPs$^a$ xix 13–16) or (2) human tendencies. When the speaker is strengthened to resist spirits (l. 35), he is enabled to persevere by the spirits given by God (l. 29). That spirits are resisted by insight and knowledge (l. 33) may indicate that these are human tendencies rather than external evil spirits. However, in line 37 the subject who rules over the psalmist is lost to the lacuna, but given the context it is likely רוחות.

1QH$^a$ iv 35b–37

35 ... Strengthen [his] loi[ns that he may sta]nd against spirits
36 [... and that he may w]alk in everything that you love and despise everything that [you] hate, [and do] what is good in your eyes.
37 [...]their [domi]nion in his members; for your servant (is) a fleshly spirit. [...] *vacat* [...] *vacat*

In this column, and the hymns generally, God chooses those who are delivered from sin to act in accordance with God's will (iv, 33–34: "As for me, I understand that (for) the one whom you have chosen you determine his way and through insight [... you] draw him back from sinning against you").[37] The ability to resist sin and evil may be attributed ultimately to election.[38] Despite the psalmist's election and

[36] That these "spirits" are explicitly related to the dominion of "Belial" is unlikely; see Davies 2010, 8.

[37] Cf. 1QH$^a$ viii 28; xii 5.

[38] As Brand 2013, 59–67.

divine support, in line 37 he still expresses that he is a "fleshly spirit."[39]

1QH$^{a}$ v 12–vi 18 is reconstructed by Puech as a hymn of the Maskil, and it is here that the other two uses of "fleshly spirit" are found (1QH$^{a}$ v 15, 30).[40] A prominent theme is knowledge of the mysteries of God.[41] Mortals, including the elect, are "fleshly spirit" (רוח בשר), and what differentiates them from the rest of humanity is the granting of true knowledge through the divine spirit.[42] In the hymns, humanity, including the author, is described as fashioned of dust and water and, as such, he asks what "fleshly spirit" is to understand all these matters and to have insight into God's counsel; the answer is that the holy spirit placed within the elect enables them to know mysteries.

1QH$^{a}$ v 12–20

12 [A psalm for the In[structor, that he may prostrate himself befor]e God . . .] deeds of God
13 [. . .]and that the simple may understand [. . .] [. . .] [. . .]*y* forever
14 [. . .]*t* and that humankind may understand concerning [. . .] flesh and the council of the spirits of [. . .] they walk.
15 [. . . Blessed are] you, O Lord, [. . .]*r* a fleshly spirit (רוח ב֯שר) *bb* [. . .]through your mighty strength
16 [and the abundance of]your [kind]ness together with your great goodness [and the cup of]your wrath and [your] zealous judgme[nts . . . unsea]rchable. All
17 [. . .]*t* all insight and in[struction] and the mysteries of the plan and the beginning[. . .]you [es]tablished
18 [. . .] holiness from a[ges] of old [and] to everlasting ages you yourself resolved [. . .]holy ones
19 [. . .] and in your wonderful mysteries [you] have instructed [me for the s]ake of your glory, and in the depth [. . . source of] your insight not
20 [. . .]you yourself have revealed the ways of truth and the works of evil (דרכ֯י א֯מ֯ת֯ ו֯מעשי רע), wisdom and folly[. . .] righteousness.

God grants the Maskil of these lines insight into the mysteries of his plan. The revelation of mysteries is intertwined with the ways of truth and evil

[39] Cf. Rom 7–8, esp. 8:9 (tensions of spirit/flesh), 8:24–25 (expectation of deliverance from the body).

[40] Puech 1988, 63. [41] Newsom 2004, 217.

[42] Cf. 1 Cor 2:14 where "natural man" (ψυχικὸς ἄνθρωπος) does not receive the gifts of the spirit; 1 Cor 3:1 where Paul contrasts spiritual (πνευματικός) with fleshly (σαρκίνος) people.

(l. 20), which accords well with the Vision of Hagu. Later in the same column, after the second occurrence of "fleshly spirit" (רוח בשר), the means by which understanding is given is the spirit (l. 36).

1QH$^a$ v 31–36a

30 for everlasting ages. In the mysteries of your understanding [you] apportioned all these in order to make known your glory. [But how i]s a fleshly spirit to understand
31 all these things and to discern *bs*[...] great [...]? What is one born of woman amid all your [gre]at fearful acts? He
32 is a thing constructed of dust and kneaded with water. Sin[ful gui]lt is his foundation, obscene shame, and a so[urce of im]purity. And a perverted spirit rules
33 him. If he acts wickedly, he will become[a sign for]ever and a portent for dis[ta]nt generations of flesh. Only through your goodness
34 can a person be righteous, and by [your] abundant compas[sion ...]. By your splendor you glorify him, and you give [him] dominion [with] abundant delights together with eternal
35 peace and long life. For [... and] your word will not turn back. And I, your servant, know
36 by means of the spirit (ברוח) that you place in me [...] and all your deeds are righteousness. And your word will not turn back. ...

The "fleshly spirit" in the Thanksgiving Hymns is equated with the obtuse part of humanity unable to gain insight without God's spirit. As Flusser comments, the gift of the spirit elevates the Qumran elect from the realm of the flesh even if the psalmist still declares that he is among mortal humanity.[43] Later in the hymns, in 1QH$^a$ xix 12–17, the psalmist exults that instruction in truth leads to purification from sin and a place among angelic beings.

## 3 CONCLUSION

At the very least, the shared use of rare vocabulary in the hymns and 4QInstruction suggests a common cultural milieu. Similar material could be explained as the work of bricoleurs gathering available materials for their own bricolage. However, a small amount of verbatim material found in 1QH$^a$ xviii and 4Q418 55 may indicate direct knowledge of the other composition.[44] Goff argues that the "Hodayot exhibits a degree of

[43] Flusser 2007, 288–90. Cf. 1QS xi 15–22, which echoes similar sentiments.
[44] See e.g. Strugnell et al. 1999, 272.

reliance on the sapiential tradition" and that "their thematic correspondences and terminological overlaps suggest a direct relationship."[45] While the authorial speaker in each exhorts his addressees to study, to whom revelation is disclosed and the degree to which it is indebted to a deterministic worldview differs between these writings. Moreover, in 4QInstruction the speaker does not make the same claims to revelation as does the psalmist of the hymns.

Thematic and terminological correspondences between 4QInstruction and other traditions have been explored by several scholars. For instance, Stuckenbruck assesses 4QInstruction's relationship to Enochic authors, though he does not posit a direct literary relationship between them.[46] Rey concludes that Sirach and 4QInstruction derive from the same scribal school.[47] Within the hymns, Enochic literature, and Sirach intriguing commonalities are found, and yet so too are sharp differences (e.g. Sirach identifies "wisdom" with "torah," although 4QInstruction never mentions "torah" nor thematizes it; Enochic literature centers upon the ascent of a righteous figure who then descends and transmits wisdom, which contrasts with 4QInstruction). If 4QInstruction is viewed as a "non-Yaḥad" composition, as opposed to a "pre-sectarian" one, this removes the perception of a clear trajectory and evolutionary development toward "sectarianism"; it allows for the possibility that 4QInstruction is part of a wider pattern of religious thinking that spans a longer period of time than is often viewed. The hymns draw upon a wider tradition (e.g. Enochic literature, Jubilees) of which 4QInstruction is a representative, but differences between these compositions need to be taken into account when assessing their relationship.

Both 4QInstruction and the Thanksgiving Hymns use "fleshly spirit" (רוח בשר) to express distance from the divine; the difference between these texts is how this distance comes about. This chapter has considered human nature. This opens up different perspectives on the disclosing of revelation to the elect. In the hymns, humanity is viewed as generally corrupt and spirit elevates the psalmist so that he can access mysteries. In 4QInstruction the order of spirit and corruption is reversed. There is only one humanity in 4QInstruction, who are bequeathed spirit and revelation from the outset, and the challenge is to maintain spirit through

[45] Goff 2004, 287. [46] Stuckenbruck 2002. [47] Rey 2009, 334.

diligent pursuit of the "mystery of existence." In 4QInstruction it is the failure to maintain spirit that leads one to become a "fleshly spirit." Furthermore, 4QInstruction emphasizes that the exalted Maskil-like figure is separated from the "fleshly spirit" (4Q418 81+81a). By contrast, in the hymns the psalmist emphasizes that even with the divinely granted spirit he remains "fleshly spirit." The granting of spirit in 1QH$^{a}$ iv is a matter of "chosen-ness," an idea that is absent from 4QInstruction.[48] Thus, those who receive revealed wisdom are considerably fewer in the hymns than in 4QInstruction.

4QInstruction may have influenced the hymns, but the hymns do not share the same view of humankind, election, or determinism. If the hymns were familiar with 4QInstruction, then changes occur in regard to accessing wisdom; there is a shift from all Israel to a narrow, elect group. In the hymns not only is revelation disclosed, but also the psalmist is in an extraordinary position of authority. The theological shifts in the hymns match well with an evolution of a worldview that, because of discontent and marginalization, seeks to limit and control access to revelation. 4QInstruction seeks to explain who is among the faithful and who is not in a less severe manner; indeed, it is weighted toward merit rather than election. In contrast, the hymns project a negative anthropology that defines "us" and "them." In the hymns the only way to rise above the continuing situation of the "fleshly spirit" in order to gain understanding is God's election; in 4QInstruction the addressees are not lifted from the "fleshly spirit," but rather if one forsakes the study of the "mystery of existence," then one becomes a corrupted spirit.

Despite these differences, some similarities suggest a closer relationship between the hymns and 4QInstruction than previously observed. A dualistic framework for 4QInstruction is only found in an unconvincing interpretation of two creations and two peoples in the Vision of Hagu passage. Neither 4QInstruction nor the hymns are dualistic. Of the more than sixty uses of רוח in the hymns, none is within binary opposites (e.g. good/evil). Even when "light" and "dark" are contrasted in 1QH$^{a}$ xx 4–10 they do not express a dualistic cosmology and they are not in opposition.[49] 4QInstruction too is entirely absent of opposing and antithetical categories, there is no "spirit" and "flesh," "light" and

[48] The root בחר occurs twice without meaningful context (4Q418 45 ii 1; 4Q418 234 2) and once as an indictment on the wicked who do not choose what God delights in (4Q418 55 5).

[49] Davies 2010, 8–9.

"darkness"; nor is an evil *yeṣer* opposing a good *yeṣer*. However, both texts enter into an emerging tradition of demonizing sin. Both have a "positive" *yeṣer* that does not function within a binary model. There is an evil *yeṣer* in both; in 4QInstruction it leads one astray and away from the pursuit of wisdom, whereas in the hymns it is present from the beginning and the psalmist gives thanks for not being left to its devices.

The "fleshly spirit" is ultimately the same description for the unenlightened and base human being. However, in the hymns and 4QInstruction it operates within very different anthropologies. The use of "vessel of flesh" (יצר בשר) is a much more straightforward circumlocution for (a segment of) humanity than the oxymoronic "fleshly *spirit*."

# 5

# Theological Anthropology in the Enochic Tradition

Loren Stuckenbruck

## 1 INTRODUCTION

The creation of "Adam" by God in Gen 2:7 is nowhere cited or alluded to in 1 Enoch. Nevertheless, among the early materials of 1 Enoch, especially the Book of Watchers, a comparable theological anthropology can be discerned. The following discussion will argue that the significance of the human being within the Enoch tradition can be profitably placed in conversation with the early chapters of Genesis. In particular, we shall take the core units of the Book of Watchers (1 Enoch 6–11 and 12–16) as a point of departure, before examining its reception in several further texts found in other parts of 1 Enoch.

## 2 ELEMENTS SHARED BY THE BOOK OF WATCHERS AND GENESIS

Let us begin with the opening chapters of Genesis.[1] Humans have much in common with the animal world: they share the status of a "living being" (נפש חיה, ψυχὴ ζῶσα, Gen 2:7; cf. Gen 1:20, 24),[2] are instructed "be fruitful and multiply and fill the earth" (Gen 1:28; cf. Gen 1:22; 9:1, 7), and are, according to the Yahwist, created "from the ground" (Gen 2:7; cf. Gen

[1] See Hendel 2004 (on Gen 6:1–4).

[2] No doubt driven by the need to distinguish humanity from the animal world, the Targums emphasize that Adam (i.e. and not the animals) could speak. See Hayward 2010. One may ask whether this presupposes an awareness and rejection of the tradition that both humans and animals were initially created with the ability to speak (Jub 3:28; Philo, *Opif.* 156; Josephus, *Ant.* 1.41).

2:19). But in both the Priestly and Yahwist accounts the human being occupies a distinctive place within the created order. In the Priestly account it is the human being who is fashioned in the image of God (Gen 1:26–27), while the Yahwist narrative marks out humanity as a species upon whom God has bestowed "a breath of life" (Gen 2:7). Moreover, the instruction to "be fruitful and multiply" is accompanied by the further statement that humans can "subdue and have dominion" over the animals (Gen 1:28), while replenishing plants and fruit trees are given as food supply (Gen 1:29). The Priestly account's commission of humans to act as stewards of other parts of the created order is echoed by the Yahwist's account, in which Adam is commissioned to work the ground (Gen 2:15; cf. Gen 2:5).

The characteristics that originally distinguished humanity from the other creatures persist after Adam and Eve's disobedience, specifically the human ability to engage in agricultural activity (Gen 3:23) and, significantly, the ongoing status of humans as being in the image of God (Gen 5:1; cf. Gen 9:6).[3] New developments, however, manifest themselves. Now the bearing of children (Gen 3:16) and the tilling of soil (Gen 3:17–19; 5:29) are accompanied, respectively, by pain (עצב, λύπη) and toil (עצבון, λύπη). As the narrative unfolds, readers become aware of rising conflict among humans (Gen 4:1–16) and of the human origination of culture (Gen 4:20–22). Although this biblical story offers no obvious value-judgment on the emergence of human culture, it does arise in the wake of the stories about disobedience (by Adam and Eve) and murder (of Abel by Cain). Thus the events leading up to the narrative of the Great Flood (Gen 5:28–6:22) create the setting for Noah's birth to be presented as "relief" (the meaning associated with his name) from "the hard labor of our hands" associated with tilling the ground that God had cursed (Gen 5:29). Corresponding to these developments in the narrative, conditions just prior to the Deluge are fraught with the increase of evil manifested through violence among humans (Gen 6:5–7, 11–13). Within this context, the description of the activities of the "sons of God" as they sired offspring through "the daughters of humanity" remains noticeably neutral in tone (Gen 6:1–2, 4).[4]

[3] Though the term דמות ("likeness") replaces צלם ("image"; cf. Gen 1:27), it derives from Gen 1:26 כדמותנו ("according to our likeness"), where it stands in parallel with כצלמנו ("according to our image").

[4] The extent to which the "sons of God" and their progeny are considered evil depends in part on the character of the traditions underlying it. Cf. Hendel 2004, 23–32 (discussion of the Canaanite, Phoenician, Mesopotamian, and Greek myths).

A number of the features just described occur also in the Book of Watchers (1 En 1–36) in the Ethiopic version,[5] supported by the Greek[6] and, occasionally, the fragmentary Aramaic manuscripts.[7] First, the events associated in Genesis with the Garden of Eden have their equivalent in "the paradise of righteousness" in the Book of Watchers (1 En 32:3–6). In the Enochic text the Garden is briefly and vaguely referred to in a statement that includes the note that the aged father and aged mother (i.e. Adam and Eve in Genesis) were driven from the Garden when they learned wisdom by eating from the magnificent tree of wisdom. Unlike the Genesis account (Gen 3:16–19), however, nothing is stated about any consequence of this. Second, the introduction of culture is directly assigned to the seditious "angels, the sons of heaven" (6:2 – Eth. and Gr. Cod. Pan.), who instruct humans in the fashioning of metals for jewelry and weapons, beautification techniques, herbal medications, and the reading and interpretation of prognosticating signs (7:1; 8:1–3). In contrast to Gen 4:20–22, these expressions of culture are unambiguously regarded as negative developments. Third, in the Enochic tradition the deterioration of culture and violence against the created order run in parallel. While the fallen angels instruct humans how to engage in reprehensible activities, their offspring, the giants, make impossible demands of humans, whom they compel to feed them (1 En 7:3–5). The giants force humans into agricultural slavery, but when the land's produce does not satisfy their voracious appetites, the giants begin destroy animals (1 En 7:5); they even turn to cannibalism and devour one another's "flesh"[8] and to drink "blood" (see Section 3).[9] The result of all this is little less than an environmental catastrophe.[10] In its complex narrative about events leading up to the Great Flood,[11] the Enochic tradition of the Book of Watchers, in contrast to the Genesis 6, gives more emphasis to the notion

[5] See Stuckenbruck 2007, 19–26; Stuckenbruck and Erho 2011. The translations adhere where possible to the Eth. I recension; unless otherwise indicated, they are my own.

[6] Citations of Gr. Codex Panopolitanus (hereafter Cod. Pan.) are based on Black 1970. The text from the Syncellus fragments is based on Mosshammer 1984.

[7] See Milik 1976, and Stuckenbruck 2000a. For the citations from the Book of Giants, see Puech 2001 and Stuckenbruck 2000b.

[8] The text of 4Q201 iii 21 has בסר[הן (Cod. Pan. ἀλλήλων τὰς σάρκας).

[9] Extant in 4Q202 1 ii 25a (supralinear) שתין דמ]א (Cod. Pan. τὸ αἷμα ἔπινον). On the giants' internecine fighting cf. 1 En 88:2; Jub 5:9; 7:22.

[10] See the discussion below on 4Q531 2, which expands the catalogue of victims in 1 En 7:3–5.

[11] The combination of three distinguishable strands in the present form of 1 En 6–11 has been noted by a number of scholars. See, e.g., Nickelsburg 1977; Newsom 1980; and Nickelsburg 2001, 171–72.

of human beings as victims of oppressive forces represented by the fallen angels' offspring; with less emphasis, the tradition acknowledges humans as complicit insofar as they adopt and carry out the angels' instructions (1 En 7:1; 8:1–3), which the writer(s) regarded as objectionable.

## 3 1 ENOCH 6–16: THE THEOLOGICAL ANTHROPOLOGY OF GIANTS AND HUMANITY COMPARED

The details given about the giants' physique (1 En 7:3) and the "flesh" that they devour from one another (1 En 7:5) suggest that the tradition draws a limited, though significant, analogy between the giants and humanity. Here, the Enochic tradition, especially through the divine speech in 1 Enoch 15–16, presents an understanding of the human being based on how this contrasts with the nature embodied by the giants. In order to clarify the theological anthropology sustained at this point in the Book of Watchers, we should first review what the texts state about the giants.[12]

Within the context of his visionary encounter in the heavenly throne room, Enoch is instructed by God what to say in response to the rebellious angels' pleas for mercy (1 En 15:1–16:4). According to the speech, these angels (called "watchers of heaven," 1 En 15:2) have violated the created order, which God had originally set up in two distinct parts with boundaries between them: the heavenly sphere of "spirits" (1 En 15:6, 10), and the earthly (human) sphere of "flesh" and "blood" (1 En 15:4, 6). By abandoning their heavenly dwelling and impregnating human women, they sired a hybrid race of giants, an act which, as we have seen, had disastrous consequences. The gargantuan race, produced through an intermingling of "flesh" (from the earthly sphere) and "spirit" (from the angelic sphere), embodies spheres intended to be separate. Illegitimate by their very nature, the giants are branded *mamzerim* (1 En 10:9 – Cod. Pan. μαζηρέους).[13]

Although the giants are regarded as misfits within the created structures of the cosmos, they share with humans a bipartite existence. For example, by virtue of being sired by the angels, the giants consist of "spirit" (cf. 1 En 15:8–16:1).[14] A similar dimension is attributed to humans (1 En 9:3, 10–

[12] For an analysis of the giants' nature, see esp. Wright 2005, esp. 96–177; Stuckenbruck 2003.

[13] The Greek transliterates ממזרים (Heb.) or ממזריא (Aram.); ממזרים sometimes refers to the "spirits" of the giants which are regarded as demonic beings: cf. 4Q510 1.5; 4Q511 35.7; 48+49–51.2–3; 4Q444 2 i 4.

[14] Eth. uses pl. *nafest*, *nāfesāt*, and *manāfest* interchangeably; Gr. Cod. Pan. and Syncellus have πνεύματα.

Eth. *nafesāt*, Gr. Cod. Pan. αἱ ψυχαί[15] from Heb./Aram. נפשת).[16] It is significant that Cod. Pan. withholds the term ψυχαί ("souls") from the giants,[17] unless it is further qualified by "flesh" (cf. 1 En 16:1). When standing alone, ψυχή is applied exclusively to (deceased) humanity (1 En 22:3 *bis*), a distinguishing feature that was lost when the text was translated into Ethiopic. Thus the vocabulary used in Cod. Pan. differs from the Greek translation tradition for Genesis in which "living soul" is applied to the animal world as well (cf. Gen 1:21, 24; 2:19).

With respect to physical existence, both the giants and human beings inhabit bodies. The physical frame of the giants could be called either "body" (1 En 15:9 – Cod. Pan. σῶμα,[18] Eth. *segā*) or "flesh" (7:5, בשר in 4Q201 1 iii 21 and 4Q202 1 ii 25a; 1 En 16:1, in a more qualified sense: Cod. Pan. ἡ ψυχὴ τῆς σαρκὸς αὐτῶν; Eth. *nāfesāta segāhomu*). For both the giants and humans, "flesh" and "blood" can be associated. This may already be the case for the giants in 1 En 7:5, where they are said to have "devoured the flesh of one another and to drink blood from it [viz. their flesh]."[19] The clearest analogy, however, occurs in 1 En 15:4, where the twinning of "flesh" and "blood" applies to both humans and giants:

> You were holy ones and spirits living forever.
> You have defiled yourselves with women and
> have sired offspring through *the blood of flesh*.
> And you have desired the blood of humans,[20]
> and you have brought forth *flesh and blood*
> – as they do it – who die and are destroyed.

The first occurrence of "flesh" and "blood" in 1 En 15:4 (αἷμα σαρκός, Eth. *dama segā*) refers to the women with whom the Watchers mated,

[15] Both Syncellus recensions read τὰ πνεύματα αἱ ψυχαί. An expansion.

[16] Cf. 4Q202 1 iii 11 to 1 En 9:3 (נפש]ת). In addition to "soul," πνεῦμα describes the post-mortem existence of humans, especially in the Book of Watchers: see 1 En 22:3 (with "souls"), 5–7, 9–13.

[17] Cod. Pan. designates the fallen angels as πνεύματα only (1 En 19:1).

[18] Syncellus: τὸ σῶμα τῆς σαρκός. An expansion (cf. 1 En 9:3; 10).

[19] So the Eth. Version. The Gr. Cod. Pan. has a more ambiguous reading: "And they began to sin against birds and animals and reptiles and fish, and to devour the flesh of one another, and they drank blood." 4Q201 1 iii 19–21 + 4Q202 1 ii 25 (frags *j*, *k*) may be reconstructed to have had a similar text (on which see below). Gr. Syncellus preserves no corresponding text for 1 En 7:4–6.

[20] Nickelsburg (2001, 271–72) interprets this as a reference to blood pollution (through sleeping with women during their menstrual period, forbidden for priests in Lev 15:19–24).

while the second instance (σάρξ καὶ αἷμα; Eth. *segā wa-dam*) refers to their progeny (the giants). For both the giants and humans these terms, where they occur together, underscore mortal existence, which in the case of humans is regarded as a given (hence humans need to procreate) and in the case of the giants is the result of a needless desire on the part of the Watchers to procreate (cf. also 1 En 15:5–7).

What were the differences between the giants and human beings within the early Enochic traditions? The first, the unsanctioned half-breed existence of the giants, was a function of their questionable origin. The spirits and bodies of the giants originated from a forbidden comingling of their rebellious fathers and their ravaged human mothers.[21] The mix of spirit/soul and flesh in humanity is of a different sort and, significantly, reflects what God bestowed upon humans from the start. This essential difference is underlined by the divine speech of 1 Enoch 15 and 16 (esp. 15:8–10).

Second, human beings are portrayed as essentially innocent, whereas the giants are regarded as culpable. Whereas in the Asa'el tradition, which is concerned with the angels' teachings, human beings become complicit in the dissemination of reprehensible skills and practices,[22] in the Shemihazah strand of the tradition they fall victim to the giants' insatiable appetites. The giants, whose nature is out of step with the created order, carry out a series of violent acts against innocent victims, thus posing a threat to the existence of what God created. This is made clear in a sustained way in 1 En 7:3–5 (cf. also Book of Giants at 4Q531 frags 1 and 2–3). One can discern the following information about what the giants do:

- They consume the "labor of all humanity" who, in turn, are unable to satisfy them (v. 3). The object of consumption here is the produce resulting from the agricultural work (cf. 1 En 11:1) to which, according to Gen 2:5, 15, humans were assigned.
- They begin to kill humankind and to eat them (v. 4; Gr. Syncellus[a] places this note after 1 En 8:3: to eat "flesh of humanity"). Humans

[21] On the hybrid nature of the giants, see esp. Alexander 1999, 337–41; Eshel 2003; Wright 2005; Coblentz Bautch 2009.

[22] The additional text for 1 En 8:1 in Syncellus ("the sons of men made for themselves and for their daughters, and they transgressed and led astray the holy ones") is probably not original (*contra* Nickelsburg 2001, 195–96; Bhayro 2005, 28–30; and Coblentz Bautch 2008). The last visible line of 4QEn[b] (= 4Q202) 1 ii contains the text "concerning antimony and eye shadow" while the line below it is left blank; text corresponding to 1 En 8:2 probably belongs to the top of col. iii (frags *p* and *r*). It is very unlikely, therefore, that Syncellus's lengthier text could have appeared below the last visible line of text on col. ii (frags *j*–*o*).

become victims of the giants' cannibalistic activity, with the result that their "souls" (1 En 9:4, 10) are left.

- They begin to sin against animals (v. 5; cf. the longer Aramaic text[23] 4QEn$^{a}$ 1 iii 20–21).
- They eat "flesh" (4Q201 1 iii 21 בשר) and drink "blood" (4Q202 1 ii 25a דמ]א).[24] This represents the endpoint of the escalating violence that began with the consumption of agricultural produce. When this was not enough, the giants began to be carnivorous.

A further description of the giants' destructive deeds is preserved in several fragments from the Book of Giants (4Q531 1 i–ii; 2–3; 1Q23 9+14 +15 cf. also Jub 5:2; 7:24). According to 4Q532 1 ii + 2.9 they (the context suggests the subject to be the "nephilim" 4Q532 2.3) "inflicted a great injury on [the] ea[rth]" and according to 1Q23 9+14+15.4 they (probably also the giants) "killed many." Most significant, however, is a catalogue of parts of the created order detrimentally affected by the antediluvian atrocities found in 4Q531 fragment 2. The text supplies an even lengthier and more detailed list of victims (e.g. the moon, all kinds of wheat, trees), than the Aramaic text to 1 En 7:5. The giants' activities, then, threaten the survival of that which God has created.

Thus, together with the Book of Giants, the early Enochic tradition emphasizes that the giants are misfits in the world by virtue of their mixed nature, and that their activities are bent on effecting an "environmental meltdown" as befits their nature. The ultimate purpose for humanity, by contrast, works in the opposite direction. In the eschatological scene following the punishment and destruction of evil (1 En 10:4–16a), the text anticipates a time when righteous humanity will enjoy reproductivity, long life, and agricultural replenishment and blessing (1 En 10:16b–19; 11:1; cf. Book of Giants at 1Q23 1+6+22; 2 Bar. 29:5–7).

Third, in an ironic twist, God-given developments among humanity provide the basis for the angels' wayward response that leads to cosmic disarray. Taking up a tradition also found in Gen 6:2, 1 Enoch 6 opens by setting the scene for the angelic rebellion: "when the sons of men had become numerous in those days, *beautiful and attractive* daughters were born to them; and the angels, the sons of heaven saw them and desired

[23] Milik 1976, 150–51.

[24] The Aramaic text breaks off without making clear whose flesh was devoured (4Q201 iii 21). Cod. Pan., followed by the Ethiopic, furnishes the rest of the sentence: they ate "the flesh of each other and they drank blood."

them" (vv. 1–2a).[25] The angels' sinful response to humanity emerges from two features in the text. First, the procreativity of humanity. Humans, not the angels, are commissioned to procreate (Gen 1:28; 9:1, 7), not angelic, spirit-beings (1 En 15:5–7a). By seeking to participate in the reproductivity of humanity, the angels bring about events that undermine this mechanism. Second, the Watchers deem the women's beauty that had attracted them to begin with as insufficient. Consequently, the instructions given by the Watchers to humanity are made to include how to fashion jewelry, the use of cosmetics, and "all manner of precious stones and dyes" (1 En 8:1). The God-given beauty with which women were endowed is subverted, replaced by techniques that the world was not created to yield.

## 4 THE BOOK OF WATCHERS' UNDERSTANDING OF HUMANITY: IMPLICATIONS FOR ESCHATOLOGY

The above review has attempted to show that the earliest Enoch traditions underline the essential integrity of humanity within the created order, doing so by setting up the giant offspring of the rebellious angels as a foil. But this theological anthropology is not presupposed, at least among the writings composed until the end of the second century BCE. The vision of eschatological bliss in 1 Enoch 10–11 is pivotal: it not only offers a conclusion to the initial fallen angels narrative in chapters 6–11, but also supplies a tradition that influences what several later passages in the Enochic corpus have to say about humanity.

For the moment, we take the vision of humanity in 1 En 10:20–22 as a point of departure. The text, in which God is speaking to the archangel Michael (cf. 1 En 10:11), reads:[26]

(20) But as for you, cleanse the earth from all uncleanness,
and from all injustice,
and from all sin and godlessness.
And eliminate all the unclean things that have been done on the earth.
(21) And all the children of humanity will become righteous,
and all the peoples will serve and bless me,
and they will all worship me.[27]

[25] The translation is my own, based on Cod. Pan. and the Eth. I recension.

[26] Translation is my own, based on Eth. I recension with the corresponding Greek terms from Cod. Pan inserted.

[27] Cod. Pan., through *homoioarcton* (και εσονται … και εσονται) omits the first line and reads, "and all the peoples will be serving, and all (will be) blessing and worshiping me" (και εσονται παντες λατρευοντες οι λαοι και ευλογουντες παντες μοι και προσυνουντες).

(22) And the entire earth will be cleansed
from all defilement and all uncleanness.
And no wrath or torment
will I ever again send upon them,
for all the generations of eternity.

This passage follows an account in which Michael and other prominent angelic figures are commissioned to enact a series of punishments against Asa'el (1 En 10:4), the giants (1 En 10:9–10, 15[28]), and Shemihazah and his wayward companions (1 En 10:11–14). In addition, the story tells of the destruction of "wrongdoing and every evil work" (1 En 10:16a; cf. further 1 En 10:20, 22). The account of divine punishment in 1 En 10:4–16a appears to be concerned with the time of the Flood (cf. 1 En 10:1–3). This time of punishment and divine intervention, however, does not altogether do away with evil. Whereas the giants are destroyed (1 En 10:15; though see 1 En 10:9–10), Asa'el is kept in a temporary subterranean abode (1 En 10:4–5) and Shemihazah and companions are bound in a fiery abyss (1 En 10:11–14) until the final judgment, at which time they will be done away with. Although the text is looking back to the period of the Noachic Flood, its concern with eschatological punishment and the appearance of a "plant of righteousness and truth" (1 En 10:16b) shows that this account about a past event (*Urzeit*) is paradigmatic for what will happen in the ultimate future (*Endzeit*). This time, from the point of view of the writer(s), the event is eschatological, and the question emerges: what grounds are there for the text to reach its conclusion that in the eschatological all humanity will "become righteous"[29] and worship God?

Despite the large amount of scholarly attention paid to 1 Enoch chapters 6–11 and 12–16, surprisingly little has been done to offer a sustained reading of how the motif of eschatological restoration and reconstitution of humanity relates to its immediate literary setting. Instead, commentators have mostly treated this vision of the future by either noting how it coheres with biblical traditions regarding the fate of the nations or by observing its influence on the later Enochic texts (see Section 5).[30] In an overview of apocalyptic ideas that he attributed to the second century

[28] The text reads "spirits of the half-breeds" (τῶν πνεύματα τῶν κιβδηλων, Eth. *manfāsāta tawnēt*), which is to be taken as a synonym for the giants (cf. 1 En 9:9–10; 10:9–10; 15:11) *contra* Dillmann 1853, 101; cf. Nickelsburg 2001, 219.

[29] So the Eth.; the phrase is omitted in Cod. Pan. through *homoioteleuton*; see further Nickelsburg 2001, 219.

[30] See esp. Black 1985, 140; Nickelsburg 2001, 224, 228; Uhlig 1984, 531–32 ; and Olson 2004, 40.

BCE, Charles commented that, "according to I Enoch x. 21, all the Gentiles are to become righteous and worship God."[31] Though Charles' interpretation of the passage has been largely retained,[32] little has been done to explain the ideological basis for such an outcome.

In light of the attempt above to isolate distinguishing features of humanity in 1 Enoch 6–16 (Sections 2 and 3), we may ask how 1 En 10:20–22 relates to the fallen angels mythology and to the literary context in chapters 12–16 that immediately follows.

The framework for addressing these questions regarding 1 En 10:20–22 (within 10:17–11:2) is determined by four factors: (1) how it relates to traditions in the Hebrew Bible which refer to the eventual recognition of Israel's God among the nations; (2) its role and function within the Book of Watchers; (3) its take-up in traditions that similarly anticipate a turning to or worship of God among the nations (Animal Apocalypse at 1 En 90:37; Apocalypse of Weeks at 1 En 91:14; Epistle of Enoch at 1 En 100:6; 105:1; Tob 14:6); and (4) its conceptual relation to late Second Temple traditions that signal a basic recognition by the nations of Israel's God (Ps Sol 17:29–32, 34; Book of Parables in 1 En 48:5; 50:2; 62:1–12; 63:1–12; Dan 7:14).

## 4.1 The Nations' Ultimate Recognition of the God of Israel in the Hebrew Bible

A number of biblical texts express the belief that the nations of the earth will worship Israel's God. A brief overview of these traditions enables us to discern particular features in 1 Enoch 10. In the Hebrew Bible the response of the nations to the God of Israel is expressed in a variety of ways. The nations will:

- come to Jerusalem to be instructed and "walk in his paths" (Isa 2:3; Mic 4:2);
- bring gifts and wealth to Jerusalem (Isa 18:7; 45:14; 60:5, 11);
- supplicate God (Isa 19:22; Zech 8:21–22);
- be subservient to Israel (Isa 45:14; 60:10, 12);
- recognize that the God of Israel is unique (Isa 45:14–15; 66:18–19; Ps 102:15);

[31] Charles 1963, 246.

[32] Except there is now wide agreement that the Book of Watchers dates to at least the third century BCE.

- recognize the special status of Israel amongst the nations (Zech 8:23; cf. Isa 60:3);
- "turn" to God (Ps 22:27);
- worship God in Jerusalem (Isa 66:23;[33] Zech 14:16–19; Ps 22:27; 86:9; cf. Zech 14:16–19).
- They are also exhorted to praise God for his justice and mercy (Ps 67:3–4; 117:1).

Why is the motif of the nations' eventual recognition of God so important? These texts are primarily motivated by the conviction that what happens to Israel – whether it be exile or restoration – forms part of God's grand design for the rest of the world.[34] They are thus a way of reenforcing the supremacy of Israel's faith. This motif reflects an outcome that emerges logically from a fundamental conviction that Israel is the elect people of a God who is Creator of the cosmos.[35] However nationalistic or ethnic the expressions of Israel's faith may be, God is held to be at work throughout the world in a way that affects the other nations which, though not elect, are nevertheless subject to God's rule (e.g. Ps 22:28; 47:8; 86:9). One way of doing this was to subordinate the deities of other nations to Israel's God, who is assigned to the pinnacle of an assembly called "gods" (*'elohim*: cf. Exod 15:11; Deut 32:43 MT; Ps 29:1–2; 46:6–7; 50:1; 82:1 [LXX]; 97:7) or "sons of God" (see Job 1:6).[36] Especially significant is Ps 82:6–7. The text (both Heb. and Gr.) has God say, "You are gods, and all of you are sons of the Most High. Nevertheless, you will die like men, and fall like *any* one of the princes" (NASB). The language of the tradition evolves in a number of texts during the Second Temple period, so that references to "gods" or "sons of God" could be identified as subordinate "angels" (so the Greek translation tradition) with whom the nations were associated (cf. Deut 32:8 LXX; 32:43 LXX; Ps 96:7).

Second, the motif of the nations' worship of God expresses a hope for the reversal of the conditions of subjugation, which Israel presently suffers. The nations will eventually acknowledge Israel's God with the result that they – and not Israel – will become the subservient ones (see esp. Isa 60).

Third, Jerusalem (and the Temple in particular) is the unmatched place of the divine presence. In the proper order of things, when Israel is restored

[33] The Greek translation to Isa 66:23 adds εν Ιεροθσαλημ, making clear what can be inferred from the context.

[34] Cf. Wright 1992, 268.

[35] The twinning of these ideas is reflected in Exod 19:5–6.

[36] See Mullen 1980, 192–93.

from her dispersion among the other nations to worship in the place where God is actually present, the nations will recognize the futility of their gods and follow in tow (e.g. Jer 16:19).

## 4.2 1 Enoch 10:20–22 as an Eschatological Conclusion to Chapters 6–11

What, then, sets the eschatological scenario in 1 Enoch 10 apart? First, in the Hebrew Bible the nations as such remain without a special covenant. They do not enjoy the status of being "elect" or "chosen," and the term "righteousness" is never associated with them. Correspondingly, they are at best only indirectly involved in the Temple cult (i.e. through the offering of their wealth, through submission, or through compliance) and do not perform or participate in any priestly function. On the other hand, it is possible that 1 En 10:21 implies that they take part in or adhere to the Jerusalem cult. In addition, the text looks forward to a time when "all the children of humanity will become righteous." This state is envisioned as possible because the earth that the nations inhabit will have been cleansed from all impurity (1 En 10:20; cf. v. 22). The awaited eschatological purity stands in stark contrast to the impurity that characterizes the illegitimate bastards, the giants, whose days are numbered and who will be destroyed (1 En 10:9–10). Nevertheless, though there is no overt attempt to steer away from Jerusalem as the center of worship, the complete lack of emphasis on Jerusalem, in contrast with biblical traditions and elsewhere in the Book of Watchers (1 En 25–27)[37] and Animal Apocalypse (cf. 1 En 90:28–36), is conspicuous.[38] The cleansing of the earth (1 En 10:20, 22) widens the horizon for ritual purity beyond Jerusalem to at least "the land," if not "the earth" as a whole (Grk. η γη par. Eth. *medr* can carry either meaning). This broader context suggests that the writer of 1 En 10:20–22 envisioned a scenario on a scale so grand that the worshipers of God will not simply consist of a more narrowly defined Jewish group (cf. 1 En 10:16). Put succinctly, the tradition is at this point concerned with humanity as a whole. If so, it remains to be discerned how is it that the text, which begins with an inner-Jewish group, can contemplate a more

[37] It is probably Jerusalem that is regarded as "the centre of the earth" (1 En 26:1 cf. 1 En 25:4–7; 26:4–27:2); cf. Nickelsburg 2001, 317–19.

[38] Corresponding to λατρεύοντες, the Eth. MSS traditions in 1 En 10:21 have *yāmlek* (lit. "to be subject to"), a term with no obvious cultic connotation. This, however, is a secondary development within the tradition.

inclusive vision that includes all human beings. To consider this, it is necessary to refer back to the text's treatment of the figure of Noah at the beginning of 1 Enoch 10.

The appearance of Noah in the text should not come as a surprise. Although as a literary unit 1 Enoch 6–11 is casually referred to as belonging to "Enochic tradition," unlike much of the rest of 1 Enoch it makes no mention of the patriarch Enoch.[39] Since Noah is the only human featured in this part of the Book of Watchers, Charles argued that chapters 6–11 originally belonged to a now lost "Apocalypse" or "Book of Noah."[40] Whether or not Charles is correct, the function of Noah within these chapters should not escape notice.

That the figure of Noah is connected with the story about the rebellious angels is appropriate in terms of biblical chronology. In the biblical tradition the mating of "the sons of God" with women on earth serves as a prelude to the Great Flood narrative (Gen 6:5–9:17), while the few verses mentioning Enoch (Gen 5:21–24) are left behind. It is known, too, that traditions about Noah circulated in several sources that date back to at least the second century BCE.[41] Two of these sources preserve Midrashic tradition about Noah's birth (Genesis Apocryphon at 1Q20 ii 1 – v 26; Birth of Noah at 1 En 106:1–107:3). In addition, the Book of Giants (see Section 3) also preserves material related to the theme of Noah's escape from the Great Flood (see 6Q8 2). Furthermore, within the wider socioreligious, Hellenistic context, we may note the appearance of the figure of Noah in Euphemeristic tradition. Under the name Belos, the biblical Noah features among the so-called Pseudo-Eupolemos fragments preserved in Eusebius, *Praeparatio Evangelica* 9.17.1–9 and 18.2. Of these fragments, the second identifies Belos, who "escaped death" and built the tower of Babel, as a giant.[42] In complete contrast, any such link between the biblical Noah and the giants is vigorously denied in the Enochic and related traditions just mentioned. Indeed, chapters 6–11 of the Book of Watchers, the Birth of Noah (1 En 106–107), and the Genesis

[39] For exceptions, see the Noachic fragments in the Book of Parables at 1 En 60:1–25; 65:4–12; and 67:1–68:5; see Hannah 2007.

[40] Especially Charles 1913, 13–14. Since the time of Charles a number of Hebrew and Aramaic texts that show an explicit interest in Noah (or preserve documents that do) have been recovered: see *inter alia* Stuckenbruck 2007, 606–89; Stone 2010; Amihay and Machiela 2010; Pfann 2010; Eshel 2010.

[41] See Hannah 2007.

[42] The text similarly traces Abraham's ancestry back to the giants.

Apocryphon adopt a position that distances the identity and purpose of Noah as much as possible from the antediluvian agents of evil.[43]

The presence of an underpinning Noachic framework for chapters 6–11 makes sense not only because of the reference to Noah (as "the son of Lamech" 1 En 10:1–3) but also because of the motifs in chapter 10 that derive from the story of the Great Flood (Gen 5:28–32, 6:5–9:17; cf. 1 En 10:16a, 17a, 20, 22). In its present form the Noachic storyline is introduced as a divine response to cries of lament that have been raised by the souls of the giant's murdered victims and relayed to God by angels (1 En 8:4–9:11). Within a narrative about the destruction of the created order through the unsanctioned offspring of the rebellious angels, the introduction of Noah is significant. Noah's parentage is legitimate: he is from Lamech, not from one of the rebellious angels (cf. 1Q20 ii 1 – v 27 and 1 En 106–107), and Noah's being stands in diametrical opposition to the composite nature of the giants (1 En 10:9, see Section 3). It is Noah as a representative human being to whom the announcement about a coming catastrophe is addressed. The message announces three things: (1) the imminent destruction of "the whole earth" through a deluge (1 En 10:2); (2) Noah's survival of the coming cataclysm (1 En 10:1, 3); and (3) the procreation of a "plant" through Noah (so the Eth. and Gr. Syncellus; Cod. Pan. has "seed"), a plant that will "remain forever" (1 En 10:3 – Gr. Syncellus and Cod. Pan.; most Eth. MSS "for all generations").

Once Noah has been introduced, those familiar with Genesis 5–6 might anticipate a retelling of the Flood story (Gen 6:5–8:22). The writer or redactor of the text, however, has more in sight than rehearsing the remote antediluvian past. The time of the Flood serves up paradigmatic imagery that inspires the description of what the writer thought would take place in the imminent future (1 En 10:17–11:2). Thus the narrative elaborates an analogy between the Noachic period and what is present and imminently future. While the Noachic storyline does not entirely disappear,[44] the ensuing events in 1 En 10:4–13 have to do with punishments meted out against the notorious evildoers already known from chapters 6–8: Asa'el (1 En 10:4–6), the giants (1 En 10:9–10; cf. 1 En 7:5), and "Shemihazah and his companions" (1 En 10:11–13). This act of divine judgment is carried out by the chief angelic emissaries Raphael, Gabriel, and Michael, the same group of angelic beings (1 En 10:1, 4, 9, 11) that conveyed the

43 See Stuckenbruck 2007, 633–41, 648–55.

44 Motifs relating to the Genesis Flood story occur again from 1 En 10:14.

human souls' appeals for justice to heaven (1 En 9:1, 4), so the story of Noah is woven into that of the rebellious angels.

Given the writer or editor's concern with the eschatological future, the punishment of evil in the Noachic past is proleptic. Noah's story is not only linked back to the foregoing antediluvian events about angels and giants. The reference to "plant" to come from Noah "forever" (1 En 10:3) and the anticipation of the final judgment of the angelic evildoers (cf. 1 En 10:5–6, 12–13) correlate the judgment and escape from the Flood in Noah's time (*Urzeit*) with its counterpart in the future when God's design for creation will be fully realized (*Endzeit*). Within 1 Enoch 6–11 it is not until chapter 10 that the story about the fallen angels, now anchored in the Noachic period, has an impact on how the writer(s) conceived of the future and, vice versa, how this understanding of the future shapes what is being stated about the text's present. Significantly, the scope of this correlation between *Urzeit* and *Endzeit* includes all humanity, for whom Noah stands as a representative. The story begins with the procreativity among the mass of humanity (1 En 6:1–2) who are then overwhelmed by the rebellious angels' violation of the cosmic order when the Watchers breed with the human women. Through Noah, it is this victimized humanity whose survival as a species is assured, not only now but through to the eschatological time. It is thus fitting that all humanity, as part of the created order, should be expected to worship God (1 En 10:20–22).

The path from Noah to the worship of God by all humanity in 1 En 10:20–22 is, however, not straightforward. The condemnation of the Watchers and slaughter of their offspring (1 En 10:14–15) is in force during the writer's present: it is brought into effect in the past through the announcement of the Flood[45] and will reach its climax through a destruction of evil in the future. This present is understood as an intervening period when evil, though essentially defeated, is allowed to persist alongside the emergence of "the plant of truth and righteousness" (1 En 10:16). Though this second "plant" alludes to the "plant" associated with Noah's offspring in 1 En 10:3, it no longer represents the human species as such and hints at a narrower group of people. This group's function in the present time is pivotal for the writer. The "plant"

[45] However, the Flood does not constitute the punishment of the Watchers or giants (in contrast to the perishing of the giants in 1 En 89:1; 4Q370 i 6; Wis 14:6; 3 Bar 4:10; 3 Macc 2:4). Instead, Deluge imagery relates to the theme of Noah's escape (1 En 10:3), the elimination of iniquity and impurity from the earth (1 En 10:16, 20, 22), and the escape of the righteous in the eschaton (1 En 10:17).

experiences a world in which evil has the upper hand while, at the same time, it (or, at least the writer of the text) is fully aware that this very same evil stands condemned and has already suffered defeat.

Who or what is this "plant of truth and righteousness"? The narrative is concerned with those who are obedient to the covenant – that is, a community with whom the writer(s) would have identified. Significantly, this community is characterized by "works of righteousness"[46] (1 En 10:16). As such, they are the ones who, presumably as Noah before them had done during the Flood, will "escape" in the future when "all iniquity" and "*every evil work*" are destroyed (1 En 10:16; cf. 1 En 107:1[47]). Read in relation to the story about the iniquitous "sons of heaven," the text draws an analogy between the destruction and eternal punishment of the angels and giants (cf. 1 En 10:9–14) and the final destruction of iniquitous activities. Given the angelic (i.e. non-human) source of the antediluvian evils, punishment is not anticipated for human beings as much as it is to be carried out against the reprehensible deeds and knowledge which they have acquired and which the text traces back to the angels (1 En 7:3–5; 8:1–3).[48]

The categorical distinction between humans, on the one hand, and the giants (and their angelic progenitors), on the other (see Section 3), has implications for the interpretation of the activities described as evil in 1 Enoch chapters 7 and 8. With some justification, George Nickelsburg and David Suter, for example, have regarded the "fallen angels" and "giants" as decipherable metaphors, respectively, for the late fourth- and early third-century BCE Diadochi (in the wake of Alexander the Great's death), or for wayward priests who had taken on objectionable practices deemed to be irreconcilable with covenant faithfulness.[49] While the notion of an unsanctioned incursion by bearers of Hellenistic culture may provide a plausible sociopolitical and religious setting in which to locate the fallen angels myth, the theological perspective offered in 1 Enoch 6–11 operates on a more profound level. Demonic forces are not only at work in those human beings who have adopted forms of knowledge and skills under the influence of powerful outsiders, they are even regarded as being at work behind those humans

[46] Eth.; omitted in Cod. Pan. through *homoioteleuton*. The longer reading is supported by the Aramaic text in 4QEn[c] 1 v 1. See Nickelsburg 2001, 218; Milik 1976, 189.

[47] Cf. Stuckenbruck 2007, 682.

[48] In this way, the tradition's focus on the culpability of the Watchers and giants is nuanced: it does not imply that humans who have been taught by them are not held responsible.

[49] Nickelsburg 1977, 2001, 170; Suter 1979.

who introduced them in the first place. The demonic and the sociopolitical oppressors of humanity are not mirror images of one another. For all its rejection of aberrant culture and of the oppression that comes through it, this story's essentially mythic character creates an extraordinary openness between a community of obedient Jews in the present and the larger enclave of humanity that in itself is not held responsible for setting the world down the wrong path (hence the emphasis on the destruction of "works" and deeds, 1 En 10:16, 20), despite being currently aligned with the demonic world. The Enochic tradition at this point may be lamenting and responding to tyrannical domination of culture on the part of groups such as the Ptolemaic or Seleucid overlords and their allies in the Jewish priesthood. However, the text does not descend into a reductionistic demonization of these groups: they remain human beings who, though they are to be punished for their acts of cultural and military domination, do not provide any warrant for a destruction of humanity as a whole. 1 Enoch 6–16 does not, then, present a thoroughgoing "social dualism" that pits one group of humans against another. Instead, the discontinuity lies between humans, on the one side, and the Watchers, on the other. It is the Watchers who have breached the boundaries that distinguish the heavenly from the earthly sphere (implied in 1 En 6:3–6, 10:7; explicated in 1 En 15:7–10) while the non-human giants (1 En 10:9) exist as a *malum mixtum* (i.e. a hybrid of spheres that ought to have remained separate). The fundamental distinction between human nature (a *bonum mixtum*) and the demonic (which by its very nature is a perversion of the created order) keeps humanity in principle and as a whole within the purview of divine purpose of redemption. For all the atrocities people commit against one another, there is something in human nature that can still be reclaimed by God, who was and remains their creator. In the Enochic tradition in the Book of Watchers, the "all" who will worship God embraces the cosmos as defined and determined by God, and it excludes those who have taken themselves out of it (the Watchers) and those whose very existence does not go back to God's creative activity (the giants).

Is there anything, then, that helps us to account for the worship of God by all humanity in 1 En 10:21? A distinction certainly remains in chapter 10 between "the plant of truth and righteousness" (1 En 10:16, i.e. elect Jews) and "all the children of men" (1 En 10:21). The former are promised a limitless period of reproductive and agricultural life (1 En 10:17–19) that reverses the annihilation and oppression suffered in the time before the Flood (1 En 7:3–5). The preserved Ethiopic and Greek texts do not specify that this bliss will include all humanity, nor do any of the recensions state precisely how the special "plant" is related to the rest of humanity. However, the arena of what "the righteous" will enjoy is "all the earth." While the idea of a new beginning evokes the Noachic covenant following the Deluge (Gen 9:1–17; note the allusion to Gen 9:11 in 1 En 10:22), the passage also draws conceptually on the language of Isa 65:17–25 and Isa 66:22–23, which refer to God's creation of a "new heaven and earth," the former passage associating this with images of fertility (cf. 1 En 10:17–19; 11:1) and the latter anticipating a world order in which "all flesh" will "worship God" (cf. 1 En 10:21). The Isaianic tradition provides the writer(s) with grounds to blur the line of demarcation between "the plant of truth and righteousness" in 1 En 10:16 and "all the children of men" in 1 En 10:21, so that the latter are admitted into the arena in which God's purpose for humanity as a whole is realized.

We have already noted above that, unlike Isaiah, the conclusion in 1 Enoch 10 does not specify Jerusalem as the locus for the eschatological worship of God. There are two further respects that distinguish 1 Enoch 10 from its antecedents in Isaiah. First, unlike Isaiah, eschatological expectation is articulated within a Noachic framework. The new beginnings envisioned in Isaiah 65 and 66 is recast in 1 Enoch 10–11 through a reading of tradition found in Gen 6:1–4, a reading that highlights the "otherworldly" dimension of evil. Second, 1 Enoch 10 projects the activity of divine salvation onto the world stage. Thus, whatever its precise status, "the plant of truth and righteousness" in 1 En 10:16 is of necessity linked with the entire human race that has also been subjected to and suffers from oppression by demonic power.

How is it that the worship of God by all humanity will come about? The text in 1 En 10:14–11:2 does not draw an unbroken direct line of continuity between "the plant of truth and righteousness" and the deliverance of humanity from destruction; "the righteous" do not, for example, bear witness to anything that results in a turning of all people to God. Instead, to the extent that the Isaianic paradigm is operative, past acts of divine punishment herald another definitive act by God that puts an end to evil as effective power. Thus eschatological worship by the nations will take place once all "uncleanness" and godless activities have been eradicated from the earth. This worship is not so much the agency for the establishment of a new world order as it is that very activity that reflects it. The period after the Flood (Gen 9:1–17) serves as an archetype for this "new beginning" of humanity in the coming era (1 En 10:22).

### 4.3 Summary of the Argument Thus Far

By placing 1 Enoch 6–16 into conversation with Genesis 1–9, I have attempted to draw attention to dimensions of theological anthropology as it was understood in the Book of Watchers. Unlike Gen 6:6–7, there is no regret on God's part in the Book of Watchers for having created humanity. The tradition in 1 Enoch 6–11 and, by extension, chapters 12–16, adapts the view found in the early chapters of Genesis that humanity occupies a unique position in creation. Genesis expresses the special place of human beings within the created order by assigning to them "the breath of life" (Gen 2:7) and specifying that they bear "the image of God" (Gen 1:26–27). In the Enoch tradition, the nature and importance of humanity is underlined by contrasting humans and the gigantic offspring of the watchers. This contrast is served by the Noachic storyline, according to which Noah, unlike the rebellious angels and giants, is given the means to survive the Flood without being harmed (1 En 10:1–3). The Enochic text assumes that since their creation humans have always been and, come what may, will always be integral to the created order. Although people are held to account for their deeds, as a species they are in the world to stay. On the other hand, evil, which is not regarded as derived from God in any way, has neither legitimate place nor any other recourse in this world than annihilation. The angelic and gargantuan actors in the narrative should not, therefore, be entirely decoded as if they simply function as metaphors for people, whether they are identified as sociopolitical oppressors or a wayward priesthood. The underlying cause and human agency for sin are distinct.

As after the disobedience in Eden recounted in Genesis 3, the early Enoch tradition allowed for humans to remain legitimate creatures: they continue to embody features that distinguish them from other forms of life. However, in 1 Enoch 6–11 and 12–16 the notion of a malevolent angelic world enabled the writers and early editors of the tradition during the third century BCE to adopt a worldview which, even more than those traditions preserved in Genesis, drove a wedge between the nature of evil and the nature of humans who, nonetheless, can fall victim to it.

## 5 THE RECEPTION OF 1 ENOCH 10:20–22 WITHIN THE ENOCHIC CORPUS

The Book of Watchers, in its received form of thirty-six chapters in Ge'ez, is framed around the core myth of the rebellious angels, especially as told in chapters 6–11. This tradition is one to which subsequent Enochic writers in

1 Enoch frequently return, not only through explicit references to the angels and their offspring,[50] but also through literary allusions to these chapters.[51] Let us turn our attention to the Enochic reception of this myth.

### 5.1 1 Enoch 12–16

The Noachic literary unit of chapters 6–11 was soon appended by a storyline in which the patriarch Enoch takes center stage. The incorporation of Enoch into the narrative functioned to reinforce how the wayward angels learned that the punishment for their and their giant offspring's misdeeds was irreversible. Enoch's status as one who "walked with *ha-elohim*" – whether *elohim* refers to God (Gen 5:22, 24) or to angelic beings (cf. 1 En 12:2) – qualified him as an ideal figure during the time of the Flood through whom to communicate God's definitive pronouncements against the primary bearers of evil in the world (1 En 15:1–16:3). Whereas Noah is the object of activity that salvages humanity as an integral part of the created order, Enoch is an agent of divine punishment. Enoch functions as one who mediates a divine pronouncement against the angels, the longest speech attributed to God in the entire 1 Enoch corpus (1 En 15:3–16:4). In this speech attention is given to activities of demonic spirit-beings, the residue of the giants whose bodies were destroyed. As we have seen (Section 3), the angelic rebellion is reflected on in relation to human nature and, indeed, cosmology itself (the distinction between "heaven" and "earth," things created as "spirit" and things created as "body"). The distinction between the angels and giants, on the one hand, and human beings, on the other, is spelled out in a way that is consistent with what we have inferred on the basis of chapter 10. In addition to the claim that God has already assigned evil to a state of punishment, the particular concern with theological anthropology in 1 Enoch 12–16 stands out as one recognizes therein the absence of eschatology, compared to chapter 10. The focus is more on the etiological explanation for why humans suffer even though personified forces of evil have been held to account.

### 5.2 1 Enoch 17–36

The twenty chapters that remain in the Book of Watchers, in its present form, take both the anthropological and eschatological discourse in

[50] See 1 En 54:5; 55:4; 64:2; 67:4; 69:2–14; 86:3–89:7; 91:15.
[51] See Stuckenbruck 2007, 206–09.

a different direction from chapters 6–16. In chapters 17–19 and 20–22 the Enochic seer journeys through the cosmos to those places in which the wayward stars (cf. 1 En 81–82) and fallen angels are undergoing punishment (so 1 En 18:11–16; 19:1–2; and 21:1–10). If read as a follow-up to chapters 6–16, the vision of retribution against the stars and angels does not describe what will happen in the eschatological future, but presents the state of things, as already seen by Enoch, at the time of the real author. During the course of the second journey the seer observes four chambers inhabited by four classes of souls of the deceased, belonging to (1) the righteous, (2) sinners of the first rank, (3) victims of sinners, and (4) a lesser rank of sinners (1 En 22:8–14). The text focuses more than it does in chapters 6–11 and 12–16 on the consequences of human participation in sin, while the significance of the fallen angels tradition is relegated to a position of lesser prominence. This increased interest in the post-mortem state of humans is retained not only in the remaining chapters of the Book of Watchers but also in much of the rest (and later composed parts) of 1 Enoch.

## 5.3 1 Enoch 5:4–9

A parallel tradition to the eschatological events described in chapter 10 re-enters the Book of Watchers. Chapters 1–5 comprise what was probably the latest section of the Book of Watchers, added to serve as an introduction to a growing tradition (1 En 6–36) that had become inextricably linked to the figure of Enoch. At this point, remnants of the Watcher tradition, with the possible exception of 1 En 1:5, have all but disappeared, while the spotlight is cast on the sinners and the righteous among humanity. The wicked, assumed to be human beings and without prospect for salvation, are cursed (1 En 5:4–6a, 7b). By contrast, the destiny of the righteous "chosen ones" is described in several ways: they will be given "light and grace" and "wisdom," they will no longer "sin," and they, "the wise ones," shall "complete the full number of the days of their lives. Their lives will grow in peace. The years of their joy will increase in gladness and eternal peace throughout the days of their lives" (1 En 5:9). Thus precisely the bliss associated with all humanity when they worship God in chapter 10 is here delimited to those who are wise. There is no hint that "sinners" – a wider group of humanity outside the covenant – will be transformed, and neither is it likely that the writer imagines that disobedient Jews (if the label "sinners" applies to them) will become righteous in the end. Indeed, if there is any eschatological metamorphosis at all, it is "the chosen ones" who undergo it and who alone will enjoy eschatological blessings.

## 5.4 1 Enoch 85–105

Traditions that accrued to the Enochic corpus during the second century BCE[52] – especially Apocalypse of Weeks (1 En 93:1–10; 91:11–17); Epistle of Enoch (1 En 92:1–4; 93:11–105:2); and Animal Apocalypse (1 En 85:1–90:42) – simultaneously stress how the righteous, not the wicked, will be rewarded and, under the influence of 1 Enoch 10, leave the way open for a turning to God among Gentiles, or at least of a recognition by them of the wisdom associated with Israel's God. Here we consider several passages in these texts briefly in turn.

## 5.5 1 Enoch 91:14

The Apocalypse of Weeks, composed between the Hellenistic crisis and the start of the Maccabean Revolt, schematizes sacred history into ten parts called "weeks." The period described as "the seventh week" is that of the author, who refers to a community of "chosen ones from the eternal plant of righteousness" who will be given special "sevenfold instruction" (1 En 93:10). The writer anticipates the imminent punishment of "the wicked"; this event is assigned to the rest of week seven and to week eight. In the near future, "the righteous" are given a role to play as agents of divine wrath against "the wicked" (1 En 91:11–12). Week eight concludes with the righteous being rewarded and with the reestablishment of the Temple for eternity (1 En 91:13). With punishment and reward having taken place, the text describes week nine as follows: "And after this, in the ninth week, the righteous judgment will be revealed to all the world, and *all the works of the wicked will depart from the whole earth*. And the world will be written down for destruction, and *all people will look to the way of upright-ness*" (1 En 91:14). Whereas the eighth week is concerned with the elect of Israel and the ultimate restoration of the Temple cult, the ninth week takes up eschatological events on a broader stage that in week ten will be extended even further to encompass the cosmos as a whole. This increasingly broader arena of divine activity suggests that the wicked whose deeds are expunged from the earth are not the same group as the oppressors mentioned in week eight. Whereas in week eight "the wicked" themselves are destroyed (i.e. they constitute the author and his community's inimical opponents or oppressors), in week nine it is "all the works" (Eth.; Aram. text from 4QEn$^{g}$ is lost at this point) of the wicked which will

[52] See Stuckenbruck 2007, 9–16.

be removed. If this is the correct reading of the text, then the Apocalypse may be picking up on a distinction implicit in 1 En 10:16, that is, one between iniquitous activity and the human beings who engage in them (cf. Birth of Noah at 1 En 107:1 and Exhortation at 1 En 91:6–8).[53] The wicked who are destroyed in week eight are treated as inseparable from the deeds that they have done, while the wicked whose works are done away with are treated as belonging to a humanity that can and will be saved. If the presentation of events in weeks eight and nine in Apocalypse of Weeks is aware of 1 Enoch 10, it offers a more transparent nuance regarding the fate of the wicked than the tradition it received.

The clearing out of wicked activities makes it possible for the text to anticipate that all humans "will look to the way of uprightness."[54] Thus their conversion or turning toward uprightness is not so surprising as it denotes a proper conclusion (cf. Isa 49:6) to a narrative in which God, the Creator of the world and the one who has fixed each of the weeks from the beginning, renews and realigns the created order to its original purpose. While sharing with chapter 10 the emphasis on the destruction of wicked deeds and the subsequent righteousness of humanity, the Apocalypse of Weeks places much less emphasis on the wickedness of the Watchers, who play hardly any role in the narrative until a possible allusion to them in the tenth week (1 En 91:15).[55] The Apocalypse also picks up on biblical tradition by having the transformation of humanity follow restorative events associated with the Temple (1 En 91:13); with the eschatological Temple in place, God's rule manifests itself in a new way.[56] This event sequence introduces a logical tension into the narrative that is less apparent in chapters 6–11: on the one hand, the wicked are destroyed by the sword (1 En 91:11–12) while on the other, in the wake of the justice and judgment brought about by God's kingly rule, "all people will look to the way of uprightness" (1 En 91:14). The writer's more immediate concern for justice against contemporary apostates involved in oppression (1 En 93:9, 11) is resolved by the slaughter of humans, whereas the punishment of the fallen angels and their offspring in chapter 10 leaves the ultimate

[53] A similar distinction is operative in the Treatise on the Two Spirits in 1QS iii 13–iv 26, esp. iv 15–16, 18–21).

[54] Though Isa 2:3 and Mic 4:2 may lie in the background, there is no mention here of any instruction through which this is to happen; see, by contrast, the Epistle at 1 En 105:1–2 (discussion below).

[55] On the textual problem, see Olson 2004, 222.

[56] According to 1 En 91:13 in 4QEn$^{g}$ 1 iv 17–18, the Temple is described as being "of the kingdom of the Great One."

destiny of humanity more open. The pattern within 1 En 91:14 itself, however, retains the influence of its Enochic predecessor.

## 5.6 1 Enoch 100:6 and 105:1–2 (Epistle of Enoch)

The texts mentioned here are found, respectively, in the main body and the conclusion of the Epistle of Enoch. Though the literary productions in which these texts occur probably do not stem from the same author,[57] they share an emphasis that juxtaposes the motif of Gentiles attaining correct understanding with the vilification of "sinners" for whom eschatological punishment is deemed irreversible.[58] The texts, extant in Ethiopic (with only 1 En 100:6 extant in Greek), may be translated as follows:

> In those days, says the Lord, they will summon and give testimony to the children of the earth from their wisdom. Show (it) to them, for you are their leaders and the rewards upon the whole earth. (2) For I and my son will join ourselves with them forever on the ways of righteousness during their lives. And you will have peace. (1 En 105:1–2)
>
> And men among the wise will see what is true, and the children of the earth will understand the entire discourse of this book, and they will know that their wealth cannot save them during the collapse of their sin. (1 En 100:6)

These passage share the hope that "the children of the earth" will eventually comprehend the wisdom that has been disclosed to the author and his community. Moreover, the writer of 1 En 105:2 expects that humanity will embark "on the ways of righteousness" (cf. 1 En 91:14). Even more than what we observed in the Apocalypse of Weeks, however, the field of vision has narrowed. The message of the Epistle is overwhelmed by a conflict between the author's community and "the sinners," who are repeatedly denounced through a series of invectives (mostly woe-oracles and oaths).[59] This is especially true of 1 En 100:6, in which "the children of the earth" are, in effect, treated as "the sinners" who can attain little more than the recognition that the Enochic revelation is true. The function of this acquired understanding, then, is the validation of Enochic revelation rather than any turn-around among the nations as such. This is much in contrast to the derivation of evil in the Book of Watchers from

[57] On the source-critical distinction between the main body and frame of the Epistle, see Stuckenbruck 2007, 213–15.

[58] This juxtaposition is analogous to the tension attributed to the Apocalypse of Weeks above (Section 5.5).

[59] See Stuckenbruck 2007, 193–97.

rebellious angels (esp. 1 En 6–36). In the body of the Epistle the blame for oppression and false teaching is laid so completely at the feet of "the sinners" that the writer claims that "sin was not sent to the earth, but the people have created it by themselves, and those who commit it will be subject to a great curse." Clearly, the human dimension of sin in 1 En 5:4–6a, 7b lies more in the background than the angelic rebellion myth of 1 Enoch 6–11; accordingly, unlike 1 Enoch 10 (and the Animal Apocalypse), there is no real distinction between deeds and the human beings who commit them.

What, then, of 1 En 105:1–2? Within what framework is the coming to wisdom of humanity to be understood? Unlike the earlier Enochic counterparts, the writer of 1 En 105:1–2 (which closes the Epistle) draws a direct line of development between the righteous community and "the children of the earth" to whom "the ways of righteousness" will be brought. The text assumes that the righteous themselves will be active agents in the dissemination of their revealed knowledge in the world.[60] While in the other Enochic texts the role of the pious is either non-existent (so 1 En 10; 91:14;[61] cf. discussion of the Animal Apocalypse in 1 En 90 below), here it is expected that the righteous will dispense their wisdom to others, and even do so with success. If we take the preceding verses (1 En 104:12–13) into account, the means by which the divine revelation would be brought to the world is conceived as the faithful copying and translation of the Enochic tradition. To this extent, it is possible that the writer probably thought that he himself was participating in passing on the testimony to which he refers in 1 En 105:1. In this case, "the righteous" functions as a narrow reference to the author and those whom he deems faithful to the Enochic tradition that he espouses. By focusing on human agency, the writer gives an answer to the problem of how all people come to the point of worshiping God, as raised in 1 Enoch 10.

Thus the authors of the Epistle at 1 En 100:6 and 105:1–2 had different outlooks regarding the eschatological future of "the children of the earth." In the former text their association with "sin" seems irreversible, and their understanding does not relate to any salvific outcome. 1 En 105:1–2 is less clear. While the righteous play a vital role in transmitting wisdom, and retain a role of leadership in the society envisioned for the

[60] Though the references to instruction and paths of righteousness are influenced by the language of Isa 2:3 and Mic 4:2, the Enochic writer is giving the Enochic community a more explicit role in the dissemination of the instruction. Cf. n. 54 above.

[61] The phrase "will be revealed" denotes divine activity rather than human meditation.

future, the wisdom given to the children of the earth results in their inclusion within that society. This future is more in line with those anticipated in 1 Enoch 10 and 91, though it is more specific with regard to how the inclusion of non-Jews will come about.

## 5.7 1 Enoch 90:30, 37 (Animal Apocalypse)

Composed during the mid-to-late 160s BCE, the Animal Apocalypse adopts a position comparable to the ones we have outlined for the Apocalypse of Weeks and, especially, the Epistle. The work, which is a much more elaborate recounting of sacred history than the Apocalypse of Weeks, draws on zoomorphic symbols to represent human characters from the time of Adam all the way to the Maccabean Revolt under Judas Maccabeus.

In 1 En 90:16–38, which comes near the conclusion to the document, the Enochic author sketches eschatological scenes of judgment and reward which build on symbolism that has already featured in the narrative.[62] Here Gentile nations, which have usually been symbolized as oppressive "wild animals," "birds," or other such animals, in the previous part of the vision (cf. esp. 1 En 89:10, 42–44, 49, 55–56, 66; 90:2–4, 8–9, 11–12, 13), come to feature in an increasingly positive manner (cf. 1 En 90:16, 18, 19, 30, 33, 37–38). The negative presentation of the Gentiles reaches its climax in the battle of Beth-Zur in 1 En 90:13–15 (cf. 2 Macc 11:6–12). The description of this battle merges with initial stages of what the writer presents as an imminent eschatological future (1 En 90:16–19) during which the righteous "sheep" are given a "big sword" with which to kill "all the wild beasts" as an act of retribution (v. 19; cf. Apocalypse of Weeks at 1 En 91:11–12).

Whether these slaughtered animals specifically represent the Seleucid armies or Gentiles more generally,[63] what follows in the vision takes a different turn. The consistency of the document's "anti-Gentile" perspective in the allegory gives way to scenes that involve some measured inclusion of Gentiles. This happens in three stages, in 1 En 90:28–30, 90:33, and 90:37–38. The first stage describes the Gentiles as "falling down and worshiping those sheep, and entreating them and obeying them in every command" (1 En 90:30). This is an image of subjugation along lines familiar from the biblical tradition (Isa 45:14; 60:10, 12 – cf. Section

[62] On the place of Gentiles in the Animal Apocalypse see Herms 2006, 120–36.
[63] See Nickelsburg 2001, 401.

4.1); the Gentiles' submission follows the reestablishment of a "new house" – probably a reference to the restoration of Jerusalem as the place of eschatological blessing and rest. Thus, as in the Apocalypse of Weeks (1 En 91:13–14) and the book of Tobit (13:11–17; 14:5–6), the reestablishment of Jerusalem (and the Temple) in all its intended glory provides the essential prelude to the inclusion of Gentiles in the eschatological future. While it is tempting to think that the subjugated Gentiles are those who did not oppress Israel and thus have escaped judgment,[64] the textual evidence does not support such a precise reading (cf. 1 En 90:19). This submission of the nations to the righteous does take the narrative in a decidedly new direction; however, this submission does not involve activity in which the Gentiles worship God.

The second stage gets underway when "all those who had been destroyed and dispersed, along with all the beasts of the field and all the birds of heaven, gathered together in that house, and the Lord of the sheep rejoiced with great joy because they had all become good, and they had returned to his house" (1 En 90:33).[65] Those who were destroyed and scattered could refer to either the Gentiles slaughtered by the sword in verse 19 or to the "blinded sheep" (apostate Jews) who were judged by fire in verses 26–27 (hence, the verb "returned"), or to both groups (as seems most likely). The inclusion of Gentiles with the statement "they had all become good" ensures that, alongside Jews to be restored, Gentiles will be included as objects of divine joy.

The third and final stage of Gentile inclusion in the vision occurs with the appearance in 1 En 90:37 of "a white bull" with big horns (cf. 1 En 85:1–3). Initially, the author emphasizes the Gentiles' subservience, though this time they fear the white bull "and made continual petition before it."[66] This activity leads to a surprising event. In 1 En 90:38 the text states, "As I watched, all of their species *were transformed*: they all [i.e. the beasts and birds mentioned in v. 37] became white bulls. ... The Lord of the sheep rejoiced over these and over all of the cattle." This conversion of the Gentiles takes place through a divine act of recreating the human race. Here this event takes place as a proper conclusion to the reconstitution of Israel.

The Animal Apocalypse does not entertain the possibility that the righteous might play a role in the salvation of humankind (in contrast to the Epistle at 1 En 105:1–2). Instead, it picks up the new creation motif

[64] So Tiller 1993, 377.
[65] For the Animal Apocalypse I follow the translation of Olson 2004, 211.
[66] The second and third stages have their closest contemporary parallel in Dan 7:14.

implied in the Apocalypse of Weeks (1 En 91:14, 16) and set forth in the Book of Watchers (1 En 10:17–11:2). The Animal Apocalypse also shares the predominant concern behind chapters 6–11 in the association of Gentiles with oppressive conditions for Israel, albeit in a different way. We have noted that in chapters 6–11 the bearers of Hellenistic culture – perhaps those who held power and had sway over the cultural ethos of Jerusalem and the Land – are not referred to in any way other than by allusion through the fallen angels. The Animal Apocalypse, by contrast, adopts a discourse that distinguishes both the demonic and the bearers of sociopolitical power. The vision describes the demonic or wayward angelic world as "stars" and "shepherds" while the Gentiles are symbolized as wild animals and birds. In this way the Animal Apocalypse explicates what the earliest tradition in the Book of Watchers implies: though heinous deeds have been carried out against God's people, those who have committed them are not entirely demonized. The ultimate establishment of God's rule in creation demands that human beings who are part of this creation be restored. *Endzeit* reflects Adamic *Urzeit*. However, the Animal Apocalypse moves away from 1 Enoch 10's focus on the destruction and punishment of the fallen angels and the giants. The author of the vision wanted to have it both ways: not only have beings who originated in heaven made a mess of the world; humans too (both Gentiles and unfaithful Jews) are held responsible and punished for their wrongdoing. The crucial distinction between humans and their deeds in the Book of Watchers – picked up in the Animal Apocalypse – is lost, replaced by a more contradictory image of total punishment (1 En 90:16–19, 26–27) and total restoration and conversion (1 En 90:33, 37–38).

## 6 CONCLUSION

This study has attempted to demonstrate that although Gen 2:7 is never quoted or alluded to in the early Enochic traditions, its focus on the integrity of human nature within the cosmos nevertheless lies in the background. In addition, nowhere in 1 Enoch is the negative anthropology expressed in Gen 6:3 in evidence, even in the Epistle of Enoch, at a point when humans are essentially blamed for the introduction of sin into the world (1 En 98:4–6). The broad correlation between the Book of Watchers at 1 Enoch 6–16 (cf. also 1 En 32) and Genesis 1–9 enables us to understand better why it is that the Enoch tradition insisted that humanity should persist as a species, even when things have gone wrong. However, the different emphases of Genesis and the Enoch tradition correspond to varying nuances with regard to the place of human beings within the created order. On the one hand, Genesis insists on the enduring status of humans as made in the image of God (Gen 1:26–27; 5:1) and focuses on human responsibility before God – whatever the role of the serpent in the Garden may have been. Thus, the human situation can be described in such negative terms that the text expresses divine regret that humanity was ever created (Gen 6:5–6)! Without appealing to humans being made in God's likeness, the Enoch tradition reflects at greater depth on the essential nature of evil, finding therein a foil against which the nature and purpose of humanity stands out in sharper relief. The emphasis in the Book of Watchers on heavenly beings as agents of evil does not deny human responsibility so much as make room for the possibility that humans can be victims as well. In contrast to Genesis, there is therefore no hint of regret regarding the creation of humanity in the Book of Watchers or the entire Enochic tradition.

The attribution of evil to non-human powers in 1 Enoch 6–16 has the eschatological worship of God by all peoples as its corollary. This expectation has no equivalent in Genesis. Against the backdrop of Genesis, the vision that includes all humanity within the ambit of the divine will for the created order is remarkable for several reasons. First, it forms an integral part of the narrative of 1 Enoch 6–11 in which it is embedded, and so is a function of its context rather than simply a preservation of an already established tradition. Prior to their integration into the Enochic tradition, these chapters were Noachic in character and transmitted a mythological discourse, inspired by a tradition similar to the one found in Genesis 6–9. The account of evil in 1 Enoch 6–9, which is not only protological but also carves out a vision for its ultimate destruction, translates into an account about God's design for creation, which is likewise protological (1 En 6:1–2) and eschatological (1 En 10:17–22).

Second, the eschatological inclusion of "all people" is noteworthy since it contrasts with the complete eradication of evil, inaugurated at the time of the Great Flood and brought to conclusion at the end. The narrator who anticipated the eschatological transformation of humanity was determined to provide a theocratic counterpart to the destruction of forces that had rebelled against God. This counterpart was based in a return of humanity to the flourishing enjoyed at the beginning (1 En 6:1–2), to which the worship of God was added; *Urzeit* relates to *Endzeit*.

Third, the categorical distinction between humanity and the demonic world is rooted in the author's theological anthropology. The angelic rebellion runs counter to the way God has organized the cosmos. The giants are the very embodiment of this breach, so have no place in the created order. Though some among them are complicit in the instructions of the angels, human beings as a species can be understood as victims. Whatever part they have had in reprehensible practices, people as a whole remain a constituent part of creation. Hence the motif of Noah's rescue and escape from the Deluge not only serves as a type for a community of the righteous called "the plant of truth and righteousness," but also makes it possible for this literary unit of 1 Enoch to conclude with the full restoration of humanity.

These features of the core angelic myth in the Book of Watchers serve as points of departure to which other early Enochic traditions return time and again. The other Enochic traditions do not bypass the Book of Watchers so as to draw on the biblical tradition; instead of linking themselves to tradition preserved in Genesis, they assume the primacy of the fallen angels myth in the received Enoch tradition as a resource for language and theological ideas that enabled them to address new challenges in their own time (e.g. the Hellenization and Maccabean Revolt in the 170s and 160s BCE). Though shifts within the Enochic tradition were many, the shadow cast by Genesis upon its earliest expression in 1 Enoch 6–11 was resilient enough to leaves its mark on the later traditions, especially the Apocalypse of Weeks, Animal Apocalypse, and the frame of the Epistle. Thus, rather than espousing an exclusive faith-perspective that denied non-Jews a part in the divine economy, the Enoch traditions remained remarkably open in outlook as far as the end of history is concerned: salvation would not be the outcome for only the very few.

The writers (or compiler) of 1 Enoch 6–11 reflected a worldview not entirely absorbed by intramural conflicts among Jewish groups.[67] The message was rooted in a Jewish appropriation of sacred history that attempted to address directly the wider challenges that Hellenization posed for Jewish self-definition. As such, its themes provided a language around which the subsequent Enochic traditions surveyed would be oriented. With respect to the place of Gentiles in the eschaton, 1 Enoch 10 was not alone during the third century BCE; the book of Tobit, which presupposes a Diaspora setting, similarly attempts to reconcile the strict preservation of Jewish piety with an outlook that ultimately embraces the Gentiles (cf. Tob 14:5–6). More than in Genesis or Tobit, however, the Book of Watchers based its vision of the future on a view of human nature that served to define and determine the salvific activity of God.

[67] This outlook shifts in the main body of the Epistle: cf. Stuckenbruck 2007, 211–15.

# 6

# The Perils of Philosophical Persuasion: Philo on the Origin of Moral Evils

Sharon Weisser

When raising the question of the origin of evil, we first need to distinguish between two meanings of the term. Evil can refer to phenomena such as diseases, earthquakes, natural disasters, and the like, or it can refer to "moral evils" – that is, to human beings' wrongdoings, improper conduct, or vices. Since the concept of an Evil Inclination, as defined by the editors of this volume, relates to moral agents and not to a bad state of affairs, it undoubtedly fits into the second category. This does not mean that Philo did not attempt to deal with natural evils. In two of his philosophical treatises – both entitled *On Providence* – he addresses this issue in connection with the question of theodicy.[1] In these books, as in many other places, Philo insists on the blamelessness and flawlessness of God, who cannot be considered as the source of any evil, nor of what deviates from nature (*Prov.* 1:92, 2:82, and 2:102). However, his various explanations of the existence natural evils, such as secondary consequences of a well-organized order (*Prov.* 2:86–102) or punishments for wicked men (*Prov.* 2:32, 104 and 1:42–44), look very much like a compendium of commonplaces and are far less engaging and elaborate than his insights on the origin of moral evil.

The purpose of this chapter, then, is to analyze Philo's thinking on the issue of the origin of moral evils. In order words, it aims to answer the question of how Philo accounts for the origin of evil human intentions or acts. In order to answer this question, it is first necessary to elucidate what amounts to "moral evil" in Philo's thought, and then to consider what he regards as its cause.

[1] See Hadas-Lebel 1973, 23–57; also Runia 2003; Frick 1999, esp. 139–75.

Most of the scholarly works that have delved into this issue usually approach it from the perspective of Philo's anthropology or ontology. My contention is that the focus on one of these aspects of his thought does not capture the complete picture. In order to understand how Philo conceives of the process by which evil originates in the soul and conduct of human beings, it is necessary to take into account the profound connection between his view on the soul's moral status and his epistemology. The position I shall defend here is that the epistemic condition of the agent plays an important function in accounting for his wrongdoings. Furthermore, I shall claim that Philo considers the philosophical practice characteristic of his own days as an important factor in what imperils the soul's epistemic and thereby moral status.

My discussion will be divided into two parts. First, I shall lay out the psychological framework that underlies Philo's reflection on the origin of vices and passions, while focusing on the interplay between sense-perception, the irrational parts of the soul, and the evaluative aspect of irrational conduct. I shall then turn to the question of what imperils the soul's epistemic status.

## 1 PSYCHOLOGY AND THE ORIGIN OF MORAL EVILS

For Philo, following the lines of Aristotle and of the Hellenistic schools of philosophy, the *telos* of human existence is to achieve happiness. Happiness is equated with the virtuous life, which represents the fulfilling of human nature.[2] This end is achieved by following the law of nature – that is, by keeping the commands of the Torah, which Philo considers to be the written expression of the law of nature.[3] At the opposite of virtue stands vice, which is directly associated with evil: "evil is vice and the actions inspired by vices" (*Opif.* 75).

Vices and passions (*pathē*) are closely connected in Philo's writings, as passions are held to bring about vicious dispositions and conduct.[4] The close association and even, at times, assimilation between passions and vices is best attested by the countless occurrences of the formula "passions and vices" in his writings, as well as by the interchangeable use that he makes of these terms.[5] The appeal to eradicate one's passions appears frequently in Philo's oeuvre, as he repeatedly reflects on the possibility, or even on the necessity, to completely liberate the soul from

[2] *Cher.* 96; *Migr.* 127–31; *Ebr.* 20–21; *Det.* 114. [3] *Opif.* 3; *Mos.* 2:48. Najman 2003.
[4] *Her.* 245; *Fug.* 152. [5] E.g. *Congr.* 59, 85; *Deus* 111–16; and see *Leg.* 3:21–22.

its passions.[6] In Philo's eyes the aim of the moral life – that is, of the life according to the Laws of Moses – is the abstention from passions and vices: "The law holds that all who adhere to the sacred constitution established by Moses, must be free from every irrational passion and every vice" (*Spec.* 4:55).

Not only are numerous biblical verses read in terms of eradication of the passions, but Jewish festivities or practices are also interpreted as an invitation to suppress the passions of the soul. Thus Passover symbolizes the necessity to unlearn the passion (ἀπομαθεῖν τὸ πάθος), and circumcision is interpreted as the excision (ἐκτομή) of the pleasures and of all the soul's passions (*Migr.* 92).[7] Philo also compares the soul's cultivation to the complete uprooting of the tree of passions, thereby adopting a metaphor commonly found in philosophical treatises of the Hellenistic and Roman periods.[8] Suppression of the passions is thus a fundamental tenet of Philo's thought insofar as passions are held to be the source of the rejection of the law of nature.[9]

Since passions are considered to be the cause of moral evils, the next question to be addressed is what accounts for the existence of passion in the human soul. Philo presents his reader with a twofold account of the origin of the passions: sometimes he maintains that passions derive from sense-perception, whereas at other times he claims that they are produced by the irrational parts of the soul. Instead of accusing him of inconsistency, I shall claim that these two accounts are in fact compatible when the cognitive aspect of *pathos* is taken into account – an aspect of Philo's concept of passion which has not yet received due attention in Philonic scholarship.

## 1.1 Passions and Sensation

The passions relate to the embodied condition of the human soul. To put it simply, passions exist because human beings have bodies equipped with sense-perception. Philo holds that the association of the mind with the body through sense-perception brings forth the passions – that is, the irrational motions of the soul. In that, Philo clearly follows Plato's

6 E.g. *Agr.* 10; *Gig.* 4; *Det.* 28, 105; *Plant.* 98; *Mut.* 72; *Somn.* 2.266.
7 *Congr.* 162; *Leg.* 3: 94, 194, and 236; *Migr.* 25, 151, 25; *Her.* 255.
8 *Agr.* 17 and *Det.* 105.
9 For a defense of Philo's endorsement of eradication of the passions see Weisser forthcoming.

treatment of the human soul in the *Timaeus*. There Plato describes the way in which the "immortal principle," handed down by the Demiurge to the inferior gods for the creation of the mortal animal (man), was planted by necessity into their bodies. The binding of the immortal soul with the body gave rise first, necessarily, to sensations, depicted as violent movements which throw the regular motions of the soul into confusion (*Tim.* 43a–b). The trouble of sensations caused the passions of the soul and impaired its cognitive functioning (44a). The passage in which the Demiurge addresses the younger gods clearly states that the paradigmatic passions (love, fear, *thumos*, etc.) follow upon sensation:

So, once the souls were of necessity implanted in bodies, and these bodies had things coming into them and leaving them, the first innate [capacity] they would of necessity come to have would be sense-perception (αἴσθησις), which arises out of forceful disturbances. This they all would have. The second would be love, mingled with pleasure and pain. And they would come to have fear and temper as well, plus whatever goes with having these [passions], as well as all their natural opposites. And if they could master these, their lives would be just, whereas if they were mastered by them, they would be unjust.[10]

In *On the Creation of the Cosmos according to Moses* – a work greatly indebted to the *Timaeus* – Philo not only endorses Plato's idea concerning God's collaborators in the creation of the irrational soul (so God cannot be held accountable for vice and vicious activities of human beings),[11] but he also takes up the close connection between sense-perception and the origin of passions. According to Philo's interpretation of the Garden of Eden episode, before the creation of the woman, the first man in Paradise enjoyed an uncorrupted rational nature, free of weakness, disease, and passion (*Opif.* 148–150). The creation of the woman, who symbolizes sensation, spelled the demise of the previous perfect rational activity. The encounter of the man with the woman brought about "a desire for bodily pleasure, which is the starting-point of wicked and law-breaking deeds" (*Opif.* 151; trans. Runia).

The close association between sensation and passions is frequent. In the *Allegories of the Laws* 2:7–9, for instance, Philo claims that sensation and passions form the "parts and products" of a single soul, and calls the passions the "offspring of sensation." Sometimes he labels sense-perception the cause of the passions (*Leg.* 2:50), or again, explains

[10] *Tim.* 42a–b; trans. Zeyl, slightly modified. See Reydams-Schils 1999, 62–65. Cf. *Tim.* 69c–d.

[11] *Opif.* 74–75. See Winston 1986; Runia 1986, 242–49.

that passions "arise out of what we see or hear or smell or taste or touch" (*Abr.* 238).[12]

Although Philo considers sensation as what causes the passions, he is also ready to give sense-perception a more positive function. Espousing the Stoic model of sense-perception, he sometimes argues that sensation is necessary for any form of knowledge, as it provides the intellect with information concerning the sensible world, from which it is possible to rise to the knowledge of the intelligible world.[13] However, most of the time, Philo emphasizes the negative aspect of sensation. According to this model the interplay between soul and sensation, seen as a direct consequence of embodiment, is responsible for the irrational passions. The cause of irrational behavior is thus framed in terms of a conflict between the soul and the body. This linkage between embodied condition and passion explains the fact that in Philo's eyes, passions are an inherent phenomenon, a necessity, or even a constraint of the embodied human condition, understood as an intellect trapped in a body.[14]

## 1.2 The Passions and the Irrational Parts of the Soul

In other instances, Philo designates the irrational parts of the human soul – that is, the appetite and the spirit – as the *locus* of irrational behavior. In a manner reminiscent of Plato's depiction of the soul in the *Republic*, for Philo, the irrational parts of the human soul have their proper objects of pursuit (such as food or sexuality, for the appetite part; honor or love of strife and disputes, for the spirited one). Time and again, Philo warns against the perils of these objects of pursuit, which become increasingly complex as the individual advances in a life ruled by passions: from the desire for simple food, to the devastating and more complex desires for luxury and delicacies.[15]

How is it then possible to reconcile these two models of the origin of passion? Should passions be considered as emerging from sensation or from the irrational parts of the soul? Reydams-Schils has convincingly argued that whereas the first model – that is, the linkage between sensation and irrationality – is based on Socratic psychology, which emphasizes the

[12] See also *Abr.* 147–50, 236–9 and references in Reydams-Schils 2008, esp. 177–79 (B4, B8, and B.ii.2).

[13] E.g. *Opif.* 139 and 166; *Her.* 53; *Somn.* 1:187–88 and *Congr.* 21.

[14] See *Gig.* 15; *Leg.* 1:108; *Sacr.* 950; *Ios.* 71; *QG* 4:77; *Migr.* 21; *Virt.* 76.

[15] Plato, *Resp.* 435c–441c, 580d–592b. Philo, *Opif.* 158–59; *Spec.* 4:82 and 112–13.

division between soul and body, the second model has a more Platonic bearing. As she has shown, a similar tension is already found in Plato's dialogues, and even within the *Timaeus* itself.[16] Following Reydams-Schils's reading, I argue that there is no fundamental contradiction, but rather a shift of emphasis. First of all, there is no doubt that the second model of the origin of passions still preserves the soul–body duality, insofar as the irrational and inferior parts of the soul form a link between the soul and the body: they are the parts of the soul that are in a body. Second, and most importantly, the two models can be combined, I shall claim, via the cognitive aspect of passion – that is, through the evaluative element contained in *pathos*.

The agent's valuation lies at the heart of Philo's understanding of passion. Through sense-perception the embodied intellect encounters sensible and external objects, but it is the valuation of these objects that leads the irrational parts of the soul to pursue them. By that I do not mean that Philo adopts the intellectualist stance of the Stoics, who equated passion with opinion (or judgment) on what seems to the agent to be good or bad or, in other words, who claimed that passion can be defined as an erroneous or unstable predication of good or bad (see below). Nonetheless, Philo's passions should not be seen as mere erratic movements of the soul, deprived of any cognitive features. Ultimately, they depend on what the agent values as worthy of concern and pursuit. *Pathos* results from the valuations of the physical object which have provoked a pleasurable or painful experience. An epistemically deficient agent is easily led to believe that what has aroused pleasure is worthy of concern whereas what causes an unpleasant feeling should not be pursued. Valuation therefore functions as the bridge between a first bodily or basic *pathos* (such as the pleasure experienced in eating) and the pursuit of the objects identified as likely to arouse it. In other words, for Philo one cannot desire delicacies without believing that they are worth pursuing; but on the other hand, one cannot hold the belief that delicacies are a proper object of concern without having experienced a basic form of bodily desire toward food, and some pleasure and gratification in achieving it. It seems therefore that for Philo *pathos* is at the same time both the basic bodily motivation that leads to the pursuit or avoidance of external objects and the more complex cognitive phenomenon resulting from the valuation of these experiences. Concern for material objects such as food, money, and so forth, based on value-beliefs, leads to the pursuit of these

[16] Reydams-Schils 1999, 62–65.

objects and, at the end, to the valuation and pursuit of the passions themselves. Philo's interpretation of the snake of Eden spells out the way in which sensation (the woman) allures the intellect by means of bodily pleasure (the serpent):

> Pleasure encounters and consorts with the senses first, and through them it deceives the ruling intellect as well. Each of the senses is seduced by its charms. They rejoice in what is set before them, sight responding to varieties of colour and shape, hearing to melodious sounds, taste to the sweetness of flavours, and smell to the fragrances of exhaled vapours. On receiving these gifts, in the manner of female servants, they offer them to reason (*logismos*) as their master, taking persuasion (πειθώ) along as their advocate so that none of the offerings whatsoever would be rejected.[17]

This passage shows that passions develop in the human soul as a result of a defective intellect which subscribes to the value-appearances of sensible experiences relayed by sense-perception. According to this reading, sensation is responsible for the passions in providing the intellect with the stimulus from external objects, while the irrational soul is accountable for the formation of the irrational motions which are the passions. Therefore, at times Philo emphasizes the body–soul distinction, stating that *aisthēsis* is the cause of the passions, while at others he chooses to accentuate the difference between the parts of the soul. The adoption of by Philo of both models of the origin of the passions likely explains why, when he subscribes to the Stoic model of the soul, he designates the five senses as what constitute, together with speech and reproduction, the irrational part of the soul.[18]

To conclude, up to now I have argued that vicious conduct results from the passions of the soul and that the existence of the passions is explained by two interconnected reasons: the embodied condition of man on the one hand, and an impaired epistemological state of the agent on the other. Passions constitute an irrational response to sensible particulars perceived by the intellect through sense-perception, and result from a wrong valuation of bodily experiences and of physical reality.

The question that naturally follows is what, in addition to the obvious pleasure and pain associated with sensible experiences, causes the agent to subscribe to the value-appearances of his experiences? Answering this question is the task of the second part of this chapter. I shall first argue that Philo considers mistaken beliefs regarding divine causation as the inception of a wrong valuation of the physical realm. Second, I shall

[17] *Opif.* 165; trans. Runia, slightly modified. [18] As in *Her.* 232 or *Migr.* 3.

suggest that improper philosophical argumentation constitutes, in his eyes, one of the main causes of ignorance and hence of irrational and vicious conduct.

## 2 THE SOUL'S EPISTEMIC STATUS

### 2.1 Error Concerning Divine Causation

For Philo, true knowledge is knowledge of God. The question of the various aspects and levels of this knowledge and of the possibility of apprehending God's essence is a complex issue which cannot be properly addressed here. Nevertheless, a prerequisite minimal form of knowledge of God requires the recognition that God is the creator of the world, or in other words, that he is its cause.[19] God's ontological primacy is thus chiefly interpreted in terms of causal primacy, which implies that the physical reality should be understood as emerging from God as its cause: "For it suffices for man's reasoning (*logismos*) to advance as far as to learn that the cause of the universe is and subsists" (*Post.* 168).[20] The possibility to gain such a knowledge is conveyed to Moses' disciples:

> For whatever benefit accrues from the most respected philosophy to its students accrues to the Jews through their laws and customs, namely, knowledge of the highest and oldest cause of all things and rejection of the error associated with created gods. For no created thing is a god in truth, but in opinion only, since it lacks the necessary quality of eternality.[21]

In this context, it comes as no surprise that Philo describes piety, "the queen of virtues" (*Spec.* 4:147), in terms of knowledge of the creator of the cosmos[22] and as the source of all other virtues (*Decal.* 52), whereas impiety is often associated with atheism.[23]

Philo insists, however, that attributing causation to God should not lead one to believe that he can be considered as the cause of evil.[24] In fact, it is of paramount importance to Philo to warn against the dangers of errors concerning the divinity conveyed by different types of people. Thus, for example, the king of Egypt represents the atheistic disposition of the

[19] See for example, *Opif.* 21; *Her.* 201, 301; *Leg.* 3:35, 100–02; *Post.* 168, 175; *Plant.* 93; *Deus* 56, 201; *Prov.* 2:72. See Sterling 2007; Calabi 2008, 3–56.

[20] See also *Fug.* 161–65 and *Spec.* 1:32–50, probably following Plato, *Tim.* 28a; *Decal.* 51–52, 64; *Post.* 175; *Mos.* 2:24 and *Prov.* 2:72.

[21] *Virt.* 64–65, trans. Wilson 2011 . Cf. *Spec.* 1:345 and *QE* 1:23.

[22] *Mut.* 76; *Conf.* 132; *Spec.* 2:63; *Decal.* 52; Sterling 2006.

[23] As in *Conf.* 114; *Ebr.* 41–45; Sterling 2006, n. 67.

[24] *Agr.* 129; *Plant.* 127–29.

soul,[25] whereas the reptile with many feet of Lev 11:42 symbolizes the polytheist one (*Migr.* 69). Errors concerning the transcendent cause of the universe – “the most excellent support of the soul” (*Decal.* 67) – leads to countless philosophical mistakes: from thinking the world unbegotten, or conceiving a plurality of worlds, and up to the divinization of heavenly bodies or even of shapeless matter.[26] It appears, thus, that for Philo the misapprehension of God’s primary causality not only brings forth misconceptions concerning God but also, and more importantly, a misevaluation of the created world and of its constituents. Error on the first cause leads one to misapprehend the organization of the cosmos and to wrongly evaluate the sensible and corruptible reality. In Philo’s opinion there is only one small step from misconceiving God’s causation to considering bodily and external goods (such as wealth, honor, glory, and so forth) as worthy of pursuit.[27]

## 2.2 Decline of Wisdom

Since error concerning God’s causal primacy brings forth many misconceptions concerning the sensible world, the next question that should be addressed is what causes the agent to endorse a set of incorrect beliefs, which ultimately will produce passions and vicious conduct. In the following, I shall argue that Philo considers the persuasiveness of improper philosophical arguments and doctrines as one of the main incentives for the agent’s endorsement of erroneous beliefs.

Philo’s view of wisdom should not be read through the dichotomy of Jewish versus Greek. For Philo, philosophy and wisdom are not ethnically determined. Philosophy is not Greek, just as wisdom is not Jewish. Philo’s concept of wisdom and philosophy are better situated in a historical dichotomy: ancient wisdom – that is, that of Moses[28] – then followed by Pythagoras and Plato, as opposed to the contemporary one, which has diverted from the truth.[29] One of the most obvious manifestations of the deterioration of philosophical practice is found in the many disagreements between the philosophical schools and among philosophers. In a fragment

[25] *Leg.* 3:212; *QG* 5:87.
[26] *Conf.* 173; *Migr.* 179, 184–89; *Leg.* 3.7. On the hierarchy of polytheisms see *Decal.* 52–57; *Spec.* 1.13–31, 1.324–32. See also *Opif.* 170–71; *Praem.* 39–40, 44.
[27] *Decal.* 9; *Det.* 4, 109–10; *Her.* 242–43; *Sobr.* 67.
[28] *Post.* 102; *Spec.* 2:165–67; *Opif.* 8.
[29] This would become a Platonic commonplace, first attested in Celsus: see Frede 1994, 5193–98.

which has been brought to scholarly attention by D. Runia,[30] Philo argues that the "clear proof" that the schools of philosophy have failed to reach an understanding of the principles of nature is the many disagreements (διαφωνίαι), dissensions (διαμάχαι), and differences of opinion (ἑτεροδοξίαι) existing among them. However, the *diaphonia* existing between the various systems of thought is not the main danger to the soul in search of wisdom. The persuasiveness, or the convincing character, of their philosophical argumentations constitutes an even greater peril. The persuasive character of a discourse that is not based on the truth leads the intellect to endorse fallible opinions concerning the proper value of the objects of this world.

## 2.3 The Dangers of *pithanos*

The analysis of the instances of the term "persuasive" (*pithanos*) in Philo's oeuvre clearly displays his distrust of the persuasive and convincing character of some discourses. First, persuasiveness is very often associated with sophistry, with rhetorical skills and maneuvers. The sophists, represented among others by the sorcerers of Egypt, are condemned for deceiving the soul and for upholding "mythical plausibility" in higher esteem than truth.[31] Interpreting Gen 15:16, Philo associates the "sins of the Amorites" with "sophistical discourses" that have the power to seduce and allure the soul by means of their persuasiveness (*Her.* 300–08, at 302). "Likely and persuasive sophisms" (εἰκόσι καὶ πιθανοῖς σοφίσμασιν; *Det.* 1) are also used by Cain – another representative of sophistry – in order to deceive his brother. Whereas Abel represents the doctrine of the love of God, i.e. the only road to virtuous life, Cain symbolizes the love of the self and the care of the body – a presumptuous doctrine of men dedicated to wealth, honors, and to "the pleasures which bring pleasant experiences to their all-welcoming soul by means of every sense" (*Det.* 34).[32] Against those cunning fighters who use specious arguments and sophistic tricks, the innocent and untrained Abel could not win.

It is not necessary to enter here into the intricate question of the identity of the Sophists in Philo's corpus. In his *Philo and Paul among the Sophists*, B. Winter considers Philo as one of the first witnesses of the Sophistic

[30] *Quaestiones in Genesim et in Exodum: fragmenta graeca*, frag. 4 (Petit 1978, 284); Runia 1999a, 126. See also *Her.* 246–48; *Ebr.* 198–202.

[31] *Migr.* 76; LXX Exod 7:11: see *Mut.* 208–09; *Det.* 38–40; Pearce 2007, 163–67.

[32] See *Migr.* 72–84.

movement which flourished in first-century Alexandria.[33] Other scholars have claimed that Philo's use of the term 'sophist' is not limited to the professional guild of rhetoricians, but rather targets a philosophical school, some pointing at the Sceptics, others at the Peripatetics, or even at the Stoics.[34] Nevertheless, it is important to keep in mind that the accusation of engaging in sophistry as opposed to philosophy is a very common device used in philosophical polemical discourses. Since Plato's condemnation of the Sophists for building arguments from probabilities and likelihood, for relying on mere appearances or illusions, and for leading the soul away from truth,[35] the term sophist has become the hallmark of a form of erudition deprived of any substantial knowledge. We should therefore not expect Philo to be systematically and exclusively committed to one of the senses of this term, as he may sometimes underline its historical aspect, and at others use it as an eristic tool.

In a passage in which Philo lists the opposing opinions concerning the genesis of the cosmos, the nature of things, and the validity of sensible perception, it is to "the didactic quarrels of the sophists" that he refers.[36] The dialectical and doxographical exposition of contradictory opinions reflects the tenets of the Sceptics, the Stoics, and the Peripatetics. Although one might think that these various opinions foster the soul's development, insofar as they investigate the nature of things, they in fact bring forth intense conflicts, as they convincingly present contradictory points of view. What Philo wishes to stress here is the danger of the persuasiveness of such arguments and conjectures, which are in fact remote from truth.

> The philosophical issues have become full of disagreement (διαφωνίας), because truth evades the easily persuaded and conjecturing mind (τὸν πιθανὸν καὶ στοχαστικὸν νοῦν). For it is the difficulty in finding and tracking the truth that, in my view, has produced these dialectical disputes.[37]

This passage, in which Philo adopts the Sceptical mode of exposition of disagreements,[38] shows that although the deceitful use of persuasive arguments is probably one of the hallmarks of what Philo consider as sophistry, it is likely not limited to it alone.[39]

[33] Winter 1997, 60–112. [34] See review in Winter 1997, 60–82.

[35] *Theaet.* 162e: πιθανολογίᾳ τε καὶ εἰκόσι; see also *Resp.* 515a; *Soph.* 232a–236d.

[36] *Her.* 246 (Gr. τὰς σοφιστῶν δογματικὰς ἔριδας). Philo's *dogmatikos* refers to something instructive or didactic: *Her.* 141, 292; *Sacr.* 42; *Leg.* 3.215.

[37] *Her.* 248. [38] See Mansfeld 1988; Runia 2008.

[39] Other instances in which plausibility is associated to sophistry are *Agr.* 16, 96; *Congr.* 18 and 26–29; *Opif.* 45.

More generally, conjectures and probabilities mark the terrestrial realm, full of confusion and disorder, overshadowed by opinions that are fallible in nature. It is important to note that Philo's overall suspicious attitude toward the persuasive character of some arguments does not imply that he radically rejects them. On some occasions he qualifies his own exegesis as "likely conjecture" (εἰκός στοχασμός) or as "likely plausibilities." These can be used by the exegete especially in cases where only God knows what the true reasons are.[40] Nevertheless, persuasive arguments or conjectures are bound to remain in the realm of opinions, characterized by the uncertainty and instability inherent in the relationship between the mobile nature of sensible reality and the agent apprehending it.[41]

In this context, it is useful to recall Plato's characterization of the stochastic *technai* (such as medicine or navigation) in terms of their dependence on circumstances external to the expertise itself, as opposed to other *technai*, which are guaranteed to achieve their goal.[42] In *On Joseph*, Philo argues that the statesman, symbolized by Joseph, should be guided by likely conjectures (εἰκός στοχασμός) and probable persuasiveness (εὔλογος πιθανότης; *Ios.* 143) in order to elicit the moral values out of the visions and appearances characteristic of the changing nature of political matters. It seems that Philo's association in *On Joseph* of conjectures and persuasiveness with the political realm reflects a current tenet that can be traced back to Plato's distinction, and that is furthermore found in later authors such as Hermagoras, who described the role of rhetoric as addressing political questions in the most persuasive way possible.[43]

Aside from Philo's acceptance of persuasiveness in some matters of biblical exegesis and in the realm of politics, the persuasiveness of arguments is, most of the time, perceived as jeopardizing the soul's epistemological status. First, the linkage between the misconception concerning God and the persuasive character of erroneous beliefs is clearly spelled out in *On the Creation of the Cosmos according to Moses*. Philo explains that in order to prevent man's future mistake of attributing the causation of earthly growth to heavenly bodies, God first provided the earth with adornment (that is, with plants, grass, crops, and fruit) and only afterwards created the heavenly bodies. The possibility of such a mistake concerning the cause of growth is directly associated with the nature of man's thought and with its

40 *Decal.* 18; *Opif.* 72, 157; *Plant.* 165; *Spec.* 1:214 *Prov.* 2.72; and *Her.* 224.
41 *Ios.* 140–47; *Praem.* 28–30; *Sacr.* 12.
42 Plato, *Phileb.* 55e–56c.
43 Hermagoras, *Test.* 12 and 13 (Woerther).

tendency to rely on appearances rather than on God. Admiring sophistry rather than wisdom, it aims at "what is likely (εἰκότων) and persuasive (πιθανῶν), and in which there is much reasonable (τὸ εὔλογον; *Opif.* 45)." Similarly, in *On the Confusion of Tongues*, the tower of Babel is interpreted as the building of persuasive arguments that aim at alienating the mind from the true honor due to God (*Conf.* 128–32). These passages clearly indicate that, for Philo, a persuasive discourse can easily lead one to err about the cause of the universe.

Philo not only assumes that persuasiveness supports error concerning divine causation but he furthermore spells out a precise linkage between the danger of persuasion and the passions of the soul. Thus, in *On Dreams* he describes the sophists of Egypt as devisers of "arguments on behalf of pleasure and desire," who fight against divine virtues by means of their "persuasiveness which advocates the cause of passion" (*Somn.* 2:279). In *On Cultivation* the serpent of Eden is said to deceive the woman by means of "seductive persuasiveness" (*Agr.* 96) and, in a similar manner, in *On the Creation of the Cosmos* the woman – that is, sense-perception, who has been allured by the serpent (pleasure) – in turn enslaves the intellect by means of persuasion (*Opif.* 165, quoted above). In *On Drunkenness* the "persuasiveness of arguments" (λόγων πιθανότητες) is what the "drunk man" – who symbolizes the person disobedient not only to the command of right reason but also to that of education and conventional laws – contributes toward the destruction of virtue.[44] It is, says Philo, this kind of guilty and blameable reasoning (*logismos*) that each of us needs to eradicate, suppressing from the mind "every evil disposition": "For it is in ourselves that the reprehensible and culpable reasoning reside and lurk, and when they are incurable, it is necessary to cut them away and to destroy them completely" (*Ebr.* 28). This passage shows the relationship between the persuasiveness of argumentation and the dangerous thoughts or reasoning (*logismos*) of human beings. This is not the only place in which Philo underlines the far-reaching implications of the dangers of the human *logismos*. In the context of a discussion concerning the dangers of sensation, Philo contrasts human reasoning or calculation with truth and faith (*pistis*) in God. Faith in human *logismos* leads to the destruction of truth. "It is better," says Philo, "to put one's trust in God, and not in uncertain reasoning (τοῖς ἀσαφέσι λογισμοῖς), or unsure conjectures" (ταῖς ἀβεβαίοις εἰκασίαις: *Leg.* 3:228).

[44] *Ebr.* 29 and 34.

The association between the unstable apprehension based on images, formed by the human *logismos*, which presumptuously puts faith in itself, and the irrational passions is clearly spelled out in the following passage:

> To believe in God is the true doctrine, while the false one is to trust our vain reasoning (τοῖς κενοῖς λογισμοῖς). But irrational impulse (ἄλογος δὲ ὁρμή) comes to be frequent and proceeds from both the reasoning and from the mind which corrupts the truth. ... So to trust either persuasive reasoning (λογισμοῖς πιθανοῖς) or a mind destructive of the truth is irrational.[45]

In the rest of the passage (*Leg.* 3:330–35), Num 21:27–30 is interpreted in terms of the destruction of the miserable mind (Moab) by false opinion, as the dissolution of its particular enthymemes (the pillars of Arnon: Num 21:28), as the flight of its particular *logismoi* (the sons of Moab: Num 21:29), as the captivity of its judgment by deceptive sophistry (the daughters captive to Seon, king of the Amorites: Num 21:29) and, finally as the burning of the mind by sense-perceptions (the women kindling a fire against Moab: Num 21:30). As the passage quoted above makes plain (*Leg.* 3:229–30), the passions are not said to emerge from the irrational parts of the soul, nor derive from sensation, but rather they are issued by the agent's own *logismos*. The persuasive character of human reasoning is what produces "the irrational impulse" in the soul or, in other words, is what produces passion. Philo's association between passion and reasoning, through the intermediary of persuasive argument, is perhaps to be seen as the origin or, at least, as a first step in the process of "demonization" of the human *logismos* – an association that would have far-reaching implications in later Christian thought.[46]

These passages show that in Philo's eyes the persuasive character of certain types of beliefs has the power to mislead the soul. The persuasiveness of a discourse that is not based on the truth but on what only appears as true has the power to cause the mind to endorse erroneous beliefs concerning divine primacy, and thereby to lead the agent astray in the determination of his choices and objects of pursuit.

## 2.4 The Sceptic Background and the *modus philosophandi*

My last question concerns what stands behind Philo's repeated warnings against the danger of persuasion. Does Philo's dislike for persuasiveness solely echo the old quarrel between philosophy and rhetoric? My

[45] *Leg.* 3:229–30.

[46] E.g. Evagrius Ponticus, *Octo. spir.* (PG 79:1145–64); Athanasius, *Vit. Ant.* 23; Origen, *Princ.* III.2.4.

contention is that, although Philo recruits the long-familiar association between persuasion and rhetoric,[47] he enriches it with an additional layer. Indeed, the familiar criticism leveled against rhetoric is redirected at the contemporary practice of philosophy – a practice which is associated with that of the Sceptics.[48] The association between the contemporaneous philosophical culture, the Sceptic tradition, and the persuasiveness of some opinions can be based on three grounds: the use of and reluctance for doxography; the integration of some Sceptic tenets; and finally the use of the term *pithanos* itself.

First of all, it should be noted that the practice of doxographical and dialectical exposition of opposite claims – a method endorsed and developed by the Sceptics (first by the Academics and later on by the Pyrrhonians) as an integral part of the philosophical inquiry – gained widespread popularity by the time of Philo, while still remaining connected, albeit remotely, to the Sceptics. As we saw earlier, Philo was himself, in a perhaps paradoxical manner, committed to this genre.[49] Whereas the goal of the Sceptic philosophers in listing the contrasting opinions of different schools or philosophers was to lead to suspension of judgment on the grounds of their improvability, the doxographical exposition of the different views on one subject was, in Philo's time, a valid mode for learning and practicing philosophy. The important role it came to play in the dissemination of philosophical doctrines and culture likely explains why Philo endorses this practice even though he finds it dangerous.

Second, as it has been noted by commentators, Philo's indebtedness to Scepticism appears clearly in *On Ebreitate* 166–205. This passage not only bears a valuable testimony to Philo's use of doxographical exposition (here, related to the creation of the world and the nature of the good: *Ebr.* 198–202), but it shows a deep connection with the Sceptic tradition. The passage, which presents the ten modes of Aenesidemus,[50] is not only suffused with distinctive Sceptic terminology, and with the standard set of examples usually used in the refutation of the valid character of sense-perception,[51] but it moreover defends suspension of judgment on the

[47] See Plato, *Gorg.* 453a–454b; Quintilian, *Inst.* II.15.1–15.

[48] In the following, Scepticism refers to the Sceptic tradition as a whole. The distinction between Pyrrhonian and Academic Scepticism will be drawn when relevant.

[49] Runia 2008; Runia 1999b, esp. 45–51; Mansfeld 1999, esp. 17–19 ; also Mansfeld 1989, 1990.

[50] Cf. Diogenes Laertius 9.78–88 and Sextus Empiricus, *Pyr.* 1.36–163.

[51] See Cicero, *Luc* 19.79; Seneca, *Nat.* I.3.9, I.5.6, I.7.2; and Reid 1985, 269.

ground that human intellect cannot gain a firm grasp of the changeable and moving physical reality (*Ebr.* 166–205). Note that Philo does not himself contend with reproducing the tropes, but uses them in order to condemn the insensibility (ἀναισθησία) of an intellect that presumptuously thinks that it has the power to evaluate by itself the truth of the impressions emerging from the sensible realities – that is, an intellect that guesses at uncertainties and uses conjectures (στοχασμός) instead of the truth (*Ebr.* 166–68). In this respect, the philosophers are especially to be blamed. Divided "into troops and companies," their unstable beliefs are attested by the many "contradictory and often opposite doctrines" on most important subjects such as the creation of the cosmos, providence, and the nature of the good (*Ebr.* 198–202).[52]

It seems, therefore, that the perception of philosophical inquiry as a mere dialectic game of opposing contradictory opinions can be seen as one of the consequences of the popularization of the doxographical method of practicing and learning philosophy. Philo was not the only intellectual to formulate these complaints. Similar criticism can be found in the sarcastic remarks of Lucian or Diodorus of Sicily, and later appears as a recurrent theme in the writings of many early Church Fathers striving to present Christianity as the true philosophy.[53]

The last link with the Sceptic tradition in my discussion is found in Philo's repeated distrust of *pithanos*. In the history of the Sceptic tradition, *pithanos* is associated with the second-century Academic philosopher Carneades, who, in articulating a more moderate form of Scepticism than that of Arciselaus, argues that "persuasive impression" (*pithanē phantasia*) can serve as a criterion for knowledge and action.[54] The question of whether Carneadean probabilism constitutes an ad hoc step in an overall attempt to challenge Stoic epistemology or whether it forms a more substantiated doctrinal tenet does not affect our present discussion. The important point here is that the doctrine according to which impressions reaching a sufficient level of persuasiveness could serve as a basis for rational procedure and action became strongly associated with the Sceptic Academy, in its Carneadean version.[55]

[52] See Runia 2008, 29–31; Lévy 2005, 85–102. The question of the reliability of Philo's report does not affect our present discussion. See Hankinson 1995, 120–21 and Striker 1983.

[53] Diodorus Siculus, *Bib. hist.* II.29.6; Lucian: e.g. *Icar.* 5–10, 29–31; *Tim.* 9; Church Fathers: e.g. Justin, 2 *Apol.* 13; Lactantius, *Inst.* 3.4; Eusebius, *Praep. ev.* 14.2.

[54] See Sextus Empiricus, *Math.* 7.159–89; Sextus Empiricus, *Pyr.* 1.230–31; Cicero, *Luc.* 99–101, 148.

[55] Cicero, *Luc.* 32–35.

As we have seen, the few exceptions mentioned above notwithstanding, Philo's position on the value of the *pithanos* differs radically from that of Carneades. Should Philo's concern with the persuasive character of some arguments be seen as a response to a certain form of Carneadean probabilism? First, it should be noted that the adoption of the terminology of one's thinker or school cannot be considered sufficient proof of influence. The spotting of a philosophical identity on the basis of terminological reminiscence often constitutes a superficial oversimplification of complex historical and dialectical processes by which a specific terminology and a philosophical group come to be intertwined. Furthermore, as we have already observed, *pithanos* is also clearly associated with what Philo considers as sophistry, and of course, the Sophists were also widely known for their appeal to "what is probable" (*eikos*). Although Philo explicitly associates the Academics with the Sophists in *Quaest. Gen.* 3:33, it does not seem to constitute a sufficient indication of a systematic identification between the Sophists and the Academics.[56] Furthermore, this passage, like others bearing a Sceptic imprint, more likely reflects a remote debt to a form of popularized Scepticism rather than a direct familiarity with the complex epistemological issues discussed by the Sceptic philosophers. As has been noted, Philo's endorsement of Sceptical terminology, themes, and methods on some occasions is imported into a radically different underlying epistemological framework. Scepticism serves as an intermediary step which enables Philo to emphasize all the more the limitation of human knowledge and the need to put one's firm and stable faith (*pistis*) in God alone (*Fug.* 136). As noted by C. Lévy, Scepticism is in Philo at the service of faith.[57]

These three elements discussed above suggest that Philo warns not so much against the most fundamental claims of the Sceptics but rather against the *modus philosphandi* with which the Sceptics were associated. The *diaphonia*, which characterizes the contemporaneous philosophical culture, is, as we have seen, for the dogmatism of Philo, a sign of deviation from the truth. The existence of many contradictory opinions among philosophers on most important issues constitutes proof that truth – which is characterized by uniqueness – has escaped the philosophical arena. One of the main dangers in the dissemination of contradictory opinions is that they are persuasive: they have the power to allure the soul and to instill erroneous beliefs which will ultimately lead to passions and a vicious disposition.

[56] Lévy 2008, 106–08. [57] Lévy 1986, 35; Lévy 2008.

Therefore, it can be assumed that the reaction against the persuasiveness of the many argumentations is a rejection of the kind of philosophical practice and culture with which Philo was familiar and in which he was embedded – a weariness of the many opinions, so to speak. Against the plurality of views on such important matters as God, the world, or the good, Philo champions a new kind of dogmatism, based on his own concept of truth – a truth which was handed down by God to Moses and which it is the task of the exegete of the biblical text to reveal. As the opposite of the heterogeneous aspect of contemporaneous philosophy, the philosophy of Moses is characterized by consistency and concordance (*Det.* 81). Moses' followers do not side with perspectival opinions since they make the benevolent, omnipotent, and omniscient cause of the universe the unique source of truth. They neither confuse an apparent good with a real one, nor do they consider any gratifications coming from sensible reality, such as bodily pleasures or social satisfactions, as worthy objects of pursuit.

## 2.5 A Final Remark on Philo's Concept of Passion

Before concluding, one further comment needs to be made. The stress on the cognitive aspects of Philo's concept of passion might lead us to believe that Philo is leaning toward a Stoic understanding of *pathos*. Despite his indebtedness to the Stoic theory of emotions, reflected in his use of the terminology and of the classification of the Stoics, Philo's understanding of the passions is not that of the Stoa.[58] Philo does not go as far as to consider every irrational motion of the soul in terms of an unstable predication of goodness or badness to an object or to a potential action. In fact, the evaluative aspect of the irrational motions of the soul can be traced back to Plato's exposition of the divided soul in the *Republic*, provided that we consider the Platonic tripartition not only in terms of psychological and motivational conflicts but also in terms of cognitive ones. In her valuable contribution to these issues, J. Moss has argued that the two prima facie different principles of division of the soul that appear in book 4 and book 10 of the *Republic*[59] can be reconciled when understood in terms of cognitive conflict.[60] On her reading, the irrational parts of the soul are characterized less by their objects of pursuit than by the unreflective way in which they accept appearances. Because the appetitive

[58] E.g. *Decal.* 143–46; *Praem.* 71; *Mos.* 2:139.

[59] See *Resp.* 602c–603a and 603e–605c. [60] Moss 2008.

and spirited parts of the soul accept how things struck them rather than how they are (since they do not have the ability to calculate), they are inclined not only to believe that a submerged stick is bent, but also that pleasurable experiences are good. The crucial point here is that the irrational passions of the soul are a response to how things appear, and an acceptance of the false perceptive value of things as good or bad.

As we have seen, Philo's understanding of human irrational behavior can be seen along these lines. For Philo, a passion constitutes a response to the value-appearance of sensible realities. In this sense, passions are closely related to the realm of opinion. Whereas he does not utterly reject the realm of opinions they nevertheless belong to an inferior cognitive state, which is that of appearance. A well-articulated false opinion has the appearance of a true one, and as such it has the dangerous power to seduce us, and to lead us to wrongly evaluate sensible reality. As we have seen, misconceptions concerning the sensible world are what cause passions and vices. Therefore, a persuasive wrong opinion imperils the soul's epistemological status, and leads it to passions and vices. Many different opinions held by different philosophical schools, presented in a persuasive or manner, are closer to sophistry than to true philosophy. Persuasive opinions lead us astray from truth, and hinder the acquisition of perfect rationality.

## 3 CONCLUSION

I started this inquiry by raising the question of the origin of moral evils in Philo's thought. I have argued that for Philo the origin of vice lies in the passions of the soul which are connected to the embodied human condition (i.e. sensation). Whereas the constraints of human materiality function as a necessary cause of the passions, it does not constitute the sufficient condition for their existence. In the account of moral corruption, the epistemological state of the agent also has to be taken into consideration. The adoption of a wrong set of beliefs, which originates ultimately from a wrong conception of God's causation, leads to an improper evaluation of the sensible and material realm. The persuasiveness of philosophical argumentation is one of the main causes accounting for the agent's endorsement of false beliefs. For Philo, the many divergent beliefs held by the different philosophical schools show that philosophy has strayed from the path of the truth and that it is now entangled in multiple contradictory opinions. For the agent to gain back rationality and to oppose the recalcitrance of his material condition, the best path is to endorse the true philosophy – that is, the Law of Moses. The gift of the Torah, which is the best and most detailed expression of the law of nature, thus expresses the infinite benevolence of the creator of the universe. Indeed, in contrast to the other philosophical systems, which lack a right constitution for mankind, the Jewish people have received the invaluable gift of the Torah, which provides right upbringing and education. At the junction between the naturalistic vantage point of ancient philosophy and that of the momentary particularism of Jewish philosophy, Philo conceives the Torah as that which can save humanity from its chaotic materiality, providing the set of rules that allow one to impose order upon his disorderly materiality. The concept of a true philosophy, which is not based on human reasoning, on conjectures, illusions, or perspectival opinions but on the truth of the revealed *logos*, is then the dogmatic solution provided by Philo for the corrupted characters of both the soul and of contemporary philosophy.

# 7

# The Evil Inclination (*yeṣer ha-ra'*) in Tannaitic Literature: Demonic Desires and Beyond

Ishay Rosen-Zvi

In this chapter I am going to do two, hopefully complementary, things: to summarize my findings on the Tannaitic *yeṣer*, and then to offer some methodological reflections about it, especially ones that were developed as a result of a recent critique of my *Demonic Desires*.[1]

## I YEṢER HA-RA' IN TANNAITIC LITERATURE

Let us open our quest for the Tannaitic *yeṣer* with a homily from Sifre Numbers, which retells the biblical story of the nocturnal encounter between Boaz and Ruth on the threshing floor. This event, the focal point of the entire book of Ruth, transforms the heroine from a childless refugee to the intended wife of Boaz and eventually the matriarch of the royal line of David. Concealing more than he reveals, the narrator describes this meeting in a laconic and enigmatic fashion. But here as elsewhere the Midrash uncovers what Scripture hides. The following homily unfolds the entire erotic drama played out that night on the threshing floor, at which the Bible only hints. To the reader's great surprise, however, the drama in this retelling is not between Boaz and Ruth at all, but between Boaz and himself; to be more precise, between Boaz and his evil *yeṣer*:

"As the Lord lives! Lie down until morning" (Ruth 3:13) – Because his evil *yeṣer* sat and importuned him the entire night. It said to him: You are unmarried and you want a woman, and she is unmarried and she wants a man (teaching that a wife is

[1] Rosen-Zvi 2011.

acquired by sexual intercourse). So go and have intercourse with her, and she will be your wife. He took an oath against his evil *yeṣer*: "As the Lord lives!" – I shall not touch her; and to the woman he said: "Lie down until morning."[2]

Beyond its interpretive creativity and dramatic eroticism, we should also note the arresting and highly sophisticated nature of the argument advanced by the evil *yeṣer* as it seeks to persuade Boaz to sleep with Ruth. The *yeṣer* does not simply entice Boaz to sexual sin, it makes a persuasive and cogent legal argument. It appears as a learned Torah scholar who sets forth a full halakhic claim, beginning with a description of the legal situation ("you are unmarried ... and she is unmarried"), and ending with the evident conclusion: "Go and have intercourse with her, and she will be your wife."[3] Indeed, Boaz is incapable of contending with such a convincing argument, and so must bind himself using a vow. The image of the evil *yeṣer* depicted here is not one of blind and unbridled passion, as scholars too often tend to assume. Rather, it is the image of a sophisticated enticer that cleverly tries to lead humans astray. Based on pseudo-halakhic arguments the *yeṣer* draws people to illicit acts.

Additional sources show that this is not an isolated literary instance, but a consistent anthropological model which presents the evil *yeṣer* as an independent entity, which is distinct from humans though it resides in their bodies. This externalization is highly significant for characterizing the image and character of humans in Tannaitic literature. Boaz does not lust for Ruth; the initiative to sleep with her comes from the evil *yeṣer* alone. From the very beginning Boaz is cast on the other side of the equation: as battling with his *yeṣer* and successfully taming it.

The struggle on the threshing floor between Boaz and his evil *yeṣer* appears in yet another Tannaitic homily in Sifre Deuteronomy. Here, however, it appears within a longer list of sins against which an oath in the name of the Lord is a useful preventive remedy:

"[Let these words that I command you today be] on your heart" (Deut 6:6) – This was the source of R. Yoshia's saying: A man must adjure his *yeṣer* (להשביע את יצרו). For you find everywhere that the righteous adjure their *yeṣer*: Abraham says (Gen 14:22), "I lift up my hand to the Lord." Boaz says (Ruth 3:13), "As the Lord lives! Lie down until morning." David says (1 Sam 26:10), "As the Lord lives, the Lord

[2] Sifre Num 38, p. 88.

[3] Although the homily does not specify why Boaz refused the *yeṣer*'s legal advice, it seems clear that it assumes that the *yeṣer* uses the legal claim as a "pretext of permission" for sexual licentiousness. Indeed, Rav, an early third-century Babylonian rabbi, is said to have flogged whoever married through intercourse (b. Yebam. 52a, b. Qidd. 12b, and the Talmud's explanation there "due to licentiousness").

Himself will strike him down." And Elisha says (2 Kgs 5:16), "As the Lord whom I serve lives, I will not take anything."[4]

This is a classical "index homily," a collection of a series of verses with a common motif. In our case, the shared motif is the formula for swearing by the Lord's name, which is read by the homilist as a technique to struggle against the *yeṣer*. This index may help us correct a common mistake with regard to the rabbinic *yeṣer*. In the case of Boaz and Ruth the evil *yeṣer* seemed to appear within a sexual context. The list in Sifre Deuteronomy, however, shows that the picture is more complicated. The evil *yeṣer* draws one to all possible sins: it draws Boaz to intercourse, just as it draws David to murder, and Abraham and Elisha to theft. The shared motif is the very antinomistic characteristic of the *yeṣer*.

We may be even more precise than that. Adjuration is a well-known technique against demons.[5] The picture of Boaz and the other biblical righteous "adjuring their *yeṣer*" indicates that the *yeṣer* has gained a demonic or quasi-demonic character in rabbinic literature. This impression is confirmed by additional sources. The *yeṣer* is structured by the early rabbis as a demon residing in humans' hearts and taking control of them, dragging them to sin.

A sophisticated battle must thus be waged against the *yeṣer*. The sources offer different strategies by which one can free oneself from the *yeṣer*'s wiles and exhortations. Adjuration is one such tool, but the most popular one is of course Torah study. This idea, appearing in several sources, is specified meticulously elsewhere in Sifre Deuteronomy:

"Therefore impress these My words upon your heart" (Deut 11:18) – This tells us that the words of Torah are like an elixir of life. (סם חיים). It is comparable to a king who was angry with his son, struck him a violent blow, and placed a bandage on the wound. He told him: My son, as long as this bandage remains on your wound, you may eat whatever you please and drink whatever you please, and bathe either in hot or cold water, and you will come to no harm. But if you remove it, it will immediately fester. Thus the Holy One, blessed be He, said to Israel: I created your evil yeṣer, and there is nothing more evil than it, (but) "If you do right, there is uplift" (Gen 4:7) – be occupied with words of Torah and it will not reign over you. But if you abandon words of Torah, then it will gain mastery over you, as it is said (ibid.), "Sin (חטאת) crouches at the door, its urge is toward you" – it has no business other than with you. But if you wish, you can rule over it, as it is said

[4] Sifre Deut 33, pp. 59–60.

[5] On adjuration as the quintessential magical practice, see Harari 2010, 132–34. On adjurations in Qumran, see Eshel 2003, 403. On Byzantine amulets, see Naveh and Shaked 1987. For possible connections between the two corpora, see Bohak 2008, 111–12.

(ibid.): "Yet you can be its master: If your enemy is hungry, give him bread to eat . . . you will be heaping live coals on his head" (Prov 25:21). The evil yeṣer is evil, the one who created it [himself] testifies that it is evil, as it is said, "Since the yeṣer of man's heart is evil (from his youth)" (Gen 8:21).[6]

This is a highly sophisticated homily, presenting the evil *yeṣer* as a nasty blow (מכה רעה) and the Torah as the bandage (רטייה) serving as its ultimate remedy (סם תם), an efficient medicine. Yet the doctrine presented in it is pretty simple, and may be summarized in a few basic points:

(a) Humans have a single *yeṣer* (only one!) given them by God, which is evil in nature.
(b) Humans are in a constant struggle with their *yeṣer*, which seeks to dominate them, specifically ensnaring them to sins.
(c) The *yeṣer* may be overpowered with the aid of the Torah; the Torah however works as a talisman, which helps only when it is actually worn.

I suggest that the single evil *yeṣer* of the rabbis is a result of their rejection of the two prevalent models for explaining the source of human sinfulness in pre-rabbinic literature. The first is the simple (or naive) biblical model of free will, adopted and developed especially by Sirach (15:12–17). The other is the cosmological (thus also dualistic and deterministic) model prevalent in Qumran and related sources, where sin is attributed to external cosmic forces ruling humans. Rabbinic Midrash argues against the former that sin is not a simple consequence of human free will, but is caused by an independent entity. But against the latter the rabbis claim that the *yeṣer* is not an external cosmic force, and that humans are capable of prevailing over it. This twofold repudiation led to the birth of a complex and distinctive model aimed at explaining the human tendency to sin without compromising individual agency. Sin is caused by the evil *yeṣer* that dwells within people, who nonetheless have the ability to fight it and prevail.

But if so, where did the good *yeṣer* come from, and why do we need it? Can a man not struggle against his evil *yeṣer* himself, just as Boaz and the other righteous did? The answer to the riddle of the good *yeṣer* may also lie in the cryptic and fragmentary scrolls from Qumran.[7] True, there is no good *yeṣer* there (or anywhere else before the rabbis), but we do find an evil *yeṣer*, which is part of a dualistic system, a cosmic struggle between demonic and angelic forces. It is thus fair to assume that the exceptional

[6] Sifre Deut 45, pp. 103–04. [7] See Tigchelaar 2008.

dual *yeṣer* structure in rabbinic literature is an amalgam of the single *yeṣer* doctrine together with a dualistic paradigm. Indeed, the only dual *yeṣer* homily in all of Tannaitic literature, at the end of Mishnah Berakhot, espouses a clear anti-dualistic polemical tone.[8]

A very similar phenomenon may be found in contemporaneous Christian discourse about the *daimones*.[9] Thus, in the third book of *On First Principles*,[10] Origen employs the theory of evil angelic beings to explain the dynamics of human sinfulness and the way to resist it. According to Origen, demons are intruders who invade the minds of humans and possess them: "By a certain kind of action or a certain kind of inaction a 'place' in the mind is given to the devil with the result that, when once he has entered our heart he either takes possession of us, or at any rate pollutes the soul" (*Princ.* III.2.4). Sin is thus a result of a combination of natural weakness and demonic taking over:

> We derive the beginnings and what we may call the seeds of sin from those desires which are given to us naturally for our use. But when we indulge these to excess and offer no resistance to the first movements towards intemperance, then the hostile powers, seizing the opportunity of this first offence, incite and urge us on in every way, striving to extend the sins over a larger field; so that while we men supply the occasions and beginnings of our sins, the hostile powers spread them far and wide and if possible endlessly.[11]

A similar dynamic is narrated in rabbinic literature, thus Genesis Rabbah: "When he [the evil *yeṣer*] sees a man rub his eyes, fix his hair,

[8] The focus of the last chapter of m. Ber. is the obligation to praise God for bad and good events alike. The second mishnah there rules that for good tidings one says, "Blessed is [He], the benevolent and the benefactor (הטוב והמטיב)," while for bad tidings one must say: "Blessed is [He], the true judge (דיין האמת)"; the third mishnah rules that "a man should say a benediction on misfortune just as on good fortune"; and the fifth mishnah cites the biblical source for these obligations. Our two-*yeṣarim* homily appears here. This context makes polemic with dualistic doctrines quite fitting, and may account for its exceptional picture of two *yeṣarim*. A dual *yeṣer* structure internalizes dualism, and submits it to the free will of the person hosting the *yeṣarim*. In this polemical, anti-dualistic context it is quite understandable that the same homily that presents a rare dualistic model also presents an exceptionally dialectic one. The evil *yeṣer* is not necessarily an enemy, for it too can be enlisted in God's service.

[9] And sometimes "devils." See Justin *1 Apol.* 58: "they who are called devils attempt nothing else than to seduce men from God." In other places, Justin ascribes the same tendency to demons.

[10] The English translation is taken from Butterworth 1966. The third book is among the parts of the Origenic corpus that were not preserved in the original Greek, but only in Rufinus's Latin translation. For the reliability of this quite liberal translation, see Butterworth 1966, xlvi–lii.

[11] Origen, *Princ.* III.2.2.

hang upon his heels [examples of immodest behaviour], he says: this one is mine" (הדין דידי) (Gen. Rab. 22.6, pp. 210–13). Origen also details the specific tactic of the demons: "One that is negligent and slothful, being less cautious, gives a place to those spirits which, like robbers (*latrones*) lying in ambush, contrive to rush into the minds of men whenever they see a place offered to them through slackness" (*Princ.* III.3.6). A remarkably identical metaphor appears in Genesis Rabbah, where the *yeṣer* appears as a "robber" waiting to seize weak people: "R. Abba b. Yudan said: It is like a powerless robber (לסטים שפוף) on a crossroads. He would tell all the passers-by: give me everything you have got. A clever man went by and saw he was useless (שאין בו תוחלת) and began to beat him" (Gen. Rab. 22.6, p. 211). Both patristic and rabbinic literatures repeatedly use the image of the cunning yet impotent robber to characterize the plots of the *yeṣer*/demons. The fact that we had to move mainly to Amoraic literature for our comparison exposes the development in the image and function of the rabbinic *yeṣer*.

These comparisons however also highlight the distinctiveness of the rabbinic *yeṣer*. For the rabbis there is a definite division between the *yeṣer* discourse and the treatment of "classic" demons. Demons are an integral part of their "normal" experience,[12] but they have no role in their account of the source of human sinfulness.[13] Only the demonic-yet-fully-internalized *yeṣer* appears in this context. The rabbis developed a sophisticated division of labor, in which external demons account for external dangers such as illness and suffering, while the (internal) *yeṣer* accounts for human sinfulness. Thus, while Origen and his followers discuss a variety of demons, appearing both as individuals and in groups, the rabbis know of only one, single *yeṣer*, penetrating humans. It is this

[12] For a list of demons in rabbinic literature, see Margalioth 1987. Demons, spirits, and evil angels function in rabbinic literature mainly as pests – causing harm, illnesses, and death (therefore named מזיקין) – or as heavenly adversaries, against individuals, Israel, or humanity at large. For the former, see Harari 2010, 302–09, and for the latter, see Urbach 1987, 166–83, and Schäfer 1975. On the vast occupation with defensive magic in rabbinic literature, see Bohak 2008, 351–425.

[13] Satanic incitements to sin (in the manner we find in Mark 1:13 [=Luke 22:3], 1 Cor 7:5, and the like) are extremely rare in rabbinic literature. They appear almost exclusively in the Babylonian Talmud, and do not depart much from their biblical precedents (see b. Ber. 62b [following 1 Chr 21:1]; b. Giṭ. 52a; b. Qidd. 81a–b; B. Bat. 15b–16a [following Job 1]; b. Sanh. 89b, 107a. On possible Persian influence on the demonology of the Bavli, see Kohut 1866). Most rabbinic sources that mention Satan, including the Bavli, portray him as a harmful pest (מזיק) or an adversary (מקטרג) rather than as an inciter (מסית).

move that made the *yeṣer* so popular in rabbinic literature and in many (probably most) subsequent Jewish moral discourses to this very day.

Let us summarize our findings thus far:

a Unlike the prevalent consensus of rabbinic scholarship, the Tannaitic *yeṣer* is evil, not dialectical. It is the name the rabbis give for the human drive toward all sin, not for the sex drive. The *yeṣer*'s dark character in early rabbinic literature is a direct result of the role it plays there as the source of human sinfulness.

b Both the dialectic *yeṣer* and its sexual nature are innovations of later rabbinic literature which in turn reformed the image of the *yeṣer* in earlier literature. A dialectic *yeṣer* can be found in Amoraic *aggadah* ("and it was very good – this is the evil *yeṣer*"), while the sexual *yeṣer* only occurs in the later strata of the Babylonian Talmud.[14]

c The *yeṣer* is a demon-like figure, and should be read as part of the Jewish demonological tradition. It is thus like the demons of Origen and his students, but more radically internalized.

These are the main theses; and now some thoughts to follow up on developments since the book.

## 2 WHAT IS A COMPARISON?

How should we interpret the similarities between rabbinic and Christian literature? This ever-pertinent question affects the *yeṣer* as well. I found various similarities between rabbinic – Tannaitic and Amoraic – literature and patristic texts, both in the character of *yeṣer/daimones* and the manner in which they are dealt with. Specific description, such as an "impotent robber" (לסטים שפוף; *astenes lestes*), or a guest who takes over the house, are found in both corpora. Should we assume a literary dependence? Some kind of genetic relationship, oral or written? Michal Bar-Asher Siegal recently posits a genetic literary relationship between the *Apophthegmata Patrum* – "The sayings of the Desert Fathers" – and the Babylonian rabbis, who were allegedly exposed to the Syriac translation of the collection.[15] I did not pursue this path in my book, but focused instead on phenomenological similarities between the central issues that disturbed Alexandrian monastics and the sages of the *beit midrash* and the solutions they offered.

[14] See Rosen-Zvi 2009. [15] Bar-Asher Siegal 2014.

Differences notwithstanding, both rabbis and early monks dedicated their lives to learning, which was for them a fundamental religious activity rather than just an intellectual endeavor – and associated study with ascetic practices. Both also connected their practices to the special war they in particular must fight against the *yeṣer*/demons. Compare b. Sukkah 52a: "[The *yeṣer*] leaves the other nations and attacks only Israel . . . Abaye said, [the *yeṣer* attacks] sages more than anyone (ובתלמידי חכמים יתר מכולן)" to Athanasius's *Life of Antony*: "The demons, therefore, if they see all Christians – monks especially (μάλιστα δε μοναχούς), labouring gladly and advancing, they first attack and tempt them" (*Vit. Ant.* 23). It is thus not surprising to find that both literatures developed a similar body of *cardiognosis*, knowledge of the heart.

Specific comparisons like those detailed above may hint at more direct connections. The comparison with fourth-century Athanasius and Evagrius is even more compelling if we consider that these images become increasingly radical and developed in Amoraic literature. Nonetheless, I incline less to genetic relations and "influence" and more toward a dialogic space of the kind analyzed by several scholars.[16]

## 3 THE PHYSIOLOGY OF THE YEṢER

In my book I made a point of reading the physical descriptions of the *yeṣer* quite literally. I suggested that these descriptions, especially the ones in b. Ber. 61a, offer a "physiology of the *yeṣer*," similar to the early Stoic physiology of sin.[17] In both corpora, sin is connected to a movement of the soul in the wrong direction – that is, against its nature. But why take at face value descriptions such as "your *yeṣer* moved upon you (זע יצרך עליך)" or "the *yeṣer* looks like a fly and sits between the two openings of the heart"?

By way of comparison, consider this academic tale from several decades ago. Judah Liebes created a scandal at the Hebrew University when he published an article entitled "*De natura dei*: On the history of Jewish Myth."[18] His central claim was that rabbinic stories are based on a stable mythical core – a monotheistic myth, based already in Scripture – according to which God has a love–hate relationship with his people. Since God has no wife or family, he is needy of human love and affirmation. Liebes

[16] See esp. Boyarin 1999; Hasan-Rokem 2003.

[17] See Galen, *PHP* 4.2.12, *SVF* 3.462. For the Stoic physiology of feelings, see Inwood 1985, 155–65; Long and Sedley 1987, 410–23; Annas 1992, 106–08.

[18] Liebes 1994a. Cf. Liebes 1994b.

uses this myth to explain the stories of the patriarchs in Genesis, the prophetic admonishments against Israel as a wayward wife, as well as the entire system of the commandments which are aimed at having humans incessantly dote on God alone. The rabbis, according to Liebes, developed this biblical myth in a theurgical direction, and this became mechanized and systematized in Kabbalah. Liebes' colleague Shalom Rozenberg responded with a scathing critique, accusing Liebes of a "Karaitic" interpretation of stories that were clearly intended to be read figuratively.[19] Liebes responded that Rozenberg was continuing the Maimonidean tradition of reading allegorically in an attempt to purify religion from the mythical. Liebes pithily explained the essence of their dispute: "the Midrash says 'when Israel do the will of the Omnipresent they add might to the [divine] Power,' Rozenberg explains that human action cannot influence God's power, but only his will; while I insist that 'divine power' means just that: divine power."

Liebes' presentation of the dispute can be nuanced, of course, but I believe that the basic argument stands. Attempting to read these sources as devoid of any literal meaning is often a product of rationalist apologetic. As Michael Fishbane insists in his *Biblical Myth and Rabbinic Mythmaking*, the key issue is coherence.[20] An image that repeats itself in various sources and contexts in the rabbinic corpus is likely to be not a metaphor, but a myth. In our case as well, the anthropology of the *yeṣer* in the entire Amoraic corpus includes images of movement, and so the *yeṣer* should be understood as affecting the human body through this movement. The similarity to the Stoic physiology of *hamartia* adds considerable weight to this reading.

## 4 SECOND TEMPLE LITERATURE AND THE TANNAITIC CONTRIBUTION

Menachem Kister traces the development of various prayers for the purification of bodily organs from sin that cleaves to them in Sirach, Qumran, Paul, and rabbinic literature. The evil *yeṣer* is part of this tradition, and in this context he offers a critique of my claim about the novelty of Tannaitic *yeṣer*.

> The key to the rabbinic image [of the *yeṣer*] is in my opinion found in the concept of the evil appetites found in Sirach, which was just one opinion among many on

[19] Rozenberg 1998. See Liebes' response: Liebes 1998. [20] Fishbane 2003.

the relationship between the external demonic forces and the internal psychological ones. The term *yeṣer ra'*, derived from Scripture, becomes crystallized in the Second Temple period, although available data suggest that it was not used as a fixed term until Tannaitic literature, and clearly does not carry the import it has in rabbinic literature. However, various formulations on the evil *yeṣer* in rabbinic literature are based on earlier, Second Temple formulations. If we combine Sirach's appetites with Jubilees' *yeṣer* and Qumranic *yeṣer ra'*, then the result is remarkably similar to rabbinic anthropology and their use of the term *yeṣer ra'*. Could certain Second Temple circles have achieved this combination? It is not impossible, in my opinion, although we lack the proper documentation at this time. But even without engaging in speculation, it is safe to say that the discrete components of the rabbinic perception are found in Second Temple literature. Ishay Rosen-Zvi recently suggested that the image of the evil *yeṣer* was created in the Tannaitic school of Rabbi Ishmael. In his opinion, the exceptional character of the *yeṣer*, and the fact that in this school it is internal to humans but separate from them, points to a rejection of the dualistic and cosmological model offered at Qumran. However, in my opinion, all the processes which allowed for the creation of this term, especially the dynamic of internalization, are found hundreds of years before rabbinic literature, and they are not a response to Qumranic dualism.[21]

Where do Kister and I differ? My claim about the relationship between the rabbis and Qumran is based on the fact that only these corpora contain the fixed term *yeṣer ra'* in an explicitly demonological mode. It is further strengthened by my reading of m. Ber. 9:5, where a two-*yeṣer* model makes an appearance in an explicitly anti-dualistic context of praising God for both good and bad.

But the kernel of the polemic is methodological: Kister thinks the various components of the *yeṣer* existed in Second Temple times, making it ancient. I believe that the central novelty is the composite creation, which is "new" and rabbinic. None of the sources Kister cites has a rabbinic-like *yeṣer*. It is only the combinations of these sources that creates it. But combinations and constellations of this kind are exactly the manner in which novel concepts are introduced in the history of religious thought.[22]

Put differently, the history of ideas is the history of the realization of potentials. Ecclesiastes 3:21 asks: "Who knows whether the human spirit goes upwards and the spirit of animals goes downwards to the earth?" This idea is clearly based on a dualistic reading of the creation story of Genesis 2, in which the Lord God breathes a spirit into Adam's earthly

[21] Kister 2010, 266–67.

[22] For the identification of new constellations as a tool in the study of ancient Judaism see Najman 2014.

form. Thus Eccl 12:7: "And the dust returns to the earth as it was, and the breath returns to God who gave it." So who is the innovator of this radical claim, Genesis or Ecclesiastes?

A good example for this is the subject currently on my desk – the birth of the goy.[23] The distinction between Jew and his other, the Gentile, has been so central to Jewish history that the vast scholarship dedicated to Jewish–Gentile relations has treated the category of the Gentile as self-evident and has never questioned its history. In a recent monograph, my colleague Adi Ophir and I attempt to show that this category was in fact born at a particular moment, that it replaced older categories of otherness, that it reorganized the relations of the Jews to their God and history, and that it was both informed by and embedded in new modes of separation of Jews from non-Jews. In fact, we strive to show that the consolidation of the category of the goy – as a binary opposition to the Jew, which signifies any individual who is not Jewish, erasing all ethnic and social differences among different others – did not take place before the Tannaitic literature.[24]

Now here too there are many precursors, but we insist that the rabbinic goy is a consolidation, or constellation, of various ingredients that existed separately in pre-rabbinic texts, and that it is exactly this consolidation that marks the birth of the goy.

It is this kind of move that brought me to the conclusion that the evil *yeṣer* can be treated as a rabbinic innovation, a conclusion that I still stubbornly cling to today.

23 See Rosen-Zvi and Ophir 2011; Rosen-Zvi and Ophir 2015; Rosen-Zvi 2013.

24 Ophir and Rosen-Zvi 2018 .

# 8

# Conflicting Intrapersonal Powers in Paul's Letters

Daniel Schumann

## 1 INTRODUCTION

Present-day attempts to examine the conceptual and theological similarities between the Pauline and rabbinic understandings of the origin of sin have revisited some of the major questions raised by Sandmel in his seminal work, "Parallelomania."[1] What is the relationship between the sources in question (i.e. the Pauline epistles and Tannaitic literature)? And what constitutes a parallel between these corpora? Referring to Kuhn, Sandmel argues that in terms of dependency and influence it may be appropriate only to speak of "Traditionszusammenhang,"[2] that is, a common Jewish tradition shared by Paul and the rabbis.[3] Equally, we must heed Sandmel's admonition that "if we make him [i.e. Paul] mean only what the parallels mean, we are using the parallels in a way that can lead us to misunderstand Paul."[4] Consequently the sources should be considered separately in their scriptural, historical, and theological contexts without rushing into unsubstantiated conclusions or, worse, *eisegesis*.

As well as an approach orientated toward tradition-historical questions, an emphasis on synchronic methods is also necessary. Did Paul "make[s] use of the yēser concept,"[5] or is he a witness to a different strand of Jewish tradition that deals with the anthropological issue of a human "inclination" in a similar yet distinct way? Whether or not Paul is adopting and adapting the *yeṣer* concept appears to depend on the identification

[1] Sandmel 1962. [2] Kuhn 1961, 337, 339. [3] Cf. Sandmel 1962, 6.
[4] Sandmel 1962, 5. [5] As e.g. Marcus 1986, 8.

of lexemic counterparts in his letters. This is challenging since Paul is not making any use of translation lexemes employed in LXX Genesis (Gen 6:5; 8:21),[6] nor does he show any affiliation with Sirach's concept of *yeṣer* (rendered διαβούλιον, "free choice, deliberation," in Greek). I therefore propose to apply the method of text-linguistic semantics, which analyzes paradigmatic and syntagmatic relationships between lexemes.[7] The decisive question for identifying a Pauline counterpart to the rabbinic *yeṣer* is how these sources conceptualize the human tendency to sin and whether the patterns of conceptualization show fundamental similarities or differences. The analysis of "word-fields" addresses this essential question by asking, Where do the sources locate this tendency in the human body? How do they conceive of its origin? In what way are human beings able to prevail over this tendency?

A first word-field, which we might label "the deeds of the Evil Inclination," contains terms such as "idolatry, narcissism, fornication, murder, or theft" (cf. t. Naz. 4:7; Sifre Num 88, pp. 14–17; Sifre Deut 33, pp. 59–60). A second word-field, concerned with "how to prevail over the Evil Inclination," encompasses actions such as praying, vowing, swearing, and Torah study (cf. t. Naz. 4:7; Sifre Deut 45, pp. 103–04). The terms "heart" and "thoughts" constitute a word-field focused on the "realm of the inclination's agitation." Finally, a word-field consisting of terms such as "demons, Satan, spirits, or angels," largely absent from Tannaitic literature,[8] but present in Second Temple Jewish demonology, may show how rabbinic discourse on the origin of sin distinguishes itself from other Jewish concepts.

The results of this analysis need to be set within the larger context of the "co-text"[9] and the various religious, sociocultural, and situational contexts[10] in which the sources are embedded. Since Paul's letters address specific situations, it is necessary to evaluate each separately.

## 2 THESSALONIANS

The first letter to the Thessalonians is the earliest of Paul's writings and the earliest correspondence of the entire New Testament. If Acts is to be trusted, Paul met Silas and Timothy in Corinth in the course of his second missionary journey (Acts 18:1–5; cf. 1 Thess 3:6), shortly

[6] See Aitken, Chapter 3 in this volume. [7] See Barthes 1964, 53–78.
[8] Cf. Rosen-Zvi 2008, 530. [9] See Brown and Yule 1983, 46–50.
[10] See Doering 2006, 39.

after his sojourn in Thessalonica (Acts 17:1–10; cf. 1 Thess 2:17), and there wrote his letter to the Thessalonians around 50 or 51 CE.[11] First Thessalonians makes repeated references to Paul's earlier missionary proclamation, albeit with limited detail; Paul's instructions were probably more elaborate when first given orally (cf. 1 Thess 2:9; 4:1–2; 5:1–2). Since Paul is praising the members of the Thessalonian community as those who "turned to God from idols, to serve a living and true God" (1 Thess 1:9), a predominantly Gentile composition can be assumed for the Thessalonian congregation.[12] Doubts about the letter's integrity and unity[13] have not been widely accepted.[14]

In a long exhortation (1 Thess 4:1–5:22) Paul admonishes his readers not to be careless in brotherly love (vv. 9–10), to follow their own business quietly, to make a living with their own hands (vv. 11–12), and, with particular emphasis, to abstain from fornication (vv. 3–8):

> [3] For this is the will of God: Your sanctification; separate yourselves from sexual immorality, [4] each of you know how to possess his own wife (lit. "vessel") in sanctification and honor, [5] not in the lust of eager desire just as the Gentiles who do not know God. [6] That no one sin against and take advantage of his brother in any matter, because the Lord is an avenger concerning all these things as we also told you beforehand and solemnly testified. [7] For God did not call us to uncleanness but in sanctification. [8] Therefore, who rejects this does not reject a human being but God who gives his Holy Spirit to you.

What is meant by "the will of God," defined as "your sanctification," is explicated in a threefold manner: 1) to separate oneself from immoral sexual conduct (v. 3b), most likely, from forbidden sexual relations with relatives,[15] from homosexuality,[16] and from extramarital intercourse;[17] 2) to acquire one's own "vessel" (vv. 4–5), a euphemism for sexual intercourse with one's own wife;[18] and 3) not to defraud one's brother in legal and economic matters.[19] Marcus identified ἐπιθυμία ("desire") in 1 Thess 4:5 as comparable to the rabbinic *yeṣer* concept, but his pronouncement, "Although *epithymia* is not always a translation

[11] Cf. Landmesser 2013, 166; Riesner 1991, 297–349.
[12] Cf. Landmesser 2013, 166.
[13] For an overview see Collins 1998, 398–400.
[14] E.g. Johanson 1987; Schnelle 2005, 65–66; Pokorný and Heckel 2007, 302–03.
[15] Cf. 1 Cor 5:1; see further Lev 18:8; Jub. 33:10–14; Ps.-Phoc. 179.
[16] Cf. Rom 1:26–27; see further Philo, *Mos.* 1:300; *Sib. Or.* 3:764.
[17] For further details, see Konradt 2001, 128–29; Vahrenhorst 2002, 406–07.
[18] Cf. Baltensweiler 1963, 4; Konradt 2001, 134 with n. 28.
[19] Cf. Reinmuth 1985, 22–41.

for *yēser* in Paul, it is so in the present case"[20] is an overstatement. It is not an anthropological *terminus technicus* for an evil intrapersonal force, since Paul uses the term positively elsewhere in the same letter (1 Thess 2:17). Marcus gives the impression that there is an unbroken tradition of understanding the *yeṣer* as a force that compounds human proclivity to sexual immorality that runs from the Hebrew Bible (Gen 6:1–5), through subsequent Jewish literature (e.g. T. Jud. 11:1–2; CD ii 16), to Paul and the later rabbis.[21] However, the most that can be said is that illicit sexuality is one of many expressions of sinful human behavior condemned by the Torah and later Jewish writings.[22] To trace every act of sexual immorality back to a single concept, a dispositional Evil Inclination, does not do justice to the variegation in our sources. Even Stoic philosophers can warn against the volition called *epithymia*, a form of irrational "emotion" (πάθος) based on a mistaken opinion about the true value of things.[23] This position is close to Paul's argument about sexual desire in Romans 1 (see below). Epictetus, a pupil of Paul's contemporary Gaius Musonius Rufus, for instance, can caution against *epithymia* as an unnatural and voluntary desire (*Diatr.* 2.18.8),[24] in contrast to *prothymia* (προθυμία), the natural and involuntary desire that shows the artificer's order of creation (*Diatr.* 1.6.9).[25] For the refined and wise person who desires only what is pleasant insofar as it is necessary, *epithymia* has come to an end (*Diatr.* 4.1.84), and with its destruction one acquires freedom for oneself (*Diatr.* 4.1.175).

The Jewish sources upon which Marcus relies are so idiosyncratic that one should avoid placing them too hastily within an overarching scheme. The phrase "youthful impulses" (διαβούλιον τῆς νεότητος) in T. Jud. 11:1–2, for example, designates something that is limited to a person's youth, and thus is contrasted with Judah's wisdom of age. Furthermore, the judgment of youth is negatively affected by the intoxication of wine and influenced by evil spirits under the dominion of Beliar. These "youthful impulses" corresponds to the "ignorance of youth" (ἄγνοια νεότητος) in T. Reu. 1:6, and belong to the dangers of youth that lead to sin.[26]

[20] Marcus 1986, 8. Cf. Marcus 1982. [21] Cf. Marcus 1986, 18 n. 9.

[22] E.g. Lev 18:22; 20:13; *Let. Aris.* 152; *Sib. Or.* 3:184 ff.; Jub. 25:1; m. 'Abod. Zar. 2:1; t. 'Abod. Zar. 3:2; see further Porton 1988, 236.

[23] For the Stoic theory of desire and emotions see SVF III 386 ff., 391 ff.; Brennan 1998, 30–32.

[24] Cf. Bonhöffer 1890, 278–80; Malherbe 2006, 60–61.

[25] Cf. Bonhöffer 1890, 248–49. [26] Cf. Hollander and De Jonge 1985, 90.

As these brief examples from Stoic philosophy and Jewish testamentary literature show, a purely phenomenological approach can lead to unsatisfactory results, or even "parallelomania." A close reading of 1 Thess 4:3–8 and the recognition of the various contexts helps us to clarify the textual strategy, the semantic range of *epithymia*, and its theological meaning. In its syntagmatic relations, *epithymia* is qualified by "with great" (ἐν πολλῇ) in 1 Thess 2:17, implying that it is something capable of varying degrees of intensity. It plausibly indicates a deficiency that is caused by an abrupt breakup of social relations. In the case of 1 Thess 2:17, Paul sees himself like a father bereft of his children (ὀρφανός).[27] In 1 Thess 4:5, as a *genitivus qualitatis*[28] adjunctive to "lust" (πάθος) and as explication of "sexual immorality" (πορνεία; 1 Thess 4:3), *epithymia* expresses a passionate sexual desire. For Paul, this sort of sexual desire is a vice of Gentiles who know neither God, his will (1 Thess 4:3), nor the order of creation. This suggests that humans are capable of controlling their *epithymia*. This way of acting upon illicit sexual urges is contrasted with a different attitude toward sexuality designated by the expression "in sanctification and honor."

In terms of textual pragmatics then, the Thessalonians are obliged not to fall back into old habits nor to embrace social mores that mirror a dominant, promiscuous pagan culture[29] and its cults.[30] Sexual conduct therefore serves as a boundary marker.[31] In conclusion, for Paul ignorance is the reason why *epithymia* causes sexual immorality. As such, Paul shows a close affinity with the Stoic theory of emotion. It is therefore probably better to understand the term as an adoption from the common philosophical milieu with which Paul's Gentile addressees would probably have been familiar.

## 3 GALATIANS

The letter to the Galatians, written around the mid-fifties CE, echoes theological rifts within the early Christian missionary efforts, mainly represented by Paul himself and his "gospel to the uncircumcised" on

[27] Cf. Seesemann 1954, 486–88.

[28] Cf. BDF §165. *Pace* Michaelis 1954, 928, who regards ἐπιθυμίας as *genitivus originis* and thus the source of πάθος.

[29] Cf. Kirchhoff 1994, 54–68.

[30] Cf. Donfried 1985; Jewett 1971, 126–33, and the critical response of Koester 1994, 394–96.

[31] Cf. Weima 2014, 246.

the one side and the "gospel to the circumcised," represented by Peter, on the other (Gal 2:7). The date of the founding of the Galatian communities and their geographic location is vigorously debated due to Paul's vague "to the churches of Galatia."[32]

When trying to identify allusions to the rabbinical concept of an Evil Inclination, the similarities between the word-field "the deeds of the Evil Inclination" and Paul's exposition on "works of the flesh" (Gal 5:19–20) is striking.[33] The exposition is embedded in a section that centers on a plea to live by the Spirit:

> [16] But I say, walk by the Spirit and you will not fulfill the desire of the flesh. [17] For the flesh sets its desire against the Spirit, and the Spirit against the flesh. For these are opposed to one another, so that you do not do the things that you wish to do. [18] But if you are led by the Spirit, you are not under the Law. [19] The works of the flesh are manifest ... [22] But the fruit of the Spirit is love, joy, peace, patience, kindness, goodness, faith, [23] gentleness, self-control. Against such things there is no law. [24] But those who belong to Christ Jesus have crucified the flesh with its passions and desires. [25] If we live by the Spirit, let us also walk by the Spirit.

The apparent contradiction between verses 16 and 24 – that is, the demand to walk in accordance with the "spirit" (πνεῦμα) in order not to fulfill the deeds of the "flesh" (σάρξ) and the conclusion that those who belong to Christ are already freed from the desires of the "flesh" – is part of the Paul's strategy to persuade the Galatians to accept his understanding of the gospel of Christ. Such a paradox is typical of Pauline ethical discourse.[34]

Paul attempts to present what he believes is the turbulent inner struggle of human volition,[35] in which "flesh" and "spirit" are pitted against each other, resulting in inconsistency in humans' volitional decisions.[36] It is, however, this "spirit" that releases the freedom obtained through the Christ-event. This freedom breaks down the boundaries between Jewish and Gentile Christ-believers,[37] affords deliverance from the law,[38] and enables people to serve one another in love.[39]

[32] See, e.g., Schnelle 2005, 114–16. [33] Cf. Davies 1980, 17–35; Marcus 1986, 9.
[34] Cf. Landmesser 2009; Zimmermann 2007, 2013.
[35] Cf. b. Ned. 32b, in which "a small city and a few people within it" (Eccl 9:14) is interpreted as the human body in conflict with it Good and Evil Inclinations.
[36] Corresponding to a well-known *topos* in antiquity: see Theissen 1983, 213–23; von Bendemann 2004, 35–63. Cf. Mark 14:38b.
[37] Cf. Schäfer 2004, 185–86; Konradt 2010, 66–68.
[38] Cf. for instance Lührmann 2001, 80–86. [39] See Konradt 2010, 70–72 .

Paul's argumentation is teleological, in that it contrasts the way of the "flesh" and the way of the "spirit," with "love" (ἀγάπη) as the primary aim of his ethical discourse.[40] While Paul is clearly referring to the work of God's Spirit in human beings (cf. Gal 6:8), the meaning of "flesh" is more problematic. "Flesh" is not identical with the inner human being nor does it dwell in a person. Betz's understanding of "spirit" and "flesh" as "impersonal forces" is questionable: the evidence of Gal 6:8, where the reflexive pronoun ἑαυτοῦ ("his own [flesh]") functions in relation to "flesh" as a predicate, speaks in favour of an anthropological understanding.[41] Although Paul's reference to the *epithymia* of the flesh (Gal 5:16) reminds us of his discourse in 1 Thess 4:5, its integration into the dualistic concept of "flesh" and "spirit" makes it very different to the Greek philosophical concept that he develops in 1 Thessalonians. His expressions in Galatians are rather an amalgamation of Jewish and Greek philosophical ideas that are influenced by his experience of the Spirit.

Crucial for the interpretation of Gal 5:16–25 is whether we take Paul's considerations as a characterization of the anthropological situation of Christ-believers in general, or whether we try to understand Paul's assertions with a stronger focus on the background of the Galatian conflict. The antithesis of "flesh" and "spirit" is introduced for the first time in the *probatio* (Gal 3:1–5)[42] and echoes throughout the letter. By indirectly taking up the accusation from Gal 1:6–10, Paul asks by whom the Galatians were bewitched that they were hampered from following the Spirit and finishing in the flesh. The opposition between "flesh" and "spirit" occurs again in Gal 4:23 and 29, but this time framed in an allegorical interpretation of the Abraham story: Abraham and Hagar try to establish an heir by way of the flesh; in contrast, Sarah's miraculous conception is a way of fulfilling the divine promise according to the Spirit (Gal 4:21–31). Furthermore, Paul identifies the women with two covenants: Hagar signifies the covenant from Mount Sinai, which led to slavery, and Sarah the one from heaven, which led to freedom. The antithesis is presented for the fourth and last time in the letter's exhortation (Gal 6:8). Paul tells the Galatians that placing hope in the flesh in order to procure justification (cf. Phil 3:4–9) is not only futile but will, as sure as the harvest follows the sowing, result in final damnation. The implication is that the cultivated field determines the fruit, not the seed. It is not said explicitly

[40] See Weder 1998, 129–45. [41] Betz 1979, 279.
[42] Regarding the letter's composition, see Betz 1979, 16–23.

whether God created human "flesh" with a sinful tendency or whether the human "flesh" became irreversibly corrupted by the influence of "sin."

In sum, the occurrences of "flesh" in Galatians depict human beings' ways of acting arbitrarily and trusting in their own abilities regarding fulfillment of the works of the law.[43] The Galatians seem to have been fooled into believing in the capability of humans to practice Torah observance as the intrinsic precondition for justification. Paul argues instead for the primacy of divine agency, in particular the Spirit, upon which the Christ-follower's belief and moral conduct is dependent. The human agent is not thereby condemned to passivity but is responsible for letting the divine agent take the lead (Gal 5:16, 18, 25). One of the reasons why Paul considers Torah observance an impossible endeavor is because he believes that "flesh," as the executive agent when humans choose to act autonomously, is corrupted and driven by desire. Circumnavigating this trajectory is even more fruitless, since the Spirit does not support or empower the Galatians in their attempt to observe the Torah.

It is difficult to shake off the notion, common in New Testament scholarship,[44] that Paul did not identify "flesh" with the physical body but rather with an evil and God-opposing force. But since the human body was not part of the transformation process initiated with the reception of the Spirit and was still joined to the fading cosmos (cf. 2 Bar 49:3), an identification with the physical body seems probable. Furthermore, Paul could count on the Galatian community of Gentile Christ-believers understanding his expression against the backdrop of the demotion of the physical body in Stoic and Platonic philosophy.[45] Thus, the corrupted physical body with its desires was believed to have an impact on the human formation of will,[46] but only insofar as the Galatians continued to confide in the flesh instead of letting the Spirit take the lead. The portrayal of flesh and Spirit as diametrically opposed (Gal 5:16–25) robs the Galatians of a potential source of hope: not even a synergy of both might have a favorable effect. On the contrary, both flesh and Spirit constantly stand in conflict with one another, so that the Galatians are deprived even of their will. To illustrate this to the Galatians, Paul presents a list of vices.

[43] See further Doering 2014.

[44] Cf. Strecker 1976, 494; Frey 1999, 75; Martyn 1997, 492–93.

[45] Cf. Plato, *Symp.* 211e; Bonhöffer 1890, 33–40; Engberg-Pedersen 2014, 42–48. In the Jewish tradition cf. Jer 17:5; 1QH[a] vii 24; 1QS xi 7, 9–11; 1QM iv 4; xii 12.

[46] Philo's views on the oppression of the soul by the flesh (*Gig.* 29–31; *Her.* 268) are comparable.

Paul's antithetical flesh–Spirit discourse is, however, so distinctive that some further issues need to be addressed. Several suggestions have been proposed in the last decades, some with a stronger emphasis on a Jewish background, others with a stronger emphasis on a Hellenistic background. For instance, Brandenburger interpreted Paul's dualism of flesh and spirit with a view to Jewish Hellenistic wisdom literature from Alexandria, represented by the Wisdom of Solomon and Philo of Alexandria.[47] But the sections examined are better understood as showing a notion of "flesh" signifying a person's earthly existence (e.g. Sir 14:17), as is the case with 1QH[a] xii 29. For example, in Wis 7:1–6 "flesh" is used to describe the development of the human being from conception (v. 2) to embryo. The opposition of "flesh" and "spirit" in Philo's writings usually serves as a distinction between the material, sensuous world on the one hand and the immaterial, spiritual world on the other.[48]

Kuhn pointed to the reference to "flesh" (בשׂר) in 1QH[a] xii 29 as reflecting the same tradition behind the Pauline usage, while noting that it picked up a notion from the Hebrew Bible (human beings as "flesh," over against the "Spirit" of YHWH).[49] But "flesh" in the Hodayot does not represent an evil force. Instead, in its immediate linguistic context it is in synonymous parallelism with "creature of clay" (*yṣr ḥmr*), indicating merely human mortality.

The works of de Boer and Frey are likewise focused on a probable Jewish tradition-historical context.[50] De Boer identified the Pauline "flesh" with the Evil Inclination "known from Jewish thought."[51] Like Marcus (see above), de Boer postulates a widespread and congruent concept of an Evil Inclination, which he also sees realized in locutions such as "the evil thought," "the evil heart," "the evil root," and "the grain of evil seed"[52] known from 4 Ezra. But he reaches this conclusion, *inter alia*, because of a misinterpretation of the reference *yṣr bśr* (יצר בשר) in 1QH[a] xviii 23. He disregards the phrase's context and translates "inclination of the flesh."[53] The hymnist, however, distinguishes between the refuge he takes in the creator of his spirit ("You have formed the spirit of your servant") and the refuge he refuses to take in a "creature of flesh," which he subsequently explicates as a reference to heroes who draw their strength from luxury and live in abundance (1QH[a] xviii 22–32). *yṣr bśr*,

[47] Brandenburger 1968. [48] Frey 1999, 49–53. [49] Kuhn 1950, 200 n. 11.
[50] De Boer 2011, 335–52; Frey, 1999, 2002. [51] De Boer 2011, 335.
[52] De Boer 2011, 339. [53] De Boer 2011, 337–38.

therefore, cannot be considered an "exact linguistic parallel"[54] to the Pauline expression "desire of the flesh" (ἐπιθυμία σαρκός) in Gal 5:16.

De Boer further claims that Paul's introduction of "flesh" is a response to the new preachers (Gal 1:6–9) in the Galatian communities.[55] According to this view, Paul's proclamation of the Torah-free gospel had, according to his opponents, left "a moral vacuum in the lives of the new Gentile believers ... leaving them completely vulnerable to the Evil Inclination."[56] But this reconstruction of the communities' situation as the background of Gal 5:16 is not without difficulties. First, if "desires of the flesh" (ἐπιθυμία σαρκός) is a locution that Paul's opponents used to denote the "Evil Impulse,"[57] why did these Christian Judaizers[58] locate this impulse in the flesh rather than the heart (cf. Gen 6:5; 8:21; 4Q370 1 i 3; m. Ber. 9:5)? Moreover, Paul does not react to the charge against his gospel and a consequential "moral vacuum." Quite the opposite. Paul's focus on the desire of the flesh is explained by the Galatians' apparent refusal to continue to walk in the spirit and to "end" their efforts "in the flesh" (Gal 3:3), which will eventually entail the deeds of the flesh (Gal 5:19–21). What makes an identification of "desires of the flesh" with the Evil Inclination (understood in rabbinic terms) ultimately unlikely is that the will of human beings is so impaired by "flesh" that they are actually unable to make decisions and withstand their "flesh," either by their own capacities or by the Torah. According to Paul, the believer is in constant need of divine agency. This is alien to the rabbinic *yeṣer* discourse. The Tannaim had a positive view of the human nature[59] and took the existence of a "good inclination" for granted,[60] but Paul did not share such optimism. Later, in the letter to the Romans (Rom 7:18), he would even admit that there is nothing good dwelling in his "flesh." These fine details make an equation of the rabbinic *yeṣer* with the Pauline "flesh" improbable.

Frey is similarly focused on a probable Jewish tradition-historical context, but he bases his argument predominantly on Qumranic evidence.[61] He leaves aside Yahadic writings (e.g. 1QS; 1QH$^{a}$) since, in his view, Paul was unfamiliar with their writings and their arcane traditions. Instead, he places the focus on pre-Yahadic writings and introduces the phrase "spirit of flesh" (רוח בשר) from wisdom literature (i.e. 4Q416–418; 4QInstruction) into the discussion. Stuckenbruck, commenting on Frey, has rightly stressed that 4QInstruction, as well as the Hodayot, is

[54] De Boer 2011, 337. [55] De Boer 2011, 338. [56] De Boer 2011, 335.
[57] De Boer 2011, 338. [58] Cf. Elmer 2009, 151. [59] Cf. Rosen-Zvi 2011, 26.
[60] Cf. m. Ber. 9:5; t. Ber. 7:7; Sifre Deut 32, p. 55. [61] Frey 1999, 2002.

rather calling attention to the dualism of two opposing spirits, "one that corresponds to the human's obedience and submission to God and one that is 'depraved', iniquitous, and conditioned by the 'flesh'."[62] The conceptualization is therefore quite different from Paul's flesh–Spirit antithesis, even if they are wrestling with similar concerns.

In conclusion, the dualism of "flesh" and "Spirit" in Paul correlates strongly with Paul's *kerygma* of the soteriological significance of Jesus' death and resurrection in Galatians. The Christ-believer is not constantly assailed by the disturbing influence of the flesh, but only insofar as he hones in on his own capabilities in the pursuit of justification rather than trusting in and living by the Spirit. He falls back into the old patterns of his un-redeemed former existence (cf. Rom 7:14–25). The believer is empowered by God's spirit and called upon to mortify the deeds of his body. Put succinctly, Paul's sometimes contemptuous assessment of the flesh-and-blood physical body is alien to rabbinic anthropology and therefore not comparable to the rabbinic *yeṣer*.

## 4 ROMANS

Paul's letter to the Romans, written around 56 CE during his last sojourn in Corinth, is peculiar with regard to its purpose and Paul's relationship with its addressees. Rome was supposed to be a port of call for further missionary activities in the western Mediterranean, especially in Spain (Rom 15:24, 28). The community, unlike those in Thessalonica and Galatia, did not go back to Paul's missionary initiative, although he clearly knew several of its members and was familiar with its communal life (Rom 16:3–15). Consequently he could not build on prior oral instruction and therefore had to present an overall picture of his gospel, illustrating the fall of human beings, the power of sin, God's righteousness, and the justification of humans. The community was apparently struggling with tensions between the weak and strong in faith (Romans 14–15) and between Jews and non-Jews (Rom 1:18–3:20; 9–11).

From the first chapter, we encounter terms corresponding to the word-field "the deeds of the Evil Inclination," such as idolatry and illicit sexual conduct. In a wide-ranging discourse about God's wrath over Gentiles and Jews alike (Rom 1:18–3:20), Paul underlines the inexcusability of ungodliness and unrighteousness among Gentiles, since God had made himself known to them through his creation (Rom 1:20–21). Hence, Paul

[62] Stuckenbruck 2011, 167 . Cf. Tigchelaar 2009; Wold 2015.

promulgates God's verdict over Gentiles in a threefold manner: the darkening of their hearts; the handing over of their hearts' desires to degrading passions; and finally, to their depraved minds (Rom 1:21, 24, 26, 28). Not quite as drastic is Paul's judgment on his fellow Jews, who had been entrusted with God's words (Rom 3:2), adopted as sons, and to whom the glory, covenant, promises, and Temple (Rom 9:4) had been granted. Yet now they are inexcusably entangled in sin (Rom 2:17–29) and in need of justification, which does not come by works of the law but by faith in Jesus Christ.

The root of this downfall is ascribed to Adam's original sin (Rom 5:12–21). His transgression brought "sin" into the world; sin brought death in its wake to all humankind, affecting it thenceforth. This cosmological evil force is in its singularity (Rom 3:9) distinguished from individual transgressions such as transgressions against the precepts of the Torah (Rom 2:12) or human actions not founded in faith (Rom 14:23).[63] Tradition-historical lines for such a particular usage of "sin" can be traced back to Sir 21:2, 27:10, and 1QH[a] xii 30–31. It is questionable that Paul's concept of sin with its focus on a single evil "power from without human beings" would resemble the rabbinic notion of sin, as Davies claimed (the common rabbinic term for sin, עבירה, implies a transgression of a boundary set forth by the Torah, not an abstract evil power).[64] Williams even went so far as to identify as "picturesque and paraphrastic names" for the evil *yeṣer* a number of Pauline expressions in Romans, such as "sin," "our old self" (6:6), "the body of sin" (6:6), "the body of death" (7:24), "the sinful passions aroused by the law" (7:5), and "setting one's mind on the flesh" (8:6).[65] Now one may wonder why Paul's remarks on the matter lack a uniform terminology, and why he prefers to refer to the Evil Inclination in so many different ways. It is unsatisfactory to resolve this problem by simply assuming that Paul was aware of the phenomenon and the discourse about it, though not of its particular designation. The inadequacy of this explanation should be obvious from each phrase's immediate context and horizon of meaning. The "old self," for example, is a designation for the believers' former existence that was characterized by their enslavement under sin; it has come to an end by their conversion, their unification with Christ in baptism, and their spiritual rebirth, qualified as walking "in newness of life" (ἐν καινότητι ζωῆς; Rom 6:4).[66] This

[63] See Böttrich 2013, 389–90. [64] Davies 1980, 24. [65] Williams 1927, 150.

[66] Cf. the rebirth motif in connection with God's spirit in Jos. Asen. 8:9. Cf. Luke 15:24; Rev 3:1.

motive of re-creation during a person's lifespan is peculiar to Paul (cf. 2 Cor 5:17; Gal 6:15) and unknown in rabbinic thought.[67]

In an analogous manner to the indwelling and interaction between the human and the divine spirit (Rom 8:16; cf. 1 Cor 6:17), Paul can refer to the existence of "sin" as a force dwelling in human "flesh" (Rom 7:18, 20), "sin" is a power rather than a mere metaphor or personification.[68] The law, according to Paul, came *ad interim* not to contain sin but to reveal and increase it (Rom 5:20), so that grace might abound and prepare the coming of the last Adam, i.e. Christ. The fruit of his righteousness and obedience is the gift of justification (Rom 5:16, 18), and with it eternal life is obtained by becoming united with Christ in his death and resurrection (Rom 6:5) through baptism. The involvement with his death signifies the crucifixion of the believer's old self, which has thus become dead to sin (Rom 6:2, 6) and its slave no more.

The topic of human existence under the law and the enslavement to sin is raised again in Rom 7:7–25, but this time with the main emphasis on existential questions relating to the individual. With the help of two rhetorical questions (Rom 7:7, 13) and a change of tense from aorist to present, the section is structured in two parts: the first (Rom 7:7–12) outlines why the law cannot be equated with sin, whereas the next (Rom 7:13–25) shows the doomed human's condition of being sold under sin.[69] Through both parts Paul draws an ambivalent picture of the law, on the one hand denoting it as holy and good (Rom 7:12–13), spiritual (Rom 7:14), and delightful to the inner human being, while on the other hand picturing it as a "stirrup holder" for the rising of sin (Rom 7:8–11). The awakening and the subsequent rising of sin are connected to humanity's confrontation with the law (i.e. its noetic perception[70]), which induces the passion that the law actually prohibits (Rom 7:5, 7, 9). In contrast, Tannaitic literature portrays the engagement with the Torah – not its observance but its study – as a means for mastering the influence of the Evil Inclination.[71] This is made explicit in Sifre Deut 45 (pp. 103–04, on

[67] Gen. Rab. 14.5 (128–29) speaks of two creations of man: one with the creation of the cosmos, one in the world to come. Other rabbinic sources speak of ungodly persons as (metaphorically) dead (e.g. y. Ber. 2:3, 4d, 3–7; cf. Epictetus, *Diatr.* 3.23.28).

[68] Cf. the similar idea of spirits dwelling in the flesh in 1QS iv 20–23.

[69] Cf. Schröter 2013, 208.

[70] Evident from the cognitive vocabulary in Rom 7:7: e.g. "know" (οἶδα), "come to know, recognize" (γινώσκω).

[71] However, the Evil Inclination can lure those who are engaged in the Torah away from their study: Sifre Deut 43, p. 96; Mek. R. Ish., Amalek 2, p. 201.

Deut 11:18), which compares the Evil Inclination with an inflicted wound and the Torah with a bandage.

The reference to the coming of the law in Rom 7:9 should therefore not be equated with the revelation of the Torah to Moses at Mount Sinai, but rather individually with the moment of human beings' instruction in the law and their willingness to become subordinate to it.[72] The understanding of "desire" (ἐπιθυμία) presented in these verses in Romans differs from its use in the Stoic theory of emotions and even from Paul's own remarks in 1 Thess 4:5. The right judgment to which the Torah can lead (Rom 7:7, 12) does not stifle human desires. On the contrary, the law is a loophole through which sin becomes alive and kills (Rom 7:11). Thus, the law is not an antidote or a helpful instrument against an evil inclination, but rather a catalyst.

Paul's expressions on the law must be understood in the context of his attempt to promote his understanding of the gospel of Jesus Christ, as he did in the letter to the Galatians; but this time he omits the harsh tone because he does not want to alienate Jewish Christ-believers in the Roman community, to whom the Torah probably had a vital part in God's salvific plan. For this reason, Rom 7:7–25 is not "an unnecessary interruption and digression in Paul's train of thought"[73] but a vital preliminary clarification. In that respect, after discussing the subjection of humankind to sin (Rom 1:18–3:20), Adam's original sin (Rom 5:12–21), and the Christ-believer's existence in the state of grace (Rom 6:1–23), Paul answers the question why the Torah had to make way for the law of the Spirit of life in Christ. Paul concludes that the Torah was not able to eliminate sin because of the weakness of the flesh (Rom 8:3).

Two further questions regarding Rom 7:7–25 still preoccupy New Testament scholarship: first, whether the human situation envisioned by Paul concerns the status before or after conversion (namely baptism); and second, how the "I" should be identified. Although the view that Paul's portrayal is a retrospect of the Christ-believer back to his former unredeemed existence[74] has been contested by some supporters of the New Perspective on Paul,[75] several indications speak in favor of this interpretation. First of all, the conflict of will between the "I" and sin (Rom. 7:20) is a fact that would indicate a person's pre-baptismal situation prior to possession of the Spirit (contrary to Gal 5:16–25). As

[72] Somewhat similar Deissmann 1925, 73. [73] Dunn 1975, 260.

[74] E.g. Bultmann 1924, 1967; Kümmel 1974.

[75] E.g. Dunn 1975; Sanders 1995, 121–28.

a consequence, "mind" (νοῦς) and "flesh" are enmeshed in a struggle leading the "I" into captivity (Rom 7:23). This interpretation is not contradicted by Rom 7:25.[76] The thanksgiving in verse 25a does not conclude Paul's argument (as "through Jesus Christ our lord" does in Rom 5:11, 21, 6:23, and 8:39),[77] but it resolves the rhetorical question, "who will deliver me from this body of death"[78] (Rom 7:24)[79] by giving thanks to God who has already freed him. Romans 7:25b thus summarizes Rom 7:14–24. Second, Paul qualifies the Christ-believer's existence in Rom 6:15, 18 (in contrast to Rom 7:17) as being no longer under the law and freed from sin. Third, the mere reference to the inner human being in Rom 7:22 is by no means a clear reference to the renewed believer, as is the case of 2 Cor 4:16[80] since, according to Rom 7:15, the "I" still seems to be blinded and not able to determine and understand its actions. The "I" even confesses that there is nothing good dwelling in its flesh. Although the "I" knows what is good and actually has the will to carry it out, it fails completely by doing the very opposite.[81] Fourth, the "I" is still conflicted between the law of God and the law of sin (Rom 7:25b), a condition that is resolved by the Christ-believer's subordination to the law of the Spirit of life in Christ (Rom 8:2).

The debate surrounding the second question has rested mainly on appraising whether the "I" in Romans 7 is to be understood in an autobiographic[82] or in a fundamental sense,[83] or even as a reference to Adam.[84] It is however misleading to narrow the evidence down to one of the interpretations mentioned above: the "I" serves most probably as a rhetorical device to focus the reader's attention. Rather than outlining the issue impersonally, Paul portrays himself as the one who became deceived and killed, counting on his readers' empathy and the knowledge that his Jewish companions in Rome have suffered the same fate. He thereby combines autobiographical, paradigmatic, and anthropological

[76] Problematized by Dunn 1975, 262–63. Several scholars identify Rom 7:25b as a secondary gloss; see Schröter 2013, 207 n. 76.

[77] E.g. Schröter 2013, 207. [78] Cf. Epictetus, *Diatr.* 2.19.27.

[79] Cf. Rom 1:25; 9:5; 11:36; 2 Cor 11:31; see further Rom 6:17; 1 Cor 15:57.

[80] A view held by Dunn 1975, 262.

[81] A similar motif to the inner struggle of the "I" (Rom 7:7–25) can be witnessed in the story of Medea (cf. Euripides, *Med.* 1043–52, 1076–80; Plato, *Prot.* 352b; Aristotle, *Eth. nic.* 7.3; Epictetus, *Diatr* 1.28.6–8, 2.26.1–4; Ovid, *Metam.* 7.17–22; Seneca. *Med.* 939–44, 988–92; further Byrskog 2015). It may be that Paul's addressees were familiar with her tragic fate and that Paul alluded to it to make clear what is at stake.

[82] See for instance Jewett 2007, 441–53. [83] See Schröter 2013, 210.

[84] See Hofius 2002; Lichtenberger 2004; Dochhorn 2009.

references,[85] in the service of his efforts at persuasion. Keeping this in mind the change of tense from the aorist in Rom 7:7–13 to the present tense in Rom 7:14–25 becomes all the more comprehensible. Paul and his Jewish addressees can already look back to the moment of subordination and turning to the Law in their hope of receiving life (hence using the ingressive aorist); but some in the ambit of the community still attached God's grace and their redemption to the observance of the Torah, resulting in the ongoing strife he portrays with the use of the typological "I" (hence the switch to the present tense).

In Rom 8:1 Paul takes up his argument from Rom 7:6 (signaled by ἄρα) where he stopped at the declaration of the Christ-believer's deliverance from the Law. Paul builds on the expression of the Christ-believer dying unto the Law by partaking in Christ's death, and his ensuing deliverance from the dominion of the Law in Rom 7:1–6. In Rom 8:3–4 he adds the fundamental rationale that Christ's incarnation came about in order to condemn sin in the flesh and to fulfill the righteousness that is required by the Law for those obtaining it by their walking "according to the Spirit."

In conclusion, his use of "sin" is the conspicuous peculiarity of Paul's hamartiology in Romans. "Sin" as alien to God's creation found its entrance into the cosmos through Adam's sin. The ensuing condemnation of all humankind under sin is described by Paul using the image of a master–slave relationship whereby it seizes the human "flesh" to wield its power and to accomplish its nefarious aims. Like the rabbinic *yeṣer*, "sin" in Romans is an antinomian entity that is dependent on man's sensual and noetic perceptions. Significant differences are, however, its nature and its capabilities. Whereas *yeṣer* is an anthropological entity, "sin" is a cosmic evil force that disables man's ability to act autonomously and which cannot be overcome except by the intervention of divine agency.

## 5 CONCLUSION

In his letters, especially Romans, Paul reflects on the inner struggle of human volition under the conditions of sin, human beings' unsuccessful attempts at achieving what is good, and the final realization that deliverance from evil and the attainment of freedom and justification are God's free gift of grace. Thereby, having both protology and eschatology in view, Paul portrays the history of salvation from Adam's transgression,

[85] Cf. Berger 2005, 331–32; Löhr 2007, 177 n. 75.

via Christ's obedience and act of redemption from the enslavement of sin through to the believer's transformation into a spiritual and imperishable being at the end of this aeon.

The aim of this study was to evaluate this evidence with a special focus on possible links to the rabbinic concept of an Evil Inclination. In terms of lexematic counterparts to *yeṣer*, three terms were subject to detailed examination: "desire" (ἐπιθυμία), "flesh" (σάρξ), and "sin" (ἁμαρτία). Although it has been shown that Paul drew on many different traditions and concepts from Jewish thought (as well as Greek philosophical thought), no close affinity to the rabbinic *yeṣer* could be found. This discovery leads to the conclusion that Paul either did not know of the rabbinic *yeṣer* concept or, if he knew it, he chose not to use it in expressing his own thought.

# 9

# The "Two Inclinations" and the Double-Minded Human Condition in the Letter of James

George van Kooten

## 1 INTRODUCTION

The rabbinic notion of "the two inclinations" has long been connected in scholarship to the notion of the δίψυχος, the double-minded nature of human beings in the Letter of James (1:8; 4:8). Oscar J. F. Seitz, for example, notably argued, first, that James' depiction of human nature as double-minded (δίψυχος) "is intended to convey the Hebrew idea of a 'double-heart,' expressed by the peculiar idiom 'belev walev'," as found in 1 Chr 12:33 and Ps 12:2,[1] and, second, that its "real antecedent ... is to be found in the rabbinic conception of a double heart or two hearts, which is generically related to the idea of two *yeṣarim* [i.e. inclinations], and in particular to that of the *yeṣer ha-ra'* [i.e. the Evil Inclination] which leads man to sin."[2] Seitz later reiterated his view, supporting it by references to the recently published Dead Sea Scrolls, and asserting that, probably already prior to James, "some Greek translator of a Hebrew document coined this adjective [i.e. δίψυχος], with its cognates διψυχία ['double-mindedness'] and διψυχεῖν ['being double-minded'], to represent the concept of the double or divided heart."[3]

A serious complication, however, is that if this were to be the full, comprehensive background to James' anthropological characterization of humankind as "double-minded" (δίψυχος), it would have been much more natural for James to depict this human condition as an existence ἐν καρδίᾳ δισσῇ, "in a twofold, double, divided heart," as Sirach does (Sir 1:28), or to depict it as διπλοκαρδία, "double-heartedness," as the Epistle of

[1] Seitz 1944, 134; cf. Seitz 1947, 211. [2] Seitz 1947, 214. [3] Seitz 1958, 331.

Barnabas (20.1c) and the Didache (5.1) do. However, James does not use this "cardiac" terminology, but rather the "psychological" terminology of the soul and mind, and in this he differs from the terminology that is applied in Jewish traditions of the human inclinations. The biblical texts that provide the basis for the Jewish notion of the Evil Inclination, Gen 6:5 ("every *inclination* of the thoughts of their *hearts* was only evil continually") and Gen 8:21 ("the *inclination* of the human *heart* is *evil* from youth"), link this inclination to the human heart. From these texts onward the primary link in Jewish texts seems to have been between the evil inclination and the heart, rather than with the human soul, to which James' terminology of "double-minded" (δίψυχος) belongs. Even if Seitz were correct in concluding that "the Greek term δίψυχος ['double-minded'] and its cognates represent an attempt to convey the notion of a divided or double heart, literally 'two hearts,' which the rabbinic writers associate with certain biblical texts where the word *levav* is used in place of *lev* [e.g. Deut 6:5],"[4] it would still be relevant to raise the question why James chose the psychological terminology of δίψυχος (or even coined it, as he is the first to use it in all extant Christian writings in Greek) instead of cardiac terminology. The aim of this chapter is therefore to consider how the Jewish notion of the two inclinations may relate to a Greek notion of double-mindedness.

This attention to the Greek discourse of a "divided self" will also serve to confirm the fruitfulness of the direction recently taken by John Kloppenborg in his article on James in the context of Hellenistic psychagogy, to which I will return below.[5] For the moment, however, I draw attention to an alternative approach taken by Guy Stroumsa on the notion of two souls and the divided will in Manicheism. Stroumsa also applies a Greek perspective to the notion of a divided self, but assumes that the Greek notion of a divided self ultimately evolved from a dualistic Iranian anthropology. In Stroumsa's view the notion of two human souls, which the fifth/fourth-century BCE Greek philosopher Xenophon ascribes to the Persian sage Araspes, may well have been an Iranian notion that also influenced Jewish anthropology. According to Stroumsa, "the Iranian tradition reported by Xenophon is presented by the history of scholarship as at the origin of the Greek conception about the duality of the human soul. ... Since the Hellenistic period, Iranian anthropological ideas also had a strong influence upon Jewish conceptions."[6] He goes on to refer to the Dead Sea Scrolls and the rabbinic notion of the two inclinations as

[4] Seitz 1947, 216. [5] Kloppenborg 2010. [6] Stroumsa 1998, 201.

evidence for the impact of such Iranian ideas on Judaism. This approach would imply that James' notion of the divided soul sits equally well in both the Iranian–Greek trajectory and the Iranian–Jewish trajectory. I will first discuss the passage in which Xenophon introduces Iranian dualistic anthropology. Although it is historically possible that Xenophon operated as a channel of Iranian influence on Greek philosophy, this nevertheless seems unlikely. The reason for this is that there appears to be a notable difference between Iranian dualistic anthropology as recorded by Xenophon and the Greek notion of the divided human self. I then examine the Greek development of the notion of the duality of the soul, followed by an overview of the Jewish trajectory, before coming to my assessment of James' position in these trajectories.

## 2 THE GREEK AND JEWISH TRAJECTORIES OF THE DIVIDED SELF

### 2.1 Xenophon and Plato

We begin with the passage from Xenophon to which Stroumsa refers. In the *Cyropedia* ("The Education of Cyrus," an investigation into leadership technique in the form of a biography of Cyrus the Great) we find a reference to Iranian dualistic anthropology, ascribed to the Median Araspes (or Araspas), a friend of Cyrus.[7] According to Xenophon, Araspes believed that human beings have "two souls":

> I evidently have two souls (Δύο [...] σαφῶς ἔχω ψυχάς). [...] For if the soul is one, it is not both good and bad at the same time, neither can it at the same time desire the right and the wrong, nor at the same time both will and not will to do the same things; but it is obvious that there are two souls (ἀλλὰ δῆλον ὅτι δύο ἐστὸν ψυχά), and when the good one prevails, what is right is done; but when the bad one gains the ascendency, what is wrong is attempted.[8]

Araspes thus ascribed the right and wrong actions of the soul to the existence of two separate souls within human beings that are in conflict with one another. In Stroumsa's view, "this doctrine, Iranian in origin, would then have infiltrated Greek philosophy, as this reappears not only in Plato's *Laws*, but also in such late representatives of the Platonic tradition as the fragments of Numenius or the *Chaldean Oracles*."[9]

[7] Cf. Tuplin 2012 ; Gärtner 2006. [8] Xenophon, *Cyr.* 6.1.41. [9] Stroumsa 1998, 200.

Historically speaking, such a reception of Iranian thought by Xenophon would be possible. Xenophon took part in internal Persian–Iranian political affairs by enrolling as a mercenary with Cyrus the Younger, who revolted against his elder brother Artaxerxes II in 401 BCE. When Cyrus was defeated, the Greeks started their long repatriation, which is described in Xenophon's *Anabasis*.[10] The contact between Xenophon and the Persian–Iranian world is therefore well established and far more tangible than alleged visits of Greek philosophers to the East to study with the Magi.[11] Of course there were also pre-Hellenistic Greek communities in Babylonia, so that early contacts between the Greek and Persian–Iranian worlds are feasible, although a stronger Greek presence in the East was only realized from the Hellenistic period onward, enduring through the Parthian period.[12]

But although Xenophon's life offers clear evidence of contact between Greek and Persian–Iranian culture, the difference between Iranian dualistic anthropology and Greek anthropology seems to be notable. Araspes' anthropology, at least as reported in Xenophon, clearly asserts the existence of two souls (plural) within human beings: "it is obvious that there are two souls." This is rather different from the Greek view of a (mere) duality within the human soul (singular). Greek philosophical sources speak of a divided self, rather than of two separate souls. This can be demonstrated from, for instance, Plato's writings.

In Book IV of his *Republic*, Plato differentiates between "two forms" (δύο … εἴδη) which exist in the soul, (1) the rational (τὸ λογιστικόν), whereby the soul "reckons and reasons," and (2) the irrational and appetitive (τὸ ἀλόγιστόν τε καὶ ἐπιθυμητικόν), with which the soul feels desires (ἐπιθυμίαι) (*Resp.* IV 439d–e).[13] One might question whether the passionate (τὸ θυμοειδὲς) is part of the appetitive (τὸ ἐπιθυμητικόν), "that part of the soul which is the seat of the desires and affections" (LSJ), or even constitutes a third form in the soul, but it is nonetheless clear that at least two forms are distinguished within the human soul.

This duality also comes to the fore in book VIII, when Plato comments on a particular deteriorated, although by no means fully degenerated, psychic type of human being that is never free from internal strife (*Resp.* VIII 554c–e), and is hence "a 'double person', by comparison with the 'single-minded and harmonious psyche' of the truly just person."[14]

[10] See Briant 2012; Lazenby 2012; Tuplin 2012. [11] See van Kooten 2015, 503–04.
[12] See van Kooten 2015, 507–19. [13] Cf. Kloppenborg 2010, 50.
[14] Gill 2006, 319; cf. Kloppenborg 2010, 50 n. 27.

> Such a man, then, would not be free from internal dissension (οὐκ ἄρ' ἂν εἴη ἀστασίαστος ὁ τοιοῦτος ἐν ἑαυτῷ). He would not be really one (οὐδὲ εἷς), but in some sort a double man (ἀλλὰ διπλοῦς τις). Yet for the most part, his better desires would have the upper hand over the worse.... And for this reason, I presume, such a man would be more seemly, more respectable, than many others; but the true virtue of a soul in unison and harmony with itself would escape him and dwell afar (ὁμονοητικῆς δὲ καὶ ἡρμοσμένης τῆς ψυχῆς ἀληθὴς ἀρετὴ πόρρω ποι ἐκφεύγοι ἂν αὐτόν).[15]

Compared with Xenophon's report on Araspes' view that human beings have two souls, it is noteworthy that Plato talks of the double (διπλοῦς) existence of a particular type of human being. The view is repeated in the reflections of Book X of Plato's *Republic* on the multiplicity of the human soul. The discussion comes up in the context of an analysis of the old quarrel between philosophy and poetry (605b–c; 607b), the latter destabilizing the balance between the different parts of the soul. This quarrel illustrates the soul's agonizing conflict (608a–b) of reason and law (λόγος καὶ νόμος) over against emotions (τὸ πάθος) (*Resp.* X 604a ff.). It is this duality that even gives rise to the talk of two men (or things?) within the human soul: "And where there are two opposite impulses (ἐναντίας δὲ ἀγωγῆς) in a man at the same time about the same thing we say that there must needs be two" (604b).[16] The talk of "two" resembles Xenophon's "two souls," yet never expressing such a fully dualistic view. Rather, the human soul (singular) is said to be differentiated in two parts, (1) "the best part (τὸ βέλτιστον) of us," which is willing to conform to what is reasonable (ὁ λογισμός), as opposed to (2) "the irrational (ἀλόγιστόν) and idle part of us" (604d).

This duality of the soul distorts its original simplicity. This is exemplified in the figure of the sea-god Glaucus in *Resp.* X 611b–613b. The true nature of the soul, when it is "not marred by communion with the body" but "when it is purified," can be gleaned from the condition of Glaucus, whose original nature (ἀρχαῖα φύσις) has become disfigured by many accretions because of his continuous immersion under water. Similarly, only when the soul is "raised by this impulse (ὁρμή) out of the depths of this sea in which it is now sunk" does its real nature (ἡ ἀληθὴς φύσις) become visible, which is not of many forms (πολυειδής), but simple, of one form only (μονοειδής) (*Resp.* X 611b–612a). The soul is therefore said to cast off its unnatural, secondarily acquired multiplicity and regain its original simplicity when it is purified from its

[15] Plato, *Resp.* VIII 554d–e. [16] Cf. among others Shields 2010.

accretions and unified again with the divine, immortal, and eternal, for which it yearns and to which it is akin. This is distinctively different from Araspes' view that there are two souls; instead of an anthropological dualism, according to Plato the soul is clearly one, the original simple nature of which, however, is distorted into its present divided, multifarious, discordant status.

In his *Timaeus* Plato shows how this duality of the human soul started at the moment of its allocation to a body, when "the immortal principle of soul" (ἀρχὴ ψυχῆς ἀθάνατος), created by the Demiurge, was received by the lower, planetary gods who gave it a body and, by doing so, mingled it with "another form of soul" (ἄλλο … εἶδος … ψυχῆς), "the mortal kind of soul" (τὸ τῆς ψυχῆς θνητὸν γένος), in which the passions (παθήματα) reside (Plato, *Tim.* 69c–e). According to this perspective, the two forms or types of soul are allocated in different parts of the human body: the immortal (form/kind of) soul in the head, the mortal (form/kind of) soul within the chest, separated from the head by the neck to ensure that the two types of soul remain apart and the lower form of soul does not pollute the immortal, divine soul (*Tim.* 69d–e). Read in conjunction with what Plato said earlier about the creation of the cosmic soul, it becomes apparent also that the divine cosmic soul itself is a composition of two sorts of soul, an indivisible and a divisible type of soul (*Tim.* 35a). This view on the duality of the cosmic soul is also echoed in Plato's *Laws*, where it is assumed that there are not less than two souls, "the beneficent soul and that which is capable of effecting results of the opposite kind" (*Leg.* X 896e). As we shall see, the Platonic view of the duality of the soul runs through the writings of Platonists such as Plutarch and Plotinus. Although in the latter passages (and especially in his *Laws*) Plato comes close to a dualism of two opposing souls, as expressed by Xenophon's Araspes, his other passages and his actual argumentation show that Plato is rather concerned with the pluriformity and the ambiguity that the single (cosmic and human) soul acquires in the course of its development and are characteristic of its present status. The Platonic opposition is never between two souls of equal power or quality; nor, in the case of the human soul, is it a permanent opposition, but a duplicity that will be brought back to its original simplicity. The implied logic is that the divided human self should regain its original homogeneity and single-mindedness by withdrawing itself from the distorting influences of the body and thus restore its original and true nature. This clear contrast with the full anthropological dualism of Xenophon's Araspes makes it unlikely that Plato's refined theory of the divided self is grounded in an Iranian conception of two souls. Plato's view on the divided human self also offers a relevant explanatory model for James' notion of the δίψυχος.

## 2.2 Inner-Stoic Tensions

The Platonic statement about the soul's current internal dividedness differs greatly from the Stoics' fully monistic view of the soul, which emphasized instead the unity of the human soul (even in its current state). Even in a Stoic philosopher such as Epictetus, who Platonized his Stoic anthropology by stressing the tension between the soul and the body,[17] it is clear that the soul itself is unified and not divided, and that this soul has different inclinations. Speaking about the body and the soul, Epictetus says:

> Inasmuch as these two elements were commingled in our begetting, on the one hand the body, which we have in common with the brutes, and on the other, reason and intelligence, which we have in common with the gods, some of us incline (ἀποκλίνουσιν) toward the former kinship (συγγένεια) [i.e. the kinship with the body], which is unblessed by fortune and is mortal, and only a few toward that which is divine and blessed [i.e. the kinship with the soul].[18]

Epictetus' differentiation between two inclinations does not imply that the human soul itself is divided. To the contrary, the soul itself is seen as undivided but is regarded as subject to two opposing inclinations. This is relevant for our assessment of James' view that human beings are double-minded, since double-mindedness is a distinctively un-Stoic notion.

Not all Stoics, however, maintained such a unified view of the soul. There seems to have been a rift within the Stoic school in this respect, since Posidonius (ca. 135–ca. 51 BCE) heavily criticized his fellow Stoic Chrysippus (ca. 280–207 BCE) on these issues. In his anti-Chrysippean polemics, preserved in Galen's *On the Doctrines of Hippocrates and Plato*, Posidonius insists on the division within the self between "the daimon in oneself, which is akin and has a similar nature to the one which governs the whole universe" and "what is worse and beast-like," "the irrational and unhappy, that is, what is godless in the soul (τὸ ἄλογον τε καὶ κακόδαιμον καὶ ἄθεον τῆς ψυχῆς)."[19] According to Posidonius, emotions emerge and threaten human happiness when one does not follow the former, "the daimon in oneself," but is swept along with the latter, "the irrational." Galen (129–216 CE), himself a Platonist,

[17] See Long 2002, 158. [18] Epictetus, *Diatr.* 1.3.3; cf. 1.3.7.

[19] Posidonius, frg. 187 ed. and trans. Kidd, part A, *apud* Galen, *On the Doctrines of Hippocrates and Plato*, 5.6.4–5.

interprets Posidonius' criticism of Chrysippus in a Platonizing way and states that Posidonius shows himself in line with what Plato taught: "since we have in us a better part of soul (τὸ βελτίων τῆς ψυχῆς μέρος) and a worse part (τὸ χείρων), he who follows the better part could be said to live in harmony with nature, while he who follows the worse part rather, in discord; the latter lives by emotion (πάθος), the former by reason (λόγον)."[20] In this way Galen shows that not all Stoics viewed the soul as a unified self that followed one of its inclinations, but that some Stoics, such as Posidonius, resembled Plato closely in their view on the divided nature of the self.[21]

## 2.3 Platonists

This duality seems indeed an important characteristic of the Platonic school, as can be illustrated by examples drawn from Platonists such as Plutarch (b. before 50 CE, d. after 120 CE) and Plotinus (205–269/70 CE). Plutarch, in his *De virtute morali*, picks up on the compounded nature of the soul, both cosmic and individual. In a sense it is Plutarch, by drawing the comparison between the individual and cosmic soul, who renders explicit what had remained implicit in Plato. According to Plutarch:

> Plato ... comprehended clearly, firmly, and without reservation both that *the soul* (ἔμψυχον) *of this universe of ours* is not simple (ἁπλοῦν) nor uncompounded (ἀσύνθετον) nor uniform (μονοειδές)[22] ... and also that *the soul of man*, since it is a portion or a copy of the soul of the Universe and is joined together on principles and in proportions corresponding to those which govern the Universe, is not simple (ἁπλῆ) nor subject to similar emotions, but has as one part the intelligent and rational (νοερὸν καὶ λογιστικόν), whose natural duty it is to govern and rule the individual, and as another part the passionate and irrational (παθητικὸν καὶ ἄλογον), the variable and disorderly, which has need of a director.[23]

In Plutarch's synthesis of the cosmological (*Tim.* 34b ff.) and anthropological (*Tim.* 69c ff.) sections on the soul in Plato's *Timaeus*, it becomes clear that the human soul has not only become compound when linked with a body by the lower, planetary gods, but that already the cosmic soul itself is ambiguous; the duality of the human embodied soul only reflects,

[20] Posidonius, frg. 187 ed and trans Kidd, part B, *apud* Galen, *On the Doctrines of Hippocrates and Plato*, 5.6.8.

[21] On Posidonius' dualistic psychology, cf. Pépin 1971, 157–58. On the monism of Stoic psychology, cf. Gill 2006; Kloppenborg 2010, 50.

[22] See Plato, *Tim.* 35a ff. Cf. Plutarch, *An. procr.* 1012B ff.

[23] Plato, *Tim.* 69c ff.; Plutarch, *Virt. Mor.* 441F–442A.

to a greater extent, what is already ambiguous in the make-up of the soul of the cosmic body. In that sense, the soul of the cosmic body is also divided, and it is apparently only God himself who is truly simple and beyond division.

Such is Plutarch's awareness of the duality of the human soul that he even picks up, from the poetic philosopher Empedocles (ca. 492–432 BCE), the talk of "two fates (μοῖραι)" or "spirits (δαίμονες)" that sow the seed of their affections into human nature:

> For it is not true, as Menander says, that "By every man at birth *a spirit* stands . . . " (Menander, frag. 551); but rather, as Empedocles affirms, *two fates, as it were, or spirits* (διτταί τινες . . . μοῖραι καὶ δαίμονες), receive in their care each one of us at birth and consecrate us . . . [followed by quotation of Empedocles] (frag. B122). The result is that since we at our birth received the mingled seeds of each of these affections (σπέρματα τῶν παθῶν ἀνακεκραμένα), and since therefore our nature possesses much unevenness (ἀνωμαλία), a man of sense prays for better things, but expects the contrary as well, and, avoiding excess, deals with both conditions.[24]

On this view, the uneven human nature is severely morally challenged by the effect of these two opposing spirits, something which later resonates in the view expressed in the *Corpus Hermeticum* that "Mind conceives every mental product: both the good, when mind receives seeds from god, as well as the contrary kind, when the seeds come from some demonic being" (IX.3).[25] Empedocles' talk of two spirits, adopted by Plutarch, is a view that is rather similar to the notion of two spirits in the Community Rule of Qumran (see 2.4 below) in respect of its dualism. With the aid of the dual, opposing principles that are characteristic for Empedocles' philosophy, Plutarch reinforces the ambiguity that he encountered in Plato's reflection on the duality of the human soul by ascribing it to two spirits.

Plotinus, too, extensively echoes Plato's dual psychology. In *Enn.* 1.1.12 Plotinus quotes *Resp.* X 611d–612a (part of the passage discussed above). Plotinus develops this passage by differentiating between the "single and simple soul" and "the other form of soul," the soul that becomes compound during its descent in the process of coming-to-be (1.1.12). In *Enn.* 2.3.9 Plotinus also draws on *Tim.* 69c–d (discussed above), about the engendering of the second soul by the lower, planetary gods, which becomes home to the passions. In line with this view, Plotinus differentiates between "the higher soul," which is "outside the body," and

[24] Plutarch, *Tranq. an.* 474B–C.

[25] Cf. Dillon 1996, 173 and 221. In *Corp. herm.* IX.3, however, the mind is rather depicted as a "passive matrix for divine or demonic seeds" (Copenhaver 1995, 151), and not so much as engaged in a struggle.

the composite soul, "a sort of soul bound to body." In this way Plotinus further develops his own views on the higher and lower self; the higher self is the self that is separable from the body, "the separable soul," or "the undescended soul."[26] In this view the duality of the two souls is maximized, as Plotinus believes that these souls have also separate memories, the memories of the lower soul fading away when the higher soul returns to heaven and leaves its lower soul behind in Hades (*Enn.* 4.3.27; cf. 6.4.16). This seems to be one of the most extreme consequences of the Platonic doctrine of the duality of the soul.

## 2.4 Philo of Alexandria

Philo of Alexandria also shows awareness of the Platonic doctrine of the duality of the soul. But does Philo belong to the Greek and/or Jewish trajectory sketched by Stroumsa? Two passages in Philo's writings seem particularly relevant.

(a) In his *Questions and Answers on Exodus*, Philo states:

Into every soul at its very birth there enter *two powers* (δυνάμεις), the salutary and the destructive. If the salutary one is victorious and prevails, the opposite one is too weak to see. And if the latter prevails, no profit at all or little is obtained from the salutary one. Through these powers the world too was created.[27]

According to John Dillon, this passage reflects "a remarkably dualist, almost Gnostic doctrine (cf. e.g. *Corp. herm.* IX.3), which can, however, be connected (at least remotely) with that of Plato in *Laws* X, 896e ff. ... the destructive power ... has here become an evil principle, akin to the Persian Ahriman and to the Evil Soul of *Laws* X."[28] Indeed, it seems that Plato's *Laws* X (discussed above) constitutes the background to Philo's reflections. Moreover, the view that "Into every soul at its very birth there enter two powers" is also similar to the view which we saw expressed in Plutarch's *On Tranquility of Mind* (474B–C), that two spirits stand by every man at birth (see above). This view also comes remarkably close to the anthropology of the Treatise on the Two Spirits in the Community Rule among the Dead Sea Scrolls:

He [i.e. God] has created man to govern the world, and has appointed for him *two spirits* in which to walk until the time of His visitation: the spirits of truth and injustice. ... The nature of all the children of men is ruled by these (two spirits),

[26] See further Sorabji 2005, 93–99, section 3(e); Pépin 1971, 96. [27] Philo, *QE* 1.23.
[28] Dillon 1996, 173.

and during their life all the hosts of men have a portion of their divisions and walk in (both) their ways. And the whole reward for their deeds shall be, for everlasting ages, according to whether each man's portion in their two divisions is great or small. For God has established the spirits in equal measure until the final age. . . . Until now the spirits of truth and injustice struggle in the hearts of men.[29]

This view of the two spirits is rather similar to Plutarch's two Empedoclean spirits, Philo's two powers, and the two souls of Plato's *Laws* X.[30] As in Plato's *Republic* this dualistic anthropology is not permanent but will eventually be removed, either – according to Plato – at the soul's ascent to God, or – according to the author of the Treatise on the Two Spirits – at the end of time, when God will "purify every deed of man with His truth; He will refine for Himself *the human frame* by rooting out all spirit of injustice from the bounds of his *flesh*" (1QS iv 20–21). According to both Plato and the author of the Treatise on the Two Spirits the duality of spirits or souls, which currently "struggle in the hearts of men" (1QS iv 23) and occasion an agonizing conflict within the soul (*Resp.* X 608a–b), will be overcome by removing the negative principle that is so closely related to the body (also called "the human frame" and "flesh"). There is surprisingly little difference between the anthropologies of Plato and the Treatise on the Two Spirits, and this may explain why Philo can be understood from both a Greek and a Jewish environment. It is important, however, to question Stroumsa's suggestion that both backgrounds are the product of one and the same sort of Iranian dualism, that is subsequently transmitted through two long separate trajectories, Iranian–Greek and Iranian–Jewish. As we have seen, the thread from Xenophon's Araspes to Plato is rather thin. Moreover, recently the direct Iranian background to the dualism of the Treatise on the Two Spirits has been called into question.[31] If this is correct, then it is unlikely that in Philo's dualistic anthropology the Iranian–Jewish and Iranian–Greek trajectories converge again. Given his knowledge of Middle Platonic anthropology, and his confirmed acquaintance with Empedocles,[32] it seems that Philo's connection with a Greek anthropological discourse is particularly strong.

(b) Another passage, in Philo's *Who Is the Heir of Divine Things*, illustrates how Philo can find confirmation for his Platonic view of the duality of the soul in the Pentateuch:

[29] 1QS iii 17–19; iv 15–23; trans. Vermes.

[30] Dillon 1996, 173–74, incl. 174 n. 1, and 221.

[31] See Brand 2013, 271–73.

[32] See Lincicum 2014.

We use "soul" in two senses (ψυχὴ διχῶς λέγεται), both for the whole soul (ἥ τε ὅλη) and also for its dominant part, which properly speaking is the soul's soul (ψυχὴ ψυχῆς). ... And therefore the lawgiver [i.e. Moses] held that the substance (τὴν οὐσίαν) of the soul is twofold (διττὴν), blood (Lev 17:11) being that of the soul as a whole, and the divine spirit (πνεῦμα; Gen 2:7) that of its most dominant part.[33]

Philo's point of departure here is the Greek differentiation between two types of soul, which are both called soul (one in a stricter sense, and the other in a broader sense), which he brings into interplay with different passages from the Pentateuch.[34]

If Philo is so thoroughly acquainted with a Greek anthropological discourse, and links up with it in his reading of the Jewish Scriptures, the question whether the author of the Letter of James can be understood in a similar way needs to be addressed.

## 3 JAMES' POSITION

Noteworthy in James' description of the double-minded (δίψυχος) condition of human beings is the way he contrasts it with God's nature, which is characterized as simple: God is willing to give wisdom "simply" (ἁπλῶς) to those who lack it and ask him for it by putting their trust in him, and who do not allow themselves to be further decomposed (διακρινόμενος) and disintegrated because of a doubtful, wavering attitude, "for the doubter, being double-minded (δίψυχος) and unstable (ἀκατάστατος) in every way, must not expect to receive anything from the Lord" (Jas 1.5–8). Here the antithesis is implied between the δίψυχος nature of human beings and the simplicity of God.

This reminds us of the same antithesis that Plato forged between the true original nature of the human soul, in which it is akin to the divine, and the secondary accretions that the human soul attracts when immersed in its earthly life; it is to this divine simplicity that the human soul is restored when it is no longer of many forms (πολυειδής), but of one form only (μονοειδής) (*Resp.* X 611b–612a). At the same time, however, this movement from a compound being to a simple being is also reminiscent of the anthropology of the Treatise on the Two Spirits, according to which human beings, in whose hearts the spirits of truth and injustice still struggle, will finally be liberated from the evil spirit. Yet James' antithesis in terms of divine simplicity versus human double-mindedness seems to indicate that he does partake in a specific Greek discourse of divine

[33] Philo, *Her.* 55–56. [34] See further van Kooten 2008, 283.

simplicity as opposed to human ambiguity, a discourse that is heavily colored by the Platonic notion of the divided self. Kloppenborg pays much attention to the Stoic background of the unstable (ἀκατάστατος) nature of human beings,[35] but James' other qualification of this human nature as double-minded (δίψυχος) is rather un-Stoic, because the Stoics emphasize the unified nature of the human soul[36] (as Kloppenborg acknowledges), whereas it is the Platonists who are deeply interested in the divided self as we have seen above.[37]

It seems that James actually resembles Philo in his application of Platonic thought. James' notion of δίψυχος is rather similar to Philo's statements about "the twofold nature of the soul" (διττὴ ... ἡ οὐσία ... ψυχῆς), discussed above. This twofold nature consists of (a) the spirit as the most dominant part of the soul, "the soul's soul," and (b) the lower part of the ψυχή; the term ψυχή is used both for the soul in its entirety or, when contrasted with the πνεῦμα, for the lower soul. This differentiation between spirit (πνεῦμα) and soul (ψυχή), supplemented with the body (σῶμα) as a third constituent of human life, is the typically Jewish adaptation of the Greek, Platonic differentiation between mind (νοῦς), soul (ψυχή) and body (σῶμα),[38] and an adaptation that we also find in James' Letter. James, too, differentiates between spirit (πνεῦμα) and body (σῶμα; Jas 2:26), regarding the πνεῦμα as the leading part of human existence, directly connected with God (Jas 4:5; cf. Isa 63:11), whereas the ψυχή refers both to the entire soul, which is in need of salvation (Jas 1:21; 5:20), and to the lower soul (cf. Jas 3:15), which is devoid of spirit. It is therefore very likely that James' notion of being "double-souled" (δίψυχος) reflects the Platonic concept of a bipartite soul that consists of the higher mind (πνεῦμα) and the lower soul (ψυχή) of passions.

The impression that James participates in a Greek, and particularly Platonic, discourse is reinforced by his depiction of the tension between God's simplicity and the double-minded nature of human beings, in which he elaborates on God's nature. God, who is fully remote from evil, is not the source of human temptation (Jas 1:13); rather, God is the source of what is good and perfect (Jas 1:17a). This simple goodness does not show any variation (Jas 1:17b):

> No one, when tempted, should say, "I am being tempted by God"; for God cannot be tempted by evil and he himself tempts no one. But one is tempted by one's own desire (ἐπιθυμία). ... Do not be misled, my beloved. Every generous act of giving,

[35] Kloppenborg 2010. [36] Cf. Gill 2006. [37] See also Shields 2010; Barney et al. 2012.
[38] See van Kooten 2008, chap. 5.

with every perfect gift, is from above, coming down from the Father of lights, with whom there is no variation (παραλλαγὴ) or shadow due to change (τροπῆς ἀποσκίασμα).[39]

It is exactly this view that we find expressed in Plato's *Republic*:

Then there is no motive for God to deceive (ψεύδοιτο).
None.
So from every point of view the divine and the divinity (τὸ δαιμόνιόν τε καὶ τὸ θεῖον) are free from falsehood (ἀψευδὲς).
By all means.
Then God is altogether simple (ἁπλοῦν) and true in deed and word, and neither changes himself nor deceives others by vision or words or the sending of signs in waking or in dreams.[40]

James thus shares with Plato the specific view that God is not the source of evil, seduction, and deception, but in his simplicity is thoroughly good and unchangeable.

It is against this background that James' and Plato's depiction of the human soul as δίψυχος ("double-minded," Jas 1.8; 4.8) and πολυειδής ("of many forms," *Resp.* X 612a) gains significance. James' stress on God's unchangeability is clearly Platonic, as the Stoics entertained a rather dynamic understanding of God, which the Platonists regarded as irreverent.[41] As James subsequently explains (1:21–25; cf. 2:8–12), the double-minded (δίψυχος) human condition can only by lifted through reason (λόγος) and law (νόμος). Just as in Plato's *Republic* the human soul experiences the agony (608a–b) between reason and law, on the one hand, and emotions (τὸ πάθος), on the other (*Resp.* X 604a ff.), so, also according to James, the soul only gets rid of the vices through reason and law. These notions of reason and law in James are partly Stoically colored, as the reason is "the implanted, innate logos" (ὁ ἔμφυτος λόγος, Jas 1:21) known from Stoicism,[42] which as "the logos of truth" is able to engender human beings anew (Jas 1:18), while the law is "the kingly law" (Jas 2:8) and "the law of freedom" (Jas 1:25; 2.12), which has its closest parallels in Platonic and Stoic sources.[43] It is only by welcoming "the implanted logos" (Jas 1:21) and by fulfilling "the law of liberty" (Jas 1:25; 2:12)

[39] Jas 1:13–17. [40] Plato, *Resp.* 382e–383a.
[41] Cf. Plutarch, *E Delph.* 388C–389D, 393E–394A. Kloppenborg acknowledges this resemblance with Plato (Kloppenborg 2010, 67), but does not notice the difference between Platonists and Stoics on God's (un)changeability, on which see van Kooten 2014a, 309–310.
[42] Though ἔμφυτος was also used in Platonism: see, e.g., Plutarch, *Quaest. plat.* 1, 1000E.
[43] As noted by Dodd 1935, 39–40.

and "the kingly law" (Jas 2:8) that human beings can save their souls (Jas 1:21). For this it is essential that human beings not only receive the implanted reason but also act in accordance with it, otherwise they would be "like those who look at themselves in a mirror; for they look at themselves and, on going away, immediately forget what they were like" (Jas 1:23–24). This imagery of failing to remember one's true nature after one has seen oneself in a mirror is Platonic and is found in Plato's *Alcibiades major* (132c–133c).[44]

## 4 CONCLUDING REFLECTIONS

All this accumulative evidence of James' acquaintance with a Platonic discourse demonstrates that, like Philo, James partook in Jewish and Greek discourses at the same time. It is no wonder then that, if James were familiar with the Jewish concept of the two *yeṣarim*, he transferred this notion not into the Greek terminology of double-heartedness (διπλοκαρδία), but into that of double-mindedness (διψυχία). A Jewish anthropology of two *yeṣarim* proved compatible with the Greek reflections on a divided self. Particular Jewish and Greek anthropological traditions turn out to be far from incompatible, and the frequent claims of a fundamental opposition between Jewish anthropological holism versus Greek anthropological dualism seem unjustified.

Finally, a note on what this dichotomic doctrine of two inclinations (*yeṣarim*) or a double-minded (δίψυχος) human condition means for the question of the extent of the sinfulness of the human condition. In the description of the theme of the conference out of which this book emerged it was stated that in rabbinic thought the explanation of the existence of sin in the world by the existence of an Evil Inclination implies that "nobody is *sinful by nature*, but all are led to sin by the Evil Inclination" (emphasis mine). This implication also holds true for the anthropology of double-mindedness that characterizes the Letter of James, as James is very careful not to identify the double-minded (δίψυχος) human condition with sin as such. As he explains, human beings only sin when they actively give way to their desire by allowing it to conceive: "one is tempted by one's own desire, being lured and enticed by it; then, when that desire has conceived, it gives birth to sin, and that sin, when it is fully grown, gives birth to death" (Jas 1:14–15).[45]

[44] See Denyer 1999. [45] Cf. van Kooten 2014b, 400–02.

However, although the double-minded (δίψυχος) human condition is not in itself sinful, it is clear that human souls can only be saved when they, through the implanted divine Logos, orient themselves again fully toward God's simplicity and receive his wisdom. As we have seen, according to Plato, too, the soul's true nature is simple and "of one form only" (μονοειδής), and its current many forms are the result of the many accretions to its simple nature during its earthly life (*Resp.* X 611b–612a); its simple nature will be restored through purification. It is noteworthy that this understanding is repeated by Tertullian. In his *A Treatise on the Soul*, he feels attracted to the Platonic view of the divided human self, on the condition that this dividedness is not seen as the soul's natural, original condition, but that the lower soul is seen as a secondary accretion to the higher, actual soul:

That position of Plato's is also quite in keeping with the faith, in which he divides the soul into two parts – the rational and the irrational (cf. Plat. *Resp.* IV 439d–e). To this definition we take no exception, except that we would not ascribe this twofold distinction to the nature [of the soul]. It is the rational element which we must believe to be its natural condition, impressed upon it from its very first creation by its Author, who is Himself essentially rational. For how should that be other than rational, which God produced on His own prompting; nay more, which He expressly sent forth by His own afflatus or breath? The irrational element, however, we must understand to have accrued later (cf. Plat. *Resp.* X 611b–612a), as having proceeded from the instigation of the serpent – the very achievement of (the first) transgression – which thenceforward became inherent in the soul, and grew with its growth, assuming the manner by this time of a natural development, happening as it did immediately at the beginning of nature.[46]

Tertullian, thus, explicitly confirms that the "natural" condition of human beings is their rational condition in which they resemble their creator, and that therefore nobody is sinful "by nature"; the sinfulness of human beings is seen as an accretion to their true nature.

[46] Tertullian, *An.* 16. Cf. Waszink 1947. Cf. also Tertullian, *An.* 10.

10

# An Evil Inclination in the Early Targums to the Pentateuch and Prophets?

Hector M. Patmore

The Targums are translations of the Hebrew Bible that combine into one seamless text straightforward translation and exegetical embellishments. In this chapter I will examine those texts in the Targums to the Law and the Prophets (according to the traditional division of the Hebrew canon) that discuss a *yeṣer* and which belong to a stratum of the Targum that is likely to be early, by which I mean that their substantive forms are likely to have their origins in the Tannaitic period.[1]

This chapter takes as its starting point the recent work of Rosen-Zvi on the *yeṣer*.[2] Rosen-Zvi has mapped out the chronological and geographical variations in the characterizations of the *yeṣer* within classical rabbinic literature. His conclusions can be summarized as follows: Tannaitic sources speak of a single *yeṣer* that resides in the human heart, and yet is often described as independent of it. The majority of Tannaitic sources view the *yeṣer* as an evil force, which drags humans to sin and against which they must ceaselessly struggle using various techniques (such as Torah study). In Amoraic sources the *yeṣer* is more clearly a reified figure, a wily and dangerous foe. This characterization is further developed in Amoraic material in the Babylonian Talmud, which ascribes physical characteristics to the *yeṣer* so that it becomes comparable to other demonic figures. The vast majority of Palestinian sources continue to speak of only one *yeṣer*; it is only in late Babylonian sources that the

[1] Pseudo-Jonathan and the Tosefta Targums to the Prophets are therefore excluded (except where Tg Ps.-J. shares material with Palestinian Targums). Both have interesting things to say about the *yeṣer*, but both are substantially post-Tannaitic and often derivative.

[2] Rosen-Zvi 2011.

two-*yeṣarim* model becomes more pronounced, and only in the post-Amoraic discursive stratum of the Babylonian Talmud ("the Stam") that the *yeṣer* begins to be identified almost exclusively with sexual appetite.

This provides us with a framework against which we can compare the Targumic material. In this chapter we will examine Targums Onqelos and Jonathan as well as Palestinian Targum traditions (preserved in Targum Neofiti, Fragment Targums, and Cairo Genizah manuscripts). There is a reasonably broad consensus in Targum studies that Onqelos and Jonathan were first committed to writing in Palestine in the second century CE and then subsequently revised in the Babylonian academies, while the proto-Palestinian Targum began to crystallize perhaps a century or so later, before undergoing a long and complex transmission history that has left us with a diverse array of recensions. These Targums have grown by accretion. Comparing what the Targums have to say about the *yeṣer* with the development of rabbinic views about it should allow us to establish whether the material in these Targums stems from earlier or later – and, in the case of Targums Onqelos and Jonathan, Palestinian or Babylonian – strata.

As well as helping us to date Targumic materials – one of the most vexed aspects of the study of the Targums – this comparison will also help us to address another major challenge in the field of Targumic studies, namely the nature of the relationship between the Targums and mainstream rabbinic Judaism and its literature.

In making such a comparison we need to take some precautionary steps to eliminate false positives. In other words, is any resemblance substantial or merely superficial? Where similarities exist between the Targums and rabbinic literature we must first consider whether or not the Targum could have arrived independently at the same conclusion. So we need to consider carefully the Targum's peculiar *modus operandi* (i.e. its translation and exegetical techniques). Given the nature of Targum (i.e. embellished translation), we must also consider carefully questions of *Vorlage* and possible translation equivalents. The ancient Versions are of particular importance in this regard. We also need to look at how the verses in question were interpreted in other ancient Jewish sources in order to establish what may be novel and what may be derived from earlier traditions.

## 1 TARGUMS ONQELOS AND JONATHAN

Let us begin with Targums Onqelos and Jonathan, which probably contain the earliest stratum of the written Targumic material (I will say something more about their origins below). Their common compositional and editorial history makes it appropriate to treat them together.

## 1.1 Genesis 6:5 and 8:21

Genesis 6:5 and 8:21 are keys texts in the discussion of the evil *yeṣer* in rabbinic literature, a tradition first attested in Sifre Deuteronomy 45 (Gen 8:21 only), and widely cited in the Amoraic sources.[3] Yet Targum Onqelos is conservative in its handing of both texts. The Masoretic text of the two verses reads:

The Lord saw that mankind's evil on the earth was great and every *yeṣer* of the thoughts of his heart (כל יצר מחשבת לבו) was only evil the whole day long. (Gen 6:5)

The Lord smelt the pleasing scent and the Lord said in his heart, 'I will never again curse the ground on account of mankind because the *yeṣer* of the human heart (יצר לב האדם) is evil from his youth and I will never again smite all that lives as I have done.' (Gen 8:21)

In both cases the *yeṣer* of the heart is best understood as that which is formed by the heart or the thoughts of the heart – that is, the product or result – which might imply the action undertaken.

In both cases Onqelos closely reflects the underlying Hebrew, reading the cognate Aramaic noun יצרא. It adds only by way of specification in Gen 8:21 that the ground would no longer be cursed on account of "the *sins of* mankind." Although Onqelos is essentially a word-for-word translation with typical Targumic modifications, it is worth bearing in mind that the Targum could have translated the Hebrew *yeṣer* (יצר) here differently.[4] Its choice of the cognate noun (יצרא) is therefore significant. Clearly the translator of Onqelos felt that in this context there was no better way of expressing the concept of the Hebrew *yeṣer* in Aramaic than by using an Aramaized form of the word. But what did translator of Onqelos understand by the Aramaized form of the word? The limited contemporary

[3] E.g. b. Sukkah 52a; b. Qidd. 30b; b. B. Bat. 16a (in which the evil *yeṣer* is equated to Satan and the Angel of Death on the basis of Gen 6:5).

[4] E.g. Tg. Isa.26:3 renders יצר סמוך with לבב שלים. The principal Greek versions of Gen 6:5 and 8:21 render *ad sensum*, so no direct equivalent of Hebrew יצר is given. A much later source (ca. 475–538 CE), Procopius of Gaza (*Comm. Gen.* 95, ed. Migne 1860), argues that the Hebrew should be translated τὸ πλάσμα τῆς καρδίας, as Aquila on Deut 31:21. On Jerome's treatment of יצר in Gen 6:5 (*cuncta cogitatio cordis intenta esset ad malum*) and Gen 8:21 (*sensus enim et cogitatio humani cordis in malum prona sunt;* also Deut 31.21 *cogitationes eius* = יצרו) see Hayward, Chapter 15 in this volume. Cf. Cohen Stuart 1984, 84–85.

Aramaic evidence and the fact that the Aramaic noun is itself a Hebrew loanword[5] makes it difficult to establish the extent to which the meaning of the Hebrew has carried over into the Aramaic on the one hand, and the extent to which we should rely on usage in Aramaic texts from other dialects and other periods to ascertain its semantic range in the Aramaic of Onqelos on the other.

Certainly, if we accept that there is some evidence that the *yeṣer* was understood as an entity in some measure ontologically distinct from humans already in the late Second Temple period then it becomes plausible to imagine that the Targumist could have understood the reference to the *yeṣer* in these verses in those terms. If such an characterization of the *yeṣer* is applicable in 4QInstruction[c] ("Do not let the thought of evil *yeṣer* deceive you" 4Q417 1 ii 12), which allude to Gen 6:5 – or for that matter Rom 7:18–20 – then the case for assuming such a signification in Targum Onqelos would be strengthened.[6] Equally, it is possible that Onqelos knew some of the material now found in Sifre Deuteronomy, our earliest rabbinic source connecting Gen 8:21 to the evil *yeṣer*,[7] though there is no direct evidence for this in Onqelos's rendering of Gen 8:21. All of this, however, remains conjecture.

Targum Onqelos mentions the *yeṣer* only once again (Deut 31:21, see below), where it simply translates the cognate Hebrew term again without any elaboration of significance. So there is really nothing in Onqelos itself that enables us to determine what the Targumist understood by the *yeṣer*. There are, however, two (only two!) uses of the term יצרא in Targum Jonathan (Isa 62:10 and Ezek 20:25). Since Targum Jonathan shares a common history with Onqelos – to the extent that it can justifiably be regarded as Onqelos's counterpart for the Prophetic books – it may shed some indirect light on the meaning of יצרא in Onqelos.

Let us look first at Isa 62:10.

## 1.2 Isaiah 62:10

The immediate narrative context of Isa 62:10 in the Masoretic Text is an oracle that promises the renewal of Jerusalem and the land (e.g. Isa 62:4),

[5] Nöldeke 1886, 722.

[6] See Rosen-Zvi 2011, 44–53 (on 4Q417, 46) and Tigchelaar 2008, 350–52. Cf. Brand's critique (2013, 46–47).

[7] Drazin 1982, 8–10, 43–47. Cf. also Origen, *Fr. Eph.* 9, commenting on Eph 2:3, who cites Gen 8:21 (ὅτε ἐνέκειτο ἡμῶν ἡ διάνοια ἐπὶ τὰ πονηρὰ ἐκ νεότητος) to explain how the corruption of humankind's initial pristine state was effected; Gregg 1902, 404, l. 222).

and the redemption and restoration of the people (e.g. Isa 62:12). The oracle is found in Trito-Isaiah (i.e. Isaiah 56–66), which probably dates from the decades shortly after the return from the Babylonian exile.[8] The oracle is addressed to those who "cause the Lord to remember" (המזכרים את יהוה), exhorting them to continue to entreat the Lord until he reestablishes Jerusalem (e.g. Isa 62:6–7). It is to this group that the verse with which we are concerned is addressed:

Pass through, pass through the gates! Prepare a path for the people (פנו דרך העם)! Build up, build up (סלו סלו), the highway! Clear it of rocks! Raise a banner over the peoples! (Isa 62:10)

Targum Jonathan develops the oracle as a whole into a clear expression of a theology of rewards for the righteous when they accomplish the Divine will (cf. Tg. Isa. 62:6, 11). This is in line with the theology of the Isaiah Targum as a whole, which presents exile (and the removal of the Shekinah – the two concepts are connected) as a just punishment for Israel's apostasy, yet promises restoration and reward should Israel repent.[9] This theological framework explains the Targum's expansive rendering of Isa 62:10 (showing variations from the Hebrew in italic):

O *prophets*, pass through and turn in at the gates! Turn (אפנו) *the hearts of* the people *to a proper* path! Proclaim good news and consolation *to the righteous who removed the disturbing thought of the yeṣer* (דסליקו הרהור יצרא), *which is like* a stumbling block (כאבן תקלא)! Raise a banner over the peoples![10]

Here we have something to get our teeth into.

To understand the Targum's meaning here, we need to have a sense of how it arrived at its exegesis. The clause "who removed the disturbing thought of the *yeṣer*, which is like a stumbling block" is derived from the two words in the Hebrew translated "Clear it of rocks!" (סקלו מאבן). This is achieved by means of two interpretative devices that are ubiquitous in Targum Jonathan. First, the letters of the Hebrew סקלו, meaning contextually "to clear of stones," are reordered, a technique sometimes referred to as *'al tiqrei*,[11] to create the Aramaic סליקו, whence "they removed". Second, the Targumist creates a simile in order to allow "the stones" to be understood metaphorically. In this new simile "the stones" (i.e. the tenor

[8] For an overview see Goldingay 2014, 1–9.

[9] See Ribera Florit 1988b, 41–42, 46–48, 52; Chilton 1987, xiv–xx.

[10] Following the edition of Ribera Florit 1988a.

[11] Ribera Florit 1988b, 27–29.

of the simile) are compared to the *disturbing thought of the yeṣer* (i.e. the vehicle),[12] to which we will return shortly.

These stones (used in this context as a noun of species, so grammatically singular in the Hebrew[13]) are further qualified as a stumbling block (אבן תקלא) by the Targum. This may reflect an alternative *Vorlage*,[14] but it seems more likely that the Targum's exegesis is actually derived from an association with Isa 57:14, a verse with which Isa 62:10 has very clear verbal parallels. Isa 57:14 begins:

Build up, build up (סלו סלו)! Prepare a path (פנו דרך)!

Then continues:

Remove any stumbling block (מכשול) from my people's path!

Targum Jonathan renders this:

*Teach and admonish!* Turn *the hearts of the people to a proper* path! Remove the stumbling block *of the wicked* (סליקו תקלת רשיעיא) from the path of *the congregation of* my people!

The verbal resonance between the two verses is even stronger in the Targum than in the Hebrew, suggesting that the Targumist has indeed coordinated the two verses (i.e. "associative" translation).[15]

The resonance between these two verses is of particular relevance to the current discussion because Isa 57:14 is one of the proof texts employed in the homily on the seven names of the evil *yeṣer* attributed to R. ʿAwira (Palestinian *amora* of the third and fourth century) or some say (איתימא) R. Joshua b. Levi (Palestinian *amora* of the first half of the third century CE) in the Babylonian Talmud (b. Sukkah 52a). There we are told that Isaiah called the evil *yeṣer* "a stumbling block" (מכשול; cf. Num Rab 15.16). Is the comparison of the *yeṣer* to a stumbling block in Targum Isa 62:10 connected to this tradition? Probably not. If it were, we might expect a reference to the *yeṣer* also in the Targum to Isa 57:14. Consequently, one must conclude that the comparison of the *yeṣer* to

12 Comparable is Jerome's explanation: *Lapides qui in uia sunt, et proici iubentur, peccata nostra sunt* (*Tract. Ps.*, LXXXIIII, l. 211). On the terms "tenor" and "vehicle" see Richards 1936, 95–138.

13 Joüon and Muraoka 2013, §135.

14 1QIsa[a] סקולו מאבן הנגף "Clear it of stumbling blocks!" (Cf. Isa 8:14); Burrows 1950, *ad loc.*

15 See Alexander 2004, 227–28; Klein 2011.

a stumbling block is entirely the result of the "associative" translation within the Targumic tradition itself.[16]

Returning to Targum Isa 62:10, we note that in addition to being likened to a stumbling block the *yeṣer* is said to generate "disturbing thoughts." In Targum Jonathan (as well as Onqelos) a *disturbing thought* (הרהור) indicates a thought that leads one astray, usually to apostasy (e.g. Tg Isa 57:17; Tg Jer 9:13; 13:10), implying an antinomian character to the *yeṣer* (it is worthy of note that the belief that the *yeṣer* leads to idolatry is a mainstay of rabbinic thinking).[17] But we have little else to go on in terms of defining the *yeṣer* more precisely here: the term הרהור is nowhere else associated with the *yeṣer* in the early Targumim,[18] nor in rabbinic literature, with the exception of a saying recorded in Avot of Rabbi Nathan (version A, 20). In this text the *yeṣer* is identified as evil and its disturbing thoughts (הרהורי יצר הרע) appear in a long list of types of thought that can be abolished by taking to heart of the words of the Torah: thoughts of hunger (הרהורי רעב), idle thoughts (הרהורי דברים בטלים), foolish thoughts (הרהורי שטות), licentious thoughts (הרהורי זנות), and so on. The thoughts listed are predominantly carnal, though not universally so; this gives us a sense of the realm that the evil *yeṣer* occupies even if it is difficult to deduce a precise characterization of the *yeṣer* from this passage. In any case, although this tradition is attributed to Hananiah (second century CE) or Nehunya b. ha-Kanah (mid-end of the second century or earlier? see Addition B to Version A 6), the extant form of the text may be post-Talmudic,[19] so that its value for evaluating the *yeṣer* in Targum Isaiah is limited.

Although the "disturbing thought" is not connected to the *yeṣer* anywhere else in Targum Jonathan, it is frequently connected to the heart, and the heart in question is often qualified as "evil" (e.g. Tg. Jer. 3.17; 7.24; 11.8; 16.12).[20] This suggests a certain equivalence between the "heart" and the *yeṣer* (cf. also Tg. Isa. 26:3) – an equivalence, it should be noted,

[16] Hence the inclusion of אבן ("stone") as one of the seven names given in the enumeration of b. Sukkah 52a on the basis of Ezek 36:26 ("I [the Lord] will remove the stone heart [לב האבן] from your flesh and I will give you a heart of flesh") is also unrelated to the Targum's exegesis.

[17] See Rosen-Zvi 2011, 25, 30–32, 88–89.

[18] The reading הרהור in place of יצרא in Tg. Onq. Gen 6:5 in the First Rabbinic Bible is certainly secondary. The two terms may be parallel in Tg. Ps.-J. Gen 49:24; cf. Tg 1 Chr 28:9, 18.

[19] Stemberger 1996, 225–27.

[20] On "evil heart" see Prov 25:20; 26:23; 4Q393 3, 3b–5a; 4 Ezra 3:20–22. See Brand 2013, 52–54, 128–43.

already implied in some Qumran texts.[21] If we are right in seeing such an equivalence, then we are more in the realm of *yeṣer* as a normal human tendency than as an independent being living within the individual.

## 1.3 Ezekiel 20:25

The second reference to a *yeṣer* in Targum Jonathan occurs in Ezek 20:25. In the Hebrew text this verse belongs to a narrative context (Ezek 20:1–26) in which the Lord rehearses the deliverance from Egypt and the giving of laws, and laments the people's rejection of his statutes, profanation of the Sabbath, and idolatry (e.g. Ezek 20:24). The oracle goes on to promise that the Lord will restore his chosen people to the land after the transgressors have been purged from their midst (e.g. Ezek 20:38). But immediately before that promise of ultimate restoration the Lord makes the following unexpected confession:

I also gave them statutes that were not good, and judgements by which they could not live. I defiled them by means of their own gifts – when [they] devoted (בהעביר, as a fire-offering?[22]) every first born of the womb – so that I might destroy them,[23] so that they might know that I am the Lord. (Ezek 20:25–26)

These two verses are extremely problematic from the point of view of theodicy: the Lord, they imply, has led the people astray, and now intends to punish them for it.

This theological problem is overcome in the Targum (a tendency found elsewhere in Targum Ezekiel):[24]

I also, *because they rebelled against my word* (במימרי) *and did not want to accept my prophets*, I removed them *and handed them over to the control* (ביד) *of their stupid yeṣer* (יצרהון טפשא). *They went and they made* decrees *that* were not proper and laws by which they could not live (יתקיימון i.e. be preserved). I defiled them by

[21] E.g., 1QS v 5 where, if it is correct to understand the text as a reversal of Gen 6:5 (i.e. יצר מחשבת לבו), the *yeṣer* replaces the heart (i.e. מחשבת יצרו): see Brand 2013, 86–87; Rosen-Zvi 2011, 45–46 (esp. n. 7); and Mizrahi, Chapter 2 in this volume. Cf. Cohen Stuart 1984, 223–25.

[22] Cf. Ezek 20:31; 2 Kgs 16:3; Deut 18:10. See Allen 1990, 12 and references there.

[23] Greenberg (1983, 369) rightly rejects the common translation "so that I might horrify them," which softens the theodicy problem. Several ancient versions, working from an unvocalized text, connect the form to אשם: Theodotion, ἕνεκεν πλημμελείας αὐτῶν, "on account of their sinful error"; Symmachus, ἵνα πλημμελήσωσιν (retroverted from Syro-hexapla), "because they committed a sinful error." But LXX already had (correctly) ὅπως ἀφανίσω αὐτούς, "so that I might destroy them," supporting the vocalization of MT.

[24] Ribera Florit 2004, 44.

means of their own gifts – when [they] devoted (באעברא) every first born – so that I might destroy them, so that they might know that I am the Lord.[25]

God transfers control to the *yeṣer* and the *yeṣer* does its work of leading the people astray.[26] The antinomian character of the *yeṣer* is again clear here, since it is the people who make their own decrees and laws,[27] an activity that is defined as folly, hence the "stupid *yeṣer*." But is the *yeṣer* here ontologically independent or just a normal human tendency? Certainly that image of "handing someone over to someone's control" (מסר + ביד) is an image normally – though not always[28] – employed in contexts of physical oppression by one's opponents, often military opponents (e.g. Tg Ezek 16:27; 21:16), which implies a certain autonomy to the *yeṣer*.

## 2 TARGUMS ONQELOS AND JONATHAN: CONCLUSIONS

These two cases are the only two references to a *yeṣer* in Targum Jonathan. How do they fit into the schema of the *yeṣer*'s development in rabbinic thought as Rosen-Zvi has mapped it out? Most obviously, we are dealing with a single *yeṣer*, fitting the dominant picture in Tannaitic sources. In both cases from Targum Jonathan the *yeṣer* is antinomian in nature. This fits best with the school of R. Ishmael. But unlike the school of R. Ishmael there is no clear characterization of the *yeṣer* as an independent being: we come closest to this in the Ezekiel passage, though it is disputable, and in the Isaiah text the *yeṣer* is more or less synonymous with the "heart," rather than being an independent being residing within it. Here it aligns more closely with the portrayal of the *yeṣer* associated with R. Akiva, in Mishnah tractate Avot, and in some passages of the Tosefta, where it is understood simply as a character trait.[29]

Speaking of the evidence from the Dead Sea Scrolls, Tigchelaar observes that "there is not always a clear distinction between virtues

[25] Following the text of Ribera Florit 1988a. The variants in the Rabbinic Bibles (ביד שנאיהון ובתר יצרהון), which Levey follows in his translation (1987, 62–63), are almost certainly secondary (cf. Tg Ezek 39:23).

[26] Cf. Sir 15:14 (MS T.-S. 12.863: Beentjes 1997). Cf. Brand 2013, 93–106, citation at 101, and Hadot 1970, 91–103. Cf. Cook 2007, 82–87.

[27] See the note in Smolar and Aberbach 1983, 40.

[28] In Tg. Isa. 64:6 the people are handed over to *their sins*, a subject that can hardly be thought of as a personified being.

[29] See Rosen-Zvi 2011, 14–35.

and vices, and spirits as personifications of those virtues and vices."[30] Such an observation is also apt in the case of Targums Ezekiel and Isaiah. So, although Targums Jonathan and Onqelos cohere sufficiently with rabbinic ideology to conclude that they took shape within a broadly rabbinic milieu, their portrayal of the *yeṣer* is not a precise match with any particular Tannaitic school or corpus of literature. This is perhaps unsurprising since Tannaitic literature itself exhibits a significant degree of diversity, and all the sources are laconic and oblique in their references to the *yeṣer*. Nonetheless, there are also parallels between the Targum and the characterization of the *yeṣer* at Qumran, as we noted above. On the basis of these observations we might venture to place the exegesis of these specific verses in Targum Jonathan, and perhaps also Onqelos, in the early Tannaitic period, before the influence of the characterization of the *yeṣer* of the school of R. Ishmael began to become pervasive,[31] and perhaps even before the association of Gen 8:21 with the *yeṣer* was made in Sifre Deuteronomy 45.

Such a conclusion is in line with the commonly held and plausible consensus that Targums Jonathan and Onqelos took shape in Palestine in the early Tannaitic period before being reworked into its current form in Babylonia in the Amoraic period. The extent of the reworking is unclear: some new material was certainly introduced, but the reworking may have been limited at many points to adjusting the language to Babylonian Aramaic. This certainly seems to be case as far as its presentation of the *yeṣer* is concerned, so there seems little reason to doubt that we are dealing with material from the Targums' Tannaitic stratum in these verses.

## 3 PALESTINIAN TARGUM TRADITIONS

Let us turn our attention now to other early Palestinian Targum traditions.

### 3.1 Genesis 6:5 and 8:21

We have already discussed Onqelos's rendering of Gen 6:5 and 8:21 above and, as is common, Targum Neofiti is close to Onqelos, but has a plus in both of these verses that is of interest. In Gen 6:5 Neofiti reads:

[30] Tigchelaar 2008, 352. [31] Rosen-Zvi 2011, 34.

every *yeṣer* (יצר) of the thoughts of their hearts was only an evil *meditation* (הגיין)[32] the whole day long.[33]

The same word is added again in Gen 8:21:

because the *yeṣer* of the human heart is an evil *meditation* (הגיין ביש) *{for them}* (להוון) from their youth.[34]

Although it is difficult to be precise about the semantic range covered by this additional lexeme (i.e. הגין), the verbal root (הגי) seems to be closer to the English "to meditate, to reflect, to reason" (often in connection with the Law) rather than "to think," hence "meditation."[35] There is no obvious connection between this root and the *yeṣer* in rabbinic literature, yet the cognate verbal root is used to describe the activity of the heart already in biblical texts (e.g. Isa 33:18; Prov 15:28; 24:2) and this association probably explains its appearance here in Neofiti. Indeed, by introducing this lexeme Neofiti seeks to explain how exactly the *yeṣer* of the heart should be understood in these contexts, namely, that the *yeṣer* of the heart is actually the heart's reasoning or meditation. Since this particular lexeme (i.e. הגין) is so often connected with meditating on the Law or deducing a principal from the Law, Neofiti may also be hinting at the *yeṣer*'s antinomian character, though such a conclusion remains speculative.

## 3.2 Deuteronomy 31:21

There are two other places in Targum Neofiti in which the *yeṣer* is explicitly qualified as evil (Gen 4:7; Deut 31:21). Deuteronomy 31:21

[32] It is possible to read this as a participle (i.e. הָגֵיין) – also at Tg Neof Gen 8:21 (הגיין) and Tg Neof Num 11:1 (הגין), as Díez Macho (1968) has done, treating יצר as conveying the plural ("pensamientos"). A nominal function (הגין Emph. הגינא) is a better fit with the syntax in all three verses.

[33] A marginal note reads וכל יצר מחשבות טובא הגיין ביש כל יומיא (perhaps: "every *yeṣer* of thoughts of goodness [was only] an evil meditation all the days"). Probably an error, based on Gen 8:21 (MT ויאמר יהוה אל לבו; Tg Neof ואמר ייי במחשבת לבה; Tg Neof margin ואמר ייי במחשבת לבה טובה).

[34] Golomb considers להוון (unique in Tg Neof) to be a learned copyist error derived from Babylonian Talmudic Aramaic (1985, 170) and therefore to be read as third masculine plural imperfect peal of הוה, taking הגיין to be a participle. This is surely incorrect. As Díez Macho has proposed in his critical edition of the text (*ad loc*) the form להוון is almost certainly a scribal error: a corruption of לבהון, which would easily be explained as a dittography since this morpheme occurs three words earlier.

[35] E.g. Tg. Jos. 1:8; cf. y. Ber. 5.9a in some versions; Tg. Ps.-J. Deut 6:7; 30:14. The attestations at Qumran (4Q531 39.1; 4Q541 2i.6(?)) are too fragmentary to allow precision concerning their contextual signification.

belongs to an address by the Lord to Moses, in which the Lord informs him of his imminent death and explains that the people will "play the harlot" once he is dead. Moses' response is to write a song so that, as the Hebrew text has it, "when many evils and afflictions have come upon [them] then this song shall bear witness before them – for it shall not be forgotten from the mouths of their descendants – because I know their *yeṣer*, which they have already formulated (יצרו אשר הוא עשה היום), [even] before I have brought them to the land that I swore [to them]." The translation is awkward because the Hebrew is problematic: it is not clear how best to translate *yeṣer* here, or for that matter the verb (עשה, rendered "formulate" in the translation just given) of which the *yeṣer* is the object. Among the ancient Versions, Aquila reads τὸ πλάσμα, i.e. something formed or molded,[36] the route followed by many modern translations.[37] The Septuagint, however, renders the relevant clause by "for I know their evil (design)" (ἐγὼ γὰρ οἶδα τὴν πονηρίαν αὐτων; cf. LXX Exod 32:12). This is clearly interpretative – an attempt to resolve the obscurity of the Hebrew[38] – but it is a striking coincidence with what we find in Neofiti. With the exception of some typical Targumic features, such as the avoidance of anthropomorphic depictions of God,[39] Onqelos's translation is fairly literal, and Neofiti (and Pseudo-Jonathan) stand extremely close to Onqelos at this verse, with one notable exception: the *yeṣer* in Neofiti is identified as the *evil yeṣer*.[40]

As far as the problematic Hebrew verb (i.e. עשה) is concerned, Neofiti translates with an Aramaic verb (עבד) that has an almost identical semantic range. Interestingly, however, this Aramaic verb on rare occasions carries over the meaning of its Hebrew homograph, yielding the sense "to serve" (e.g. Deut 28:48; we would expect the verb (פלח).[41] At something of a stretch, then, we might translate Targum Neofiti "because their evil *yeṣer*, which they are *serving* today, is revealed before me." If (and it is a big if) intended, this is a brilliant sleight of the translational hand.

The three verses just discussed are the only verses that discuss the *yeṣer* in Neofiti that are not also attested in other genuinely Palestinian Targums

[36] Cf. Wevers' (1995) retroversion of Theodotion from the Syro-Hexapla: *semen eorum*.

[37] E.g. JPS, RSV, TOB. [38] Dogniez and Harl 1992, 318; Wevers 1995, 503.

[39] E.g. "It has been revealed before me" (Tg. Onq.) instead of "I know" (MT). Another example would be Onqelos's adjustment of the grammatically singular forms (with implied plural sense) to grammatically plural forms.

[40] I.e. Tg. Neof.: יצרהון בישה; Tg. Ps.-J.: יצרהון בישא; Tg. Onq.: יצרהון.

[41] More frequently in this sense the quadriliteral root שעבד (e.g. Tg. Neof. Gen 15:13, 14; Exod 21:6). Related nouns (עבד "servant, slave," עבדותא "slavery") are common.

(excluding Onqelos).[42] Sadly, they do not give us a great deal to go on in terms of characterizing the *yeṣer*, only that it is evil and that it is an activity of the mind (idiomatically, the heart).

We will return to Neofiti's understanding of the *yeṣer* below. Before we do, let us look at a Targumic tradition that is not only attested in Neofiti (along with its marginal glosses), but also in the Genizah manuscripts of Palestinian Targum, and the (so-called) Fragment Targums. These distinct sources share a common textual tradition to Gen 4:7.

## 3.3 Genesis 4:7

In the Hebrew text of Gen 4:7 the Lord addresses Cain following his rejection of (or more accurately, disregard for) Cain's offering in favor of that of his brother, Abel:

"Surely, if you do right, there is uplifting,"[43] the Lord says, "but if you do not do right sin couches at the door; its urge is toward you, yet you can rule over it."

This translation follows the Hebrew text, with the major grammatical problems – always rich fodder for the ancient exegete – ironed out (as we will see). The grammatical problem that interests us concerns the clause "its urge is toward you" (ואליך תשוקתו). The pronoun ("its") is masculine, but "sin" (חטאת) is feminine, so to what does the pronoun refer? The Palestinian Targum tradition has an answer: the evil *yeṣer*.

Dating Palestinian Targum traditions is notoriously problematic, but I am going to begin with the text as it is found in our oldest manuscript, a fragment from the Cairo Genizah collection of what was probably once a continuous manuscript of the entire Pentateuch, dated around 1000 CE.[44] This is a good place to start since the Genizah fragments of the Palestinian Targum to the Pentateuch generally contain fewer scribal errors than Neofiti, and hence are a more reliable witness.[45] In the Palestinian Targum preserved in this Genizah manuscript the address to Cain is transformed into:

Surely if you improve your deeds in this world, it will be pardoned and forgiven you in the world to come; but if you do not improve your deeds in this world, then your sin is retained for the day of judgment. Indeed at the gate of the heart, sin

[42] Frg Tgs do not cover these verses and they have not been preserved among the Genizah manuscripts of Palestinian Targum to the Pentateuch.

[43] Possibly "forgiveness" (cf. verb נשא in Gen 18:24, 26; Exod 32:32; 34:7; Num 14:18, 19; also נשא עון Isa 33:24; נשא פשע Ps 32:1).

[44] MS Antonin Ebr. III B, Saltykov-Schedrin collection, Leningrad, according to Klein 1986.

[45] Flesher and Chilton 2011, 76.

couches, but in your hands I have placed control over the evil *yeṣer* (מסרת רשותיה דיצרא בישא), and you shall rule over it [the *yeṣer*][46] whether to sin or to be innocent.

As one might expect, the same text is preserved in the Fragment Targums[47] and in Targum Neofiti with some minor variants.

The reference to the evil *yeṣer* here needs to be read in a broader narrative context to be properly understood. All the sources expand the following verse (Gen 4.8) to create a dialogue between Cain and Abel that enables these Targums to explain the apparent arbitrariness of God's action. In the fullest version of this discussion, which is recorded in the Fragment Targums, Cain denies the existence of judgment, a judge, a world to come (עלם אוחרן), reward for the righteous, and retribution for the wicked. He concludes that the world was not created nor is it governed (מדבר) with mercy (ברחמין), and this explains why Abel's offering was accepted and his not. Abel refutes each of these claims in turn and concludes by explaining that it was "because the fruits of [my] deeds were better than yours, [that] my offering was favourably accepted."

Neofiti and the Genizah manuscript offer a substantially shorter version of this disputation with some variations that need not concern us here[48] since the concluding point remains the same: namely, that God did not act arbitrarily. Rather, each of the brothers was repaid according to the merit of his deeds.[49] Indeed, this is the very same point made in the Divine address to Cain in the preceding verse (cited above):

if you improve your deeds in this world, it will be pardoned and forgiven you in the world to come; but if you do not improve your deeds in this world, then your sin is retained for the day of judgment.

The themes are much the same as those that we encountered in the verses we examined from Targum Jonathan (i.e. theodicy, reward for the righteous),[50] but the narrative here is clearly didactic – and this is where

[46] The Hebrew is ambiguous, and probably corrupt. The noun "sin" (חטאת) in both form and by common usage is feminine, yet it appears to govern a masculine participle (רבץ "couches"). The indirect object pronoun (בו) is masculine, so could mean "you can rule over it" (but with no clear referent) or "you can rule over him," namely Abel. The Targum opts for the former as does, e.g., Symmachus and Jerome: Hayward 1995, 121–22. Cf. Gen. Rab. 22.6. LXX and Theodotion, on the other hand, opt for the latter: see Harl 1986, 114–15.

[47] According to Klein 1980. [48] See, e.g., Marmorstein 1931, 235–37; Bassler 1986.

[49] Cf. Heb 11:4; 1 John 3:12. See McNamara 1978, 156–60. Cf. also T. Benj. 7.4–5.

[50] There are even echoes in the vocabulary: Tg Isa 62:11 talks of the reward (אגר lit. "wages") of "those who perform his word," the same term used in the Fragment Targum, i.e. "good reward for the righteous" (Frg. Tg. Gen 4.8 אגר טב לצדיקיא).

the evil *yeṣer* comes into play: if you control the evil *yeṣer* so that you perform good deeds, then you will be counted innocent and rewarded; give your evil *yeṣer* free rein and it will lead you to sin, which will be met with punishment. The text clearly implies that Cain has the power to choose (and of course, this lesson is intended for the whole audience, not just Cain). Nothing is said explicitly about Cain's choice or the *yeṣer* in the description of Abel's murder, which follows, so it is left to the reader to speculate that Cain followed the prompting (if that is the right term) of the *yeṣer* down the path of sin to murder.[51]

Let us return to the question of date. How ancient might this tradition be? In the case of Gen 4:7 we are dealing with an ancient Palestinian tradition that has been preserved in three different sources with only very minor variations. The similarities – in both the elements of translation and the expansions – are such that we must assume a common written source (i.e. a proto-Palestinian Targum). But exactly how old this textual tradition might be is difficult to ascertain. The Genizah manuscript provides a *terminus ante quem* (ca. 1000 CE) for this tradition. One source that might help us date this material is Targum Onqelos. The text of Onqelos and the Palestinian Targums to the first half of Genesis 4:7 are sufficiently similar for us to assume that they are textually related: the proto-Palestinian Targum probably developed from proto-Onqelos – that is, in the first stage of Onqelos's composition (the Tannaitic phase). Yet there is no reference to the *yeṣer* at this point in Targum Onqelos, which offers a much simpler interpretation of the passage in terms of sin and repentance (i.e. "Surely if you improve your deeds it will be forgiven you, but if you do not improve your deeds then the sin [some vss. your sin] is retained for the day of judgment"). This would appear to support the conclusions reached earlier concerning Onqelos's development and date (though, of course, we cannot know what Onqelos knew but chose not to include), particularly since Gen 4:7 is already connected to the evil *yeṣer* in Sifre Deuteronomy (45), a Tannaitic source.[52] This suggests that the common Palestinian Targum source from which all our versions of Palestinian Targum have been derived (i.e. a proto-Palestinian Targum), post-dates the Tannaitic layer of Onqelos and expands upon it.

What can be said of the Palestinian Targums' characterization of the *yeṣer*? For a start, the *yeṣer* is certainly singular. If we are right in

[51] On the *yeṣer* leading to murder see Rosen-Zvi 2011, 54–55, 66, 102, 104. Cf. also Wis 10.1–3.

[52] For translation and discussion see Rosen-Zvi 2011, 21–22.

perceiving a certain equivalence between the sin couching at the door and the "evil *yeṣer*" in the Targums' rendering,[53] then the physicality of the image ("*couching* at the door") would imply that the *yeṣer* is an independent being. Furthermore, the clause "you shall rule over it whether to sin or to be innocent" makes clear that the *yeṣer* can be overpowered, though no indication is given concerning how it is to be overpowered (Torah study is the usual method advocated in classical rabbinic sources).[54] The same clause also implies judicial categories (i.e. "innocent" or "sinful")[55] and, as such, suggests its antinomian character. Taken together, this characterization aligns closely with what we find in the Tannaitic homily in Sifre Deuteronomy 45 and in other sources from the school of R. Ishmael,[56] and certainly a late Tannaitic or early Amoraic date is at least plausible for the material common to the Palestinian Targums.

Returning to the material attested in Neofiti, but not found in other Palestinian Targums (excluding Onqelos; Tg. Neof. Gen 6:5; 8:21; Deut 31:21), we seem to be faced with a slightly different picture. Neofiti's rendering of Gen 6:5 and 8:21 would seem to rule out an understanding of the *yeṣer* as an independent being. This would fit more comfortably with the presentation of the *yeṣer* in the Mishnah, where the term marks a negative human trait.[57] That a single text contains different stances is not inexplicable, if we assume that Neofiti has added material – either of the author's invention or from another source – to the proto-Palestinian Targum source.[58]

[53] Cf. Sifre Deut 45; b. Ber. 61a (a tradition attributed to R. Samuel that cites Gen 4:7 in support of the view that the evil *yeṣer* is like a kind of wheat – a pun, i.e. חטאת "sin" versus חטה "wheat" – probably alluding to a tradition that identified the forbidden fruit eaten by Adam as wheat: see b. Ber. 40a).

[54] E.g. b. Qidd. 30b (specifically connected to Gen 4:7). Cf. Midr. Pss. [Buber] 119.64; b. Sanh. 91b; Avot R. Nat. A 16. The concept of Torah as an effective countermeasure against the human tendency to sin has ancient foundations: see Brand 2013, 130–31.

[55] On quite different grounds, the Septuagint understands the problem with Cain's offering in judicial terms, specifically of ritual fault: "If you brought correctly but did not divide [the offering] correctly, then have you not sinned?" If Rufinus' Latin translation is to be trusted, Origen (*Hom. Exod.* 13.4) develops an exegetical point from the wording of the Septuagint, arguing that, while one's own understanding and personal discipline constitutes a proper offering, it is not sufficient unless shared, hence the text says not only *recte offert* but also *recte dividit*.

[56] Rosen-Zvi 2011, 18–28. [57] Rosen-Zvi 2011, 29–30.

[58] See further Flesher and Chilton 2011, 71–129, 151–66; McNamara 1992, 1–46.

## 4 CONCLUSION

Let me offer some comments by way of conclusion. The first thing that strikes us when examining the *yeṣer* in these early strata of Targumic literature is that the *yeṣer* is largely absent: none of the Targums studied has much to say about it. This may in part be a question of genre: the Targums are after all limited to some extent by the constraints of translation. Nonetheless, what we have appears to fit fairly comfortably into the characterization of the *yeṣer* in Tannaitic literature, particularly when we consider the question of reification. This in turn, appears to fit with a scholarly consensus (not universally held, admittedly) concerning the Targums' dates: namely, that Onqelos and Jonathan were committed to writing in Palestine in the second century CE and then subsequently revised in the Babylonian Academies, while the proto-Palestinian Targum began to take written form about a century later, before undergoing a fluid transmission history that has resulted in a diverse array of recensions.

11

# "Gnostic" Theologies of Evil

Timothy Pettipiece

The second century CE saw the rise of the first wave of speculative Christian theologies. Leading thinkers in this group, such as Valentinus, Ptolemaeus, Marcion, and Basilides – working in cultural centers like Alexandria, Antioch, and Rome – sought to address some of the core theological quandaries of their day such as the nature of creation, emergent Christianity's relationship to its Jewish heritage, and the origin of evil – issues which are all inextricably linked. Unlike their later proto-orthodox rivals who would seek the genesis of wickedness in the movements of the human will, members of the first wave opted for largely metaphysical solutions to the problem of evil. As such, these thinkers had a very different understanding of cosmology and anthropology than their rivals who eventually sidelined them as purveyors of "false *gnosis*" and heresy. As such, this chapter will explore some of the "gnostic" explanations for evil and the human inclination to evil based on a range of ancient, albeit fragmentary, sources.

While a great deal has been and continues to be written on the concept of Gnosticism and how to define its characteristics,[1] there can be no doubt that the basis for many of the theologies which writers such as Irenaeus and Hippolytus[2] condemned as "false *gnosis*"[3] were a radical reimagining of the traditional Genesis creation story. At some point, probably in the late first century CE, the traditional Judaic notion of a more-or-less benign creator

[1] Williams 1996; King 2003; Brakke 2010. [2] Vallée 1981.

[3] Something that has often been overlooked in discussion of the "gnostic" label is just how proto-orthodox writers used the term. The problem was not that some Christians claimed to have *gnosis*, which was a well-established spiritual gift, but that the content of such revealed knowledge was judged to be false (see Pettipiece 2018).

god was turned inside out. Instead, the creator of the world was condemned as an impostor who wickedly conspired to prevent human beings from acquiring knowledge of the true god hidden in the divine realm beyond the cosmos. This malevolent Demiurge, as he was often called, was said to be the product of a disastrous degeneration of divine being, and the world that he fashioned, including human beings themselves, was seen as deficient if not outright evil. According to this radical "protest exegesis,"[4] as it has been called, the Jewish god came to be seen as an adversary rather than an advocate and the Garden of Eden as a prison rather than a paradise.

Whether or not Jews or Christians (or some mixture thereof) first developed this alternate narrative remains an open question.[5] It was, however, rapidly integrated into the speculative theologies of several important second-century Christian teachers, including those that Irenaeus, in his work *Against the Heresies*, labeled followers of Valentinus.[6] Little is known of Valentinus himself,[7] other than that he was a second-century Egyptian theologian who spent time in Rome, where he was nearly elected bishop. A small number of fragments have been attributed to him, drawn largely from the writings of Clement of Alexandria. One of these deals with the Evil Inclination:

> And one there is who is good! His free act of speaking is the manifestation of the son. And through him alone can a heart become pure, when every evil spirit has been put out of the heart. The many spirits dwelling in the heart do not permit it to become pure: rather, each of them performs its own acts, violating it in various ways with improper desires. And in my opinion the heart experiences something like what happens in a caravansary. For the latter is full of holes and dug up and often filled with dung, because while they are there, people live in an utterly vulgar way and take no forethought for the property since it belongs to someone else. Just so, a heart too is impure by being the habitation of many demons, until it experiences forethought. But when the father, who alone is good, visits the heart, he makes it holy and fills it with light. And so a person who has such a heart is called blessed, for that person will see god.[8]

Using a typically evocative image, Valentinus compares the human heart – which we might understand as the seat of intention – to a squalid merchant camp crowded by conflicting desires, which he calls "evil spirits." Only when the Father enters the heart can it be purified and the desire to

[4] Rudolph 1983, 54; Williams 1996, 54–57.

[5] The only plausible circumstance is a radical reimagining of the Genesis narrative in reaction to the destruction of the Jewish Temple by the Romans in 70 CE (Grant 1966, 34)

[6] Thomassen 2006. [7] Lampe 2003; Markschies 1992; Dunderberg 2008.

[8] Clement of Alexandria, *Strom.* II.114.3–6, trans. Layton 1987 (frg. H).

do evil dispelled. Yet this would seem to be an act of grace, since it is only when the Father decides to "visit the heart" that such a purification can occur. This fits with the generally deterministic outlook of Valentinian thought, which divided humanity into three classes: spirituals, psychics, and material (Irenaeus 1.6). According to the Valentinian *Tripartite Tractate*[9] from the Nag Hammadi codices:

> The spiritual substance is one and a single image [. . .] its sickness is the condition [. . .] form. As for the substance of those who are psychical, its condition is double, because it has an understanding of what is superior, and confesses it, but it is <also> inclined toward evil on account of the inclination of the presumptuous thought. And as far as the material substance is concerned, its impulses are diverse and take many forms. It was a sickness that assumed many kinds of inclinations. The first human, then, is a mixed molding and a mixed creation, and a depository of those on the left and those on the right, as well as of a spiritual Word, and his sentiments are divided between each of the two substances to which he owes his existence.[10]

According to this Valentinian anthropology, human beings are mixed creatures, with differing proportions of the three basic substances. Those with a high degree of spiritual substance have easy access to knowledge and salvation, while those who are material are lost in the world of idolatry and error. The middle class, the psychics, are somewhere in between. They may have a limited access to saving knowledge, but are still inclined to follow their evil impulses. In this way, the presence or absence of an evil inclination in the individual is largely the result of the cosmic order that has allotted the basic elements in differing proportions. As Clement of Alexandria remarks, Valentinus "supposes that there is a people that by its (very) nature is saved."[11]

A similar idea is expressed by Heracleon, alleged to have been a student of Valentinus. Heracleon,[12] who authored the first known commentary on the Gospel of John, explained Jesus' statement in John 8:44 ("You are from your father the devil, and you choose to do your father's desires") as referring not to the materials, who are the devil's children "by nature," but to the psychics, who are the devil's children "by intent" (Origen, *Comm. Jo.* 20.24). Heracleon seems to have equated the materials with traditional polytheists and the psychics with "the Jews" of John's Gospel, although he likely had in mind proto-orthodox Christians who sought to

[9] Thomassen and Painchaud 1989.
[10] *Tri. Trac.* 106 (NHC I; trans. Thomassen); (Meyer 2007).
[11] Clement of Alexandria, *Strom.* IV.89.2–4 (trans. Layton, frg. F).
[12] Pettipiece 2002; Brooke 1891.

maintain a link with Jewish tradition. As a result, the Valentinians seem to have drawn a link between an individual's capacity for sin and their ability to receive divine *gnosis*. While the materials cannot even gain access to divine knowledge, the spirituals receive it by default – one group is inherently sinful, the other is inherently redeemed. The psychics, however, occupy the middle ground in being offered *gnosis* but then willfully rejecting it. Thus we have something that verges on a doctrine of free will, yet at the same time deterministically excludes most people from exercising any kind of personal agency.

Basilides too, another second-century Egyptian theologian, discussed the human impulse to commit evil in vivid metaphorical terms, also preserved by Clement:

> A newborn baby, then, has never sinned before; or more precisely, it has not actually committed any sins, but within itself it has the activity of sinning. Whenever it experiences suffering, it receives benefit, profiting by many unpleasant experiences. Just so, if by chance a grown man has not sinned by deed and yet suffers, he suffered the suffering for the same reason as the newborn baby: he has within himself sinfulness, and the only reason he has not sinned (in deed) is because he has not had the occasion to do so. Thus not sinning cannot be imputed to him. Indeed, someone who intends to commit adultery is an adulterer even without succeeding in the act, and someone who intends to commit murder is a murderer even without being able to commit the act.[13]

Basilides saw the capacity to sin as an inherent part of the human condition and embraced Jesus' dramatic emphasis on the will to sin from the Sermon on the Mount. The mere desire to sin constitutes a sin in and of itself. Therefore, evil need not be actualized, it simply has to be intended. Lack of intention, however, can lead to forgiveness. As he says, "not all sins are forgiven ... only those committed involuntarily and out of ignorance" (Clement of Alexandria, *Strom.* IV.153.4). As we might expect, the connection between sin and ignorance is a theme explored by several "gnostic" theologians. Yet, as the previous fragment seems to imply, suffering serves as evidence of sinfulness even if the sufferer is not aware. It could even be that those sins were committed in a previous life (Clement of Alexandria, *Strom.* IV.83.2). Like Valentinus and Heracleon, Basilides taught that only those who were "by nature faithful and elect" (Clement of Alexandria, *Strom.* V.3.2–4) could hope to be redeemed, which, according to Clement, caused him to view the old and new covenants as "superfluous." Salvation depended solely on one's essential nature, not in one's attitude or actions.

[13] Basilides, frg. G (Clement of Alexandria, *Strom.* IV.82.1–2 [trans. Layton]).

One of the more unusual of the so-called gnostic teachings is Hippolytus' summary of a treatise known as *Baruch* by the teacher Justin, which is a peculiar blend of Jewish and Greek mythological motifs. According to this work, the world was created by a pair of divine powers known as Elohim and Eden. When Elohim decided to return to the divine realm, Eden was left abandoned and in her anger caused discord and sin among human beings:

Then Eden, knowing that she had been abandoned by Elohim, in her grief set her own angels beside her and adorned herself becomingly, in the hope that Elohim might fall into desire and come to her. But as Elohim, held fast by "the Good," came down no more to Eden, Eden commanded Babel (who is Aphrodite) to effect adulteries and divorces among men, in order that, just as she herself had been separated from Elohim, so also the spirit of Elohim might be pained and tormented by such separations, and suffer the same as the abandoned Eden.[14]

Here too suffering and sin is an externally imposed consequence of cosmic preconditions. The alienation and anger of Eden also causes one of her angels, named Naas (from the Hebrew for "snake") to rape both Adam and Eve, thereby causing further transgressions of the law (Hippolytus, *Haer.* 5.26.23). In an attempt to remedy this situation, Elohim sends Baruch, his revelatory spirit, to select a series of prophets – who include not only Moses and Jesus, but Heracles (!) – to enlighten humanity about the wickedness of Eden. Yet, just as in the Valentinian teaching, some are more naturally receptive to this message than others, since Justin is also said to have divided human beings into spirituals, psychics, and materials (Hippolytus, *Haer.* 5.26). In such a scenario, human beings are little more than pawns in a vast incomprehensible struggle between cosmic powers.

It was not only the creation and paradise stories that were subject to radical revision. Other parts of the biblical narrative were also reappraised. For example, Epiphanius claimed that the "Sethians"[15] believed that angelic powers had sneaked Ham onto the Ark in order to perpetuate wickedness: "Inasmuch as the angels recognized that their entire people was going to be obliterated by the flood, by trickery they secretly added the aforementioned Ham in order to preserve the evil people, which had been made by them."[16] In this way, wickedness is maintained by the perpetuation of a particular genetic lineage that the Deluge failed to make extinct.

[14] Hippolytus, *Haer.* 5.26.19–21 (trans. Wilson), in Foerster 1972. [15] Turner 2001.
[16] Epiphanius, *Pan.* 39 (trans. Layton); Williams 1987.

The Sethians, or "Seed of Seth," however, are also connected by many scholars to one of the classic articulations of the demiurgical myth – the *Secret Book of John*. This work, of which we have four copies, takes the form of a revelation discourse delivered by the savior to John, which recounts the nature of the divine realm, the fall of divine Wisdom, and the rise of the Demiurge's hegemony over the cosmos. Moreover, it offers a rather negative evaluation of the human condition, since it states that the cosmic rulers "made all creation blind so that the deity above them all might not be recognized. And because of the bond of forgetfulness, their sins became hidden (to them)" (*Ap. John* 28 [trans. Layton]). Thus we see the connection again being made between sin and ignorance. From this perspective, human beings are locked into the dark enchantment of the Demiurge and unaware of their sins. Only saving knowledge – that is, *gnosis* – can break this fateful spell. In another inversion of the Genesis account, the Secret Book of John also states that it was the Demiurge and his minions who planted the tree in the Garden of Eden:

> Its root is bitter; its branches are deadly; its shade is hateful; deception resides in its leaves; its blossom is the anointing of wickedness; its fruit is death; its seed is desire; and it is in the dark that it blossoms. The dwelling place of those that eat of it is Hades, and the darkness is their realm of repose.[17]

The image of the "evil tree" is a commonplace in so-called gnostic speculations. We find a similar motif in the Gospel of Philip, also from Nag Hammadi:

> For so long as the root of evil is hidden it is mighty. But as soon as it has been recognized it has perished and as soon as it has appeared it has ceased to be. For this reason scripture says that "even now the axe is laid to the root of the trees" ... Let each one of us, too burrow for the root of evil that is within, and root it up from his or her heart. It will be rooted up when it is recognized. But if we are ignorant of it, it sinks its roots within us, and yields its crops within our hearts; dominates us; we are its slaves; it takes us captive, so that we do the things we do not want, and do [not] do the things that we want; and [it] grows powerful because we have not recognized it.[18]

Here the author uses Pauline language to evoke the seemingly insurmountable power of sin. But evil is said to be rooted in ignorance, and only recognition of the true nature of reality, by means of *gnosis*, can allow one to dig it out.

[17] *Ap. John* 21–22 (trans. Layton); Waldstein and Wisse 1995; King 2008.
[18] *Gos. Phil.* 104 (trans. Layton); Ménard 1967.

The image of the tree was also a favorite in western Manichaean speculation of the third and fourth centuries. In fact, Manichaeans drew one of their preferred archetypes for the doctrine of the two radically opposed natures of Light and Darkness from an exegesis of Matt 7:17–20. Thus, the second chapter of the theological compendium known as the *Kephalaia* is called "The Second, on the Parable of the Tree." Here, the biblical citation comes in the form of a question from Mani's disciples:

> We implore you, our / Lord, that you [teach us] and interpret for us these / two trees [which Jesus] proclaimed to his disciples, as is written / in the [Gospel, where he said]: The good tree produces / [good fruit,] although [the] evil tree produces bad fruit /[. . . There is no] good tree that produces bad fruit, / [nor is there an evil tree that] produces good fruit. / [Every tree is known by] its fruit.[19]

One of the principal points of this chapter is the fact that even though the two natures are in total ontological opposition, they are structurally similar, since they each possess the same set of five qualities, known to Manicheans as "Limbs": (1) Mind, (2) Thought, (3) Insight, (4) Counsel, and (5) Consideration. Nevertheless, the fact that the good and evil natures are structurally identical means that one can really only distinguish them by an evaluation of their "fruits," i.e. their impact on the world. As an illustration, the compiler of the chapter chooses Luke 22:3 to show how Judas "was counted among the [twelve], / but, in the end, because it is written about him that Satan [entered him] / he handed the Saviour over to the Jews" (19.1–3). Similarly, chapter 2 alludes to 15:9 by stating that "[it is written about] / Paul that he was a persecutor at first . . . the church / of God, as he persecuted . . . " (6–8). This furnishes additional proof that people, and by extension natures, are not always what they appear to be. Judas seemed good, but turned out to be evil; Paul seemed evil, but turned out to be good.

Manicheans were also keenly aware of the vicissitudes of salvation. For, even if someone received the gift of enlightenment, which Manicheans called the "Light-Mind," constant vigilance was necessary to combat the rebellious nature of sin. After all, in Manichean thought Sin is a personified cosmic force and darkness is a substance that makes up part of humanity's mixed nature. It always retains the ability to reassert itself and reawaken the Evil Inclination. Borrowing from Paul, they used the image of the Old Man and the New Man. However much the New

[19] *Kephalaia* (Berlin) 17.2–9 (trans. mine), see Pettipiece 2009; Schmidt et al. 1940.

Man may suppress the Old Man, sin and evil can sometimes overpower. *Kephalaia* Chapter 38 describes just such a situation:

> But if he does not strengthen this watch, (Sin) (will) come back and put on and disturb his Mind, which was originally at rest. It (will) disturb his love for his Teacher and his instructor. It (will) remove from his heart the love for the Church and fill it totally with hate, and all his brothers (will) become hateful to him. His brothers and his beloved and his companions, who love him, they (will) be like enemies to him. Now, if this man is disturbed in this way, and he abandons his love and his desire to change himself, (then) this man (will) become, in turn, a lost vessel and he (will) leave the Church and he (will) reach his end in the world. The Mind which was in him (will) be dispersed from him and return to the Apostle who sent it. He becomes filled with evil spirits and they play with [him], drawing him here and there, and he, in turn, becomes like an worldly man, changing and being like a bird plucked of its feathers {and becomes earthly}.[20]

As this passage so poignantly describes, even an elite member of the Church, an Elect, can fall victim to the pressures of sin and become an apostate alienated from the community. Such an understanding represents a more developed view of sin than we seem to have in the earlier gnostic speculations. Whereas teachers such as Valentinus and Basilides tended to view salvation as a byproduct of one's essential nature, leaving little room for the will, Manicheans acknowledged the continued need for vigilance and effort in the face of sin's continued power. For Manicheans, then, evil is a matter of both nature and will.

It should not be surprising, then, to find echoes of the Manichaean formulation of the Evil Inclination in one of Augustine's treatments of the same topic. For, in Book 14 of the *City of God* we read:

> Accordingly God, as it is written, made man upright, and consequently with a good will. For if he had not had a good will, he could not have been upright. The good will, then, is the work of God; for God created him with it. But the first evil will, which preceded all man's evil acts, was rather a kind of falling away from the work of God to its own works than any positive work. And therefore the acts resulting were evil, not having God, but the will itself for their end; so that the will or the man himself, so far as his will is bad, was as it were the evil tree bringing forth evil fruit.[21]

Augustine here seems to suggest that human beings, although created good, are still mixed creatures in the sense that they possess both good and evil wills. For him, evil is not a substance but an absence. Should the

[20] *Kephalaia* (Berlin) 99.2–17 (trans. mine).

[21] Augustine, *Civ.* 14.11 (trans. NPNF).

will turn away from the good and to evil, then the individual is alienated from God and brings forth fruit of the evil tree.

A liminal figure in so many ways, Augustine was in a rather unique position. A former Manichaean "Hearer" now turned champion of Nicene orthodoxy, he spent a great deal of energy trying to disentangle himself from his Manichaean past and provide a way into orthodoxy for his former Manichaean friends. But, as Jason BeDuhn has persuasively argued in the second volume of his work *Augustine's Manichaean Dilemma*, many of the bishop of Hippo's core theological positions were developed while wrestling with his Manichaean past, including the notion of "original sin."[22] Augustine, however, did not provide Manichean answers to Catholic questions, as some ancient and modern commentators have accused him of doing, but Catholic answers to Manichean questions.

In this way, Augustine's thought conforms to the general pattern of Christian theology since the second century. More often than not, proto-orthodox authors found themselves reacting to previously formulated positions that they viewed as flawed or problematic. Therefore, when Irenaeus, Clement, and later Origen sought to lay out the parameters of early Christian thought, they were doing so in response to a series of highly developed speculative theologies. Ultimately, this first generation of Christian theologians, with their radical revision of Genesis and deterministic sense of human nature, were repudiated in favor of a more positive and inclusive view of the world and humanity's place in it. At the core of this process was the question of evil, and, without the bold and adventurous answers sought by the so-called heretics, the orthodox position would have never formed.

As was stated at the outset, the questions of cosmogony, continuity with Judaism, and evil were all inextricably linked. The gnostic rejection of the creation and the Jewish god came at a delicate time for early Christians. It is precisely in the second century that the early Christian movement was increasingly coming to the attention of Roman authorities, who accused Christians of (among other things) abandoning the ways of their ancestors. In order to counter this claim, it was important for apologetic purposes for Christians to maintain a link to their Jewish heritage – particularly its scriptures. As a result, a new way to solve the problem of evil had to be put forward, one which exonerated divinity and

[22] BeDuhn 2013.

implicated humanity; one which made sin and evil not a matter of nature but of will.

Finally, I would like to suggest that in most instances the rhetoric of sin and evil has more to do with sectarian group dynamics than purely theological abstraction. These categories were used to delineate who was inside and who was outside a given religious community. In the sources presented above, those who accept a particular cosmological myth can claim to have *gnosis* and the status of the "spiritual" elite. Those who do not are said to be lost in the outer darkness. Thus, the "Evil Inclination," whatever it might be, is ultimately the impulse that draws the individual away from the community and serves as an effective instrument for religious groups of various sorts to police their boundaries and determine membership.

# 12

# The Rabbinic "Inclination" (*yeṣer*) and the Christian Apocrypha

Monika Pesthy-Simon

If one wishes to look for parallels to the rabbinic *yeṣer* in Christian Apocrypha one must first know what these Apocrypha are. This, however, is far from easy. According to the most widespread understanding of the word, "the (Christian) apocrypha are texts with the ambition of belonging to the biblical writings but without being included into the canon."[1] This meaning of the word "apocryphon" originated with Protestants in the seventeenth century during the theological debates with Catholics and, as time went on, a corpus (we could almost say, a canon) of apocryphal writings came into being. The notion, however, raises a number of problems: the majority of Apocrypha were not intended to become "canonic" (their titles were often added only afterwards); when the early Apocrypha were written the canon had not yet been created; according to this definition no Apocryphon could have been written after the closing of the canon, but many writings composed much later are considered as such; this notion is not an academic but a theological one, and its meaning varies according to the theological conviction of a given religious community (e.g. OT Apocrypha are not the same for Catholics and Protestants).[2] As P. Tóth puts it: "The interpretation of the apocrypha according to the biblical canon … seems very questionable in terms of academic objectivity."[3]

[1] Tóth 2011, 45.

[2] In the 5th edition of the *NT apocrypha* Schneemelcher tries to circumscribe more cautiously what Christian apocrypha are, but the basic elements remained the same (Hennecke and Schneemelcher 1991, 1:61).

[3] Tóth 2011, 49.

To remedy these shortcomings, Bovon and Geoltrain, in the preface to the collection edited by them, characterize (Christian) Apocrypha as follows: "(They are) texts which conserve memorial traditions about biblical personalities and events, about the figures of Christianity or Jewish tradition. They are writings of various literary genres and of divers origins preserved in numerous manuscripts and in a great variety of languages."[4] According to them, it is not their origin but their future fate that distinguishes the Apocrypha from the canonical writings: while the latter are unchangeable, the former were continually rewritten, transformed, and translated. This definition (or rather description), however, opens the door too wide: homilies of unknown origin elaborating on biblical scenes also fit it,[5] and as no time-limit is given, medieval texts equally found their way into the corpus of Apocrypha. The discussion concerning the meaning of Apocrypha continues, but no useful and unambiguous definition has been found so far.[6]

As for the adjective "Christian," here again we face some difficulties, because in several cases (some of them quite important) it cannot be determined with certainty whether a document is Jewish or Christian, or to what extent is it Jewish or Christian.[7] And we should not forget that also OT Apocrypha can be Christian.[8]

Another question is whether we should include Gnostic texts in our corpus (we leave aside the equally debatable question of what exactly "Gnostic" means). The Gospel of Philip and the Gospel of Truth can surely be called Christian Apocrypha, but generally they are treated under the heading of "Nag Hammadi texts." As for the Acts of Thomas, which unquestionably belongs to the Apocrypha, the extent to which it can be considered Gnostic is still under discussion. The Acts of John, another well-known Apocryphon, is surely not Gnostic, but contains some very markedly Gnostic passages (chs. 94–102) inserted into the text later.

Naturally, it is not our task to resolve these problems. Rather, I wanted to point out that no thorough treatment of the rabbinic *yeṣer* (or simply

[4] Bovon and Geoltrain 1997, xx.

[5] Some were included in the second volume of the collection (Geoltrain and Kaestli 2005, 63–74, 103–04, 1555–78) while the vast majority of the homiletic material was completely disregarded: cf. Tóth 2011, 79–80.

[6] See Tóth 2011.

[7] E. g. T. 12 Patr.; Ascen. Isa. was thought to contain both Jewish and Christian parts, until Norelli showed that the whole writing is Christian: Norelli 1994.

[8] E.g. Odes Sol.

the origin of sin) in Christian Apocrypha can be made until we know exactly what Christian Apocrypha are. The writings called by this name display such diversity that it is hazardous to pronounce general statements about them. Nonetheless, these texts constitute a very important part of early Christian literature and cannot be left out of consideration when we want to understand the development of Christian ideas.

After these preliminary remarks, I propose to examine some passages which I consider relevant for our topic, found in such writings which are conventionally called Christian Apocrypha. We shall treat only second- or third-century texts, because this period constitutes the transition between the NT and the systematic patristic thinking about the origins and causes of sin.

The *yeṣer* as such does not appear in Christian Apocrypha, but they contain some very interesting passages describing how evil operates in our world. These passages deserve our attention: we intend to look for similarities with the *yeṣer*,[9] and, if such similarities are found, to ask ourselves about their meaning and origin.

## 1 ACTS OF ANDREW

The Acts of Andrew was probably composed between 150 and 200, the third century being the *terminus ad quem*. The place of origin is unknown, but Alexandria has been proposed as a possible intellectual milieu.[10]

A difficult passage, containing lacunae, describes the methods used by the devil against humanity (Acts Andr. 49–50).[11] Andrew explains to his disciples that before the coming of Christ the whole of humanity was in the power of the devil, who could therefore appear in a friendly guise; but since he has been unmasked by Christ, he now has to fight openly. The second phase of the cosmic battle, in which the devil attacks Christians through external evils such as persecutions, is not really interesting for us, but the description of the first phase contains some useful details (we quote only the most important portions):

> Thinking that he (i.e. the devil) will keep them (i.e. human beings) in his power and rule over them forever, he attacks them in such a way that he makes the enmity

[9] Concerning the *yeṣer* I rely on the writings of Rosen-Zvi (2008, 2009, 2011) without always expressly mentioning them.

[10] Cf. J.-M. Prieur, *Actes d'André*, in Bovon and Geoltrain 1997, 881.

[11] It is part of a longer speech delivered by Andrew in the prison. For the very problematic text we possess only a single manuscript. See also the English translation in the *NT apocrypha* (Hennecke and Schneemelcher 1991, 2:133).

between them resemble friendship. For he often depicted certain things of his own (τὰ ἴδια), which he suggested (ὑπερβάλλων) to them [and] by which he expected to dominate them, as delightful and deceptive. So, he did not appear openly as an enemy but feigned friendship worthy of them.[12]

The subject is always the devil; the other (designated sometimes in singular, sometimes in plural in the Greek) attacked by him is humankind, or the spiritual element in humans. What tactic does the devil employ?

He presented a person with his suggestions as if they were coming from within (the verb used for this – ὑπερβάλλω – would become a *terminus technicus* of demonic suggestion in monastic literature), and when he was unmasked by Christ he had to change tactics. This corresponds exactly to the machinations of the *yeṣer*: "The *yetzer*, just like the demons, can work only incognito. Therefore identifying a specific argument as the advice of the *yetzer* neutralizes its effect."[13]

The suggestions are delightful and deceptive; so are the things presented by the *yeṣer*, we only have to think of the case of Boaz.

He shows friendship (φιλία); we have an interesting parallel to this in b. Ḥag. 16a, a text to which we shall return below.[14] In later monastic writings the demons always attack by means of thoughts; the *yeṣer*, on the contrary, prefers deeds. Here the question is left open: the devil suggests "his own" (τὰ ἴδια).

He offers gifts.[15] The text presents the transformation of an internalized enemy into an external one. This latter, attacking only Christians, shows some similarities with the "national enemy" of the Israelites, but his attacks are external: he causes pain and trouble to the believers. In Judaism these external evils are attributed to demons, and not to the *yeṣer*.

In the first phase of his history the devil behaves very much like the *yeṣer* in its later Amoraic form: he is a cunning deceiver working inside the human being, and his machinations aim at depriving the latter of eternal bliss. The image of the *yeṣer* as a totally internalized, sophisticated enticer characterizes the Amoraic literature in particular, but even in the early Tannaitic Midrash Sifre Num 88 the *yeṣer* of Boaz acts in more or less the same way.[16]

[12] According to the Greek text: ed. J.-M. Prieur, CCSA 6, 503–05.
[13] Rosen-Zvi 2011, 99. [14] Rosen-Zvi 2011, 93.
[15] Cf. Rosen-Zvi 2011, 87: "Being fully internalized, the evil yetzer cannot use direct coercion."
[16] Cf. Rosen-Zvi 2011, 18–19.

## 2 ACTS OF PETER

The Acts of Peter was composed at the end of the second century, but its place of origin cannot be determined – Rome or Asia Minor seems most probable. In chapter 8 Peter addresses the devil as follows:

> O what manifold arts and temptations of the devil! O what contrivances and inventions of evil! He prepares for him a great fire in the day of wrath, the destruction of simple men, the ravening wolf, the devourer and waster of eternal life! Thou hast ensnared the first man in lustful desire and bound him by thine ancient wickedness and with the chain of the body; thou art the fruit of the tree of bitterness, which is all most bitter, including lusts of every kind. Thou hast made Judas ... do wickedly and betray our Lord Jesus Christ ... Thou didst harden the heart of Herod and provoke (*coëgisti*) Pharaoh, making him fight against Moses, the holy servant of God; thou didst give Caiaphas the boldness to hand over our Lord Jesus Christ to the cruel throng, and even now thou dost shoot at innocent souls with thy poisoned arrows. Thou wicked enemy of all ... like a firebrand thrust out from the hearth thou shalt be quenched by the servants of our Lord ... For thou, devouring wolf, wouldst carry off sheep which are not thine, but belong to Christ Jesus, who keeps them with the most careful care.[17]

The devil in this text remains an independent personality pursuing his aims through human history. Though he is not a "demon that inhabits human hearts,"[18] and though he cannot be identified with the rabbinic *yeṣer*, some remarkable similarities to it can be detected. He is wicked and cunning; he strives to induce men to sin, and in order to achieve this he uses various devices;[19] his aim is to deprive humans of eternal life; although evil originated from sexuality, the sins that followed afterwards at the instigations of the devil were not sexual ones but acts such as betrayal, attacks against the righteous, and murder; the devil is the "enemy of all" but has power only over those who belong to him;[20] these latter, it seems, have no chance of resisting him (cf. *coëgisti* – you have *compelled* the Pharaoh); the text fluctuates between the image of an external enemy and that of an internalized one. The expression "like a firebrand thrust out from the hearth thou shalt be quenched by the servants of our Lord ..." could have been used concerning the *yeṣer* as well.[21]

[17] Acts Pet. 8 (trans. Prieur and Schneemelcher): Hennecke and Schneemelcher 1992, 295.
[18] Rosen-Zvi 2011, 36. [19] Cf. Rosen-Zvi 2011, 19 (Boaz), 24–25 (deceiver).
[20] Rosen-Zvi 2011, 106–07.
[21] Cf. the sages controlling their *yeṣer*: Rosen-Zvi 2011, 187.

## 3 ACTS OF THOMAS

### 3.1 Acts of Thomas 32

The Acts of Thomas, written at the beginning of the third century, is an important witness of early Eastern Christianity. It was composed in Syriac and translated into Greek shortly afterwards. We have both the Syriac and Greek versions, but their relation is far from clear. According to the *communis opinio* the Greek in its present form is closer to the original, the Syriac having been revised in order to become more "orthodox."

Chapter 32, influenced by Acts of Peter 8, contains an expanded list of the misdeeds of Satan and his kin. The serpent, "baleful son of a baleful father," unmasked by Thomas, proudly enumerates his achievements perpetrated through human (and cosmic) history. There are two new motifs, not present in Acts of Peter 8, which merit our attention: (1) The mention of Cain: "I am he" – says the serpent – "who kindled and inflamed Cain to slay his own brother." In Gen. Rab. 20.7 we read: "The urge of the evil *yeṣer* is for none but Cain and his associates."[22] (2) Instigation to idolatry: "I am he who led the multitude astray in the wilderness, when they made the calf"; one of the main occupations of the *yeṣer* is to induce the children of Israel to *avodah zara*, "foreign worship."[23]

The Greek and Syriac versions of this passage diverge on several points, two of which are perhaps of some interest.

Verse 2 reads in Greek as follows: "I am son of him who hurt and smote the four standing brothers" – an allusion whose meaning remains hidden to us. The Syriac, however, is completely clear: "I am the son of him to whom power has been given over the creatures and who disturbs them."

Verse 13 Greek: "I am he who inhabits and possesses the abyss of Tartarus"; Syriac: "I am he to whom power has been given in this world." The evil figure of the Syriac version seems to be closer to the *yeṣer* than his Greek counterpart. While the latter seems to be a rebellious and fallen angel banished to the underworld, the former is a demonic being installed by God in this world in order to "disturb" (i.e. to test and lead astray) people.[24]

[22] Quoted by Rosen-Zvi 2011, 103–04.

[23] Cf. Rosen-Zvi 2011, 103–04. According to Jewish as well as Christian tradition, idolatry was instituted by the demons, cf. Jub 11:4–5. For the Church Fathers the point of departure was Ps 95:5 (LXX): "For all the gods of the peoples are δαιμόνια." On the pagan gods and demons, see, e.g., Tertullian, *Cor.* 7.7–9; *Apol.* 23.

[24] In Acts Thom. 34:5 (Syriac) the devil is called the "disturber" of men.

## 3.2 Acts of Thomas 34:1a–d

In my opinion this curious passage of the Acts of Thomas, found only in the Syriac version, comes the closest to the description of the *yeṣer*. The third part of the Acts of Thomas relates the story of a young man killed by a serpent. Thomas, seeing what happened, declares, according to the Syriac: "This could not have happened without the instigation of the enemy who is wont to do such things. The enemy would not have dared to commit this against someone who is a stranger to him but only against someone who had submitted himself to him."[25] At this, a huge serpent appears and explains that he has killed the young man because he made love (moreover on Sunday!) to the girl with whom he, the serpent, was also in love. Then he enumerates all his former misdeeds (we have seen the list above), and finally Thomas compels him to suck his poison out of the young man, whereupon the serpent bursts and dies, and the young man revives. According to the Syriac version, on this occasion he pronounces a glorification to God which in the Greek has no counterpart. He says, among other things:

> Glory to you, merciful, great and glorious God, maker and creator of all the creatures! You established limits and measures for every creature which you have created, and gave them differences (or: varieties /ܫܘ̈ܚܠܦܐ/) which help their natures. You made man with the work of your hand according to the will of your Divinity so that he should reign over everything. And you created for him another creature (ܒܪܝܬܐ ܐܚܪܝܬܐ, fem.) that he should fight with it (fem.) according to the freedom you gave him. But man forgot his free nature and became the slave of his companion (ܠܘܬܗ, masc. or fem.). When this latter discovered that he forgot his freedom, he became his enemy. And the enemy was glad that he found admittance to his companion and hoped to become lord over all the slaves.[26]

According to Poirier and Tissot, the "other creature" who becomes the enemy of his (or her?) companion is the woman, while the enemy who hopes to subdue humanity is the devil. This interpretation seems unacceptable to me because on the basis of the Syriac it is evident that the word "enemy" (occurring twice in our passage) refers to one and the same being. The solution of S. Naeh is more nuanced: for him the enemy is the sexual instinct personified by Eve.[27]

[25] Acts Thom. 30:3. The Greek has: " . . . he has made use of no other form and wrought through no other creature than that which is his subject."

[26] Acts Thom. 34:1b–c. Syriac text: Bedjan 1968 [1892], 35–36.

[27] See Bovon and Geoltrain 1997, 1360 ; Naeh 1997.

The interpretations of Tissot and Poirier as well as that of Naeh are based on the supposition that the expression "created him another creature" alludes to Gen 2:18: "I will make him a helper as a partner (כנגדו עזר)." It is true that the word translated by "partner," כנגדו, can equally mean "standing in front of him," "opposing him,"[28] and some rabbinic writings interpreting Gen 2:18 actually exploited this double meaning of the preposition נגד, as for example: "if he is favoured, she will be a help, if not, she will be against him."[29]

I strongly doubt, however, that our text should be based on this kind of interpretation. First of all, this is possible only in Hebrew, but not in Greek or in Syriac; Gen 2:18 as we have it in the Septuagint and the Peshitta cannot be understood this way. The Syriac word for "his companion" (ܚܒܪܬܗ) is not that used by the Peshitta in Gen 2:18.[30] Second, such extreme misogyny (woman = Satan) is very rare in early Judaism[31] and attested nowhere in early Christianity (only later, in some monastic writings, do women acquire truly diabolical traits). As far as I know not even the most misogynistic author had ever declared that woman was expressly made for man to struggle against. Third, the Apocryphal Acts of the Apostles are markedly encratic, but absolutely not misogynistic; on the contrary. Their protagonists (beside the apostle, of course) are women of very strong character (in addition to being rich, noble, and beautiful) who free themselves from their respective husbands and betrotheds, and take their lives into their own hands.[32] The Acts of Thomas represents women in a notably positive way, and they never appear as temptresses. In our scene the young man was killed because of a girl, but she plays no role in the story and nothing indicates that she had seduced the young man. Finally, we must keep in mind that the word "creature" used in our passage cited above, though feminine in Syriac, can refer equally to female and male beings.

Therefore, in my opinion, the creature with whom man has to struggle is not the woman, but the devil as a cosmic enemy (he wants to subdue

[28] Jastrow 1903, 872.

[29] b. Yebam. 63a; Yal. Gen 23; cf. Gen. Rab. 17:6, quoted in Jastrow 1903, 872.

[30] Naturally we do not know what Syriac biblical text the author of this insertion could have used.

[31] Rosen-Zvi 2011, 122–23 brings some examples from rabbinical writings in which woman is implicitly identified with the evil *yeṣer*.

[32] In the last thirty to forty years this has been largely exploited by feminists, some of whom even supposed that the Apocryphal Acts of the Apostles was written by women: cf. Bremmer 1995.

everybody) and as a personal one (every human being has to fight his own battle against him). The passage does not concern the sin of Adam, and there is no primordial "fall" – the struggle begins all over again.

The central idea of the third part of the Acts of Thomas is the power of evil over humanity (we saw the list of misdeeds committed by the serpent). The real problem, however, is how it became possible that Satan should acquire such a power over humankind. Acts of Thomas 30:3 according to the Syriac version (quoted above) tries to resolve this by maintaining that the serpent could have killed the young man only because he submitted himself to its will.[33]

The meaning of our passage is thus the following: humankind was free by nature, and, in order to be able to exercise that freedom, was confronted by God with the Evil One. However, instead of struggling against him, humanity voluntarily submitted to him. The idea that Satan was expressly created for this reason, though not a very widespread one, can be found in some Second Temple writings,[34] and is not completely unheard of in Christianity either. It appears in the Pseudo-Clementines, but the most interesting parallel to our passage can be found in Lactantius, in the famous "dualistic" addition of *The Workmanship of God* 19 *bis*.[35]

The evil being of our passage has very much in common with the *yeṣer*: He is a creature of God. He is no fallen angel, and did not become evil by his own choice, but was created as such. As we read in Sifre Deut 45: "I created your evil *yeṣer* and there is nothing more evil than it."[36] He was created with the purpose that man should fight against it; against the *yeṣer* humans have to struggle all their lives. The enemy was created as a companion to humankind – the *yeṣer* accompanies humans throughout their lives and grows with them (it is a subject of discussion when exactly

[33] The Greek text does not even raise the question: cf. n. 24 above.

[34] First of all in 1QS iii 18–iv 1, but Mastema in Jub and Belial in T. 12 Patr. play similar roles, though their respective origins remain hidden.

[35] 1 Dedit ei et constituit *aduersarium* nequissimum fallacissimum spiritum, *cum quo* in hac terrestri vita sine ulla securitatis requie *dimicaret*. Cur autem deus hunc *uexatorem generi hominum* constituerit breviter exponam. 2 Ante omnia *diuersitatem* uoluit esse ideoque uulgo non aperuit ueritatem, sed eam paucissimis reuelauit: quae diuersitas omne arcanum mundi continet. Haec est enim quae facit esse uirtutem, quae scilicet non modo esse, sed ne apparere quidem <posset>, quia uirtus esse non poterit, nisi fuerit compar aliquis, in quo superando uim suam uel exerceat uel ostendat. 3 Nam ut uictoria constare sine certamine non potest, sic nec uirtus quidem ipsa sine hoste. Itaque quoniam uirtutem dedit homini, stauit illi ex contrario inimicum, ne uirtus otio torpens naturam suam perderet (Perrin 1974, 210–12; I have indicated in italic the most obvious parallels to our text).

[36] Quoted by Rosen-Zvi 2011, 65.

the *yeṣer* of a person comes into being); it can actually be considered a companion. As Rosen-Zvi puts it, "Amoraic *yetzer* ... grows with humans and develops in stages to become a dangerous foe (cf. 'first sweet and then sour', y. Shab. 14:3, 14c)."[37] The enemy who gains admittance to his companion and hopes to become master over all the servants is very near to the *yeṣer* who is first a visitor and then becomes master of the house (Gen. Rab. 22:6).[38] A person who takes care can rule over his/her *yeṣer*. This positive attitude concerning the *yeṣer* mainly characterizes the Babylonian tradition. This enemy is at the same time a personal and a cosmic one, just as the Amoraic *yeṣer* increasingly resembles the great demonic princes such as Belial or Mastema, and is even identified with Satan.[39] In short, the description of the Amoraic *yeṣer* given by Rosen-Zvi fits perfectly with the evil being in our passage: "Amoraic *yetzer* is more developed, reified, and demonized; it acquires a distinct character and even a physical shape"[40] – our enemy, as we have seen, appears in the form of a huge serpent.

The most interesting parallel to our text is produced by b. Ḥag. 16a in which R. Judah in the name of Reish Lakish relates the "friend" mentioned in Mic 7:5 to the evil inclination: "'Trust not a friend' (Mic 7:5), and friend (רֵעַ) means none other than the evil *yeṣer*, for it is said: 'For the *yeṣer* of man's heart is evil' (רַע Gen 8:21)." This interpretation rests on the similarity between the words "friend" and "evil," and is therefore possible only in Hebrew. Furthermore, since the dating of rabbinic tradition is quite difficult we cannot be sure if it precedes the composition of our text (the date of which is equally unknown). It cannot be excluded, however, that the author of the Syriac insertion was acquainted with it.

As we have seen, the enemy of Acts Thom. 34:1a–d is very similar to the Amoraic *yeṣer*, especially as it appears in the Babylonian sources. We now have to ask ourselves whether the enemy is sexualized or not, in other words whether we are dealing with the sexual instinct or simply with instigation to sin in general. The sin committed by the young man (lying with a girl, and especially on Sunday) is a sexual one, but the sins committed on the instigation of the enemy (the serpent) are not sexual ones, as becomes clear from the list given earlier. After his resurrection the young

37 Rosen-Zvi 2011, 70. 38 Cf. Rosen-Zvi 2011, 69.

39 As Reish Lakish puts it according to the Bavli (this is present only in the Bavli): "Satan is yetzer hara, the angel of death": cf. Rosen-Zvi 2011, 79.

40 Rosen-Zvi 2011, 82.

man declares himself liberated from the "acts of corruption," but this does not necessarily mean a vow of chastity.[41]

On the basis of these similarities I would venture to say that here we are actually dealing with the *yeṣer*.

## 4 APOCALYPSE OF PAUL

In general, I shall not treat Gnostic texts, but here we make an exception for an interesting passage of the Gnostic Apocalypse of Paul (NHC V,2). I feel entitled to do so because the passage itself is not Gnostic at all, and in my opinion it goes back to Jewish sources. Klauck considers it an addition to the Apocalypse of Paul[42] because if we omit it the logic of the whole work remains undisturbed.

We must keep in mind that two Apocalypses of Paul are known, a Coptic Gnostic one found among the Nag Hammadi writings, and another which is not Gnostic at all. The two are completely independent except for a short scene of the non-Gnostic apocalypse which has been probably influenced by a similar scene in the Gnostic one. Regarding the date of origin of the Gnostic Apocalypse, Murdock and MacRae proposed the second half of the second century, while according to Funk, however, it can be dated only somewhere during the period between the middle of the second century and the beginning of the fourth.[43] It was probably written in Greek, but we do not know in what measure the extant Coptic text corresponds to the original. The place of origin is unknown.

The Apocalypse of Paul describes the heavenly journey of Paul. The starting point is given by Galatians 1–2, which recounts Paul's ascent to Jerusalem to meet his fellow apostles. In our text this ascension becomes a heavenly journey that ends in the tenth heaven. In the fourth heaven Paul is present at a judgment scene: avenging angels bring a soul before a judge (the toll-collector,[44] *telōnēs*), who reproaches the soul for the lawless deeds he had committed. The soul, however, does not admit his guilt but demands witnesses. Then the witnesses actually arrive:

[41] Concerning the encratism of the Acts Thom. see Tissot 1981 and 1988.

[42] Klauck 1985, 175. [43] Murdock and MacRae 1979 ; Funk 1991, 695–96.

[44] This toll-collector, in my opinion, is neither a Gnostic archon nor a hostile power of Hellenistic astrology, but simply a doorkeeper who has to decide whether a soul can enter the fourth heaven or not. The closest parallel to this figure can be found in Ascen. Isa. 10: cf. Pesthy 2007, 201–02.

**20**
. . . And
the three witnesses came.
The first spoke, saying:
"Was I [not]
in the body the second hour
[]? I rose up against you

**21**
until [you fell] into anger [and]
[rage] and envy." And
the second spoke, saying:
"Was I not
in the world? I entered at
the fifth hour, and saw you
and desired you. And behold,
then, now I charge you with the
murders you committed."
The third spoke saying:
"Did I not come to you at
the twelfth hour of the day when
the sun was about to set? I gave you darkness
until you should accomplish your sins."[45]

The soul is then cast down into a body.

The judgment scene has been interpreted by scholars in quite different ways. Murdock and MacRae called it "the result of a popular syncretism influenced by Jewish apocalyptic literature and Greek mythology."[46] Kasser sees here old Egyptian influence,[47] while Carozzi connects it to Jewish Egyptian apocalyptic literature.[48] In an earlier paper I have argued for Jewish and Jewish Christian influence on the judgment scene,[49] but here I want to treat only the three witnesses. They are not identical with the Evil Inclination: they are demons – three different, personal, and quite individual demons. Their methods, however, have much in common with those of the *yeṣer*. All three of them contributed to the committing of the same crime(s). The first demon incited the sinner to anger, rage, and envy; as we know, to evoke anger and envy belongs to the fundamental "tasks" of the *yeṣer*, and the Tosefta vividly depicts the fits of rage caused by the evil *yeṣer* (t. B. Qam. 9:31).[50] The second demon induced the sinner to

[45] Trans. in Murdock and MacRae 1979. [46] Murdock and MacRae 1979, 48.

[47] Kasser 1965, 77–78. [48] Carozzi 1994, 70. [49] Pesthy 2007.

[50] Cf. Rosen-Zvi 2011, 30. Moore 1997, 1:492 quotes an "anonymous Tannaite authority" with reference to Job: "Satan comes down and misleads a man, then goes up and stirs up God's wrath, and obtains permission and takes away his soul."

murder, and naturally the evil *yeṣer* is also responsible for such severe sins as murder and idolatry. As for the third, who brings darkness in order to facilitate the crimes, here I do not know any parallels.

But the most surprising fact is the double role played by the demons: they incite people to sin and then accuse them of the sins committed. This detail, as far as I know, has no parallel in early Christian literature, but corresponds precisely to the description of the *yeṣer* given by a homily in the Babylonian Talmud: "R. Samuel b. Nahmani in the name of R. Jonathan said: 'The evil *yetzer* entices man in this world, and testifies against him in the world to come.'"[51] The *yeṣer* acts here exactly as the three demons do in our text.

The roots of this concept reach very far back. Satan, as we know, was originally the accuser and, as such, an important member of the divine court. He exercises his legal function in Job 1–2 and is hindered from doing so in Zech 3:2. Later on, as he gradually becomes the Enemy, the Evil One, his role of accuser is relegated to the background (we find it, however, even in the NT: in Rev 12:10 he is called κατήγωρ, "accuser," and in 1 Pet 5:8 ἀντίδικος, "adversary in a lawsuit"). Christianity makes of him a fallen angel, and in consequence he definitively ceases to be the accuser (he can exercise this function only as long as he is the subordinate of the Lord and not a rebel angel).

As a direct connection between the quoted passage of the Apocalypse of Paul and the homily in the Bavli seems quite improbable, the similarity, in my opinion, can best be explained through common origins reaching back to the writings of Second Temple Judaism. Jubilees 1:20 reads as follows (Moses is praying): "May your mercy, Lord, be lifted over your people. Create for them a just spirit. May the spirit of Belial not rule them so as to bring charges against them before you and to trap them away from every proper path so that they may be destroyed from your presence."[52] This idea reappears in our Apocalypse almost in its original form (with the only difference that the judge is not God, but the toll-collector), while the Bavli, quite naturally, replaces Belial with the evil *yeṣer*.

## 5 CONCLUSION

Rosen-Zvi argues that the unique rabbinic *yeṣer* is "part of a longer move toward placing demons inside the human psyche."[53] This process took

[51] Quoted by Rosen-Zvi 2011, 107. [52] Trans. in VanderKam 1989, 5.
[53] Rosen-Zvi 2011, 128.

place in Late Antiquity, and characterizes rabbinic Judaism as well as early Christianity, in which it arrives at its fulfillment by Origen, Evagrius, and other monastic writers.

The relevant passages of the Christian Apocrypha we have reviewed above fit perfectly into this process and represent an intermediate state: Satan or the demons are not really internalized, but they act inside human beings and instigate them to sin from within.

Let us now consider if we can establish some closer relationship between these passages and the rabbinic writings. Unfortunately, the place of origin is unknown for the majority of apocryphal writings.

The Acts of Thomas constitute a lucky exception to this, because we know that it was written in East Syria, perhaps in Edessa. The beginnings of Christianity in Edessa are not clear at all,[54] but it is generally admitted that it had a definitely Jewish-Christian character and it is attested that an important Jewish community lived there. The situation is complicated by the fact that we do not know when Acts Thom. 34:1a–f was composed and inserted into the Acts but, as I have tried to argue above, a direct Jewish influence cannot be excluded: it seems probable that the author of the short inserted passage was acquainted with contemporary Mesopotamian Jewish tradition. This is all the more interesting because it supports the hypothesis of Rosen-Zvi according to which the sexualization of the *yeṣer* appeared quite late in Mesopotamian Jewish literature.[55] The Acts of Thomas, like Aphrahat, is very much interested in sexuality and show encratic tendencies but, notwithstanding this fact, the "enemy," whose figure was probably constituted under Jewish influence, is not identified with sexual desire.

In the case of Apoc. Paul 20:25–21:14, although it shows an interesting similarity to some rabbinic texts, common roots rather than direct connections seem most probable. It is possible that the passage comes from earlier – perhaps Jewish – writing. As I have argued above, the ideas expressed in this passage correspond to a very ancient notion of Satan and the demons, which disappeared completely from Christianity, and was transferred to the *yeṣer* by rabbinic Judaism.

The Acts of Andrew 49–50 describes a sophisticated enticer who feigns friendship and entraps human beings with his "gifts," which seem highly desirable but are in fact deceitful. This very early text presents

[54] See Brock 2004, 162. The story told in the Abgar legend was written later and probably lacks historicity.

[55] Rosen-Zvi 2011, 117–18.

a thoroughly developed image of the enemy which can be paralleled only with later Amoraic texts, though it also shows similarities to the *yeṣer* of Boaz. In this case, it seems, Christianity went ahead of the rabbinic tradition.

As for the two other texts which we have examined (Acts Pet. 8 and Acts Thom. 32), the similarities we found were rather general. They are therefore probably not a result of Jewish influence but rather witness to the development of ideas, which took place in parallel in both Judaism and Christianity.

At the beginning I stated that because of the diversity of the so-called Christian Apocrypha we cannot hope to arrive at general conclusions. Notwithstanding this fact, we can establish some general similarities between the demonic being that we encounter in the Apocrypha and the rabbinic *yeṣer*:

The person to be tempted is not aware of an external enemy; he does not even realize that the instigation comes from an enemy.

The demon, like the *yeṣer*, is interested in (sinful) deeds, not in thoughts, contrary to the demons of Origen and the later monastic writings.

Human beings have to struggle against the demon; they are free, and have the power and the possibility to overcome it or to submit to it.

The struggle is not a psychological one between two parts of a person; the human being, as a whole fights against the demon.

The demon is not connected to the body, although it makes the body its instrument.

The demon is not sexualized; the sins committed on its instigation are murder, treachery, idolatry, and, naturally, also fornication.

Although these texts know about the "fall" of Adam, the idea of "original" sin is completely foreign to them. Sin does not originate from (fallen) human nature, but from (external) demonic powers which act inside the human being.

13

# Origen on the Origin of Sin

Riemer Roukema

In a volume on the origin of sin a contribution about Origen should not be missing, but this is not because his name has anything to do with the term "origin." Although in other languages his name is sometimes erroneously spelled Origines, which suggests a relationship with the Latin word *origo* (gen. *originis*), Origen's name (Ὠριγένης, Ōrigenes in Greek) derives from the Egyptian god Horus and means "son of Horus." A variant of his name is aspirated by the editors as Hōrigenes, showing more clearly the derivation from the name Horus.[1] Our Origen was born in Alexandria around 185 CE, and according to his early fourth-century biographer, Bishop Eusebius of Caesarea,[2] his parents were Christians, but this had not kept them from giving their son a pagan name;[3] however, they may also have converted to Christianity after the birth of Origen, who was their eldest child. Since there is no mention of Origen's baptism as a young adult, he may have been baptized as an infant.[4] Eusebius says that Leonides, Origen's father, gave his son a thorough Christian education. He also relates that, during the reign of the emperor Severus, when the Alexandrian authorities unleashed a wave of persecution against Christians, Leonides was one of the martyrs. This occurred around 201 CE, when Origen was sixteen years old. Since he appeared to be a gifted young man, when he was eighteen his bishop, Demetrius, asked him to assume the catechetical instruction of his church,

[1] POxy 2595 (third century CE), in Barns et al. 1966, 155.

[2] *Hist. eccl.* VI.1–3, 6–8, 14–39 (LCL 265). See the analyses by Nautin 1977, 31–98, and McGuckin 2004, 1–23.

[3] In ca. 177 CE the apologist Athenagoras writes in his *Leg.* 2.2 (PTS 31) to the emperors Marcus Aurelius and Commodus that for Christians a name is not bad or good in itself.

[4] See Crouzel 1985, 21–22.

since other teachers were not available due to the persecution. Apart from his activities as a catechist, Origen continued to study both the Scriptures, including apocryphal Jewish writings, and Greek philosophy. Over the years his fame as a learned and philosophically trained interpreter of Scripture increased. His convert Ambrose, a former Valentinian Gnostic, urged him to compose commentaries on Scripture, which he did, besides many other works.

The real reason why Origen should be included in a volume on the origin of sin is that during his life and in the subsequent centuries he became, and remained, a most influential, though controversial, Christian scholar, who is unequaled in Greek Christianity. In this contribution I will investigate his views – or rather, speculations – on the origin of sin, and I will briefly draw a conclusion about the possible relationship between Origen's anthropology and the rabbis' view of *yeṣer hara*ʿ.[5]

For the theme of the origin of sin it is relevant that at the end of the 220s Origen started to write his *Commentary on Genesis*, in which he must have dealt with the fall of the rational creatures from heaven – to which I will come back – but this work has only been preserved in fragments and other testimonies, in which this primordial fall is not commented on.[6] Much later, years after he had settled in Caesarea Maritima because of a conflict with his Alexandrian bishop, he delivered a series of sermons on Genesis, which have been preserved in a Latin translation made by Rufinus of Aquileia (in 400–404 CE). However, in the first sermon, on the six days of the creation of the world, the origin of sin is not expounded, and the second sermon discusses Noah and the Flood.[7] This story might have induced Origen to explain why humankind had turned so evil that God intended to destroy it except for Noah and his family, but in this sermon he does not go into this question.

The first volumes of his *Commentary on Genesis* probably contributed to Bishop Demetrius's growing suspicion of his intelligent catechist. Although in his later works Origen clearly drew on Greek philosophy for his exposition of Scripture and the Christian faith, he rarely referred to philosophers explicitly;[8] most of his arguments consisted of biblical references. But people who were acquainted with philosophy would recognize

[5] In this chapter I draw on Roukema 2018. I have also discussed the theme of the present chapter in Roukema 2003 (Dutch version, 2004).

[6] See Metzler 2010. [7] See de Lubac and Doutreleau 1976; English trans. Heine 1982.

[8] Only in his apology against the Platonic philosopher Celsus (ca. 248 CE), to which I will return, did he regularly refer to Greek philosophers explicitly.

that he made use of it for his theological investigations and interpretative methods. However, Christians such as Demetrius could not appreciate his approach. It was probably in reaction to such suspicions that Origen wrote his fundamental work *On First Principles* (Gr. *Peri Archōn*, Lat. *De Principiis*), in which he explored and expounded the Christian faith (in his words, "the apostolic preaching") and his view of Scripture more or less systematically. The title refers to a Greek genre, since there are more authors who wrote such books entitled *Peri Archōn.*[9] In *On First Principles* Origen deals with the creation of the world and therefore with the origin of sin, among other themes. In this fundamental work he probably intended to justify his expositions of the first chapters of Genesis, which had provoked the criticism of his bishop. He completed this work around 230 CE, when he was still working in Alexandria.

Unfortunately, however, most of the Greek version is lost, but it is still known in an adapted Latin translation made by Rufinus of Aquileia (from 398 CE) and through other, shorter testimonies in Latin and Greek. Rufinus' translation is the most important source of Origen's view of the origin of sin. It is a free translation, and sometimes Rufinus subtly adapted the Greek text to late fourth-century Catholic orthodoxy, but for our purpose it is most valuable because it obviously transmits the gist of Origen's ideas on this matter.

In order to expound Origen's view of the origin of sin, we have to go back to the very beginning of creation and the primordial disaster that happened then.[10] In his view – or rather, hypothesis – God first created spiritual, rational creatures (φύσεις λογικαί) or minds (νόες), who should contemplate and love God in heaven. These creatures lived through their spirit (πνεῦμα) and had spiritual bodies. In spite of their proximity to God and contemplation of God, to different degrees almost all spiritual creatures were overcome by negligence. God had created them with a free will, but as a consequence of this gift they fell away from him. However, God's Logos and only Son, Christ, was the sole exception who remained faithful to his Father in heaven. As a consequence of their fall, the rational creatures were attached to bodies that differed according to the gravity of their fall. Some creatures became angels; they remained relatively close

9 For the title see Lies 1992, 8–14. I use the edition by Görgemanns and Karpp 1976. John Behr later published another edition and translation (Behr 2017).

10 Origen discusses the following events in *Princ.* I.4–8, II.8–9. See the analyses by Daniélou 1948, 207–17; Crouzel 1985, 267–84; and Gasparro 2000a, 2000b. I do not agree with those scholars who downplay Origen's speculations that were inspired by Greek philosophical questions, such as Laporte 1970; Edwards 2002; Tzamalikos 2007.

to God and kept their spiritual, angelic bodies. Another category consisted of the devil and his angels, the demons, whose bodies were transformed correspondingly. Other creatures turned into heavenly bodies such as the sun, the moon, and the stars, which were therefore considered animate beings. An important category of rational creatures cooled down to become human souls, and were incarnated in human bodies. This interpretation of ψυχή ("soul") in the sense of ψύχεσθαι ("to cool down") was known in contemporaneous philosophy,[11] and Origen found a confirmation of this explanation in Matt 24:12, where Jesus says in his apocalyptic discourse, "And because of the increase of lawlessness, the love of many will grow cold (ψυγήσεται)." Other texts that he quoted from Scripture in order to underpin his view of a fall of the creatures were Ezek 28:1–19 and Isa 14:12–22 which deal with the kings of, respectively, Tyre and Babel, who are said to have fallen from heaven. In Origen's interpretation these kings were originally angels who had been with God in heaven but were not satisfied with their position. Origen considers them as images of Satan, the devil, about whom Jesus said that he watched him fall from heaven (Luke 10:18). In Satan's wake, almost all other spiritual creatures removed themselves from their original proximity to God as well, each according to the gravity of his sin.

But what was the primordial, original, sin, in Origen's view? In Isa 14:12–13 we read that the heavenly king of Babel, the Day Star or Lucifer, wanted to ascend to heaven and set his throne above the stars of God. In Ezek 28:16–17 we read that the angelic king of Tyre filled his storehouses with lawlessness so that he sinned, and that his heart was exalted because of his beauty. However, for his analysis of the origin of sin Origen does not employ these texts in *On First Principles*. He explains that in the beginning the rational beings were created, so they had not existed beforehand. The consequence of the fact that they came into being after their initial non-existence is that they were changeable (*convertibiles et mutabiles*). This means that everything that God gave them can also be taken away from them, and disappear. What happened is that the movement of the *noes*, the minds or rational creatures, did not go in the right direction. The Creator had given them a free will so that they might choose and preserve what is good, but instead of this, Origen writes according to Rufinus, "sluggishness (*desidia*), disgust (*taedium*) with the effort to preserve goodness, an aversion to and a negligence (*aversio ac neglegentia*) of the

[11] See e.g. Plato, *Crat.* 399DE; Aristotle, *De an.* 1.2 (405B); *SVF*, §§ 804–07; Philo, *Somn.* 1.31 (LCL 275).

better things caused the beginning of moving away from goodness" – which is God himself. He continues, "But moving away from goodness is nothing else but finding oneself in evil."[12] In anticipation of his discussion of the primordial fall in *Princ.* II.9, Origen had already pointed to negligence (*neglegentia*) as the reason of the fall of the rational creatures in book I.[13] Later on, Origen – in Rufinus' rendering – refers to it again (*defectum per neglegentiam*).[14]

Twice Rufinus also uses the term *satietas*, "satiety," when he translates a consideration about the various stages that lead to the eschatological perfection of human beings, thanks to the ceaseless efforts of the Father, the Son, and the Holy Spirit, through which in the end "we [humans] can contemplate the holy and blessed life." When, after much struggle, humans reach this blessed life, they have to persevere in it, "so that no *satiety* of that goodness may ever seize us." He mildly adds that even if satiety should seize someone who had already reached the highest stage of perfection, such a creature will not be removed immediately, but will slide down gradually and little by little, so that he may quickly come to his senses and return.[15] To be sure, these considerations – or speculations – concern the eschatological restoration of God's creatures and not their primordial fall, but we may suppose that at the same time they refer to the reason why the rational creatures originally fell away from God: this was because of their negligence and disgust, to which the term "satiety" corresponds. This is confirmed by the first denunciation of Origen's teachings that was formulated in Greek by the emperor Justinian in 543 CE. It reads:

> If someone says or holds that the souls of human beings were preexistent in that they used to be minds (νόες) and holy powers, but were struck by satiety (κόρος) of the divine contemplation and were changed for the worse and therefore cooled down from God's love, and hence were called "souls" and for punishment were sent down to bodies, let he be anathematized.[16]

For the present investigation it is important that in this imprecation the original Greek term for *satietas*, κόρος, has been preserved with regard to the original fall of the preexistent minds. This implies that according to Origen's speculation the reason why the rational creatures fell away from

[12] Origen, *Princ.* II.9.2. [13] Origen, *Princ.* I.3.8–4.1. [14] Origen, *Princ.* II.9.5.

[15] Origen, *Princ.* I.3.8. It is noteworthy that Origen's Alexandrian predecessor Clement had already written that in the end the holy souls' contemplation will be insatiable (ἀκόρεστος): *Strom.* VII.13.1 (SC 428).

[16] Görgemanns and Karpp 1976, 822; also in Schwartz 1940, 213; cf. 191.

God is that they were negligent and had enough of God's goodness. In other words, they were bored with it, as may happen to believers who attend weekly worship or discover that they no longer feel at home in the faith in which they were raised.

This hypothesis raises the following question: If God's creatures can get bored with God's goodness, could it be that God's goodness is the reason for this boredom or satiety, just as some preachers are boring because of the style in which they lead worship? Marguerite Harl has thoroughly examined this theme and concludes – rightly, in my view – that the fault lies with the creatures' negligence, not with God's goodness. Therefore she proposes that this satiety has to be interpreted as "weariness" ("lassitude"), not as "saturation" which is provoked by God.[17] With reference to Marguerite Harl's article, Cinzia Arruzza emphasizes that in Origen's view it is negligence, which she opposes to satiety, that provoked the creatures' fall,[18] but quite rightly Harl did not introduce this opposition and interpreted satiety as "lassitude," which she considered in agreement with negligence.

In conclusion, this implies that according to Origen the origin of sin can be found in the first events in heaven and comes down to negligence and the satiety of God's goodness that arose in the spiritual, rational creatures, so that they removed themselves from God and fell away from him. As a consequence, the falling creatures were attached to bodies that differed according to the gravity of their fall.

Before I deal with the question of the origin of this hypothesis, I note that Origen rarely comes back to it in his other extant works. This is probably due to the criticism he encountered after publishing *On First Principles*. Although the details of the controversy that arose around his person and work are not clear, the result was that a synod of the Alexandrian Church condemned him, so that he was forced to leave his native town and settled in Caesarea Maritima, as I noted above. Caesarea had a bishop, Theoctist, who, like his colleague Alexander of Jerusalem, could appreciate Origen's approach and investigation of the Christian faith, ordained him a priest, and gave him the scholarly freedom that he deserved.[19] However, the fact that in his subsequent works, as far as they have been preserved, his hypothesis about the primordial sin can hardly be found, does not imply that he abandoned it. In 248 CE, almost two decades after he had written *On First Principles*, he composed a lengthy

[17] Harl 1966, 390–95. [18] Arruzza 2009.

[19] Crouzel 1985, 38–46; McGuckin 2004, 12–16.

apology *Against Celsus*, in which he refuted the attacks on Christianity that had been published by the Platonic philosopher Celsus seventy years before, in a book entitled *The True Doctrine* (*Alēthēs Logos*). Incidentally, in this apology Origen regularly refers to Greek philosophers explicitly. When he deals with the Hebrew word Satan, he explains that it means ἀντικείμενος, "adversary." In a passage which contains mainly biblical but also a few Platonic terms he maintains:

Every man who has chosen evil (κακία) and to live an evil life so that he does everything contrary to virtue is a Satan, that is, an adversary to the Son of God who is righteousness, truth, and wisdom. But speaking more strictly, the Adversary is the first of all beings that were in peace and lived in blessedness who lost his wings[20] and fell from the blessed state. According to Ezekiel he walked blameless in all his ways until iniquity was found in him, and being "a seal of likeness and a crown of beauty" (Ezek 28:11) in the paradise of God he became, as it were, sated with good things (κορεσθεὶς τῶν ἀγαθῶν) and came to destruction, as the Word tells us which mysteriously says to him: "Thou didst become destruction and shalt not exist forever" (Ezek 28:19).[21]

Origen's use of the verb κορέννυμι, which is related to κόρος, proves that in the course of his life he did not give up his view of satiety of divine goodness as the reason why the first creatures fell away from God, although in this apology he cautiously introduces it with "as it were," οἱονεί, as if he were suggesting that he did not presume to describe the actual events with complete certainty, but was aware that he was putting forward a sort of metaphor.

However, in book 20 of his *Commentary on the Gospel of John*, where he comments on Jesus' saying – as the Fourth Gospel presents it – to his Jewish audience that "you wish to accomplish the desires of your father," the devil (John 8:44), he adds that this inclination to give in to such sinful desires is common to people in general. There Origen explains that the devil was the first χοϊκός, i.e. the first being who belonged to the dust of the earth (cf. 1 Cor 15:47, 49) because he was the first to fall away from the better things (in heaven) and thus became the beginning of the material creation;[22] but in this context Origen does not refer to the devil's satiety of

[20] This is a Platonic notion. In Plato's *Phaedrus* Socrates compares the soul with the combined force of two winged horses and a charioteer (246A). The soul traverses heaven, but if it is unable to persevere in the contemplation of God, it grows heavy through forgetfulness and evil, loses its wings, and falls down to the earth where it puts on an earthly body (246C, 248C).

[21] Origen, *Cels.* VI.44 (SC 147); trans. Chadwick 1980, 361–62.

[22] Origen, *Comm. Jo.* XX.176–82 (SC 290).

God's goodness. He wrote this book a few years after he had settled in Caesarea.[23] In his later *Homilies on Numbers* he quotes Isa 10:13–14 and 14:13–14 as testimonies to the devil's pride, but without referring to the reason of his fall, according to Rufinus' translation.[24] In his *Homilies on Ezekiel*, however, which roughly date to the same period, Origen quotes Isa 10:13–14 again and there – in Jerome's translation – he does refer to the devil's conceit, pride, and arrogance as the reason for his fall out of heaven to the earth, but again without mentioning any satiety of God's goodness.[25] Perhaps he just thought that it was not necessary to mention the idea of the primordial satiety of God's goodness in his *Commentary on John* and in these homilies, but it may also be that he consciously refrained from mentioning it because he did not want to stir up controversy again.

Historians always like to investigate the possible source of an idea. Did Origen have any predecessors from whom he took over his hypothesis about negligence and satiety as the origin of sin in heaven? As far as I know, among previous authors whose works have been preserved, Philo of Alexandria is the only one who testifies to this view. In his work *On the Giants,* Philo discusses the Platonic view of a descent of souls from heaven, which he associates with the descent of God's angels according to LXX Gen 6:2. In Platonic terms he describes how one category of souls descended to human bodies and might also, against the current, return to the place from which they came.[26] In this work Philo does not give a reason of the descent of this category of souls, but he does give one in another work, *Who Is the Heir?* There he comments on LXX Gen 15:11, "And birds came down on the bodies, the half-pieces"; these bodies are the carcasses of animals that Abram had taken and divided in two because God had told him to do so.[27] Philo interprets the birds as symbols of those souls "which, although they were raised in the air and the most pure ether, could not bear the satiety (κόρος) of the divine good things, and migrated to the earth, the region of the things mortal and evil."[28] So in Philo's view these souls descended to human bodies on earth because they were sated

[23] McGuckin 2004, 29–30.

[24] Origen, *Hom. Num.* 12.4 (SC 442). For the date see Nautin 1977, 403, 411. In Isa 10:13–14a Origen interprets the proud words of an Assyrian king ("I will . . . take with my hand the whole world like a nest" [NETS]) as the devil's brag. For Isa 14:13–14 see above in this chapter. See also Bostock 2011, 114.

[25] Origen, *Hom. Ezech.* 9.2; cf. 13.2 (SC 352). For the date see again Nautin 1977, 403, 411. For a broader discussion of these texts see Patmore 2012, 59–66.

[26] Philo, *Gig.* 12–13 (LCL 227), with allusions to Plato, *Tim.* 43A and *Phaed.* 248C.

[27] Philo, *Her.* 227 (LCL 261).

[28] Philo, *Her.* 239–40; translation mine.

with God's goodness. Marguerite Harl suggests that Philo drew on an existing interpretation of Plato's *Phaedrus* 247–48,[29] which held that the fall of the souls was instigated by their satiety, because they could not stand the feast of immortality. This would imply that according to this tradition the souls did not move away from God out of their free will, but because of an innate deficiency. Harl emphasizes that this last element, however, cannot be found in Origen.[30]

Having established how Origen explained the cause of the rational creatures' fall from their original bliss, and the sources on which he drew, we might wonder how he related his view to the story of Adam and Eve's fall in paradise. Although Origen's commentary on the first chapters of Genesis is lost, fragments and other references to these chapter have survived. In his apology *Against Celsus* he says that the description of paradise in Genesis 2 has to be interpreted allegorically. Subsequently he compares Adam and Eve's ejection from paradise with the Platonic doctrine of the descent of the soul, hinting at the mysterious meaning of the garments of skin with which God clothed Adam and Eve when he cast them out (Gen 3:21).[31] Unfortunately, in his extant works Origen does not elaborate on this interpretation of Adam and Eve's first sin in terms of the descent of the souls. Concerning the garments of skin, we read in his *Homilies on Leviticus* that they referred to the sinner's mortality, and his fragility caused by the corruption of the flesh.[32] Later authors such as Methodius of Olympus, Epiphanius of Salamis, and Jerome accused Origen of interpreting the garments of skin as the material bodies in contradistinction to the original creation of the human being in an immaterial body. According to a catena fragment, however, Origen disagreed with the following two interpretations: first, that the garments of skin are the material bodies; second, that they refer to the mortality of human bodies.[33] In recent decades much has been written about Origen's notion of a twofold creation of the human being, but these studies do not shed any more light on his view of the primordial inclination to evil.[34]

[29] See note 20 above.

[30] Harl 1966, 378–83. My search in the *Thesaurus Linguae Graecae* did not yield any other texts that testify to this interpretation.

[31] Origen, *Cels.* IV.39–40. For Origen's allegorization of Gen 2–3, see Hanson 2002, 269–72; Pisi 1987; Tzvetkova-Glaser 2011.

[32] Origen, *Hom. Lev.* 6.2, l. 106–15 (SC 286).

[33] Origen, *Sel. Gen.* 3:21, in Petit 1986, 124–25; cf. Metzler 2010, 190–97.

[34] See, e.g., Dupuis 1967, 38; Vogt 1987, 83–87; Hennessey 1992, 373–75; Uthemann 1999, 408–09; Heine 2003, 72–73; Noce 2003, 679–80; Tzvetkova-Glaser 2010, 102–05.

An important source for this theme might be Origen's interpretation of Paul's epistle to the Romans (Rom 5:12), which reads, "just as sin came into the world through one man and death came through sin, and so death spread to all because all have sinned," and the following verses, in his lengthy *Commentary on Romans*. Here once again we have to content ourselves with Rufinus' translation, made around 405 CE. In his Latin text, which, as Rufinus admits, is an abridged version of the original Greek, Origen does sometimes allude to the fall of the preexistent creatures,[35] but undoubtedly Rufinus had grown aware that it was preferable not to dwell on this tricky theme for which Origen had been fiercely criticized in the preceding years.[36] We may assume that Origen's Greek text was a little more explicit about this relationship between the fall of the preexistent creatures and the coming of sin into the world. What can be learned from the Latin translation, however, is that in Origen's thought human beings are sinners. He considered this to be the case not only because they were in Adam when he sinned and was banished from paradise, which, in some way, would include their ejection from the primordial bliss in heaven, but also because they are sinners by instruction, since children imitate their parents. As so often, Origen does not express his preference for one interpretation over another.[37]

To conclude, the following question remains to be discussed. After the spiritual creatures – in other words, the minds in their spiritual bodies – fell away from God and cooled down to be souls who attached themselves to material human bodies, what constitution do they have on earth, according to Origen? It is clear that they are sinful beings, but how did Origen assess their continued inclination to evil? For this question I follow the detailed study of Jacques Dupuis. In Origen's anthropology, in the human being whose mind (νοῦς) has cooled down to soul, his spirit (πνεῦμα) has survived the fall, although it is weakened by sin. This means that the soul finds itself between the spirit and the body or flesh, and can orient itself to either of them – or, to put it another way, to either the inner or the outer man (ἄνθρωπος: 2 Cor 4:16).[38] Referring to the apostle Paul, in the human being Origen perceives an antagonism between the flesh and the spirit (Gal 5:17: "For the flesh has desires against the

[35] Origen, *Comm. Rom.* V.1.511–19, 538–48; V.4.30–32 (AGLB 33; also in PG 14, 1018A–1019A, 1029CD); trans. in Scheck 2011. See Roukema 1988, 44–52.

[36] See Clark 1992, 95, 109–10, 133–35.

[37] Roukema 1988, 45–50; Heither 1990, 104–14, 120–25.

[38] Dupuis 1967, 36–40. Cf. Crouzel 1955.

spirit, and the spirit against the flesh, and these are opposed to each other"). One's flesh draws the soul to vices, but one's spirit inspires it to virtues, so that the soul has to choose between the two. In this struggle, it has the capacity to make good choices thanks to its free will, so that ultimately the human being will be celestial and spiritual, not terrestrial and carnal.[39] Although Ishay Rosen-Zvi has shown us that the presumed rabbinic concept of the two *yeṣarim*, one good and one evil, is in fact marginal in Tannaitic literature since we usually read there about only one *yeṣer*,[40] we might observe that Origen's view of the antagonism between good and evil in human beings seems to correspond more closely with the rarely found Tannaitic teaching of two inclinations.

However, it is unlikely that there is a direct relationship between Origen's anthropology and the alleged rabbinic teaching of two inclinations, although he did have personal contacts with Jews both in Alexandria and in Caesarea, and was interested in Jewish interpretations of Scripture.[41] Concerning their respective theories on the Evil Inclination in the human being it is hardly relevant that, like the rabbis, Origen drew on the Jewish Scriptures. Unlike the rabbis, however, for his view on the origin of sin and the Evil Inclination in human beings he was inspired by Plato, the Platonic Jew Philo, the apostle Paul, and the Gospels about Jesus Christ. To be sure, Paul's exposition of the evil inclination of sinful flesh is paralleled by a similar view in pre-rabbinic and rabbinic Judaism.[42] Yet, if there is any resemblance between Origen's anthropology and the rabbinic view of the Evil Inclination, this is due to the epistles of the Jew Paul, not to a direct borrowing from the rabbis Origen met.[43]

39 Dupuis 1967, 42–51.

40 Rosen-Zvi 2008. The single exception that he refers to (525) is found in m. Ber. 9:5 and its parallels t. Ber. 6:7 and Sifre Deut 32.

41 See, e.g., Bietenhard 1974; de Lange 1976; Sgherri 1982; Brooks 1988; Blowers 1988; Tzvetkova-Glaser 2010; Stemberger 2013; Dorival and Naiweld 2013.

42 de Boer 2011, 337–39.

43 It is noteworthy that the scholars who studied Origen's contacts with contemporaneous Jews (see n. 41 above) do not refer to the topic of the *yeṣer hara'*.

# 14

# Augustine on the Diabolical Suggestion of Sin

Sophie Lunn-Rockliffe

In debate with his theological opponents, especially the Pelagians, Augustine came to formulate an account of the natures and origins of two different kinds of human sin: "original sin," and individual, personal sins.[1] The former referred to Adam and Eve's primal disobedience, which was biologically transmitted to all their descendants through concupiscence, and guilt for which was shared by all from birth.[2] The latter encompassed the wide range of sins committed individually by humans. Augustine took care to distinguish between these two categories of sin, as, for example, in a treatise dating to about 411, *On the Deserts of Sinners and Infant Baptism*.[3] In this, he distinguished between "the sins which are peculiar to every man (*propria cuique peccata*), which they themselves commit and which belong simply to them," and "that one sin, in and by which all have sinned."[4] He also attacked those who said that infants must be baptized for the remission of the sins which they had themselves committed; on the contrary, he asserted, infants were blameless as far as their conduct in life was concerned, and baptism was only necessary to cleanse them of their inherited sin.[5] While pointing out the differences between these two kinds of sin, Augustine acknowledged that they were causally connected, on the grounds that original sin had had various

[1] On original sin, see Beatrice 1978 and Mann 2001; on individual and "personal" sins, see Wiley 2002, 56–75.

[2] On concupiscence, see Nisula 2012.

[3] *De peccatorum meritis et remissione, et de Baptismo Parvulorum*, ed. Urba and Zycha 1913, 3–151 (trans. NPNF[1]).

[4] Augustine, *Pecc. merit.* I.10.11.

[5] Augustine, *Pecc. merit.* I.17.22.

weakening effects on post-lapsarian humans, which in turn increased the likelihood that they would commit their own personal sins.[6]

This chapter tackles Augustine's treatment of this second category, of individual, personal sins, and focuses in particular on his argument that these sins were sometimes suggested to humans by the devil, a diabolical hamartiology which relates to a model developed elsewhere by Augustine for how human emotions could be stirred up by demons. It explores the relationships in Augustine's thought between demonic and psychological etiologies for emotions and sins, and between philosophical (especially Stoicizing) and theological–exegetical explanatory models. It shows how scriptural exegesis of two particular biblical stories – the serpent's temptation of Adam and Eve in Genesis, and the devil's instigation of Judas's betrayal of Jesus in the Gospels – shaped Augustine's thinking about diabolical suggestion. He regularly expounded these distant scriptural anti-exempla to reveal a timeless truth about the process through which Satan continued to suggest sins to humans: as in Eden, so in the present day. Rather than establishing a strict causal connection between humanity's first sin and all subsequent individual sins, this argument offered instead a looser, analogical comparison between them. Furthermore, Augustine balanced the notion of the diabolical suggestion of human sin with a more spontaneous, self-generating notion of sin which was exemplified by the devil's own first sin – something which could not have been suggested to him by some hostile external agent, since his fall was, in Augustine's cosmology, the first.[7]

This chapter thus pursues a subject – demonic etiologies for sin – that has received relatively muted interest among some notable scholarly treatments of Augustine's ideas of theodicy, his notions of the emotions, and his theory of motivation.[8] Here, I draw comparative inspiration from Rosen-Zvi's recent rehabilitation of a demonological interpretation of the rabbinic "evil inclination" (*yeṣer ra'*) against the dominant scholarly

[6] On the weakening consequences of the fall, see Wetzel 2008. [7] Lunn-Rockliffe 2013.

[8] Byers (2013, 36–37 and nn. 81–83) downplays the significance of demons, pursuing a sophisticated analysis of Augustine's Stoic–Platonic thought which emphasizes its classical antecedents. Sorabji (2000, 347–48) flags up the non-Stoic novelty of the introduction of demons to discussions of "first movements" and "bad thoughts" by Christians from Clement to Antony via Evagrius, as well as by Porphyry; however, he does not discuss the role of the demonic or the diabolical in Augustine's ideas about first movements. Accounts of Augustine's demonology in his *City of God* can be found in Evans (1982, 98–111) and Kelly (1974, 108–14), who compare some demonological passages of Augustine with later medieval writings. Two recent articles by Wiebe (2017) and Smith (2017) considerably refine our understanding of Augustine's demonology (in the *City of God* and across Augustine's oeuvre respectively).

tendency to interpret it in psychological terms, a comparison to which I return in my conclusion.[9] Throughout, I will highlight the aspects of this subject about which Augustine expressed aporetic doubt, including questions of how demons were able to learn humans' barely conceived thoughts, and how demons and the devil suggested sins to humans through thoughts and bodily senses. Here, it becomes apparent that the operation of evil spirits was more mysterious to Augustine than the motivations of his fellow self-sabotaging, sinful human beings.

As we will see, there are some striking resonances between Augustine's thinking on demonic and diabolical causes of emotions and sins and discussions of this topic in Origen's *On First Principles* and Evagrius' *On Thoughts*.[10] However, it is difficult to reconstruct the patterns of textual transmission, as well as the more diffuse influence of orally disseminated ideas, which might explain these resemblances. Evagrius himself owed a great deal to Origen, making it hard to determine whether apparently "Origenist" ideas have been derived firsthand.[11] Scholars disagree about the depth of Augustine's acquaintance with Origen and Evagrius.[12] If Augustine was not linguistically equipped to read independently and extensively in Greek, then he would only have been able to read works by Origen and Evagrius in their Latin translations by the likes of Rufinus; but if we take a more generous view of Augustine's competence in Greek, it is possible to imagine that he had read the original versions of some works by Origen and Evagrius, whose works were in circulation in the west during his lifetime.[13] Augustine's treatment of the external suggestion of sin to humans was not, then, altogether novel, and should be read against a longer tradition of (particularly monastic) thought which similarly blended Stoicizing philosophy with scriptural exegesis.

[9] Rosen-Zvi 2011, 5–8.

[10] The main points of comparison are to be found with Origen, *Princ.* III.2.1–7, ed. and trans. H. Crouzel and M. Simonetti, *SC* 252–3, 268–9, 312 (1978–84); and Evagrius, *On Thoughts*, ed. A. and C. Guillaumont and P. Géhin (1998) ; see also Sinkewicz 2003, 136–82.

[11] On Evagrius' debts to Origen (among others) in the area of demonology, see Stewart 2005.

[12] For a restrained account of Augustine's knowledge of Origen, see Edwards 2012, 223–24; for a more generous evaluation, see Heidl 2003. As to Augustine's knowledge of Evagrius, Byers (2013, 151) states that Evagrius was "not an important influence on Augustine," while Sorabji (2004, 103–04) argues that "Augustine had surely read Evagrius."

[13] On Augustine's linguistic capabilities, see Courcelle 1969, 149–65; Burton 2012, 115–16. On Rufinus and his translations of Origen's works into Latin, see Clark 1992, 158–93. On the circulation of Evagrius' works and their translation into Latin, see Casiday 2013, 42–44.

## 1 DEMONIC AGITATION

Let us start by examining Augustine's early thinking on the subject of the demonic agitation of human emotions. In 389 Nebridius wrote to his close friend Augustine, who had returned to North Africa after his recent baptism in Milan, and who would go on to be ordained at Hippo in 391.[14] Nebridius asked with some urgency how celestial powers were able to reveal things to humans by dreams in their sleep. He asked whether they influenced human minds by thoughts (*per cogitationes*), and whether higher powers actually exhibited in their own body (*in suo corpore*) or in their imagination (*in sua phantasia*) the things that humans dreamed. If they did things in their own body, then humans must surely have another set of eyes that allowed them to see such things even while they slept. But if they did these things in their own imagination, and were thus able to impress human imaginations, why was it, Nebridius asked, that he could not similarly cause a dream in Augustine? After all, he observed in puzzlement, even our bodies have the power of originating dreams in us, compelling us to repeat by imagination and in sleep things that we have already experienced, such as hunger or thirst.[15]

In his response, Augustine subtly adjusted the terms of his correspondent's questions.[16] Where Nebridius had asked about the operations of higher, heavenly powers (*superiores* and *coelestes potestates*), he answered about the activities of higher powers or demons (*superioribus potestatibus vel daemonibus*), and of aerial or ethereal beings (*aeriis aethereisve animantibus*; *qui aerio vel aethereo corpore … agunt*); in Augustine's usage, "aerial beings" generally referred to evil demons, "ethereal beings" to angels.[17] He also side-stepped Nebridius' proposed range of solutions, which speculated about the mode of operation of heavenly powers, and instead concentrated on the human subject. He explained that every emotion (literally "movement of the rational soul," *motus animi*) affected the human body, and that even if these bodily effects, "footprints of (the soul's) motion" (*vestigia sui motus*), were not discernible to humans, they were discernible to higher powers or demons, whose powers of perception were

[14] Brown 2000, 125–30; on Nebridius, see Brown 2000, 57 and 125–28.

[15] Augustine, *Ep.* 8, ed. Goldbacher 1895; trans. Parsons 1951, 20.

[16] Augustine, *Ep.* 9, ed. Goldbacher 1895; trans. Parsons 1951, 21.

[17] On "aerial" and "ethereal" beings, see O'Daly 1987, 122 and n. 32, and Elliott 1998, 128–30 and 240–41. On demons as aerial beings, see, e.g., Augustine, *Civ.* 8.16, 9.3 (citing Apuleius, *De deo Socr.* 8), 9.18.

far superior to those of humans.[18] These effects remained impressed on the body with the force of a habit, ready to be stirred up and so to force thoughts (*cogitationes*) and dreams onto us according to the will (*voluntas*) of the power stirring them up. He then gave a medically derived example of this process which, rather paradoxically given the preceding discussion, did not contain any external agents, demonic or other. Rather, Augustine characterized the internal cycle of human anger reflexively as "a turbulent appetite" (*turbulentus appetitus*): anger increases bile, and increased bile increases our tendency to anger. He concluded that that which the soul, by its motion, effects in the body is able reflexively to move the soul again.

About a decade later, in his *On the Divination of Demons*,[19] Augustine drew on his earlier account of demons' ability to discern and stir up the bodily inscribed traces of human emotions in a description of their ability both to identify and play on human thoughts. Indeed, his use of the same vivid analogies in both texts makes it very likely that he had the argument of his earlier letter in mind, or even to hand, when writing the treatise.[20] In *On Divination*, as in his letter to Nebridius, Augustine stated that demons had superior powers of movement and perception because of the aerial quality of their bodies.[21] However, he provided more detail about the mechanics of demonic persuasion than he had to Nebridius: through the subtlety of their bodies, demons could enter human bodies undetected and "mingling (*miscendo*) themselves with their (i.e. humans') thoughts (*cogitationibus*) through certain imaginary impressions (*per quaedam imaginaria visa*)," they could persuade them in "mysterious and invisible ways (*miris et invisibilibus modis*)."[22] Echoing the explanation offered to Nebridius, he argued that demons could discern human intentions (*dispositiones*) – not only those spoken, but even those merely conceived in thought – since certain signs from the rational soul (*ex animo*) were expressed in the body.[23]

18 For the use of *motus animi* to mean *passiones*, *affectiones*, and *perturbationes*, translating Greek *pathê*, see Augustine, *Civ.* 9.4, discussed below.

19 *De divinitate daemonum*, ed. Zycha 1900; trans. Brown 1955, 415–42.

20 Both texts make striking comparisons between the operation of demons and the marvelous spectacle of rope-dancers (*funambuli*) and other musical and theatrical performers: see Augustine, *Div.* 4.8 and *Ep.* 9.3. The association of these kinds of performers with the demonic had, of course, a strong moral point; see Webb (2008, 197–276) on Christians and the theater.

21 Augustine, *Div.* 3.7.

22 Augustine, *Div.* 5.9. See also Augustine, *Div. quaest. LXXXIII*, 12, in which he reports the words of a learned pagan, Fonteius of Carthage, about the dangers of a "wicked spirit" (*malignus spiritus*) intermingled with the senses (*sensibus immixtus*) polluting the soul and clouding the light of the mind.

23 Augustine, *Div.* 5.9.

Nebridius' letter to Augustine, Augustine's response to that letter, and his reflections on demons in *On Divination* all contain intriguing echoes of Evagrius' *On Thoughts*, although it is unclear if and how Nebridius and Augustine would have been able to access this work, and of course resemblances to it can be explained by their sharing some other common source. Nebridius' question about the precise operation of spiritual powers in dreams recalls Evagrius' discussion of the demonic manipulation of human dreams.[24] Augustine's explanation of how demons could "read" human bodies resembles Evagrius' account of how demons examined humans' bodily movements and gestures carefully in order to discern what kinds of mental representations they harbored in their hearts, and as a basis for attacking them.[25] Augustine's hesitancy to reveal the mechanics of demons' operations also chimes with Evagrius' coyness on the subject. In his *Retractations*, Augustine expressed regret about his *On the Divination of Demons*, stating that he had spoken on "an obscure subject" (*rem occultissimam*) – namely how demons could discern humans' thoughts through the expression of those thoughts in their bodies – with more confidence than he should have; he explained that although it had been discovered through experience that such thoughts come to the notice of demons, it was very unclear whether this was through signs furnished by the bodies of those thinking these thoughts, or whether demons learned these things through "another spiritual power" (*alia vi et ea spiritali*).[26] This shares something with Evagrius' refusal to go into detail about how demons recognized the mental representations in human hearts on the basis not just of words but also movements of the body; Evagrius explained that "our holy priest" Macarius of Alexandria had forbidden him from explaining these matters any further, as inappropriate for a general audience.[27]

Augustine's interest in the demonic contribution to human emotions was not unwavering or consistent. As we have already seen, his letter to Nebridius initially foregrounded the role of demons, before abandoning them altogether in his discussion of emotions such as anger. In book 9 of his monumental *City of God*, in which he

[24] Cf. Evagrius, *Octo. spir.* 4; see also 27–9 on dreams. Nebridius, like Evagrius, invokes sensations such as thirst in sleep.

[25] Cf. Evagrius, *Octo. spir.* 37.

[26] Augustine, *Retract.* 2.56, ed. Knöll 1902; trans. Bogan 1968.

[27] Evagrius, *Mal. cog.* 37; see *Mal. cog.* 16, where he also refuses to write in more detail about the machinations of demons, out of concern for the "more simple" of his readers.

reported and evaluated a large body of "pagan" philosophical wisdom about demons and investigated the issue of the genesis of the emotions (*animi motus*) or passions (*passiones*), Augustine also showed varying interest in the demons.[28] To begin with, he drew on the Platonist Apuleius' account of demons in his *On the God of Socrates*, presenting them as creatures who were disturbed by storms of turbulent emotions, which he also characterized in moralizing terms as "depraved" (*pravis*).[29] He compared the demons unfavorably to the wise man, before moving on to discuss the Stoic claim that emotions did not affect the wise man, in a long chapter in which the demons disappeared from view altogether.[30] Here, he attempted to argue that the substance of the Stoics' own arguments in fact tended closer to the views of their Platonist opponents, namely, that although emotions did affect the wise man, he was nonetheless not subject to them.

In this context he paraphrased a section of Aulus Gellius' *Attic Nights* that narrated a philosopher's reactions to a storm at sea, and reported his subsequent exposition of Epictetus. Sorabji has convincingly shown that first Gellius and then Augustine confused Stoic "pre-passions" with "emotions" proper.[31] This has the result that Augustine's reportage of the Stoic position stressed that man could not control whether and when "impressions" (*visa* or *phantasiae*) struck and moved the rational soul (*animus*). Indeed, these impressions could move the rational soul of even the wise man, which inevitably produced a visible bodily effect, so that he briefly grew pale (*expalluit*) from fear. We have, of course, already encountered this last idea, of human emotions producing bodily effects, in Augustine's letter to Nebridius, but there it was integrated into an account of demonic agitation; here, no demons are involved. Augustine stressed in *City of God* that although humans had no control over whether or not they received "impressions," they did have control over whether they assented to them. This is a theme that we shall encounter shortly in various other of his works, although there it is thoroughly "diabolized," that is, cast as a moral choice to accept impressions from the devil.

[28] Augustine, *City of God*, ed. Dombart and Kalb 1955; trans. Dyson 1998.

[29] Augustine, *Civ.* 9.3. Although Augustine's account of the emotions is often morally inflected, he was careful not to elide "sin" with "emotion," as for example in his discussion in *Div. quaest. LXXXIII*, 77, "is fear a sin?"

[30] Augustine, *Civ.* 9.4.

[31] On Gellius' and Augustine's transformation of Stoic ideas of the pre-passions, see Sorabji 2000, 72–84; Wetzel 2007, 352–55. On Augustine's "Stoicism" more broadly, see, for example, Colish 1985, 2: 142–238; Byers 2013.

## 2 DIABOLICAL SUGGESTION

In the second part of this chapter, I will examine a number of Augustine's exegetical, homiletic, and didactic works which integrated Stoicizing ideas of the emotions and of "motivating impressions" with readings of key passages of Scripture to provide an account of the stimulation of human sins by evil spiritual agency. However, where Augustine identified these agents as plural demons in his letter to Nebridius and *On Divination*, in these other texts he rather emphasized the intervention of the devil alone. This difference can be explained in part by these texts' more decisively exegetical character, which saw them homing in on key scriptural episodes of diabolical suggestion: the satanic serpent in Eden, and the devil who entered Judas. It also probably reflects Augustine's appropriation of the work of earlier exegetes. It is quite possible that he had read some portions of Origen, whether directly or in translation, which tackle diabolical instigation with reference to scriptural exempla; he might also have drawn on exegetical works by writers such as Ambrose, who had in turn quarried generously from Origen.[32]

Augustine's *On Genesis against the Manicheans* was, as its title suggests, both a polemical and an exegetical treatise, written in Africa at the turn of the 380s and 390s, at about the same time as the correspondence with Nebridius discussed above.[33] His commentary *On the Sermon on the Mount* was written a little later, a year after his ordination to the episcopate at Hippo in 395.[34] In the first work Augustine described the coming to be of sin (*peccatum*), which he then outlined in pithier and more precise terms in the later text as a threefold process that moved from suggestion, through delight and desire, to consent: in much the same way that, on the Stoic model, emotions were only elicited if assent was given, sin was only committed if reason consented to the delight generated by the initial suggestion, or "motivating impression." In both texts Augustine moved between scriptural past and contemporary predicament, collapsing the boundary between exegesis and moral instruction. Sinners from the scriptural past, Adam and Eve and Judas, thus became figures of timeless relevance who could illuminate and exemplify the long history of postlapsarian human sinning, up to and including Augustine's present. In both

[32] Origen, *Princ.* III.2.1 discusses a number of scriptural examples. On Augustine's "Origenism," see Bammel 1992 and Heidl 2003.

[33] Augustine, *On Genesis against the Manicheans*, ed. Weber 1998; trans. Teske 1991, 47–141. On the dating of this text, see Augustine, *Retract.* 1.10.1, and Teske 1991, 4.

[34] Augustine, *Sermon on the Mount*, ed. Mutzenbecher 1967; trans. Kavanagh 1951.

texts Augustine identified the source of evil suggestion as the devil, and suggestion as operating either through thought and memory (*cogitatio* and *memoria*) or through the bodily senses (*corporis sensus*).

In book 2 of his commentary on Genesis, tackling the introduction of the serpent and temptation story in chapter 3 of Genesis, Augustine performed a bravura piece of allegorical exegesis that seems to have been inspired in part by the sermons he had heard Ambrose preach in Milan and which circulated as treatises on the days of creation, and on paradise.[35] According to Augustine's figurative interpretation, the serpent in Eden signifies the devil, but he should not be thought to have been literally "in" paradise, for paradise was not an actual place but rather a state, the "life of bliss" (*beata vita*); furthermore, the devil did not make his approach to Adam and Eve "in bodily fashion" (*corporaliter*), but "as a spirit" (*spiritaliter*).[36] Augustine then moved into the present tense to ask how the serpentine devil deceives humans in general: "Surely, then, he does not appear to them visibly (*visibiliter*), nor does he approach those in whom he works as if through a kind of physical space (*quasi corporeis locis*)?" Augustine's answer was also couched in the present tense, signaling the movement from the exposition of Scripture into the revelation of timeless truths about the devil's mode of operation. It emphatically excluded the possibility that Satan approaches humans visibly or in physical space, diverging from Augustine's earlier explanation to Nebridius that demons' exceptionally subtle constitution allows them to stir up humans in the body without our perceiving it. Instead, he asserted that the devil "suggests" (*suggerit*) things "through thoughts" (*per cogitationes*) to people, although he highlighted the obscure operation of this process by noting that this worked "in mysterious ways" (*miris modis*).

Augustine then departed from the text of Genesis to introduce a New Testament case of diabolical suggestion: Judas. Here, again in the form of question and answer, Augustine addressed the issue of "how" (*quomodo*) the devil approached Judas when he persuaded him to betray Jesus: "Surely he (the Devil) was not seen in a (physical) place (*in locis*), nor was he seen (visibly) with these eyes by him (Judas)? Of course not; as it says, he (the Devil) entered into his (Judas's) heart (*intravit in cor eius*)." Augustine's question reprised what he had just outlined of the more general approach of the devil to humankind (that he was not seen visibly or in physical places), and thus "physical" is implied of "place" here, and

[35] Ambrose, *Hexameron* and *On Paradise*, ed. Schenkl 1897; trans. Savage 1961.

[36] Augustine, *Gen. Man.* 2.14.20.

"visibly" of his appearance. In his emphatic denial of this possibility, Augustine stressed the secretive quality of Satan's entry in a phrase that conflated two distinct verses from an Old Latin text of the Gospel of John, providing us with an example of Augustine's habit of (what Houghton dubs) "flattening" his "mental" text of the Bible.[37] It is hard to reconstruct the precise Old Latin text of John used by Augustine for his commentary on Genesis,[38] but it appears that he mixed the content of two verses of John (13:2, where the devil "put it into Judas' heart" to betray Jesus; and 13:27, where Satan "entered into Judas" after he had received bread from Jesus) to coin a new phrase: "he (the devil) entered into his (Judas') heart" (*intravit in cor eius*).[39] Although the language of thought and deliberation is absent from Augustine's description of the devil's entry into Judas, it is arguably implied by mention of *cor*, the heart; in Christian Latin usage this often denoted the seat of cognitive faculties of thought and deliberation, and so the very place of *cogitatio*.[40] Indeed, in his *Tractates on the Gospel of John*, written some two decades later, Augustine made it clear that the devil's suggestion to Judas was made through thought, not in speech, commenting of John 13.2 that "Such a putting (*missio*) is a spiritual suggestion (*spiritalis suggestio*): and enters not by the ear, but through thought (*per cogitationem*); and through this not bodily, but spiritually."[41]

In the next section of his commentary on Genesis, Augustine again used the present tense to assert that the drama in Eden had eternal descriptive power for the process of sin:

37 See Houghton 2008, 67–69; and 139–40 on the text of John in *On Genesis against the Manicheans*.

38 In his later *Tractates on the Gospel of John*, Augustine's *lemmata* provide witnesses to his dependence on a Vulgate text type of John: *Tract. Ev. Jo.* 55.3 quotes John 13:2 (*et coena facta, cum diabolus iam misisset in cor, ut traderet eum Iudas Simonis Iscariotes*); *Tract. Ev. Jo.* 62.1 quotes John 13:27 (*et post panem tunc introivit in illum satanas*).

39 Houghton 2008, 308, cites other instances of such conflation: Augustine, *Enarrat. Ps.* 3.1; *Serm.* 313E.4; *Enarrat. Ps.* 136.9.

40 Old Latin and Vulgate texts of the Bible used *cogitatio cordis* to render the idea of man's plotting wickedness in, among others, two key passages of Genesis (6:5 and 8:21). On the heart as seat of deliberation, see Byers 2013, 35 and n. 88; cf. van Kooten and Hayward, Chapters 9 and 15 in this volume.

41 Augustine, *Tract. Ev. Jo.* 55.4. It is notable that Augustine here interprets "the heart" (*cor*) in his Latin text of John 13:2 as referring to "the heart of Judas" (*cor Judae*), not the devil's own heart; there is variation between manuscripts of the Greek text of the Gospel here which could support the latter reading. See Barrett 1978, 439.

Even now, when someone slides down into sin (*cum ad peccatum quisque delabitur*), nothing else takes place but what then occurred with those three; the serpent, the woman and the man. For first suggestion is made, whether by thought (*per cogitationem*) or by the senses of the body (*per sensus corporis*), by seeing or touching or hearing or tasting or smelling.

Here, Augustine provided an alternative to the model of the operation of suggestion outlined in the previous section; where the devil tempted Judas through thoughts (*cogitationes*), Adam and Eve had implicitly been tempted through bodily senses (*sensus corporis*). He concluded: "When this suggestion (*suggestio*) has been made, if our desire (*cupiditas*) is not moved towards sinning, the cunning of the serpent will be shut out. If, however, it is moved, it will be as though the woman were already persuaded."[42] In this phrase, as elsewhere in this passage, Augustine's representation of delight and desire moving toward sin both drew on and transformed Stoicizing models of the emotions and passions: "suggestion" (*suggestio*) in Augustine's usage has been argued persuasively by Byers to represent the Stoic idea of "motivating impression" (*phantasia hormêtikê*).[43] However, whereas "motivating impressions" in Stoic thought were not the property of supernatural powers, Augustine claims that "suggestion," working through thoughts, could be diabolical.

Augustine gave further precision to his account of the process of sin in his slightly later *Commentary on the Sermon on the Mount*, in a passage discussing Jesus' warning in Matthew that "everyone who looks at a woman with lust has already committed adultery with her in his heart (*in corde suo*)"[44] – yet another scriptural instance of the idea that thought was an activity associated with the human heart. Elaborating on this saying, Augustine enumerated the three stages by which sin was completed (*impletur peccatum*) as suggestion, delight, and consent (*suggestio*, *delectatio*, and *consensio*), a scheme which might owe something to Origen.[45] As in his *Commentary on Genesis*, Augustine divided suggestion into two modes: that which took place "through memory" (*per memoriam*) – that is, by a mental, imaginative capacity – and that which worked "through the bodily senses" (*per corporis sensus*) of sight, hearing, smell, taste, and touch. "Suggestion" presented itself to the soul or mind, as in the example of how, when fasting, the sight of food stirred the

[42] August. *Gen. Man.* 2.14.21. [43] See Byers 2013, 30–35 and O'Daly 1987, 106–08.

[44] Matt 5:28, cited in Augustine, *Serm. Dom.* 1.12.33.

[45] Augustine, *Serm. Dom.* 1.12.34. On the derivation of this model from Origen, see Heidl 2003, 155–58, and Teselle 1990.

appetite with delight. Augustine then provided an account of the steps (*gradus*) of suggestion, comparing it to something made "as if by a serpent (*quasi a serpente suggestio fiat*), that is, by a slippery and spinning – that is, a temporal – movement of bodies." He juxtaposed "images (*fantasmata*) turning about within, inside the soul," which were derived from "the body, from outside," and "hidden movement of the body," including the five senses, which "touches the soul." He concludes that "the more secretly it glides in, so as to take hold of thought (*ut cogitationem contingat*), the more aptly is it compared to a serpent."[46]

This description of bodily movement impressing mental images on the soul reverses the idea explored in his letter to Nebridius and *On Divination*, whereby the movements of the soul leave an impression on the body. Although Augustine clearly outlined in this passage the two routes, mental and corporeal, through which suggestion worked, he was rather more allusive about its source: he used serpentine figurative language to describe it, but did not name it as Satan. Suggestion here is figured in a passive construction with an ablative agent, which rather distances the serpent from the act; indeed, it is not presented as made directly by a particular serpent, such as the devil in Eden, but only operates "like," or "in the manner of" (*quasi*), a serpent. In the next few lines of this passage, Augustine clarified the inspiration for the serpentine comparison. He wrote that the three stages of sin "resemble that transaction which is described in Genesis," and again presented suggestion and persuasion (implicitly "to sin") in a passively constructed analogy, as "made as if by the serpent" (*quasi a serpente fiat*). He located "delight" (*delectatio*) and "consent" (*consensio*) to sin, in, respectively, the carnal appetite of Eve and the reason of Adam, reprising the gendered presentation of the stages of sin from the *Commentary on Genesis*. Satan is not named at any point in this passage, but his presence is implicit in the slippery serpent of Eden, long interpreted by Christians as a diabolical disguise.[47]

## 3 VOLUNTARY SIN

So far we have seen that Augustine's explanation of human sin, derived in part from readings of Scripture, regularly traced it back to the suggestion

[46] Augustine, *Serm. Dom.* 1.12.34.

[47] On the Genesis serpent as Satan, see Forsyth 1987, 304–05, Kelly 2006, 147–59, and Gilhus 2006, 162–63, 240–42.

of Satan. However, Augustine vigorously denied that this understanding of the devil's operation in any way excused humans from responsibility for their own sins. In the same way that a Stoic account of the emotions insisted on the key of assent to "motivating impressions," so Augustine insisted on the significance of consent to sin. He made this case particularly strongly in a more philosophically and less exegetically focused kind of text, *On the Free Choice of the Will*, the first book of which was begun at Rome in the 380s shortly after his conversion, and books 2 and 3 of which were completed at Hippo by 395.[48] This work dealt with the origins of evil, a hoary question posed by his interlocutor Evodius, and the subject of broader ongoing debate with the Manicheans. It included, toward the end of book 3, an explanation of the "sources of sins" (*origines peccatorum*), which presents a rather different taxonomy from that which we have so far encountered.

Augustine distinguished between sin that came from our own spontaneous thought (*spontanea cogitatio*) and that which came from the persuasion of another (*persuasio alterius*). He stressed that both were voluntary: a person who sins from their own thoughts does not do so unwillingly (*invitus*), and similarly a person who consents to the evil persuasion of another still sins by their own will (*voluntate*). Augustine's identification of two different sources of sins here might be related to the threefold distinction found both in Rufinus' Latin translation of Origen's *On First Principles* and in Evagrius' *On Thoughts*, although it somewhat modifies those etiologies.[49] Augustine stressed that sin by one of these routes was more blameworthy than by the other: it was more serious to sin by one's own thinking, without the persuasion of another. It was also more serious to be an agent persuading someone else to sin through envy and trickery (*invidentia dolusque*) than to be led into sinning by persuasion; mention of two of the key characteristics imputed to Satan show that Augustine had in mind the devil as the key example of an agent persuading sins in others. This becomes clearer still in the next part of this passage, where Augustine characterized the devil as one who made humanity his subject through evil

[48] Augustine, *On the Free Choice of the Will*, ed. Green 1970; trans. King 2010.

[49] Origen, *Princ.* III.2.4 (Rufinus' Latin translation): "Thoughts (*cogitationes*) sometimes come from us ourselves, sometimes are stirred up by hostile powers (*a contrariis virtutibus*), and sometimes are introduced even by God or the holy angels." He went on to reassure his readers that it was possible, when an evil power (*maligna virtus*) has begun to incite us to evil, for us to repel wicked suggestions (*pravas suggestiones*). See Heidl 2003, 155, and Sorabji 2000, 346, 355, and 372–73. Rufinus' translation was probably made during his stay in Rome in 398, and might have reached Augustine.

persuasion. That is, Augustine made it clear that the devil sinned more seriously than a human being on the second charge.[50] As we will see, Augustine's account of the genesis of the devil's first sin also condemned him on the first charge, as one who sinned without the persuasion of another.

In a later passage of book 3 of *On Free Choice*, Augustine explained that nothing except some kind of impression (*aliquod visum*) attracts the will to do something, and that although a person has no power over what impression touches them, they do have the power to take up or reject that impression, and misery or happiness thus deservedly follow.[51] This resembles Augustine's report in *City of God* of Stoic ideas of impressions (*visa* and *phantasiae*), which also distinguished between the fact that it was not in human power whether or when such impressions struck the soul, unlike consent to those impressions; again, we see the application of philosophical theories of "impressions" begetting emotions to a more exegetically slanted account of the suggestion of sins by Satan. In *On Free Choice* Augustine then elaborated on the two different kinds, or indeed sources, of these impressions: they might be derived from "higher things" (*ex superioribus*), as in the case of God's command to Adam in Eden, or from "lower things" (*ex inferioribus*), as in the case of the suggestion of the serpent (*suggestio serpentis*). Here we have a clear example of how Augustine equated "impression" (*visum*) with diabolical suggestion (*suggestio*). He also stressed that although the man in Eden had no control over the content of God's command, or over the serpent's suggestion, he was nonetheless completely free to choose to resist them.[52]

Augustine raised a further problem with this: the first man had clearly received impressions (*visa*) from either side, so where did the counsel of impiety come from that was suggested to the devil himself, counsel which he took and by which he fell from the privileged heights of heaven?[53] Augustine explained that one who wills "has to will something," and "unless this something is either advised externally by bodily sense (*extrinsecus per sensum corporis admoneatur*), or arrives within the mind in hidden ways, he cannot will it."[54] This seems to pick up on the oft-stated contrast between suggestion as communicated through bodily senses and through thought, although there is an aporetic quality to Augustine's qualification that mental suggestion happens "in hidden ways" (*occultis*

[50] Augustine, *Lib.* 3.10.29.104–06.
[51] Augustine, *Lib.* 3.25.74.255.
[52] Augustine, *Lib.* 3.25.74.256–57.
[53] Augustine, *Lib.* 3.25.75.258.
[54] Augustine, *Lib.* 3.25.75.259.

*modis*), reminiscent of a similar expression of doubt about the operation of demons in his earlier letter to Nebridius.

Augustine then identified the most important distinction as the source (rather than the operation) of the two kinds of impressions (*visa*):

> Hence we should distinguish between two kinds of impressions, of which one is that which comes from the will of someone trying to persuade (*a voluntate suadentis*), like that of the devil to which Adam consented when he sinned, and the other comes from things subject either to the attention of the rational soul (*animus*) or to the bodily senses.[55]

This refines the distinction made earlier in this text between sin that comes from one's own spontaneous thought (*spontanea cogitatio*) and sin that comes from the persuasion of another (*persuasio alterius*). Adam's sin was the latter, and, as we soon learn, the devil's was the former. Augustine explained that among things subject to the attention of the rational soul (*animus*) was first of all the rational soul itself. In a difficult passage he discussed how, in contemplating the highest wisdom, the rational soul somehow looks on itself, and, in a reflexive maneuver, enters into its own mind (*mens*); if it then fails to act with sufficient humility, and to remember that it is nothing compared to God, but tries to imitate God and desires to be greater, then this is pride, the first sin of all.[56] It thus emerges that the devil's first sin was not suggested to him by another, but by some kind of internal cycle of spontaneous self-contemplation that engendered pride.[57] This rendered his sin more serious than that of Adam, persuaded to sin by another. Augustine ends this discussion by returning to the here and now, and to the sincere wish that no impressions (*visa*) from lower things (*ex inferioribus*) should wrench us away from the higher vision.

Despite differentiating between more or less serious kinds of sin on the grounds of whether it was suggested by persuasion or one's own thought, Augustine insisted that both were voluntary; his relative hierarchy of sin did not excuse a person from responsibility for consenting to diabolical impressions or suggestions. However, against the background of the Pelagian controversy, Augustine increasingly emphasized humankind's need for divine grace in resisting such suggestions. This can be seen in his discussion of suggestion in *Tractate 55 on the Gospel of John*, in which he contrasted diabolical suggestions (*diabolicae suggestiones*) with good suggestions (*bonas suggestiones*), and claimed that the human mind (*mens*

[55] Augustine, *Lib.* 3.25.75.259–60. [56] Augustine, *Lib.* 3.25.75.260–63.
[57] Lunn-Rockliffe 2013, 122–26.

*humana*) was either helped by grace (*adiuta per gratiam*) or abandoned by divine help (*divino auxilio deserta*) in consenting to one or the other.[58]

The concern to acknowledge divine help in the fight against sin is also visible in Augustine's *On Continence.* This was for some time dated to early in his career because of its supposedly anti-Manichean themes. However, it also contains some anti-Pelagian concerns, and a later dating is now preferred.[59] In chapter 10 Augustine warned his listeners not to presume on their own strength and to watch "those snares of the suggestions of the devil" (*illas diabolicarum suggestionum insidias*).[60] He returned to the devil's "deadly suggestions" (*mortiferae suggestiones*) later in this text, which he further specified as those "whereby he further urges the sinner to excuse rather than accuse his own sins."[61] He decried those who complained that they were compelled by various forces to sin, including those who "refer all the evil that they do to the devil, nor do they wish to have even a share (sc. of responsibility) with him." This recalls the scathing criticism made by Origen of "simple" Christians who think that all men's sins are caused by "the persistent efforts of these opposing powers exerted upon the minds of sinners ... For if, for example, there were no devil, no single human being would go astray."[62] Augustine expressed incredulity about a similar argument: "Although they are able to imagine that [the devil] has persuaded them to evil by secret suggestions (*occultis suggestionibus*), they are not able to doubt that they themselves have yielded to those suggestions no matter whence they came."[63] Here Augustine attacked the idea that because a sin had been suggested by Satan, this absolved the sinner from responsibility for it. Such people gave over the totality of their ill-doing to him, but failed to realize that the devil's power of suggestion was not irresistible.

Augustine's characterization of the devil's suggestions as "secret" (*occultus*) here perhaps applied not just to their being hidden from sinners, but also to their being mysterious in their genesis and operation to Augustine himself. We have seen a number of these kinds of aporetic markers, by which suggestions were said to work *miris modis* and *occultis modis*. Sometimes they took the form of unanswered questions, as in his *Tractate 55 on the Gospel of John*: "But how are such things done, so that

[58] Augustine, *Tract. Ev. Jo.* 55.4.

[59] Augustine, *On Continence*, ed. Zycha 1900, 139–83; ed. and trans. Kearney and Hunter 1999.

[60] Augustine, *Contin.* 10. [61] Augustine, *Contin.* 13. [62] Origen, *Princ.* III.2.2.

[63] Augustine, *Contin.* 14.

devilish suggestions (*diabolicae suggestiones*) should be introduced, and so mingle (*misceantur*) with human thoughts (*humanis cogitationibus*) that a man accounts them his own (*ut eas tanquam suas deputet homo*), how can a man know?"[64] Here, Augustine reprised an idea developed in his slightly earlier *On Divination*, where he wrote about the mingling (*miscendo*) of demons with human thoughts through imaginary impressions. However, in this tractate he alerted readers to a further problematic effect of this mixing, which is that it was done in such a way that a man judged the demonically affected thoughts to be his own. This, in turn, returns us to the recursive, reflexive picture of demonic emotions which Augustine outlined early on in his letter to Nebridius, where demons were able to get inside humans to activate lingering bodily traces (the "habit") of earlier mental activity.

## 4 CONCLUSION

We have seen that Augustine repeatedly asked questions about the genesis of human sins: what kinds of impressions or suggestions motivated or affected sin? What was the source of that impression, and how was it conveyed? At what point did humans' and demons' assent to an impression tip over into the conception, however secret and interior, of a sin? If sin could be suggested from without by an external agent, did that excuse the sinner from responsibility for sinning? In tackling these questions, he seems to have drawn on Stoic ideas of the genesis of the emotions and passions, and to have used ideas that resemble those found in works by Origen and Evagrius; both of these writers had integrated Stoic notions of motivating impressions with demonic etiologies for sin, and Origen in particular had explicated the diabolical suggestion of sin through notorious anti-exempla from Scripture such as Judas, Adam and Eve. In commenting on these last cautionary tales, Augustine repeatedly and explicitly collapsed the boundary between the sinners of the Bible and contemporary sinners: as then, so also now.

Although it is tempting to systematize Augustine's thought, it is important to remember that much of it developed in response to texts or ideas to which he objected: against Manicheism in the earlier phase of his episcopate, and against Pelagianism after about 411. This helps to explain why Augustine's writings on sin can seem somewhat paradoxical in their emphases. On the one hand, he was keen to repudiate anything

[64] Augustine, *Tract. Ev. Jo.* 55.4.

reminiscent of Manichean anthropology which suggested that there had been, from the moment of their creation, something rotten in the matter of humans. On the other hand, he was eager to stress to the Pelagians that Adam and Eve's sin had so weakened humanity's ability to will the good that they were particularly liable to the effects of diabolical temptation, and thus in need of God's grace to resist it. It is striking, then, that across his lifetime, and in a range of works of varying theological colors, the diabolical suggestion of sin appears to have been a relatively stable and significant feature of Augustine's hamartiology. He consistently stressed Satan's role in Scripture as suggester and tempter; not just of Adam, or Judas, but even of Christ. Indeed, Augustine described the devil making "suggestions" to Christ in one homily on the New Testament, echoing language we have observed elsewhere of the devil's suggestions to ordinary human sinners.[65]

In my introduction, I suggested that Augustine's thinking on the idea of demonic and diabolical suggestion could be compared with the rabbinic idea of the evil *yeṣer*. Of course, it is unlikely that Augustine had directly encountered this notion, given the relatively limited opportunities for personal contact with Jewish thinkers and communities during his brief rhetorical career at Rome and Milan in the 380s, and then during his long tenure of the bishopric at Hippo in North Africa from 395 to 430.[66] Unlike Jerome, Augustine never learned to read Hebrew, and thus had no direct access to rabbinic learning.[67] Instead, his access to Jewish teaching was likely mediated through the works of learned Christians: some, like Origen, had had direct contact with the rabbis of Alexandria and Caesarea, and had learned Hebrew,[68] and many, like Ambrose, had read Philo.[69] Furthermore, the evil *yeṣer* is absent from most strands of Jewish wisdom that might have been transmitted to him indirectly, although it is possible that traces of it can be discerned in the good and bad inclinations of pseudepigraphal literature such as the Testament of Asher.[70] Perhaps the closest encounter Augustine had with anything resembling *yeṣer hara'* was in the dualist anthropology of Manicheism, a system to which he was affiliated in his younger days as a "hearer,"

[65] Augustine, *Serm.* 73.2 on the New Testament.
[66] On Augustine's contact with Jewish communities, see Fredriksen 2010. On allusion to Jewish oral tradition, see Horbury 2010, 8–9.
[67] Burton 2012, 115.
[68] On Origen and rabbinic thought, see de Lange 1976; Rosen-Zvi 2011, 38–40.
[69] See Runia 1993.
[70] On the reception of the evil *yeṣer* in pseudepigraphical literature, see Stewart 2005, 4.

a low-grade initiate, but which he finally and definitively rejected for a Platonizing kind of Christianity in 386. That rejection is very visible in, for instance, his treatise *On Two Souls*, where he attacked a Manichean teaching that resembles the *yeṣer hara'*, although cast in psychic terms: the presence of two souls, one good, one evil, within each human being (a notion which itself had complicated origins).[71]

Although Augustine did not directly receive the rabbinic idea of the evil *yeṣer*, his devil bears comparison with this figure. Much as Rosen-Zvi analyzes contemporary demonological discourse from the world of Christian monasticism to demonstrate that the *yeṣer* "functions in the very same way as demons in contemporaneous literatures," we can try to compare Augustine's suggestive devil with the rabbinic *yeṣer* to establish how far it should be viewed as a demonological, and how far a psychological entity.[72] Augustine's devil is a single external creature who can nonetheless insinuate himself inside humans so that his thoughts mix with their own, and who provides tempting impressions and persuasive suggestions; when humans assent, whether in thought or deed, they commit sins. This devil shares some features with the evil *yeṣer*, itself a demonic being distinct from self but nonetheless residing inside the human heart, and an "antinomian enticer" who draws humans to sins. However, the devil is also a "cosmic being" with a developing biography, personality, and set of ambitions, and this separate and external personality looks rather different from the "internalized" *yeṣer*; indeed, it may be telling that there are only very limited examples of the assimilation of Satan to *yeṣer hara'* in rabbinic literature.[73]

The Christian devil shares an interesting grammatical singularity with the evil *yeṣer*, which, although as manifold as the humans who have it, is always referred to in the singular. Here, Augustine's insistence in his didactic and exegetical texts on the singularity of the devil who suggests sins to humans notably diverges from his emphasis on the work of the plurality of demons in manipulating the emotions in the letter to Nebridius, and in *On the Divination of Demons*. This difference of emphasis can partly be explained by the different focuses of and influences on the two kinds of texts: Augustine's exegetical and didactic treatises

[71] Augustine, *On Two Souls*, ed. Zycha 1891, trans. Newman 1887, 95–107. Of course, Augustine might not have given an accurate account of Manichean anthropology for polemical reasons. See Wetzel 1992, 88–96; BeDuhn 2013, 103–21.

[72] On comparative methodology, see Rosen-Zvi 2011, 36–43.

[73] On these characterizations of *yeṣer hara'*, see Rosen-Zvi 2011, 6–7; on rabbinic assimilation of Satan and the *yeṣer*, see Rosen-Zvi 2011, 161–62.

circled around scriptural examples of Satan's suggestion of sin to Adam and Eve, and to Judas, while his letter to Nebridius and *On Divination* eschewed scriptural exegesis in favor of a Stoicizing account of the emotions. However, I would also argue that, overall, Augustine evinces a more consistent preoccupation with the suggestion of sin by the Devil as a singular being, compared to earlier and contemporary writers who tackled the topic and whose works he might have read. Origen had yoked together and treated almost interchangeably the influence of plural "opposing powers" (*contrariae virtutes*) and a singular opponent, the devil.[74] The work of Evagrius that seems to be closest to Augustine, *On Thoughts*, focuses almost exclusively on the demons. We also find a greater variability in accounts of the suggestion of sin in Cassian's Latin *Conferences*:[75] he reports conversations between Germanus and Moses, and between Germanus and Serenus, which tackle the singular diabolical and plural demonic suggestion of sin respectively.[76] Although Cassian and Augustine were contemporaries, it is unlikely that they were drawing on each other's work, for it has been shown that the two make only veiled references to each other, and that the influence is often negative.[77] Instead, any resemblances between the two are better explained by their drawing on common sources, principally Origen, Evagrius, and Stoic philosophy. It remains to be determined whether Augustine's deployment of ideas from these sources in his hamartiology was direct or indirect, but it is clear that his synthesis was distinctively diabolical.

74 See Origen, *Princ.* III.2.1–7 *passim.*

75 Cassian, *Conferences*, ed. Pichery 1955–59. On the date of Cassian's *Conferences*, probably before 426, see Pichery 1955, 28–30.

76 On Cassian's knowledge of Origen and Evagrius, see Marsili 1936; Pichery 1955, 58–59; Stewart 1998, 35–37. On Cassian's Stoicism, see Colish 1985, 2: 115–22.

77 On Cassian's attitude to Augustine, see Ramsey 1993a, 1993b; Stewart 1998, 35–37, 82–83. For an argument suggesting that Augustine had read some Cassian, see Duchrow 1963.

# 15

# Jerome and the "Inclination" (*yeṣer*): The Evidence of the Vulgate

C. T. R. Hayward

By the time of Jerome's birth in the first half of the fourth century CE, the rabbinic Sages had become well accustomed to speaking of the bad *yeṣer* and the good *yeṣer* as constituent elements in the make-up of the individual human being.[1] The two expressions are already found side by side at m. Ber. 9:5, interpreting Deut 6:5. Their place in what is an exegetical setting illustrates that the idea of the *yeṣer* had its home not in speculation, but in learned exposition of Scripture.[2] While rabbinic writings later than the Mishnah continue to speak of both the good and the bad *yeṣer*, references to and discussion of the latter, simply designated "the *yeṣer*," often predominate to the exclusion of the good *yeṣer*.[3] Questions such as the origins of this *yeṣer*, its precise nature, its *raison d'être*, the moment in a person's existence at which it makes its first appearance, and many others are debated; and antidotes to it are prescribed. In our own day, students of rabbinic Judaism have emphasized the complexity of the thinking that attaches itself to the bad *yeṣer*, and have attempted rigorously to analyze the variety of situations in which the Sages invoked it. Their researches have tended to distance the *yeṣer* from association with sin, an association favored by older scholarship, and to view it as bound up especially with sexual desire, whose promptings the observant Jew must bring under control.[4]

[1] The date of Jerome's birth is debated. Kelly 1975, 337–39, cautiously accepts 331 BCE, the date given by Prosper of Aquitaine. Recent scholars (e.g. Rebenich 1992, 22–23) tend to agree on 347 BCE.

[2] As Porter 1901, 108; Schechter 1961, 242–47; Schofer 2003, 26–27; Schofer 2007, 328–33.

[3] See Stiegman 1979, 526.

[4] See Rosen-Zvi 2008 (esp. 513–16); Rosen-Zvi 2011; Boyarin 1993.

Jerome first visited the East on a pilgrimage to Jerusalem in 372 CE. For some years (ca. 375–77) he lived near Antioch in the desert of Chalcis,[5] before resuming his travels to Constantinople and Rome, and finally settling in the Land of Israel at Bethlehem from 386. He remained there until his death in 420 CE. He had begun his studies of Biblical Hebrew some time before his return to Rome in 382; and once he had settled in Bethlehem he was in regular, if not daily, contact with his Jewish teachers and instructors. Whereas it was once fashionable in certain quarters to call into question Jerome's knowledge of Biblical Hebrew, any lingering doubts about his competence in the language should be set aside in light of the weighty studies of Kamesar, Graves, Kedar-Kopfstein, and others.[6] These scholars have also demonstrated the remarkable erudition that Jerome displays in his translation of the Hebrew Scriptures, and the extraordinary care which he lavished on this enterprise as it dominated his life for some fifteen years before its completion in 405–06 CE.[7] That Latin translation will be the principal concern of this chapter, since it offers direct evidence for Jerome's understanding of the word *yeṣer* in Biblical Hebrew, and may also afford insights into his explications of the term which might conceivably be indebted to views of his Jewish contemporaries. Since Jerome's Bible translation was completed before the outbreak of the Pelagian controversy, in which he was belatedly to become involved, we may be reasonably confident that it was generally unaffected by the ecclesiastical disputes over the nature of human beings that began to affect the Western Church from 411 CE onwards.[8]

Jerome would certainly have been aware of the noun *yeṣer*, which is mentioned in Biblical Hebrew on nine occasions. The consonants *yodh*, *tzade*, and *resh*, which constitute its "stem" or "root," have the general sense of "to form" or "to fashion"; and Jerome's usual translation of this root in verbal formations other than the active participle *qal* is by means of the Latin *formare*, "to shape, fashion, mould."[9] God is the subject of this verb except on two occasions, Isa 44:10 and 12, where the subject is a human manufacturer of idols. Less frequently, Jerome employs the verb *plasmare*: this has the same general semantic range as *formare*, but is evidently related to the Greek verb πλάσσω, a regular translation

[5] See Rebenich 1992, 12–20.

[6] See Kamesar 1993; Graves 2007; Kedar-Kopfstein 1994.

[7] See Kelly 1975, 283–85.

[8] Jerome seems to have been aware of the writings of Pelagius before the controversy was fully developed: see Cain 2009, 91, 162–66.

[9] Thus Gen 2:7, 8, 19; Isa 43:7, 21; 44:10, 12, 21; 45:18; Jer 10:16; Pss 95(94):5; 104-(103):26; 139:16 translated from LXX; Ps 139:16 according to the Hebrew.

equivalent in LXX of Hebrew יצר.[10] Jerome has recourse to *plasmare* at 4 Kgdms 19:25 and its parallel in Isa 37:26; at Ps 74(73):17 in his translations of both the Hebrew and Greek of this verse; and in his translation of the Hebrew of Pss 95:5 and 104:26. In all these verses, God is subject of the verb. Jerome's decision on occasions to opt for this verb is of some interest, given the importance of the nouns *plasma*, "an image, figure, creature," and *plasmatio*, "a forming, fashioning, creating," which should become apparent as we proceed.[11] Two remaining instances of the verb יצר he renders *creare* ("to create," Isa 46:11) and *facere* ("to make," Jer 51:19): both have God as their subject.

The active participle *qal* of יצר may, depending on its context, mean a potter, or one who fashions objects out of some crude material. In such cases, Jerome may translate it as *fictor*, "maker, inventor, sculptor";[12] or by means of some form of the verb *fingere*, "to form, shape, mould, model."[13] In like manner he uses *figulus*, "potter," to translate יוצר at Isa 45:9. His selection of this word at Isa 29:16, where the root יצר occurs three times in various forms, will need to be examined later. In the majority of these cases, God is the One who is depicted as the potter or fashioner, either of the universe, or of items in the world, or of Israel His unique people. Only rarely, and strikingly, do active participial *qal* forms of יצר have human beings as subjects; and then they are fashioners or formers of idols (Isa 44:9; Hab 2:18). One final observation on verbal formations from root יצר is in order. The overwhelming majority of them are to be found in the books of Isaiah, Jeremiah, and the Psalter. In the Pentateuch they are found only at Gen 2:7, 8, and 19, where the Almighty "fashions" the Adam and the animals from the ground. Consequently, it is probable that information found in the books of the Prophets and the Psalms was in Jerome's mind as he translated the Books of Moses, that section of the Hebrew Bible that he left until last in his translation project.[14]

10 See, for example, LXX Gen 2:7, 8, 19; 4 Kgdms 19:25; Pss 32:15; 73:17; 93:20; 94:5; 103:26; 138:16; Isa 27:11; 29:16; 43:1, 7; 44:2, 9, 10, 21, 24; 45:18; 49:5, 8; Jer 10:16; 18:11; 19:1; 28:19; 40:2; Hab 2:18.

11 *Plasma* is a Greek word taken over into Latin, while *plasmatio* represents a distinctively Latin formation developed from it. For the meanings of these nouns in Latin, see Lewis and Short 1879, 1385.

12 See Isa 45:9; 64:7; Amos 7:1; Hab 2:18 (x2). He once translates the active participle of יצר with *operator*, "worker," with reference to God (Isa 22:11).

13 See Jer 18:11; Zech 12:1; Pss 33(32):15; 94(95):9, 20 in his translations of the Hebrew and LXX, all except the last verse with God as subject.

14 See Kelly 1975, 283–84.

The comparatively uncommon noun *yeṣer*, however, presented Jerome with a wider range of concerns. Three of its nine occurrences were straightforward for him. The first of these, Ps 103:14 with its statement that the Lord knows יצרנו ("our formation") and remembers that we are dust, recalls the divine action in forming of the human being described in Gen 2:7–8, and appears in his translation of the Psalms according to the Hebrew as *ipse enim novit plasmationem nostram recordatus est quia pulvis sumus* ("for He Himself knew our fashioning: He remembered that we are dust"). Here the emphasis is on God's fashioning and forming the human creature.[15] The second, Hab 2:18, speaks of the fashioning of an idol, whose maker has confidence in יצרו, "its formation." Jerome translates: *speravit in figmento fictor eius* ("the one forming it hoped in the thing formed"),[16] representing the maker's trust in the "image, production, or creation" resulting from the making of the idol. He adopts the same translation of יצר in the third of these verses, Isa 29:16, *et figmentum dicat fictori suo*, "and may the thing formed say to its fashioner?" The remaining six verses mentioning *yeṣer*, however, required of Jerome deeper consideration.

Preeminent among them are three verses from the Books of Moses; and these would have brought Jerome into direct contact with key texts considered by the rabbinic Sages in their discussions of the bad *yeṣer*. The two verses Gen 6:5 and 8:21 provide, in a manner of speaking, a frame for the great Flood in the days of Noah. The first of them gives God's reason for bringing about the Flood, and according to the Masoretic Text declares as follows (the translation of *yeṣer* here as "formation" is provisional, and intended in a quite neutral sense):

> And the Lord saw that great was the evil of humanity upon the earth; and all the formation of the thoughts of his heart (וכל יצר מחשבת לבו) was only evil all the day (רק רע כל היום).

The account of the Flood concludes with the note in Gen 8:21 that God accepted Noah's sacrifice and declared "to his heart (אל לבו)" that he would never again curse the ground on account of humanity, "because the formation of the heart of humanity is evil from his youth (כי יצר לב האדם רע מנעריו)." It is at once apparent that both verses share items of vocabulary, and that the word *yeṣer* is directly juxtaposed with the human heart, the seat of the mind

[15] LXX of this verse, Ps 102:14, had translated יצרנו as τὸ πλάσμα ἡμῶν, which Jerome represented accurately as *figmentum nostrum*, "our formation, figure, image, production," emphasizing the object made rather than the process of its creation.

[16] The Hebrew text known to Jerome apparently lacks the suffix on יצרו present in MT (cf. יצריו at 1QpHab xii 11).

and will. In Gen 6:5, furthermore, it is set side by side with מחשבת, a term expressive of thought, design, purpose, or plan. In these two verses, therefore, a less physical and concrete, more abstract or intellectual sense of *yeṣer* seems to be indicated. At the same time, a certain ambivalence is still present: the significance of *yeṣer* as something that is formed does not necessarily disappear altogether from these verses; and the word מחשבה, too, can indicate in certain contexts the "invention" or product of a craftsman.[17] Jerome would have known that the noun *yeṣer* is used only twice in the Chronicler's writings, at 1 Chr 28:9 and 29:18; and that in both these verses it is juxtaposed to מחשבות, as it is in Gen 6:5. He would also have been aware, however, that the Chronicler employed מחשבה on just two further occasions, at 2 Chr 2:13 and 26:15, where it has the sense of "invention."

These were not the only considerations confronting Jerome as he came to translate Gen 6:5 and 8:21 into Latin. The consonantal Masoretic Text of Gen 6:5 which we have today states:

וירא י״ כי רבה רעת האדם בארץ וכל יצר מחשבת לבו רק רע כל היום

and the Lord saw that the badness of humanity was great on the earth, and all the formation of the thoughts of his heart were only bad from his youth.

No variants are attested in the Samaritan Pentateuch or in Qumran manuscripts.[18] The translations of Aquila, Symmachus, and Theodotion have not survived; but LXX has left us with a quite distinctive rendering of its Hebrew *Vorlage*,[19] which runs:

And the Lord God, seeing that the evils of human beings had multiplied upon the earth, and every individual meditates in his heart diligently (καὶ πᾶς τις διανοεῖται ἐν τῇ καρδίᾳ αὐτοῦ ἐπιμελῶς) upon evil things all the days.

Several points should be noted here. First, the Greek translators have replaced the opening main verb of the Hebrew with a participle, whose subject is "the Lord God." Second, they have read the word רבה as a verb, with רעת האדם as its subject, the first word in this compound expression being treated as a plural form, to yield "the evils of human beings," which are consequently said to have increased. Third, they appear to have represented יצר מחשבת לבו by means of a verb, διανοεῖται, providing it with a subject derived from Hebrew וכל to yield "and every individual meditates in his heart." As John Wevers remarks, at this point they have

[17] See esp. Exod 31:4 (*fabre* for מחשבת); 35:32 (*opus?*), 33 (*fabre*); 2 Chr 2:14 (*scalptura*); 26:15 (*diversi generis machinas*).

[18] All citations of MT Genesis from Tal 2015.

[19] Citations of LXX Gen 6:5; 8:21 from Wevers 1974.

created a pattern different from that found in the Hebrew.[20] Having done this, they needed to supply a preposition to precede לבו to give the intended sense "and every individual meditates in his heart." Finally, they put for the Hebrew רק, "only," an adverb meaning "diligently" or "carefully";[21] understood רע as a species of collective meaning "evil things"; and translated the expression "all the day" as a plural.

Jerome's translation is remarkable on a number of counts, not least in its provision of a paraphrastic element whose presence may be construed as explication of a Hebrew particle.[22] His version has:

videns autem Deus quod multa malitia hominum esset in terra et cuncta cogitatio cordis intenta esset ad malum omni tempore

Moreover, God seeing that the badness of human beings was great on the earth, and all the thought of their heart was bent toward evil at all time.

The initial participle *videns*, and the divine descriptor *Deus*, are virtually the only points of contact in terms of structure that Jerome's translation has with LXX. The clause "that the badness of human beings was great on the earth" replicates exactly the Hebrew in our current Masoretic Text, with רבה accented *milra'* as an adjective "great" or "much," and רעת understood as a singular form.[23] This may be a coincidence; or it may reflect one or more of the translations of Aquila, Symmachus, and Theodotion (now lost); or it may have originated in information passed to Jerome by one of his Jewish interlocutors.[24] The last possibility should at least be considered, especially in light of what follows: "and all the thought of their heart was bent toward evil." Here Jerome translated the compound phrase יצר מחשבת with the single word "thought," *cogitatio*. LXX had already signaled that the expression was concerned with human meditation and thinking; but Jerome's approach differs considerably from that of the Greek translators.[25] That he was capable of understanding both יצר and מחשבה as meaning "thought" is not in doubt: when יצר occurs on its own at Deut

[20] See Wevers 1993, 78–79.

[21] This word in uncommon in LXX, and only here translates Hebrew רק. It appears again at Gen 8:21, however, where it seems to have no equivalent in the Hebrew: see further below.

[22] Citations of the Vulgate from Weber et al. 1994. Translations are mine.

[23] On the Masoretic accentuation of רבה, see Spurrell 1896, 75. LXX had accented the word *mil'el*, giving a third-person feminine singular perfect *qal* of the verb רבב.

[24] See Jerome's *Epist.* 75.19: Hennings 1994, 120–21.

[25] On LXX Gen 6:5, see Harl 1986, 61, 127 . LXX appear not to have translated יצר here.

31:21, he has no hesitation in so translating it;[26] and *cogitatio* is far and away his most common translation equivalent of מחשבה.[27]

At this point, other evidence needs to be considered. First, attention should be paid to Jerome's translation of phrases resembling those found in Gen 6:5 in the books of Chronicles, which he had finished translating before completing his work on the Pentateuch, and whose Hebrew text he had studied with Jewish assistance when he had first undertaken his work of translation.[28] At 1 Chr 28:9 we encounter the expression וכל יצר מחשבות, where Jerome translates each word individually as *et universas mentium cogitationes*. In this verse יצר appears in Latin as *cogitatio*, and מחשבות is treated separately, appearing as *mentes*, to yield "and all the thoughts of minds." First Chronicles 29:18, however, has the phrase ליצר מחשבות לבב עמך, "the formation of the thoughts of the hearts of your people." For this, Jerome put *hanc voluntatem cordis eorum*, "this will, inclination of their heart," omitting "your people," supplying "heart" with a third-person suffix, and treating the compound ליצר מחשבות as a single expression, now translated as "will" or "inclination," *voluntas*.[29] All this seems to indicate that Jerome could associate *yeṣer* directly with the mind on the basis of 1 Chr 28:9; and that the shared vocabulary of Hebrew 1 Chr 28:9 and 29:18 would also allow him to bring *yeṣer* into association with the will of human beings. With regard to 1 Chr 29:18 in particular, it is worth pointing out that Jerome never employs *voluntas* as a translation equivalent of מחשבה – unless, of course, he has done so on this single occasion.

Returning to Gen 6:5, we must explore further, and attempt to account for, the presence of the words *intenta esset ad*, "was bent toward." No such words are found in the Hebrew. They may express, however, and serve to articulate Jerome's intellectual preoccupations at the time when he was working on his translations. On adopting the ascetic life, Jerome had famously renounced his reading and study of the great Latin Classical authors. This "vow" he claims to have kept for

[26] God declares to Israel: "for I know יצרו which he is going to do today ... "; Jerome translates: *scio enim cogitationes eius quae facturus sit hodie*. Targums Neofiti and Pseudo-Jonathan specify that God knows "their evil *yeṣer*."

[27] E.g. Isa 55:7, 8, 9; 65:2; 66:18; Jer 4:14; 6:19; 18:11, 12, 18; 29:11; Ezek 38:10; Prov 15: 22, 26; 16:3; 19:21.

[28] See Kelly 1975, 158–59, 190, 283.

[29] The Lucianic recension of LXX 1 Chr 29:18 renders ליצר מחשבות with ἐν διανοίᾳ, "in (the) thought, mind," reflecting either a different Hebrew *Vorlage* or a decision of the translators that the two Hebrew terms are more or less equivalent in sense with one Greek expression.

some fifteen years; but in the early 390s – at the very time when his translation of the Hebrew Bible was occupying him intensely – he took up his study of the classics once more. This was demonstrated some time ago by Harald Hagendahl, and has been emphasized in the recent researches of Michael Graves and Megan Williams.[30] Among the Latin works that he studied at this time were Cicero's philosophical writings, a matter of some interest given that Cicero could use the word *cogitatio* in the quite specific sense of "the reasoning power, faculty of thought" in human beings, and forms of *intentus* to describe the direction of human thought toward specific objects.[31] There arises the possibility that Jerome may have entertained some such sense of the words when translating Gen 6:5.

Whether this is so or not – and further investigation into this matter is required – it seems clear that Jerome envisaged Gen. 6:5 as saying something about *cogitatio cordis* which required further explication. The trigger for this may be found in the presence of the Hebrew particle רק, "only," which brings us into contact with the world of rabbinic exegesis. It is well known that the school of R. Akiva understood particles like את ,רק and אך as significant for the interpretation of the biblical text: they are taken to indicate *mi'ut* – that is, a restriction or limitation of sense in the verse or phrase in which they occur.[32] Whether or not Jerome was aware of this particular rabbinic hermeneutical principle, he certainly comprehended the exegetical significance of particles: this much is evident in his extended analysis of the meaning of אך at Jer 32:30 before opting for an interpretation of the word given by Symmachus.[33] Michael Graves' observations on this point are directly applicable to our investigation, not only since Jer 30:32 speaks of Israel and Judah as doing הרע, "what is bad," but also because it alerts us to the importance of another scriptural verse, Deut 28:29. This last puts אך in close proximity to "all the days," whose singular form "all the day" closes Gen 6:5. A little later, Deut 28:33 uses words very similar to those found at 28:29, but this time using the particle רק. The context is one of divine punishment for misdeeds following Israel's failure to obey the commandments.[34] Indeed, a survey of Jerome's treatment of the particle רק in his translation of the Pentateuch suggests that he treated it

[30] See Hagendahl 1958; Graves 2007, 15–16; Williams 2006, 161–65.

[31] On Cicero's philosophy see Steel 2013, particularly the chapters by Schofield and Zetzel.

[32] See, for example, b. Pes. 22b; Gen Rab 22:4.

[33] See Jerome, *Comm. Jer.* on Jer 30:32a. [34] See Graves 2007, 185–88.

with great care, providing no standard equivalent for it,[35] and on occasions other than Gen 6:5 opting to paraphrase to convey its sense.[36]

All this needs to be borne in mind as we consider Gen 8:21, which records God's acceptance of Noah's sacrifice after the Flood, and His promise not to curse the earth again because of humanity:

כי יצר לב האדם רע מנעריו
because the formation of the heart of humanity is bad from his youth.

As is the case at Gen 6:5, the translations of Aquila, Symmachus, and Theodotion are not extant for this verse; and LXX elaborate the clause about the *yeṣer*, reading: "because the mind of humanity diligently involves itself in evil things from youth," ὅτι ἔγκειται ἡ διάνοια τοῦ ἀνθρώπου ἐπιμελῶς ἐπὶ τὰ πονηρὰ ἐκ νεότητος. The Hebrew of Gen 6:5 and 8:21 clearly share items of vocabulary; but LXX creates an even closer relationship between the two verses by employing the adverb "diligently" in translating both of them.[37] Jerome's treatment of this clause is striking: *sensus enim et cogitatio humani cordis in malum prona sunt ab adulescentia sua*, "for the disposition and thought of the human heart are inclined to evil from its youth." He has apparently translated יצר as *sensus*, a term with a wide range of possible meanings; these can include "understanding," "feeling," "sentiment," "inclination," "disposition," "sense," and "frame of mind." He employs this noun only here in his translation of the Pentateuch.[38] The word *cogitatio*, "thought," may represent either a second translation of יצר (reasons for thinking that this may be so should be clear from what we have seen above), or an explication of the word "heart." Either way, the human heart is presented in the Vulgate of this verse as the seat of *sensus* and *cogitatio* which are inclined, *prona sunt*, to evil, an amplification of the Hebrew not found in any other ancient version.[39] Elsewhere, Jerome

[35] In Genesis: *dummodo* (19:8); *forsitan* (20:11); *tantum* (24:8; 41:40); *praeter* (47:22); *absque* (47:26).

[36] See Gen 26:29; Deut 17:16. Cf. Deut 12:5.

[37] See Wevers 1993, 111–12; Harl 1986, 139 ; Aitken, Chapter 3 in this volume.

[38] Elsewhere in his translations of the Hebrew Bible *sensus* renders קשב, "sign of life" (lit. "attentiveness") (4 Kgdms/2 Kgs 4:31); בינה, "understanding" (1 Chr 22:12); קירות, "walls" of the heart (Jer 4:19); Aramaic מנדע, "knowledge" (Dan 4:31, 33); Aramaic פשר, "interpretation" (Dan 5:15); in a paraphrase of the Hebrew, signifying the senses (2 Kgdms/2 Sam 19:35[36]). It appears in Old Latin Gen 8:21: see Fischer 1951, *ad loc.* This may, therefore, be one of those verses where Jerome found the older Latin versions to be of use.

[39] None of the Old Latin witnesses cited by Fischer 1951 uses the words *cogitatio*, *humanus*, or *pronus*; their translations follow closely the text of LXX. In implicit references to Gen 8:21, however, Jerome can adopt language similar to that of the Old Latin traditions: see, for example, his *Comm. Jon.* 1:2, *depravatus est homo propria voluntate et a pueritia*

application of the results of his formal training in youth as a *grammaticus*.[47] This he evidently appropriated for his analysis of Classical Hebrew texts: Michael Graves has described his procedures for working, many of which are on display here. These began with a concern for *lectio*, the correct pronunciation of a text, and the proper division of words and phrases into intelligible segments (called *distinctio*).[48] A crucial aspect of *lectio* is the identification of voices and speakers in the text.[49] The *grammaticus* must then engage in *enarratio*, a process of interpretation which may involve the resolution of linguistic and grammatical problems and the provision of background information.[50] This might well involve παράφρασις (paraphrase), a clarification of difficult expressions using simpler and more direct language to produce the *sensus*, the clear meaning of the text.[51]

Jerome thus explains Isa 26:1–4 as a conversation involving several different speakers. Verse 1 he puts into the mouth of the chosen people, telling of their city and its fortifications. Verse 2 Jerome attributes to the Almighty, who is addressing the angels, instructing them to open the gates of the city for the just to enter. In this scheme of things, verse 3 is spoken by the people, while verse 4 relays the prophet's response to the people's declaration. Armed with this information, we are now able to consider what Jerome has to say about his translation of Isa 26:3.

> After God's speech, the people reply in Hebrew IESER SAMUCH, which Aquila and Symmachus have translated alike as πλάσμα ἐστηριγμένον, that is, "our error has been taken away," or "our thought has been made steady" – our thought which beforehand used to waver between You and the idols, such that we should no more be carried about by the wind of every teaching, but believe with our whole mind in You, the Lord, the Saviour. In place of this expression we have given the translation "the ancient error has departed," so that the meaning (*sensus*) should be clearer (manifestior).[52]

The ultimate source for his treatment of this verse he names as the versions of Aquila and Symmachus, both of whom had put πλάσμα for יצר. Evidently Jerome took πλάσμα in this context to signify "thought," *cogitatio*, paraphrasing it to obtain a clearer meaning (*sensus manifestior*). His commentary also reveals how integral to his explication of יצר is the word *mens*, "mind." But Aquila and Symmachus, with their translation of יצר as πλάσμα, have, it seems, allowed Jerome to operate on two levels. First, he

[47] See Graves 2007, 13–75. [48] See Graves 2007, 31. [49] See Graves 2007, 33–34.
[50] See Graves 2007, 35–50. [51] See Graves 2007, 51; Jay 1985, 159, 133 n. 25.
[52] Jerome, *Comm. in Isaiam* VIII.15.

can use πλάσμα to signify "an image, figure, created thing," and thus idols (*idola*). But he can also use it in a more abstract sense as "thought," closely associated with *mens*, "mind." Although Hebrew יצר can signify both a manufactured object and a purpose or design of the mind, Greek πλάσμα cannot properly be pressed into service to mean "thought" or "mind."[53] How, then, might Jerome's interpretation of Aquila and Symmachus be explained?

A possible answer to this question takes us back to Gen 6:5 and 8:21 by way of the commentary of Eusebius of Emesa (ca. 300–ca.359 CE) on these verses. Jerome certainly knew the writings of Eusebius, one of a very small number of Christian scholars who had some slight knowledge of Hebrew, and whose native tongue was Syriac.[54] The Greek of Eusebius' Commentary on Gen 8:21, which is the language in which Jerome would most likely have known his work, survives to our day, and has been studied in depth by Bas ter Haar Romeny. Here is his translation of the relevant passage.[55]

> Now the Hebrew, instead of mindfully [ἐπιμελῶς of LXX], (says): "A natural[56] (inclination) of man (is directed) towards bad things from his youth"; but this is conceived by them (i.e., the Hebrews) also in this way; "the formation [πλάσμα] of man's heart (is directed) to bad things from his youth." Surely then he does not say "natural (inclination)" but "formation [πλάσμα] of the heart, that is, that the mind possessing free will is involved in, and takes pleasure in, bad things from youth.[57]

Jerome does not mention Eusebius in his commentary on Isaiah; but his general knowledge of Eusebius' writing, and the latter's explicit invocation of "the Hebrew" to explain a particularly important word confronting Jerome in Isa 26:3, deserve notice. There were, it would seem, two possible sources which could inform Jerome that the Greek πλάσμα could mean both "idol" and "thought" or "mind": the commentary of Eusebius, and ὁ Ἑβραῖος to whose words Eusebius himself appeals.[58] The "ancient error" which Jerome highlights in this verse is idolatry and

[53] It can be used in the sense of a "forgery" or "fiction," and of an affected style of speech or writing, a sense it may also bear when it is used in Latin.

[54] He refers to Eusebius in *Vir. ill.* 91; 119; *Epist.* 70:4.4; 73:2.2; 112:4.4; *Qu. hebr. Gen.* 22:13, and other places: see Petit et al. 2011, xxiii n. 4.

[55] See ter Haar Romeny 1997, 277.

[56] The Greek has φυσικόν.

[57] Eusebius of Emesa, *Comm. Gen.* Frg. xxv on Gen 8:21, 9:4–5, in ter Haar Romeny 1997, 277. On the textual situation and exegesis of the Fragment, see ter Haar Romeny 1997, 280–85.

[58] See ter Haar Romeny 1997, 47–64.

the "thought" or "mind" that go in tandem with it. It has gone away, to be replaced with confidence in "the Lord, the Savior."

Idolatry as an aspect of the possible meanings of Hebrew יצר could, therefore, be defended by Jerome on both philological and exegetical grounds, as his commentary on Isa 26:3 demonstrates, and his translation of Exod 32:22 strongly implies. His association of idolatry with יצר might also reflect, or even reproduce, information derived directly from Jewish conversation partners. Significant in this regard is a teaching ascribed to R. Jannai, a distinguished Palestinian Sage of the early third century CE, reported at *y. Ned.* 9:1, 41b.

R. Jannai says, Everyone who listens to (obeys) his *yeṣer* is as if he practises idolatry (כל השומע ליצרו כאלו עובד ע"ז). What is the reason? "There shall not be in you (בך) a strange (foreign) deity (אל זר): and you shall not worship a strange god" (Ps 81:10). זר (the strange thing) which is within you do not make king over you.[59]

It should be observed that in both Jerome's comments on Isa 26:3 and in R. Jannai's statement idolatry is depicted as an element within the human being. Furthermore, R. Jannai exhorts his hearers not to let the *yeṣer*, as a foreign element, rule as king over them; and Jerome envisages the "just people" of Isaiah's song, from whom the "ancient error has departed" believing *tota mente* that God is their Lord. This is not, of course, to claim that Jerome had access to R. Jannai's teaching directly; rather, the Talmudic statement confirms that, already in Jerome's time and in the geographical location where he lived for over thirty years, Jews could interpret יצר as referring to idolatry, and that such an interpretation could be ascribed to a well-known authoritative figure. It should be noted that it matters little whether R. Jannai himself was indeed the source of this teaching; rather, the mere fact that it could be put into the mouth of such a revered and famous Sage alerts us to its significance for the redactors of the Yerushalmi.

Jerome's Latin translation of the Hebrew Bible, we may conclude, reveals rather more than a concentration on matters philological when it is a question of his treatment of the noun יצר. There is no doubting the importance of philological concerns for Jerome's work: we have noted how carefully he treated verbal forms deriving from the root יצר, and his discrimination in rendering those six biblical verses where the noun *yeṣer* has to do with the human heart. His selection of the Latin words *cogitatio*, *mens*, *sensus*, and *voluntas* we have surveyed, albeit briefly; and his

[59] See also b. Sabb. 105b, and discussion in Moore 1997, 1:469–70. Cf. Tg. Ps.-J. Deut 17:3.

translations of Gen 6:5 and 8:21 have set before us the vocabulary he considered most appropriate to convey the meaning of the Hebrew text's conviction that the human *yeṣer* has an inclination to what is bad. When he encounters an event in which a group of people does, indeed, find itself *pronus ad malum*, it is idolatrous worship that is in view; and his philological and exegetical treatment of *yeṣer* in the difficult verse Isa 26:3 brings together his perceptions of *yeṣer* in human beings as both internal "thought" and external "idolatry." In none of this does Jerome offer for our inspection a "system," or organized arrangement of "concepts"; just as the Bible might be viewed as "unsystematic," so are Jerome's observations as he endeavors to give the *sensus* of the sacred text. Each verse, each segment of each verse, requires analysis in its own right. Jerome's perception that Isa 26:3 refers, among other things, to idolatry is certainly remarkable, given R. Jannai's declaration; for both the Jewish Sage and the Christian ascetic, it would appear, idolatry is still a threat, lurking in the hidden recesses of the human personality, to be opposed and overcome.

# 16

# Rabbinic Inclinations and Monastic Thoughts: Evagrius Ponticus' Doctrine of Reasoning (*logismoi*) and Its Antecedents

Augustine Casiday

## 1 INTRODUCTION

In a book exploring the Jewish concept of the Evil Inclination and its influence, a chapter focused on λογισμοί (roughly, "thoughts") in the writings of Evagrius Ponticus might seem counterintuitive, at least initially: contemporary scholarship has preferred to search Evagrius' writings for evidence of Classical and post-Classical Greek philosophy and, to a lesser extent, antecedent Christian literature. In terms of this agenda, exploring Evagrius' connections with Jewish thinking would seem at best a low priority and at worst a fool's errand. A minor, but typical, indication of these preconceptions at work can be seen in discussions regarding the attribution of a brief tract "On the Tetragrammaton" preserved in Christian scholia on Job. Despite an early and unambiguous attribution to Evagrius, two scholars reattributed it to Origen (a reattribution laconically endorsed by *Clavis Patrum Graecorum*), based on an argument no more substantial than noting that Evagrius' reputation as a heretical, Neoplatonizing exegete is at odds with an interest in establishing some basic information about Hebrew usages for the benefit of Christians.[1] I have argued against the reattribution and made a provisional inventory of some evidence that Evagrius did indeed have an informed interest

[1] Devreese 1954, 108–11; Guillaumont 2004, 148–49; Geerard 1983, 179, item 1503 (10). For the early attribution, see MS Vat Gr 749, f. 8. Note, too, that J. B. Cotelier attributed the work to "Evagrius, monk of Skete," publishing it amidst other texts by Evagrius and one about Evagrius (see Cotelier 1686, 68–120). I am aware of no authority for Migne's decision, when reprinting Cotelier's work, to attribute the text to Evagrius of Antioch (see PL 23.1273).

(albeit one very difficult to characterize with any confidence or specificity, at least at this stage in research) in Hebrew language and in Jewish practices.[2] That argument may not carry the endorsement of a standard reference book, but it appears to have been tacitly endorsed in a least one specialist publication.[3] The study of Evagrius' relationship to Jewish thinking and Hebrew language is in its infancy, with numerous basic questions as yet unaddressed. Ishay Rosen-Zvi's extensive engagement with Evagrius' works in adducing patristic parallels to rabbinic uses is an encouraging inducement to continue this work,[4] and this chapter attempts to make a modest contribution to it. The point of departure for this chapter is an argument, published several decades ago but largely neglected, by Antoine Guillaumont about Evagrius' λογισμός. This chapter will develop and qualify Guillaumont's argument, not least by updating it with reference to subsequent scholarly findings. In doing so, it is intended to contribute to an ongoing project of research into Evagrius' writings that respects their historical complexity and eschews arbitrarily simplifying them.

## 2 THE SEMANTIC FIELD OF EVAGRIUS' λογισοί AND ITS ANTECEDENTS

The first modern critical edition of a text by Evagrius surviving in the original Greek – his *Praktikos, or the Monk* – was edited by Antoine and Claire Guillaumont and published in 1971. Inaugurating, as they put it, "an edition of the works of Evagrius Ponticus which we intend to continue and, if possible, see through to completion,"[5] the edition benefited from a substantial introduction amounting to a volume of roughly 470 pages. Along with Mme Guillaumont's meticulous critical study, the introduction provides M Guillaumont's "Historical and Doctrinal Study" in four chapters.[6] It is in Guillaumont's treatment of the "theory of the eight principal thoughts" that we find a significant argument about the semantic field of the Evagrian λογισμοί. Guillaumont's claims in two domains are most important: first, how Evagrian λογισμοί relate to uses of that term in earlier Greek literature; second, how they relate to *yeṣarim*.

[2] Casiday 2013, 36 n. 20, 102–13.

[3] Ramelli (2015, 24) claims that, "in his scholia on Job, [Evagrius] demonstrates an attention for the philological establishment of the text." Meanwhile, without noting the debate about its attribution, Wilkinson incorporates Evagrius' text into his analysis (2015, 128–29).

[4] See Rosen-Zvi, 2011, especially ch. 2.

[5] Guillaumont 1971, 5.

[6] Guillaumont 1971, 21–125. Unless otherwise specified, in what follows, by "Guillaumont" I mean Antoine Guillaumont, not Claire Guillaumont.

Guillaumont situated the Evagrian λογισμός with reference to evidence from multiple provenances, chiefly philosophical and theological, from the Greek records. His claims about the theological sources have been retrenched, as we shall see, though his position about the philosophical sources cannot be straightforwardly accepted. That position he stated succinctly in accounting for various terms that appeared in that most valuable of earlier sources for Evagrius, the Holy Scriptures in Greek. Aggregating several Greek terms found in that literature (διάνοια, ἐνθύμια, ἐννόημα, ἔννοια), Guillaumont remarked that "their variety proves the difficulty that the Greek language had in finding, in its vocabulary related to the intellectual life, a word which could easily take a negative sense; [...] The word λογισμός, designating intellectual activity *par excellence*, 'reasoning,' 'reason,' was the most refractory."[7]

The sanguine assessment of λογισμός implied in these comments is firmly restated and extended in the introduction to a subsequent critical edition where that term is immensely important, Evagrius's Περὶ λογισμῶν.[8] The editors affirm that "Evagrius is no longer dependent on the Greek philosophical tradition, for which the word λογισμός can only have a positive semantic content."[9] That claim presupposes a startling and implausible consensus on the part of Greek philosophers, perhaps through overreliance upon Plato and Aristotle,[10] and a confidence in the optimism of Greek philosophy that is unjustified. We can find disconfirmation in Epicurus' *Letter to Menoeceus*, where he advocates νήφων λογισμός ("sober calculation");[11] why stipulate sobriety if, in the Greek philosophical tradition, calculation or reasoning "can only have a positive semantic content"?

Kevin Corrigan has mounted a broader-based criticism of Guillaumont's decision to preclude Hellenistic philosophy from consideration.[12] Corrigan draws attention to evidence from Plotinus' *Enneads*, building on Filip Karfik's analysis which explicates how the

[7] Guillaumont 1971, 60–62, with the general claim that the term λογισμός is used positively by Philo and in 4 Macc.

[8] Guillaumont, Guillaumont and Géhin 1998, 9–144. In this volume, the authorship of the introduction is not specified.

[9] Guillaumont et al. 1998, 27.

[10] E.g., Plato, *Resp.* 4.439d, 10.602e–604d, at 603a: ἀλλὰ μὴν τὸ μέτρῳ γε καὶ λογισμῷ πιστεῦον βέλτιστον ἂν εἴη τῆς ψυχῆς; Aristotle, *Metaph.* 1.980b28: τὸ τῶν ἀνθρώπων γένος [ζῇ] 'καὶ τέχνῃ καὶ λογισμοῖς.'

[11] Bailey 1926, 88, 132.4.

[12] Corrigan 2009, 77–78, 80; the whole of ch. 5 is dedicated to an exploration of Evagrius' sources that is significantly independent from Guillaumont's publications and that benefits from Corrigan's expertise in ancient philosophy.

physicality and temporality of the embodied soul are limitations that necessitate the exercise of reasoning and that impact upon its operating.[13] According to Plotinus, practical exercises of calculation and reasoning are unnecessary to the divine – indeed, are incompatible with its very mode of existence: "What calculation [λογισμός], then, can there be or counting or memory when intelligence [φρονήσεως] is always present, active and ruling, ordering things in the same way?"[14] The very process of reasoning or calculating, notes Plotinus, betrays a lack of understanding: "for when he finds what is needed, he stops calculating [λογιζόμενος]; and he comes to rest because he has entered into knowledge."[15] These claims are importantly qualified and critical. Two features of Plotinus' λογισμός can serve to illuminate the way Evagrius uses the word. First, by attending to the temporal and physical conditions of λογίζομαι (i.e. λογισμοί and how humans use them), Plotinus' usage elicits an aspect of Evagrius' usage that is often obscured in modern translations: like a Plotinian λογισμός, an Evagrian λογισμός should be understood as an extended occurrence or a process within time – thinking more than thought.[16] Indeed, for Evagrius the λογισμός is typically linked to iterative, if not habitual, actions. Second, Plotinus' claim that reasoning ceases when one achieves knowledge corresponds to the "inexhaustible ignorance" that Evagrius identifies as mind's blessedness when it abides with God.[17]

For Corrigan's purposes, these arguments contribute to a sophisticated and plausible case for renewed attention to the Platonic and Aristotelian aspects of Evagrius' terminology (as against the general trend to find in that terminology almost exclusively Stoic influence).[18] A recent publication by Kathleen Gibbons has established that this approach is fruitful,[19] though pursuing these developments would go beyond the remit of this chapter. Even so, further study of Evagrius' works by ancient philosophers would undoubtedly make significant contributions to our understanding of those works.[20] In the matter at hand, provisional findings are enough to

13 Karfík 2011–12. See also White 1985, 244–45 n. 67; and Caluori 2015, 91–110.

14 Plotinus, *Enn.* 4.4[11], trans. Armstrong 1984, 165.

15 Plotinus, *Enn.* 4.4[12], trans. Armstrong 1984, 167.

16 Corrigan's translation of λογισμός as "reasoning" draws out this aspect of the Evagrian λογισμός more clearly than most translations: cf. "pensée" in SC; "thoughts" in Sinkewicz 2003, *passim*; "Gedanken" in Bunge 1992; and "pensieri" in Lazzeri 2005 (an Italian translation of the Antirrhetikos), *passim*.

17 Hausherr 1959; cf. Corrigan 2009, 170.

18 Corrigan 2009, 199.

19 Gibbons 2015, 297–330. Gibbons surveys the preference for Stoicism at 298 n. 3.

20 Thus, Peter Adamson calls for greater integration of Christian sources into the study of ancient philosophy (2015, 215–16).

justify the claim that there is no great distance between the way Evagrius used the term, on the one hand, and the way other philosophically competent Greeks used the term in Late Antiquity, on the other, as Guillaumont claimed.

As for Christian sources, Guillaumont identified two major theological influences upon Evagrius' use of the term λογισμός, namely, the *Life of Anthony* and Origen's comments and homilies on biblical texts (according to a liberal standard which includes Tobit, Ben Sirach, and the Testaments of the Twelve Patriarchs).[21] Columba Stewart consolidated and extended Guillaumont's preliminary findings by focusing especially on antecedent demonologies, with particular attention to the Hellenistic sources; in this way, Stewart draws out the links in Evagrius' works between the manipulation of λογισμοί and the demons – and so, by extension, the cosmos of rational beings among whom humans live and act.[22] Stewart rightly notes the importance in Origen's writings of the angels who contend against the demons,[23] but his claim that Evagrius and other monastic authors had inherited from Origen a "shift in emphasis to a psychological pathology" is less than self-evidently true.[24] Stewart also complements Guillaumont's references to the *Life of Anthony* by drawing on Samuel Rubenson's landmark research into Anthony's *Letters*.[25] Rubenson has established beyond reasonable doubt Anthony's authorship of seven surviving letters, which now stand as an invaluable source for the adaption of themes from Origen by Anthony and thus for their proliferation among Anthony's followers. For purpose of this chapter, there are important teachings in Anthony's *Letter* 6.46–48, where his comments situate λογισμοί within his teaching about demons and wrongdoing in terms that foreshadow Evagrius' more systematic teaching:

> In truth, my children, I tell you that every man who delights in his own desires, *and who is subdued to his own thoughts* (prostratus a cogitationib⁹ propriis) and sticks to what is sown in his own heart and rejoices in it and thinks in his heart that it is some great chosen mystery, and through it justifies himself in what he does, the soul of such a man is the breath of evil spirits and his counsel towards evil, and his body is a store of evil mysteries which it hides in itself: and over such a one the demons have great power, because he has not dishonoured them before all men.[26]

[21] Guillaumont 1971, 57–60. [22] Stewart 2005. [23] Stewart 2005, 8–9.
[24] Stewart 2005, 10. [25] Stewart 2005, 13–14, citing Rubenson 1995.
[26] Anthony, *Letter* 6.46–48 (trans. Rubenson 1995, 219), emphasis added; the Latin is from Champier 1516, fol. XVI.

This "great power" is horrifyingly realized, according to Anthony, when humans become the demons' "bodies, and [...] our soul receives their wickedness; and when it has received them, then it reveals them through the bodies in which we dwell."[27] How the demons can interact in this way with humans is disclosed shortly thereafter, when Anthony teaches the monks of Arsinoë that the "spiritual essence" of all reasoning creatures – demons, angels, and humans alike – is one and that the differentiated status of each creature corresponds to "the deeds of each one."[28] This essential compatibility between demons – and, for that matter, angels – enables them directly to exert tremendous influence over humans. And Anthony's explanation for the diversity of rational beings (which is echoed by an eschatological passage in one of Evagrius' letters)[29] is a familiar theme from Origen's writings.[30]

As for Origen's writings as such and their influence on Evagrius, despite the extensive circumstantial evidence that Evagrius' life put him in frequent contact with people who were studying Origen,[31] the entanglement of Evagrius' reputation with Origen's, particularly during the Second Origenist Controversy,[32] and the fruitfulness of scholarly comparisons of Origen's and Evagrius' writings,[33] much work remains to be done toward positively establishing Evagrius' actual knowledge of Origen's thinking and writings. Even so, Guillaumont has catalogued several passages by Origen that indicate his broad familiarity with Hellenistic Jewish thinking about the influence of spiritual agents upon humans – particularly the Testaments of the Twelve Patriarchs, from which Origen expressly claims to have derived his sense that "specific Satans should be understood for specific sinners."[34] According to Guillaumont, the influence of Jewish traditions such as these accounts most satisfactorily for the features of Evagrius' λογισμός that fall beyond the prevailing norms of Greek philosophical usage (as Guillaumont identified those norms). However, one need not

27 Anthony, *Letter* 6.51 (trans. Rubenson 1995, 219).

28 Anthony, *Letter* 6.56–63 (trans. Rubenson 1995, 220); on the οὐσία νοερά, see Rubenson 1995, 61–62.

29 Evagrius, *Ep.* 64.[1].24, 26 (trans. Casiday 2006, 68–69). This letter is known traditionally as the "Ad Melaniam," but according to a more accurate and more recent convention it is known as the "Great Letter."

30 See Gasparro 2000a. 31 See Casiday 2013, 9–27. 32 See Hombergen 2001.

33 See, e.g., Ilaria Ramelli's comparisons between Evagrius' writings and works by Origen and Nyssen (2013, 471–508).

34 Origen, *Hom. Josh.* 15.6 (Baehrens 1921, 392), cited by Guillaumont 1971, 59–60. In this connection, Baehrens noted *T. Reu.* 2.1–3.7, but see too *T. Ash.* 1.3–9 (de Jonge et al. 1978, 3–5, 135–36).

subscribe to his characterization of Greek philosophy in order to accept the value in looking to Jewish antecedents that illuminate Evagrius' use of the term λογισμός.

Even though Guillaumont's sense of λογισμός within Greek philosophy seems overly simplified, he nevertheless plausibly identified themes from Jewish sources that correspond in a meaningful way to Evagrius' use of that term. Guillaumont's estimation of the relevance of *yeṣarim* for Evagrian λογισμοί was remarkably positive, noting in particular "the personal, and wicked, character of the *yetzer*" (e.g. in several versions of Sir 15:14) and a few occurrences in texts from Qumran.[35]

The narrow basis of Guillaumont's evidence introduces complications into his argument that Evagrius was influenced by a "traditional Jewish concept." In the case of the Testaments of the Twelve Patriarchs, it is unclear whose views those pseudepigrapha represent. Guillaumont took the Testaments as the basis for making far-reaching claims about the Jewish provenance of the terms and concepts that interested him,[36] but he prescinded from discussing their origins. Subsequent research has plausibly argued that the complexity of these texts indicates that they were written within religious settings that do not satisfactorily fit into tidy modern categories. The proliferation and continued existence of such "religious subcultures" would have increased the points of contact that Evagrius may have had with Jewish traditions,[37] and so it behoves researchers into Evagrius' sources to take a broad view when considering his knowledge of or relationship to Jewish thinking. This consideration in turn raises the question which Jewish tradition Guillaumont believed had provided concepts with explanatory power for our interpretation of the Evagrian λογισμός. It could well be the case that the semantic overlap noted by Guillaumont was a fortuitous instance not particularly representative of Jewish tradition. Echoing Rosen-Zvi, we might say that Guillaumont's claim for the traditional Jewishness of Evagrius' sources (based chiefly on the Testaments) exhibits the "methodological fallac[y of] basing conclusions on only a selection of sources."[38]

Given that Guillaumont engaged with a very small sampling of Jewish tradition roughly contemporaneous to Evagrius, Rosen-Zvi's work on Tannaitic *yeṣer* has significantly advanced the state of research beyond Guillaumont's preliminary remarks. Rosen-Zvi based his claims on a systematic survey of the rabbinic literature, incorporating late ancient

[35] Guillaumont 1971, 60–62; also restated briefly in Guillaumont 2004, 212–13.
[36] Thus, Guillaumont et al. 1998, 27. [37] Frankfurter 2007. [38] Rosen-Zvi 2008, 516.

evidence from Jewish and from Christian sources to disclose significant and intriguing practical and conceptual similarities across contemporaneous religious texts. The Tannaitic and monastic sources that Rosen-Zvi has studied feature a recurrent preoccupation with sacred scriptures (the sacredness of many of which the late ancient authors would have accepted, regardless of their religious loyalties, even or perhaps especially if they contested their meaning) that are exposited using broadly common techniques. His productive comparison of these sources justifies moving beyond well-documented recourse to Hebrew by Evagrius' predecessor Origen and contemporary Jerome,[39] and interrogating the functional similarities between the concepts λογισμός and *yeṣer* for the insights they might offer into late ancient exegesis, cosmology, and casuistry.

Rosen-Zvi's research into the Tannaitic *yeṣer* is a good basis for a brief catalogue of similarities to the Evagrian λογισμός. Thus, the *yeṣer* is "not a natural disposition or a simple embodiment of human desires, but an antinomian entity residing within men and inciting them against the Torah."[40] This statement corresponds to the demonic λογισμός in Evagrius' writings insofar as he presents the λογισμός as practically interchangeable with the demon who uses it to seduce humans.[41] Evagrius does not regard λογισμοί as reifications or personifications of psychological experiences, but rather as the manifestations of attempts by independent rational agents to interact with humans.[42] However, there are limitations to this specific similarity.

Because Evagrius categorized λογισμοί into generic types, and because he typically referred to ὁ λογισμός of one or another of those types, it seems unlikely that he regarded each λογισμός as a distinct person. Rather, he likely considered each λογισμός as the action of a personal agent, namely, a demon with particular oversight for a specific type of sin working under the authority of Satan.[43] Furthermore, it is to be noted that Evagrius identifies λογισμοί as the demons' preferred tool for use against monks.[44] Thus he made a distinction in principle between λογισμοί and demons,

39 On which, see Salvesen 2007. 40 Rosen-Zvi 2008, 520.

41 Thus, Guillaumont 1971, 57–60.

42 For the moment, I am reserving consideration of human λογισμοί.

43 Cf. Evagrius' description of "the demons who learn from the Devil" (*scholion* 150 on Prov 16:28; all references to the text of Géhin 1987).

44 Evagrius, *Praktikos* 48 (Guillaumont and Guillaumont 1971, 608 ): "Against seculars the demons prefer to fight using things [πραγμάτων], but more often by thoughts [λογισμῶν] against the monks."

however often he collapsed that distinction in practice. This distinction marks a difference between the *yeṣer* and the λογισμός.

There are other points of similarity. Rosen-Zvi has found that (according to the majority view) the *yeṣer* acts so as to create "a duality and division within the human heart, thus preventing the singularity that is necessary for serving God. One cannot serve the Lord with all his heart when the evil *yetzer* resides in it. The *yetzer* thus must be extirpated in order to attain the desired unity."[45] Demonic thoughts, according to Evagrius, attack the monk's purity of heart, and in doing so work against the pursuit of that integrity which is corollary of blessedness; put otherwise, one who is pure in heart has nothing to fear from demonic thoughts: "The imperturbable person 'is calm without fearing' any evil λογισμός."[46]

To further its work, the *yeṣer* does not simply incite, but seduces through "a persuasive and cogent legal argument."[47] The *yeṣer* operates through intellectual seduction effecting cognition rather than, for instance, though the simple perversion of appetites and desires. The λογισμός similarly interacts with human understanding. Evagrius' writings make a practical distinction between, say, understanding the utility or acknowledging the beauty of gold on the one hand and being overwhelmed by the λογισμός of greed on the other.[48] This distinction is paralleled in other cases (e.g. one could be hungry or tired without necessarily being in thrall to the λογισμοί of gluttony or sloth). The λογισμοί try to secure a shift in human cognition as a necessary element in their attempt to build up a stable disposition that includes mental habits, and that results in an enduring pattern of behavior. As such, they are set apart from the subjective experience of physical needs that can, but need not, become opportunities for demonic λογισμοί to strike. The origins of the λογισμοί from personal natures (rather than from minds as such) and their typically persuasive character serve to distinguish them from other terms, chiefly in the semantic field of the term νοῦς (e.g. διάνοια, νόημα, νόησις), that Evagrius uses to describe other cognitive events and processes.

These shared features are so many and so significant that Rosen-Zvi has made a strong case that one should "read the rabbinic *yetzer* and monastic demonology as a shared formation."[49] While the foregoing survey of

45 Rosen-Zvi 2008, 526.

46 Evagrius, *scholion* 17 on Prov 1:33; on these terms and their relationships, see further Driscoll 2005, 76–93.

47 Rosen-Zvi 2008, 522.

48 Cf. Evagrius, *Mal. cog.* 19 (references to text from Guillaumont et al. 1998).

49 Rosen-Zvi 2011, 129.

themes from Evagrius tends to confirm Rosen-Zvi's findings in this matter, which can themselves be seen as deepening and confirming Guillaumont's earlier intuitions about Evagrius' sources, there is more to be said. The shift from comparison with the monastic λογισμός (as I have been doing) to Rosen-Zvi's comparison with monastic demonology is, I suggest, not inconsequential. In fact, I think that the most important divergence between Evagrian λογισμοί and rabbinic *yeṣarim* is probably signaled in the focus on Evagrius' writings as evidence for monastic demonology. As I will argue in the following section, although Evagrius' usage of the term is characteristically negative and implies that demons are involved, Evagrian λογισμοί are nevertheless not inherently evil. To the contrary, Evagrian λογισμοί strictly speaking are natural and, although they assuredly admit of corruption, perversion, or misdirection, they are good in and of themselves.

## 3 "NO λογισός IS EVIL FROM NATURE"

In recent years, much has been written in the study of Evagrius' demonology.[50] By contrast, advances in the scholarly understanding of Evagrian anthropology have been topical, and thus restricted;[51] and exceedingly modest gains have been made with respect to Evagrian angelology.[52] The relative balance of scholarly attention is arguably justified by the evidence from Evagrius' writings, which proportionally favors attention to moral danger. This claim is borne out by his *Antirrhêtikos*, or "Book of Responses," which consists in eight books (one for each of the evil "generic" λογισμοί) and, within each book, works through holy scriptures identifying texts to be memorized and recited in hypothetical circumstances – a sophisticated and practical handbook with remarkable implications for casuistry.[53] The relative proportions for these responses can be taken as roughly indicative of Evagrius' priorities: of 498 responses,[54] by

[50] See Brakke 2006, 48–77.

[51] E.g., Richard Sorabji's excellent treatment on emotions according to Evagrius (2000, 357–71).

[52] E.g., Evagrian angels feature prominently in Muehlberger 2013, but her interpretation is in service of a problematical contrast. The contrast presents Evagrius as a type (a monk advocating personal transformation and permanent mutability) and Augustine as a type (a bishop advancing institutional stability and the cultural supremacy of Christianity); see Muehlberger 2013, 29–32.

[53] This work survives in Syriac translation: Frankenberg 1912, 472–545; Brakke 2009. For ease of referencing, I refer to Brakke's numbering.

[54] Brakke 2009, 173 n. 21.

my count 146 directly address the reader and human, or "the soul's," λογισμοί (29.3 percent);[55] two, angels and angelic λογισμοί (0.4 percent);[56] 47, the Lord (9.4 percent);[57] and the remaining 303 responses – an overwhelming majority – address demons and demonic λογισμοί (60.8 percent). Evagrius' comments about demonic λογισμοί provide a wealthy fund for modern research, but for completeness we must attend to the λογισμοί originating from humans and from angels, too. After all, the comparatively rarer mentions of angels in his writings do not indicate that Evagrius thought that angels were less prominent, important, or numerous. To the contrary, recalling Elisha's servant whose eyes were opened, Evagrius claims that "the air is filled with holy angels that help us and are not visible to the demons"[58] – and it would be as inadvisable for Evagrius' scholarly readers to ignore them as he clearly considered it was for his monastic readers to do so.

Returning then to Guillaumont's commentary, he acknowledged that the linkage between λογισμοί and demons in Evagrius' writings is statistically normative without therefore being necessary. To be sure, Evagrius uses the term λογισμοί "in a pejorative sense" so frequently that, "in the absence of any adjective (πονηροί, δαιμονιώδεις), the word λογισμοί suffices, on its own, to designate evil thoughts."[59] Even so, Guillaumont documented that not every λογισμός inhibits progress toward the knowledge of God, and that there are angelic and human λογισμοί as well as demonic λογισμοί.[60] Guillaumont's analysis proceeds along the commonest usage, with the observation that Evagrius appears to have used the terms "thought" and "demon" interchangeably: "From this practical equivalence, the *logismos* finds itself, as it were, hypostasised, and he speaks of it as of the demon itself."[61] Even so – and here we return to

[55] Evagrius, *Antirrhêtikos* 1.9, 45, 46, 48, 50, 51; 2.6, 8, 11, 12, 13, 16, 18, 20, 22, 26, 30, 31, 36, 38, 41, 43, 44, 47, 53, 56, 57, 62, 63, 64; 3.12, 13, 14, 15, 19, 20, 27, 43, 45, 53; 4.1, 3, 5, 7, 10, 11, 12, 13, 14, 16, 17, 18, 19a, 19b, 21, 22, 26, 27, 32, 40, 42, 44, 46, 51, 52, 56, 57, 60, 61, 62, 65, 66, 67, 68, 69, 71, 72, 75; 5.1, 7, 8, 9, 10, 21, 25, 27, 28, 29, 30, 36, 39, 45, 46, 48, 54, 55, 58, 61, 62, 64; 6.3, 4, 6, 9, 10, 14, 15, 16, 17, 19, 20, 31, 34, 36, 37, 38, 44, 45, 51, 52, 54, 56, 57; 7.3, 7, 8, 17, 22, 24, 37; 8.4, 7, 11, 14, 17, 19, 20, 32, 43, 46, 49a, 49d, 49f, 50, 56, 60.

[56] Evagrius, *Antirrhêtikos* 2.14, 42.

[57] Evagrius, *Antirrhêtikos* 1.43, 44; 2.19, 21, 24, 25, 27, 50, 51, 52, 54; 3.16, 24; 4.8, 15, 29, 31, 35, 36, 37, 41, 43, 45, 49, 63, 64; 5.12, 33; 6.11, 21, 22, 23, 27, 39, 42; 7.25; 8.6, 10, 21, 22, 23, 24, 25, 28, 48, 49b.

[58] Evagrius, *Antirrhêtikos* 4.27 (trans. Brakke 2009, 106).

[59] Guillaumont 1971, 56.

[60] Guillaumont 1971, 21–125, with references to Evagrius, *Kephalaia Gnostika* 6.83 and *Mal. cog.* 7.

[61] Guillaumont 1971, 57.

the limits of comparing Evagrian λογισμοί and rabbinic *yeṣarim* – there are unmistakably indications that Evagrius made a real distinction between the λογισμός and the demon who corresponds to it.

Thus, he defines the demonic λογισμός not as the immediate presence of a demon, but as a collaborative venture between the demon who inspires it and the human, vulnerable through moral failures, who accedes to that inspiration and enacts it: "A demonic thought is an image [εἰκὼν] of the perceptible person, composed by that understanding with which the mind in impassioned motion says or does something illicitly in secret, having been banished by it toward the idol that has crept in."[62] The terms Evagrius used in that definition are perhaps not what one might expect to find, but he does use them similarly in other passages to analyze moral aspects of the human inner life. That other usage clarifies, in some measure, what this definition means: the demonic thought is a distorted image of the physical human, whose deliberation is impassioned and thus misdirected (i.e. toward an idol), which the human mind uses in morally significant actions.[63] By that standard, it is a joint venture on the part of a demon and a human.

Evagrius' teaching in this matter was not wholly innovative. The passage from Anthony's sixth letter, quoted above, makes a similar point: a man who "delights in his own desires" and is "subdued by his own thoughts" has made his own the impulses of the demons. Evagrius' definition and Anthony's admonition build upon the ethical analysis of thoughts (including thoughts that are inspired by demons, angels, and God) found in Origen's *On First Principles*.[64] That Evagrius believed human thoughts were susceptible to demonic influence in this way is further confirmed in his *Antirrhêtikos*, where his responses to the human intellect, or the soul's thoughts, that have acceded to the demons' suggestions are uncompromisingly adversarial. Some modern interpreters have affirmed (following well-trodden paths) that Evagrius believed humans could become demons; a more modest claim that accounts for the evidence from his writings is that Evagrius believed demons and humans could reach a concord of wills, resulting in what we might want to classify as cases of demonic possession.[65]

62 Evagrius, *Skemmata* 26 (= ps.-Supplement 14), ed. Muyldermans 1931, 54.

63 On Evagrius' uses of the term εἰκών elsewhere, see Casiday 2013, 168–85.

64 Cf. Origen, *Princ.* III.2.4 (Koetschau 1913, 250–51).

65 *Pace* Brakke 2006, 77. The idea that souls can progress and decline along grades of divinity was certainly available in Late Antiquity, as witnessed by Plutarch (see *Def. orac.* 415B–C); although the similarities between Plutarch's *obiter dictum*, on the one hand,

Although demonic thoughts have a human substrate, this does not mean that all human thoughts naturally incline toward evil. Evagrius regards human thoughts as basically poised to "introduce to the understanding the bare form" (εἰς τὴν διάνοιαν ... τὴν μορφὴν εἰσφέρει ψιλήν) of what the person sees, or by extension otherwise physically encounters, and to do so without any passion.[66] That the human λογισμός naturally operates without passion reinforces a key stipulation in the definition of the demonic λογισμός as considered above, namely, that in such a case the mind's movement is impassioned. Human λογισμοί emerge naturally from human nature and, given the fundamental goodness of nature as a creation by God, they are disposed by that nature toward natural virtue. Evagrius provides a clear example of the connection between human λογισμοί and natural virtue in another letter. More generally, this letter provides illuminating remarks about the different kinds of λογισμοί and offers an explanation of how an evil λογισμός is established and comes to have power over the person in which it is established:

1. Against the demonic thought there are three opposing thoughts that cut it off if it endures in our thinking. They are the angelic thought, the thought that is influenced by our resolve for the better, and the thought given by human nature in keeping with which even pagans are moved to love their own children and honor their parents. 2. But against the good thought there are only two opposing thoughts. They are the demonic thought and the thought that comes when our resolve is inclined toward the worst. No thought is evil from nature; for we were not evil from the beginning, as indeed the Lord sowed good seed in his own field [cf. Matt 13.24]. 3. Thus the thoughts cut off and are cut off. That is, the good cut off the bad and again are cut off by them. The Holy Spirit therefore looks upon the intention of the first thought and condemns or justifies us. 4. This is what I am saying: a thought of hospitality for the Lord's sake arises in me, but the Tempter cuts it and puts in it the intention of vainglory. And again, a thought of hospitality to please people arises in me, but it too will be destroyed by the good thought that by the Lord is working righteousness in us. 5. If then we hold fast to the first thought by good works and are tempted by the second, then we will receive the reward for the first thought because, being human and struggling with the demons, it is impossible to keep the upright thought incorrupt. And yet we are able to have a wicked thought without attempting it, because of the remnants of virtue abiding

and the system of beliefs attributed to Evagrius and others by those who condemned them, on the other, may be evocative, this does not amount to an argument about how best to interpret Evagrius' writings.

[66] Evagrius, *Mal. cog.* 8; cf. *Evagrii discipulorum kephalaia* 159 (references to text from Géhin 2007).

in us. But if a thought remains hindering someone instead of being abolished, then it persists and the person's power goes to this thought.[67]

In this letter Evagrius evaluates the operation of λογισμοί in moral terms. Of great importance is the repeated affirmation that human intentionality matters: the resolve and intention of the human, known to and judged by God, aligns human λογισμοί with the angels or with the devils. But that resolve can be proven or else corrupted by the person's response to λογισμοί coming from without. Even so, it is worth noting that Evagrius counts the λογισμοί that emerge from human nature among the λογισμοί that oppose the work of the demons. Human resolve can incline toward the angels or the demons; human nature is an intrinsic good, created robustly enough to act virtuously even from its fallen condition.

As for the angelic λογισμοί, several considerations need to be registered. First, Evagrius believed that holy angels and saintly humans are kindred (ὁμόφυλοι).[68] God created both humans and angels for fulfillment by Christ as children of God through the spirit of adoption.[69] Furthermore, λογισμοί are by nature good.[70] Now Evagrius' disciples recounted his teaching that the same mechanisms used by demons for evil purposes can be used by angels for holy purposes.[71] But a contrast suggests itself. Since λογισμοί are naturally good, the evil of demonic λογισμοί is parasitic upon their reality, whereas the goodness of the angelic λογισμοί accentuates their reality. Moreover, demonic λογισμοί work against the natural inclination of reality and angelic λογισμοί work with it. It seems therefore reasonable to conjecture that Evagrius would have believed angelic λογισμοί to be more efficacious than demonic λογισμοί.

## 4 CONCLUSION

Antoine Guillaumont's pioneering comments on the λογισμοί in Evagrius' writings have aged well. Subsequent research has corroborated and extended his claims; for instance, whereas Guillaumont looked to the *Life of Anthony* for Anthony's teachings that had informed Evagrius, it is possible following Samuel Rubenson's research to look to Anthony's

[67] Evagrius, *Ep.* 18 (Syriac: Frankenberg 1912, 578), using the internal divisions of the German translation (Bunge 1986, 230–31). *Mal. cog.* 8.31 preserves the Greek text for *Ep.* 18.1–2 and is therefore used as the base for that section.

[68] Cf. Evagrius, *Or.* 40 (trans. Casiday 2006, 190).

[69] See Evagrius, *scholia* 163 and 164 on Prov 17:17 and cf. *scholion* 189 on Prov 19:4.

[70] See Evagrius, *Ep.* 18.2.

[71] *Evagrii discipulorum kephalaia* 75.

letters, too, for evidence of his teachings and to find in them further corroboration of Guillaumont's argument. In some cases, researchers have chipped away at the edges of Guillaumont's claims, and in doing so have only sharpened his argument as a whole. Here, a good example is Corrigan's incorporation of Plotinus' *Enneads* into the analysis of Evagrian λογισμοί, which Guillaumont overlooked in his survey. Corrigan has established that the word λογισμός, as used by Evagrius' near-contemporaries, was not as unambiguously positive as Guillaumont had indicated. The value of Corrigan's argument, however, is that it situates Evagrius more precisely and securely within intellectual history, which is exactly the project that I think Guillaumont's work initiated.

But perhaps the most striking case of advances in the scholarship are relevant to Guillaumont's evocative comparison of λογισμοί with Jewish *yeṣarim*. Through his publications on the *yeṣer* in Tannaitic sources, Ishay Rosen-Zvi has illuminated some inadequacies in Guillaumont's initial statement, but more importantly he has also made major strides in comparatively evaluating Evagrius' writings with reference to the biblical sources, and especially writings by R. Akiva. Rosen-Zvi has distinguished those two sources from the emergent consensus in rabbinic literature that identifies *yeṣarim* chiefly as evil. The fact that R. Akiva and Evagrius agree, as against that trend, in finding that inclinations are natural and as varied as human experience is intriguing to say the least. As I have demonstrated, Evagrian λογισμοί are not necessarily evil (indeed, all λογισμοί are basically good) and they are distinct in principle from the personal agents who generate them. The dissimilarities between R. Akiva and Evagrius, on the one hand, and the broader trend surveyed by Rosen-Zvi, on the other, introduce an important qualification to Guillaumont's basic claim that the *yeṣarim* are meaningful antecedents to Evagrius' λογισμοί. It is not possible at this stage of research to advance upon Rosen-Zvi's claim that the *yeṣarim* he studied and the monastic thoughts have importantly similar morphologies. It would be gratifying to be able to posit direct interaction, though evidence for this is lacking; more likely, the similarities between R. Akiva's position and that of Evagrius demonstrate spontaneous parallels based on a common fund of religious texts. But even that more modest claim is an important advance on complacently assuming that, for instance, Evagrius was in thrall to Platonic philosophy to the exclusion of other influences and sources. To the contrary, these preliminary considerations indicate that in his expression of a concept central to his writings Evagrius was moving (whether he knew it or not) along a path already trodden by R. Akiva.

# 17

# "Inclination" (*yaṣrā*) in the Syriac Tradition

David G. K. Taylor

The Syriac term *yaṣrā*, "inclination," "urge," "wilfulness," and its use in Syriac texts, has not until recently been the subject of any detailed study,[1] and this is perhaps surprising not only because of its interest for an understanding of early Syriac Christian thought, but also for its potential contribution to discussions of the origins and development of Jewish concepts of the *yeṣer*.

As will be evident, Syriac *yaṣrā* is a cognate of Hebrew *yēṣer*. But in Syriac, as in Aramaic more generally, there are no corresponding verbal forms from the root *y-ṣ-r*, which in Hebrew (*qal* יָצַר) means "to form, fashion." When the verbal root *y-ṣ-r* is used in the Hebrew Bible it is usually rendered in the Syriac Peshitta by *g-b-l* ("to form, fashion")[2] or by *b-r-ʾ* ("to create"),[3] although other verbal roots are also occasionally used.[4] This led Nöldeke to conclude, as long ago as 1886,[5] that Syriac *yaṣrā* and the Targumic Aramaic *yiṣrā* (יִצְרָא) were both loan words from Hebrew, and Sokoloff's various dictionaries of Aramaic and Syriac agree with this judgment.[6] It is less clear, however, whether Syriac *yaṣrā* was a direct borrowing from Hebrew, or was introduced via a Jewish Aramaic dialect, as were various other examples of Jewish religious terminology such as

[1] Since this chapter was written an excellent study of *yaṣrā* in the writings of Narsai has been published by Becker 2016. The term was briefly first studied by Brock 1979, 221.

[2] See Gen 2:7, 8, 19; Isa 43:1, 7 (43:21 read *g-b-l* for *g-b-ʾ*?); 44:2, 21, 24; 45:7, 18; 46:11; 49:5; Jer 40:2; Ps 93:20; 94:5.

[3] See Isa 43:10; 45:18; Zech 12:1; Ps 73:17; 93:9; 104:26.

[4] For example: *ʿ-t-d* ("to prepare") in 2 Kgs 19:25 and Isa 37:26; *ʿ-b-d* ("to make") in Isa 44:9, 10; *g-l-p* ("to engrave, fashion") in Isa 44:12 and Hab 2:18; *t-q-n* ("to construct, equip") in Isa 54:17; *ṣ-w-r* ("to fashion, depict") in Jer 1:5 (note *ketiv* and *qere* in the MT).

[5] Nöldeke 1886, 722. [6] Sokoloff 2002, 540; Sokoloff 1990, 243; Sokoloff 2009, 580.

*kāhnā* (Levitical priest), *kumrā* (non-Levitical priest), and *ʾorāytā* (Torah). The existence of a small number of Hebrew and Jewish Aramaic loan-words in Syriac should not be surprising: after all, the Syriac Peshitta Old Testament was translated from Hebrew by multiple Hebrew-reading scholars who also incorporated various haggadic and halakhic elements, and who are thus likely to have been Jewish or of Jewish origin.[7] It is also evident that numerous Jewish exegetical traditions were early absorbed by Syriac-speaking Christianity in northern Mesopotamia, either through conversion of Jewish individuals or communities to Christianity or through intellectual contact.[8] This raises the possibility, prima facie, that early Syriac Christian understanding of *yaṣrā* reflected contemporary Jewish use of the term in Mesopotamia.

The starting point for a study of Syriac usage of *yaṣrā* is the small collection of biblical passages in the Peshitta that use the word, namely Gen 6:5, 8:21b, and Deut 31:21a. In each of these passages Syriac *yaṣrā* renders Hebrew *yēṣer*. It is also found in three passages in Sirach, which was included in the Peshitta biblical canon, and was translated into Syriac from Hebrew (rather than Greek).[9] In the first of these, Sir 15:14, the Hebrew text is preserved, and includes the term *yēṣer*. In the other two passages, Sir 17:31 and 21:11, the Hebrew is now lost. However, the presence of *yaṣrā* in these passages is strong evidence that the lost Hebrew verses also contained *yēṣer*. This is significant, not just because it adds a few more references to our list of citations, but also because these verses provided early readers with further information about the *yaṣrā*. While the Genesis passages emphasize the habitual and protracted wickedness of the human *yaṣrā*, Sir 17:31 introduces the possibility that the *yaṣrā* can be subdued (*kbaš*) – and this I presume is also the origin of the rabbinic tradition that the *yeṣer* can be subdued (כבש) – and Sir 21:11 states that the one who keeps the law restrains (*ʿāleṣ*) his *yaṣrā*.

There are no passages where the Peshitta translates from Hebrew and uses *yaṣrā* without *yēṣer* being found in the underlying Hebrew passage. However, there are several passages where the Hebrew biblical text has *yēṣer*, but the Peshitta does not use *yaṣrā*. In Isa 26:3 the structure of the Hebrew proved problematic for the Peshitta and the Septuagint, and both took the opening words of the verse as a continuation of the previous verse, and made the necessary textual adjustments. In Isa 29:16, Hab 2:18, and Ps 103:14, *yēṣer* is used in its primary sense as "fashioning, formation, makeup, thing fashioned," and so the Syriac renders this in the first and

[7] See Weitzman 1999; Maori 1995. [8] Brock 1979; Kronholm 1978; Hidal 1974.

[9] The origins of the Syriac version of Sirach are still a topic of debate: Nelson 1988; van Peursen 2011; Owens 2011.

last passage with the Syriac equivalent, *gbiltā* (from *g-b-l*), and in the second it paraphrases the Hebrew. Finally, in 1 Chr 28:9 and 1 Chr 29:18 *yēṣer* is used in passages where the translation "inclination" would be justifiable, and so one might have expected to see Syriac *yaṣrā*. Instead, despite the fact that Weitzman has argued that the Syriac translation of Chronicles is heavily influenced by Jewish religious thought, the translator has very freely paraphrased the verses, in a way that is typical of his work.[10]

The presence of *yaṣrā* in some Peshitta translations of Hebrew biblical books clearly raises the issue of the dating of these translations. The Peshitta versions of these books vary greatly in translation style, lexical choices, and competence, and close analysis led Michael Weitzman to argue persuasively that at least fifteen different translators were involved, and less persuasively that they all belonged to a single community or school.[11] It is usually thought that the Pentateuch was translated first, and then the Prophets, and then the Writings, though the duration of this process is difficult to estimate. The earliest Peshitta manuscripts date to the fifth century CE, but all of the biblical books, including Sirach, are cited in their Peshitta form by Aphrahat, a bishop in the Iranian empire, who wrote his twenty-three treatises or "demonstrations" between 337 and 345 CE. This suggests that the Peshitta translations must have been completed by 300 CE at the latest. Weitzman was himself persuaded by an article by Joosten that the Gospel harmony of Tatian, usually dated to around 170 CE, and widely (but not universally) thought to have been composed in Syriac rather than Greek, quoted the Old Testament from the Peshitta version.[12] Joosten's arguments are problematic, however, since much of his evidence is drawn from the Persian and Arabic Gospel harmonies which are of much later date, and whose texts have been vulgatized,[13] which leaves him only one Syriac Old Testament citation, Zech 9:9, which is extracted from the Diatessaron commentary of Ephrem (d. 373). Joosten's evidence is far more convincing, however, when he argues that citations of the Old Testament in the Old Syriac Gospels (usually dated after 200 CE) are influenced by the Peshitta text, rather than following the underlying Greek.[14] This suggests that the Peshitta translations of the Hebrew biblical books were produced in the late second or early third century, although we still lack the evidence necessary to provide greater accuracy.

[10] See Weitzman 1999, 111–21; Weitzman 1998; Dirksen 1995.
[11] See Weitzman 1999, 164–205. [12] See Weitzman 1999, 248–58; Joosten 1990.
[13] See Petersen 1994, 133–138, 259–263; Joosse 1999; Joosse 2002.
[14] Joosten 1990; Joosten 2001; Joosten 2006.

One further Syriac biblical passage needs to be mentioned here, 4 Macc 3:4, since it too includes *yaṣrā*, in the form *marirut yaṣrā*, "bitterness of *yaṣrā*," which renders κακοήθειάν, "bad character, malignity." 4 Maccabees was translated from Greek into Syriac, perhaps by the early fourth century,[15] and is included in the Syriac biblical canon in manuscripts such as 7a1.[16] 4 Maccabees 3:4 observes that the *yaṣrā* cannot be removed, but the mind (*reʿyānā*) can help prevent it from overpowering the individual.

So *yaṣrā* is not used in the Peshita as a mechanical translation equivalent for Hebrew *yēṣer*, but is only used in passages that involve mental activity or moral inclination. The Syriac translators of the books of the Pentateuch and of Sirach had access to other vocabulary to express such concepts, but have instead borrowed a technical term from Jewish anthropology, whether from Hebrew or from Jewish Aramaic. This is in stark contrast to the Septuagint's translation of the same passages, where there is no consistent rendering of *yēṣer* (reflecting the fact, no doubt, that the concept had only developed into a technical term in Jewish thought during the years that separated the two translations). When writing of the Hebrew usage of *yēṣer*, Piet van der Horst stated: "The concept of an evil inclination is typically rabbinic. This notion does not occur in the Bible, but the rabbis did derive it from biblical texts (esp. Gen 2:7; 6:5; 8:21)."[17] In the Syriac-speaking context, by contrast, the Jewish concept of *yeṣer* does occur in their Bible, and its usage there would heavily influence subsequent interpretation by later Syriac Christian writers. We must be cautious, however, about asserting that *yaṣrā* in the Peshitta corresponds to a particular later stage of its development in rabbinic thought, since this cannot be discerned from the biblical passages under investigation.

As the usage in 4 Maccabees suggests, the term *yaṣrā* was rapidly taken up by Syriac translators and writers, and used in contexts other than the translation of Hebrew. Table 1 provides an overview of its usage in Syriac literature.[18]

[15] It appears to have influenced the wording of Ephrem in his *Sermon on Our Lord*, XLIV (cited below).

[16] See Bensly and Barnes 1895; Hiebert 2005. Hiebert adopts Bensly and Barnes' dating of the manuscripts, which is far from accurate, and should be updated by reference to the Peshiṭta Institute's *List of Old Testament Peshiṭta Manuscripts* (1961), 110, 114.

[17] van der Horst 1999. For an examination of pre-rabbinic development of the concept of *yeṣer*, see Tigchelaar 2008.

[18] The "Church" column indicates whether the text/author belonged to the "West Syriac" Syrian Orthodox Church (W), or the "East Syriac" Church of the East (E). The final column, "All?," indicates whether or not the entire text/corpus has been searched.

TABLE 1 *Distribution of* yaṣrā *in Syriac sources*

| Text/Author | Date | Number of uses noted | Church | All? |
|---|---|---|---|---|
| Peshitta OT | c. II/III | 7 (3 in Torah; 3 in Sirach; 1 in 4 Macc) | | ✓ |
| Acts of Thomas | c. III | 2 | | ✓ |
| Aphrahat | *fl.* 337–345 | 7 | | ✓ |
| Ephrem | d. 373 | 16 (3 in C. Gen)[19] | | ✓ |
| *Liber Graduum* | late c. IV | 4 | | ✓ |
| Titus of Bostra (trans.) | pre-411 | 2 | | ✓ |
| Eusebius, *Martyrs of Palestine* (trans.) | pre-411 | 1 | | ✓ |
| Persian Martyr Acts | early c. V | 3 | | ✗ |
| Isaac of Antioch | c. V | 9 | | ✗ |
| *Life of Rabbula* | c. V | 1 | W | ✓ |
| Barsauma of Nisibis | c. V | 1 | E | ✗ |
| Narsai | d. 502 | 255 | E | ✓ |
| Jacob of Sarug | d. 521 | 1 | E | ✗ |
| Philoxenos of Mabbug | d. 523 | 1 | W | ✗ |
| Nestorius (trans.) | c. VI | 1 | E | ✗ |
| *Kalila w-Dimna* (trans.) | c. VI | 1 | E | ✗ |
| Cyrus of Edessa | mid-c. VI | 3 | E | ✗ |
| Ishoyahb III | d. 659 | 1 | E | ✗ |
| Shemun d-Taybuteh | late c. VII | 2 | E | ✗ |
| Ioḥannan bar Penkayē | late c. VII | 1 | E | ✗ |
| Jacob of Edessa | d. 708 | 2 | W | ✗ |
| Timothy I | d. 823 | 10 | E | ✗ |
| Ishodadh of Merw | mid-c. IX | 8 (5 in C. Gen) | E | ✓ |
| Anton of Tagrit | c. IX | 1 | W | ✗ |
| Bar Salibi | d. 1171 | 10 (3 in C. Gen, 2 in C. Ben Sirach) | W | ✗ |
| Michael the Syrian | d. 1199 | 2 | W | ✓ |
| John of Mosul | d. 1281 | 2 | E | ✗ |
| Bar Hebraeus | d. 1286 | 4 | W | ✗ |
| Abdisho bar Berika | d. 1318 | 2 | E | ✗ |

19 Occurrences in commentaries ('C.') on Genesis, Sirach, etc., are clearly generated by the biblical text, and so are noted in the table, though included in the totals for each author.

I must emphasize that the figures provided in the column for the "number of uses noted" are intended only to be indicative of the usage of *yaṣrā*, and are not absolute. In some cases I have been able to check through an entire text such as the Peshitta Old Testament or the *Liber Graduum*, or through the entire published corpus of a writer, such as Aphrahat, Ephrem, and Narsai.[20] For other authors I have simply relied upon chance encounters in texts, or references in lexica which I have cross-checked with the critical editions. Some texts will have escaped my attention altogether.

The table also excludes other lexical forms which were produced as a result of the full integration of *yaṣrā* into Syriac. For example, an adjectival form, *yaṣrānā*, was produced and used as early as the fifth century CE by the East Syriac poet Narsai (ca. 399–ca. 502).[21] An abstract noun, *yaṣrānuṯā*, was used in the acts of the Church of the East synod of the catholicos Mar Ezekiel, held in 576.[22] Again, in the thirteenth century, Bar Hebraeus (d. 1286) appears to have produced (or perhaps simply employed) a denominative verb, *'eṯyaṣar* ("to act wilfully," "to be inclined to act badly").[23] Finally, I have excluded terminology that may be thought to parallel or reflect the influence of *yaṣrā/yēṣer*, such as *meṣṭalyānuṯā*, "inclination," which is particularly common in texts translated from Greek, since these terms deserve a separate study.

The table draws our attention to several noteworthy features of the use of *yaṣrā* in Syriac. First, there is continuous use of the term from the very beginnings of Syriac Christian literature, and the date of these texts is contemporaneous with the early rabbinic texts that use *yēṣer*. Second, although many scholars have argued convincingly that the ideology of *yeṣer* lies behind various passages in the epistles of Paul, especially in his letter to the Romans,[24] no Syriac New Testament text, in any version, includes mention of the *yaṣrā*. Third, with a few rare exceptions such as the profoundly Hellenized *Book of the Laws of the Countries* written by

[20] In the case of Narsai I have also examined a number of unpublished texts, still in manuscript.

[21] See Mingana 1905, 2: 94.6. The mid-tenth-century lexicon of Bar Bahloul includes the adjectival form *yaṣrāyā* (Duval 1888–1901, 849), but the apparatus of Duval reveals that other manuscripts of this lexicon, and the earlier lexicon of Bar 'Ali (see Hoffmann 1874, 171, #4492), read *yaṣrānā*. It seems likely that *yaṣrāyā* is simply a scribal error.

[22] See Chabot 1902, 122.8.

[23] See Payne Smith 1868–1901, 1: 1620. A citation is given (from the 1619 manuscript lexicon of the Maronite George Karmsedinoyo) to one of Bar Hebraeus' poems on the soul, but I have been unable to identify the source text in any of the editions available to me.

[24] See, for example, Davies 1980, ch. 2.

a pupil of Bardaisan (d. 222), it is found in almost all early Syriac writers. Fourth, from the fifth century on there is particular interest in the term in East Syriac authors, that is, authors of the Church of the East writing in the Sassanian Empire, rather than the West Syriac, Syrian Orthodox, authors of the Roman Empire. The poet Narsai's use of *yaṣrā* is particularly remarkable in its frequency, far outnumbering the use of the term in all other Syriac authors combined.[25] By contrast, Narsai's West Syriac contemporary Jacob of Sarug, who has a similarly voluminous poetic output, uses the term only once. I will argue below that this was for doctrinal reasons. Fifth, it should perhaps be mentioned, as will become self-evident in a moment, that only a small number of these occurrences are found in exegetical literature expounding the biblical citations already mentioned. Sixth, as we have already seen with the citation in 4 Maccabees, the term is taken up and used in early Syriac translations of Greek texts such as the anti-Manichean work of Titus of Bostra, and Eusebius of Caesarea's *Martyrs of Palestine*, both preserved in a manuscript of 411 CE.[26]

In some of the earliest Syriac uses of *yaṣrā*, the "inclination" seems to be understood as being morally neutral. For example, the fourth-century writer Aphrahat seems to regard the *yaṣrā* as being subject to human control and self-discipline, and thus capable of being directed toward the good through righteous behavior. In his *Demonstration* 14 he describes an ideal wise and just individual:[27]

[Understanding] depicts wonderful things in his heart,
and the eyes of his senses see across the oceans,
and all creatures are enclosed within his thought,
and his *yaṣrā* is wide open to receive,
and he is the great temple of his Maker,
and the King on High enters and dwells in him.

Again, in his demonstration on fasting (*Dem.* 3), he writes:[28]

And one fasts from meat and wine
and certain foods;
and one fasts so as to make a fence for his mouth,

[25] See now Becker 2016. [26] BL Add. 12,150. [27] Parisot 1894, 661.13.
[28] Parisot 1894, 100.1.

so as not to speak hateful words;
and one fasts from anger,
and subdues his *yaṣrā* so as not to be defeated.

Here there is clear influence from Sirach 17:31. And in *Demonstration* 9, on humility, he echoes Sir 21:11:[29]

And all their thoughts are set on their Lord
and they travel and journey on the way that is narrow and strait,
and they enter the strait gate of the kingdom,
they restrain their *yaṣrā* to keep the Law.

Ephrem (d. 373) too is clearly aware of the Sirach passages. In the Nisibene hymns (HNis 21.15) he writes:[30]

There is one who finds an opportunity and acts presumptuously,
and there is another who resists and restrains his *yaṣrā*,
one considers that judgement will be preserved,
and another that it will not even happen.

Further influence from Sirach can be found in the anonymous late fourth-century *Liber Graduum*:[31]

And everyone, to the extent that he seeks you, so he will find you.
And to the extent that he restrains his *yaṣrā* to keep the Law, so he will grow great.
And as much as he increasingly humbles himself, so he will be glorified.

And again:[32]

But if you restrain your *yaṣrā*, and pray for the one who strikes you, and make peace with him, you suffer with our Lord, and you will be glorified with him.

This is not to suggest that the early Syriac writers underestimated the tendency of the human *yaṣrā* to incline toward evil. Ephrem, who wrote a commentary on Genesis and discussed the references to *yaṣrā* there,[33]

[29] Parisot 1894, 416.17. [30] Beck 1961, 57.21. See also Beck 1975, IV.305, 58.22.
[31] Kmoskó 1926, 333.4. [32] Kmoskó 1926, 420.11.
[33] Tonneau 1955, VI.6, 57.21–31; VI.13, 62.9–12.

also regularly describes the "bitter *yaṣrā*,"[34] or, using the wording of 4 Macc 3:4, the "bitterness of the *yaṣrā*." In the *Sermon on Our Lord*, for example, he wrote:[35]

> Although our Lord knew that that Pharisee had purposed evil against him, he refuted him gently and not harshly. For sweetness descended from on high to diminish the bitterness of our evil *yaṣrā*.

Ephrem could even describe the *yaṣrā* as being like a serpent, coiled within each human being (HNis 40.4):[36]

> His *yaṣrā* is coiled up within, his jealousy hisses constantly like a serpent

And yet for Ephrem this *yaṣrā*, which tended toward evil, and could be exploited by Satan, was not in itself evil. As he wrote in his commentary on Gen 6:7 and God's statement concerning all living beings that "I am sorry that I have made them":[37]

> For if there had been any blemish in the beings made by God, He would have created a new creation, and He would not have kept within the ark any work which had caused remorse for its Maker.

It should not perhaps be a surprise that such classic and influential representatives of early Syrian asceticism as Aphrahat, Ephrem, and the *Liber Graduum* should have enthusiastically taken up the passages of Sirach that encourage self-restraint, discipline, and the subduing of the *yaṣrā*, and it perhaps provides another explanation for the popularity of this concept within Syriac literature.

A similar understanding of *yaṣrā* can be found in an early fifth-century Syriac translation of Titus of Bostra's *Contra Manichaeos*, in a passage (IV.55) only preserved in Syriac. The context is Titus' argument that God only blames those people who are wicked due to their will, and not wicked due to their nature, and hence Christ came to save those who would be healed in their will. The Syriac text then continues as follows:[38]

[34] See, for example: Beck 1970, III.45, 50.8; Beck 1972, IV.549, 46.21.
[35] Beck 1966 , XLIV, 42.26. [36] Beck 1963, XL.4, 30.20.
[37] Tonneau 1955, VI.7, 58.12.
[38] Text: Poirier et al. 2013, 370–71, trans. Roman et al. 2015, 426–27.

For also in the beginning, in Genesis, He said: "My Spirit shall not reside in these people, because they are of flesh," and "the *yaṣrā* of man is intently fixed on wickedness from his youth," and (here) He used the name *yaṣrā* instead of "will" (*ṣebyānā*). For this (reason) He blamed them from the beginning, for He would scarcely have blamed them if they had been led to evil actions by some compulsion.

Titus was citing Gen 6:3 and Gen 8:21 from the Septuagint, and the Syriac translator mostly follows the distinctive wording of the Greek Bible (hence the inclusion of *ḥpiṭā'iṯ* = ἐπιμελῶς, "intently"). But, as often with this translator, he was also influenced by his knowledge of the Peshitta,[39] and so rendered διάνοια, "mind," by *yaṣrā*. Having done so, he then added a gloss explaining that *yaṣrā* was used here instead of "will," the key word in this discourse. This would not have been necessary in the original Greek, and so this gloss must be the work of the translator, added either to keep the argument about "will" coherent or because he thought the reader might not understand this non-native word.

At first glance a very similar equation of the two terms is to be found in the ninth- and tenth-century Syriac lexicographers Isho' bar 'Alī[40] and Abū'l-Ḥasan ibn Bahlūl.[41] The latter reads: "*yaṣrā* i.e. will (*ṣebyānā*) that behaves wickedly and impudently." Closer examination, however, clearly reveals that there is a significant difference in their glosses. For the translator of Titus of Bostra *yaṣrā* appears to be a neutral term, a term that describes the human will that is not in itself wicked but is far too often set on wicked practices, whereas for the medieval lexicographers it is by definition will that acts wickedly (apparently, particularly in relation to anger and aggression rather than sexual misbehavior or theft).[42] Similar developments are well known from rabbinic texts, but it is less easy to determine whether these are independent phenomena, due in part to reflexion upon the biblical source texts available to each community, or whether the Syriac understanding of *yaṣrā* developed in response to continued contact with Jewish thought.

[39] See Baumstark 1933; Poirier 2010. [40] Hoffmann 1874 (rpr. 1886), 171, #4491.
[41] Duval 1888–1901, 849.
[42] See the citation of the 1619 manuscript lexicon of the Maronite George Karmsedinoyo in Payne Smith 1868, 1:1620, where there is an expanded definition: "*yaṣrā*, *yaṣrē*. i.e. will (*ṣebyānā*) that behaves wickedly and impudently, such as anger, rage, threatening, fraud, profiteering, calumny, fury, censure."

The possibility that influence from post-biblical Jewish thought did on occasion play a role in the Syriac understanding of *yaṣrā* is raised by an examination of Syriac texts which touch upon the topic of the origin of the human *yaṣrā*. The only clear statements I have found relating to this date to the fifth and early sixth centuries. The East Syriac writer Narsai (d. 502) is clear that the *yaṣrā* was included in God's creation of the first humans. He writes (in *Hom.* 7):[43]

You created him from the dust, as it pleased You,
and together with his clay You mixed the longings of the weak *yaṣrā*.
Your (Divine) Command compounded the weak *yaṣrā* with his dust,
and he cannot bind together the weakness of his clay without you.

Narsai's starting point here is clearly Gen 2:7, which describes God forming Adam from the dust. In the Hebrew the verb used is *y-ṣ-r*, and this provides an obvious link with *yēṣer* for rabbinic exegetes. In both the Peshitta and here in Narsai, the verb used is *g-b-l* ('to form, fashion'), and so there is no etymological link in Syriac between the *yaṣrā* and this description of the creation of Adam. So either Narsai's belief that the *yaṣrā* has been an integral part of the human being since the creation led him to link the *yaṣrā* with Gen 2:7, or alternatively Narsai (or his teachers) knew that contemporary Jewish thought linked the *yeṣer* with Gen 2:7. Both alternatives are possible, but the latter seems to me a more plausible explanation.

The proposition that the *yaṣrā* was of divine creation potentially raises many theological problems. Is God ultimately responsible for our sins? If humanity was created in God's likeness and image (Gen 1:26), how does the *yaṣrā* fit into this model? What of free will? Narsai's response is that God's overriding purpose was to train and educate human reason and discernment. Narsai, following Theodore of Mopsuestia, believed that humans were created mortal by God, and childlike.[44] They needed to be prepared and educated for the existence that would follow their expulsion from paradise, an event which the omniscient God anticipated. So he writes (*Hom.* 36):[45]

[43] Mingana 1905, 1: 131.16.
[44] See Frishman 1992, 58; Gignoux 1968, 449–52, 482–84, 488–92; Salvesen 2003.
[45] Mingana 1905, 2: 203.14; Gignoux 1968, 548.355.

He created Adam from the dirt, and called him His image,
and He made his dust in the likeness of the dust of mortality.
He placed this in the composition of his body from the beginning,
that he might travel in the path of mortality so as to demand life.
He did not decree the curses and the pains of childbirth out of anger,
And He did not bring death to mortals out of remorse.
The natural properties which He placed in the nature of mortality
He reformulated them as a threat, for the aid of humans.
He knew the dust of Adam before it came into being,
that death would unbind and put an end to the composition of his body.
It was clear to Him that he would surely sin through desire of the fruit,
and He knew the evil *yaṣrā* of his discernment.
Through testing He wished to make his reason wise,
so that his discernment would not lack exercise.
Through the commandment He devised a means to teach Adam,
that he should keep the statute of the commandment of his Lord.
Through the tree the veil of his discernment was removed,
through the eating of the fruit he demonstrated the power of his reason.

Narsai is also keen to assert the free will of humanity, and to deny that evil formed any natural part of human nature (*Hom.* 14):[46]

My mind made me repent, for I remembered that your evil is not of (your) nature.
The creator created you free, and made you the master of your will,
and these two things are yours, to discern truth from deceit.
Lord, do not reckon this against me, that I rashly complained,
and accused the evil *yaṣrā* which causes bitter envy to grow.

Narsai may wish to affirm the key Christian doctrine of human free will, and the sovereignty of the human soul, but as he admits rhetorically in this passage, his first instinct is always to blame the *yaṣrā* for human wrongdoing.

A striking contrast with Narsai's thought can be found in the writings of his contemporary Jacob of Sarug (d. 521), who was writing in the Roman Empire and belonged to the non-Chalcedonian miaphysites, the Syrian Orthodox. Jacob believed that Adam and Eve were created both mortal and immortal – that is, with the potential for both. In this he was

[46] Mingana 1905, 1: 236.1.

following the teachings of Ephrem, rather than Theodore and the Antiochenes.[47] He was also determined to affirm the reality of the free will (*ḥīrutā*) given to humanity – who were created as adults, not children – and indeed to Satan and the demons.[48] He argues that it is blasphemous to suggest that Adam's fall was predestined by God, or that he commissioned Satan to tempt Adam and Eve.[49] Their transgression of the commandment was a consequence of their exercise of adult free will in response to Satan's decision, made through his free will and envy, to tempt them. So Jacob frequently makes use of "free will" (*ḥīrutā*), and the neutral term "will" (*ṣebyānā*), and avoids using *yaṣrā* – presumably because the latter would imply that God was responsible at best for human moral frailty and at worst for an evil inclination within human nature. His one use of the term *yaṣrā* is thus very instructive. In a homily on the Theotokos, Mary, he writes:[50]

He sanctified her body and made her without hateful desire,
just as the virgin Eve was before she desired.
The sin which entered the house of Adam through the motions of desire,
the Holy Spirit removed from her when he came to her.
That addition which the serpent made, the evil *yaṣrā*,
he cleared away from her, and filled her with holiness and innocence.

From this passage it appears that Jacob considered the *yaṣrā* to be a product of Satan's corruption of the original pure human nature.[51] In another passage[52] he refers to the serpent's venom corrupting the clay fashioned by God, and perhaps it is this that he has in mind.

Adam was a vessel of clay, and when [God] had fashioned him,
the serpent bit him, and since he was weak, he was corrupted.

Just as there was disagreement over the origins of the *yaṣrā*, so also the exact location of the *yaṣrā* seems not to have been fixed in the Syriac tradition. The Genesis passages refer to "the *yaṣrā* of the thought of his heart" (Gen 6.5) and "the *yaṣrā* of the heart of man" (Gen 8.21), in which the Hebrew/Syriac "heart" corresponds to the mind. Unsurprisingly, this

[47] See Bou Mansour 1993. [48] Alwan 1989, III.30. [49] Alwan 1989, II.115–44.

[50] Bedjan 1902b, 634.21; Jacob's poems were reprinted separately as Bedjan 1902a, 22.21; and Bedjan 2006, vol. 6.

[51] In one manuscript there is a minor textual variant, "*and* the evil *yaṣrā*."

[52] Alwan 1989, I.1164.

location is repeated by many subsequent Syriac writers and texts, such as the Testament attributed to Ephrem:[53]

For evil people are going to come to you after me,
they are dressed in the skin of lambs, but within they are rapacious wolves.
The words of their mouths are sweet, but the *yaṣrā* of their hearts is bitter.
They are wrapped in the habit of good people, but they are like satans.

Narsai too can refer to the heart/mind as the locus of the *yaṣrā* (*Hom.* 17):[54]

He who would give the peace to his brother in church
must cleanse his heart of all anger and rage and *yaṣrā*.

However, in several places Narsai seems to state that the *yaṣrā* is located within the soul, rather than the mind. This is particularly clear in the following passage (*Hom.* 14):[55]

For neither does our *yaṣrā* exist substantially apart from the soul,
it is the discernment within the soul that acts in all ways.
The soul is the mistress of man, for she rules over the emotions and senses,
And she guides nature, as her will wishes.
In our soul these two are set equally, good and evil,
and she chooses, according to her testing, to do this rather than that.

For Narsai the adversary of the *yaṣrā* appears to be the human will (*ṣebyānā*), and he has an entire homily that recounts their struggle (*Hom.* 9). It begins:[56]

Mortal nature is too weak to approach perfection,
he who is of flesh and blood is not able to inherit the future life.
The *yaṣrā* of his thought is set upon evil from the beginning,
and when his will desires the good, his *yaṣrā* drags it to the evil.
And although two contrary thoughts are set in his nature,
his *yaṣrā* conquers his nature, and drags it towards enticements.

[53] Beck 1973, 59.565. [54] Mingana 1905, 1: 278.1. [55] Mingana 1905, 1: 236.8.
[56] Mingana 1905, 1: 149.15.

His free will is enslaved to the service of the desire of the flesh,
and it is entirely led by force by the passions of mortality.
His will is not able to perform the good he wishes,
but his *yaṣrā* compels him to perform the evil he does not wish.
He is constantly thrown into struggle, fighting with his *yaṣrā*,
and battling against enticements, with the weapon of his free will.
Everyone is defeated by his *yaṣrā*, and is enslaved by desires,
and his willpower does not withstand the onslaught of the desire of the flesh.

After this rather bleak start to his homily, Narsai goes on to say that while our free will is powerless when it stands alone against the *yaṣrā*, nevertheless, with God's aid and mercy, the *yaṣrā* can be controlled and defeated.[57]

By the strength of your aid [that] ravening tyrant, the *yaṣrā*, will be defeated,
who battles against our soul, with the weapon of our free will.
May your grace, Lord, which seeks out the lost, return us to the fold of life!

This is not in total contrast to the passages discussed earlier from Aphrahat, Ephrem, and the *Liber Graduum*, in which the righteous individual is able to subdue and restrain his *yaṣrā*, and yet there is a clear shift toward the need for divine grace to defeat this Evil Inclination. In the Latin West in the early fifth century such issues had been at the heart of the fierce disputes over the teachings of Pelagius (d. 418), who was famously refuted by Augustine. Although Pelagius was condemned at the Council of Ephesus in 431 (following an earlier condemnation at Carthage in 418, during his lifetime), the controversy over his ideas appears to have had little impact among the Eastern Christian communities. And yet it is hard not to think that some ripples must have spread east across the Mediterranean, and that in the writings of Narsai we see the traces of a general shift in Christian theological approach which increasingly placed an emphasis on the individual's need for divine grace, and the inadequacy of unaided human acts of righteousness.

As we have seen, Narsai in particular is interested in the consequences of humanity as a whole possessing and struggling with an innate *yaṣrā*, but some other texts mention it in association with perceived enemies of the Church. The Syriac translator of Eusebius' *Martyrs of Palestine* – a translation produced before 411 CE – used it of a pagan judge putting Christians to death:[58]

[57] Mingana 1905, 1: 164.11. [58] Cureton 1861, 47.20.

"The officers seized [Julianos] and took him before the judge. And that judge commanded that which his evil *yaṣrā* conceived, and they delivered this man also to a slow fire."

Narsai himself applies it to heretics in his homily on the Evangelists:[59]

They were tested through the evil *yaṣrā* of the heretics
who tear asunder the beautiful robe of the faith.

A far more common use is to apply it to the Jews, both the Israel of old and the opponents of Jesus. To some extent this simply echoes Deut 31:21, but of course it also went hand in hand with a Christian polemic which claimed that the Jews willfully refused to acknowledge that Jesus was the Messiah and the Son of God, an act which was itself seen as just one episode in a long history of continuous rebellion against God. The earliest example of this in Syriac is to be found in the third-century Acts of Thomas:[60] "And Israel was not persuaded because of their evil *yaṣrā*." And it appears again in the following century in Aphrahat (*Dem.* 19):[61]

And because God knew their evil *yaṣrā*
he did not compel them to go up from Babylon.

This rather depressing use of *yaṣrā* in anti-Jewish polemic clearly became such a standard trope that it could lend itself to whimsical satire. The learned Church of the East catholicos Timothy I (d. 823) made unexpected play with the concept of "the bitterness of the *yaṣrā* of the Jews" (a phrase that again clearly derives from 4 Macc 3:4) in one of his letters:[62]

If authority over heaven and earth is due to the cross, yet the cross is due to the bitterness of the *yaṣrā* of the Jews, then the authority of Christ over all was born from the bitterness of the *yaṣrā* of the Jews. And if the bitterness of the *yaṣrā* of the Jews is the cause of the cross, and the cross is the cause of death, and death is the cause of the resurrection, and the resurrection is the cause of the kingdom of heaven, and the kingdom of heaven is a good thing that is exalted and raised up above all, so then the bitterness of the *yaṣrā* of the Jews is the cause of a good thing that is most glorious. The bitterness of the *yaṣrā* then is an evil, and one to be praised!

59 Shimun 1970, 231. The homily is listed as no. 9 in Mingana 1905: 1: 26.
60 Wright 1871, 240. 61 Parisot 1894–1907, 848.21.
62 Braun 1914, Letter 2.7, 70.21.

Occasionally, as in the Acts of the Persian Martyrs, this hostile sense is played with by Christian authors, so that Christian martyrs, such as Martha daughter of Pusai,[63] are reproached by their Iranian judges for their stubborn and willful *yaṣrā*:[64]

And now you [Martha], do not persist in your *yaṣrā* like your father, but do the will of Shapur the King of Kings and Lord of all the quarters [of the earth].

In attempting this introductory survey to the concept and use of *yaṣrā* in Syriac literature, including numerous authors and texts spread over a thousand years, there is clearly a danger of overlooking key passages and themes, and regional or temporal variations. Nevertheless, it seems reasonable to draw several provisional conclusions from the material presented.

1. *Yaṣrā* is a loan-word in Syriac that ultimately derives from Hebrew, and was first introduced into Syriac by biblical translators of Jewish origin, for whom this was a key concept that could not be expressed in native Syriac vocabulary.
2. In addition to Gen 6:5, 8:21, and Deut 31:21, the Syriac translation of the Hebrew of Sirach 15:14, 17:31, 21:11, and of the Greek of 4 Macc 3:4, also played a key role in establishing the early Syriac understanding of *yaṣrā*, including the possibility that it could be restrained or subdued through righteous behavior.
3. The prolonged contact of Syriac Christian scholars with Jewish exegetes, and the occasional conversion of Jews to Christianity in Mesopotamia, leaves open the possibility that Syriac Christian understanding of *yaṣrā* did not develop in total isolation from the developing Jewish ideology of *yeṣer*, but evidence for this specific influence is limited (perhaps to one passage in Narsai). Nevertheless, within Syriac texts *yaṣrā* has its own distinctive development within the context of Christian exegesis and theology.
4. There is no evidence in Syriac sources that Syriac writers knew of the possibility of there being two *yeṣarim*, a good *yeṣer* and an evil *yeṣer*.[65] Only a single *yaṣrā* is ever mentioned, and no passage has yet been

[63] The martyrdom of Martha occurred in the late fourth century, and was known in Greek to the historian Sozomen (d. ca. 450). The oldest surviving Syriac manuscripts to contain the text date to the eleventh and twelfth centuries. See Brock 2008.

[64] Bedjan 1891, 235.4. [65] See Rosen-Zvi 2008.

found in Syriac which mentions a "good *yaṣrā*," although the *yaṣrā* is sometimes said to be capable of effecting good behavior.

5. The earliest Syriac texts regard this *yaṣrā* as being morally neutral, capable of inspiring good or bad behavior, and subject to restraint. This appears to have been combined with the belief that most commonly the *yaṣrā* provoked bad behavior. By the medieval period the *yaṣrā* was normally treated as a source of evil.
6. There is no evidence that Syriac sources particularly linked the *yaṣrā* to sexual misbehavior.[66]
7. Ironically, the Jewish concept of *yeṣer* was later frequently used by Syriac Christians in polemical contexts to explain the willfulness of the Jews in not accepting Jesus as the Messiah and Son of God.
8. Syriac Christians believed strongly in the negative role played in the world by Satan and a great variety of demons, with no attempt to demythologize them, and so it is perhaps unsurprising that there seems to have been no attempt to personify the *yaṣrā* as in some Jewish texts.[67]
9. From the fifth century on *yaṣrā* was far more popular in East Syriac writers than in West Syriac writers. Particularly notable in the former group is Narsai, for whom *yaṣrā* was a key anthropological and philosophical concept which helped to explain humanity's tendency from the beginning to do that which was forbidden, and to explain why this tendency could not be overcome except with the aid of divine grace. By contrast, West Syriac writers such as Jacob of Sarug rejected any concept that undermined the autonomy of human free will and divine justice, or which suggested that in God's creation of humanity He inbuilt a tendency for humans to sin. Jacob, and others in his tradition, thus prefer to talk of human will, *ṣebyānā*, rather than *yaṣrā*.

[66] Although Narsai's negative attitude towards women leads him close to this (Becker 2016, 189). For links to sexual desire in Jewish texts, see van der Horst 2006; Rosen-Zvi 2009.

[67] In poetic texts Ephrem, for example, was perfectly happy to personify Sin and Death for rhetorical purposes (see HNis 41, 53), and Narsai could portray his own *yaṣrā* speaking against him in a lawsuit: see Mingana 1905, 1: 167.10; for a translation of the opening passage, see Becker 2016, 184.

# 18

# Evil, Sin, and Inclination (*yeṣer*) in Jewish and Christian Poetic Disputes between the Body and Soul

Ophir Münz-Manor

This chapter examines a group of liturgical poems in Hebrew, Jewish Palestinian Aramaic, and Syriac that focus on the issues of evil, sin, and *yeṣer*. The poems portray a dispute between the body and the soul, each of whom tries to convict the other of responsibility for the person's sins. Each side in the dispute addresses its opponent, and at times also God, and brings proofs and arguments that exemplify its own innocence and the other's guilt. The poems, Jewish and Christian alike, share the same verdict: both body and soul are responsible for sins, and both should be punished. These poetic disputes are one more example of the rich interaction between Jewish and Christian liturgical poetry in the late antique Near East, and their roots go back to ancient Mesopotamian literature.[1] The Syriac disputes that I examine here are well known, especially to those interested in Syriac Christianity.[2] In contrast, most of the Jewish poems were only discovered and published recently, and they are presented here for the first time in English translation.[3]

As will be discussed below, while the notion of *yeṣer* is employed in the Hebrew poems it is by no means a prominent theme in them. This in itself is indicative of the nature and status of the *yeṣer* in late antique liturgical texts in general, and the difference between this and its prominence in rabbinic literature will be discussed toward the end of the chapter. It is

[1] For a comparative outlook on Jewish and Christian liturgical poems from the Near East see Münz-Manor 2010.

[2] See, for example, Brock 1999.

[3] For the critical edition of the Hebrew texts see Münz-Manor 2013. The translations on pp. 6–9 were prepared for this chapter by Michael Rand and Ophir Münz-Manor, and those on pp. 15–20 by Michael Rand.

worthwhile mentioning in this context that in general wrongdoing is only mentioned once in the statutory Jewish prayer. The sixth benediction of the *amidah* prayer reads: "Forgive us Father for we have sinned before You. Wipe and forgive our sins since You are merciful. Blessed are You, Lord, who forgive abundantly."[4] It is self-evident that not much can be concluded from this general statement, which was recited daily by the congregants. In contrast, in the Babylonian Talmud there are several personal, apotropaic prayers, some of which refer explicitly to evildoing and the *yeṣer*.[5] Some of these prayers were added in the Middle Ages to the liturgy as supplements to the statutory text, but again they are not attested in liturgical sources from Late Antiquity. One could assume perhaps that the almost total lack of references to evildoing and *yeṣer* in the statutory prayer gave rise to these personal prayers. The only exception to this rule in Jewish liturgy are liturgical poems for the Day of Atonement. These contain occasional references to the *yeṣer*, and to the question of sin and forgiveness. As noted above, the dispute poems between the body and the soul are the classic example of interest in such questions. It is worth noting that evil and sin played a more pronounced role in Christian liturgy as a result of their centrality in Christian theology; but again, they appear most often in the Lenten liturgy.

## I THE DISPUTE BETWEEN BODY AND SOUL IN SYRIAC, JEWISH ARAMAIC, AND HEBREW LITURGICAL POETRY

The first poetic reference to the dispute between the body and soul, although not a dispute proper, is found in a poem by Ephrem the Syrian, who wrote the following:

> Body and Soul go to court / to see which caused the other to sin
> The wrong belongs to both / for freewill belongs to both.[6]

In these two lines Ephrem presents the attitude of Syriac Christianity (and also that of rabbinic Judaism, as we shall see) to the question of the relationship between body and soul: namely, that they are both liable. Robert Murray summed up this point very cleverly: "questions of responsibility and imputability will always be acute for religious traditions which, like both Judaism

[4] For the textual variants of this blessing see Ehrlich 2015. At a later stage in the development of Jewish prayer, sometime in the early Middle Ages, more extensive sections that relate to evil, sin, and forgiveness were added; but they fall outside the scope of this chapter.

[5] See b. Ber. 16b–17a.

[6] Carmina Nisibena 69:5. The Syriac text was published by Beck 1963, 111, trans. Brock 1999, 32.

and especially Syrian Christianity, strongly emphasise human free will."[7] The next dated poem featuring the dispute between body and soul dates to the fifth century, but before analyzing it I shall explore Syriac and a Jewish Aramaic poems because of their linguistic proximity. Two Syriac disputes have come down to us from the sixth century, in which the dispute between body and soul is related in an expansive manner. Here are some key strophes from one of the poems, which was recited on the third Sunday of Lent:

Soul and Body fell into dispute
and became engaged in a great struggle.
Let us now listen to what they are saying
in the great contest in which they are engaged . . .

When I was asleep and you were on guard,
who was the adulterer in that still sleep?
You are the guard, why then did you not prevent
that adulterous dream from defiling me? . . .

I did not consent when you did wrong,
so I will be far away when you are beaten.
You will be punished in your dust,
while I will find delight in the sky . . .

Both of you now have acted together
and a single judgement is reserved for you.
Join one another and do not be separated,
for there is no division between you.[8]

After an introductory strophe, the dispute itself begins. First, the body accuses the soul of urging him to perform forbidden deeds, claiming that without her he would have been incapable of sinning at all. The soul then accuses the body of being the exclusive source of bad deeds. It is worthwhile noting that the poem presupposes a hierarchy between the soul and the body, as the latter seems to accept the superiority of the soul over him and the soul quite clearly patronizes the body.[9]

A Jewish Palestinian Aramaic dirge for a man from roughly the same century is very similar to the Syriac poem. The poem opens with general pronouncements on the death of a human being, on the soul's leaving the body, and on the judgment in store for the two of them. The seventh strophe of the poem contains an introduction leading up to the dispute:

[7] Murray 1995, 182. [8] Trans. Brock 1989, 58–63.

[9] In the second dispute poem (attributed to Jacob of Sarug) we also an implicit hierarchy of body and soul. See Drijvers 1991.

The King exalted / glorious and unequalled / He will judge / body and soul as one
Soul and body / contend at law together / rendering an account / of every deed.

After a statement to the effect that God is to judge the body and the soul together, and a description of the setting of the dispute, follows the dispute itself. Below are two strophes in which the body and the soul accuse one another:

The body cries out / woe, woe is me / you are the one that broke me / and sapped my strength
My spirit when I rendered / my speech fled / neither talk nor beauty / have I not had enough?
Then begins the soul / to say to the body / you are the one that performed / every evil deed
Beneath the dust / your corpse is held fast / locked up and placed / in the house of imprisonment.

As is customary in this genre, the dispute is organized in the form of direct speech quoted from the two contestants, each of whom speaks in turn. In the sample quoted above the body addresses the soul, claiming that it is she who is to be held responsible, and submitting as evidence the fact that from the moment the soul left him he lost the power of speech, which here represents life itself. The soul accuses the body of performing all manner of forbidden acts, even claiming, quite cleverly, that his earthen grave is in fact a prison, and hinting thereby that he has in any case already been consigned to the place that is appropriate for him who has been legally convicted. After an additional round of arguments comes the concluding strophe, which reports the verdict of the judge:

The Mighty One sees / all the acts of mankind / and says to the body / and to the soul
You both / will be judged / for every deed / on the day of reckoning.[10]

The poet thereby unambiguously proclaims that the body and the soul are one unit, indivisible, and that the two of them must bear the consequences of their joint activity.

The earliest Hebrew liturgical poetry presenting the dispute between body and soul was recited on the Day of Atonement and dates to the fifth century; it thus stands in between Ephrem's poetic allusion to the dispute and the dispute poem just quoted. The Syriac and Hebrew poems share not only the content of the dispute and its conclusion but also literary features: both have an alphabetic acrostic; both are strophic and use similar metrical schemes. The major

[10] The Aramaic texts were published by Yahalom and Sokoloff 1999, 300–05.

difference between them is that the Syriac poem does not feature a refrain. These resemblances exemplify once more how interrelated Jewish and Christian liturgical poetry were in the late antique Near East, both in terms of form and content.[11] Key strophes from the Hebrew dispute read as follows:

When You set forth judgment, You call to the heavens to render the soul,
Thus also the earth You call from below to raise up the flesh.
When they are examined, "Who sinned unto Me?" You say, and
each other they reprove.

The soul is Yours and the body Your making, Have mercy on your creatures!

The lump declares: "While the soul was within me she condemned me
Indeed she was for me like a stumbling block on the path before the blind.
Then when she flew from me I was thrown to the worms like a dumb stone."

The soul is Yours and the body Your making, Have mercy on your creatures!

The soul speaks: "Surely I am pure as when I was in-breathed,
I became as the lump, like the pure with the wicked living in a common home.
He joyed in making me sin, deception and theft in his mouth, yet did not sate me."

The soul is Yours and the body Your making, Have mercy on your creatures!

The flesh declares: "The soul led me on a crooked road –
Fancies of the heart, visions of the eye, rousing of the appetite.
She was taken from me, [leaving] no form and no speech and no sin in me.

The soul is Yours and the body Your making, Have mercy on your creatures!

And the soul says: "You dare condemn me that you may be justified?
When you were eager with the gain of oppression to fill your trunk!
And ever since I withdrew I have tasted no food – Here I am, confront me!

The soul is Yours and the body Your making, Have mercy on your creatures!

He from on high at them mocks for the deception they harbour.
The one with the other, exchanging arguments to be saved from judgement.
Summoned one against another, they place hand on mouth for there is naught to
answer.

The soul is Yours and the body Your making, Have mercy on your creatures!

They are likened to a pair, the lame and the blind, guardians of a king's orchard.
The fruits were stolen by the efforts of both, but they deceived in the admission.
The king hastened to expose their deception in the court, so he combined and
convicted them.[12]

[11] See Münz-Manor 2010. [12] For the Hebrew text see Yahalom 2005, 133–34.

The poem opens with an interesting allusion to Ps 50:4: "He calls to the heavens above and to the earth, that he may judge his people." The poet modifies the verse as if indicating that God summons the soul and the body from the heavens and the earth respectively. The verse serves here as an introduction to the entire dispute and, as we shall see below, other liturgical poems and Midrashic prose always use this verse in a similar manner. At any rate, we can discern that the body, referred to here as "the flesh" (בשר), and in one place lump (גולם), accuses the soul (נפש), claiming that because of her insinuations he was forced to act as an accessory to sin, and provides as evidence the fact that without her he is not capable of acting at all.

The imagery used in the poem is fascinating. For example, at the beginning of the dispute the body uses the following metaphor: "Indeed she was for me like a stumbling block on the path before the blind" (גם היתה לי כמכשול עלי אורח לפני עור). The image is expanded by the reference to Lev 19:14 ולפני עור לא תתן מכשול (You shall not ... place a stumbling block before the blind).[13] Moreover, the imagery is cleverly developed in the next line, in which the body describes himself as a dumb stone. The soul, naturally, claims the exact opposite: from the moment that I left the body, she says, I was no longer forced to engage in material matters, which according to her are the root of evil. Here we can also notice the role of gender in the dispute, since body is linguistically masculine and soul feminine. Indeed some of the arguments build, at least rhetorically, on this gender distinction, although ultimately the two are regarded as equals, as much as sin is concerned.[14]

The second notable feature of the poem is the use of refrain; the refrain is the point at which the congregation joins the poet–cantor and responds to and engages with the poem. By using the refrain the poet invites the community to partake in the performance of the poem and to become a part of its discourse.[15] More importantly, the refrain reaffirms the unity of body and soul, and concludes with a plea for mercy.

[13] In b. ʿAvod. Zar. 6a–b this verse is interpreted as a warning against causing someone to sin.

[14] The situation is quite similar in the Syriac disputes, since Syriac shares the same linguistic differentiation of body as masculine and soul as feminine.

[15] On that feature of late antique liturgical poetry, see Arentzen and Münz-Manor 2019.

In the fourth strophe in which the body speaks he states that the soul lead him astray to the path of "fancies of the heart, visions of the eye, rousing of the appetite" (הרהור הלב / ומראית העין / והערת יצר). The *yeṣer* (translated here poetically as *appetite*) is presented here as an organ of the body alongside the heart and the eye; it is represented as a concrete figure.[16] To each of these organs an action is attached: הרהור הלב (contemplation of the heart);[17] מראית העין (vision of the eye) and הערת יצר (rousing of the *yeṣer*). It is quite clear that the actions are negative, yet the organs themselves seem to be rather neutral. Another allusion to the *yeṣer* appears later in the poem as the poet describes the resurrection of the body and the injection of the soul using the simile כשאור לעיסה (like leaven to dough), an expression that in the Talmuds (both Palestinian and Babylonian) serves as an epithet to *yeṣer hara*ʿ.[18]

It is worthwhile noting that, despite the great similarities between the Jewish and Christian Syriac poems (in both form and content), there are also differences. The Jewish poems are less expansive than their Christian counterparts. It is not only that they are shorter: what characterizes them is their focus on the concrete mechanism of human wrongdoing, whereas the Syriac poems are more theological in nature and offer a more developed and "psychological" outlook on the human being. This contrast should be seen in light of the difference in discursive trends between Jewish and Syriac texts. Rabbinic discussions are usually fragmented and present a variety of viewpoints, whereas the Syriac corpora are based on the writings of several authors, most notably Ephrem. Many of Ephrem's works were written in verse; thus his poetry, and the poetry of his successors, is more abstract and theoretical in its essence. In contrast, Hebrew liturgical poetry focused mainly on ritual and performance in public, hence it is less scholarly and contemplative. In sum, the Hebrew and Aramaic and the Syriac poems draw and reflect, on the one hand, on their distinctive traditions, but present similar attitudes toward the shared culpability of body and soul, flesh and spirit, on the other.

[16] The sixth-century Hebrew poet Yannai enumerated the organs of the body that cause sin, and among them (between the heart and the kidneys) he mentions the yeṣer: "We did not subdue yeṣer" (לא כפפנו יצר). On that feature of the yeṣer see Rosen-Zvi 2011, 174–75.

[17] As I have learned from Noam Mizrahi's comment, this is a rendition of שרירות הלב.

[18] The simile appears in one of the prayers mentioned above in n. 5 and in its parallel in y. Ber. 4:2.

## 2 THE PARABLE OF THE LAME AND THE BLIND IN JEWISH AND CHRISTIAN SOURCES

In the concluding strophe of the Hebrew dispute the poet alludes to a parable about a lame person and a blind person. This parable is known from other Hebrew sources (in verse and prose alike); it also appears in Epiphanius' *Panarion* and, since it is an important feature of the disputes, I shall now discuss it at some length. The earliest textual witness to the parable of the lame and the blind is found in the Midrashic compilation known as the *Mekhilta de-Rabbi Shimon bar Yochai*, a set of homilies on the book of Exodus, which dates to the third century CE. The text reads:

Antoninus asked this of Rabbi, saying to him, "After a person dies, and his body is entirely destroyed, does the Holy One, blessed be He, bring him to justice?" He said to him, "You have asked me about the body, [which] is impure. Ask me about the soul, which is pure!" They told a parable: To what is the matter alike? "It is like a human king who had an orchard, and in it were appealing first fruits. He placed in it two guards, one lame and one blind. The lame one said to the blind one, 'I am looking at appealing first fruits!' The blind one, 'As if I can see!' The lame one said to him, 'as if I can walk!' [So] the lame one rode on the back of the blind one, and they took the first fruits. After a few days, the king came and sat in judgment over them. He said to them, 'Where are the first fruits?' The blind one said to him, 'As if I can see!' The lame one said to him, 'as if I can walk!' The king was clever. What did he do? He made the one ride on the back of the other, so they were walking about. The king said to them, 'This is what you did, and you ate them!'" Likewise, the Holy One, blessed be He, brings the body and the soul, and stands in judgment over them. He says to the body, "Why did you sin before me?" It says before him, "Master of the World, from the day that the soul departed from me, I've been cast to the ground like a stone!" He says to the soul, "Why did you sin before Me?" It says before Him, "Master of the world, is it I who sinned? It is the body that has sinned! from the Day that I departed it, haven't I been pure before you?" The Holy One, blessed be He, brought the soul and placed it inside the body, and judged them both as one. As it says in Scripture, "He summoned the heavens above" (Ps. 50:4) – [meaning,] to bring the soul. And afterward, " . . . and the earth, (for the trial of the people)" (Ps. 50:4) – [meaning,] to bring the body, and afterward to judge the one with the other.[19]

The context of this Midrash is a discussion of Exod 15:1: "Horse and driver He has hurled into the sea." Here too the question of the responsibility of the Egyptian and his horse is discussed; ultimately God convicts both. In the *Mekhilta* text, as in Ephrem's verses and in the Hebrew

[19] Trans. Nelson 2006, 125–28. The texts have received much scholarly attention over the years; see Luitpold 1941, 1943; Kister 2007, 254–59.

dispute poem, the body and soul are said to be an indivisible unit. Interestingly, the Midrashic text concludes with an allusion to Ps 50:4, the same verse that opens the Hebrew poem discussed above. In fact, the order of things in the poem is inverted in comparison to the *Mekhilta* text where the order is (1) parable, (2) dispute, and (3) biblical prooftext. Given the chronology of both texts, it is quite clear that the Hebrew poem is alluding to the Midrashic text and combines it in a smooth manner into the new liturgical context of the poem.

As many scholars have noted, a parallel version of the parable appears in Epiphanius' *Panarion*. According to Epiphanius the parable is quoted from a certain *Apocryphon of Ezekiel*, a vague and disputed attribution. Before elaborating on the relationship between Epiphanius' version and its Jewish counterparts, let me quote from the text:

> To give a symbolic description of the just judgement in which the soul and the body share, Ezekiel says, A king had made soldiers of everyone in his kingdom and had no civilians but two, one lame and one blind ... And the blind man said: "Let's go into the garden and ruin the plants there." But the lame man said, "And how can I, when I'm lame and can't [even] crawl?" And the blind man said, "Can I do anything myself, when I can't see where I'm going? But let's figure something out ... " By so doing they got into the garden, and whether they did it any danger or not, their tracks were there to be seen in the garden afterwards. And the merry-makers who entered the garden on leaving the wedding were surprised to see the tracks in the garden ... What did the righteous judge do? Seeing how the two had been put together he put the lame man on the blind man and examined them both under the lash, and they could not deny the charge ... Thus the body is linked with the soul and the soul with the body, for the exposure of their joint work, and there is a full judgement of both, the soul and the body; they are jointly responsible for the things they have done, whether good or evil.[20]

Epiphanius shares with Ephrem, a contemporary of his, and with the rabbis the notion that body and soul have mutual responsibility for sins. Epiphanius' employment of the parable is, however, unparalleled, to the best of my knowledge, in other Christian texts. The uniqueness of Epiphanius' parable and its similarities to the parable in the *Mekhilta* have led many scholars to examine their relationship.[21] The most comprehensive and updated study was carried out by Marc Bregman, who concluded that despite Epiphanius' attribution of the parable to Ezekiel its source cannot be the so-called *Apocryphon of Ezekiel*. According to Bregman the parable in the *Panarion* echoes a rabbinic homiletical

[20] Epiphanius, *Pan. against Origen*, 70.6–17, trans. Williams 2013.
[21] On the matter see Mueller 1994; Bauckham 1996; Chazon 2000.

Midrash that builds upon the parable as it appears in the *Mekhilta*. In his words: "It therefore seems most likely that the author of the passage quoted by Epiphanius was a Christian who borrowed and reworked homiletical traditions current in the cultural milieu of rabbinic Judaism."[22] Bregman's assertion seems convincing, but the discovery of three additional versions of the parable in Hebrew liturgical poems complicates the picture, since in one of them there are references to some details only known from Epiphanius' version.[23] The poem, which dates to the sixth or seventh century, presents the following version of the parable:

A fanciful parable / about vineyard keepers – / a lame one and a blind:
The lame one holds / speech with the blind / proposing a scheme.
The blind one retorts / reprimanding his fellow, / the lame one and his plot.
  The soul is Yours / and the body Your creature. / Your works cry "Mercy!"

The lame one replied, / "How does the lame / gird on a sword?"
I am lame, / come bear me / and I'll fill my garment's bosom.
The two were joined / and between them took / all their heart's desire.
  The soul is Yours / and the body Your creature. / Your works cry "Mercy!"

A wayfarer stood, / saw the burden / and cried out to the king.
Their lord saw / that the fruit was gone / and said to them thus:
Branches and tree!/ Who wrecked them, / and who took the fruit?
  The soul is Yours / and the body Your creature. / Your works cry "Mercy!"

The two intriguing details that are paralleled in Epiphanius' version appear in the second and third strophes. In the second strophe the lame man describe himself as someone who cannot carry a sword – namely, that he is not a soldier. This notion, which does not appear in any of the other dispute poems (or any other prose version of the parable), is found in Epiphanius' version ("A king had made soldiers of everyone in his kingdom and had no civilians but two, one lame and one blind"). In the following strophe it is the figure of the wayfarer that discovers the mischief of the lame and the blind, again a motif that appears only in Epiphanius ("And the merry-makers who entered the garden on leaving the wedding were surprised to see the tracks in the garden"). The textual evidence of this poem makes us wonder whether it is based on the version in Epiphanius or on a "lost" Jewish Midrash à la Bregman. Frankly, it is impossible (at least at this point in time) to reconstruct the genealogy of the parable, if such a genealogy is at all possible, but at any rate it

[22] Bregman 1991, 137. [23] Two of these poems are discussed below.

exemplifies the complexity of the literary relationships between Jewish and Christian texts in verse and prose.

## 3 THE YEṢER IN HEBREW DISPUTES

Generally speaking, the *yeṣer* is only rarely mentioned in late antique Jewish liturgical poetry and, as noted above, it is almost entirely absent from contemporary statutory prayers. The *yeṣer* is mentioned here and there in the poetic works of the fifth-century Hebrew poet Yose ben Yose, who writes in one place: "See the leaven of our hearts, the inclination of youth" (ראה שאור לבבנו, יצר הנעורים).[24] As noted above, leaven in dough is a common metaphor for the Evil Inclination in rabbinic sources and liturgical poetry.[25] Yose ben Yose's predecessor Yannai also alludes to the dispute between body and soul, and he too mentions the *yeṣer* and the parable of the lame and the blind. As noted above, most of the Hebrew liturgical poems that relate to the *yeṣer* were written for the service of the Day of Atonement, but Yannai mentions it in a different liturgical setting. Yannai composed a poetic cycle for the triennial lectionary according to the Palestinian rite and his poem about sin, *yeṣer*, and forgiveness was written for the reading of Leviticus 4 that opens with the verse "If a soul shall sin." Here is the relevant part of his poem:

So being from a place of justice and a place of judgment
and a place of Law, the soul is submitted to judgment.
Hence when it sins it will give a reckoning
when You pass [. . .] on the day of reckoning.

If the body sins it's from a place of sin.
But how can the soul sin, as it's from a place of no sin.
. . .

The soul will say, "The flesh brought me to sin."
And the flesh will retort, "The soul brought me to sin."
The Judge of their deeds will laugh at them,
for He is their Maker and knows their make.

The two together are like a lame one and blind,
who had their abode in the king's garden.

[24] Mirsky 1991, 154. Blazer birabi Qilir, a celebrated liturgical poet of the seventh century, also made use of this metaphor in a composition for Rosh Hashanah, in which he wrote: "The stink of the evil leaven" (צחן רוע שאור): Münz-Manor 2015, 175.

[25] See also n. 18 above.

They ruined the fruit as one hoisted another.
The king will judge them hoisted on one another.

Yannai opens the poem with a declaration that the soul alone will be responsible for the sins of a person. Yannai makes this unusual claim because of the liturgical context: since the Torah reading begins with a verse that talks about a soul that sins, it is only natural for Yannai to follow that figure of speech. But soon afterwards Yannai balances the account and states that both soul and body are accountable for the sins of a person.

Yannai also integrates the *yeṣer* in the discussion as he writes: "for He is their Maker and knows their make" (כי הוא יוצרם יודע יצרם), a formulation that plays on the root יצר, thus connecting the creator (יוצר) with the inclination (יצר).[26]

In another Hebrew dispute also from the sixth century an additional allusion to the *yeṣer* appears:

Indeed flesh too will impute to his soul the punishment for his crime.
"I rehearsed your praises before Him . . . like one misdirecting the blind.
A sure scourge for one placing a stone to trip passers-by, a stumbling block on the way."

"Can I relent in the face of this?" the faithful Judge will answer and say.
Now his soul within him mourns and says, "What's your charge?
[ . . . . . . . . . . . . . . . . . . ] makes her nest alongside the pit's mouth.
It was your nature misled me bit me like a viper [ . . . . . . . . . . . ] "
So the Creator answers her, "Whence [ . . . . . . ] was not created."

Here too the evidence is not entirely clear because of the lacunae in the manuscript, yet even what remains is rather interesting. In this instance the soul accuses the body (whereas in the former example it was the opposite): "It was your nature that misled me, bit me like a viper" (ויצרך השאני כמו פתן נשכני). That the *yeṣer* here is evil is beyond any doubt, as it is likened to a poisonous snake. Moreover, the *yeṣer* is not only deadly here, it is also actively tempting the soul. The imagery of this line is also very suggestive, as it alludes to the temptation story of Adam and Eve. It is not only the image of the serpent but also the phrase ויצרך השאני ("It was your nature that misled me") that alludes to Gen 3:13: ותאמר האישה הנחש השיאני ואוכל ("The serpent duped me and I ate").

The climax of the use of the *yeṣer* is reached in a dispute from the eighth century. Here the *yeṣer* made its way into the refrain that reads:

[26] The parable of the lame and blind is briefly mentioned, but how it relates to the rest of the material is unclear as the manuscript cuts off at this point.

"You know our nature. / Forgive us, Creator, / our God and Keeper!" (ידעתה יצרינו / סלח לנו יוצרינו / אלוהינו נוצרינו).[27] The inner logic of the refrain can be summed up in the following way: (1) God is aware of (perhaps also responsible for) the human *yeṣer*; (2) hence the people beg God, the creator, to forgive; (3) and the refrain concludes with a vocative address to God, to save the congregation. There is yet another intriguing appearance of *yeṣer* in this poem:

> Sickness in his life, / his myriad desires / filling his brief days.
> Here today, / gone with the wind tomorrow, / nowhere to be found.
> Can he find a reply, / to say "My heart's been made pure" / before his speaking Creator?

The most noteworthy feature here is the use of *yeṣer* in a unique plural form יצרותיו, which came into being, beyond doubt, because of the rhyme pattern (שנותיו / ימותיו / יצרותיו). But the rhyming scheme in itself cannot explain this form since the poet actively seeks to amplify the force of the *yeṣer* as he adds the word רוב. Moreover, the poem seems to refer to medical aspects of the *yeṣer*. In this respect it is possible that the *yeṣer* was understood to cause suffering: the use of דוי (sickness) to describe a consequence of the *yeṣer*'s activity is particularly striking in this regard.

From the discussion of the Hebrew liturgical poems that relate to the *yeṣer* the following conclusions can be drawn. First and foremost, the *yeṣer* is rather marginal in payytanic literature. This fact should, however, be viewed in context. *Piyyut* in general is characterized by its focus on the narration of biblical accounts, and only in rare cases does one find halakhic discussion or treatments of concepts or beliefs. Indeed, the poems cited in this chapter are quite unusual in their contemplative nature, which relates directly to their liturgical context of sin, penance, and redemption. That being said, one can make the following observations on the nature of the *yeṣer* in *piyyut*: it is internal to the human body, and in general it is associated with sin. However, it is evident that for the poets the question of the relations between body and soul is independent from the question of the *yeṣer*, a picture that emerges also from rabbinic literature, particularly in Palestinian sources.[28] Interestingly, in one place (in the serpent imagery) the *yeṣer* has a demonic nature. Furthermore, we note that there is no reference to the two *yeṣarim* paradigm (i.e. an evil and

[27] Here again we find the artful use of יצר and יוצר.

[28] Rosen-Zvi 2011. This should not surprise us since piyyut is also a Palestinian phenomenon.

a good inclination),[29] nor is the *yeṣer* sexualized. Finally, there is some intensification of the role and nature of the *yeṣer*, which becomes more corporal and evil in the later poems, a fact that dovetails nicely with developments in later rabbinical sources. We can safely conclude then that the picture that emerges from the examination of Hebrew liturgical poems from late antique Palestine corroborates Rosen-Zvi's conclusions concerning the *yeṣer* in rabbinic culture.[30]

## 4 CONCLUSION

Poetic disputes between body and soul concerning the responsibility for a person's sins were popular in the late antique Near East. The poetic and thematic similarities between the Jewish and Christian accounts highlight once more the interrelations between the two religions and the importance of a comparative study of them. There are many discursive ways to approach questions concerning evil and sin. Most of the Midrashic texts, which took shape inside the study hall, have a learned nature, for example. In contrast, the presentation of these topics in contemporary liturgical poems was aimed at a much more diverse audience and overall they were less scholarly. Liturgical poems, to be sure, also have didactic and intellectual traits, yet their primary purpose was to create a ritual experience for the congregants, especially the lay or unlettered. Therefore, I argue that liturgical texts should be studied first in their own right and second together with rabbinic (or patristic) literature, as two components of one religious and cultural system. By doing so we will enrich our understanding of these cultures, and we will produce a more nuanced picture of the societies we seek to explore and understand.

[29] In theory one could argue that the form יצרותיו (his inclinations) relates to this concept, although I do not think it is the case, as discussed above.

[30] Rosen-Zvi 2011.

# 19

# The Wizard of Āz and the Evil Inclination: The Babylonian Rabbinic Inclination (*yeṣer*) in Its Zoroastrian and Manichean Context

Yishai Kiel

## 1 INTRODUCTION

The rabbinic *yeṣer*[1] (or *yeṣer hara'*)[2] is situated at the crossroads of psychology and demonology. On the one hand, it conceptualizes the internal human desire to sin and, on the other, it personalizes and reifies evil.[3] Thus, while the *yeṣer* is imagined in rabbinic sources as an internal disposition or inclination toward sinfulness, it is, at the same time, portrayed as a very "real" demonic entity intruding into the bodies and souls of humans.

Both the psychological and ontological manifestations of the rabbinic *yeṣer* were previously contextualized with ancient Jewish and Christian constructions of evil and sin.[4] Without denying the importance of these contexts, I presently seek to expand this comparative framework by

* I would like to thank Prods Oktor Skjærvø, Ishay Rosen-Zvi, and Adam Becker for their comments on this chapter.

1 For the *yeṣer* (variously translated as inclination / tendency / disposition / instinct / desire) in rabbinic culture, see Boyarin 1993, 61–76; Schofer 2003; Alexander 2002; van der Horst 2006; and Rosen-Zvi 2011.

2 For Boyarin 1993, 64–67, 74–76, the term *yeṣer* (as opposed to *yeṣer hara'*) is emblematic of a dialectical anthropology of a single inclination that is neither evil nor good in itself, while the use of the term *yeṣer hara'* is reflective of a dualistic anthropology that assumes two inclinations. A third model of a single inclination that is wholly evil is preferred in Rosen-Zvi 2008, 1–27.

3 Rosen-Zvi 2011, 3–8 describes a paradigmatic shift in scholarship from the *yeṣer* as an embodiment of evil to the *yeṣer* representing an internal psychological struggle. Rosen-Zvi offers a demonic interpretation of the *yeṣer*, but concedes that "the *yetzer* cannot be fully explained in the framework of ancient demonology either. Unlike Mastema and Satan it is not a cosmic being but a fully internalized entity that resides inside the human heart" (2011, 7).

4 See, e.g., Cohen Stuart 1984, 94–100; Boyarin 1993, 67–70; Satlow 2003, 209–12; Rosen-Zvi 2011, 36–64; Becker 2016, 202–05.

considering the possible impact of Iranian culture on Babylonian rabbinic representations of the *yeṣer*. My discussion, to be sure, will not weigh on the complex and long-debated issue of earlier Iranian influence on pre-rabbinic and especially Qumranic forms of metaphysical and psychological dualism.[5] Regardless of whether, and to what extent, Iranian thought had already influenced the doctrine of the two spirits at Qumran,[6] I presently seek to situate the distinctive construal of the *yeṣer* that emerges in Babylonian rabbinic culture in the context of the indigenous Zoroastrian and Iranian Manichean traditions of the Sasanian period.

Notwithstanding previous attempts to connect certain aspects of the rabbinic *yeṣer* with Iranian traditions,[7] in what follows I shall argue that distinctly Babylonian rabbinic constructions of the *yeṣer* ought to be examined, first and foremost, in the light of Zoroastrian and Manichean portrayals of the Middle Persian demon Āz[8] – a psycho-demonic embodiment of human desire, which assumes cosmic dimensions of evil and occupies a central position in the diabolic hierarchy alongside the Evil Spirit himself.

The nature of "desire," to be sure, differs significantly in the rabbinic, Zoroastrian, and Manichean systems. In rabbinic culture the *yeṣer* is manifested mainly through human desire to sin (although, as we shall see, in Babylonian rabbinic culture there is a pronounced emphasis on sexual sin in particular); in Zoroastrianism Āz is manifested through gustatory, sexual, and acquisitive forms of human desire; and in

5 I refer here to the notion of the two spirits/inclinations and not to body–soul dualism. For the extent of the Iranian impact on Qumranic dualism see, e.g., Shaked 1972; de Jong 2010.

6 For ethical–psychological and metaphysical–ontological manifestations of the doctrine of the two spirits at Qumran see, e.g., Levison, 2006; Kister 2009; Xeravits 2010; Stuckenbruck 2011, 162–66; Popović 2016; Brand 2013.

7 See, e.g., Kohut 1866, 66–67. Elman (2007, 148) speculated that the Talmudic portrayal of the *yeṣer* as a fly situated in one's heart (b. Ber. 61a) engages the Zoroastrian image of the corpse-demoness (*nasuš*), which is described as having "the form of a disgusting fly" (*Videvdad* 7.2). He further suggests that the Talmudic identification of the *yeṣer* with Satan and the Angel of Death (b. B. Bat. 16a) may be related to Iranian conceptions of the Evil Spirit as an embodiment of evil in the human psyche.

8 The apparently female demon Āz (Av. Āzi masc.) is known from a variety of Zoroastrian and Manichean sources and is derived from the verb *āz*- ("to strive for, long after"). See Bartholomae 1904, cols. 342–43. The name has been translated variously as "avidity," "lust," "desire," "hunger," "craving," "covetousness," "acquisitiveness," "concupiscence," and so forth. Here, I will use the term "desire" rather loosely, so as to designate the three main aspects of human desire associated with Āz, namely hunger, sexual lust, and greed. For previous discussions of this demon see Zaehner 1955, 166–83; Schmidt 2000; Choksy 2002, 38–44; Sundermann 2003; Lincoln 2012, 35–36; Asmussen 2011.

Manicheism Āz, which constitutes the Iranian equivalent of Greek Hylē (Matter) found in Western Manicheism and other gnostic traditions, is manifested primarily through bodily desire for sexual mingling (see below). What makes these distinctive notions of "desire" comparable, therefore, is not so much the nature or object of said desire, nor its underlying anthropological assumptions, but rather the fact that in all three cultures it is similarly reified as a psycho-demonic entity, which assumes cosmic dimensions of evil.

While proposing a broad phenomenological comparison of the functions of the *yeṣer* and Āz in their respective cultures, I shall center on a close reading of a lengthy Talmudic story (b. Yoma 69b; b. Sanh. 64a) concerning the eschatological imprisonment and incapacitation of the *yeṣer* (projected back onto the returnees from the Babylonian exile),[9] in the light of Zoroastrian and Manichean depictions of the imprisonment of Āz at the end of days.[10] In this context, we shall see that several peculiar and idiosyncratic details in the Talmudic story are illuminated by a comparison with the Iranian traditions.

Moving beyond analogical correlation, I posit that the rabbinic, Zoroastrian, and Manichean accounts of the eschatological defeat of the *yeṣer*/Āz are intimately and cognately related: in all three accounts, a figure that functions essentially as a psycho-demonic embodiment of human desire assumes cosmic dimensions of evil and, in this capacity, is destined to be defeated at the end of days; it is connected with human death and identified, in one way or another, as a demon/angel of death; a divine message pertaining to prayer and truth plays a significant role in its imprisonment; it is confined to a restricted area (a prison of some sort) and is sealed with molten metal; it is imagined as a fiery lion-shaped figure; its sexual dimensions emerge as a separate demonic entity that warrants "special treatment"; and, finally, its obliteration is tied to the cessation of procreation.

Although some of the parallels presented here are, admittedly, of a generic nature (e.g. the depiction of desire in terms of burning fire), the significance of the evidence lies not in the relative conviction one attaches to one or another point of similarity, but rather in the

[9] For previous readings of this Talmudic story, see Boyarin 1993, 61–63; Rosen-Zvi 2011, 119.

[10] For the Pahlavi accounts of this event see *Selections of Zādspram* 34.32–45; *Mēnōy ī Xrad* 8.15–16; *Pahlavi Rivāyat* 48.90–96; *Bundahišn* 34.27–30. The Manichean accounts quoted below stem, for the most part, from Middle Persian fragments of Mani's *Šābuhragān* found at Turfan.

cumulative effect of the data. The existence of multiple thematic and literary parallels between the Talmudic and Iranian accounts of the eschatological imprisonment and defeat of desire would seem to point to a more intimate relationship, which goes beyond mere phenomenological affinity.

That said, the intimate connections between the Talmudic and Iranian accounts were facilitated, no doubt, by a more fundamental phenomenological resemblance that Āz and the *yeṣer* exhibited in earlier layers of their respective traditions. The functional resemblance of these figures (insofar as they represent a psycho-demonic manifestation of human desire), therefore, is not necessarily a distinctive product of Sasanian culture, as this feature can be discerned in earlier layers of the Jewish and Iranian traditions. I submit, however, that the basic affinity between the Jewish and Iranian representations of demonic desire enabled, in turn, the fostering of more intimate connections between the *yeṣer* and Āz in the context of the interreligious exchange that took place in Sasanian Babylonia – the birthplace of Mani and Manicheism, seat of the Sasanian throne, home to Babylonian rabbinic culture, and a major center of Zoroastrianism. It is in this particular cultural setting that the eschatological fate of the *yeṣer* was recast in the image and likeness of Zoroastrian and Manichean portrayals of Āz.[11]

I further argue that the syncretistic currents that pervaded Sasanian culture more broadly, and particularly the documented tendency to converge and equate mythical figures from the Judeo-Christian and Iranian traditions,[12] enhanced the identification of the *yeṣer* and Āz in the minds of the Babylonian rabbis and, perhaps also, in the minds of their Iranian contemporaries. The Babylonian rabbinic story of the imprisonment of the *yeṣer* reflects, therefore, not merely the adaptation of isolated motifs from the surrounding cultures to an existing rabbinic thread, but rather a novel construction, which seeks to thoroughly integrate the Zoroastrian and Manichean demon Āz into the rabbinic discourse on the *yeṣer*.

[11] Although the Zoroastrian traditions are preserved, for the most part, in Pahlavi works composed in the ninth and tenth centuries, the Manichean evidence adduced below (dated to the early Sasanian period) strengthens the assumption that the Zoroastrian traditions date back to the Sasanian period and, therefore, can inform the emergence of similar traditions concerning the *yeṣer* in rabbinic Babylonia.

[12] For cross-cultural identifications of mythical figures in rabbinic, Zoroastrian, and Manichean traditions in the Sasanian period, see Kiel 2015a, 2015b, and 2019.

## 2 THE YEṢER AND IRANIAN DEMONOLOGY: A PHENOMENOLOGICAL PERSPECTIVE

Before I turn to a detailed comparison of the Babylonian rabbinic and Iranian accounts of the imprisonment of the *yeṣer* and Āz at the end of days, I must first address the more basic phenomenological resemblance of these figures as psycho-demonic manifestations of human desire. This basic resemblance constitutes the cultural backdrop against which I propose reading the eschatological traditions pertaining to these figures, which were preserved in the Babylonian Talmud and Zoroastrian and Manichean literature.

Demons and evil spirits occupied a central place in Jewish, Christian, and philosophical thought in Late Antiquity, and were believed to possess, harm, and affect humans in various ways.[13] The significance of the rabbinic *yeṣer* (as well as similar constructions of the Evil Inclination found in patristic and monastic literature) lies not in the place it occupies as a harmful supernatural being, but rather in its distinctive role as a "demon of desire" that operates both from within and from without the human psyche.[14]

Unlike many Jewish Hellenistic and Greek Christian authors, who imagined the internal struggle against sin in terms of a quarrel between mind and body, logos and desire, or rational and irrational facets of the self, for the rabbis, who generally adhered to a monistic and unified self,[15] the struggle was, first and foremost, against external demonic forces that attempted to infiltrate the human body and soul. The body, according to the rabbinic scheme, was not perceived as the source of sin or sinful desire, but rather as a "neutral battle-ground,"[16] which the demons sought to dominate. Thus, the Amoraic rabbis imagined the hostile invasion of the human body by the *yeṣer* in terms of a city under siege (b. Ned. 32b),[17] while the *yeṣer* was likened to a highway robber who attempts to seize hold of a house (the human body or soul).[18]

13 Martin (2004, 187–206) has traced a paradigmatic shift in the perception of demons in the Roman East during the third and fourth centuries. Authors such as Porphyry, Iamblichus, and Origen (and, one might add, the rabbis) began to accept the notion rejected by several of their predecessors, according to which the demon (or rather the *daimōn*) is not merely an intermediary divine being, but an evil power that causes actual harm to humans.

14 Rosen-Zvi 2011, 1–8.

15 For rabbinic notions of the self and the relationship of body and soul, see Stiegman 1979; Rubin 1989; Boyarin 1993, 5–6, 31–35; Goshen-Gottstein 1994; Rosen-Zvi 2012, 59–67; Balberg 2014, 8–12.

16 See Rosen-Zvi 2011, 2.

17 This passage seems to express a dualistic system of two inclinations. See Rosen-Zvi 2011, 1–2.

18 Gen. Rab. 22:6 (ed. Theodor-Albeck, 210–13). Rosen-Zvi 2011, 66–72, notes that Origen describes the demons in very similar terms (e.g. *Princ.* III.3.6). St. Anthony

This basic feature of the rabbinic *yeṣer*, which is hardly limited to rabbinic Babylonia, is reminiscent of Pahlavi notions of the interaction of demons (or, at least, the psycho-ontological "class" of demons) and humans.[19] In Zoroastrianism, the Evil Spirit and his demonic companions are said to belong essentially to the other world (*mēnōy*) and have no concrete existence in this world (*gētīy*).[20] Not unlike the demonologies of Porphyry, Origen, and the rabbis, the Pahlavi authors maintained that demons can gain embodied existence by penetrating the bodies of humans, lodging in them in a parasitic fashion and manifesting themselves through the kinds of sinful and harmful behavior they propagate. Demons who thus break into the bodies of humans corrupt them both physically (via bodily decay) and spiritually (via sin). The only way to defeat these demons is by denying them access to the body and soul. In this scheme, the human body represents the ultimate battleground between the forces of good and evil and, therefore, humans are enjoined to protect and preserve their bodies as much as possible from demonic invasions.[21]

The following Pahlavi texts will serve to illustrate the means by which the demons ought to be fought against:

It has been said: Being on one's watch is the following: one who makes this body like a fortress and who places watch over it, keeping the gods inside and not letting the demons enter.[22]

When it comes to possessing "manly virtue," the following is best: One who struggles with the demons of the other world, whoever they may be, and in

likewise stresses that demons intrude the body like "robbers in the house." See Brakke 2006, 20–21.

[19] On Zoroastrian demonology in general see Christensen 1941; Calliere 2001; Colpe 2003, 316–26, 470–72, 567–602; Pirart 2007; Lincoln 2012, 31–42. Zoroastrian demonology is not limited to the realm of psychological traits, as it encompasses "an unflinching attempt to name, comprehend, and defend against all that threatens, frightens, and harms us" (Lincoln 2012, 31). The longest and most comprehensive list of demons is found in *Bundahišn* 27.14–50. Compare also *Videvdad* 10.9–17, 19.40–47; *Yašt* 3.5–17; *Bundahišn* 5.1–3; *Dādestān ī Dēnīg* 36.31, 37–46; *Bundahišn* 27.6–12. See Lincoln 2012, 40–42; Pirart 2007, 34–55.

[20] For the notions of *mēnōy* and *gētīy* in Iranian literature, see Shaked 1971; Stausberg 2002, 1: 333–38. For the demon's lack of embodied existence in this world see, e.g., *Dādestān ī Dēnīg* 18.2 (ed. Jaafari-Dehaghi, 72–73). Cf. *Dādestān ī Dēnīg* 36.51 (ed. Jaafari-Dehaghi, 130–31); *Dēnkard* 5.71–2.

[21] See, e.g., *Dēnkard* 6.264 (trans. Shaked 1979, 103; Williams 1997, 159); *Dēnkard* 3.199 (trans. Shaked 2001, 583; Williams 1997, 159; de Menasce 1973, 209); *Dēnkard* 6.236 (ed. Shaked, 92–93); *Dēnkard* 6.302 (ed. Shaked, 116–17).

[22] *Dēnkard* 6.E.34a (ed. Shaked, 202–03).

particular does not let these five demons into his body: Desire (Āz), Envy (Arešk), Lust (Waran), Wrath (Xešm), and Infamy (Nang).[23]

Much like the rabbinic *yeṣer*, the Pahlavi texts classify the demons (or, at least, the "psychological" class thereof) as highway robbers (*rāhdāran*) who attempt to infiltrate the human body and dominate it. The human body is likened to a fortress (*diz*)[24] that requires constant guarding against demonic intruders. Also, like the rabbinic perception of Torah as a remedy for, and a means to battle, the *yeṣer*,[25] the Pahlavi texts emphasize that wisdom (*xrad*)[26] and the religious Tradition (*dēn*)[27] ought to be raised up against these demons.

Āz, the psycho-demonic manifestation of human desire, is described in several Pahlavi texts as the fiercest of demons and the one most difficult to conquer,[28] having divided itself into three categories, corresponding to human cravings for food, sex, and worldly possessions:

And Āz, being of one "nature," was unable to sully the creations that had been scattered, and so,[29] in order that (its) powers in unison(?) might be propagated among the creations, was divided into three: that which is "by nature" (*čihr*), that which is "out of (exceeding?) nature," and that which is "outside of nature."

"By nature" is when (Āz) is in edibles (?), to which one's life-soul (*gyān*) is tied.

"Out of nature," is wish for (sexual) mingling, which is precisely what is called Lust (Waran), which, by looking out, what is inside is aroused, and (thus) the nature of the body is suppressed.[30]

"Outside of nature" is desire (*ārzōg*) for whatever good thing one sees or hears.

Each layer is divided into two: "by nature," that is hunger and thirst; "out of nature," that is "the one who pours" and "the one who receives" (the semen);

[23] *Dēnkard* 6.23 (ed. Shaked 10–11, slightly modified). Cf. *Dēnkard* 5.7 (trans. Skjærvø 2011, 201).

[24] This word is often presented with the Aramaeogram KLYTA (from Aramaic קרתא\קריתא "city"), paralleled by the homily on the "little city" in b. Ned. 32b.

[25] See, e.g., Sifre Deut 45 (ed. Finkelstein, 103–04); Gen. Rab. 22:6 (ed. Theodor-Albeck, 212–13); Gen. Rab. 54:1 (ed. Theodor-Albeck, 575); b. Qidd. 30b.

[26] Cf. Mani's claim in the *Šābuhragān* (M 49) to teach "wisdom and knowledge (*gnosis*)" (xrd ʾwd dʾnyšn), so as to redeem humanity from Āz and Ahriman (Sundermann 2003, 330).

[27] For the power of the religious Tradition (*dēn*) to defeat the demons see, e.g., *Dēnkard* 9.2.4–16; *Bundahišn* 1.29–31 (15–16); *Dēnkard* 7.4.63 (= the Pahlavi version of *Yašt* 19.80): *Dēnkard* 9.2.18; Vevaina 2010, 126–27.

[28] See, e.g., *Dēnkard* 6d2 (ed. Shaked, 176–79; quoted below): "Then Ādur-Narsē said to Ādur-Mihr: 'O Priest, what demon is the fiercest (*stahmagtar*) . . . ' Ādur-Mihr said: 'The one demon that is fiercest is Āz.'"

[29] Thus, Schmidt 2000, 522, n. 5: *ā-š* for <ZYš> *ī-š* in the unique MS.

[30] Cf. *Dādestān ī Dēnīg* 30.11: *awištāb ī az āz* ("the oppression that is from Āz"), quoted below.

"outside of nature," that is accumulating (wealth) by robbery and not giving because of stinginess.[31]

In the *Bundahišn* Āz is described as follows:

The demon Āz is that which swallows things.

When, due to deprivation there is nothing at hand, then it eats from (any? its own?) body. It is such a demon that, if all the property of this world were given to it, it does not store (any of it, but immediately devours it), yet does not become satiated.[32]

While the Manichean Āz is primarily and emphatically sexual (see below), it has been noted that, not unlike its Zoroastrian counterpart, it too is characterized by insatiable hunger.[33] In the Manichean tradition the insatiable hunger of Āz can be best illustrated through the myth of the swallowing of the offspring of their fellow demons by the incarnations of Āz.[34]

Similarly to the rabbinic *yeṣer*, which is not associated with sexual desire in particular,[35] Āz was perceived as an embodiment of desire in a broad sense and in relation to different types of human cravings. By drawing attention to these similarities I am not arguing for genealogical dependency, not merely because the basic psycho-ontological duality of the demonic sphere is broadly attested across cultures, but also because the nature of said "desire" is fundamentally different in the rabbinic, Zoroastrian, and Manichean systems. In this section I merely wish to have pointed out that a similar phenomenology of psycho-demonic desire, intruding into the human body and soul from without, can be discerned in the rabbinic and Iranian systems. This, I shall argue, facilitated the formation of more intimate connections between the Babylonian rabbinic *yeṣer* and the Zoroastrian and Manichean Āz – which in turn assumed cosmic dimensions of evil and occupied a central position in the diabolic hierarchy alongside the Evil Spirit – a process which resulted in the emergence of cognate stories pertaining to their eschatological defeat.

31 *Selections of Zādspram* 34.36. Cf. Gignoux and Tafazzoli 1993, 122–23; Zaehner 1955, 351–52.

32 *Bundahišn* 27.34. Cf. b. Sukkah 52b (and t. Hor. 1:4).

33 Sundermann 2003, 328–29. Cf. Zaehner 1955, 170; Schmidt 2000, 521.

34 See Skjærvø 1982.

35 I assume with Rosen-Zvi 2011, 14–35, 65–86, that, prior to the redactional layer of the Babylonian Talmud, the rabbinic *yeṣer* is not specifically sexual. Cf. Boyarin 1993, 61–76; Schofer 2003; van der Horst 2006.

## 3 THE IMPRISONMENT OF THE YEṢER IN THE BABYLONIAN TALMUD

In a rather bizarre Talmudic story (b. Yoma 69b; b. Sanh. 64a) the Babylonian rabbis attempt to communicate their insights into the psychology of human desire and the nature of temptation and sin, by imagining the capturing and imprisonment of the *yeṣer* and its sexual offshoot. The story is set in the early post-exilic period and purports to describe the history of the Judean returnees from the Babylonian exile, who sought to rid themselves of the Evil Inclination once and for all.

"And they cried with a loud voice unto the Lord their God" (Neh 9:4) – What did they say? Rav Yehudah, others maintain it was R. Yohanan,[36] said: "Woe,[37] woe (is us),[38] it is that which destroyed his house, burnt his Temple, slew the righteous, and exiled Israel from their land.[39] Have you not given it to us that we might be rewarded (for withstanding its temptation)? We wish neither it nor its reward (for overcoming it)." They fasted for three days,[40] praying; hereafter a note that had [the word] "truth" written on it descended to them from Heaven. R. Hanina[41] said: this demonstrates that the seal of the Holy One, blessed be He, is truth. It came out, shaped as a fiery lion cub, from the Holy of Holies. The Prophet said to them, "that is it."[42] As they held it fast, a hair fell from it, and its roar was heard for four hundred parasangs. They said: what shall we do?[43] The prophet said to them: cast him into a cauldron[44] and cover it with lead, so as to absorb its voice,[45] as it is written, "that is wickedness; and thrusting her down into the tub, he pressed the leaden weight into its mouth" (Zech 5:8). They said: since the time is propitious, let us pray regarding desire for (sexual) sin.[46] So, they prayed and it was delivered into their hands. They imprisoned it for three days; after that they sought an egg for the ill[47] and could not find one. They said: what shall we do? Shall we pray for half (=that its power be partially destroyed)? Heaven will not grant that. So, they blinded its eyes. This was effective insofar that one does not lust after one's relatives.[48]

[36] Other textual traditions have R. Yonatan (Florence) or R. Nathan (Karlsruhe).

[37] This appears to be a Greek loan-word (βία) denoting an act of force or violence (LSJ 314). See Kohut 1878–1892, 2:45; Jastrow 1903, 160; Wartski 1970, 198; Fraade 2013, 188.

[38] Munich 6 and JTS add here: "(to us) from the *yeṣer* for idolatry."

[39] Munich 95, Oxford 366, and the Wien fragment add: "and still it dances amongst us."

[40] Munich 95 adds: "and three nights."

[41] Other textual witnesses have "Rav Huna."

[42] Oxford 366 has: "this is the *yeṣer* for idolatry."

[43] Munich 6 and JTS 218 add here: "if we kill it, it will raise its voice and destroy the world."

[44] Karlsruhe: "a lead cauldron."

[45] Munich 6 and JTS 218 add here: "and they set a fire under it and burned it."

[46] *yaṣra de-'avera* (lit. "the *yeṣer* for sin"). The term *'avera*, however, both here and elsewhere, often denotes sexual sin in particular. See, e.g., b. Ber. 22a; b. Meg. 12a; b. Sotah 11b.

[47] Karlsruhe and Munich 95: "a newly laid egg" (ביעתא בת יומא).

[48] b. Sanh. 64a. (according to MS Yad Harav Herzog). Cf. b. Yoma 69b.

This unique story seeks to interpret the cry of the returnees from the Babylonian Exile mentioned in Neh 9:4 ("And they cried with a loud voice unto the Lord their God") as a cry of distress over the destruction caused by an unidentified entity, which is said to have "destroyed his house, burnt his Temple, slew the righteous, and exiled Israel from their land." Although the printed editions (and some of the manuscripts) explicitly identify this entity as the *yeṣer* for idolatry,[49] most textual witnesses lack any specific identification. The assumption that this anonymous evil figure should be identified with the inclination for idolatry seems to be based on a later interpolation in the text, which sought to explain the two parts of the Talmudic narrative as pertaining to different aspects of the Evil Inclination – the desire for idolatry and the desire for sexual sin.[50]

An intertextual reading of this anonymous entity that "destroyed his house, burnt his Temple, slew the righteous, and exiled Israel from their land" in the light of another Talmudic homily (b. Sukkah 52a) leads to its identification as the quintessential *yeṣer*. In this homily, which moves back and forth from individual-psychological to collective-cosmic imagery,[51] it is said that the *yeṣer* is responsible for destroying both the First and Second Temples and for slaying the righteous.[52]

Joel called it "northerner," as it is written "I will drive the northerner (*ṣefoni*) far from you; I will thrust it into a parched and desolate land (Joel 2:20)" – Our Rabbis taught: it is called "northerner" (*ṣefoni*) since the *yeṣer* is hidden (*ṣafun*)[53] in a human's heart;[54] "I will thrust it into a parched and desolate land" – to a place where there are no humans for it to attack; "with its face towards the eastern sea" – this implies that it set its eyes[55] against the first Temple and destroyed it and

[49] Boyarin 1993, 61–63, interprets the story as an etiological myth, "which explains why the Jews of rabbinic times are no longer attracted to the worship of idols." This interpretation, however, is based on a later reconstruction of the passage as referring specifically to the *yeṣer* for idolatry.

[50] Rosen-Zvi 2011, 207, n. 99, acknowledges that the identification of the evil figure in the story as the *yeṣer* for idolatry is based on a gloss, but argues that other rabbinic sources (b. ʿAbod. Zar. 17a; Song Rab 7:8) suggest that this later gloss might be a correct interpretation of the original text.

[51] Rosen-Zvi 2011, 78–79.

[52] It is noteworthy that, according to b. Yoma 9b, the First Temple was destroyed on account of a variety of sins – idolatry, sexual transgressions, and murder – while the Second Temple was destroyed on account of "baseless hatred."

[53] Beyond the wordplay on "north" (*ṣafon*) and "hidden" (*ṣafun*), it is noteworthy that in the Iranian tradition the demons are geographically located in the north. See, e.g., *Videvdad* 19.1; Duchesne-Guillemin 1982.

[54] For the internal situation of the *yeṣer* in the heart, see also b. Ber. 61a; Gen Rab 67:8 (ed. Theodor-Albeck, 763).

[55] Compare the blinding of the *yeṣer*'s eyes in the abovementioned Talmudic story.

slew the sages therein; "and its hinder part toward the western sea" – this implies that it set its eyes against the second Temple and destroyed it and slew the sages therein.[56]

Beyond the significance of this passage as an intertext of b. San. 64a and b. Yoma 69b, insofar as both accounts seem to highlight the role of the *yeṣer* in the destruction of the Temple and the slaying of the righteous/ sages, it also underscores the implicit eschatological tone embedded in the story of the imprisonment of the *yeṣer*. Although the story is set in the early Persian period, attributing the capturing and imprisonment of the *yeṣer* to the returnees from the Babylonian exile, the ultimate hope for the eschatological obliteration of the *yeṣer* at the end of days can hardly be missed here, in the light of the eschatological scene described in b. Sukkah 52a.[57] It would seem that the exegetical stimulus of Neh 9:4 and Zech 5:8 triggered the recasting of the eschatological scene back onto the early Persian period. The intertext of b. Sukkah 52a also stresses the multifaceted role of the *yeṣer* as a psychological inclination, on the one hand, and an embodiment of cosmic evil and collective catastrophe, which will be obliterated at the end of days, on the other.

In what follows I shall endeavor to decipher some of the more peculiar and cryptic elements in the Talmudic story (e.g. the image of the *yeṣer* as a fiery lion cub emerging from the Holy of Holies; the note that came down from heaven with the word "truth" written on it; the imprisonment of the *yeṣer* in a cauldron sealed with metal; the subsequent setting of fire under it [according to some textual witnesses]; and the surprising appearance of the sexual *yeṣer* as a separate and reified demonic entity), in the light of the Zoroastrian and Manichean accounts of the imprisonment and final defeat of Āz at the end of days.

## 4 READING THE TALMUDIC STORY IN ITS ZOROASTRIAN AND MANICHEAN CONTEXT

### 4.1 The *yeṣer*, Satan, and the Angel of Death

In b. San. 64a the *yeṣer* is not merely a psycho-demonic embodiment of desire, but also, and more emphatically, a cosmic force identified with the very principle of evil ("that is wickedness") and responsible for the

[56] b. Sukkah 52a (according to MS Oxford – Bodl. heb. e. 51 [2677]).

[57] See also the related portrayal of the slaying of the *yeṣer* in the end of days in b. Sukkah 52a.

destruction of the Temple and the death of the righteous ("it is he which destroyed his house, burnt his Temple, slew the righteous, and exiled Israel from their land"). The destructive and diabolic qualities attached to the *yeṣer* are corroborated by other Talmudic passages, particularly in a Babylonian rabbinic tradition that explicitly identifies the *yeṣer* as "Satan" and the "Angel of Death."[58]

The Babylonian rabbinic elevation of the *yeṣer* to the top of the diabolic hierarchy can be illuminated by its comparison with the relative position of Āz in the Manichean and Pahlavi traditions relating the eschatological events. While in the Avesta Āzi does not seem to occupy a central position in the diabolic system,[59] and while several "philosophical" Pahlavi texts seem to regard Āz merely as a demonic manifestation of desire in the psychological sphere, in the Manichean texts and in the Pahlavi accounts of the eschatological narrative Āz assumes cosmic dimensions of evil. While it is difficult to determine if and when Āz was in fact "promoted" to be the right hand of the Evil Spirit, it is evident that in third-century Babylonia, the birthplace of Manicheism, Āz had already assumed a prominent position in the hierarchy of evil.

In the Manichean tradition Āz is classified as the "mother of all demons,"[60] on a par with Ahriman.[61] Indeed, references to "Āz and Ahriman" pervade Iranian Manichean literature,[62] in which Ahriman, as the original principle of evil, is accompanied by Āz, an embodiment of Matter (ὕλη; Hylē).[63] The couple Āz and Ahriman also occurs in the Pahlavi accounts of the eschatological narrative,[64] where Āz is appointed by Ahriman as his "captain" (*spāhbed*)[65] and eventually devours (and thus

58 b. B. Bat. 16a. This statement is attributed to a third-century Palestinian rabbi (Resh Laqish), but it only appears in the Babylonian Talmud and appears to reflect a Babylonian rabbinic perspective. Cf. Elman 2007, 148; also Gen Rab 89:1 (ed. Theodor and Albeck, 1086).

59 Schmidt 2000, 517. On the rise to prominence of Āz see Zaehner 1955, 179–80; Sundermann 1986; Skjærvø 1995, 267.

60 See, e.g., fragment S 9 (Henning, 1932); Schmidt 2000, 517, n. 1.

61 See Asmussen 2011; Sundermann 2003, 332; Zaehner 1955, 167.

62 See, e.g., M 49; MM ii, pp. 307–08; M 7984.2; M 7981.1; M 7980.2. Several examples can be found in MacKenzie 1979.

63 Āz parallels, not so much the philosophical concept of ὕλη, but rather its personification in Gnostic and Western Manichean thought as the embodiment of Matter in which the light is imprisoned. See Zaehner 1955, 168; Schmidt 2000, 517.

64 See n. 10 above.

65 *Selections of Zādspram* 34.32 (cf. Gignoux and Tafazzoli 1993, 120–21; Zaehner 1955, 351): "and then he chose a general, who was none other than Āz."

succeeds) its master.[66] Thus, the elevation of the *yeṣer* and its identification with Satan in the Babylonian Talmud can be illuminated perhaps in the light of contemporaneous Iranian traditions, according to which Āz occupied a central position in the diabolic hierarchy alongside the Evil Spirit.[67]

Furthermore, the *yeṣer* is said in b. San. 64a and b. Yoma 69b to be responsible for the death of the righteous and, as we have seen, is equated in b. B. Bat. 16a with the Angel of Death (מלאך המות) himself. This aspect of the Babylonian rabbinic *yeṣer* too is informed by Iranian traditions relating to Āz, as the latter is said to be responsible for the cutting off of human life by way of devouring their sustenance.[68] Although I am not entirely convinced by the hypothesis, proposed by Hanns-Peter Schmidt and Werner Sundermann, that Āz functioned as a full-fledged "demon of death" in the Pahlavi or Manichean tradition,[69] it is possible that the association of Āz with the cutting off of life inspired the identification of the cosmic *yeṣer* with the Angel of Death in Babylonian rabbinic culture.

## 4.2 Truth vs. Desire

Since the *yeṣer* and Āz are not merely psychological manifestations of human desire, but also cosmic embodiments of evil, they can only be defeated with divine assistance. In the Talmudic story a note descends from heaven with the word "truth" written on it, which leads the rabbis to conclude that the "seal of the Holy One is truth." But what does truth have to do with the capturing of the *yeṣer*? Is this merely a sign of divine reassurance, as suggested by the traditional commentators?[70] I submit that the appearance of truth in this context is informed by a comparison with the Iranian account of the imprisonment of Āz.

In the Pahlavi sources it is the deity Srōš (Av. Sraoša) who aids in the smashing of Āz at the end of time:

[66] *Pahlavi Rivāyat* 48.92 (cf. ed. Williams, 1: 186–187, 2: 86): "[after having devoured the other demons] the Evil Spirit will say to the demon-created Āz, and the demon-created Āz will say to the Evil Spirit: I shall devour you, ignorant one."

[67] The evidence gathered from the Manichean sources (early Sasanian period) suggests that the Pahlavi Āz too is the product of Sasanian currents.

[68] Zaehner 1955, 171–72.

[69] Schmidt 2000, 519; Sundermann 2003, 330. The suggestion that Āz was regarded as the "helper" of Astwihād (the "Bone-untier"; Av. *astō-widātu*), the Pahlavi "demon of death" par excellence (e.g. *Bundahišn* 4.24; *Mēnōy ī Xrad* 1.117), relies on shaky textual evidence. See the comments in Schmidt 2000, 519, n. 14 (regarding *Dēnkard* 9.16.2).

[70] See, e.g., R. Shlomo Itzhaqi (Rashi) on b. San. 64a and b. Yoma 69b.

Ohrmazd will stand up with Srōš-ahlīy, and Srōš-ahlīy will smite Āz and Ohrmazd (will smite) the Evil Spirit.[71]

And Srōš-ahlaw will undo the demon Āz.[72]

While Srōš is connected to the notions of "obedience" and "readiness to listen," he was also associated with prayer, closely linked to Ard (Av. Aši) and Mihr (Av. Mithra; the overseer of contracts and manifestation of truthfulness),[73] and assumed the role of divine messenger and mediator between the divine and human realms.[74] In one of the Pahlavi lists of deities lodging in human beings,[75] Wahuman, Srōš, and Ard are said to lodge in thought, speech, and action respectively. In order to protect truthfulness in speech, the original function of Srōš as "listener"[76] is described as follows: (*Dādestān ī Dēnīg* 2.16):

That Srōš lodges in speech (is manifest) from him who truthfully speaks what he is aware of and listens to what he is not aware of from truthful *dastwar*s (teachers).[77]

While far from certain, I would like to speculate that the eschatological overcoming of Āz by Srōš – in his capacity as divine messenger and mediator between the divine and human realms, associated with human prayer, and closely linked to truthful utterance and the god Mihr – can significantly inform the Talmudic story. Quite in line with the various functions of Srōš in the Pahlavi tradition, the Talmudic story relates that, as a result of human prayer, God sends the returnees a divine message, a note on which the word "truth" is written, to aid them in the overcoming of the *yeṣer*. It is at the very least possible that this Talmudic scene subtly engages the Pahlavi account of Srōš's overcoming of Āz at the end of days.

## 4.3 The Imprisonment of Desire

Next in the Talmudic story, the returnees are instructed by the prophet to cast the *yeṣer* into a cauldron and cover it with lead, so that its voice cannot be heard. While the notion of the imprisonment of demons in

71 *Pahlavi Rivāyat* 48.94 (ed. Williams, 2: 86–87). See also *Bundahišn* 34.28–29 (trans. Skjærvø 2011, 171); *Selections of Zādspram* 34.44–45.

72 Day Hordad of the Month of Frawardīn 35 (trans. Skjærvø 2011, 167).

73 On Mithra see, e.g., Schmidt 2006.

74 On these features of Srōš, see Kreyenbroek 1985; Shenkar 2014, 144–48.

75 See, e.g., *Dēnkard* 6.1b (ed. Shaked, 2–3) = *Dādestān ī Dēnīg* 93.2.

76 For Srōš as "readiness to listen," see Skjærvø 2011, 15–16.

77 *Dādestān ī Dēnīg* 2.16 (ed. Jaafari-Dehaghi 1998, 46–47); *Bundahišn* 26.121 (ed. Anklesaria, 230–33, §117).

metallic chains (often chains of iron or lead in particular) pervades magical literature in general, and Babylonian incantation bowls in particular,[78] the imprisonment of the *yeṣer* with a leaden seal at the end of days is particularly reminiscent of the Pahlavi account of the eschatological imprisonment of Āz. In the Pahlavi account the Evil Spirit and Āz scurry back into the hole through which they first entered the world of mixture, and the hole, in turn, is sealed with molten metal:

> The Evil spirit and Āz, their resources having been struck down by the ritual formula from the Gathas [i.e. the Ahuna Vairiia?], will (scurry) back to the gloom and the darkness, through the passage in the sky through which they scurried in.
> [The river of molten metal will flow into hell, which will be cleansed; then] the *hole through which the Evil Spirit had scurried will be closed by that metal.[79]

Similar descriptions of the eschatological imprisonment of Āz and the Evil Spirit at the end of days are found in Manichean literature. Thus, we read in the *Šābuhragān* that "(when) the renovation comes about, then Āz and Ahrimen and the demons and the witches shall be bound in that prison for ever beyond recovery!"[80]

In the Talmudic story the seal of lead used to confine the *yeṣer* is meant to absorb the sound of its cry. This detail might also be indebted to the Pahlavi account, as the imprisonment of the Evil Spirit and Āz and the sealing of the hole through which they scurried away is said to achieve a similar effect:[81] "And he will expel all from the sky through the hole through which they scurried in. And in that place, he will make them so stunned and senseless."[82]

Finally, in several Talmudic manuscripts (Munich 6 and JTS 218) we read that, following the imprisonment of the *yeṣer* in a cauldron and its sealing with metal, "they set a fire under it and burned it." This description would seem to echo the Manichean tradition of the "great fire" that will burn at the end of days and consume Āz along with its fellow demons and the sinners.[83]

78 See, e.g., Yamauchi 1967, 260–61 (cf. Montgomery 1913, 248). Cf. b. Ber. 6a and b. Git. 68a.

79 *Bundahišn* 34.30–31 (cf. trans. Anklesaria, 291–92). Compare *Pahlavi Rivāyat* 48.86–88 (cf. ed. Williams, 1: 186–87, 2: 86).

80 M 7981/I/V/ii/13–19. On the eschatological prison see, e.g., MacKenzie 1979, 520–21. For the imprisonment and separation of the male and female demons see the Manichean Coptic *Sermon of the Great War*, p. 41.5–10 (Gardner and Lieu 2004, no. 71, p. 226). Similarly, *Kephalaia* XLI (105, 30–34, in Gardner 1995, 110). Cf. b. Git. 68a.

81 For the howling of the demons see, e.g., *Dēnkard* 7.2.48.

82 *Pahlavi Rivāyat* 48.95 (ed. Williams, 1: 186–89, 2: 87).

83 See MacKenzie 1979, 516–21; Gardner 1995, 110.

## 4.4 "Shaped as a Fiery Lion Cub"

According to the Talmudic story, following the three-day fast and after having received the note from heaven with the word "truth" written on it, the *yeṣer* finally emerges from the Holy of Holies[84] in the shape of a fiery lion cub (גוריא דנורא). The representation of the *yeṣer* as lion shaped is significantly informed by the Manichean portrayal of the demonic incarnations of Āz as lion shaped. According to the Manichean myth, Āz assumed the form of a male and female Āsarēštār (the equivalents of Ašaqlūn/Saklas and Pēsūs/Namrāʾēl/Nebrōʾēl), who are described in turn as "lion-shaped":

Thereupon, that Āz, from all that progeny of the demons that had fallen down unto the earth from the sky, donned that male Āsarēštār and female Āsarēštār,[85] lion-shaped, *lusty and wrathful, sinful and predatory. She made them her own covering and garment and *lusted inside them.[86]

The Talmudic depiction of the *yeṣer* as a fiery figure – an image attested in other Talmudic sources as well[87] – is likewise informed by Iranian portrayals of Āz, as in both Zoroastrian and Manichean sources Āz is said to be connected with fire.[88] In *Videvdad* 18.18–19 the fire beseeches the housemaster to seek out firewood to light it, lest Āz extinguish it:[89]

(During the first third of the night, the Fire) beseeches the house-master of the house (to come) to (its) aid: House-master, get up! . . . Seek firewood, bring (them) to me! Light me with ritually clean firewood. The demon-created *āzi* seems to tear off my life thread(?) even before it has come full circle (pairi-iθna).

In the later Persian *'Ulamā'-i Islām*, the insatiable hunger of Āz is connected with the "fire that is within us":

Again, about what you asked as to how, at the resurrection, the fire that is within us will exist without food, the answer is: it is apparent that the sun is hotter than other fires, but it lives without food. It is clear that food is eaten by the demon (Āz),[90] as it is said that there are several demons intermingled in the bodies of man.

[84] The location of the *yeṣer* in the Holy of Holies appears to be in line with its earlier depiction as the one responsible for the destruction of the First and Second Temples.

[85] On the form *āsarēštār* rather than *āsrēštār*, see Skjærvø 1997, 165, n. 10.

[86] See Hutter 1992, 82–84. Cf. Asmussen 1975, 128.

[87] See, e.g., b. Qidd. 81a (in which lust is envisioned as a "fire at the house of ʿAmram"); b. Sanh. 37b.

[88] Schmidt 2000, 518; Sundermann 2003, 333–34.

[89] *Videvdad* 18.19. Cf. Moazami 2014, 406–07.

[90] Āz is mentioned here in only one manuscript, but appears again later in this passage. See Dhabhar 1932, 442, n. 5.

It is asked: "When there will be no food, how will there be any pleasure?" It should be known that when there are no (demons like) Āz and Niyāz (Want), what need is there for food? If there is no demon of heat, what need is there for shelter? If there is no demon of cold, what need is there for fire? If there is no demon of lust (Waran), what need is there for women?[91]

While the exact nature of the relationship between Āz and the internal fire in this passage is not altogether clear, in the Manichean tradition fire is the very embodiment of Āz.[92] In a Middle Persian *Kephalaia* text, it is said:

At the coming of Āz three ways of death are revealed, the hidden fire and the visible fire (both leading) to transmigration and (good) smell and flowers to paradise.[93]

It would seem, therefore, that the Talmudic portrayal of the *yeṣer* as a "fiery lion cub" is rooted in, and indebted to, contemporaneous Zoroastrian and Manichean imagery of Āz as both lion shaped and embodied in fire.

## 4.5 The Reification of Sexual Desire

While insatiable hunger is the predominant quality of Āz in the Pahlavi tradition, the Manichean sources emphasize, above all, its sexual and lustful dimensions.[94] As a counterpart of Greek Hylē (ὕλη) and Latin *concupiscentia*,[95] Āz represents in the Iranian Manichean tradition not simply Matter per se but particularly bodily lust for sexual mixing. The emphatically sexual portrayal of Āz in the Manichean tradition can be illustrated by the continuation of the passage from the *Šābuhragān*:

And just as in the beginning in that dark hell, where it itself scurried about, Āz itself had taught the demons and witches, the wrathful monsters and the Āsarēštārs, male and female, *rutting and sexual acts, thus, afterward too, Āz again began to teach in the same manner *rutting and sexual acts to those other monsters and Āsarēštārs that had fallen from the sky onto the earth so that they would *rut and have sex.[96]

The sexual covetousness of Āz is also present, albeit to a lesser extent, in the Pahlavi tradition. As we have seen, according to the *Selections of*

91 *Persian Rivayats* (Dhabhar 1932, 442); Sundermann 2003, 334.
92 Sundermann 2003, 333–34.
93 M 5750 (trans. Sundermann 2003, 335–36). The passage seems to convey the idea that Āz, who is embodied both in the internal flame within humans and in the visible fire, leads them to the cycle of rebirth (rather than salvation) by seducing them to sin.
94 See esp. Sundermann 2003, 328–29; Schmidt 2000, 521.
95 For Hylē and Āz see above. For *concupiscentia* see Zaehner 1955, 168.
96 M 7984.1 (ed. Hutter, 83–84).

*Zādspram*, a significant part of the desirous nature of Āz is defined in terms of the "wish (*kāmagōmandīh*) for (sexual) mingling, which is precisely what is called Lust (Waran), which, by looking out, what is inside is aroused."[97] Although sex itself was generally embraced in Zoroastrianism (not only in terms of fertility and procreation but also insofar as pleasure and enjoyment are concerned), sexual desire in the sense of excessive or illicit lust was believed to be dominated by the demonic sphere and embodied by Āz.[98]

The eschatological hope for eradicating sexual desire, embodied and personified in Āz, would seem to fit more naturally within the Manichean worldview, which encouraged celibacy among the Elect and avoidance of procreation among the Auditors,[99] rather than the generally anti-ascetic tendencies that characterize Zoroastrian praxis. While the Manichean avoidance of procreation (or of sex altogether) was intended, first and foremost, to reduce the harm caused to the Living Soul by further entrapping it in Matter, the notion of the final obliteration of Āz is indeed more consistent with a worldview that rejects sexual praxis. Thus, it is possible that the Pahlavi traditions pertaining to the obliteration of Āz at the end of days are the result of Manichean influence.[100] To be sure, however, notwithstanding Zaehner's attempt to resolve the internal contradiction within the Pahlavi tradition by excluding the eschatological obliteration of sexual desire from the realm of "orthodox" Zoroastrianism and attributing it instead to vestiges of "Zurvanite" lore,[101] it would seem that the Pahlavi authors simply regarded excessive and illicit forms of sexual desire (in contradistinction to sex and sexual pleasure) as linked to Āz and the demonic sphere, and thus hoped (independently perhaps of Manichean influence) for their obliteration at the end of days.[102]

Interestingly, the multifaceted nature of the covetousness of Āz – desire for food, sex, and material acquisition – was historicized and concretized in the context of the myth of its eschatological imprisonment, as Āz is said to have split itself into its distinctive demonic components. Thus, while Pahlavi Āz is not specifically sexual, in the eschatological scene Āz "gives

97 *Selections of Zādspram* 34.36 (quoted above). 98 See Kiel 2016, ch. 1.

99 Beduhn 2000, 61.

100 Sundermann (2003, 331, following Schaeder 1941, 291–92. Cf. Zaehner 1955, 183–92) has further speculated along these lines that the Pahlavi figure of Jeh, the Primal Whore, owes its very existence to the Manichean Āz, as it seems to function as a Zoroastrian substitute for the sexual and feminine dimensions of the Manichean Āz.

101 Zaehner 1955, 179–80. 102 Kiel 2016, ch. 1.

birth," as it were, to sexual lust (Waran)[103] (see the *Selections of Zādspram* 34.36 quoted above).

In what follows, I shall attempt to illuminate the nature of the relationship between the quintessential *yeṣer* in the first part of the Talmudic story and its sexual offshoot that emerges as a separate demonic entity in the second part of the story, by alluding to the distinctive relationship between sexual lust (Waran) and desire (Āz) in the Pahlavi account of the eschatological events.

In the second part of the Talmudic story the rabbis envision a reality devoid of sexual desire, by projecting back onto the Persian period a failed attempt to rid humanity of sexual desire once and for all. The personified sexual *yeṣer* informs the returnees that in its absence the ability to procreate will be undermined and, indeed, after its imprisonment for three days not even a single egg (representing fertility and procreation) can be found. Eventually, the returnees decide to blind its eyes and set it free, so as to achieve, at the very least, the elimination of sexual desire for their relatives.[104]

The focus in the second part of the narrative on the embodiment of sexual desire in particular (as opposed to the quintessential *yeṣer* in the first part) appears to be connected with a broader shift in the perception of the *yeṣer* in Babylonian rabbinic culture. Ishay Rosen-Zvi has convincingly demonstrated in this regard that the *yeṣer* – which in Tannaitic and Amoraic literature is imagined as a general inclination to sin – has been heavily sexualized in the redactorial stratum of the Babylonian Talmud.[105] The story recorded in b. Sanh. 64a and b. Yoma 69b seems to consciously map this broader shift in the conceptualization of the *yeṣer* onto a particular historical moment, by shifting the focus from the quintessential *yeṣer* in the first part of the narrative to a specifically sexual *yeṣer* in the second part.

The Talmudic reification of sexual desire as a distinct demonic figure, in the context of the eschatological narrative of the imprisonment of the *yeṣer*, can be significantly illuminated when compared to the Pahlavi account of

103 On Pahlavi Waran (Lust), see König 2010, 150–54. For the sexual dimensions of Waran see esp. *Bundahišn* 27.31–32 (cf. ed. Anklesaria, 238–39).

104 It is unclear whether this Talmudic reference to sexual desire for one's relatives echoes the Zoroastrian doctrine of *xwēdōdah* (Av. *xᵛaētuuadaθa*), which is said in the Pahlavi sources to refer to endogamous marital unions, especially of father and daughter, mother and son, or brother and sister, and is regarded as one of the most pious deeds in the Zoroastrian tradition. For the Zoroastrian doctrine see Skjærvø 2013. For Talmudic echoes, see Kiel 2014.

105 Rosen-Zvi 2011, 112–19; Rosen-Zvi 2009.

the splitting of Āz into Waran (Lust) and the other constituents of human desire in the end of days, as in both stories the demonic embodiment of desire "engenders" a separate embodiment of sexual desire.

Similar to the Talmudic story, in which it is suggested that the complete obliteration of the sexual *yeṣer* will necessarily result in the cessation of human and animal fertility, the Pahlavi narrative discloses that, in the aftermath of the obliteration of Āz and the demons, and upon the Renovation, there will no longer be need for procreation, as described in the *Pahlavi Rivāyat*: "And man and woman will have desire (*kāmag*) for one another, and they will enjoy it and consummate it, but there will be no birth from them."[106]

While this passage constitutes a typical Pahlavi description of the world to come, which in itself is not necessarily connected to the obliteration of Āz, it is noteworthy that in some of the Pahlavi versions of the *eschaton* (e.g. the *Selections of Zādspram* 34.41 quoted above), the cessation of procreation in the world to come is indeed linked to the obliteration of Āz in particular. According to the Pahlavi authors, in the renewed world there will be no need for procreation,[107] although sexual mingling and even (a purified form of) sexual desire will remain.[108] In the Talmudic story, by contrast, the returnees, who first wish to rid themselves of sexual desire altogether, eventually realize its inseparability from the procreative function and thus come to terms with its presence.[109] This difference can be explained perhaps by the fact that, unlike the Pahlavi tradition, the Talmudic story is not situated in the eschatological period (although it alludes to it), but rather recast onto an earlier period in history. Elsewhere, however, the Babylonian Talmud records a tradition according to which in the world to come (probably in the sense of after the resurrection) there will be no *piryah u-reviyah* (lit. "procreation," but perhaps also "sex" more broadly): "Rav was accustomed to say: The world to come is not like this world; in the world to come there is neither reproduction nor procreation (לא פריה ולא רביה)."[110]

[106] *Pahlavi Rivāyat* 48.106 (ed. Williams, 1: 190–191, 2: 88). Similarly, *Bundahišn* 34.24, *Selections of Zādspram* 34.41 (ed. Gignoux and Tafazzoli, 124–25).

[107] The logic of this doctrine is that humans were created in order to fight and remove evil from the world. Once that has been accomplished, procreation is no longer necessary.

[108] Cf. b. Sukkah 52a, in which it is assumed that, in spite of the death of the *yeṣer* at the end of days, a sexual drive will remain.

[109] See the interpretation suggested in Boyarin 1993, 61–64.

[110] b. Ber. 17a (according to MS Oxford 23); cf. *'Abot R. Nat.* A: 1 (ed. Schechter, 5) and parallels.

In juxtaposing Talmudic and Iranian traditions concerning sex at the end of days, I wish to point out the inherent connection exhibited in both religious traditions between the final obliteration of the psycho-demonic manifestation of sexual desire (the sexual *yeṣer* and Āz [–Waran], respectively) and the question of the persistence of the sexual and procreative functions at the end of days.

## 5 CONCLUSION

Rabbinic portrayals of the *yeṣer* were previously contextualized in scholarship with other ancient Jewish and Christian traditions. In this chapter, I hope to have expanded this comparative framework, by viewing Babylonian rabbinic representations of the *yeṣer* in the light of Zoroastrian and Iranian Manichean traditions. We have seen that the distinctive perception of the *yeṣer* that emerges from the Talmudic account of its eschatological imprisonment – namely, that of a cosmic embodiment of desire and evil on a par with Satan himself – is strikingly reminiscent of Iranian traditions relating the eschatological confinement and destruction of Āz.

The significance of these parallels lies not in the relative conviction one attaches to one or another point of affinity, but rather in the cumulative effect of the evidence. Although each thematic or literary parallel can in itself be dismissed as a reflection of phenomenological resemblance, the existence of multiple parallels between the Talmudic and Iranian accounts of the imprisonment of the demonic embodiment of desire at the end of days suggests that we are dealing with cognate stories and not merely with an accidental convergence of motifs. In this context, I have speculated that a more basic form of phenomenological affinity between the rabbinic and Iranian psychologies of desire – namely, the recasting of human desire in the image of a psycho-demonic entity, which attempts to invade the human body and dominate it by generating sinful lust – facilitated the emergence of more intimate connections that were fostered in Sasanian Babylonia. In this context, the rabbis appear to have reconfigured the *yeṣer* in the image and likeness of indigenous traditions about Āz.

# 20

# The Evil Inclination in the Targums to the Writings

Leeor Gottlieb

## 1 INTRODUCTION

The purpose of this chapter is to examine if and how the Targums to the Writings make use of the concept of the Evil Inclination (*yeṣer hara'*). Research on the Evil Inclination has focused mainly on texts from the Talmud and Midrash – and rightly so.[1] It is worthwhile, though, including the corpus of Aramaic Targums in discussions about rabbinic concepts, because these contain valuable information about Jewish interpretations of Scripture compiled over many centuries, primarily throughout the first millennium CE. As such, Targums reflect, at times, how some rabbinic concepts were perceived, thus affording one more perspective through which to understand the concept under scrutiny.[2]

It is also important, however, to be aware of what one might not expect to find in this body of literature. Targums by and large do not engage in the sort of give-and-take, question-and-answer style found in Talmudic and Midrashic texts, which record dialogues between sages striving to arrive at some sort of conclusion. One should also generally not expect to find the origin of a rabbinic concept or term in a Targum. Instead, one might expect to find the usage of a preexisting idea in a Targum, reflecting the influence and penetration of the idea's historical context on the language and scholarly milieu of the translator.

[1] Cf. Moore 1997, 1: 469–70; Urbach 1987, 415–27; Rosen-Zvi 2011.

[2] Thus, Alexander writes: "The targum had a role in the *Beit ha-Midrash* ... They were valued as convenient repositories of traditional exegesis" (2004, 241).

Thus, for example, the Pentateuch records three instances of the instruction, "You shall not boil a kid in his mother's milk."[3] In all three places Targum Onqelos famously renders the verse "You shall not eat meat with (-ב) milk." The translator's departure from the literal rendition of the Hebrew text is clearly not of his own invention, but rather reflects his desire to embed a normative application of Scripture drawn from Jewish tradition into the flow of his Aramaic translation.[4] Onqelos does not attempt to justify his non-literal translation, nor does he supply the reader with any discussion on the details or history of the law he embeds into the flow of his translation. He simply trusts that his audience understands the context. Or perhaps he wishes to encourage the manner in which this verse was understood in practical post-biblical Jewish custom by introducing it into the version of Scripture most accessible to the masses, namely the Aramaic translation.

If, therefore, we are to find mention of the *yiṣrāʾ bîšāʾ* (יצרא בישא), the Aramaic counterpart of rabbinic Hebrew's *yeṣer haraʿ*, in Targumic literature, these cases will most probably reflect inherited terminology, based on an earlier notion or even a particular rabbinic text, rather than the Targumist's independent choice of words.

## 2 TARGUMS TO THE WRITINGS AS A GROUP

For the purpose of this chapter I am grouping together all the Targums to the Writings. Nonetheless, the reader should be reminded that each of these Targums is an independent composition of its own. The Targums to the Writings differ from one another in style, language, tendency for expansion, and other qualities. Nevertheless, the methodological justification for treating this heterogeneous group of Targums as a whole is that, apart from the unique circumstances of Targum Proverbs,[5] they reflect a general affinity with rabbinic literature and Targumic practices inherited from the earlier Targums. This last statement also implies that by and large these Targums were completed relatively late in the era of Targumic composition – an era which I consider to have ended in the first part of the second millennium CE.[6]

[3] Exod 23:19; 34:26; Deut 14:21.

[4] For more examples of departure from literal translation motivated by halakah in Tg. Onq., cf. Melammed 1978, 179–98.

[5] See Alexander 1992, 326. [6] See further Gottlieb 2014.

## 3 DISTRIBUTION OF THE WORD יצר IN THE TARGUMS TO THE WRITINGS

The first step in this study is to list where the Targums mention the יצרא בישא. However, since authors sometimes used the word יצר without בישא when referring to the Evil Inclination, every usage of this word in this particular meaning must be included in our list. The word יצר meaning "inclination," "urge," "design" is found some twenty-nine times in the various Targums to the Writings, of which only two, Ps 103:14 and 1 Chr 29:18, are direct equivalents of the word יצר in the Hebrew.[7]

The breakdown of all the appearances of *yeṣer* in the Targums to the Writings appears in Table 2.

The table shows that, even if we exclude Daniel, Ezra, and Nehemiah, for which we do not possess a Targum, most of the Targums of the Writings make no mention at all of the *yeṣer*. In those who do mention

TABLE 2 *Appearances of* yeṣer *in the Targums to the Writings*

| Book | Number of Appearances | Chapter/Verses |
|---|---|---|
| Psalms | 9 | 50:14, 23; 51:7; 91:12; 101:4; 103:14; 119:70 |
| Proverbs | 0 | |
| Job | 0 | |
| Ruth | 1 | 3:8 |
| Song of Songs | 0 | |
| Ecclesiastes | 11 | 3:11; 7:8, 19; 9:14–15; 10:1, 4, 10 |
| Lamentations | 0 | |
| Esther | 0 | Including Targum Rishon and Targum Sheni |
| Daniel | – | |
| Ezra | – | |
| Nehemiah | – | |
| Chronicles | 8 | 1 Chr 4:10; 8:40; 28:9; 29:18; 2 Chr 6:14; 29:36; 33:13; 36:13 |

[7] Hebrew יצר appears three times in the Writings. In 1 Chr 28:9, however, it is translated by Aramaic הרהור.

the *yeṣer*, the distribution of the term tends to be spread out, spanning the majority of the composition, with the exception of Targum Ruth.

I will now proceed to present the actual texts, demonstrating how each Targum displays its own angle on how it perceives and applies the term יצר.[8] I have no intention of providing an exhaustive discussion for every verse. For our purposes it will suffice to indicate the manner in which the word *yeṣer* is used in each example, and thereby highlight different vantage points and portrayals of the *yeṣer* in these texts.

## 4 TARGUM PSALMS

Targum Psalms presents several different angles through which we can perceive how the author regarded the יצרא בישא.

### 4.1 The *yeṣer* as the Antagonist of Humanity

***Psalm 13:5***

*Hebrew*: Lest my **enemy** say, "I have overcome him," my foes exult when I totter.
*Targum*: Lest the **evil inclination** should say, "I have taken control of him," [lest] my oppressors rejoice because I stray from your paths.

In Ps 13:5 "the Evil Inclination" (יצרא בישא) is the Aramaic equivalent of "enemy" (Hebrew אויב). This approach is in line with several rabbinic texts, most notably b. Sukkah 52a, which provides seven names for the *yeṣer*, the fourth of which is שונא, a synonym of אויב. Bavli Baba Batra 16a equates "the Evil Inclination" (יצר הרע) with Satan, who is sometimes referred to as בעל דבבא (Aramaic for "enemy"), and with the Angel of Death.

### 4.2 Slaughtering One's *yeṣer*

***Psalm 4:6***

*Hebrew*: Offer sacrifices in righteousness and trust in the LORD.
*Targum*: Subdue your **inclinations** (יצריכון) and it will be reckoned to you as a righteous sacrifice; and hope in the LORD.

[8] Translations of the Hebrew follow NJPS. Translations of Tg. Ps, Tg. Ruth, and Tg. Qoh follow Accordance (version 5, TARG-E module). Translation of Tg. Ps.-J. follows Accordance (version 1.1, TARG3-E module). Translations of Tg. Chr from McIvor 1994. All translations have been modified as needed.

### *Psalm 50:14*

*Hebrew*: Sacrifice a thank offering to God, and pay your vows to the Most High.
*Targum*: Subdue the **evil inclination** and it will be reckoned before the LORD as a sacrifice of thanksgiving; and pay to the Most High your vows.

### *Psalm 50:23*

*Hebrew*: He who sacrifices a thank offering honors Me, and to him who improves his way I will show the salvation of God.
*Targum*: He who sacrifices the **evil inclination**, it will be reckoned to him like a sacrifice of thanksgiving, and he honors me; and whoever will remove the evil way, I will show him the redemption of the LORD.

In the three verses above in Targum Psalms we find that the Targum likens the slaughtering of sacrifices in the Hebrew text to the slaughtering of one's Evil Inclination, which in turn is equated in merit to the offering of a sacrifice. The link made here between a sacrifice and the Evil Inclination is unexpected and – based on the context of the Hebrew verse alone – frankly quite surprising to the reader. Stec explained that "Targum Psalms reflects a situation in which the nation in exile can no longer offer sacrifices, and suggests as a substitute that control of one's inclinations is equivalent to sacrifice."[9] However, this explanation does not account for the specific choice of the Evil Inclination on the part of the Targumist. Why the *yeṣer* and not any other religious idea or value? Why did he not suggest, for instance, that giving alms to the poor is equivalent to sacrifice? Why did he not propose that reciting a prayer is equivalent to sacrifice? I posit that behind this seemingly surprising comparison is a rabbinic idea that specifically designated the ultimate fate of the *yeṣer* to be slaughtered like a sacrifice, as appears in Lev Rabbah 9:1 which quotes Ps 50:23 and adds: "This is Achan who slaughtered his *yeṣer* (שזבח יצרו) like a Todah offering."[10] Bavli Sukkah 52a states that in the future God will slaughter the *yeṣer* (although not in an explicit sacrificial context).

The sixth-century Hebrew poet Yannai wrote: "he slaughtered his *yeṣer* before his Creator … " (זבח יצרו לפני יוצרו)[11] Similarly, a first-millennium halakhic composition describes how one should prostrate oneself during a certain point in prayer with the words: "he shall lie down like a lamb bound for slaughter in order to slay his *yeṣer* (כדי שיזבח

[9] Stec 2004, 32, n. 11. [10] Ed. Margulies 1993, 173–74.
[11] Line 13 of Yannai's Kedushta for Genesis, אשרי מואסי ערלה ובוחרי מילה (text according to maagarim.hebrew-academy.org.il).

יצרו) before his Creator."[12] These and other texts demonstrate that this notion of slaughtering of the *yeṣer* like a sacrifice was a common enough expression. Accordingly, the translator of Psalms embedded this idea in his work precisely in the verses that are alluded to in the rabbinic teaching.

## 4.3 The *yeṣer* Leads Humanity to Sin

The notion of the *yeṣer* being like a stumbling block, seen also in Targum Jonathan to Isa 62:10, can be found in Tg. Ps 91:12.

### *Psalm 91:12*

*Hebrew*: They will carry you in their hands lest you hurt your foot on a stone.
*Targum*: They will lift you up by their strength, lest you stumble on the **evil inclination**, which is likened to the stones at your feet.

Similarly, the *yeṣer*'s role as an enticer to sin is mentioned in Ps 103:14.

### *Psalm 103:14*

*Hebrew*: For He knows **how we are formed** (יִצְרֵנוּ); He is mindful that we are dust.
*Targum*: For he knows **our evil inclination** (יצרנא בישא) that makes us sin; in his presence it is remembered, for we are from dust.

The Hebrew verse employs the word יצר, but certainly not in the meaning of יצר הרע.[13] Still, it is ample opportunity for the Targumist to add the teachings he is familiar with: He knows our Evil Inclination that causes us to sin.

## 4.4 The *yeṣer* and the Heart

The link between the *yeṣer* and the heart, which is traced back to the language of Genesis (Gen 6:5; 8:21), is found in both Targum Pss 101:4 and 119:70:

### *Psalm 101:4*

*Hebrew*: Perverse thoughts (לֵבָב עִקֵּשׁ) will be far from me; I will know nothing of **evil** (רָע).
*Targum*: For let the twisted **heart** (ליבא עוקמנא) pass from me; I shall not know the **evil inclination**.

[12] Excerpt from the composition הלכות מסידור בנוסח ארץ ישראלי, 134 (text according to maagarim.hebrew-academy.org.il).
[13] Cf. NJPS: "For He knows how we are formed."

***Psalm 119:70***

*Hebrew*: Their **minds** (לִבָּם) are thick like fat; as for me, Your teaching is my delight.

*Targum*: The **inclination of their heart** (יצרא דלבהון) has become mindless as fat; as for me, my delight is your Torah.

## 4.5 The Nature of Sin

The *yeṣer* has been likened above to a stumbling block, and has been called an enticer to sin.[14] However, the verses above do not describe the type of sin one is led to by the *yeṣer hara'*. Such an example appears only once in Targum Psalms, and it alludes to sexual desire.

***Psalm 51:7***

*Hebrew*: Indeed I was born with iniquity; with sin my mother conceived me.

*Targum*: Behold, in iniquities my father thought to create me; and in the sin of the **evil inclination** my mother conceived me.

In Ps 51:7 the Hebrew verse describes the Psalmist's very conception as a result of sin. Targum Psalms offers two alternative translations for this verse. In the second one the Targumist goes one step further than the Hebrew text and claims that the sin stems from the Evil Inclination, thus tying the *yeṣer* specifically to the realm of sexual passion. This falls in line with rabbinic thought, in which even the term for sin, עבירה, when appearing on its own, frequently refers to sexual immorality,[15] and specifically with late rabbinic usage of the term *yeṣer*, which came to be equated with sexual attraction in "the late, probably post-amoraic, strata of the Bavli" according to Rosen-Zvi.[16] It is, therefore, not surprising that the only concrete example in the relatively late Targum Psalms of a particular sin connected to the *yeṣer* is of a sexual nature.

### 5 TARGUM RUTH

Another example of the *yeṣer* connected to sexual drive is found in the sole appearance of *yeṣer* in Targum Ruth.

[14] See Ps 91:12; 103:14; b. Sukkah 52a.

[15] E.g. b. Yebam. 78b. Cf. Jastrow 1903, 1038; Rosen-Zvi 2011, 204, n. 68.

[16] Rosen-Zvi 2011, 118.

### Ruth 3:8

*Hebrew*: In the middle of the night, the man gave a start and pulled back – there was a woman lying at his feet!

*Targum*: In the middle of the night the man was startled, and he trembled, and his flesh became soft like turnip from fear. He looked and lo – a woman lying at his feet. His **inclination grew strong** (ותקף יצריה), but he did not approach her, just as did Joseph the Righteous who refused to approach the Egyptian woman, the wife of his master; just as Paltiel bar Laish the Pious did, who placed a sword between himself and Michal daughter of Saul, wife of David, whom he refused to approach.

In Ruth 3:8 Boaz wakes up in the middle of the night and is startled to discover a woman lying at his feet. Targum Ruth elaborates on this verse and describes Boaz's physical reactions during this nocturnal encounter. In the Targum, Boaz's alarm results in the loss of his erection.[17] When Boaz regains his composure, his sexual drive immediately grows and, although he is strongly tempted by his *yeṣer* to sleep with the woman, he does not give in to his desire, and becomes a paragon of virtue, joining the ranks of Joseph and Paltiel – both of whom are depicted in rabbinic homilies as no less than heroic in repressing their sexual urge to commit adultery.[18]

## 6 TARGUM QOHELET

Targum Qohelet contains the highest number of occurrences of the word *yeṣer* – eleven – among the Targums to the Writings. In fact, the only Targum with more appearances of *yeṣer* is Targum Pseudo-Jonathan, which deserves a separate study of its own in regard to this term.

[17] This temporary erectile dysfunction is likened by the Targumist to a turnip. This surprising simile arises from the similarity of the rare Hebrew word וַיִּלָּפֵת and the noun לֶפֶת, "turnip" (see b. San. 19b). Most Talmudic commentators understood the reference to the turnip as a description of Boaz's erection upon discovering a woman lying at his feet (cf. Rashi *ad loc.*). Tg. Ruth, however, apparently understood the opposite, and explained the turnip simile as a loss of an erection. This may be due to the Targumist's understanding of the role the word ויחרד plays in the Hebrew verse, preceding וילפת. Thus, Tg. Ruth incorporates the trembling (רתיתא) from fear as the reason for Boaz's sudden dysfunction.

[18] For numerous rabbinic sources regarding the piety and sexual restraint of Joseph, Boaz and Paltiel, see Ginzberg 1925–28, 5: 340 n. 121; 6: 192 n. 60, 198 n. 85, 273–74 n. 133.

## 6.1 The *yeṣer* and the Heart

### *Qohelet 3:11*

*Hebrew*: He brings everything to pass precisely at its time; He also puts eternity in **their mind** (בְּלִבָּם), but without man ever guessing, from first to last, all the things that God brings to pass.

*Targum*: King Solomon said by the spirit of prophecy, "All things has the Lord made fitting in His (own) time." ... Moreover, he concealed from them the great Name which was written and explicitly inscribed on the foundation stone, which the **evil inclination that is in his heart** (יצרא בישא דבליבהון) known before him, which had it been transmitted to humanity, they would have used it to discover what would be at the end of days and forever and ever. The day of death is also concealed from them so that it would not be made known to man from the beginning what would be at the end.

In Tg. Qoh 3:11 King Solomon is said to have concealed the mystery of God's holy name from the Israelites, because he knew their character, and realized they would ultimately succumb to the Evil Inclination in their hearts (as seen above in Targum Psalms, influenced by the language of Genesis) and abuse the power of this divine name to reveal secrets from the future. This is another instance of submission before temptation that has nothing to do with sex, and yet it too is orchestrated by the Evil Inclination.

## 6.2 Subduing the *yeṣer*

### *Qohelet 7:8*

*Hebrew*: The end of a matter is better than the beginning of it. Better a patient spirit than a haughty spirit.

*Targum*: Better is the end of a matter than its beginning because at its beginning it is not known to a man what its end will be, but it is known to a man that the end of good things is good. And better before the Lord is a man who controls his spirit and **subdues his own inclination** (ומכבש ית יצריה) than a man who walks in a haughty spirit.

Targum Qohelet 7:8 speaks about the virtue of self-control (דשליט ברוחיה) over haughtiness. Adding another expression to the man who controls his spirit, the Targumist writes "and subdues his own inclination." This addition clearly echoes the famous statement by Shimon ben Zoma in m. Avot 4:1: "Who is strong? He who subdues his *yeṣer*!" (הכובש את יצרו).

### *Qohelet 7:19*

*Hebrew*: Wisdom is more of a stronghold to a wise man than ten magnates that a city may contain.

*Targum* (alternate translation): And **wisdom helps the sage subdue his evil inclination** (יכבש ית יצרא בישא) so that he will not sin more than the strength of the ten sons of Jacob who were in the great city Shechem when they killed every male by the sword but afterward **they did not subdue their inclination** (לא כבשו ית יצריהון) but sold their brother Joseph for twenty pieces of silver.

Targum Qohelet 7:19 includes two alternative translations for the Hebrew text. In the second one the Targumist introduces the claim that an effective tool in man's struggle to subdue his *yeṣer* is wisdom (חכמה). The point here is that ten people who were strong enough to overpower and ultimately massacre an entire city were too weak to win their own personal battle with their *yeṣer*, which led them to be consumed by greed.

### *Qohelet 10:1*

*Hebrew*: Dead flies turn the perfumer's ointment fetid and putrid; so a little folly outweighs massive wisdom.

*Targum*: And the **evil inclination**, which inhabits the gates of the heart like a fly, causes death in the world because it causes the wise one to stink when he sins, and it destroys the good name that beforehand resembled anointing oil, which produces a fragrant scent with spices. And how much more precious and beautiful than the wisdom of the wise and the wealth of the rich is a man whose foolishness is negligible!

Upon reaching Qoh 10:1, the Targumist recalled the famous teaching in b. Ber. 61a, which bases itself on this verse in Qohelet: The Evil Inclination is like a fly, and it dwells between the two openings of the heart. Consequently, he simply embedded this teaching in the Aramaic rendition of the verse.

## 6.3 The Battle between the Good *yeṣer* and the Evil *yeṣer*

The importance of wisdom in the battle against the *yeṣer* is highlighted in a fascinating lengthy translation of Qoh 9:14–15.

### *Qohelet 9:14–15*

*Hebrew*: There was a little city, with few men in it; and to it came a great king, who invested it and built mighty siege works against it. Present in the city was a poor wise man who might have saved it with his wisdom, but nobody thought of that poor man.

*Targum*: The body of a man is comparable to a small village: few within it are heroic men, just as the merits within the heart of a person are few; and the **evil inclination**, which is comparable to a great and mighty king, enters the body to conquer, and it encircles the heart so as to make it err, and it builds a site to inhabit so that he will be willing to turn aside from

> paths that are straight before the Lord in order to catch him in great nets of Gehenna in order to burn him seven times for his sins. And the **good inclination**, lowly but wise, was found within the body, and it prevailed against it [the Evil Inclination] and conquered it by its wisdom, and it saved the body from the judgment of Gehenna by its power and its wisdom, just as the hero by fighting the battle saves the inhabitants of the village by the wisdom of his heart. But afterwards no one remembers the **good inclination**, which saved him. Instead he says to himself, "I am righteous," just as the inhabitants of that village did not remember that humble person who saved them.

The Targumist contrasts the Evil Inclination with the Good Inclination (יצרא טבא), portraying both inclinations as conducting a nerve-racking battle against each other. In this battle, a person is not so much a combatant as the prize over which the two sides are fighting. In contradistinction to rabbinic descriptions of the Evil Inclination being no more than a feeble highway robber (ליסטיס שפוף),[19] in this Targum it is compared to no less than a mighty king, who is expected to be victorious in this battle, whereas the Good Inclination is described as lowly but wise (מכיך וחכים). Yet, despite its meager appearance, the Good Inclination's wisdom is enough to overcome the mighty king and ultimately save his prize – a man – from his fate had the Evil Inclination proven victorious, namely the punishment of Gehennom.

## 6.4 The Torah as an Antidote for Sin

*Qohelet 10:4*

*Hebrew*: If the wrath of **a lord** (אִם־רוּחַ הַמּוֹשֵׁל) flares up against you, don't give up your post; for when wrath abates, grave offenses are pardoned.

*Targum*: If the spirit of the **evil inclination** (רוחא דיצרא בישא) rules over you and prevails to overcome you, do not leave your good place in which you have customarily stood, for the words of the Torah were created as a cure in this world for forgiving and forgetting great sins before the Lord.

The mention of the Evil Inclination in Tg. Qoh 10:4 is inspired by the Hebrew word מושל, "one who rules," which is similar to 9:14, in which the *yeṣer* was likened to a mighty king. However, in this case the contrast to the Evil Inclination is not the Good Inclination, or wisdom in general, but rather specifically the Torah, which was intended from its inception to be an antidote for sin.

[19] An image derived from Gen 4:7 (לַפֶּתַח חַטָּאת רֹבֵץ) and developed in Gen. Rab. 22 (Theodor and Albeck 1965, 211).

### 6.5 Prevailing over the *yeṣer* as Part of Repentance

*Qohelet 10:10*

*Hebrew*: If the ax has become dull and he has not whetted the edge, **he must exert** (יְגַבֵּר) more strength. Thus the advantage of a skill [depends on the exercise of] prudence.

*Targum*: And when the people, the house of Israel, sins, the heavens become as strong as iron so as to not bring down rain, and that generation has not prayed before the Lord, all the world will be destroyed by famine because of this. But when multitudes repent, gather, **overpower their evil inclinations** (ומתגברין על יצריהון), and appoint their shepherds to seek mercy from the God of heaven, [God finds] favor in them because of [their having made] proper [use] of their wisdom.

This final example in Qohelet depicts the people of Israel finally repenting for their sins, and this repentance is coupled with the act of overpowering their *yeṣer* (מתגברין על יצריהון), which is an expansive Aramaic rendering of the Hebrew יְגַבֵּר.

## 7 TARGUM CHRONICLES

### 7.1 The *yeṣer* of the Heart

Of the eight occurrences of יצר in Targum Chronicles, six conform to the "יצר of the heart" pattern mentioned above, originating in the language of Gen 6:5 and 8:21. Most of these examples need no further explanation.

*1 Chronicles 28:9*

*Hebrew*: . . . for the LORD searches all **minds** (לְבָבוֹת) and discerns the design (יֵצֶר) of every thought . . .

*Targum*: . . . for the Lord searches out all the **inclinations of the hearts** (יצריא דלביא) and discerns all the imaginations (הרהורי) of the thoughts.

*1 Chronicles 29:18*

*Hebrew*: . . . remember this to the eternal credit of the **thoughts** (לְיֵצֶר מַחְשְׁבוֹת) of Your people's **hearts** (לְבַב) . . .

*Targum*: . . . keep this freewill offering as eternal merit, to direct the **inclination** of the **thoughts** of the **heart** (יצר הרהורי לבבא) of your people . . .

*2 Chronicles 6:14*

*Hebrew*: . . . You who steadfastly maintain the Covenant with Your servants who walk before You with all their **heart** (לִבָּם).

*Targum*: ... keeping covenant and goodness with your servants who walk in your ways and who worship before you with all the desire of their soul and with all the **inclination** of their **hearts** (יצרא דלבהון).

## *2 Chronicles 29:36*

*Hebrew*: Hezekiah and all the people rejoiced over what God had enabled the people to accomplish. ...

*Targum*: Hezekiah and all the people rejoiced because the Lord had established for the people the **inclination** of their **heart** ...

This verse connects the *yeṣer* with the heart, like the other examples here. However, the appearance of *yeṣer* seems somewhat puzzling because the word "heart" does not appear in the Hebrew. The appearance of "inclination of their heart" in this verse indicates, in my opinion, that the Targumist had before him a variant Hebrew text that contained "their heart" (לִבָּם) instead of, or in addition to, the word "the people" (לָעָם).[20] This being the case, he applied the same translation technique used in the examples above and below, and prefixed *yeṣer* to this presumed Hebrew word.

## *2 Chronicles 33:13*

*Hebrew*: –[21]

*Targum*: But immediately the mercy of the Lord of the universe prevailed, whose right hand is stretched out to receive the sinners who return to his fear and break the **inclination** of their **heart** by repentance ...

## *2 Chronicles 36:13*

*Hebrew*: ... and hardened his **heart** so as not to turn to the LORD God of Israel ...

*Targum*: ... and strengthened the **inclination** of his **heart** so as not to return to the fear of the Lord ...

The remaining two cases in Chronicles are of a different nature. The first is in 1 Chr 4:10 and it is the only appearance of יצרא בישא in Targum Chronicles.

# 7.2 Jabez Prays to be Free of the *yeṣer hara'*

## *1 Chronicles 4:10*

*Hebrew*: Oh, bless me, enlarge my territory, stand by me, and make me not suffer pain from misfortune!

[20] See Gottlieb 2016, p. 52.

[21] This entire excerpt from Tg. Chr. is part of a large expansion without equivalents in the Hebrew.

*Targum*: O that you might indeed bless me with sons, and extend my territory with disciples! O that your hand might be with me in debate, and that you might provide me with companions like myself, so that the **evil inclination** may not provoke me!

The Targumic version of the prayer of Jabez is but a reworked edition of two Talmudic homilies on this verse that appear in b. Tem. 16a. The Targumist chose elements from both Hebrew Talmudic homilies and reworked them into his Aramaic version of 1 Chr 4:10. His usage of "the Evil Inclination" is simply a translation of *yeṣer hara*ʿ, which appears in both versions of the Talmudic homily. Therefore, even this one instance of the Evil Inclination does not reflect the Targumist's own independent exegetical conclusion, but rather that of his literary source.

## 7.3 The Reward of the Ulamites for Subduing their yeṣer

The remaining instance of יצר in 1 Chr 8:40 speaks of subduing the *yeṣer*, as seen above in Qoh 7:8 and 7:19. However, the context in which this familiar expression appears calls for further elucidation.

### *1 Chronicles 8:40*

*Hebrew*: The descendants of Ulam – men of substance, who drew the bow, had many children and grandchildren – one hundred and fifty; all these were Benjaminites.

*Targum*: The sons of Ulam were men who were mighty warriors, **subduing their urges** (כבשין יצריהון) like a man who draws the bow with skill; it was for this reason that they had many sons and grandsons; their family numbered one hundred and fifty.

The original Hebrew portrays the sons of Ulam both as valiant and skilled archers and as apparently fertile procreators. The Targumist evidently felt that the relation between these two seemingly separate traits is one of cause and effect. Therefore, in the Targum the Ulamites become men of ethical valor, based on the Mishnaic teaching mentioned before: "Who is strong? He who subdues his *yeṣer*!" Thus the Ulamites' might is measured by their success in subduing their inclinations. This success is then compared to the skill of a master archer who shoots with precision. Finally, the bountiful number of children in their clan is regarded as a heavenly reward for their righteousness. This explanation of the Targum, however, leaves much to be desired. How does the subduing of the *yeṣer* resemble the action of an archer? Also, is there any correlation between the Ulamites' deed and their reward, or could they just as easily have been rewarded with economic prosperity? A more complete explanation should take into account a Talmudic reference to this verse in b. Nid. 31a–b. The Talmud cites 1 Chr 8:40, and then asks:

But does a person have the power to increase the number of sons and sons of sons? Rather, because they held themselves back in the womb so that their wives would reach sexual satisfaction first, so that their children would be male – Scripture credits them as though they were the ones to increase the number of sons and sons of sons.

It seems to me that our Targumist had this Talmudic teaching in mind when he translated the verse into Aramaic. He was also aware of the rabbinic interpretation of the word קשת (bow) as representing the male sex organ in the context of Joseph in Gen 49:24,[22] and of ejaculation being compared to the shooting of an arrow in several places in the Talmud.[23] Thus the connection between both parts of the verse is much clearer now. The abundance in children – understood by the Talmud to be specifically male children – was a direct result of the Ulamites' ability to control themselves during intercourse – and it is this self-control that was alluded to when the Targumist referred to subduing their *yeṣer*, i.e. the capability to delay their own sexual satisfaction until their wives first achieved theirs.

## 8 CONCLUSION

In this chapter we examined some twenty-nine appearances of *yeṣer* in the Targums to the Writings. In some, the *yeṣer* is called "the Evil Inclination" (יצרא בישא). In others the word *yeṣer* is associated with the word "heart" (לב), under the influence of the book of Genesis. In one instance the word was used in the context of the Good Inclination (יצרא טבא). Almost all occurrences of the word are not formal equivalents of the word *yeṣer* in the Hebrew verse. Some of the appearances were set in a sexual context, while others showed that *yeṣer* may be used in other contexts as well. Despite all this variety, all usages of the word *yeṣer* were traced back either to biblical influences or to rabbinic ones. We may conclude – in full accord with our expectation – that when the Targumists cited in this chapter used this word, they functioned not as

[22] y. Hor. 46d (col. 1420 in Sussman 2001); Gen. Rab. 98 (Theodor and Albeck 1965, 1270); Cf. Tg. Ps.-J. Gen. 49:24.

[23] E.g. b. Nid. 43a: "Any emission of semen that does not shoot out like an arrow (יורה כחץ) does not fructify."

heralds, but rather as echoes. As such, the Targums discussed here are in line with rabbinic Judaism and serve as faithful representatives thereof.

That being said, I wish to close this study with an observation about the absence of the *yeṣer* in Targum Proverbs. Several times in the discussions above I mentioned Shimon ben Zoma's famous words in m. Avot 4:1, "Who is strong? He who subdues his *yeṣer*!" The biblical source that ben Zoma cites when making this statement is Prov 16:32, "Better to be forbearing than mighty, To have self-control than to conquer a city" (NJPS). Ben Zoma's teaching was so influential that it caused the composer of Targum Qohelet to invoke it upon his arrival at a verse (Qoh 7:8) that resembled this verse in Proverbs. If a Targumist with the same background and similar tendencies had written the Targum of Proverbs, he would presumably not have missed the opportunity to insert the Mishnaic teaching into his Aramaic version of Prov 16:32. This, however, is not the case.

*Targum*: Better he who stretches his spirit [i.e. is slow to anger] than he who is mighty; and he who conquers [i.e. controls] himself is better than he who seizes a city.

The author of Targum Proverbs happens to use the same verbal root found in the Mishna (כב"ש) to translate Hebrew לכ"ד. However, his selection of a different noun (נפש) and not *yeṣer* indicates that the composer of Targum Proverbs clearly had no intention of echoing Ben Zoma's teaching in his work. This is a telling example that supports existing theories on the foreign, non-rabbinic origin of Targum Proverbs.[24] While Targum Proverbs is a member in title in the group of the Targums to the Writings, it is very different in origin and character from the other members of this group.

[24] Cf. Alexander 1992, 326. Note also the similarity between the Targum and Peshitta.

# References


Adamson, Peter. 2015. "Neoplatonism: The Last Ten Years," *International Journal of the Platonic Tradition* 9: 205–20.

Adrados, Francisco Rodríguez. 1980–. *Diccionario Griego-Espanol* (Madrid).

Alexander, Elizabeth Shanks. 2002. "Art, Argument, and Ambiguity in the Talmud: Conflicting Conceptions of the Evil Impulse in b. Sukkah 51b–52a," *HUCA* 73: 97–132.

Alexander, Philip S. 1992. "Targum, Targumim," in *The Anchor Bible Dictionary*, ed. D. N. Freedman, 6 vols. (New York), 6: 320–31.

1999. "The Demonology of the Dead Sea Scrolls," in *The Dead Sea Scrolls after Fifty Years*, ed. P. W. Flint and J. C. VanderKam, 2 vols. (Leiden), 2: 331–53.

2004. "Jewish Aramaic Translations of Hebrew Scriptures," in *Mikra*, ed. M. J. Mulder (Peabody), 217–53.

Allen, Leslie C. 1990. *Ezekiel 20–48*, WBC 29 (Dallas).

Alwan, Khalil. 1989. *Jacques de Saroug. Quatre homélies métriques sur la Création*, CSCO 508–09 (Leuven).

Amihay, Aryeh, and Machiela, Daniel. 2010. "Traditions on the Birth of Noah," in *Noah and His Book(s)*, ed. M. E. Stone et al., SBLEJL 28 (Atlanta), 53–69.

Annas, Julia. 1992. *The Hellenistic Philosophy of Mind* (Berkeley).

Anat, M. A. 1980. "The Origins of the הטוב יצר," in *Shalom Sivan Memorial Volume* (Jerusalem), 217–22 [Hebrew].

Arentzen, Thomas, and Münz-Manor, Ophir. 2019. "Soundscapes of Salvation: Resounding Refrains in Jewish and Christian Liturgical Poems," *Studies in Late Antiquity* 3: 36–55.

Armstrong, A. Hilary. 1984. *Plotinus, IV, Enneads IV, 1–9*, LCL 443 (London).

Arruzza, Cinzia. 2009. "Négligence et chute dans la pensée d'Origène," *RTP* 141: 261–72.

Asmussen, Jes P. 1975. *Manichaean Literature* (New York).

2011. "Āz," in *Encyclopaedia Iranica*, 3, Fasc. 2, 168–69 (Online: www.iranicaonline.org).

Baehrens, Willem A. (ed.). 1921. *Origenes Werke*, 17.2, GCS 30 (Leipzig).

Bailey, Cyril (ed.). 1926. *Epicurus: The Extant Remains* (Oxford).
Balberg, Mira. 2014. *Purity, Body, and Self in Early Rabbinic Literature* (Berkeley).
Baltensweiler, Heinrich. 1963. "Erwägungen zu 1. Thess. 4,3–8," *TZ* 19: 1–13.
Bammel, Caroline P. 1992. "Augustine, Origen and the Exegesis of St Paul," *Augustinianum* 32: 341–68.
Bar-Asher Siegal, Michal. 2014. *Early Christian Monastic Literature and the Babylonian Talmud* (Cambridge).
Barney, Rachel, et al. (ed.). 2012. *Plato and the Divided Self* (Cambridge).
Barns, John Wintour Baldwin, et al. 1966. *The Oxyrhynchus Papyri*, 31 (London).
Barrett, Charles K. 1978. *The Gospel According to St John*, 2nd ed. (London).
Barthes, Roland. 1964. *Eléments de sémiologie* (Paris).
Bartholomae, Christian. 1904. *Altiranisches Wörterbuch* (Berlin [repr. 1961]).
Bassler, Jouette M. 1986. "Cain and Abel in the Palestinian Targums," *JSJ* 17: 56–64.
Bauckham, Richard. 1996. "The Parable of the Royal Wedding Feast (Matthew 22:1–14) and the Parable of the Lame Man and the Blind Man (Apocryphon of Ezekiel)," *JBL* 115: 471–88.
Bauer, Hans, and Leander, Pontus. 1922. *Historische Grammatik der hebräischen Sprache* (Halle [repr. 1965]).
Baumgarten, Joseph M. 1991–92. "On the Nature of the Seductress in 4Q184," *RevQ* 15: 133–43.
Baumstark, Anton. 1933. "Das Problem der Bibelzitate in der syrischen Übersetzungsliteratur," *OrChr* ser. 3, 8: 208–25.
Beatrice, Pier Franco. 1978. *Tradux peccati*, Studia patristica mediolanensi 8 (Milan).
Beck, Edmund (ed.). 1961. *Des heiligen Ephraem des Syrers Carmina Nisibena*, 1, CSCO 218 (Leuven).
1963. *Des heiligen Ephraem des Syrers Carmina Nisibena*, 2, CSCO 240 (Leuven).
1966. *Des heiligen Ephraem des Syrers Sermo de Domino Nostro*, CSCO 270 (Leuven).
1970. *Des heiligen Ephraem des Syrers Sermones*, 1, CSCO 305 (Leuven).
1972. *Des heiligen Ephraem des Syrers Sermones*, 3, CSCO 320 (Leuven).
1973. *Des heiligen Ephraem des Syrers Sermones*, 4, CSCO 334 (Leuven).
1975. *Nachträge zu Ephraem Syrus*, CSCO 363 (Leuven).
Becker, Adam H. 2016. "The 'Evil Inclination' of the Jews: The Syriac *Yatsra* in Narsai's Metrical Homilies for Lent," *JQR* 106: 179–207.
Bedjan, Paul (ed.). 1891. *Acta martyrum et sanctorum*, 2 (Leipzig).
1902a. *Cantus seu homiliae Mar-Jacobi in Jesum et Mariam* (Leipzig).
1902b. *S. Martyrii, qui est Sahdona, quæ supersunt omnia* (Leipzig).
1968. *Acta martyrum et sanctorum syriace*, 3 (Hildesheim [1892]).
2006. *Homilies of Mar Jacob of Sarug*, 6 (Piscataway).
BeDuhn, Jason D. 2000. *The Manichaean Body* (Baltimore).
2013. *Augustine's Manichaean Dilemma*, 2 (Philadelphia).
Beentjes, Pancratius C. 1997. *The Book of Ben Sira in Hebrew*, VTSup 68 (Leiden).

Behr, John (ed. and trans.). 2017. *Origen: On First Principles I–II*, OECT (Oxford).
Bensly, Robert L., and Barnes, W. Emery. 1895. *The Fourth Book of Maccabees and Kindred Documents in Syriac* (Cambridge).
Berger, Klaus. 2005. *Formen und Gattungen im Neuen Testament*, UTB 2532 (Tübingen).
Berlin, Adele, and Brettler, Marc Z. 2004. *The Jewish Study Bible* (Oxford).
Betz, Hans. D. 1979. *Galatians*, Hermeneia (Philadelphia).
Bhayro, Siam. 2005. *The Shemihazah and Asael Narrative of 1 Enoch 6–11*, AOAT 322 (Münster).
Bietenhard, Hans. 1974. *Caesarea, Origenes und die Juden* (Stuttgart).
Black, Matthew. 1970. *Apocalypsis Henochi Graeci in Pseudepigrapha Veteris Testamenti*, PVTG 3 (Leiden).
1985. *The Book of Enoch or I Enoch*, SVTP 7 (Leiden).
Blowers, Paul. 1988. "Origen, the Rabbis, and the Bible," in *Origen of Alexandria*, ed. C. Kannengiesser and W. L. Petersen (Notre Dame), 96–116.
Bogan, Mary I. 1968. *St Augustine, The Retractations*," in *The Writings of Augustine*, FC 60 (Washington).
Bohak, Gideon. 2008. *Ancient Jewish Magic* (Cambridge).
Bonhöffer, Adolf. 1890. *Epictet und die Stoa* (Stuttgart).
Bostock, Gerald. 2011. "Satan: Origen's Forgotten Doctrine," in *Origeniana Decima*, ed. S. Kaczmarek et al., BETL 244 (Leuven), 109–23.
Böttrich, Christfried. 2013. "Selbstverständnis, Weltbild, Dämonologie," in *Paulus Handbuch*, ed. F. W. Horn (Tübingen), 385–90.
Bou Mansour, Tanios. 1993. *La théologie de Jacques de Saroug*, 1 (Kaslik).
Bovon, François, and Geoltrain, Pierre. 1997. *Écrits apocryphes chrétiens*, 1 (Paris).
Boyarin, Daniel. 1993. *Carnal Israel* (Berkeley).
1999. *Dying for God* (Berkeley).
Brakke, David. 2006. *Demons and the Making of the Monk* (Cambridge, MA).
2009. *Evagrius of Pontus. Talking Back: Antirrhêtikos* (Collegeville).
2010. *The Gnostics* (Cambridge, MA).
Brand, Miryam T. 2013. *Evil Within and Without*, JAJSup 9 (Göttingen).
Brandenburger, Egon. 1968. *Fleisch und Geist*, WMANT 29 (Neukirchen-Vluyn).
Braun, Oskar (ed.). 1914. *Timothei patriarchae I epistulae*, CSCO 74 (Leuven).
Brayford, Susan. 2007. *Genesis*, Septuagint Commentary Series (Leiden).
Bregman, Marc. 1991. "The Parable of the Lame and the Blind: Epiphanius' Quotation from an Apocryphon of Ezekiel," *JTS* 42: 125–38.
Bremmer, Jan N. 1995. "Women in the Apocryphal Acts of John," in *The Apocryphal Acts of John*, ed. J. N. Bremmer (Kampen), 37–56.
Brennan, Tad. 1998. "The Old Stoic Theory of Emotions," in *The Emotions in Hellenistic Philosophy*, ed. J. Sihvola and T. Engberg-Pedersen (Dordrecht), 21–70.
Briant, Pierre. 2012. "Cyrus the Younger," in *The Oxford Classical Dictionary*, 4th ed. (Online: www.oxfordreference.com/).
Brock, Sebastian P. 1979. "Jewish Traditions in Syriac Sources," *JJS* 30: 212–32.
1989. "The Dispute between Soul and Body," *ARAM* 1: 53–64.
1999. "Tales of Two Beloved Brothers: Syriac Dialogues between Body and Soul," in *From Ephrem to Romanos*, ed. S. Brock (Aldershot), 29–38.

2004. "The Earliest Syriac Literature," in *The Cambridge History of Early Christian Literature*, ed. F. Young et al. (Cambridge), 161–71.
2008. *The History of the Holy Mar Maʿin with a Guide to the Persian Martyr Acts* (Piscataway).
Brooke, Alan E. 1891. *The Fragments of Heracleon* (Cambridge).
Brooke, George J. 2002. "Biblical Interpretation in the Wisdom Texts from Qumran," in *The Wisdom Texts from Qumran and the Development of Sapiential Thought*, ed. C. Hempel et al., BETL 159 (Leuven), 201–22.
Brooks, Roger. 1988. "Straw Dogs and Scholarly Ecumenism: The Appropriate Jewish Background for the Study of Judaism," in *Origen of Alexandria*, ed. C. Kannengiesser and W. L. Petersen (Notre Dame), 63–95.
Brown, Gillian, and Yule, George. 1983. *Discourse Analysis* (Cambridge).
Brown, Peter A. 2000. *Augustine of Hippo: A Biography*, 2nd ed. (Berkeley).
Brown, Ruth W. (trans.) 1955. "The Divination of Demons," in *St. Augustine, Treatise on Marriage and Other Subjects*, ed. J. Deferrari, FC 27 (Washington).
Bultmann, Rudolf. 1924. "Das Problem der Ethik bei Paulus," *ZNW* 23: 123–40.
1967. "Römer 7 und die Anthropologie des Paulus," in *Exegetica*, ed. E. Dinkler (Tübingen), 198–209.
Bunge, Gabriel. 1992. *Evagrios Pontikos: über die acht Gedanken* (Würzburg).
1986. *Evagrios Pontikos: Briefe aus der Wüste* (Trier).
Burrows, Millar. 1950. *The Dead Sea Scrolls of St. Mark's Monastery*, 1 (New Haven).
Burton, Philip. 2012. "Augustine and Language," in *A Companion to Augustine*, ed. M. Vessey with S. Reid (Chichester), 113–24.
Butterworth, George W. 1966. *Origen: On First Principles* (New York).
Byers, Sarah C. 2013. *Perception, Sensibility and Moral Motivation in Augustine* (Cambridge).
Byrskog, Samuel. 2015. "Adam and Medea – and Eve: Revisiting Romans 7,7–25," in *Paul's Graeco-Roman Context*, ed. C. Breytenbach, BETL 277 (Leuven), 273–99.
Cain, Andrew. 2009. *The Letters of Jerome*, Oxford Early Christian Studies (Oxford).
Calabi, Francesca. 2008. *God's Acting, Man's Acting: Tradition and Philosophy in Philo of Alexandria*, Studies in Philo of Alexandria 4 (Leiden).
Calliere, Pierfrancesco. 2001. "In the Land of the Magi: Demons and Magic in the Everyday Life of Pre-Islamic Iran," in *Démons et merveilles d 'Orient*, ed. R. Gyselen, Res orientales 13 (Bures-sur-Yvette), 11–36.
Caluori, Damian. 2015. *Plotinus on the Soul* (Cambridge).
Carozzi, Claude. 1994. *Eschatolgie et au-delà. Recherches sur l'Apocalypse de Paul* (Aix-en-Provence).
Casiday, Augustine M. 2006. *Evagrius Ponticus* (Oxford).
2013. *Rethinking the Theology of Evagrius Ponticus* (Cambridge).
Chabot, Jean-Baptiste. 1902. *Synodicon orientale, ou recueil de synodes nestoriens* (Paris).
Chadwick, Henry (trans.). 1980. *Origen: Contra Celsum* (Cambridge).
Champier, S. 1516. *Epistolę Sanctissimorũ sequenti Codice contetæ* (Paris).

Charles, Robert H. (trans.). 1913. *The Book of Enoch or 1 Enoch* (Oxford).

1963. *Eschatology* (New York [1913]).

Chazon, Esther. 2000. "Apocryphal Fragments Attributed to Ezekiel (The Blind and the Lame)," in *The Apocryphal Ezekiel*, ed. M. Stone, SBLEJL 18 (Atlanta), 9–19.

Chilton, Bruce D. 1987. *The Isaiah Targum*, ArBib 11 (Edinburgh).

Choksy, Jamsheed K. 2002. *Evil, Good, and Gender* (New York), 38–44.

Christensen, Arthur. 1941. *Essai sur la démonologie iranienne* (Copenhagen).

Clark, Elizabeth A. 1992. *The Origenist Controversy* (Princeton).

Coblentz Bautch, Kelley. 2008. "Decoration, Destruction, and Debauchery: Reflections on 1 Enoch 8 in Light of 4QEn$^{b}$," *DSD* 15: 79–95.

2009. "Putting Angels in their Place: Developments in Second Temple Angelology," in "*With Wisdom as a Robe*," ed. M. Kõszeghy et al. (Sheffield), 174–88.

Cohen, Menachem (ed.). 2003. *Mikra'ot Gedolot 'Haketer': Psalms* (Ramat-Gan).

Cohen Stuart, G. H. 1984. *The Struggle in Man between Good and Evil* (Kampen).

Colish, Marcia L. 1985. *The Stoic Tradition from Antiquity to the Early Middle Ages*, 2 vols. (Leiden).

Collins, John J. 1999. "In the Likeness of the Holy Ones: The Creation of Humankind in a Wisdom Text from Qumran," in *The Provo International Conference on the Dead Sea Scrolls*, ed. D. W. Perry and E. Ulrich, STDJ 30 (Leiden), 609–18.

Collins, Raymond F. 1998. "The Function of Paraenesis in 1 Thess 4,1–12; 5,12–22," *ETL* 74: 398–414.

Colpe, Carsten. 2003. *Iranier—Aramäer—Hebräer—Hellenen*, WUNT I/154 (Tübingen).

Cook, Johann. 1997. *The Septuagint of Proverbs: Jewish and/or Hellenistic Proverbs?* VTSup 69 (Leiden).

2007. "The Origin of the Tradition of the יצר הטוב and יצר הרע," *JSJ* 38: 87–88.

Copenhaver, Brian P. 1995. *Hermetica: The Greek* Corpus Hermeticum *and the Latin* Asclepius (Cambridge).

Corley, Jeremy. 2008. "Septuagintalisms, Semitic Interference, and the Original Language of the Book of Judith," in *Studies in the Greek Bible*, ed. J. Corley and V. Skemp, CBQMS 44 (Washington), 65–96.

Corrigan, Kevin. 2009. *Evagrius and Gregory: Mind, Soul and Body in the 4th Century* (Aldershot).

Cotelier, Jean Baptiste. 1686. *Ecclesiae Graecae Monumenta*, 3 (Paris).

Courcelle, Pierre. 1969. *Late Latin Writers and their Greek Sources* (Cambridge, MA).

Crouzel, Henri. 1955. "L'anthropologie d'Origène dans la perspective du combat spirituel," *Revue d'ascétique et de mystique* 31: 364–85.

1985. *Origène* (Paris).

Crouzel, Henri, and Simonetti, Manlio (ed. and trans.). 1980. *Origen, Traite des principes, III–IV*, SC 268 (Paris).

Cureton, William. 1861. *History of the Martyrs in Palestine, by Eusebius, Bishop in Caesarea* (London).

Daniélou, Jean. 1948. *Origène* (Paris).
Davies, Philip R. 2010. "Dualism in the Qumran War Texts," in *Dualism in Qumran*, ed. G. G. Xeravits, LSTS 76 (Edinburgh), 8–19.
Davies, William D. 1980. *Paul and Rabbinic Judaism*, 4th ed. (Philadelphia).
Day, John. 2013. "Comparative Ancient Near Eastern Study: The Genesis Flood Narrative in Relation to Ancient Near Eastern Flood Accounts," in *Biblical Interpretation and Method*, ed. K. J. Dell and P. M. Joyce (Oxford), 74–88.
de Boer, Martinus C. 2011. *Galatians*, NTL (Louisville).
Deissmann, Adolf. 1925. *Paulus*, 2nd ed. (Tübingen).
de Jong, Albert. 2010. "Iranian Connections in the Dead Sea Scrolls," in *The Oxford Handbook of the Dead Sea Scrolls*, ed. T. H. Lim and J. J. Collins (Oxford), 479–500.
de Jonge, Marius, et al. (ed.). 1978. *The Testaments of the Twelve Patriarchs*, PVTG 1.2 (Leiden).
de Lange, Nicholas R. M. 1976. *Origen and the Jews* (Cambridge).
de Liagre Böhl, F., and Brongers, H. A. 1975–78. "Weltschöpfungsgedanken in Alt-Israel," *Persica* 7: 69–136.
de Lubac, Henri, and Doutreleau, Louis (ed. and trans.). 1976. *Origène, Homélies sur la Genèse*, SC 7$^{bis}$ (Paris).
de Menasce, Jean Pierre. 1973. *Le troisième livre du Dēnkard* (Paris).
Denyer, Nicholas. 1999. "Mirrors in James 1:22–25 and Plato, *Alcibiades* 132C–133C," *TynBul* 50: 237–40.
Devreese, Robert. 1954. *Introduction à l'étude des manuscrits grecs* (Paris).
Dhabhar, Ervad Bamanji Nusserwanji. 1932. *The Persian Rivayats of Hormazyar Framarz and Others* (Mumbai).
Díez Macho, Alejandro. 1968. *Neophyti 1, I, Genesis*, Textos y Estudios 7 (Madrid).
Dillmann, August. 1853. *Das Buch Henoch* (Leipzig).
Dillon, John M. 1996. *The Middle Platonists: 80 BC to AD 220*, rev. ed. (Ithaca).
Dirksen, Pieter B. 1995. "Some Aspects of the Translation Technique in P-Chronicles," in *The Peshitta as a Translation*, ed. P. B. Dirksen and A. van der Kooij, MPI 8 (Leiden), 17–23.
Dochhorn, Jan. 2009. "Röm 7,7 und das zehnte Gebot," *ZNW* 100: 59–77.
Dodd, Charles H. 1935. *The Bible and the Greeks* (London).
Doering, Lutz. 2006. "Parallels without 'Parallelomania': Methodological Reflections on Comparative Analysis of Halakhah in the Dead Sea Scrolls," in *Rabbinic Perspectives*, ed. S. D. Fraade et al., STDJ 62 (Leiden), 13–42.
2014. "4QMMT and the Letters of Paul: Aspects of Mutual Illumination," in *The Dead Sea Scrolls and Pauline Literature*, ed. J.-S. Rey, STDJ 102 (Leiden), 69–87.
Dogniez, Cécile, and Harl, Marguerite. 1992. *Le Deutéronome*, La Bible d'Alexandrie 5 (Paris).
Dombart, Bernhard, and Kalb, Alphonsus (ed.). 1955. *Sancti Aurelii Augustini De civitate Dei*, CCSL 47–48 (Turnhout).
Donfried, Karl P. 1985. "The Cults of Thessalonica and the Thessalonian Correspondence," *NTS* 31: 336–56.

Dorival, Gilles, and Naiweld, Ron. 2013. "Les interlocuteurs hébreux et juifs d'Origène à Alexandrie et à Césarée," in *Caesarea maritima e la scuola origeniana*, ed. O. Andrei (Brescia), 121–38.
Drazin, Israel. 1982. *Targum Onkelos to Deuteronomy* (Brooklyn).
Drijvers, Hans J. W. 1991. "Body and Soul: A Perennial Problem," in *Dispute Poems and Dialogues in the Ancient and Mediaeval Near East*, ed. G. J. Reinink and H. L. J. Vanstiphout, OLA 42 (Leuven), 121–34.
Driscoll, Jeremy. 2005. *Steps to Spiritual Perfection: Studies on Spiritual Progress in Evagrius Ponticus* (New York).
Driver, Samuel R. 1902. *A Critical and Exegetical Commentary on Deuteronomy*, 3rd ed., ICC (Edinburgh).
Duchesne-Guillemin, Jacques. 1982. "Ahriman," in *Encyclopaedia Iranica* (New York), 1: 670–73.
Duchrow, Ulrich. 1963. "Zum prolog von Augustins *de doctrina christiana*," *VC* 17: 165–72.
Dunderberg, Ismo. 2008. *Beyond Gnosticism* (New York).
Dunn, James D. G. 1975. "Rom. 7,14–25 in the Theology of Paul," *TZ* 31: 257–73.
Dupuis, Jacques. 1967. *"L'esprit de l'homme." Étude sur l'anthropologie religieuse d'Origène*, Museum Lessianum section théologique 62 (Paris).
Duval, Rubens (ed.). 1888–1901. *Lexicon syriacum auctore Hassano Bar-Bahlule* (Paris).
Dyson, Robert W. (ed. and trans.). 1998. *Augustine: The City of God against the Pagans* (Cambridge).
Edwards, Mark J. 2002. *Origen against Plato* (Aldershot).
2012. "Augustine and His Christian Predecessors," in *A Companion to Augustine*, ed. M. Vessey with S. Reid (Chichester), 214–26.
Ehrlich, Uri. 2015. *The Weekday Amidah in Geniza Prayer Books* (Jerusalem).
Elgvin, Torlief. 1997. "An Analysis of *4QInstruction*," Ph.D. thesis (Hebrew University of Jerusalem).
2004. "Priestly Sages? The Milieus of Origin of 4QMysteries an 4QInstruction," in *Sapiential Perspectives*, ed. J. J. Collins et al., STDJ 51 (Leiden), 13–47.
Elliott, Dyan. 1998. *Fallen Bodies* (Philadelphia).
Elman, Yaakov. 2007. "'He in His Cloak and She in Her Cloak': Conflicting Images of Sexuality in Sasanian Mesopotamia," in *Discussing Cultural Influences*, ed. R. Ulmer (Lanham), 129–63.
Elmer, Ian J. 2009. *Paul, Jerusalem and the Judaisers*, WUNT II/258 (Tübingen).
Engberg-Pedersen, Troels. 2014. "The Sinful Body: Paul on Marriage and Sex," in *Ehe – Familie – Gemeinde*, ed. D. Dettinger and C. Landmesser, ABG 46 (Leipzig), 41–60.
Eshel, Esther. 2003. "Genres of Magical Texts in the Dead Sea Scrolls," in *Die Dämonen*, ed. A. Lange et al. (Tübingen), 395–415.
2010. "The Genesis Apocryphon and Other Related Aramaic Texts from Qumran," in *Aramaica Qumranica*, ed. K. Berthelot and D. Stökl Ben Ezra, STDJ 94 (Leiden), 277–98.
Evans, Gillian R. 1982. *Augustine on Evil* (Cambridge).

Evans, Trevor V. 2001. *Verbal Syntax in the Greek Pentateuch* (Oxford).
Fischer, Bonifatius. 1951. *Die Reste der altlateinischen Bibel*, vol. 2: *Genesis* (Freiburg).
Fishbane, Michael. 2003. *Biblical Myth and Rabbinic Mythmaking* (Oxford).
Flesher, Paul V. M., and Chilton, Bruce D. 2011. *The Targums: A Critical Introduction* (Waco).
Flusser, David. 2007. *Judaism of the Second Temple Period*, 1 (Grand Rapids).
Foerster, Werner. 1972. *Gnosis: A Selection of Gnostic Texts*, trans. R. M. Wilson (Oxford).
Forsyth, Neil. 1987. *The Old Enemy: Satan and the Combat Myth* (Princeton).
Fox, Michael V. 2005. "LXX-Proverbs as a Text-Critical Resource," *Textus* 22: 95–128.
Fraade, Steven. 2013. "Moses and Adam as Polyglots," in *Envisioning Judaism*, ed. R. S. Boustan et al., 2 vols. (Tübingen), 1: 185–94.
Frankenberg, Wilhelm. 1912. *Euagrius Ponticus* (Berlin).
Frankfurter, David. 2007. "Beyond 'Jewish Christianity'," in *The Ways that Never Parted*, ed. A. Becker and A. Reed (Minneapolis), 131–43.
Frede, Michael. 1994. "Celsus Philosophus Platonicus," in *ANRW* II.36.7, 5183–5213.
Fredriksen, Paula. 2010. *Augustine and the Jews* (New Haven).
Frey, Jörg. 1999. "Die paulinische Antithese von 'Fleisch' und 'Geist' und die palästinisch-jüdische Weisheitstradition," *ZNW* 90: 45–77.
2002. "Flesh and Spirit in the Palestinian Jewish Sapiential Tradition and in the Qumran Texts," in *The Wisdom Texts from Qumran and the Development of Sapiential Thought*, ed. C. Hempel et al., BETL 159 (Leuven), 367–404.
Frick, Peter. 1999. *Divine Providence in Philo of Alexandria* (Tübingen).
Frishman, Judith. 1992. "The Ways and Means of the Divine Economy: An Edition, Translation and Study of Six Biblical Homilies by Narsai," Ph.D. thesis (Leiden University).
Funk, Wolf-Peter. 1991. "The Coptic Gnostic Apocalypse of Paul," in *New Testament Apocrypha*, ed. E. Hennecke et al., rev. ed., 2 vols. (Westminster), 2: 695–700.
Gardner, Iain. 1995. *The Kephalaia of the Teacher*, Nag Hammadi and Manichaean Studies 37 (Leiden).
Gardner, Iain, and Lieu, Samuel N. C. (ed.). 2004. *Manichaean Texts from the Roman Empire* (Cambridge).
Gärtner, Hans Armin. 2006. "Araspes," in *Brill's New Pauly: Antiquity*, ed. H. Cancik and H. Schneider (Brill Online: http://dx.doi.org/10.1163/1574-9347_bnp_e131320).
Gasparro, Giulia Sfameni. 2000a. "Caduta," in *Origene. Dizionario*, ed. A. Monaci Castagno (Rome), 49–53.
2000b. "Creazione," in *Origene. Dizionario*, ed. A. Monaci Castagno (Rome), 98–103.
Geerard, Maurice (ed.). 1983. *Clavis Patrum Graecorum*, vol. 1: *Patres Antenicaeni* (Turnhout).
Géhin, Paul (ed. and trans.). 1987. *Évagre le Pontique, Scholies aux Proverbes*, SC 340 (Paris).

2007. *Évagre le Pontique, Chapitres des disciples d'Evagre*, SC 514 (Paris).
Geoltrain, Pierre, and Kaestli, Jean-Daniel. 2005. *Écrits apocryphes chrétiens*, vol. 2 (Paris).
Gibbons, Kathleen. 2015. "Passions, Pleasures, and Perceptions: Rethinking Evagrius Ponticus on Mental Representation," *ZAC* 19: 297–330.
Gignoux, Philippe (ed.). 1968. *Homélies de Narsaï sur la création*, PO 34.3–4 (Turnhout).
Gignoux, Philippe, and Tafazzoli, Ahmad. 1993. *Anthologie de Zadspram*, Studia Iranica 13 (Paris).
Gilhus, Ingvild S. 2006. *Animals, Gods, and Humans* (London).
Gill, Christopher. 2006. *The Structured Self in Hellenistic and Roman Thought* (Oxford).
Ginzberg, Louis. 1925–28. *The Legends of the Jews*, 7 vols. (Philadelphia).
Goff, Matthew J. 2003. *The Worldly and Heavenly Wisdom of 4QInstruction*, STDJ 50 (Leiden).
2004. "Reading Wisdom at Qumran: 4QInstruction and the Hodayot," *DSD* 11: 263–88.
2009. "Recent Trends in the Study of Early Jewish Wisdom Literature," *CurBR* 7: 376–416.
2016. "A Seductive Demoness at Qumran? Lilith, Female Demons and 4Q184," in *Das Böse, der Teufel und Dämonen*, ed. J. Dochhorn et al., WUNT II/412 (Tübingen), 59–76.
Goldbacher, Alois (ed.). 1895. *Sancti Aureli Augustini. Opera*, II.1–5, CSEL 34.1 (Vienna).
Goldingay, John. 2014. *A Critical and Exegetical Commentary on Isaiah 56–66*, ICC (London).
Golomb, David M. 1985. *A Grammar of Targum Neofiti*, HSM 34 (Chico).
Görgemanns, Herwig, and Karpp, Heinrich (ed. and trans.). 1976. *Origenes vier Bücher von den Prinzipien* (Darmstadt).
Goshen-Gottstein, Alon. 1994. "The Body as Image of God in Rabbinic Literature," *HTR* 87.2: 171–95.
Gottlieb, Leeor. 2014. "Composition of Targums after the Decline of Aramaic as a Spoken Language," *AS* 12: 1–8.
2016. "The Hebrew Vorlage of Targum Chronicles," *AS* 14: 36–65.
Grant, Robert McQueen. 1966. *Gnosticism and Early Christianity*, 2nd ed. (New York).
Graves, Michael. 2007. *Jerome's Hebrew Philology*, VCSup 90 (Leiden).
Green, William M. (ed.). 1970. *Aurelii Augustini. Opera*, II.2, CCSL 29 (Turnhout).
Greenberg, Moshe. 1983. *Ezekiel 1–20*, AB 22 (Garden City).
Gregg, John A. F. 1902. "The Commentary of Origen upon the Epistle to the Ephesians: Part II," *JTS* 11: 398–420.
Gryson, Roger, et al. (ed.). 1994. *Commentaires de Jérôme sur le Prophète Isaïe Livres VIII–XI*, AGBL 27 (Freiburg).
Guillaumont, Antoine (ed. and trans.). 1971. *Évagre le Pontique, Traité Pratique ou Le Moine*, 1, SC 170 (Paris).
2004. *Un philosophe au désert. Évagre le Pontique* (Paris).

Guillaumont, Antoine, and Guillaumont, Claire (ed. and trans.). 1971. *Évagre le Pontique, Traité Pratique ou Le Moine*, 2, SC 171 (Paris).

Guillaumont, Antoine, Guillaumont, Claire, and Géhin, Paul (ed. and trans.). 1998. *Évagre le Pontique, Sur les pensées*, SC 438 (Paris).

Gunkel, Hermann. 1997. *Genesis*, trans. M. E. Biddle (Macon).

Hadas-Lebel, Mireille (ed). 1973. *Philon d'Alexandrie. De providentia*, I-II, Les oeuvres de Philon d'Alexandrie 35 (Paris).

Hadot, Jean. 1970. *Penchant mauvais et volonté libre dans la Sagesse de Ben Sira* (Brussels).

Hagendahl, Harald. 1958. *Latin Fathers and the Classics* (Göteborg).

Hankinson, R. James. 1995. *The Sceptics* (London).

Hannah, Darrell D. 2007. "The Book of Noah, the Death of Herod the Great, and the Date of the Parables of Enoch," in *Enoch and the Messiah Son of Man*, ed. G. Boccaccini (Grand Rapids), 469–77.

Hanson, R. Paul C. 2002. *Allegory and Event: A Study of the Sources and Significance of Origen's Interpretation of Scripture* (Louisville [1959]).

Harari, Yuval. 2010. *Early Jewish Magic* (Jerusalem) [Hebrew].

Harl, Marguerite. 1966. "Recherches sur l'origénisme d'Origène," in *Studia Patristica*, 8, ed. F. L. Cross, TUGAL 93 (Berlin), 373–405.

1986. *La Genèse*, La Bible d'Alexandrie 1 (Paris).

Hasan-Rokem, Galit. 2003. *Tales of the Neighborhood: Jewish Narrative Dialogues in Late Antiquity* (Berkeley).

Hausherr, Irénée. 1959. "Ignorance infinie ou science infinie?" *OCP* 25: 44–52.

Hayward, C. T. Robert. 1995. *Jerome's Hebrew Questions on Genesis* (Oxford).

2010. "Food, the Animals, and Human Dignity: Jewish Perceptions in a Targumic Context," in C. T. R. Hayward, *Targums and the Transmission of Scripture into Judaism and Early Christianity*, SAIS 10 (Leiden), 361–76.

Heidl, Gyorgy. 2003. *Origen's Influence on the Young Augustine* (Piscataway).

Heine, Ronald E. (trans.). 1982. *Origen: Homilies on Genesis and Exodus*, FC 71 (Washington).

2002. *The Commentaries of Origen and Jerome on St. Paul's Epistle to the Ephesians*, Oxford Early Christian Studies (Oxford).

2003. "Origen's Alexandrian *Commentary on Genesis*," in *Origeniana Octava*, ed. L. Perrone et al., BETL 164 (Leuven), 63–73.

Heither, Theresia. 1990. *Translatio Religionis: die Paulusdeutung des Origenes* (Cologne).

Hendel, Ronald. 2004. "The Nephilim Were on the Earth: Genesis 6:1–4 and Its Ancient Near Eastern Context," in *The Fall of the Angels*, ed. C. Auffarth and L.T. Stuckenbruck, Themes in Biblical Narrative 6 (Leiden), 11–34.

Hennecke, Edgar, and Schneemelcher, Wilhelm. 1991. *New Testament Apocrypha*, rev. ed., trans. R. McLachlan Wilson, 2 vols. (Louisville).

Hennessy, Lawrence R. 1992. "A Philosophical Issue in Origen's Eschatology," in *Origeniana Quinta*, ed. R. J. Daly, BETL 105 (Leuven), 373–80.

Henning, W. B. 1932. "Ein manichäischer kosmogonischer Hymnus," *NAWG*: 214–28.

Hennings, Ralph. 1994. *Der Briefwechsel zwischen Augustinus und Hieronymus und ihr Streit um den Kanon des Alten Testaments, und die Auslegung von Gal. 2, 11–14*, VCSup 21 (Leiden).

Herms, Ronald. 2006. *An Apocalypse for the Church and for the World*, BZNW 143 (Berlin).

Hess, Richard S., and Tsumura, David T. (ed.). 1994. *"I Studied Inscriptions from before the Flood": Ancient Near Eastern, Literary, and Linguistic Approaches to Genesis 1–11* (Winona Lake).

Hidal, Sten. 1974. *Interpretatio Syriaca: die Kommentare des heiligen Ephräm des Syrers zu Genesis und Exodus*, ConBOT 6 (Lund).

Hiebert, Robert J. V. 2005. "Preparing a Critical Edition of IV Maccabees," in *Interpreting Translation*, ed. F. García Martínez and M. Vervenne, BETL 192 (Leuven), 193–216.

Hoffman, Yair. 1997. "Prophecy and Soothsaying," in *Tehillah le-Moshe*, ed. B. Eichler et al. (Winona Lake), 221–43.

2001. *Jeremiah*, 2 vols. (Tel Aviv).

Hoffmann, Georg. 1874. *Syrisch-arabische Glossen* (Kiel).

Hofius, Otfried. 2002. "Der Mensch im Schatten Adams," in *Paulusstudien II*, ed. O. Hofius, WUNT I/143 (Tübingen), 104–54.

Hollander, Harm W., and de Jonge, Marius. 1985. *The Testaments of the Twelve Patriarchs*, SVTP 8 (Leiden).

Holm-Nielsen, Svend. 1960. *Hodayot: Psalms from Qumran* (Aarhus).

Hombergen, Daniel. 2001. *The Second Origenist Controversy* (Rome).

Horbury, William. 2010. "The New Testament and Rabbinic Study: An Historical Sketch," in *The New Testament and Rabbinic Literature*, ed. R. Bieringer et al., JSJSup 136 (Leiden), 1–42.

Houghton, Hugh A. G. 2008. *Augustine's Text of John* (Oxford).

Huehnergard, John. 2008. *Ugaritic Vocabulary in Syllabic Transcription*, 2nd ed., HSS 32 (Winona Lake).

Humbert, Paul. 1958. "Emploi et portée biblique du verbe *yāṣar* et de ses dérivés substantifs," in *Von Ugarit nach Qumran*, BZAW 77 (Berlin), 82–88.

Hutter, Manfred. 1992. *Manis kosmogonische Šābuhragān Texte*, StOR 21 (Wiesbaden).

Hyatt, J. Philip. 1955–56. "The View of Man in the Qumran 'Hodayot'," *NTS* 2: 276–84.

Inwood, Brad. 1985. *Ethics and Human Action in Early Stoicism* (Oxford).

Jaafari-Dehaghi, Mahmoud. 1998. *Dādestān ī Dēnīg*, 1, Studia Iranica 20 (Paris).

Jastrow, Marcus. 1903. *A Dictionary of the Targumim, the Talmud Babli and Yerushalmi, and the Midrashic Literature* (London).

Jay, Pierre. 1985. *L'Éxègese de Saint Jérôme d'après son Commentaire sur Isaïe* (Paris).

Jewett, Robert. 1971. *Paul's Anthropological Terms*, AGJU 10 (Leiden).

2007. *Romans*, Hermeneia (Minneapolis).

Johanson, Bruce C. 1987. *To All the Brethren: A Text-Linguistic and Rhetorical Approach to 1 Thessalonians*, ConB NT 16 (Stockholm).

Joosse, N. Peter. 1999. "An Introduction to the Arabic Diatessaron," *OrChr* 83: 72–129.

2002. "An Introduction to the So-Called Persian Diatessaron of Īwānnīs ʿIzz al-Dīn of Tabrīz," *OrChr* 86: 13–45.
Joosten, Jan. 1990. "The Old Testament Quotations in the Old Syriac and Peshitta Gospels," *Textus* 15: 55–76.
2001. "Tatian's Diatessaron and the Old Testament Peshitta," *JBL* 120: 501–23.
2006. "The Old Testament in the New," in *The Peshiṭta*, ed. B. ter Haar Romeny, MPI 15 (Leiden), 99–106.
2007. "The Original Language and Historical Milieu of the Book of Judith," *Meghillot* 5–6: 159–76.
2012. *The Verbal System of Biblical Hebrew*, JBS 10 (Jerusalem).
Joüon, Paul, and Muraoka, Takamitsu. 2013. *A Grammar of Biblical Hebrew*, 2nd ed., SubBi 27 (Rome).
Kamesar, Adam. 1993. *Jerome, Greek Scholarship, and the Hebrew Bible* (Oxford).
Karfik, Filip. 2011–12. "L'Âme *Logos* de l'intellect et le *logismos* de l'âme," *Χώρα. Révue d'Études Anciennes et Médiévales* 9–10: 67–80.
Kasser, Rodolphe. 1965. "Textes gnostiques, remarques à propos des éditions récentes du Livre secret de Jean et des Apocalypses de Paul, Jacques et Adam," *Mus* 78: 71–98.
Kavanagh, Denis J. (trans.). 1951. *Augustine,* Commentary on the Lord's Sermon on the Mount, *with Seventeen Related Sermons*, FC 11 (New York).
Kearney, Ray (trans.), and Hunter, David G. (ed.). 1999. *Marriage and Virginity*, The Works of Augustine, 1/9 (Hyde Park).
Kedar-Kopfstein, Benjamin. 1994. "Jewish Traditions in the Writings of Jerome," in *The Aramaic Bible*, ed. D. R. G. Beattie and M. J. McNamara, JSOTSup 166 (Sheffield), 420–30.
Kelly, Henry A. 1974. *The Devil, Demonology and Witchcraft* (London).
2006. *Satan: A Biography* (Cambridge).
Kelly, John N. D. 1975. *Jerome* (London).
Kelso, James L. 1948. *The Ceramic Vocabulary of the Old Testament*, BASORSup 5–6 (New Haven).
Kiel, Yishai. 2014. "Confessing Incest to a Rabbi: A Talmudic Story in its Zoroastrian Context," *HTR* 107.4: 401–24.
2015a. "Reimagining Enoch in Sasanian Babylonia in Light of Zoroastrian and Manichaean Traditions," *AJSR* 39.2: 407–32.
2015b. "Creation by Emission: Recreating Adam in the Babylonian Talmud in Light of Zoroastrian and Manichean Literature," *JJS* 66.2: 295–316.
2016. *Sexuality in the Babylonian Talmud* (Cambridge).
2019. "The Usurpation of Solomon's Throne by Ashmedai (bGit 68a–b): A Talmudic Story in its Iranian Context," *Irano-Judaica* 7: 439–71.
King, Karen L. 2003. *What Is Gnosticism?* (Cambridge, MA).
2008. *The Secret Revelation of John* (Cambridge, MA).
King, Peter. 2010. *Augustine* (Cambridge).
Kirchhoff, Renate. 1994. *Die Sünde gegen den eigenen Leib*, SUNT 18 (Göttingen).
Kister, Menachem. 2007. "Aggadoth and Midrashic Methods in the Literature of the Second Temple Period and in Rabbinic Literature," in *Higayon l'Yona*, ed. J. Levinson et al. (Jerusalem), 231–59 [Hebrew].

2009. "On Good and Evil: The Theological Foundation of the Qumran Community," in *The Qumran Scrolls and their World*, ed. M. Kister, 2 vols. (Jerusalem), 2: 497–528 [Hebrew].

2010. "'Inclination of the Heart of Man,' the Body and Purification from Evil," in *Meghillot: Studies in the Dead Sea Scrolls VIII*, ed. M. Bar-Asher and D. Dimant (Jerusalem), 243–86 [Hebrew].

Klauck, Hans-Josef. 1985. "Die Himmelfahrt des Paulus (2 Kor. 12.2.–4) in der koptischen Paulusapokalypse aus Nag Hammadi (NHC V/2)," *SNTSU* 10: 151–90.

Klein, Michael L. 1980. *The Fragment-Targums of the Pentateuch According to their Extant Sources*, 2 vols., AnBib 76 (Rome).

1986. *Genizah Manuscripts of Palestinian Targum to the Pentateuch*, 2 vols. (Cincinnati).

2011. "Associative and Complementary Translation in the Targumim," in *Michael Klein on the Targums: Collected Essays 1972–2002*, ed. A. Shinan and R. Kasher, SAIS 11 (Leiden), 77–88.

Kloppenborg, John S. 2010. "James 1:2–15 and Hellenistic Psychagogy," *NovT* 52: 37–71.

Kmoskó, Mihály (ed.). 1926. *Liber Graduum*, PS 1.3 (Paris).

Knöll, Pius (ed.). 1902. *Sancti Aureli Augustini. Opera*, I.2, CSEL 36 (Vienna).

Koester, Helmut. 1994. "Archäologie und Paulus in Thessalonike," in *Religious Propaganda and Missionary Competition in the New Testament World*, ed. L. Bormann et al., NovTSup 74 (Leiden), 393–404.

Koetschau, Paul (ed.). 1913. *Origenes Werke*, 5, GCS 22 (Leipzig).

Kohut, Alexander. 1866. *Über die Jüdische Angelologie und Daemonologie in ihrer Abhängigkeit vom Parsismus* (Leipzig).

(ed.). 1878–92. *Nathan ben Yehiel of Rome, Aruch Completum* (Vienna).

König, Götz. 2010. *Geschlechtsmoral und Gleichgeschlechtlichkeit im Zoroastrismus*, Iranica 18 (Wiesbaden).

Konradt, Matthias. 2001. "εἰδέναι ἕκαστον ὑμῶν τὸ ἑαυτοῦ σκεῦος κτᾶσθαι … Zu Paulus' sexualethischer Weisung in 1 Thess 4,4f.," *ZNW* 92: 128–35.

2010. "Die Christonomie der Freiheit: zu Paulus' Entfaltung seines ethischen Ansatzes in Gal 5,13–6,10 *Early Christianity* 11 60–81

Kreyenbroek, G. 1985. *Sraoša in the Zoroastrian Tradition*, Orientalia Rheno-Traiectina 28 (Leiden).

Kronholm, Tryggve. 1978. *Motifs from Genesis 1–11 in the Genuine Hymns of Ephrem the Syrian* (Uppsala).

Kuhn, Karl G. 1950. "Die in Palästina gefundenen hebräischen Texte und das Neue Testament," *ZTK* 47: 192–211.

1961. "Der Epheserbrief im Lichte der Qumrantexte," *NTS* 7: 334–46.

Kümmel, Werner G. 1974. "Römer 7 und die Bekehrung des Paulus," in *Römer 7 und das Bild des Menschen im Neuen Testament*, TB 53 (Munich), 1–160.

Kutscher, Edward Y. 1974. *The Language and Linguistic Background of the Isaiah Scroll (1QIsa*[a]*)*, STDJ 6 (Leiden).

Lampe, Peter. 2003. *From Paul to Valentinus* (London).

Landmesser, Christof. 2009. "Begründungsstrukturen paulinischer Ethik," in *Jenseits von Indikativ und Imperativ*, ed. F. W. Horn and R. Zimmermann, WUNT I/238 (Tübingen), 177–96.

2013. "Erster Thessalonicherbrief," in *Paulus Handbuch*, ed. F. W. Horn (Tübingen), 165–72.

Lange, Armin. 1995. *Weisheit und Prädestination: Weisheitliche Urordnung und Prädestination in den Textfunden von Qumran*, STDJ 18 (Leiden).

Laporte, Jean. 1970. "La chute chez Philon et Origène," in *Kyriakon*, ed. P. Granfield and J. A. Jungmann, 2 vols. (Münster), 1: 320–35.

Layton, Bentley. 1987. *The Gnostic Scriptures* (Garden City).

Lazenby, John F. 2012. "Cunaxa," in *The Oxford Classical Dictionary*, 4th ed. (Online: www.oxfordreference.com/).

Lazzeri, Valerio (trans.). 2005. *Evagrio Pontico. Contro i Pensieri Malvagi* (Magnano).

Le Boulluec, Alain, and Sandevoir, Pierre. 1989. *L'Exode*, La Bible d'Alexandrie 2 (Paris).

Lee, John A. L. 1983. *A Lexical Study of the Septuagint Version of the Pentateuch*, SBLSCS 14 (Chico).

Levey, Samson H. 1987. *The Targum of Ezekiel*, ArBib 13 (Edinburgh).

Levison, John R. 2006. "The Two Spirits in Qumran Theology," in *The Bible and the Dead Sea Scrolls*, ed. J. H. Charlesworth, 3 vols. (Waco), 2: 169–94.

Lévy, Carlos. 1986. "Le 'scepticisme' de Philon d'Alexandrie: une influence de la Nouvelle Académie?" in *Hellenica et Judaica*, ed. A. Caquot et al. (Leuven), 29–41.

2005. "Deux problèmes doxographiques chez Philon d'Alexandrie: Posidonius et Enésidème," in *Philosophy and Doxography in the Imperial Age*, ed. A. Brancacci (Florence), 79–102.

2008. "La conversion du scepticisme chez Philon d'Alexandrie," in *Philo of Alexandria and Post Aristotelian Philosophy*, ed. F. Alesse, Studies in Philo of Alexandria 5 (Leiden), 103–20.

Lewis, Charlton Thomas, and Short, Charles. 1879. *A Latin Dictionary* (Oxford).

Lichtenberger, Hermann. 2004. *Das Ich Adams und das Ich der Menschheit*, WUNT I/164 (Tübingen).

Lieber, Laura. 2010. "The Rhetoric of Participation: Experiential Elements of Early Hebrew Liturgical Poetry," *JR* 90: 119–47.

Liebes, Yehuda. 1994a. "De Natura Dei: On the Jewish Myth and Its Development," in *Massuot*, ed. M. Oron and A. Goldreich (Jerusalem), 243–97 [Hebrew].

1994b. "Of God's Love and Jealousy: The Dangers of Divine Affection," *Dimmui* 7: 30–36 [Hebrew].

1998. "Myth and Orthodoxy: A Reply to Shalom Rozenberg," *Madaei Hayahadut* 38: 145–79 [Hebrew].

Lies, Lothar. 1992. *Origenes' "Peri Archon": eine undogmatische Dogmatik* (Darmstadt).

Lincicum, David. 2014. "Philo's Library," *SPhilo* 26: 99–114.

Lincoln, Bruce. 2012. *Gods and Demons, Priests and Scholars* (Chicago).

Lipsius, Richard A., and Bonnet, Maximilien. 1972. *Acta Apostolorum Apocrypha* I–II/1–2 (Hildesheim).

Löhr, Hermut. 2007. "Paulus und der Wille zur Tat," *ZNW* 98: 165–88.
Long, Anthony A., and David N. Sedley. 1987. *The Hellenistic Philosophers*, 1 (Cambridge).
2002. *Epictetus: A Stoic and Socratic Guide to Life* (Oxford).
Lührmann, Dieter. 2001. *Der Brief an die Galater*, 3rd ed., ZBK.NT 7 (Zurich).
Luitpold, Wallach. 1941. "The Colloquy of Marcus Aurelius with the Patriarch Judah I," *JQR* 31: 259–86.
1943. "The Parable of the Blind and the Lame," *JBL* 62: 333–39.
Lunn-Rockliffe, Sophie. 2013. "The Diabolical Problem of Satan's First Sin: Self-Moved Pride or a Response to the Goads of Envy?" in StPatr 63, 121–40.
Lust, Johan, Eynikel, Erik, and Hauspie, Katrin. 2003. *Greek–English Lexicon of the Septuagint*, rev. ed. (Stuttgart).
Lyons, John. 1977. *Semantics*, 2 vols. (Cambridge).
MacKenzie, David N. 1979. "Mani's Šābuhragān," *BSOAS* 42.3: 500–34.
Maier, Johann. 1960. *Die Texte vom Toten Meer*, 2 vols. (Munich).
Malherbe, Abraham J. 2006. *Paul and the Popular Philosophers* (Minneapolis).
Mann, William E. 2001. "Augustine on Evil and Original Sin," in *The Cambridge Companion to Augustine*, ed. D. Meconi and E. Stump (Cambridge), 98–107.
Mansfeld, Japp. 1988. "Philosophy in the Service of Scripture: Philo's Exegetical Strategies," in *The Question of "Eclecticism,"* ed. J. Dillon and A. A. Long (Berkeley), 70–102.
1989. "Chrysippus and the *Placita*," *Phronesis* 34.3: 311–42.
1990. "Doxography and Dialectic: The Sitz im Leben of the Placita," in *ANRW* II.36.4, 3056–3229.
1999. "Sources," in *The Cambridge History of Hellenistic Philosophy*, ed. K. Algra et al. (Cambridge), 3–30.
Maori, Yeshayahu. 1995. *The Peshitta Version of the Pentateuch and Early Jewish Exegesis* (Jerusalem) [Hebrew].
Marcus, Joel. 1982. "The Evil Inclination in the Epistle of James," *CBQ* 44: 606–21.
1986. "The Evil Inclination in the Letters of Paul," *IBS* 8: 8–21.
Margalioth, Reuven. 1987. *Malachei Elyon* (Jerusalem) [Hebrew].
Margulies, Mordecai. 1993. *Midrash Wayyikra Rabbah* (New York).
Markschies, Christoph. 1992. *Valentinus Gnosticus?* WUNT I/65 (Tübingen).
Marmorstein, Arthur. 1931. "Einige vorläufige Bemerkungen zu den neuendeckten Fragmenten des Jerusalemischen (palästinischen) Targums," *ZAW* 49: 232–42.
Marsili, Salvatore. 1936. *Cassiano ed Evagrio* (Rome).
Martin, Dale B. 2004. *Inventing Superstition* (Cambridge, MA).
Martyn, J. Louis. 1997. *Galatians*, AB 33A (New York).
McGuckin, John A. 2004. "The Life of Origen," in *The Westminster Handbook to Origen*, ed. J. A. McGuckin (Louisville), 1–23.
McIvor, J. Stanley. 1994. *The Targum of Chronicles*, ArBib 19 (Edinburgh).
McNamara, Martin. 1978. *The New Testament and the Palestinian Targum to the Pentateuch*, AnBib 27 (Rome).
1992. *Targum Neofiti 1: Genesis*, ArBib 1A (Edinburgh).
Melammed, Ezra Z. 1978. *Bible Commentators* (Jerusalem) [Hebrew].

Ménard, Jacques E. 1967. *L'Évangile selon Philippe* (Paris).
Metzler, Karen (trans.). 2010. *Origenes: Die Kommentierung des Buches Genesis* (Berlin).
Meyer, Marvin W. 2007. *The Nag Hammadi Scriptures* (New York).
Michaelis, Wilhelm. 1954. "πάθος," *ThWNT* 5: 926–29.
Migne, Jacques-Paul. 1860. *Procopius of Gaza, Commentarii in Genesin*, PG 87.1 (Paris).
Milik, Jozef T. (ed.). 1976. *The Books of Enoch* (Oxford).
Mingana, Alphonse. 1905. *Narsai Doctoris Syri Homiliae et Carmina*, 2 vols. (Mosul).
Mirsky, Aharon. 1991. *Yosse ben Yosse: Poems* (Jerusalem) [Hebrew].
Moazami, Mahnaz. 2014. *Wrestling with the Demons of the Pahlavi Videvdad*, Iran Studies 9 (Leiden).
Montanari, Franco. 2013. *Vocabolario della Lingua Greca*, 3rd ed. (Turin).
2015. *Brill Dictionary of Ancient Greek*, English ed. by M. Goh and C. Schroeder (Leiden).
Montgomery, James A. 1913. *Aramaic Incantation Texts from Nippur* (Philadelphia).
Moore, George F. 1997. *Judaism in the First Centuries of the Christian Era*, 2 vols. (Peabody [1927–30]).
Morin, D. Germanus. 1958. *S. Hieronymi Presbyteri Opera*, vol. 2: *Opera Homiletica*, CCSL 78 (Turnhout).
Moss, Jessica. 2008. "Appearances and Calculations: Plato's Division of the Soul," *Oxford Studies in Ancient Philosophy* 34: 35–68.
Mosshammer, Alden A. (ed.). 1984. *Georgius Syncellus, Ecloga Chronographica* (Leipzig).
Muehlberger, Ellen. 2013. *Angels in Late Ancient Christianity* (Oxford).
Mueller, James R. 1994. *The Five Fragments of the Apocryphon of Ezekiel*, JSPSup 5 (Sheffield).
Mullen, E. Theodore. 1980. *The Assembly of the Gods*, HSM 24 (Chico).
Münz-Manor, Ophir. 2010. "Liturgical Poetry in the Late Antique Near East: A Comparative Approach," *JAJ* 1: 336–61.
2013. "Jewish and Christian Dispute Poems on the Relationship between the Body and the Soul," *Jerusalem Studies in Hebrew Literature* 25: 187–209 [Hebrew].
2015. *Ancient Piyyut: An Annotated Anthology* (Tel Aviv) [Hebrew].
Muraoka, Takamitsu. 2009. *A Greek–English Lexicon of the Septuagint* (Leuven).
Murdock, William R., and MacRae, George W. 1979. "*The Apocalypse of Paul*," in *Coptic Gnostic Library*, vol. 3: *Nag Hammadi Codices V,2–5 and VI with Papyrus Berolensis 8502 1 and 4*, ed. D. M. Parrot (Leiden), 47–63.
Murphy, Roland E. 1958. "*Yēṣer* in the Qumran Literature," *Bib* 39: 334–44.
Murray, Robert. 1995. "Aramaic and Syriac Dispute-Poems and their Connections," in *Studia Aramaica*, ed. J. Greenfield et al., JSSSup 4 (Oxford), 157–87.
Mutzenbecher, Almut (ed.). 1967. *Sancti Aurelii Augustini de Sermone Domini in Monte libros duos*, CCSL 35 (Turnhout).

Muyldermans, Jozef. 1931. "Evagriana," *Mus* 44: 37–68.

Naeh, Shlomo. 1997. "Freedom and Celibacy: A Talmudic Variation on Tales of Temptation and Fall in Genesis and its Syrian Background," in *The Book of Genesis in Jewish and Oriental Christian Interpretation*, ed. J. Frishman and L. van Rompay, Traditio exegetica graeca 5 (Leuven), 73–89.

Najman, Hindy. 2003. "A Written Copy of the Law of Nature: An Unthinkable Paradox?" *SPhilo* 15: 54–63.

2014. *Losing the Temple and Recovering the Future* (Cambridge).

Nautin, Pierre. 1977. *Origène. Sa vie et son oeuvre* (Paris).

Naveh, Joseph, and Shaked, Shaul. 1987. *Amulets and Magic Bowls* (Jerusalem).

Nelson, David. 2006. *Mekhilta de-Rabbi Shimon bar Yohai* (Philadelphia).

Nelson, Milward Douglas. 1988. *The Syriac Version of the Wisdom of Ben Sira Compared to the Greek and Hebrew Materials*, SBLDS 107 (Atlanta).

Newman, Albert Henry (trans.). 1887. *St. Augustin, The Writings against the Manichaeans and the Donatists*, NPNF 4 (Oxford), 95–107.

Newsom, Carol. 1980. "The Development of 1 Enoch 6–19: Cosmology and Judgment," *CBQ* 24: 310–29.

2004. *The Self as Symbolic Space*, STDJ 52 (Leiden).

2012. "Spirit, Flesh, and the Indigenous Psychology of the Hodayot," in *Prayer and Poetry in the Dead Sea Scrolls and Related Literature*, ed. J. Penner et al., STDJ 98 (Leiden), 339–54.

Nickelsburg, George W. E. 1977. "Apocalyptic and Myth in 1 Enoch 6–11," *JBL* 96: 383–405.

2001. *1 Enoch 1* (Minneapolis).

Nisula, Timo. 2012. *Augustine and the Functions of Concupiscence*, VCSup 116 (Leiden).

Noce, Carla. 2003. "Tema della nudità dell'anima," in *Origeniana Octava*, ed. L. Perrone, P. Bernardino, and D. Marchini, 2 vols., BETL 164 (Leuven), 1: 679–86.

Nöldeke, Theodor. 1886. "Review of F. Delitzsch, *Prolegomena eines neuen hebräisch-aramäischen Wörterbuchs zum Alten Testament*," *ZDMG* 40: 718–43.

Noort, Ed. 1998. "The Stories of the Great Flood," in *Interpretations of the Flood*, ed. F. García Martínez and G. P. Luttikhuizen (Leiden), 1–38.

Norelli, Enrico. 1994. *L'Ascensione di Isaia*, Origini. Nuova Serie 1 (Bologna).

O'Daly, Gerard J. P. 1987. *Augustine's Philosophy of Mind* (Berkeley).

Olson, Daniel. 2004. *Enoch* (North Richland Hills).

Otzen, Benedikt. 1990. "יָצַר yāṣar," in *TDOT*, 6: 257–65.

Owens, Robert J. 2011. "Christian Features in the Peshitta Text of Ben Sira," in *The Texts and Versions of the Book of Ben Sira*, ed. J.-S. Rey and J. Joosten, JSJSup 150 (Leiden), 177–96.

Parisot, Jean (ed.). 1894–1907. *Aphraatis Sapientis Persae Demonstrationes*, PS 1.1–2 (Paris).

Parsons, Wilfrid (trans.). 1951. *Augustine, of Hippo:* Letters I, FC 12 (Washington).

Patmore, Hector M. 2012. *Adam, Satan, and the King of Tyre*, Jewish and Christian Perspectives 20 (Leiden).

Payne Smith, Robert. 1868–1901. *Thesaurus Syriacus*, 2 vols. (Oxford).
Pearce, Sarah. 2007. *The Land of the Body: Studies in Philo's Representation of Egypt*, WUNT I/208 (Tübingen).
Pépin, Jean. 1971. *Idées grecques sur l'homme et sur Dieu* (Paris).
Perrin, Michel (ed. and trans.). 1974. *Lactance, l'ouvrage du Dieu créateur*, SC 213 (Paris).
Peshiṭta Institute Leiden. 1961. *List of Old Testament Peshiṭta Manuscripts* (Leiden).
Pesthy, Monika. 2007. "Earthly Tribunal in the Fourth Heaven (NH V,2 20,5–21,22)," in *The* Visio Pauli *and the Gnostic Apocalypse of Paul*, ed. J. N. Bremmer and I. Czachesz, Studies on the Early Christian Apocrypha 9 (Leuven), 198–210.
Petersen, William L. 1994. *Tatian's Diatessaron*, VCSup 25 (Leiden).
Petit, Francoise. 1978. *Philon d'Alexandrie, Quaestiones in Genesim et in Exodum: fragmenta graeca* (Paris).
(ed.). 1986. *Catenae Graecae in Genesim et in Exodum*, vol. 2: *Collectio Coisliniana in Genesim*, CCSG 15 (Turnhout).
Petit, Francoise, et al. (trans.). 2011. *Eusèbe d'Émèse Commentaire de la Genèse*, Traditio exegetica graeca 15 (Leuven).
Pettipiece, Timothy. 2002. "Heracleon: Fragments of Early Valentinian Exegesis," MA thesis (Wilfrid Laurier University).
2009. *Pentadic Redaction in the Manichaean Kephalaia* (Leiden).
2018. "Varieties of Christian Gnosis," in *A Companion to Religion in Late Antiquity*, ed. J. Lössl and N. J. Baker-Brian (London), 297–318.
Pfann, Claire. 2010. "A Note on 1Q19: The 'Book of Noah'," in *Noah and his Book(s)*, ed. M. E. Stone et al., SBLEJL 28 (Atlanta), 71–76.
Pichery, Étienne (ed. and trans.). 1955–59. *Jean Cassien, Conférences*, SC 42, 54, 64 (Paris).
Pirart, Éric. 2007. *Georges Dumézil face aux demons iraniens* (Paris).
Pisi, Paola. 1987. "Peccato di Adamo e caduta dei *noes* nell' esegesi origeniana," in *Origeniana Quarta*, ed. L. Lies (Innsbruck), 322–35.
Poirier, Paul-Hubert. 2010. "Pour une étude des citations bibliques contenues dans le *Contra Manichaeos* de Titus de Bostra," in *Sur les pas des Araméens chrétiens*, ed. F. Briquel-Chatonnet and M. Debié (Paris), 373–82.
Poirier, Paul-Hubert, et al. (ed.). 2013. *Titus Bostrensis. Contra Manichaeos libri IV graece et Syriace*, CCSG 82 (Turnhout).
Pokorný, Petr, and Heckel, Ulrich. 2007. *Einleitung in das Neue Testament*, UTB 2798 (Tübingen).
Popović, Mladen. 2016. "Anthropology, Pneumatology, and Demonology in Early Judaism," in *"And God Breathed into Man the Breath of Life": Dust of the Ground and Breath of Life (Gen 2.7)*, ed. J. van Ruiten and G. van Kooten (Leiden), 58–98.
Porter, Frank Chamberlin. 1901. "The *Yeçer Hara*: A Study in the Jewish Doctrine of Sin," in *Biblical and Semitic Studies* (New York), 93–156.
Porton, Gary G. 1988. *Goyim: Gentiles and Israelites in Mishnah-Tosefta*, BJS 155 (Atlanta).

Prestel, Peter, and Schorch, Stefan. 2011. "Genesis: Das erste Buch Mose," in *Septuaginta Deutsch*, ed. M. Karrer and W. Kraus (Stuttgart), 145–257.

Prieur, Jean-Marc. 1989a. *Acta Andrae: Praefatio – commentaries*, CCSA 5 (Turnhout).

(ed.). 1989b. *Acta Andrae: Textus*, CCSA 6 (Turnhout).

Puech, Émile. 1988. "Un hymne Essénien en partie retrouvé et les Béatitudes: 1QH V 12–VI 18 (=col. XIII–XIV 7) et 4QBéat.," *RevQ* 13: 59–88.

2001. "4Q530–533, 203 1. 4QLivre de Géants$^{b\text{-}e}$ ar," in *Qumrân Grotte 4 XXII*, ed. É. Puech, DJD 31 (Oxford), 9–115.

Qimron, Elisha. 1995. "The Biblical Lexicon in Light of the Dead Sea Scrolls," *DSD* 2: 295–329.

Ramelli, Ilaria. 2013. *The Christian Doctrine of Apokatastasis*, VCSup 120 (Leiden).

2015. *Evagrius's Kephalaia Gnostika*, Writings from the Greco-Roman World 38 (Atlanta).

Ramsey, Boniface. 1993a. "John Cassian: Student of Augustine," *Cistercian Studies Quarterly* 28: 5–15.

1993b. "Addendum to Boniface Ramsey, 'John Cassian: Student of Augustine'," *Cistercian Studies Quarterly* 28: 199–200.

Rebenich, Stefan. 1992. *Hieronymus und sein Kreis* (Stuttgart).

Reid, James Smith. 1985. *M. Tulli Ciceronis Academica* (London).

Reinmuth, Eckhart. 1985. *Geist und Gesetz*, TA 44 (Berlin).

Rey, Jean-Sébastien. 2009. *4QInstruction: Sagesse et eschatologie*, STDJ 81 (Leiden).

Reydams-Schils, Gretchen J. 1999. *Demiurge and Providence: Stoic and Platonist Readings of Plato's Timaeus* (Turnhout).

2008. "Philo of Alexandria on Stoic and Platonist Psycho-Physiology," in *Philo of Alexandria and Post-Aristotelian Philosophy*, ed. F. Alesse (Leiden), 168–95.

Ribera Florit, Josep. 1988a. *Targum Jonatán de los Profetas Posteriores en tradición babilónica: Isaías* (Madrid).

1988b. *El Targum de Isaías*, Biblioteca Midrásica 6 (Valencia).

2004. *Targum de Ezequiel* (Estella).

Richards, Ivor A. 1936. *The Philosophy of Rhetoric* (Oxford).

Riesner, Rainer. 1991. *Die Frühzeit des Apostel Paulus*, WUNT I/71 (Tübingen).

Risse, Siegfreid. 2005. *Hieronymus: Commentarioli in Psalmos* (Turnhout).

2003. *Hieronymus: Commentarius In Ionam Prophetam* (Turnhout).

Rofé, Alexander. 1979. "The Composition of Deuteronomy 31 in Light of a Conjecture about Inversion in the Order of Columns in the Biblical Text," *Shnaton* 3: 59–76.

Roman, Agathe, et al. 2015. *Titus de Bostra. Contre les manichéens*, CCT 21 (Turnhout).

Rosen-Zvi, Ishay. 2008. "Two Rabbinic Inclinations? Rethinking a Scholarly Dogma," *JSJ* 39: 513–39.

2009. "Sexualising the Evil Inclination: Rabbinic 'Yetzer' and Modern Scholarship," *JJS* 50: 264–81.

2011. *Demonic Desires*: Yetzer Hara *and the Problem of Evil in Late Antiquity* (Philadelphia).

2012. *Body and Soul in Ancient Jewish Thought* (Ben-Shemen) [Hebrew].
2013. "The Birth of the Goy in Rabbinic Literature," in *Myth, Mysticism and Ritual*, ed. I. Rosen-Zvi et al., Te'uda 26 (Tel Aviv), 361–438 [Hebrew].
Rosen-Zvi, Ishay, and Ophir, Adi. 2011. "Goy: Toward a Genealogy," *Dine Israel* 28: 69–112.
2015. "Paul and the Invention of the Gentiles," *JQR* 105: 1–41.
Roukema, Riemer. 1988. *The Diversity of Laws in Origen's Commentary on Romans* (Amsterdam).
2003. "L'origine du mal selon Origène et dans ses sources," *RHPR* 83: 405–20.
2004. "De oorsprong van het kwaad volgens Origenes en zijn bronnen," in *Kennis van het Kwaad*, ed. L. J. Lietaert Peerbolte and E. J. C. Tigchelaar (Zoetermeer), 103–20, 167–70.
2018. "Origen of Alexandria," in *Brill Encyclopedia of Early Christianity*, ed. D. G. Hunter et al. (Leiden).
Rozenberg, Shalom. 1998. "On the History of the Jewish Myth," *Madaei Hayahadut* 38: 145–79 [Hebrew].
Rubenson, Samuel. 1995. *The Letters of St Antony* (Minneapolis).
Rubin, Nissan. 1989. "The Sages' Conception of the Body and Soul," in *Essays in the Social Scientific Study of Judaism and Jewish Society*, ed. S. Fishbane and J. N. Lightstone (New York), 47–103.
Rudolph, Kurt. 1983. *Gnosis* (San Francisco).
Runia, David T. 1986. *Philo of Alexandria and the Timaeus of Plato*, Philosophia antiqua 44 (Leiden).
1993. *Philo in Early Christian Literature: A Survey* (Assen).
1999a. "Philo of Alexandria and the Greek Hairesis-Model," *VC* 53: 114–47.
1999b. "What Is Doxography?" in *Ancient Histories of Medicine: Essays in Medical Doxography and Historiography in Classical Antiquity*, ed. P. J. van der Eijk, Studies in Ancient Medicine 20 (Leiden), 33–55.
2003. "Theodicy in Philo of Alexandria," in *Theodicy in the World of the Bible*, ed. A. Laato and J. C. de Moor (Leiden), 576–604.
2008. "Philo and Hellenistic Doxography," in *Philo of Alexandria and Post-Aristotelian Philosophy*, ed. F. Alesse, Studies in Philo of Alexandria 5 (Leiden), 13–54.
Salvesen, Alison. 2003. "Infants or Fools in the Garden of Eden? An Ambiguity in Early Syriac Tradition," in *Hamlet on a Hill*, ed. M. F. J. Baasten and W. T. van Peursen, OLA 118 (Leuven), 432–40.
2007. "A Convergence of the Ways? The Judaizing of Christian Scripture by Origen and Jerome," in *The Ways that Never Parted*, ed. A. Becker and A. Reed (Minneapolis), 233–58.
Sanders, Ed P. 1995. *Paulus* (Stuttgart).
Sandmel, Samuel. 1962. "Parallelomania," *JBL* 81: 1–13.
Satlow, Michael L. 2003. "'And on the Earth You Shall Sleep': Talmud Torah and Rabbinic Asceticism," *JR* 83.2: 204–22.
Savage, John J. (trans.). 1961. *Ambrose, Hexameron, Paradise, and Cain and Abel*, FC 42 (Washington).

Saydon, Vered. 2010. "The Connection between Thought and Emotion in Biblical Hebrew: A Syntactic and Semantic Study of the Hebrew Verb *ḥašav*," *Leš* 73.1: 7–25 [Hebrew].

2013. "Ḥašav—Ḥavaš? A Comment on the Ancient Semantic Development of the Verb Ḥašav," *Leš* 75.1: 89–100 [Hebrew].

Schaeder, Hans H. 1941. "Der Iranische Zeitgott und sein Mythus," *ZDMG* 95: 268–99.

Schäfer, Peter. 1975. *Rivalität zwischen Engeln und Menschen*, SJ 8 (Berlin).

Schäfer, Ruth. 2004. *Paulus bis zum Apostelkonzil*, WUNT II/179 (Tübingen).

Schechter, Solomon. 1961. *Aspects of Rabbinic Theology* (New York).

Scheck, Thomas P. (trans.). 2011. *Origen: Commentary on the Epistle to the Romans Book 1–5*, FC 103 (Washington).

Schenkl, Karl (ed.). 1897. *Sancti Ambrosii. Opera*, CSEL 32.1 (Vienna).

Schmidt, Carl, et al. 1940. *Kephalaia* (Stuttgart).

Schmidt, Hanns-Peter. 2000. "Von awestischen Dämon Āzi zur manichäischen Āz, der Mutter aller Dämonen," in *Studia Manichaica IV*, ed. R. E. Emmerick et al. (Berlin), 517–27.

2006. "Mithra i. Mitra in Old Indian and Mithra in Old Iranian," in *Encyclopedia Iranica* (Online: www.iranicaonline.org).

Schnelle, Udo. 2005. *Einleitung in das Neue Testament*, 5th ed., UTB 1830 (Göttingen).

Schofer, Jonathan W. 2003. "The Redaction of Desire: Structure and Editing of Rabbinic Teachings Concerning Yeser ('Inclination')," *Journal of Jewish Thought and Philosophy* 12: 19–53.

2007. "Rabbinical Ethical Formulation and the Foundation of Rabbinical Ethical Compilations," in *The Cambridge Companion to the Talmud and Rabbinic Literature*, ed. C. E. Fonrobert and M. S. Jaffee (Cambridge), 313–35.

Schröter, Jens. 2013. "Der Mensch zwischen Wollen und Tun: Erwägungen zu Römer 7 im Licht der 'New Perspective on Paul'," in *Paulus: Werk und Wirkung*, ed. P.-G. Klumbies et al. (Tübingen), 195–223.

Schuller, Eileen M., and Newsom, Carol A. 2012. *The Hodayot (Thanksgiving Psalms)*, SBLEJL 36 (Atlanta).

Schwartz, Baruch J. 2007. "The Flood Narratives in the Torah and the Question of Where History Begins," in *Shai le-Sara Japhet*, ed. M. Bar-Asher et al. (Jerusalem), 139–54 [Hebrew].

Schwartz, Eduard (ed.). 1940. *Collectio Sabbaitica contra Acephalos et Origeniastas destinata*, ACO 3 (Berlin).

Seesemann, Heinrich. 1954. "ὀρφανός," in *TWNT*, 5, 487–88.

Seitz, Oscar J. F. 1944. "Relationship of the Shepherd of Hermas to the Epistle of James," *JBL* 63: 131–40.

1947. "Antecedents and Signification of the Term DIYUXOS," *JBL* 66: 211–19.

1958. "Afterthoughts on the Term 'Dipsychos'," *NTS* 4: 327–34.

Sgherri, Giuseppe. 1982. *Chiesa e Sinagoga nelle opere di Origene*, SPMed 13 (Milan).

Shaked, Shaul. 1971. "The Notions Mēnōg and Gētīg in the Pahlavi Texts and their Relation to Eschatology," *AcOr* 33: 59–107.

1972. "Qumran and Iran: Further Considerations," *IOS* 2: 433–46.
1979. *The Wisdom of the Sasanian Sages [Dēnkard 6]*, Persian Heritage Series 34 (Boulder).
2001. "The Moral Responsibility of Animals: Some Zoroastrian and Jewish Views on the Relation of Humans and Animals," in *Festschrift in Honor of Anders Hultgard*, ed. M. Stausberg (Berlin), 578–95.
Shenkar, Michael. 2014. *Intangible Spirits and Graven Images*, Magical and Religious Literature of Late Antiquity 4 (Leiden).
Shields, Christopher. 2010. "Plato's Divided Soul," in *Plato's Republic*, ed. M. L. McPherran (Cambridge), 147–70.
Shimun, Eshai (ed.). 1970. *Homilies of Mar Narsai* (San Francisco).
Siegert, Folker. 2001–03. *Zwischen hebräischer Bibel und Altem Testament*, 2 vols., MJSt 9 and 13 (Berlin).
Sinkewicz, Robert E. 2003. *Evagrius of Pontus: The Greek Ascetic Corpus* (Oxford).
Skinner, John. 1910. *A Critical and Exegetical Commentary on Genesis*, ICC (New York).
Skjærvø, Prods Oktor. 1982. "Āsarēštār," in *Encyclopedia Iranica* (New York), 2: 801–2.
1995. "Iranian Elements in Manicheism: A Comparative Contrastive Approach: Irano-Manichaica I," in *Au carrefour des religions*, ed. Rika Gyselen, Res Orientales 7 (Bures-sur-Yvette), 263–284.
1997. "On the Middle Persian Imperfect," in *Syntaxe des Langues Indo-iraniennes anciennes*, ed. E. Pirart, AuOrSup 6 (Barcelona), 161–88.
2011. *The Spirit of Zoroastrianism* (New Haven).
2013. "Next-of-Kin Marriages in Zoroastrianism," in *Encyclopedia Iranica* (Online: www.iranicaonline.org).
Smith, Gregory. 2017. "Augustine on Demons' Bodies," in StPatr 82, 7–32.
Smolar, Leivy, and Aberbach, Moses. 1983. *Studies in Targum Jonathan to the Prophets* (New York).
Sokoloff, Michael. 1990. *A Dictionary of Jewish Palestinian Aramaic of the Byzantine Period* (Ramat Gan).
2002. *A Dictionary of Jewish Babylonian Aramaic of the Talmudic and Geonic Periods* (Ramat Gan).
2009. *A Syriac Lexicon* (Piscataway).
Sorabji, Richard. 2000. *Emotion and Peace of Mind: From Stoic Agitation to Christian Temptation* (Oxford).
2004. "Stoic First Movements in Christianity," in *Stoicism*, ed. S. K. Strange and J. Zupko (Cambridge), 95–107.
2005. *The Philosophy of the Commentators*, vol. 1 (Ithaca).
Sperber, Alexander (ed.). 1959–62. *The Bible in Aramaic Based on Old Manuscripts and Printed Texts*, 3 vols. (Leiden).
Spurrell, George J. 1896. *Notes on the Text of the Book of Genesis* (Oxford).
Stausberg, Michael. 2002. *Die Religion Zarathushtras*, 3 vols. (Stuttgart).
Stec, David M. 2004. *The Targum of Psalms*, ArBib 16 (Edinburgh).
Steel, Catherine (ed.). 2013. *The Cambridge Companion to Cicero* (Cambridge).

Stemberger, Günter. 1996. *Introduction to the Talmud and Midrash*, ed. and trans. M. Bockmuehl, 2nd ed. (Edinburgh).

2013. "Ebraismo a Caesarea Maritima. Personalità rabbiniche e temi esegetici al tempo di Origene ed Eusebio," in *Caesarea Maritima e la scuola origeniana*, ed. O. Andrei, Supplementi Adamantius 3 (Brescia), 95–104.

Sterling, Gregory. 2006. "The Queen of the Virtues: Piety in Philo of Alexandria," *SPhilo* 18: 103–23.

2007. "The First Theologian: The Originality of Philo of Alexandria," in *Renewing Tradition*, ed. M. W. Hamilton et al. (Eugene), 145–62.

Stewart, Columba. 1998. *Cassian the Monk* (Oxford).

2005. "Evagrius Ponticus and the Eight Generic Logismoi," in *In the Garden of Evil*, ed. R. Newhauser (Toronto), 3–34.

Stiegman, Emero. 1979. "Rabbinic Anthropology," in *ANRW* II.19.2, 487–579.

Stone, Michael E. 2009. "'Be You a Lyre For Me': Identity or Manipulation in Eden," in *The Exegetical Encounter between Jews and Christians in Late Antiquity*, ed. E. Grypeou, and H. Spurling, Jewish and Christian Perspectives 18 (Leiden), 87–100.

2010. "The Book(s) Attributed to Noah," in *Noah and His Book(s)*, ed. M. E. Stone et al., SBLEJL 28 (Atlanta), 7–25.

Strecker, Georg. 1976. "Befreiung und Rechtfertigung: zur Stellung der Rechtfertigungslehre in der Theologie des Paulus," in *Rechtfertigung*, ed. J. Friedrich et al. (Tübingen), 479–508.

Striker, Gisela. 1983. "The Ten Tropes of Aenesidemus," in *The Skeptical Tradition*, ed. M. Burnyeat (Berkeley), 95–115.

Stroumsa, Guy G. and Fredriksen, Paula. 1998. "The Two Souls and the Divided Will," in *Self, Soul, and Body in Religious Experience*, ed. A. I. Baumgarten and J. Assmann, SHR 78 (Leiden), 198–217.

Strugnell, John, Harrington, Daniel J., and Elgvin, Torlief. 1999. *Qumran Cave 4 XXIV*, DJD 34 (Oxford).

Stuckenbruck, Loren T. 2000a. "201 2–8. 4QEnoch[a] ar," in *Qumran Cave 4 XXVI: Cryptic Texts and Miscellanea*, ed. S. J. Pfann et al., DJD 36 (Oxford), 3–7.

2000b. "4QEnoch Giants[a] ar, 4QEnoch[f] ar, 1QEnochGiants[a] ar (Re-edition), 1QEnochGiants[b]? ar (Re-edition), 2QEnochGiants ar (Re-edition), 6QpapGiants ar (Re-edition)," in *Qumran Cave 4 XXVI: Cryptic Texts and Miscellanea*, ed. S. J. Pfann, et al., DJD 36 (Oxford), 8–94.

2002. "4QInstruction and the Possible Influence of Early Enochic Traditions: An Evaluation," in *The Wisdom Texts from Qumran and the Development of Sapiential Thought*, ed. C. Hempel et al., BETL 159 (Leuven), 245–61.

2003. "Giant Mythology and Demonology: From the Ancient Near East to the Dead Sea Scrolls," in *Die Dämonen*, ed. A. Lange et al. (Tübingen), 318–38.

2007. *Commentary on 1 Enoch 91–108*, CEJL (Berlin).

2011. "The Interiorization of Dualism within the Human Being in Second Temple Judaism: The Treatise of the Two Spirits (1QS III: 13–IV:26) in Its Tradition-Historical Context," in *Light against Darkness*, ed. A. Lange et al., JAJSup 2 (Göttingen), 145–68.

Stuckenbruck, Loren T. and Erho, Ted M. 2011. "The Book of Enoch and the Ethiopian Manuscript Tradition: New Data," in *"Go Out and Study the Land" (Judges 18:2)*, ed. A. M. Maeir et al., JSJSup 148 (Leiden), 257–67.

Sundermann, Werner. 1986. "Mani, India, and the Manichaean Religion," *South Asian Studies* 2: 11–19.

2003. "The Zoroastrian and the Manichaean Demon Āz," in *Paitimāna*, ed. S. Adhami (Costa Mesta), 328–38.

Sussman, Yaacov 2001. *Talmud Yerushalmi: According to Ms. Or. 4720 (Scal 3) of the Leiden University Library with Restorations and Corrections* (Jerusalem).

Suter, David. 1979. "Fallen Angels, Fallen Priests," *HUCA* 50: 115–35.

Tal, Avraham. 2015. *Biblia Hebraica Quinta*, vol. 1: *Genesis* (Stuttgart).

Taradach, Madeleine. 1991. *Le Midrash*, MdB 22 (Geneva).

ter Haar Romeny, Bas. 1997. *A Syrian in Greek Dress*, Traditio exegetica graeca 6 (Leuven).

Teselle, Eugene. 1990. "Serpent, Eve, and Adam: Augustine and the Exegetical Tradition," in *Augustine: Presbyter Factus Sum*, ed. J. T. Lienhard et al. (New York), 341–61.

Teske, Roland J. (trans.). 1991. *Augustine,* On Genesis, FC 84 (Washington).

Theissen, Gerd. 1983. *Psychologische Aspekte paulinischer Theologie*, FRLANT 131 (Göttingen).

Theodor, Julius, and Albeck, Chanoch. 1965. *Midrash Bereshit Rabba*, 3 vols., 2nd ed. (Jerusalem).

Thomassen, Einar. 2006. *The Spiritual Seed: The Church of the "Valentinians"* (Leiden).

Thomassen, Einar, and Painchaud, Louis. 1989. *La traité tripartite (NH I, 5)* (Quebec).

Tigchelaar, Eibert J. C. 2001. *To Increase Learning for the Understanding Ones*, STDJ 44 (Leiden).

2008. "The Evil Inclination in the Dead Sea Scrolls, with a Re-edition of 4Q468i (4QSectarian Text?)," in *Empsychoi Logoi*, ed. A. Houtman et al., Ancient Judaism and Early Christianty 73 (Leiden), 347–57.

2009. "'Spiritual People,' 'Fleshly Spirit,' and 'Vision of Meditation': Reflections on *4QInstruction* and 1 Corinthians," in *Echoes from the Caves*, ed. F. García Martínez, STDJ 85 (Leiden), 103–18.

Tiller, Patrick A. 1993. *A Commentary on the Animal Apocalypse of 1 Enoch*, SBLEJL 4 (Atlanta).

Tissot, Yves. 1981. "Encratisme et Actes apocryphes," in *Les Actes apocryphes des Apôtres*, ed. F. Bovon (Geneva), 109–18.

1988. "L'encratisme des Actes de Thomas," in *ANRW*, II.25.6, 4415–29.

Tonneau, Raymond-Marie (ed.). 1955. *Sancti Ephraem Syri in Genesim et in Exodum commentarii*, CSCO 152 (Leuven).

Tóth, Péter. 2011. "Way Out of the Tunnel? Three Hundred Years of Research on the Apocrypha," in *Retelling the Bible*, ed. L. Dolezalova and T. Visy (Bern), 45–84.

Tuplin, Christopher J. 2012. "Xenophon," in *The Oxford Classical Dictionary*, 4th ed. (Online: www.oxfordreference.com).

Turner, John D. 2001. *Sethian Gnosticism and the Platonic Tradition* (Quebec).

Tzamalikos, Panayiotis. 2007. *Origen: Philosophy of History and Eschatology*, VCSup 85 (Leiden).

Tzvetkova-Glaser, Anna. 2010. *Pentateuchauslegung bei Origenes und den frühen Rabbinen* (Frankfurt am Main).

2011. "L'interprétation origénienne de Gen 2,8 et ses arrières-plans rabbiniques," in *Origeniana Decima*, ed. S. Kaczmarek et al., BETL 244 (Leuven), 63–73.

Uhlig, Siegbert. 1984. *Jüdische Schriften aus hellenistisch-römischer Zeit*, vol. 6: *Das Äthiopische Henochbuch* (Gütersloh).

Urba, Karl F., and Zycha, Joseph (ed.). 1913. *Sancti Aureli Augustini. Opera*, VIII.1, CSEL 60 (Vienna).

Urbach, Ephraim E. 1987. *The Sages: Their Concepts and Beliefs* (Cambridge, MA).

Uthemann, Karl-Heinz. 1999. "Protologie und Eschatologie: zur Rezeption des Origenes im 4. Jahrhundert vor dem Ausbruch der ersten origenistischen Kontroverse," in *Origeniana Septima*, ed. W. A. Bienert and U. Kühneweg, BETL 137 (Leuven), 399–458.

Vahrenhorst, Martin. 2002. *"Ihr sollt überhaupt nicht schwören": Matthäus im halachischen Diskurs*, WMANT 95 (Neukirchen-Vluyn).

Vallée, Gérard. 1981. *A Study in Anti-Gnostic Polemics: Irenaeus, Hippolytus, and Epiphanius* (Waterloo).

van der Horst, Pieter W. 1999. "Evil Inclination יצר הרע," in *DDD*, 2nd ed., 317–19.

2006. "A Note on the Evil Inclination and Sexual Desire in Talmudic Literature," in *Jews and Christians in Their Graeco-Roman Context*, ed. P. W. van der Horst, WUNT I/196 (Tübingen), 59–65.

VanderKam, James C. (ed. and trans.). 1989. *The Book of Jubilees*, CSCO 510–511 (Leuven).

van Kooten, George. 2008. *Paul's Anthropology in Context*, WUNT I/232 (Tübingen).

2014a. "The Divine Father of the Universe from the Presocratics to Celsus: The Greco-Roman Background to the 'Father of All' in Paul's Letter to the Ephesians," in *The Divine Father*, ed. F. Albrecht and R. Feldmeier, Themes in Biblical Narrative 18 (Leiden), 293–323.

2014b. "Human Being," in *The Oxford Encyclopedia of the Bible and Ethics*, ed. R. L. Brawley, 2 vols. (Oxford), 1: 394–405.

2015. "Matthew, the Parthians, and the Magi: A Contextualization of Matthew's Gospel in Roman–Parthian Relations of the First Centuries BCE and CE," in *The Star of Bethlehem and the Magi*, ed. P. Barthel and G. van Kooten, Themes in Biblical Narrative 19 (Leiden), 496–646.

van Peursen, Wido T. 2004. "The Peshitta of Ben Sira: Jewish and/or Christian?" *AS* 2: 243–62.

2011. "Ben Sira in the Syriac Tradition," in *The Texts and Versions of the Book of Ben Sira*, ed. J.-S. Rey and J. Joosten, JSJSup 150 (Leiden), 143–65.

Vevaina, Yuhan. 2010. "Enumerating the Dēn: Textual Taxonomies, Cosmological Deixis, and Numerological Speculations in Zoroastrianism," *HR* 50.2: 111–43.

Vogt, Hermann-J. 1987. "Warum wurde Origenes zum Häretiker erklärt? Kirchliche Vergangenheits-Bewältigung in der Vergangenheit," in *Origeniana Quarta*, ed. L. Lies (Innsbruck), 78–99.

von Bendemann, Reinhard. 2004. "Die kritische Diastase von Wissen, Wollen und Handeln," *ZNW* 95: 35–63.

Waldstein, Michael, and Wisse, Frederik. 1995. *The Apocryphon of John*, Nag Hammadi and Manichaean Studies 33 (Leiden).

Wartski, Isidore. 1970. *Leshon ha-midrashim* (Jerusalem).

Waszink, Jan Hendrik. 1947. *Quinti Septimi Florentis Tertulliani* De anima (Amsterdam).

Webb, Ruth. 2008. *Demons and Dancers* (Cambridge, MA).

Weber, Dorothy (ed.). 1998. *Sancti Aureli Augustini. Opera*, CSEL 91 (Vienna).

Weber, Robert, et al. 1994. *Biblia Sacra iuxta Vulgatam Versionem*, 4th ed. (Stuttgart).

Weder, Hans. 1998. "Die Normativität der Freiheit," in *Paulus, Apostel Jesu Christi*, ed. M. Trowitzsch (Tübingen), 129–45.

Weima, Jeffrey A. D. 2014. *1–2 Thessalonians*, BECNT (Grand Rapids).

Weisser, Sharon. forthcoming. *Eradication ou modération des passions. Histoire de la controverse entre Stoïciens et Péripatéticiens chez Cicéron, Sénèque et Philon d'Alexandrie* (Turnhout).

Weitzman, Michael P. 1998. "Is the Peshitta of Chronicles a Targum?" in *Targum Studies*, vol. 2: *Targum and Peshitta*, ed. P. V. M. Flesher (Atlanta), 159–93.

1999. *The Syriac Version of the Old Testament* (Cambridge).

Werman, Cana. 2002. "The 'תורה' and the 'תעודה' Engraved on the Tablets," *DSD* 9: 75–103.

2004. "What Is 'the Book of Hagu?'" in *Sapiential Perspectives: Wisdom Literature in Light of the Dead Sea Scrolls*, ed. J. J. Collins et al., STDJ 51 (Leiden), 125–40.

Westermann, Claus. 1994. *Genesis 1–11*, trans. J. J. Scullion (Minneapolis).

Wetzel, James. 1992. *Augustine and the Limits of Virtue* (Cambridge).

2007. "Augustine," in *The Oxford Handbook of Religion and Emotion*, ed. J. Corrigan (Oxford), 349–60.

2008. "Body Double: Saint Augustine and the Sexualized Will," in *Weakness of Will from Plato to the Present*, ed. T. Hoffman (Washington), 43–58.

Wevers, John W. 1974. *Septuaginta Vetus Testamentum Graecum*, vol. 1: *Genesis* (Göttingen).

1993. *Notes on the Greek Text of Genesis*, SBLSCS 35 (Atlanta).

1995. *Notes on the Greek Text of Deuteronomy*, SBLSCS 39 (Atlanta).

White, Michael. 1985. *Agency and Integrality: Philosophical Themes in the Ancient Discussions of Determinism and Responsibility* (Dordrecht).

Wiebe, Gregory. 2017. "Augustine on Diabolical Sacraments and the Devil's Body," in StPatr 82, 73–90.

Wiley, Tatha. 2002. *Original Sin* (New York).

Wilkinson, Robert J. 2015. *Tetragrammaton*, Studies in the History of Christian Traditions 179 (Leiden).

Williams, Alan. 1997. "Zoroastrianism and the Body," in *Religion and the Body*, ed. S. Coakley (Cambridge), 155–66.

Williams, Frank (trans.). 1987. *The Panarion of Epiphanius of Salamis: Book I (Sects 1–46)* Nag Hammadi and Manichaean Studies 63 (Leiden).
Williams, Megan H. 2006. *The Monk and the Book* (Chicago).
Williams, Michael A. 1996. *Rethinking "Gnosticism"* (Princeton).
Williams, Norman P. 1927. *The Ideas of the Fall and of Original Sin* (London).
Wilson, Walter T. 2011. *Philo of Alexandria, On Virtues* (Leiden).
Winston, David. 1986. "Theodicy and Creation of Man in Philo of Alexandria," in *Hellenica et Judaica*, ed. A. Caquot et al. (Leuven), 105–11.
Winter, Bruce W. 1997. *Philo and Paul among the Sophists* (Cambridge).
Wold, Benjamin G. 2015. "'Flesh' and 'Spirit' in Qumran Sapiential Literature as the Background to the Use in Pauline Epistles," *ZNW* 106: 262–79.
2018. *4QInstruction: Divisions & Hierarchies*, STDJ 123 (Leiden).
Wright, Archie T. 2005. *The Origin of Evil Spirits*, WUNT II/198 (Tübingen).
Wright, N. Thomas. 1992. *The New Testament and the People of God* (London).
Wright, William (ed.). 1871. *Apocryphal Acts of the Apostles* (London).
Xeravits, Géza G. (ed.). 2010. *Dualism in Qumran*, LSTS 76 (Edinburgh).
Yahalom, Joseph. 2005. "The World of Grief and Mourning in the Genizah," *Ginzei Qedem* 1: 117–34.
Yahalom, Joseph, and Sokoloff, Michael. 1999. *Jewish Palestinian Aramaic Poetry from Late Antiquity* (Jerusalem) [Hebrew].
Yamauchi, Edwin. 1967. *Mandaic Incantation Texts* (New Haven).
Zaehner, Robert C. 1955. *Zurvan: A Zoroastrian Dilemma* (Oxford).
Zimmermann, Ruben. 2007. "Jenseits von Indikativ und Imperativ: Entwurf einer 'impliziten Ethik' des Paulus am Beispiel des 1. Korintherbriefs," *TLZ* 132: 259–84.
2013. "Die Ethik der Kirche: Normen, Begründungen, Strukturen, Argumentation," in *Paulus Handbuch*, ed. F. W. Horn (Tübingen), 433–39.
Zurawski, Jason. 2012. "Separating the Devil from the *Diabolos*: A Fresh Reading of Wisdom of Solomon 2.24," *JSP* 21: 366–99.
Zycha, Joseph (ed.). 1891. *Sancti Aureli Augustini. Opera*, VI.1, CSEL 25 (Vienna).
1900. *Sancti Aureli Augustini. Opera*, V.3, CSEL 41 (Vienna).

# Index of Names


Arruzza, Cinzia, 206

Bar-Asher Siegal, Michal, 121
Baumgarten, Joseph M., 56
BeDuhn, Jason, 184
Betz, Hans D., 132
Billerbeck, Paul, 1
Bovon, François, and Geoltrain, Pierre, 187
Brand, Miryam, 36
Brandenburger, Egon, 134
Bregman, Marc, 288

Carozzi, Claude, 197
Charles, Robert H., 74, 77
Cohen Stuart, G.H., 35–36, 47
Corrigan, Kevin, 249, 261

Davies, William D., 137
de Boer, Martinus, 134
Dillon, John, 152
Dupuis, Jacques, 210

Elgvin, Torlief, 49

Fishbane, Michael, 123
Frey, Jörg, 134, 135
Funk, Wolf-Peter, 196

Gibbons, Kathleen, 250
Goff, Matthew J., 61
Graves, Michael, 233, 239, 243
Guillaumont, Antoine, 248, 251, 252, 257, 260
Guillaumont, Antoine, and Guillaumont, Claire, 248

Hadot, Jean, 36
Hagendahl, Harald, 239
Harl, Marguerite, 206, 209
Houghton, Hugh A.G., 221

Joosten, Jan, 264

Kamesar, Adam, 233
Karfik, Filip, 249
Kedar-Kopfstein, Benjamin, 233
Kister, Menachem, 123
Klauck, Hans-Josef, 196
Kloppenborg, John, 144, 155
Kuhn, Karl G., 126, 134

Lévy, Carlos, 111
Liebes, Judah, 122

Marcus, Joel, 128, 129, 134
Moss, Jessica, 112
Muraoka, Takamitsu, 43
Murdock, William R. and MacRae, George W., 196, 197
Murray, Robert, 281

Naeh, Shlomo, 192
Newsom, Carol A., 58

Nickelsburg, George, 80
Nöldeke, Theodor, 262

Ophir, Adi, 125

Poirier, Paul-Hubert, 192
Porter, F.C., 34–35

Rey, Jean-Sébastien, 62
Reydams-Schils, Gretchen J., 99
Rosen-Zvi, Ishay, 1, 13–14, 33–34, 47, 57, 124, 127, 159, 167, 195, 198, 211, 213, 230, 248, 253, 255, 261, 293, 312, 321
Rozenberg, Shalom, 123
Rubenson, Samuel, 251, 260
Runia, David T., 98, 101, 104

Sandmel, Samuel, 126
Schmidt, Hanns-Peter, 306
Schuller, Eileen M., 58
Seitz, Oscar J.F., 143
Sokoloff, Michael, 262
Sorabji, Richard, 218
Stec, David M., 319
Stewart, Columba, 251
Strack, Hermann, 1
Stroumsa, Guy, 144, 152, 153
Stuckenbruck, Loren T., 62, 135
Sundermann, Werner, 306
Suter, David, 80

ter Haar Romeny, Bas, 244
Tigchelaar, Eibert J.C., 56, 167
Tissot, Yves, 192
Tóth, Péter, 186

van der Horst, Pieter W., 265

Weitzman, Michael, 264
Werman, Cana, 51
Wevers, John, 237
Williams, Megan, 239
Williams, Norman P., 137
Wilson, Walter T., 102
Winter, Bruce W., 104

Zaehner, Robert C., 311
Zurawski, Jason, 47–48

# Index Locorum


**Hebrew Bible**
Genesis, 15
1–9, 4, 92
1–11, 24–25
1:20–29, 65
1:21, 24, 69
1:26, 272
1:26–27, 93
1:28, 72
2, 124
2:4–3:24, 27
2:5, , 66
2:7, 25, 65–66, , 83, 92, 272
2:7–8, 234, 235
2:8, 193
2:9, 27
2:15, 66
2:18, 27
2:19, 25, 65, 69
3:11, 27
3:13, 291
3:16–19, 66, 67
3:17–19, 26
3:21, 209
3:23, 66
4:1–22, 66
4:7, 117, 171
4:7–8, 27
4:20–22, 67
4:23–24, 27
4:26, 51
5:1, 66, 93
5:21–24, 77
5:22, 84
5:28–32, 78
5:28–6:22, 66
5:29, 26, 66
6:1–4, 82
6:1–5, 129
6:2, 71
6:3, 92
6:5, 2–3, , 24–29, , 30, 39, 135, 144, 161, 235, 274, 278, 320, 326
6:5–6, 93
6:5–8:22, 78
6:5–9:17, 77, 78
6:6, 4, 28
6:6–7, 83
6:7, 28
6–9, 93
8:21, 2–3, , 24, 27, 29–30, , 40, 118, 135, 144, 161, 195, 235, 240, 274, 278, 320, 326
9:1, 7, 65, 72
9:1–17, 82
9:6, 66
9:20–24, 29
14:22, 116
15:16, 104
49:24, 329
Exodus
15:1, 287
15:11, 75
31:4, 18
35:32, 35, 18
38:23, 18

Leviticus
4, 290
11:42, 103
19:14, 285
Numbers
21:27–30, 108
24:17, 51
Deuteronomy, 15
6:5, 144, 232
6:6, 116
11:18, 117, 139
28:29, 239
28:33, 239
28:48, 170
31:16, 21–23
31:20, 21–23
31:21, 20–24, , 29, 277, 278
32, 23
32:43, 75
Ruth
3:8, 322
3:13, 115
1 Samuel
26:10, 116
2 Kings
5:16, 117
1 Chronicles
4:10, 327
8:40, 328
12:33, 143
28:9, 236, 326
29:18, 236, 326
2 Chronicles
2:13, 236
6:14, 326
26:15, 236
29:26, 327
36:13, 327
Nehemiah
9:4, 303, 304
Job
1–2, 198
1:6, 75
4:9, 16
10:9, 16
27:16, 16
30:19, 16
Psalms
4:6, 318
12:2, 143
13:5, 318
22:27, 75
22:28, 75
29:1–2, 75
33:15, 18
46:6–7, 75
47:8, 75
50:1, 75
50:4, 285, 288
50:14, 319
50:23, 319
51:7, 321
67:3–4, 75
81:10, 245
82:6–7, 75
86:9, 75
91:12, 320
96:7, 75
97:7, 75
101:4, 320
102:15, 74
103:14, 320
117:1, 75
119:70, 321
Proverbs
15:28, 169
16:32, 330
24:2, 169
25:21, 118
Ecclesiastes
3:11, 323
3:21, 124
7:8, 323
7:19, 323
9:14–15, 324
10:1, 324
10:4, 325
10:10, 326
12:7, 125
Isaiah, 15
2:3, 74
10:13–14, 208
14:12–22, 204
14:13–14, 208
18:7, 74
19:22, 74
24:5, 23
24:19, 23
26:1–5, 242
29:16, 17
33:18, 169
41:25, 16

**Hebrew Bible** (cont.)
44:9, 234
44:10, 19
44:12, 19
45:7, 16
45:9, 17
45:14, 74, 90
45:14–15, 74
49:6, 87
56–66, , 163
60, 75
60:3, 75
60:5, 11, 74
60:10, 12, 74, 90
62:4, 162
62:7, 163
62:10, 163
62:12, 163
63:11, 155
65:17–25, 82
66:18–19, 74
66:22–23, 82
66:23, 75
Jeremiah, 16
16:19, 76
18:1–4, 16
18:1–11, 30–31
18:4, 21
32:30, 239
Ezekiel
20:1–26, 166
20:38, 166
28:1–19, 204
Daniel
7:14, 74
Micah
4:2, 74
7:5, 195
Habakkuk
2:18, 234
Zechariah
3:2, 198
5:8, 304
8:21–23, 74, 75
9:9, 264
14:16–19, 75

**New Testament**
Matthew
7:17–20, 182
24:12, 204
Luke
10:18, 204
22:3, 182
John
8:44, 207
13:2, 221
13:27, 221
Acts
17:1–10, 128
18:1–5, 127
Romans, 6, 136–41, , 267
1:18–3:20, 136, 139
5:11, 21, 140
5:12, 210
5:12–21, 137, 139
5:16, 18, 138
5:20, 138
6:1–23, 139
6:2, 6, 138
6:4–6, 137, 138
6:15, 18, 140
6:23, 140
7:1–6, 137, 141
7:7–25, 138–41
7:14–25, 136
7:18, 135
7:18, 20, 138
7:18–20, 162
7:24, 137
8:1, 141
8:2, 140
8:3, 139
8:3–4, 141
8:6, 137
8:16, 138
8:39, 140
9–11, 136
14–15, 136
14:23, 137
15:24, 28, 136
16:3–15, 136
1 Corinthians
6:17, 138
15:47, 49, 207
15:9, 182
2 Corinthians
4:16, 140
5:17, 138
Galatians, 6, 130–36
1–2, 196
1:6–9, 135

1:6–10, 132
2:7, 131
3:1–5, 132
3:3, 135
4:21–31, 132
4:23, 29, 132
5:16–25, 131, 132, 133, 135, 139
5:17, 210
5:19–21, 135
6:8, 132
6:15, 138
Philippians
3:4–9, 132
1 Thessalonians, 6, 127–30
1:9, 128
2:9, 128
2:17, 128, 129, 130
3:6, 127
4:1–2, 128
4:1–5:22, 128
4:3–8, 130
4:5, 132, 139
5:1–2, 128
James
1:5–8, 154
1:8, 6, 143, 156
1:13–17, 156
1:14–15, 157
1:18, 156
1:21–25, 155, 156, 157
2:8–12, 156
2:12, 156
2:26, 155
3:15, 155
4:5, 155
4:8, 6, 143, 156
5:20, 155
1 Peter
5:8, 198
Revelation
12:10, 198

**Jewish Apocrypha**
1 Esdras
8:19, 42
8:21,24, , 42
2 Maccabees
11:6–12, 90
4 Maccabees, 36
4 Ezra, 36, 134
Judith
8:29, 35, 38
Sirach, 2–3, , 15, 33–37, , 62, 124, 127, 251
1:28, 143
5:2, 47
14:17, 134
15:5, 36
15:12–17, 118
15:14, 253
17:6, 36
21:2, 137
27:6, 43, 44, 137
27:10, 137
32:27, 37
33:10, 37
37:3, 44
46:1, 37
49:14, 37
49:7, 38
Tobit, 251
13:11–17, 91
14:5–6, 91, 94
14:6, 74
Wisdom, 36, 48
1:12–13, 47
1:16, 47
2:1, 47
2:21–24, 47
6:23, 48
7:1–6, 134
10:5, 47
14:14, 47

**Christian Apocrypha**
Acts of Andrew, 8
49–50, 188–89, , 199
Acts of John
94–102, 187
Acts of Peter, 8
8, 190, 200
Acts of Thomas, 8, 187, 277
30:3, 192, 194
32, 191, 200
34:1a–d, 192–96
34:1a–f, 199
Apocalypse of Paul, 8
20:25–21:14, 199
NH V:2, 198
Apocryphon of John
21–22, 181
28, 181
Gospel of Philip, 187

**Christian Apocrypha** (cont.)
104, 181
Gospel of Truth, 187

**Pseudepigrapha**
1 Enoch
1–16, 4
1–36, 67
1:5, 85
1:26–27, 83
5:4–6a, 7b, 89
5:4–9, 85
5:21, 74
6–11, 77, 89, 93
6–16, 81, 92
6–36, 89
6:1–2, 72, 79, 93
6:2, 67
6:3–6, 81
7–8, 80
7:1, 67
7:3–5, 68–71, , 80, 81
7:5, 69, 78
8:1, 72
8:1–3, 67, 80
8:4–9:11, 78
9:1, 4, 79
9:3, 10, 68
10, 86, 88–90, , 94
10:1–22, 72–74, , 83
10:4–19, 71
10:9, 68
10:14–11:2, 82
10:16, 87
10:17–22, 93
10:17–11:2, 74, 78, 92
11:1, 71, 82
12–16, 84
15:1–16:4, 68–71
15:7–10, 81
17–36, 84–85
22:3, 69
25–27, 76
32, 92
32:3–6, 67
48:5, 74
50:2, 74
62:1–12, 74
63:1–12, 74
81–82, 85
85:1–3, 91
86–105, 86
89:10–66, 90
90:16–38, 90–92
90:28–36, 76
90:37, 74
91:11–12, 90
91:11–15, 86–88
91:14, 74, 88–90
91:14, 16, 92
91:6–8, 87
93:10, 86
93:9, 11, 87
98:4–6, 92
100:6, 74, 88–90
104:12–13, 89
105:1, 74
105:1–2, 88–90, 91
106–07, 78
106:1–107:3, 77
107:1, 80, 87
90:2–15, 90
2 Baruch
29:5–7, 71
49:3, 133
Animal Apocalypse *See* 1 Enoch 85–90
Apocalypse of Weeks *See* 1 Enoch 93:1–20; 91:11–17
Apocryphon of Ezekiel, 288
Birth of Noah *See* 1 Enoch 106–107
Book of Parables *See* 1 Enoch 37–71
Book of Watchers *See* 1 Enoch 1–36
Epistle of Enoch *See* 1 Enoch 91–92
Exhortation *See* 1 Enoch 91:1–10, 91:18–19
Jubilees, 62, 124
1:20, 198
5:2, 71
7:24, 71
Psalms of Solomon
17:29–32, 34, 74
Testaments of the Twelve Patriarchs, 36, 251, 252
Asher, 229
Judah
11:1–2, 129
Reuben
1:6, 129

**Septuagint**, 3, 8
Genesis
2:7, 37

2:8, 193
6:2, 208
6:3, 271
6:5, 40, 43, 48, 127, 236
8:21, 40–42, , 43, 48, 127, 240, 271
15:11, 208
24:45, 41
27:41, 41
Exodus
32:12, 170
Deuteronomy
31:21, 38
32:8, 75
32:43, 75
1 Chronicles
28:9, 43, 44
29:18, 43
Psalms
82:1, 75
82:6–7, 75
103:14, 38
118:118, 44
Proverbs
13:23, 42
Isaiah
22:11, 37
26:3, 263
29:16, 38
43:10, 37
44:10, 37
44:12, 38
45:11, 18, 37
45:b7, 9, 37
45:9, 37
46:11, 37
54:1, 38
Jeremiah
31:10, 42
40:2, 37
Amos
4:13, 37
Habakkuk
2:18, 38
Aquila, 8, 35, 236, 237, 240, 243
Symmachus, 8, 35, 236, 237, 239, 240, 243

**Vulgate**, 8
Genesis
6:5, 237, 241, 246
8:21, 240, 241, 246
Exodus
32:22, 241, 245
Deuteronomy
31:21, 237, 241
2 Kings
19:25, 234
1 Chronicles
28:9, 238, 241
29:18, 238, 241
Psalms
74:17, 234
95:5, 234
103:14, 235
104:26, 234
Isaiah
26:3, 242, 246
29:16, 234, 235
37:26, 234
44:10, 12, 233
45:9, 234
46:11, 234
Jeremiah
51:19, 234
Habakkuk
2:18, 235

**Targums**
Cairo Genizah Palestinian Targums
Genesis
4:7, 171–74
4:8, 172
Fragment Targums
Genesis
4:7, 171–74
4:8, 172
Targum Jonathan, 7, 160, 172
Isaiah
26:3, 165
57:14, 164
57:17, 165
62:10, 162–66
62:6, 11, 163
Jeremiah
3:17, 165
7:24, 165
9:13, 165
11:8, 165
13:10, 165
16:12, 165
Ezekiel
16:27, 167

**Targums** (cont.)
20:25, 162, 167
20:25–26, 167
21:16, 167
25:14, 167
Targum Neofiti, 160
Genesis
4:7, 171–74
4:8, 172
6:5, 168–69, , 174, 241
8:21, 168–69, , 174, 241
Deuteronomy
31:21, 169–71, , 174
Targum Onqelos, 7, 160, 316
Genesis
4:7, 173
6:5, 161–62
8:21, 161–62
Deuteronomy
31:21, 162
32:21, 170
Targum Pseudo-Jonathan, 12, 322
Deuteronomy
32:21, 170
Targums to the Writings, 12, 316, 329
Ruth, 318
3:8, 321–22
1 Chronicles, 12, 326–29
4:10, 328
8:40, 328
28:9, 326
29:18, 317, 326
2 Chronicles, 12, 326–29
6:14, 327
29:26, 327
33:13, 327
36:13, 327
Psalms, 12, 318–21, , 323
4:6, 318
13:5, 318
50:14, 319
50:23, 319
51:7, 321
91:12, 320
101:4, 320
103:14, 320
103:4, 317
119:70, 321
Proverbs, 330
16:32, 330
Ecclesiastes, 12, 322–26
3:11, 323
7:8, 323, 328, 330
7:19, 324, 328
9:14, 325
9:14–15, 325
10:1, 324
10:10, 326
10:4, 325

**Peshitta**, 10
Genesis
2:7, 272
2:18, 193
6:5, 263, 274
8:21, 263, 274
Deuteronomy
31:21, 263
1 Chronicles
28:9, 264
29:18, 264
4 Maccabees, 268
3:4, 265, 270, 277, 278
Psalms
103:14, 263
Sirach, 265, 270
15:14, 263, 278
17:31, 263, 269, 278
21:11, 263, 269, 278
Isaiah
26:3, 263
29:16, 263
Habakkuk
2:18, 263

**Qumran**
1QGenesis Apocryphon
1Q20 ii 1–v 26, 77
1Q20 ii 1–v 27, 78
4QAdmonition based on the Flood
4Q370 1, 1, 3, 135
4QMagical Booklet
4Q560 1 i 2–3, b1 ii 5–6, 59
4QSongs of the Maskil
4Q510 1 5–6, 59
4QEnoch, 86
4Q201,
1 iii 21, 69
4Q202,
1 ii 25a, 69
4QIncantation
4Q444 1 1–4, b2 i 4, 59

4QInstruction, 3–4, , 49, 59, 135
1Q26, 49
4Q184,
1, 17, 56
4Q415,
2 ii, 53
4Q416,
1, 49, 54–57
2, 52
4Q417,
1 i 11, 58
1 ii 12, 55, 162
1 i 13b–18, 49–52
4Q418,
2+2a, 49
55, 61
69 ii, 55
81+81a, 52–54, , 63
126 i–ii, 55
221, 2, 56
11QPsalms
11Q5 xix 13–16, 59
Book of Giants
1Q23,
1+6+22, 71
9+14+15, 71
4Q531,
1 i–ii, 70–71
2–3, 70–71
4Q532,
1 ii+2:9, 71
2:3, 71
6Q8,
2, 77
Community Rule, 135, 151
1QS
iii 13–4, 26, 57
iii 17–18, 51
iii 17–19, 153
iv 15–23, 153
iv 20–21, 153
iv 23, 153
xi 22, 58
Temple Scroll
4Q524 15, 22, 56
11Q19 66, 8, 56
Thanksgiving Hymns, 3, 135
1QH[a]
iii 29, 58
iv, 63
iv 33–37, 59
ix 23, 58
ix 37, 57
v 12–20, 60–61
v 31–33, 59
v 31–36, 61
viii 18, 58
x 11,38, 57
xi 24–25, 58
xii 14, 57
xii 29, 134
xii 30, 58
xii 30–31, 137
xiii 8, 57
xiv 35, 58
xviii 22–32, 134
xix 12–17, 61
xix 6, 58
xv 16, 19, 57
xv 6–7, 58
xviii, 61
xviii 25, 49, 58
xx 29, 35, 58
xx 4–10, 63
xxi 11, 38, 58
xxi 17, 25, 34, 58
xxi 29, 58
xxi 30, 58
xxii 12, 58
xxiii 13, 28, 58
xxiii 37, 38, 58
xxiv 6, 49, 58
xxiv 6–13, 58
xxv 31–32, 58
Treatise of the Two Spirits *See* Community Rule:1QS 3:13–4:26

**Rabbinic Literature**
Mishnah
Berakhot
9:5, 124, 135, 232
Avot, 167
4:1, 323, 330
Tosefta, 167
Nazir
4:7, 127
Bava Qamma
9:31, 197
Avot de Rabbi Nathan
Version A

**Rabbinic Literature** (cont.)
20, 165
6, 165
Tannaitic Midrash
Sifre Numbers, 115
38, 116
88, 127, 189
Sifre Deuteronomy
33, 117, 127
45, 118, 127, 138, 161, 162, 168, 173, 194
Mekhilta de-Rabbi Shimon bar Yochai, 287, 289
Talmud, 6, 12, 198, 281, 286, 315
Babylonian, 11, 159
Berakhot
17a, 313
61a, 324
Yoma
69b, 296, 302, 304, 306, 312
Sukkah
52a, 122, 164, 304, 318, 319
Hagigah
16a, 189, 195
Nedarim
32b, 298
Bava Batra
16a, 306, 318
Sanhedrin
64a, 296, 302, 304, 306, 312
Temurah
16a, 328
Niddah
31a–b, 329
Jerusalem, 245, 286
Shabbat
14:3, 14 c, 195
Nedarim
9:1, 41b, 245
Aggadic Midrash, 6, 11, 315
Genesis Rabbah
20:7, 191
22:6, 120, 195
Leviticus Rabbah
9:1, 319
Numbers Rabbah
15:16, 164

**Piyyutim**
Yannai, 290
Yose ben Yose, 290

**Philo**, 4–5, , 6, 8, 47
*Allegories of the Laws*
2:7–9, 98
2:50, 98
3:212, 103
3:228, 107
3:229–230, 108
3:330–335, 108
*On Cultivation*
96, 107
*On Dreams*
2:279, 107
*On Drunkenness*
166–168, 110
166–205, 109
198–202, 109
28, 107
*On Flight and Finding*
136, 111
*On Joseph*
143, 106
*On Providence*
1:42–44, 95
2:32, 104, 95
2:86–102, 95
*On the Confusion of Tongues*
128–132, 107
*On the Creation of the Cosmos according to Moses*, 98
8, 103
45, 107
75, 96
148–150, 98
151, 98
165, 101, 107
*On the Decalogue*
52, 102
67, 103
*On the Giants*
12–13, 208
*On the Life of Abraham*
238, 99
*On the Migration of Abraham*
69, 103
92, 97
*On the Posterity of Cain*
102, 103
168, 102
*On the Special Laws*
2:165–167, 103
4:147, 102

4:55, 97
*On the Virtues*
64–65, 102
*Questions and Answers on Exodus*
1:23, 152
*Questions and Answers on Genesis*, 42–43
3:33, 111
5:87, 103
*That the Worse Attacks the Better*
1, 104
34, 104
*Who is the Heir?*
227, 208
248, 105
300–308, 104
55–56, 154

**Early Christian**
1 Clement
4:7–8, 48
Ambrose, 220
Anthony of Egypt, 9
Letters
6:46–48, 251
*Apopthegmata Patrum*, 121
Athanasius
Life of Antony, 251, 260
23, 122
Augustine, 9–10
*City of God*, 225
14:11, 183
3, 218
*Letters*
9, 215
*On Continence*
10, 227
13, 227
14, 227
*On Genesis against the Manichees*, 219
2:14:20, 220
2:14:21, 222
*On the Deserts of Sinners and Infant Baptism*
1:10:11, 212
*On the Divination of Demons*, 219, 223, 228, 230
5:9, 216
*On the Free Choice of the Will*, 224
3:25:74:255, 225
3:25:74:256–7, 225
3:25:75:259, 225
3:25:75:259–60, 226
*On the Sermon on the Mount*, 219
*On Two Souls*, 230
*Retractions*
2:56, 217
*Tractates on the Gospel of John*
55:4, 221, 227, 228
Barnabas
20:1 c, 144
Basilides, 179, 183
Cassian
*Conferences*, 231
Clement of Alexandria, 184
*Stromata*
2:114, 177
4:153, 179
4:82, 179
4:83, 179
5:3, 179
Didache
5:1, 144
Ephrem the Syrian, 10, 274, 275, 276, 283, 286, 287
*Carmina Nisibena*
69:5, 281
*Commentary on Genesis*
VI:7, b58:12, 270
*Liber Graduum*, 270, 276
333:4, 269
420:11, 269
*Nisbene Hymns*
21:15, 269
*Sermon on Our Lord*
XL:4, b30:20, 270
XLIV, 42:26, 270
Eusebius, 201
*Martyrs of Palestine*, 268
47:20, 276
*Praeparatio Evangelica*
9:17:1–9, 77
Eusebius of Emesa
*Commentary on Genesis*, 8:21–9:5, 244
Evagrius Ponticus, 9, 122, 199, 228
*"On the Tetragrammaton"*, 247
*Antirrhetikos*, 256
4:27, 257
*Letters*
18, 260
*On Thoughts*, 214, 224, 231

**Early Christian** (cont.)
37, 217
4, 217
*Praktikos*, 9, 248
28, 254
*Skemmata*
26, 258
Irenaeus, 176, 184
*Against the Heresies*, 177
1:6, 178
Jacob of Sarug, 268, 273, 279
Jerome, 8–9, , 254
*Commentariorum in Isaiam*
VIII:15, 242, 243
Justinian, 205
Lactantius
*The Workmanship of God*
19, 194
Narsai, 10, 267, 278, 279
*Homilies*
14, 273, 275
17, 275
36, 272
7, 272
9, 275, 277
Origen, 5, 8, 9, 184, 199, 200, 228, 299
*Against Celsus*
VI:44, 207
*Commentary on Genesis*, 202
*Commentary on Romans*
V:1:511–19 538–548, 210
V:4:30–32, 210
*Commentary on the Gospel of John*, 207
20:24, 178
*Contra Celsum*
IV:39–40, 209
*Homilies on Ezekiel*
9:2, 208
*Homilies on Leviticus*
6:2, 209
*Homilies on Numbers*
12:4, 208
On First Principles, 8, 204, 214, 224
2:9, 205
3:2:2, 119, 227
3:2:4, 119, 258
3:3:6, 120
Tertullian
*A Treatise on the Soul*
16, 158
Timothy I
*Letters*
2:7, b70:21, 277
Titus of Bostra
*Contra Manichaeos*
IV:55, 270
Valentinus, 177
*Tripartite Tractate*
106, 178

**Classical Literature**
Apuleius
*On the God of Socrates*, 218
Aulus Gellius
*Attic Nights*, 218
Carneades, 110
*Chaldean Oracles*, 145
*Corpus Hermeticum*
IX:3, 151, 152
Diodorus of Sicily, 110
Empedocles, 153
*On Tranquility of Mind*
474B–C, 151
Epictetus
*Dialogues*
1:6:9, 129
2:18:8, 129
4:1:175, 129
*Discourses*
1:3:3, 149
1:3:7, 149
Epiphanius, 289
*Panarion*, 288
39, 180
Galen, 149
*On the Doctrines of Hippocrates and Plato*, 149
Hippolytus, 176
*Refutation*
5:26:19–21, 180
5:26:23, 180
Lucian, 110
Peripatetics, 105
Plato, 6, 8, 47
*Alcibiades Major*
132 c–133 c, 157
*Laws*, 145
X 896e, 148
X 896e ff, 152
*Phaedrus*
247–48, 209

*Republic*, 99
IV 379, 34
IV 382e–383a, 156
IV 439d–e, 146
IV, X, 112
VIII 554 c–e, 146
X 604a ff, 156
X 604a–d, 147
X 605b–c, 147
X 607b, 147
X 608a–b, 147, 153, 156
X 611b–612a, 147, 154, 158
X 611b–613b, 147
X 611d–612a, 151
X 612a, 156
*Symposium*
197d, 42
*Timaeus*, 98, 100
34b ff, 150
35a, 148
42a–b, 98
43a–b, 98
44a, 98
69, 34
69 c ff, 150
69 c–d, 151
69 c–e, 148
Plotinus, 6, 148
*Ennead*, 249
1:1:12, 151
2:3:9, 151
4:3:27, 152
6:4:16, 152
Plutarch, 148
*De Virtute Morali*
441 F–442A, 150
*On Tranquility of Mind*, 152
*The E at Delphi*
388 C–389D, 156
393E–394A, 156
Porphyry, 299
Posidonius, 149
Fragment 187, 149
Pseudo–Eupolemos, 77
Sceptics, 105, 109
Stoics, 34, 105
Theodotion, 236, 237, 240
Xenophon, 6, 144
*Anabasis*, 146
*Cyropaedia*
6:1:41, 145

**Persian Literature**
Abū'l–Ḥasan ibn Bahlūl, 271
Aphrahat, 10, 270, 276
*Demonstrations*
14, 268
19, 277
3, 268
9, 269
*Book of the Laws of the Countries*, 267
*Bundahisn*
27:34, 301
34:30–31, 308
*Dadestan i Denig*
2:16, 307
*Day Hordad of the Month of Frawardin*
35, 307
*Denkard*
6:E:34a, 299
*Kephalaia*, 310
17:2–9, 182
19:1–3, 182
6–8, 182
99:2–99:17, 183
*Pahlavi Rivayat*
442, 309
*Pahlavi Rivayat*
48:106, 313
48:94, 306
48:95, 308
*Sabuhragan*
M 7984:1, 310
M7981:I:V:ii:13–16, 308
*Selections of Zadspram*
34:36, 300,
311
34:41, 313
*Videvad*
18:18–19, 309

Lightning Source UK Ltd.
Milton Keynes UK
UKHW012135120121
376941UK00002B/7

9 781108 470827